1st Workshop on Customizable NLP: Progress and Challenges in Customizing NLP for Domain, Application, Group, or Individual (CustomerNLP4U 2024)

Miami, Florida, USA
16 November 2024

ISBN: 979-8-3313-0844-5

Printed from e-media with permission by:

Curran Associates, Inc.
57 Morehouse Lane
Red Hook, NY 12571

Some format issues inherent in the e-media version may also appear in this print version.

Printed with permission by Curran Associates, Inc. (2025)

Association for Computational Linguistics
209 N. Eighth Street
Stroudsburg, Pennsylvania 18360

Phone: 1-570-476-8006
Fax: 1-570-476-0860

acl@aclweb.org

Additional copies of this publication are available from:

Curran Associates, Inc.
57 Morehouse Lane
Red Hook, NY 12571 USA
Phone: 845-758-0400
Fax: 845-758-2633
Email: curran@proceedings.com
Web: www.proceedings.com

CustomNLP4U 2024

The 1st Workshop on Customizable NLP: Progress and Challenges in Customizing NLP for a Domain, Application, Group, or Individual (CustomNLP4U)

Proceedings of the Workshop

November 16, 2024

Order copies of this and other ACL proceedings from:

Association for Computational Linguistics (ACL)
317 Sidney Baker St. S
Suite 400 - 134
Kerrville, TX 78028
USA
Tel: +1-855-225-1962
acl@aclweb.org

Introduction

We are thrilled to welcome you to the Workshop on Customizable NLP (CustomNLP4U) at EMNLP 2024, held at the Hyatt Regency Miami Hotel on November 16, 2024. This workshop will explore the latest advancements and challenges in creating NLP models that can be customized for varied users, settings, and ethical considerations. CustomNLP4U aims to foster discussion and showcase research on the next generation of NLP models, which can adapt to unique user needs while addressing privacy, copyright, and personalization challenges.

This year's workshop brings together researchers, developers, and practitioners from across the NLP community. The program includes keynote talks, presentation sessions, and a poster session featuring both long and short papers. Each presentation and poster provides insights into data, modeling, evaluation, open science practices, applications, and ethical considerations in customizable NLP. These topics are crucial as we seek to build NLP systems that are not only powerful but also adaptable, transparent, and ethically sound.

Our call for papers attracted a diverse range of submissions across both academic and industry perspectives. We are grateful for the hard work and dedication of the Program Committee and the Steering Committee members, who carefully reviewed each submission. Their efforts were invaluable in shaping this year's program and ensuring high-quality presentations.

Workshop Highlights

1. Keynotes and Presentations: The program includes multiple keynote talks and oral presentation sessions covering topics such as data collection, customized model evaluation, privacy in NLP, and ethical considerations for adaptive AI. 2. Poster Session: Presentations in poster format enable more interactive engagement, offering opportunities for attendees to discuss topics like personalized AI assistants, sociolect modeling, federated learning, and chain-of-thought prompting. 3. Themes: This year's submissions reflect a growing interest in applications across sensitive domains like medical and legal NLP, as well as advancements in interpretability and control for varied use cases. Papers span topics from data privacy to interpretability, open science practices, and ethical issues in customization.

The workshop would not have been possible without the efforts of our Organizers and Steering Committee. We extend our gratitude to Sachin Kumar (Ohio State University, Allen Institute for AI), Weijia Shi (University of Washington), Chan Young Park (Carnegie Mellon University), Vidhisha Balachandran (Microsoft Research), and Shirley Anugrah Hayati (University of Minnesota, Twin Cities) for their leadership and dedication in organizing CustomNLP4U.

Our Steering Committee members—Yulia Tsvetkov, Noah A. Smith, Hannaneh Hajishirzi (all from the University of Washington), Dongyeop Kang (University of Minnesota, Twin Cities), and David Jurgens (University of Michigan)—have provided guidance and support throughout the planning process.

Thank you for joining us at CustomNLP4U 2024! We look forward to an inspiring day of discussions, insights, and collaborations, all aimed at driving the future of adaptable, ethical, and user-centered NLP systems.

Organizing Committee

Organizers

Sachin Kumar, Ohio State University, Allen Institute for AI
Weijia Shi, University of Washington
Chan Young Park, Carnegie Mellon University
Vidhisha Balachandran, Microsoft Research
Shirley Anugrah Hayati, University of Minnesota, Twin Cities

Steering Committee

Yulia Tsvetkov, University of Washington
Dongyeop Kang, University of Minnesota, Twin Cities
Noah A. Smith, University of Washington
Hannaneh Hajishirzi, University of Washington
David Jurgens, University of Michigan

Program Committee

Reviewers

Yachuan Liu, University of Michigan - Ann Arbor
Haz Sameen Shahgir, Bangladesh University of Engineering and Technology
Niloofar Ranjbar, Amirkabir University of Technology
A.B. Siddique, University of Kentucky
Satoshi Kodera, Tokyo University
Hamish Ivison, University of Washington
Prajna Devi Upadhyay, BITS Pilani, Birla Institute of Technology and Science
Noriaki Kawamae, Sophia University
Sabit Hassan, University of Pittsburgh
WenHao Wang, Zhejiang University
Jian Xie, Fudan University
Oleg Smirnov, Microsoft Gaming
Yusuke Kimura, Doshisha University
Wentao Ye, Zhejiang University
Danni Liu, Karlsruher Institut für Technologie
Sina Gholamian, Thomson Reuters
Lukas Hilgert, Karlsruher Institut für Technologie
Oxana Vitman, Universität Bremen
Bo Li, Sambanova Systems
Bodhisattwa Prasad Majumder, Allen Institute for Artificial Intelligence
Jonathan Lingjie Li, Computer Science Department, Stanford University
Ben Bogin, Allen Institute for Artificial Intelligence
Minsun Kim, KAIST
Kangil Lee, Inha University
Jacqueline He, University of Washington
Jimin Mun, CMU, Carnegie Mellon University
Klim Zaporojets, Aarhus University
Zekun Wu, Department of Computer Science, University College London, University of London
Caio Filippo Corro, Sorbonne Université
Alban Zammit, PayPal Inc.
Prajvi Saxena, German Research Center for AI
Sheshera Mysore, Microsoft
Wen Wang, Alibaba Group
Liming Xu, University of Cambridge
Hayoung Jung, Department of Computer Science
Bohan Zhang, University of Michigan - Ann Arbor
Moghis Fereidouni, University of Kentucky
Mengya Hu, Microsoft
Qingxiaoyang Zhu, University of California, Davis
Nika Amaglobeli, Texas Woman's University
Ro-ee Tal, University of British Columbia
Safoora Yousefi, Microsoft Inc
Wentao Zhang, University of Waterloo
Pradeep Dasigi, Allen Institute for Artificial Intelligence
Xin Yan, University of Waterloo
Creston Brooks, Princeton University

Jesse Atuhurra, Nara Institute of Science and Technology, Japan
Adib Mosharrof, University of Kentucky
Taro Watanabe, Nara Institute of Science and Technology, Japan
Bernal Jimenez Gutierrez, The Ohio State University
Takahiro Komamizu, Nagoya University
Akhil Arora, Swiss Federal Institute of Technology Lausanne
Dheeraj Rajagopal, Carnegie Mellon University
Mian Zhong, Johns Hopkins University
Yangyi Chen, Department of Computer Science, University of Illinois at Urbana-Champaign
Mehar Bhatia, University of British Columbia
Robert Calef, Massachusetts Institute of Technology
Ziyang Luo, National University of Singapore
Yuxi Xia, Universität Vienna
Alisa Liu, University of Washington
Agam Shah, Georgia Institute of Technology
Shangbin Feng, University of Washington
Ravi Shanker Raju, Sambanova Systems
Libby Ferland, University of Minnesota - Twin Cities
Kai Zhang, Ohio State University, Columbus
Orevaoghene Ahia, Department of Computer Science
Harsh Kohli, The Ohio State University, Columbus
Clara Na, Carnegie Mellon University
Shuyue Stella Li, Department of Computer Science, University of Washington
Anjalie Field, Johns Hopkins University
Anugunj Naman, Purdue University
Simon Yu, Northeastern University
Farhan Samir, University of British Columbia
Debarati Das, University of Minnesota - Twin Cities
Paul Röttger, Bocconi University
Michael Galarnyk, Georgia Institute of Technology
Sayantan Pal, State University of New York at Buffalo
Haneul Yoo, KAIST
WooJoo Kim, Pohang University of Science and Technology
Joonwon Jang, Postech
Petros Karypis, University of California, San Diego
Julia Mendelsohn, University of Michigan - Ann Arbor
Bin Hu, University of Minnesota - Twin Cities
Rachith Aiyappa, Indiana University Bloomington
Xiaofeng Zhu, Microsoft
Jackie CK Cheung, McGill University
Kemalcan Bora, Universitat Pompeu Fabra
Chuhong Mai, Amazon
Youngjin Lim, LG Energy Solution
Lele Cao, Microsoft (ABK)
Cesare Spinoso-Di Piano, , McGill University
Anthony Sicilia, Northeastern University
Jaya Krishna Mandivarapu, Microsoft
Yarik Menchaca Resendiz, University of Stuttgart, Universität Stuttgart
Anum Afzal, Technische Universität München
Jinwoo Jang, LG Energysolution

Table of Contents

Navigate Complex Physical Worlds via Geometrically Constrained LLM

Yongqiang Huang[1], **Wentao Ye**[2], **Liyao Li**[2], **Junbo Zhao**[2,*]
[1]College of Energy Engineering, Zhejiang University
[2]College of Computer Science and Technology, Zhejiang University
Emails: {hyq.cee, yewt01, liliyao, j.zhao}@zju.edu.cn
* **Corresponding author:** j.zhao@zju.edu.cn

Abstract

This study investigates the potential of Large Language Models (LLMs) for reconstructing and constructing the physical world solely based on textual knowledge. It explores the impact of model performance on spatial understanding abilities. To enhance the comprehension of geometric and spatial relationships in the complex physical world, the study introduces a set of geometric conventions and develops a workflow based on multi-layer graphs and multi-agent system frameworks. It examines how LLMs achieve multi-step and multi-objective geometric inference in a spatial environment using multi-layer graphs under unified geometric conventions. Additionally, the study employs a genetic algorithm, inspired by large-scale model knowledge, to solve geometric constraint problems. In summary, this work innovatively explores the feasibility of using text-based LLMs as physical world builders and designs a workflow to enhance their capabilities.

1 Introduction

LLMs acquire extensive world knowledge embedded in textual data through pre-training. This raises an intriguing question: can LLMs reconstruct and simulate the physical world using this textual knowledge? The physical world, characterized by complex geometric and physical constraints, can be abstracted into fundamental geometric shapes. Utilizing a custom-designed engine, we simplify the 3D world's geometric content into basic cube combinations. This work pioneers the exploration of text-only LLMs as potential builders of the physical world, leveraging their pre-trained knowledge to understand and generate 3D spatial representations purely from textual descriptions.

Some preliminary work on world-building has explored constructing 3D worlds at the image level. Techniques like 3D-VAE-GAN (Wu et al., 2016) and Pix2Vox (Xie et al., 2019) combine Variational Autoencoders (VAEs) (Kingma and Welling, 2013) and Generative Adversarial Networks (GANs) (Goodfellow et al., 2020) to generate high-quality 3D models with precise shape and pose control. AtlasNet (Groueix et al., 2018) approximates 3D surfaces by learning a set of 2D textures, effectively handling irregular topologies. Despite their impressive quality, these models struggle with simulating complex physical interactions and maintaining spatial consistency due to intricate and dynamic geometric constraints(Li et al., 2024).

Some methods rely on high-precision geometric libraries or external knowledge bases for human-level prior knowledge. For instance, Sun et al. (2023) and Zhou et al. (2024) use LLMs to generate 3D scene images by calling Blender APIs based on user requirements. Wu et al. (2024) proposes combining external knowledge bases to generate 3D scenes from sketches. However, these methods heavily depend on external libraries and interfaces, which lack flexibility and face challenges like resource maintenance, copyright disputes, and network security issues(Gao et al., 2014).

We explored how to leverage LLM pre-training knowledge to autonomously guide complex geometric constraints. Our evaluation compared the spatial construction and geometric relationship understanding abilities of GPT-3.5-turbo and GPT-4, revealing that GPT-4 excels in spatial construction tasks due to its superior performance. we also introduced an innovative multi-agent approach for 3D scene construction, establishing geometric conventions at three levels (center, axis, and surface) to standardize the spatial relationships of 3D objects as understood by LLMs. This multi-level graph-driven approach enhances the spatial understanding and reasoning capabilities of LLMs. The workflow ensures information consistency and uniformity, mitigating data silos and redundancy issues, while enabling LLMs to explore their ability to understand geometric relationships of physical world.

Proceedings of the 1st Workshop on Customizable NLP: Progress and Challenges in Customizing NLP for a Domain, Application, Group, or Individual (CustomNLP4U), pages 1–11
November 16, 2024 ©2024 Association for Computational Linguistics

2 Related Work

2.1 Generation Based On 3D Graphics

The application of GANs and VAEs in 3D scene generation has made notable progress in recent years. Chan et al. (2022) provides a method which can synthesize high-resolution, multi-view consistent images in real-time and also generate high-quality 3D geometry. Xie et al. (2019) proposes a context-aware convolutional neural network to reconstruct 3D voxel models from single and multi-view images. This method uses GANs to enhance the detail and structural accuracy of the generated 3D models. Wu et al. (2016) combines GAN for generating and controlling 3D objects, producing high-quality 3D models with shape control. Groueix et al. (2018) introduces a 3D surface generation method by learning a collection of 2D maps to approximate 3D surfaces, handling irregular topologies.Besides, Tang et al. (2024) find a method to use 2D diffusion model which can further control the generated content and inject reference-view information for unseen views.

These works typically offer high quality and realism, creativity, and diversity in generated content. However, they also face challenges such as high data dependency, complexity, and computational intensity.Moreover, such work often overlooks the complex geometric relationships between objects in the physical world.

2.2 Generation Based On External Libraries

The quality and availability of numerous 3D models have significantly improved. Tang et al. (2024) provide a large amount of 3D materials. And Zhou et al. (2018) provide an open-source library that supports rapid development of software for processing 3D data.It benefits research that utilizes LLMs to invoke open-source models and achieve scene graph construction. Sun et al. (2023), based on a multi-agent system, call the Blender interface to generate 3D scene images according to user requirements. SceneX (Zhou et al., 2024) employs LLMs to drive procedural modeling, utilizing Blender APIs and a vast array of procedural assets. Wu et al. (2024) offer an approach that combines user sketches with external knowledge, progressively generating 3D scenes through a scene diffusion model. Their work demonstrates how these agents can leverage external tools and model libraries to automate the construction and understanding of scene graphs.

Utilizing existing model libraries offers significant advantages in terms of efficiency, scalability, and flexibility in scene generation. However, due to the heavy reliance on external libraries and external materials, the work in question exhibits inconsistent material quality, poses high maintenance complexity, demonstrates insufficient flexibility, and involves copyright challenges.

3 Method

3.1 Graph Runs Through the Entire Workflow

Multi-agent systems have demonstrated effective performance in segmenting complex problems into numerous sub-problems and resolving them (Grossi et al., 2023), aligning with the step-by-step decomposition of three-dimensional scene concepts and the meticulous refinement of generated content at each stage in this work. And implementing information alignment between proxy groups is a huge challenge(Han et al., 2024). Inspired by Qi et al. (2023) and Ranasinghe et al. (2024), we choose graph database as the medium. In our work, we use GPT-4 (OpenAI, 2023b) as the basis for the agent and Neo4j (Neo4j, 2023) database to store our graph. By employing a graph database to capture spatial information and representing shapes and their geometric relationships with nodes and edges, complex geometric relationships can be managed flexibly. The graph database records scene information, providing a comprehensive overview of user objectives and scene graphs throughout the workflow. This ensures that generated scenes align with predefined spatial constraints and design specifications by integrating relational processing with large model generation capabilities, offering a flexible and efficient solution for managing complex spatial data and scene generation.

3.1.1 Scenery Designer

Graph databases can stably and comprehensively record object information in existing scenes, thereby reducing scene graph generation errors caused by illusions or memory problems in LLMs, such as reconstructing existing objects or using non-existent objects as reference points. By providing detailed scene information to LLMs, the graphics database helps to develop plans that are consistent

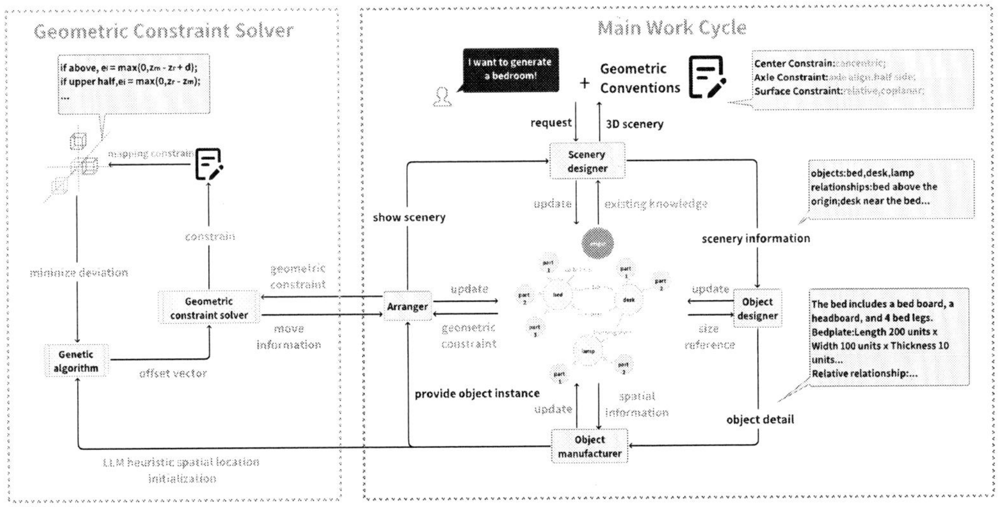

Figure 1: The entire workflow is based on geometric conventions and relies on multiple agents to carry out 3D scene construction work around the graph. The user's demand information will be refined layer by layer by designers and used to generate object instances. Finally, the arranger will use the mapping from geometric constraints to deviations and a genetic algorithm solver to determine the correct placement position of the object.

with the given semantics and do not conflict with the current scene graph. Based on this, the scene designer will mobilize their internal world knowledge to design a scene that is semantically consistent with the input, including the main objects in the scene and the spatial geometric relationships between objects.

3.1.2 Object Designer

After the scene planning is completed, the object designer needs to design objects with appropriate structure and size based on the existing reference objects in the scene. On the one hand, image databases are needed to provide background information, and on the other hand, LLMs themselves require a certain level of common sense knowledge and reasoning ability to lay a more detailed foundation for the next step of object creation.

3.1.3 Object Manufacturer

After completing the object design phase, we proceed to the construction phase. At this stage, LLMs require a thorough understanding of the descriptive statements used by object designers, particularly those describing the interrelationships between internal modules of the object. This ensures alignment between the generated objects and their descriptive statements. We have observed that models with weaker performance, such as the GPT-3.5 turbo(OpenAI, 2023a), often have poor performance in this step, regardless of the level of detail provided by the designer. Additionally, to minimize the risk of spatial divergence when using genetic algorithms in later permutation calculations, the initial position of the object should be proximate to its main reference object, typically adhering to their relative spatial relationships. Here, a graphical database becomes crucial, as it offers detailed information about the size and position of reference objects, as well as their approximate relative relationships. This information is essential to guide LLMs in utilizing their internal knowledge effectively.

3.1.4 Arranger

Following the construction of the object, further optimization of its spatial position is required to meet specific spatial requirements, such as those related to smaller particle sizes. Initially, the relationship information between the newly constructed object and the reference object must be extracted from the graph database. This information is then used to perform further inference and to supplement any missing spatial constraints. Based on these completed spatial constraints, the appropriate constraint equations can be selected for positional optimization.

The graph database provides a comprehensive understanding of global scene information at each layer of the workflow and provides necessary information for each layer to complete tasks. It can efficiently manage complex relationships and dependencies, enabling each level to accurately locate and process relevant information in complex scenarios.

3.2 Geometric Conventions

Inspired by the work of Hedau (2011) and Klein (1998), we recognize that clearly and systematically representing the relative positions of objects in space is beneficial for enhancing the spatial reasoning capabilities of LLMs. Consequently, we have devised a spatial convention that encompasses three levels of constraint relationships: geometric center, axis, and surface, with varying degrees of constraint strength.By integrating different spatial conventions, we can flexibly and accurately determine the positions of objects within a reasonable range. This set of spatial conventions is integral to our entire workflow. Through the implementation of a unified spatial convention system, we ensure consistency and standardization throughout the workflow.

An example of the spatial convention we designed is as follows:

3.2.1 Geometric Center Relationship Constrain

- Concentric relationship:

$$x_m^c = x_r^c, \quad y_m^c = y_r^c \quad \text{and} \quad z_m^c = z_r^c \quad (1)$$

3.2.2 Axle Relationship Constraint

- x align:

$$x_m^c = x_r^c \quad (2)$$

- front half:

$$x_{\mathrm{r}}^c > x_{\mathrm{m}}^c \quad (3)$$

3.2.3 Surface Relationship Constraint

- front:

$$x_r^b - x_m^f = d \quad (4)$$

- coplanar front:

$$x_r^t = x_m^t \quad (5)$$

To avoid misunderstandings, we briefly declare the following symbols:

- x, y and z represent the projections of the corresponding parts of the object on that axis
- In superscripts, f, b and t, etc. respectively represent the corresponding surfaces of the object, such as the front, back/bottom, and top surfaces. And c represents the geometric center.
- In the subscript, r and m represent the reference object and the object to be moved, respectively. And d stands for distance.

3.3 Graph Driven LLM Spatial Inference

The final layer of the workflow is called the arranger, responsible for the spatial arrangement of generated objects in the scene. Wei et al. (2024)discussed Detailed introduction on how to construct a knowledge graph of geographic spatial data, as well as how to express and infer spatial relationships. Inspired by this, this work maps the relative positional relationships of objects to a graphics database. By setting strong and weak reference objects, we provide different levels of constraints for the object to be moved. With the continuous enrichment of graphic information, our framework will provide increasingly accurate spatial constraints. After determining the spatial constraints, the LLM inspired genetic algorithm is used to solve the spatial constraints, which is used to update the spatial position of the object to be moved and dynamically update the graphic data. This layer utilizes a graphical database to store entities and their spatial relationships, establishing and updating spatial constraints at the granularity of objects. The process specifically includes several steps:

3.3.1 Graph Database Interaction

Arranger interacts with graphical databases to generate more detailed relationship information and select the correct constraint equation according to it. Based on the provided rough relationship pairs, the arranger select the strong reference object which will provides 1 to 3 constrains from the graph database and return the weak reference objects which provides 0 to 2 constrains and be associated with the strong reference object. In this way, the computational complexity of constraints can be reduced. The LLM agent will obtain various types of information about the reference object, including its dimensions and spatial positions. It will then infer and add new spatial constraints within the basic spatial constraint framework and select the correct constraint equation for genetic algorithm calculation of accurate spatial positioning.

3.3.2 Genetic Algorithm for Solving Geometric Relationships

Given the global optimization capabilities of the genetic algorithm and its effective use with heuristic initialization, we ultimately opted for the genetic algorithm to address the spatial constraints. When LLM completes spatial constraints and selects the correct geometric equation, the permutator pass the parameters to the genetic algorithm(Shapiro, 1999) solver to optimize the geometric relationships and further adjust and update the spatial position of the objects initialized by LLM.

Each object is composed of multiple blocks, with each block represented by its centroid coordinates and three-dimensional dimensions. The specific representation is as follows:

Single block representation:

$$b_i = \{c_i, d_{i1}, d_{i2}, d_{i3}\}$$

where $c_i = (x_i, y_i, z_i)$ is the centroid coordinates, and d_{i1}, d_{i2}, d_{i3} represent the length, width, and height, respectively.

Object representation:

$$O_i = \{b_{i1}, b_{i2}, \ldots, b_{in}\}$$

where O_i represents an object composed of multiple blocks b_{ij}. In addition, the spatial information of objects can also be represented as follows:

$$O_i = \{C_i, D_{i1}, D_{i2}, D_{i3}\}$$

where C_i is the centroid coordinates, and D_{i1}, D_{i2}, D_{i3} represent the length, width, and height of O_i respectively.

We define various types of spatial constraints to describe the relative spatial relationships between objects. Below are examples of above, and upper half:

$$\text{above} : z_m^b \geq z_r^t + d$$

$$\text{upper half} : z_m^c \geq z_r^c$$

To generate appropriate constraint equations, we abstract the reference object as a block and generate movable object pairs with reference part relationships for each object. Then, based on the generated relationship pairs, we generate appropriate constraint equations and pass them to the genetic algorithm for solution.

Assume we have multiple reference objects R_k and a movable object M, each pair $(R_k, \text{relation}, M)$ can be represented as a set of constraint formations:

$$e_i = \begin{cases} \max\left(0, z_m^c - z_r^c + d\right), \text{if above} \\ \max\left(0, z_r^c - z_m^c\right), \text{if upper half} \end{cases} \tag{6}$$

The optimization goal is to minimize the total error:

$$\min E = \min \sum_{i=1}^{N} e_i^2$$

To determine effective motion vectors, we employed a genetic algorithm inspired by LLM initialization. Objects are generated at specific positions based on global and reference content, partially fulfilling constraint requirements. The algorithm's initialization is then refined based on the size of both the reference object and the object to be moved, enhancing the optimization process. Each genome consists of three XYZ coordinates representing motion vectors. The total error E of each individual is calculated to assess fitness, with top-performing individuals selected for crossover and mutation. During crossover, parent DNA combines to produce new offspring, and mutations make fine adjustments to coordinates. This process iterates until a set number of generations or error convergence is achieved, gradually approaching the optimal solution.

4 Experiment

In this section, we will discuss the factors affecting the quality of the 3D scene graph generated by the LLM from two aspects. The first influencing factor is the model's ability. We test the generation performance of the base models GPT-3.5-Turbo and GPT-4 without using the framework. The second influencing factor is the degree of integration with the work framework. We set up three sets of experiments to explore the complete use of the work framework, including ablation experiments to analyze the impact of removing certain components.

4.1 Model Performance Impact

Our experiment found a strong correlation between LLM performance and spatial understanding. Evaluating GPT-3.5-Turbo and GPT-4-0125 on object and scene generation tasks, we observed that GPT-3.5 had poor spatial comprehension and simplistic outputs. In contrast, GPT-4 showed improved spatial concepts and multi-object scene generation but still used simple blocks with limited detail.

4.1.1 Object Generation

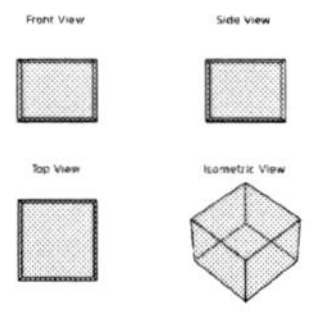

(a) Chair(3.5)

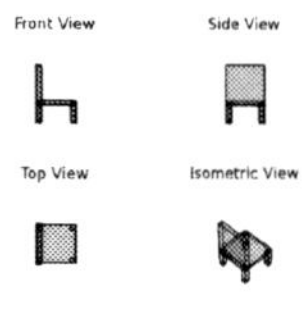

(b) Chair(4)

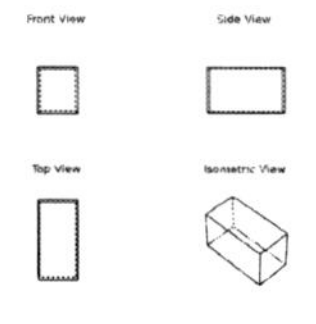

(c) Table(3.5)

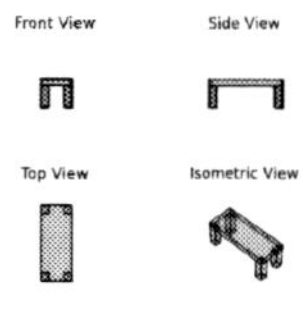

(d) Tabel(4)

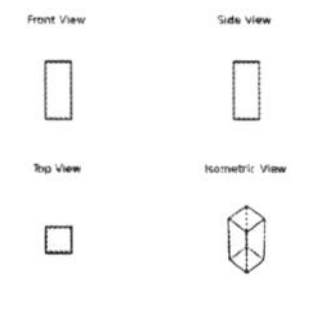

(e) Lamp(3.5)

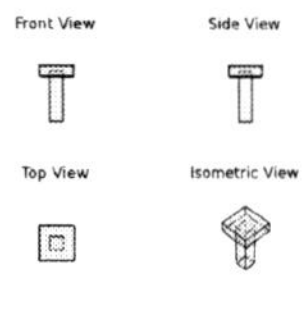

(f) Lamp(4)

Figure 2: GPT-4 produces complex structures and details and achieves better semantic alignment than GPT-3.5.

4.1.2 Scenery Generation

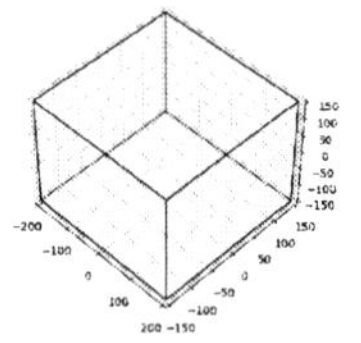

(a) Bedroom(3.5)

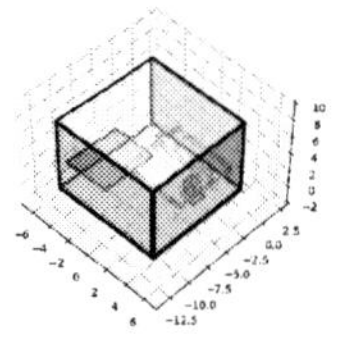

(b) Bedroom(4)

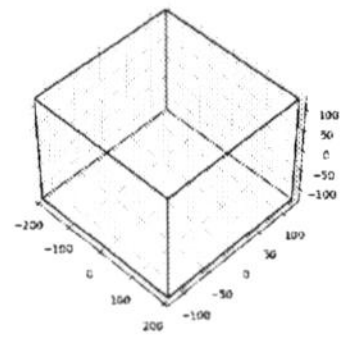

(c) Kitchen(3.5)

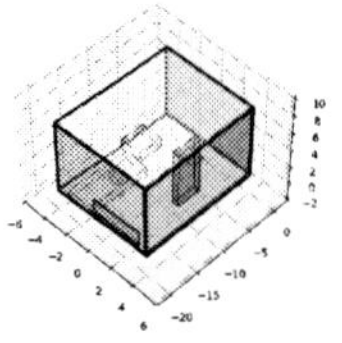

(d) Kitchen(4)

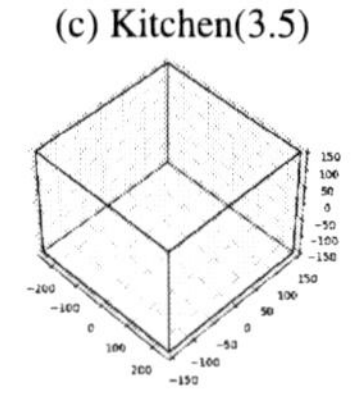

(e) Living(3.5)

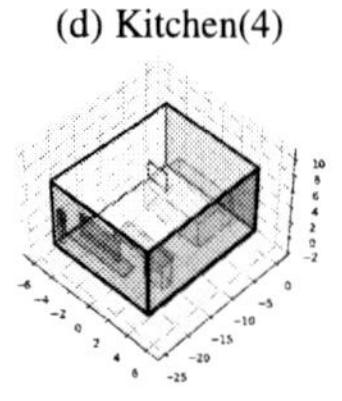

(f) Living(4)

Figure 3: GPT-4 shows better spatial comprehension and multi-object scene generation than GPT-3.5, but still uses simple blocks with limited detail.

4.2 Analysis And Comparison

Metric: We choose CLIP (Radford et al., 2021)to calculate the similarity between the generated object and scene images and text, in order to evaluate the alignment between the text and the generated content. In addition, during the experimental process, there is often a large amount of overlap or object isolation in the generated failed scene images. Therefore, for the scene, we additionally introduced overlap score and isolation score, corresponding to the proportion of overlapping volume to the total volume of all objects and the proportion of isolated blocks to the total block, respectively.

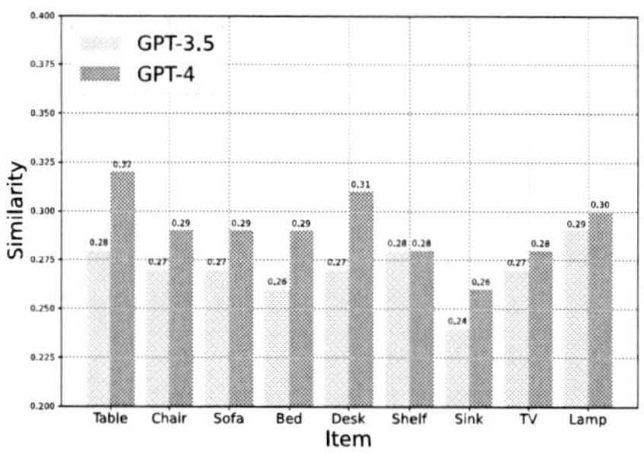

Figure 4: In object level generation tasks, the clip index of agents based on GPT-4 is generally better than ones based on GPT-3.5.

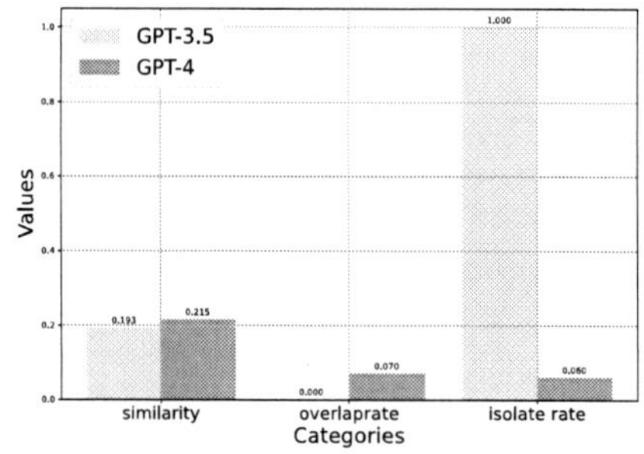

Figure 5: In the scenario level generation task, the clip index of GPT-4 group is **10.1%** higher than that of GPT-3.5 group, and its isolation rate is much better than that of GPT-3.5 group.

4.3 Framework Impact

Baseline Methods: The baseline we have chosen is a single agent without designed agents or graph driven methods, which showed in Figure 3. The base model of each agent is gpt-4-0125 preview with default temperature.

4.3.1 Ablation Study

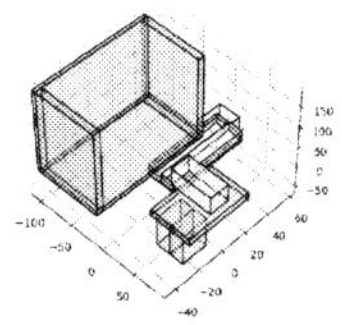

(a) Bathroom(ablation)

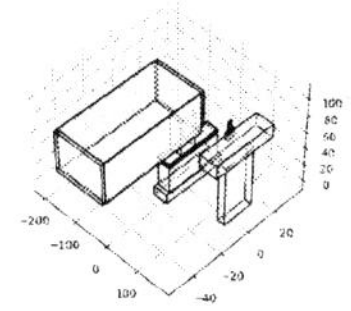

(b) Bathroom

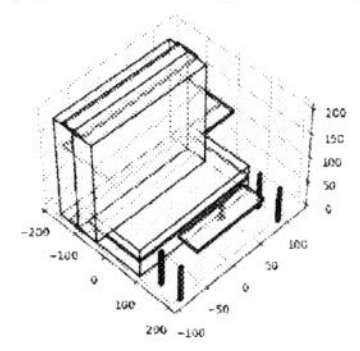

(c) Bedroom (ablation)

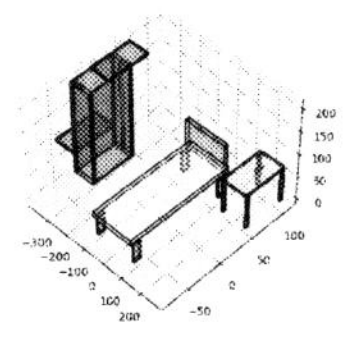

(d) Bedroom

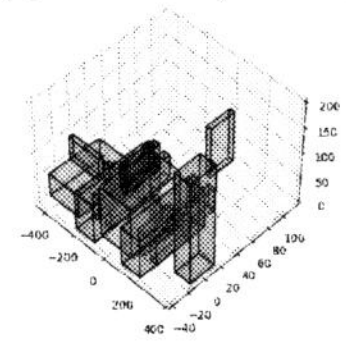

(e) Cafe (ablation)

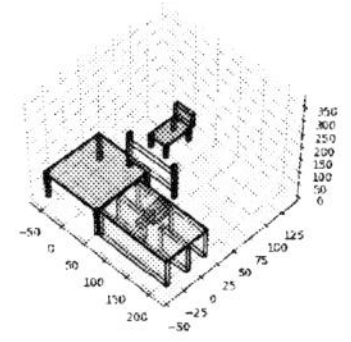

(f) Cafe

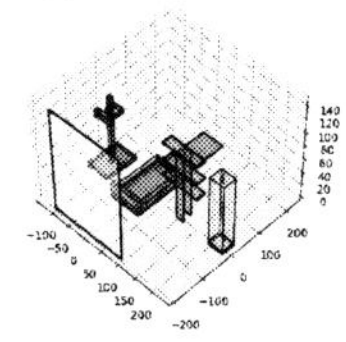

(g) Gym (ablation)

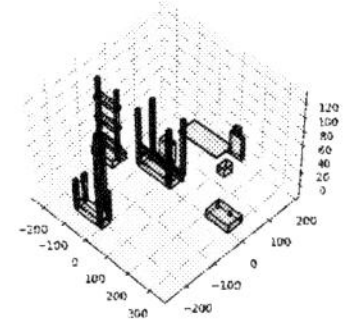

(h) Gym

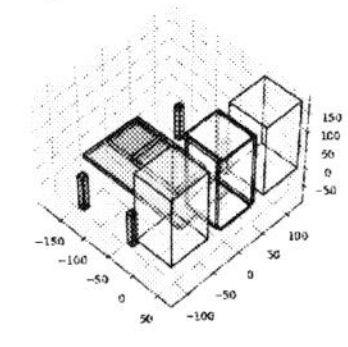

(i) Kitchen (ablation)

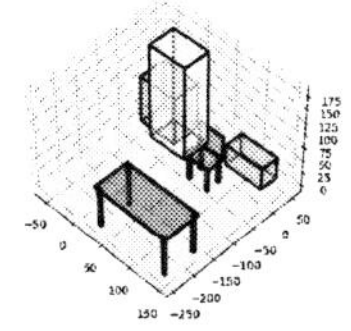

(j) Kitchen

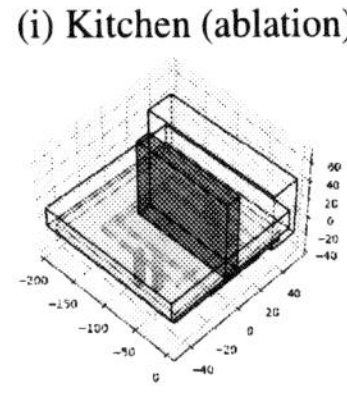

(k) Living (ablation)

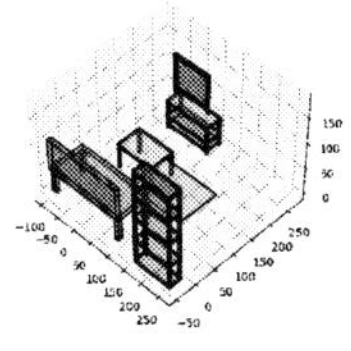

(l) Living

Figure 6: The ablation group showed detailed structures, but lacked reasonable spatial planning The non-ablated group can not only represent details of objects but also have a reasonable plan for the placement of objects.

In the ablation group experiment, we eliminated the interaction process between the graphical database and the workflow, while retaining the workflow of multi-agent collaboration. The non ablated group completely retained the graph reasoning framework.

4.4 Analysis And Comparison

The schematic diagram illustrates the performance of LLM scene graph generation in three modes. Images produced by the baseline method neglect object details but exhibit some overall spatial planning capability. The ablation group attempts to emphasize object details but lacks spatial planning, leading to overcrowded scenes. The non-ablated group excels in both object details and proper object placement.

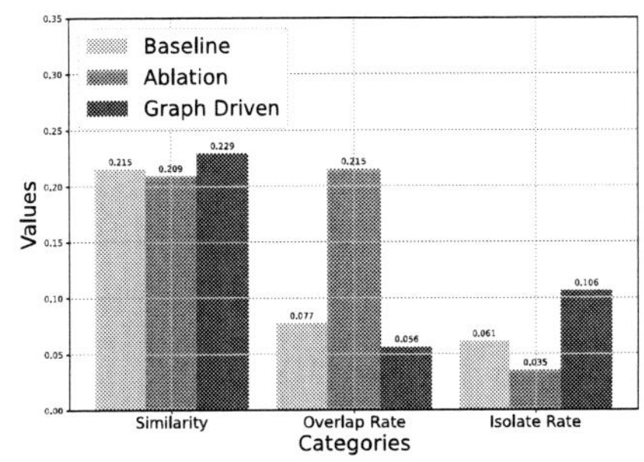

Figure 7: Comparison of metrics across different work modes indicates the following information: using graph driven workflows improves the similarity between images and text, with a decrease in spatial overlap rate but an increase in isolation rate

According to the above Figure 7, we found that in terms of clip similarity, the graph driven group performed better than both the baseline and ablation groups, and was generally better than both in a single task, with mean values **6.3%** and **8.7%** higher than the baseline and ablation groups, respectively. In terms of object overlap rate, it is lower than both, but in terms of isolation rate, it is higher than both.

5 Conclusion And Limitation

Our research provides an intuitive demonstration of the spatial understanding capabilities of LLMs and quantitatively evaluates the spatial comprehension of two distinct models. Additionally, we enhance the geometric understanding and spatial reasoning abilities of LLMs in complex physical environments by implementing well-defined geometric conventions and a graph-driven framework.

This study is conducted using a custom-developed sandbox platform, designed to present the spatial concepts understood by LLMs in a more intuitive and flexible manner. However, due to resource constraints, we are unable to test higher-performing models, which limits our ability to fully showcase the framework's potential in improving the spatial understanding of LLMs.

References

Eric R. Chan, Connor Z. Lin, Matthew A. Chan, Koki Nagano, Boxiao Pan, Shalini De Mello, Orazio Gallo, Leonidas J. Guibas, Jonathan Tremblay, Sameh Khamis, et al. 2022. Efficient geometry-aware 3d generative adversarial networks. In *Proceedings of the IEEE/CVF Conference on Computer Vision and Pattern Recognition*, pages 16123–16133.

Lin Gao, Yan-Pei Cao, Yu-Kun Lai, Hao-Zhi Huang, Leif Kobbelt, and Shi-Min Hu. 2014. Active exploration of large 3d model repositories. *IEEE transactions on visualization and computer graphics*, 21(12):1390–1402.

Ian Goodfellow, Jean Pouget-Abadie, Mehdi Mirza, Bing Xu, David Warde-Farley, Sherjil Ozair, Aaron Courville, and Yoshua Bengio. 2020. Generative adversarial networks. *Communications of the ACM*, 63(11):139–144.

Davide Grossi, Ariel Rosenfeld, and Nimrod Talmon. 2023. Advances in multi-agent systems research: Eumas 2021 extended selected papers. *SN Computer Science*, 4(5):587.

Thibault Groueix, Matthew Fisher, Vladimir G. Kim, Bryan C. Russell, and Mathieu Aubry. 2018. A papier-mâché approach to learning 3d surface generation. In *Proceedings of the IEEE Conference on Computer Vision and Pattern Recognition*, pages 216–224.

Shanshan Han, Qifan Zhang, Yuhang Yao, Weizhao Jin, Zhaozhuo Xu, and Chaoyang He. 2024. Llm multi-agent systems: Challenges and open problems.

Varsha Chandrashekhar Hedau. 2011. *3D spatial layout and geometric constraints for scene understanding*. University of Illinois at Urbana-Champaign.

Diederik P Kingma and Max Welling. 2013. Auto-encoding variational bayes. *arXiv preprint arXiv:1312.6114*.

Rüdiger Klein. 1998. The role of constraints in geometric modelling. In *Geometric Constraint Solving and Applications*, pages 3–23. Springer.

Xiaoyu Li, Qi Zhang, Di Kang, Weihao Cheng, Yiming Gao, Jingbo Zhang, Zhihao Liang, Jing Liao, Yan-Pei Cao, and Ying Shan. 2024. Advances in 3d generation: A survey. *arXiv preprint arXiv:2401.17807*.

Inc. Neo4j. 2023. *Neo4j Documentation*.

OpenAI. 2023a. Gpt-3.5 turbo.

OpenAI. 2023b. Gpt-4 technical report. *OpenAI*.

Jianzhong Qi, Zuqing Li, and Egemen Tanin. 2023. Maasdb: Spatial databases in the era of large language models (vision paper). In *Proceedings of the 31st ACM International Conference on Advances in Geographic Information Systems*, SIGSPATIAL '23. ACM.

Alec Radford, Jong Wook Kim, Chris Hallacy, Aditya Ramesh, Gabriel Goh, Sandhini Agarwal, Girish Sastry, Amanda Askell, Pamela Mishkin, Jack Clark, et al. 2021. Learning transferable visual models from natural language supervision. In *International Conference on Machine Learning*, pages 8748–8763. PMLR.

Kanchana Ranasinghe, Satya Narayan Shukla, Omid Poursaeed, Michael S. Ryoo, and Tsung-Yu Lin. 2024. Learning to localize objects improves spatial reasoning in visual-llms.

Jonathan Shapiro. 1999. Genetic algorithms in machine learning. In *Advanced Course on Artificial Intelligence*, pages 146–168. Springer.

Chunyi Sun, Junlin Han, Weijian Deng, Xinlong Wang, Zishan Qin, and Stephen Gould. 2023. 3d-gpt: Procedural 3d modeling with large language models. *arXiv preprint arXiv:2310.12945*.

Zhenyu Tang, Junwu Zhang, Xinhua Cheng, Wangbo Yu, Chaoran Feng, Yatian Pang, Bin Lin, and Li Yuan. 2024. Cycle3d: High-quality and consistent image-to-3d generation via generation-reconstruction cycle.

Bo Wei, Xi Guo, Xiaodi Li, Ziyan Wu, Jing Zhao, and Qiping Zou. 2024. Construct and query a fine-grained geospatial knowledge graph. *Data Science and Engineering*, 9(2):152–176.

Jiajun Wu, Chengkai Zhang, Tianfan Xue, Bill Freeman, and Josh Tenenbaum. 2016. Learning a probabilistic latent space of object shapes via 3d generative-adversarial modeling. *Advances in Neural Information Processing Systems*, 29.

Zijie Wu, Mingtao Feng, Yaonan Wang, He Xie, Weisheng Dong, Bo Miao, and Ajmal Mian. 2024. External knowledge enhanced 3d scene generation from sketch. *arXiv preprint arXiv:2403.14121*.

Haozhe Xie, Hongxun Yao, Xiaoshuai Sun, Shangchen Zhou, and Shengping Zhang. 2019. Pix2vox: Context-aware 3d reconstruction from single and multi-view images. In *Proceedings of the IEEE/CVF International Conference on Computer Vision*, pages 2690–2698.

Mengqi Zhou, Jun Hou, Chuanchen Luo, Yuxi Wang, Zhaoxiang Zhang, and Junran Peng. 2024. Scenex: Procedural controllable large-scale scene generation via large-language models. *arXiv preprint arXiv:2403.15698*.

Qian-Yi Zhou, Jaesik Park, and Vladlen Koltun. 2018. Open3d: A modern library for 3d data processing.

A Geometric conventions

A.1 Geometric Center Relationship Constrain

1. **concentric**: Concentric.
   - Calculation: The Euclidean distance between the centers of the two objects.

A.2 Axle Relationship Constraint

A.2.1 Align Relationship

1. **x aligned**: X-aligned.
   - Calculation: The alignment error in the x direction between the two objects.
2. **y aligned**: Y-aligned.
   - Calculation: The alignment error in the y direction between the two objects.
3. **z aligned**: Z-aligned.
   - Calculation: The alignment error in the z direction between the two objects.

A.2.2 Half Side Relationship

1. **left half**: Left half.
   - Determine if the `ref center` object is in the left half of the `mov center` object.
2. **right half**: Right half.
   - Determine if the `ref center` object is in the right half of the `mov center` object.
3. **upper half**: Upper half.
   - Determine if the `ref center` object is in the upper half of the `mov center` object.
4. **lower half**: Lower half.
   - Determine if the `ref center` object is in the lower half of the `mov center` object.
5. **front half**: Front half.
   - Determine if the `ref center` object is in the front half of the `mov center` object.
6. **back half**: Back half.
   - Determine if the `ref center` object is in the back half of the `mov center` object.

A.3 Surface Relationship Constraint

A.3.1 Relative Positioning Relationship

1. **left**: `mov center` object is to the left of the `ref center` object.
   - Calculation: The distance between the left edge of the `ref center` object and the right edge of the `mov center` object minus the given `distance`.
2. **right**: `mov center` object is to the right of the `ref center` object.
   - Calculation: The distance between the left edge of the `mov center` object and the right edge of the `ref center` object minus the given `distance`.
3. **above**: `mov center` object is above the `ref center` object.
   - Calculation: The distance between the bottom edge of the `mov center` object and the top edge of the `ref center` object minus the given `distance`.
4. **below**: `mov center` object is below the `ref center` object.
   - Calculation: The distance between the bottom edge of the `ref center` object and the top edge of the `mov center` object minus the given `distance`.
5. **front**: `mov center` object is in front of the `ref center` object.
   - Calculation: The distance between the back edge of the `mov center` object and the front edge of the `ref center` object minus the given `distance`.
6. **back**: `mov center` object is behind the `ref center` object.
   - Calculation: The distance between the back edge of the `ref center` object and the front edge of the `mov center` object minus the given `distance`.

A.3.2 Coplanar Relationship Constrain

1. **coplanar top**: Coplanar on top.
   - Determine if the top edges of the two objects are coplanar.
2. **coplanar bottom**: Coplanar on the bottom.

- Determine if the bottom edges of the two objects are coplanar.

3. **coplanar left**: Coplanar on the left.
   - Determine if the left edges of the two objects are coplanar.
4. **coplanar right**: Coplanar on the right.
   - Determine if the right edges of the two objects are coplanar.
5. **coplanar front**: Coplanar in front.
   - Determine if the front edges of the two objects are coplanar.
6. **coplanar back**: Coplanar in the back.
   - Determine if the back edges of the two objects are coplanar.

B Objects Generated With Workflow

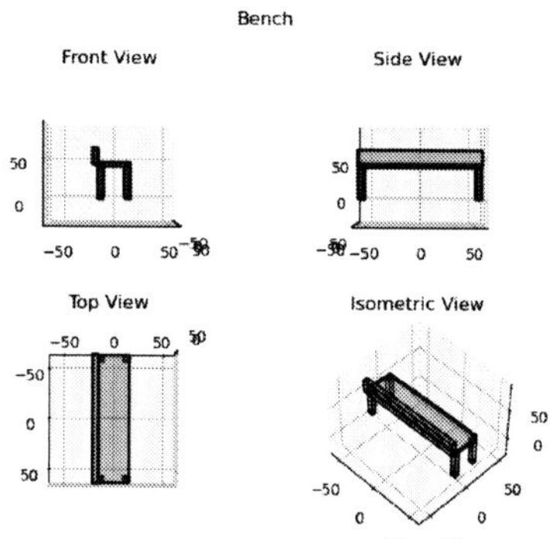

Figure 8: Bench

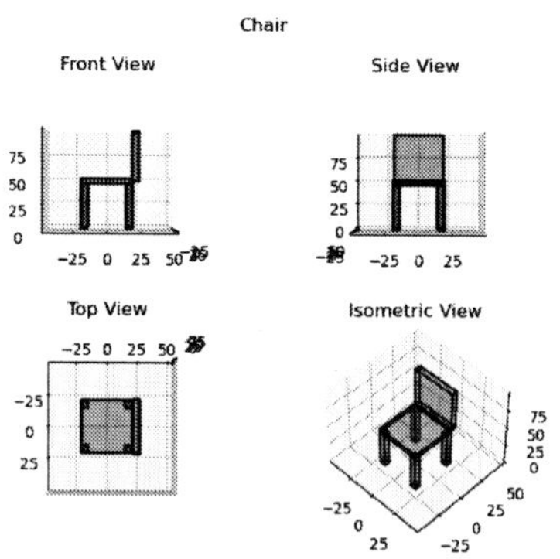

Figure 9: Chair

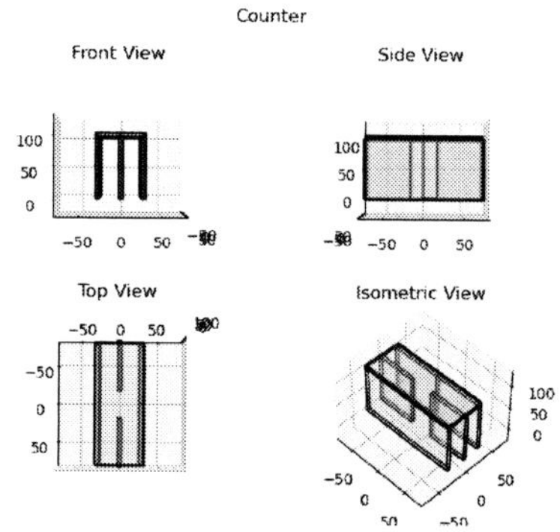

Figure 10: Counter

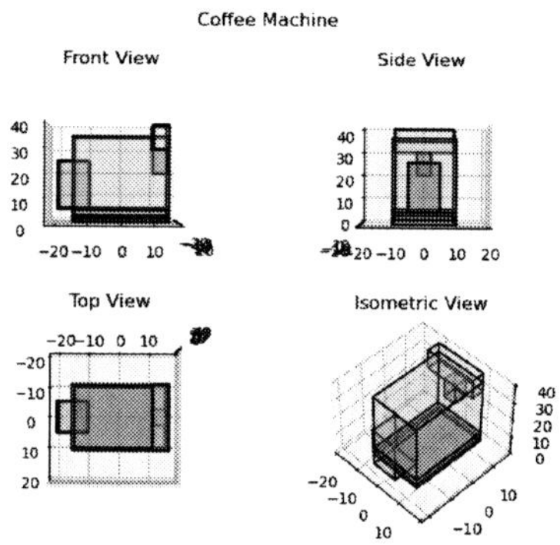

Figure 11: Coffee Machine

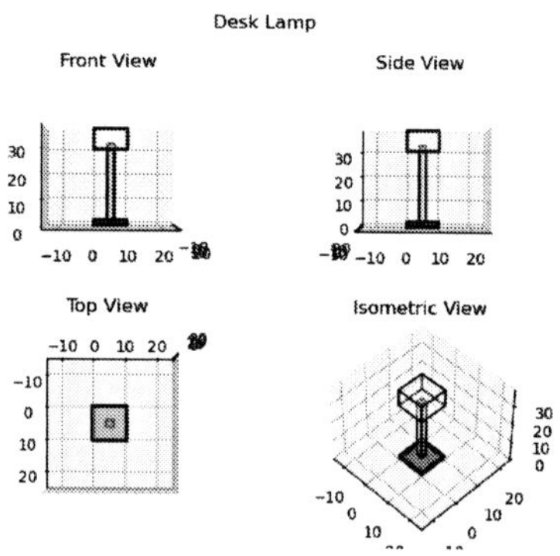

Figure 12: Lamp

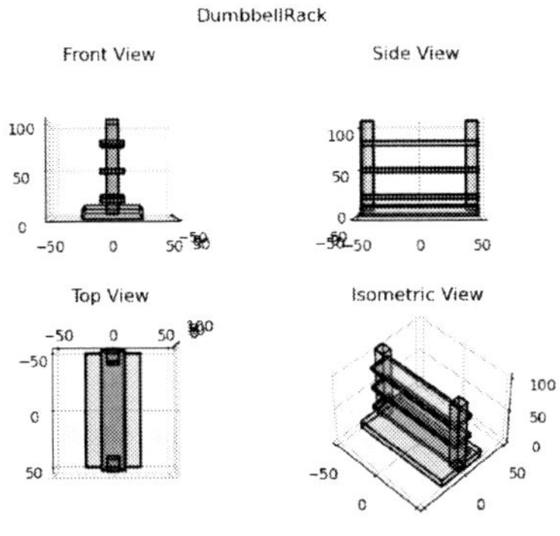

Figure 13: Dumbbell Rack

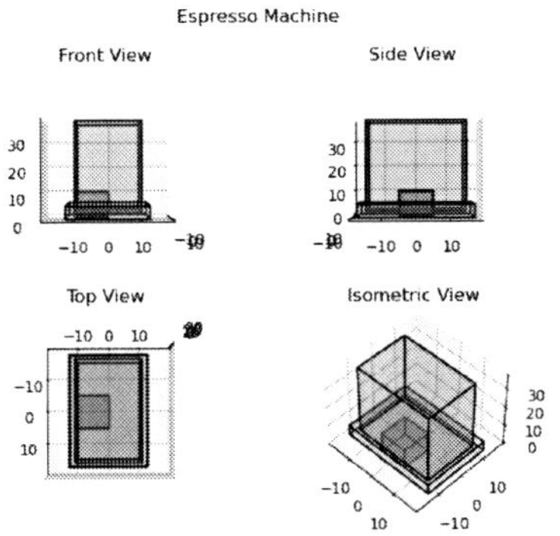

Figure 14: Espresso Machine

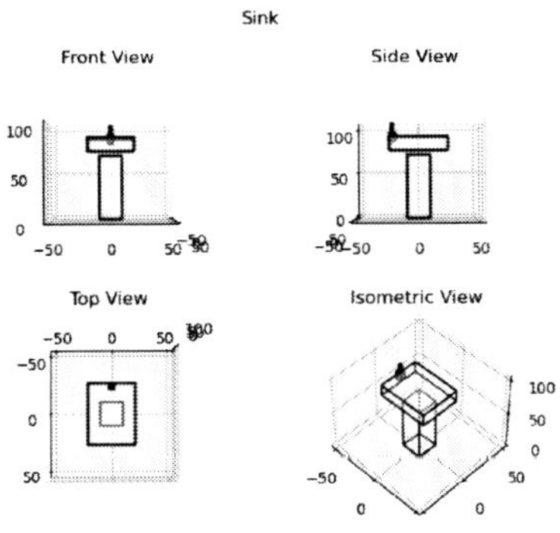

Figure 15: Sink

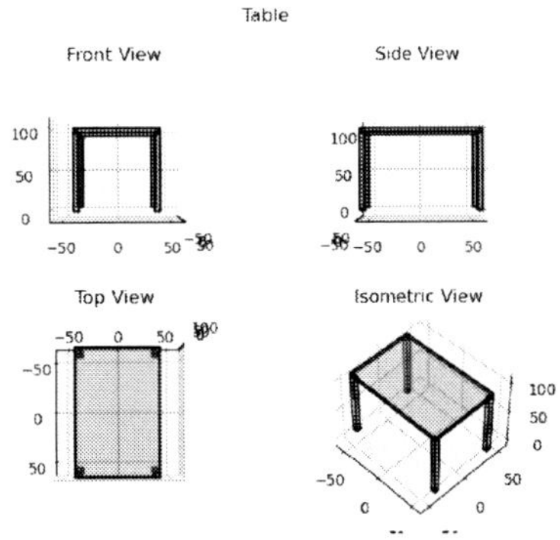

Figure 16: Table

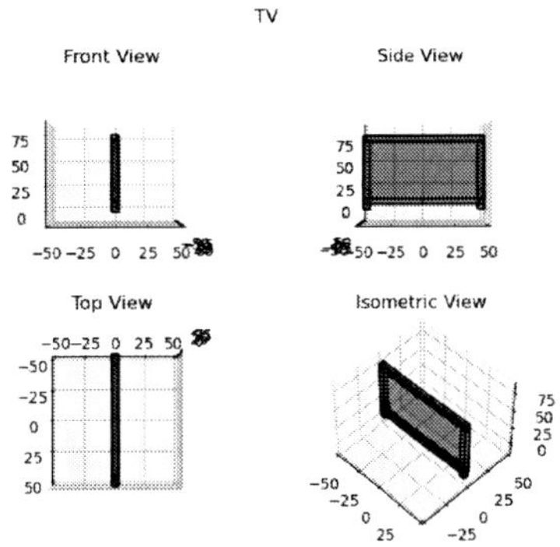

Figure 17: TV

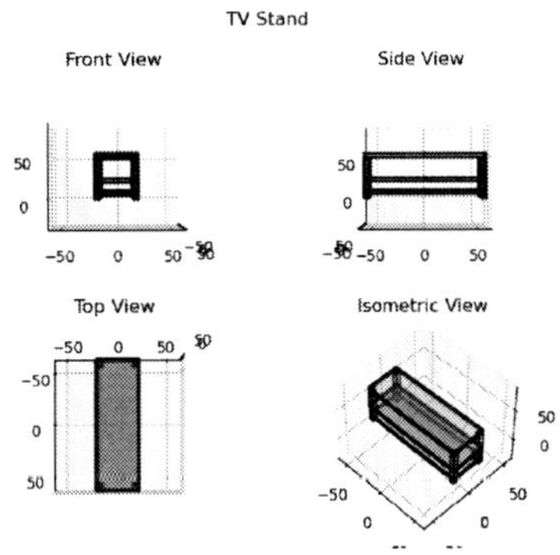

Figure 18: TV Stand

Empowering AAC Users: A Systematic Integration of Personal Narratives with Conversational AI

Sayantan Pal[†], **Souvik Das**[†], **Rohini K. Srihari**[†], **Jeffery Higginbotham**[‡], **Jenna Bizovi**[‡]
State University of New York at Buffalo
[†]Department of Computer Science and Engineering
[‡]Department of Communicative Disorders and Sciences
{spal5, souvikda, rohini, cdsjeff, jbizovi}@buffalo.edu

Abstract

Communication barriers have long posed challenges for users of Alternate and Augmentative Communication (AAC). In AAC, effective conversational aids are not solely about harnessing Artificial Intelligence (AI) capabilities but more about ensuring these technologies resonate deeply with AAC user's unique communication challenges. We aim to bridge the gap between generic outputs and genuine human interactions by integrating advanced Conversational AI with personal narratives. While existing solutions offer generic responses, a considerable gap in tailoring outputs reflecting an AAC user's intent must be addressed. Thus, we propose to create a custom conversational dataset centered on the experiences and words of a primary AAC user to fine-tune advanced language models. Additionally, we employ a Retrieval-Augmented Generation (RAG) method, drawing context from a summarized version of authored content by the AAC user. This combination ensures that responses are contextually relevant and deeply personal. Preliminary evaluations underscore its transformative potential, with automated metrics and human assessments showcasing significantly enhanced response quality.

1 Introduction

Communication is essential for sharing experiences and fostering connections, yet it poses significant challenges for many individuals using AAC (Light and McNaughton, 2012, 2014). According to recent statistics, about 5 million people in the U.S. and 97 million globally are unable to use speech for communication due to conditions like cerebral palsy and ALS (Beukelman and Light, 2020). Augmentative communication technologies (ACTs)(Light and McNaughton, 2013) have been developed to aid these individuals, offering tools like eye tracking and dynamic screen navigation to facilitate communication through text and picture selection. Despite these advancements, traditional AAC solutions(Elsahar et al., 2019) often lack the depth to express an individual's personality fully, and the slow communication rates, typically less than 10 words per minute, can lead to frustration and isolation (Waller, 2019; Beukelman and Mirenda, 2013).

Traditional AAC tools (Baldassarri et al., 2014; Light, 1988; Higginbotham et al., 2007) have been instrumental in enabling communication for many, yet often lack the finesse (Pancholi et al., 2023) needed to capture the user's personal narratives and unique experiences. Recent advancements in AI, deep learning, and language models (Thompson et al., 2004; MacDonald et al., 2021; Ghazvininejad et al., 2018) offer new possibilities for creating personalized conversational aids that adapt to the user's background and evolve with their changing needs. This paper, a collaboration between computer scientists and AAC practitioners, presents an innovative approach that prioritizes personal narratives by merging modern AI's adaptability with individual user stories.

Previous studies (Sennott et al., 2019) prioritized model accuracy over adaptability in AAC systems, focusing on technical aspects rather than individuality; this highlights the need for a new approach that values personal narratives and leverages AI to reflect each user's uniqueness. In this study, we introduced a system that does not merely optimize for speed or vocabulary variety; (1) it seeks to resonate deeply with each AAC user's individuality. (2) By leveraging a conversational dialogue dataset tailored to a specific user and integrating the knowledge from the authored content, we crafted a model that outputs responses deeply rooted in their experiences. Furthermore, (3) our dual methodology—combining the finesse of fine-tuning encoder-decoder models (Kale and Rastogi, 2020) with the grounded knowledge retrieval (Li et al., 2022) of RAG—enriches the response generation process.

Proceedings of the 1st Workshop on Customizable NLP: Progress and Challenges in Customizing NLP for a Domain, Application, Group, or Individual (CustomNLP4U), pages 12–25
November 16, 2024 ©2024 Association for Computational Linguistics

The significant out-performance of our RAG approach, validated through human and automatic evaluations, is crucial as it sets a new benchmark in AAC, emphasizing the importance of making every interaction deeply personal and contextually rich, thereby enriching the lives of AAC users through more meaningful conversations.

2 Related Work

Recent advancements in AAC have leveraged AI to improve communication for those with speech impairments, with applications like Voiceitt's Talkitt (Costanzo et al., 2023) and LIVOX (Neamtu et al., 2019) providing real-time assistance and bridging communication gaps. These innovations reflect a growing awareness of the challenges faced by differently-abled individuals (Meekosha, 2011) and show a shift in AAC research towards AI-powered mobile applications, particularly for ASD children in developing countries (Farzana et al., 2020). This transition from traditional SGD to AI applications indicates a promising direction in enhancing communication abilities for verbally challenged youth.

Google's Project Euphonia[1] uses AI to enhance speech recognition for atypical speech patterns by training ASR models (Tobin and Tomanek, 2022) and developing speech intelligibility classifiers (Venugopalan et al., 2023) on a diverse dataset of disordered speech from conditions like ALS and cerebral palsy. This initiative improves accessibility to voice-activated technologies and tackles the challenge of understanding non-standard speech patterns. Concurrently, Brain-Machine Interfaces (BMI) offers new possibilities in AAC, allowing direct brain-to-computer communication, which could transform interaction for those with severe motor impairments (Lebedev and Nicolelis, 2006).

Research highlights that augmentative communication technologies (ACTs) typically allow communication rates of under 10 words per minute (Beukelman and Light, 2020), with adaptations to improve interaction often leading to misunderstandings (Fulcher-Rood and Higginbotham, 2019). For individuals with severe motor impairments, options like brain-computer interfaces (BCIs) offer text-based communication, though speeds remain below one word per minute (Koester and Arthanat, 2017). In contrast, our work enriches AAC by focusing on the depth and richness of personal narratives, integrating real-life dialogues to enhance conversational AI. This approach aligns with projects like Euphonia and BMI-based systems, aiming to significantly improve communication effectiveness and quality of life for AAC users by merging AI advancements with practical communication needs.

[1]Project Euphonia: `https://sites.research.google/euphonia/about/`

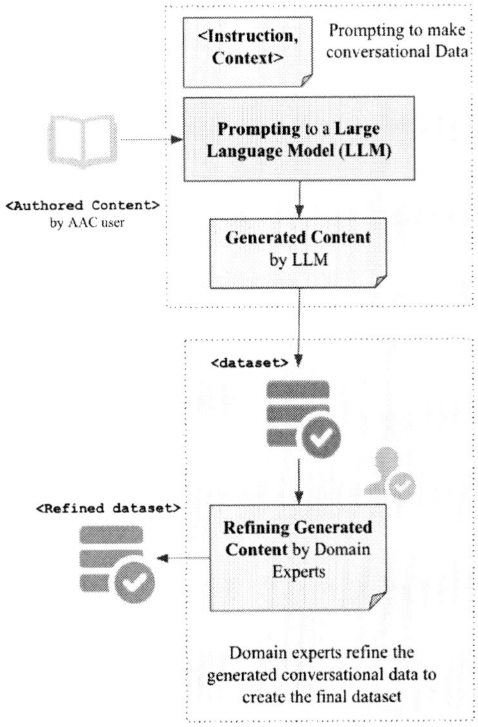

Figure 1: Overview of the Dataset Creation Process

3 Dataset

We construct a personalized dataset to enhance communication for AAC users. The primary motive of this dataset is to facilitate AAC users in sharing their life experiences more effectively and authentically with others. Generic language models often lack the nuanced understanding required for personalized interactions; our dataset plays a pivotal role in fine-tuning pre-trained language models. By doing so, we aim to equip these models with the ability to generate communication that is not only contextually rich but also profoundly personal, mirroring the individual experiences and narratives of AAC users. Information about the AAC User and the study setting can be found in Appendix A, B.

3.1 Prompt-Driven Dataset Generation

To create a dataset that resonates with the personal voice of AAC users, we initiated the process by converting the authored content, denoted by C, into initial conversation drafts. We employed Google Gemini[2] as our large language model (LLM) for this purpose:

$$D_0 = f_{\text{LLM}}(C; P) \quad (1)$$

where f_{LLM} represents the generative function of Google Gemini, applied to the authored content C, with P encapsulating the prompting strategies to generate structured drafts that mirror authentic conversational dynamics. These strategies involve setting specific contexts and instructions that guide the model's output, ensuring relevance and alignment with AAC communication needs. The prompting strategies can be found in Appendix C.

3.2 Dataset Refinement

The initial drafts D_0 are further refined by AAC domain experts to ensure that the dialogues closely align with the user's unique expression needs and remain true to their personal experiences. This refinement process involves several key guidelines:

- **Lexical Adjustments**: Experts incorporate a set of predetermined vocabulary (Beukelman et al., 1998) that maintains the professionalism and clarity required for effective AAC communication.
- **Contextual Relevance**: Each dialogue is assessed for its situational appropriateness, ensuring that the content is relevant to the scenarios typical for AAC users.
- **Authenticity Checks**: Dialogues are reviewed to ensure they reflect the personal tone[3] and style of the AAC user, modifying any content that feels inauthentic or out of character.

The refined dialogues are formalized as:

$$D = g_{\text{AAC}}(D_0, E) \quad (2)$$

[2]Google Gemini is chosen for its advanced conversational capabilities and commitment to data privacy, enabling the generation of dialogues without storing user data.

[3]This includes iterative reviews with AAC users and their close contacts to validate the emotional congruence of the dialogues, along with linguistic analyses to maintain consistency with the user's known speech patterns and vocabulary preferences.

Speaker	Generated Utt.	Expert Refined Utt.
Partner	What are your thoughts on being unique?	How do you feel about your **individuality**?
User	Many don't see my true self, only my disability.	People often overlook my individuality, just see the disability.
Partner	It's hard, but everyone should be recognized for their true self.	That's tough, everyone deserves to be seen for who they truly are.
User	I want you to know that my mind works well.	My **cognitive abilities** are fully intact, you know.
Partner	I understand. Being smart isn't just about physical skills.	I completely get that. Intelligence isn't defined by **physical ability**.
User	Many people do not understand those like me.	There's a vast misunderstanding around people like me.
Partner	Agree, understanding each other is important.	Yes, we should all strive to understand each other better.
User	Finding love is hard with a disability.	It's tough finding love when you're **differently-abled**.

Table 1: A Sample dialogue refined by experts. The highlighted words have been chosen based on the criteria defined in section 3.2. (Utt means utterances)

Topic ID	Top Words	Frequency
9	school, found, year	23
4	[N1], interaction, friend	22
1	home, group, staff	17
5	[N2], share, together	13
7	trip, experience, day	12
6	[N2], visit, bond	9
0	family, parent, home	8
8	life, experience, family	5
2	life, staff, home	4
3	together, wheelchair, visit	4

Table 2: Topics and their top words with frequencies. Any entity that could be identified has been replaced with [N(index)]

where D is the final dataset of refined dialogues, g_{AAC} is the refinement function employed by AAC experts, and E represents expert knowledge and guidelines specific to AAC communication styles.

These transformations ensure that the dataset is both authentic and aligned with the personal communication styles of AAC users. The dataset creation process, inspired by established conversational frameworks like the Daily Dialogue dataset (Li et al., 2017), is depicted in Figure 1. A sample dialogue refined by experts is shown in Table 1. Information about the data creation team is provided in Appendix D.

3.3 Dataset Statistics

Our conversational data comprises 511 dialogues, encompassing 4053 utterances, with an average of approximately 4 turns per dialogue. The average number of utterances per dialogue is 7.93, and the average utterance length is 12.19. In analyzing the content, we identified various topics, as shown in Table 2. The most prevalent words from the top topics were school, found, year, interaction, friend, and home, as derived from our topic analysis. Additionally, in assessing the dialogic nature of our content, we found that questions constituted 62.23% of the utterances, and the remaining were statements.

4 Methodology

4.1 Model Architecture

Our approach employs an encoder-decoder architecture and a Retrieval-Augmented Generation (RAG) system to enhance AAC interactions, using FLAN-T5 (Chung et al., 2022) for generating responses and a retrieval system for contextual relevance. We fine-tune language models (Melis et al., 2017) and integrate the RAG model (Azamfirei et al., 2023) to combine the strengths of fine-tuned models while reducing hallucinations, ensuring responses are grounded in factual correctness and enhancing communication authenticity for AAC users.

4.1.1 Encoder-Decoder based Model Fine-tuning and Post-processing

We initialize our conversational model using the FLAN-T5 architecture, fine-tuned on the custom conversational dataset. Let $\boldsymbol{X}$ represent the input sequence and $\boldsymbol{Y}$ the target sequence in the training dataset. The training objective is to optimize the following loss function:

$$\mathcal{L}(\theta) = - \sum_{(\boldsymbol{X},\boldsymbol{Y})\in\mathcal{D}} \log P(\boldsymbol{Y}|\boldsymbol{X};\theta) \tag{3}$$

where $\mathcal{D}$ is our dataset comprising sequences of conversational data, and θ denotes the parameters of the FLAN-T5 model. Detailed analysis of the fine-tuning parameters θ can be found in Appendix E. Furthermore, we post-processed the FLAN-T5 generated outputs using the allenai/cosmo-xl (Kim et al., 2023) model to adapt to situation-specific descriptions and roles, rendering the responses even more human-like. The prompting strategies to the model can be found in appendix F.

4.1.2 Retrieval-Augmented Generation (RAG) Prompt Fusion Model

The core objective of our methodology was to enhance factual accuracy and prevent hallucinations in generated responses by deeply rooting them in the genuine context derived from the AAC user's experiences. Our approach utilizes a dual-encoder framework in the RAG model to achieve this. The model operates as follows:

- **Input Prompt and Context Retrieval:** Given an input prompt $\boldsymbol{P}$, the retriever system, using ChromaDB (Huber, 2023), extracts the top k most relevant passages $\boldsymbol{C}_k$ from an indexed database. These passages provide the necessary context for generating a response that is both accurate and richly informed by relevant information.

- **Integration of Components:** The generation process integrates multiple components to formulate a comprehensive input for the text generation model. These components include:

  1. Dialogue history ($\boldsymbol{H}$), which captures the flow of conversation up to the current prompt.
  2. The response generated by the FLAN-T5 large model ($\boldsymbol{R}_{\text{FLAN}}$), providing a preliminary reply based on the input prompt.
  3. The top k context passages ($\boldsymbol{C}_k$), ensuring the response is contextually grounded.

  The prompt template for the generation model incorporates these elements along with specific instructions aimed at generating truthful and non-hallucinatory responses. The combined input is represented as $\boldsymbol{I}$:

$$\boldsymbol{I} = \{\boldsymbol{H}, \boldsymbol{R}_{\text{FLAN}}, \boldsymbol{C}_k\} \tag{4}$$

- **Response Generation:** The final response $\boldsymbol{R}$ is generated by the text generation model (GPT-3.5 Turbo) using the aggregated input $\boldsymbol{I}$:

$$\boldsymbol{R} = f_{\text{gen}}(\boldsymbol{I};\phi) \tag{5}$$

  where f_{gen} is the function representing the parameters of this model. Details about these parameters and their optimization can be found in Appendix G.

By formalizing the input and processing stages in the equations above, we provide a clear framework for understanding how each component contributes to the final output, thereby ensuring that the responses are both contextually rich and aligned with the actual data. This approach significantly

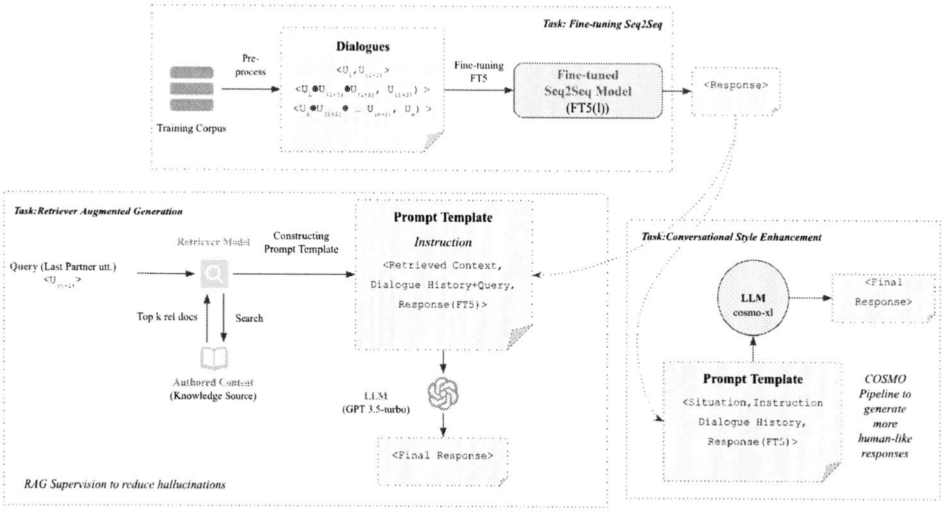

Figure 2: Overview of the Model Architectures. The block at the top shows the fine-tuned Flan-T5(FT5) model on the conversation Dataset. We use the generated response in the next two tasks to perform RAG and conversation style enhancement. Please note here, u means utterance.

reduces the likelihood of hallucinations in the generated text, a critical aspect when dealing with sensitive communication needs such as those of AAC users.

5 Experimental Setup

5.1 Baseline

We preprocess and format our data into sequences suitable for training. The data preparation steps are added to Appendix H. We initiated our experiments with a baseline using zero-shot FLAN-T5 models in three configurations: small, base, and large. The models were fine-tuned to our specific requirements, with the detailed finetuning procedure available in Appendix E.

5.2 Prompting Strategy to LLMs

Effective prompting is crucial for generating accurate and relevant outputs by large language models. Our strategy employs tailored approaches for the COSMO and RAG models:

1. **COSMO**: This model utilizes situation (s), instruction (i), and conversation history (h) to generate responses that are contextually aligned with the user's needs. The response is computed as:

$$r_{\text{COSMO}} = f_{\text{COSMO}}(s, i, h) \quad (6)$$

2. **RAG**: The response generation formula is:

$$r_{\text{RAG}} = f_{\text{RAG}}(c, q, r_{\text{T5}}) \quad (7)$$

where c is the top retrieved document, q the current query, and r_{T5} the initial response from FLAN-T5.

These strategies ensure that the outputs not only reflect the conversational context accurately but also provide a base for meaningful and personalized user interactions.

5.3 Evaluation Techniques

To rigorously evaluate the performance of our models and ensure a comprehensive understanding of their capabilities, we employed a two-fold evaluation strategy encompassing both automatic and human evaluations.

5.3.1 Automatic Evaluation

For automatic evaluation, we employed Referential Metrics including BLEU Scores (Papineni et al., 2002), which assess word and phrase matches; METEOR Scores (Banerjee and Lavie, 2005), accounting for synonyms and stems; and BERTScore (Zhang et al., 2020), which measures text similarity using BERT's contextual embeddings. Additionally, we used Rouge1, Rouge2, and RougeL (Lin,

2004) to evaluate unigram, bigram, and longest sequence matches between generated and reference texts, respectively.

5.3.2 Human Evaluation

Human-centric evaluation supplemented our automatic methods, with judges rating responses based on six criteria—specificity, sincerity, understandability, relevance, fluency, and quantity using a three-point scale. Selecting these criteria draws from interdisciplinary research involving linguistics, psychology, and computer science (Light and McNaughton, 2014). Additionally, AAC users assessed responses on a 5-point scale across five criteria: Relevance, Sincerity, Conciseness, Representativeness, and Realism, detailed in Appendix I.

5.4 Human-Centric Evaluation: A Pilot Study

5.4.1 Motivation and Aim of the Pilot Study

In AAC, effective communication should resonate with the user's experiences, making human judgment crucial for evaluating system efficacy. While automated metrics offer initial insights, they may not capture all nuances. Therefore, this pilot study aimed to compare automated scores with human perceptions of response quality, identifying gaps and refining our evaluation process. We also involved domain experts familiar with AAC contexts to ensure a human-centric assessment of the system's performance.

5.4.2 Methodology

We selected a random sample of 30 dialogues from our test set of 400 prompt-response pairs. This subset was evaluated using two human judges, who rated the responses based on six specific criteria and the previously mentioned rating scales. Additionally, the AAC user evaluated these responses on a 5-point scale.[4]

6 Results and Discussion

6.1 Automatic Evaluation Results

Our evaluation study encompassed six distinct models. The first three were versions of FLAN-T5, differentiated by their size: small, base, and large. The fourth model, named "Flan-T5 large + COSMO", enhanced the response quality of Flan-T5 by incorporating human-like interaction capabilities. The fifth, "ZeroShot COSMO", uniquely operated without specific response data, situation, or instruction, relying solely on conversation history. The final model in our evaluation arsenal was the "RAG Model", which emerged as the best. Table 3 illustrates that the RAG model demonstrated a noticeable edge, marking a substantial improvement in response generation quality over others.[5] Additionally, in figure 3, we plot line graphs to show how RAG performs much better compared to the other models.

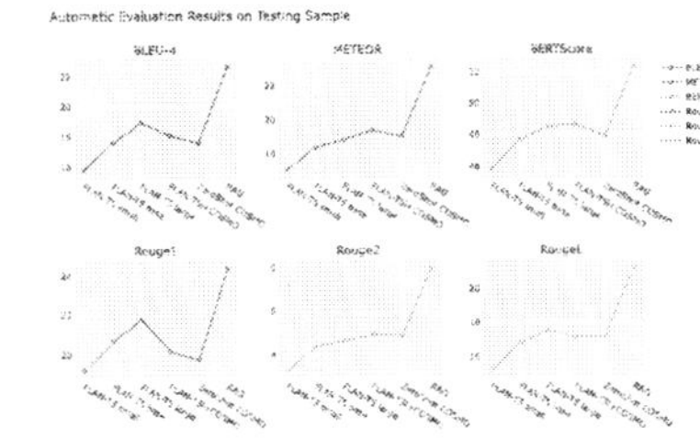

Figure 3: Automatic Evaluation Results on Testing Samples compared across different Models. All the Flan-T5 models used here are the ones that have been fine-tuned on the dataset. The RAG model uses GPT 3.5 turbo as the LLM.

6.2 Human Evaluation and Insights of the Pilot Study

Two domain experts, well-versed in the nuances and challenges of AAC, served as our evaluators. They appraised the responses based on six criteria, each reflecting a vital facet of effective communication. The evaluations for these criteria averaged across 30 data points. The average of each measure from the judges is reported in Table 4. Additionally, the AAC user scored each of these 30 data points on a 5-point scale reported in Table 5[6].

We have included a visual representation of the comparative performance across models (Figure 4). It graphically showcases the variance in scores and underscores the strengths of each model. A further

[4]Not all models underwent human evaluation. Some zero-shot models with a lower number of parameters did not generate responses of sufficient quality for meaningful evaluation. Furthermore, the human evaluation process was intensive, involving the AAC user's assessment over a three-week period, which limited the number of responses each model could feasibly be evaluated on.

[5]There is no comparison with SOTA as this is a novel work in the domain on AAC, thus RAG methodology is compared to the Flan-T5 baseline

[6]The AAC user utilized a 5-point scale for evaluation. This decision was made considering the user's familiarity with the 5-point scale and the significant time and effort required to introduce and explain an unfamiliar scale to differently-abled individuals.

Model	BLEU-4	METEOR	BERTScore	Rouge1	Rouge2	RougeL	Avg.
FT5-zero-shot (s)	10.98	10.12	42.83	12.60	02.67	11.27	15.07
FT5-fine-tuned (s)	15.78	17.08	45.78	19.21	03.29	15.29	19.40
FT5-zero-shot (b)	09.07	10.27	43.43	13.08	03.28	12.06	15.19
FT5-fine-tuned (b)	17.59	18.37	47.66	20.69	04.37	16.79	20.91
FT5-zero-shot (l)	08.09	11.06	44.11	15.13	04.25	14.28	16.15
FT5-fine-tuned (l)	18.93	18.83	48.49	21.76	04.60	17.55	21.69
FT5(l)+cosmo-xl	18.07	19.38	48.65	20.15	04.91	17.15	21.45
cosmo-xl(zero-shot)	17.56	19.02	47.91	19.74	04.87	17.21	21.05
RAG(Llama2-13B)	15.91	17.79	47.84	19.09	05.76	16.54	20.48
RAG(FT5(l)+GPT3.5t)	22.61	23.08	52.36	24.37	07.99	21.20	**25.26**

Table 3: Automatic Evaluation Results on the Testing Sample (400 Prompt-Response Pairs). FT5 is the Flan-T5 model, and s, b, and l denote small, base, and large configurations, respectively. All results reported in this table represent the best outcomes from three separate runs of each model.

Model	Specific	Sincere	Understandable	Relevant	Fluency	Quantity
FT5 (l) J1	1.130	0.900	0.730	0.970	0.800	1.070
FT5 (l) J2	1.110	0.930	0.770	1.000	0.830	1.030
FT5 (l) Avg.	1.120	0.915	0.750	0.985	0.815	1.050
FT5(l)+COSMO J1	0.930	0.930	0.870	1.000	1.030	0.970
FT5(l)+COSMO J2	0.930	0.930	0.870	1.000	1.030	0.970
FT5(l)+COSMO Avg.	0.930	0.930	0.870	1.000	1.030	0.970
COSMO(zero-shot) J1	0.930	0.830	0.870	0.830	1.100	1.000
COSMO(zero-shot) J2	1.030	0.870	0.870	0.830	1.100	0.870
COSMO(zero-shot) Avg.	0.98	0.850	0.870	0.830	1.100	0.935
RAG(FT5(l)+GPT3.5t) J1	1.300	1.230	0.970	1.300	1.400	1.000
RAG(FT5(l)+GPT3.5t) J2	1.300	0.900	0.900	1.300	1.370	1.000
RAG(FT5(l)+GPT3.5t) Avg.	**1.300**	**1.050**	**0.935**	**1.300**	**1.385**	**1.000**

Table 4: The average of each criterion from the respective judges (30 responses)

Criterion	Score
Relevant	3.30
Factual	3.40
Concise	3.40
Representative	3.00
Realistic	3.56

Table 5: The average of each criterion from the AAC User on a 5 point scale on the best model. Where 5 means highest, 1 means lowest(30 responses)

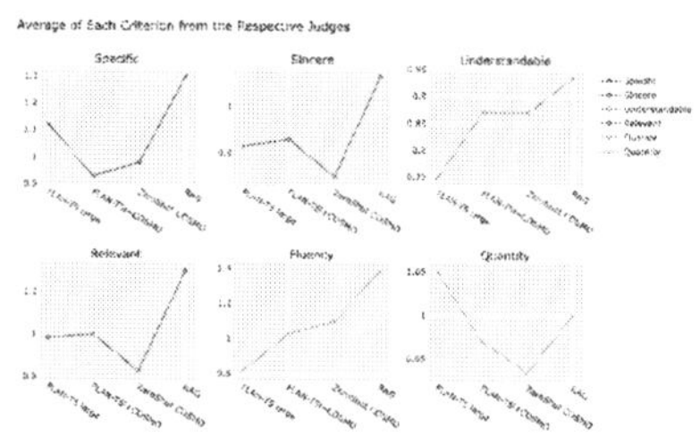

Figure 4: Average of Each Criterion from the Respective Judges compared across four different models. All the Flan-T5 models used here are the ones that have been fine-tuned on the dataset. The RAG model uses GPT 3.5 turbo as the LLM.

detailed breakdown of the observation is available in Appendix J.

6.2.1 Understanding the Generated Response

In Appendix N, we have shown 3 example prompts that help us understand crucial details about the generation quality of each of the models. Furthermore, we calculated the Inter-rater Consistency among the judges (Appendix L) and performed ANOVA test (Appendix M).

6.2.2 Feedback Synthesis

The judge's feedback revealed our evaluation process's good and bad parts. Using the less-same-greater method made rating easier than other methods. However, the different types of conversations, some not even real talks, made checking harder. Some rating parts, like 'sincerity', were used in ways that were not meant. Also, a problem in one area sometimes affects scores in other areas(this essentially means how complex each of the criteria can be for human judges to make proper evaluations). They also suggested adding up scores to understand the responses' quality better.

6.3 Ablation Study

We examined the performance of several models with an emphasis on Flan-T5 fine-tuned, Flan-T5 fine-tuned augmented with cosmo, and RAG (using GPT-3.5 turbo). The Flan-T5 fine-tuned models demonstrated substantial improvements in both automatic metrics and human evaluations across the board, compared to their zero-shot counterparts, with the large configuration (FT5(l)) showing the most significant gains as shown in Table 3 and Table 4. When enhanced with COSMO, the Flan-T5 (l) further improved, particularly in human-evaluated criteria such as fluency and relevance, indicating an enhanced ability to generate more contextually appropriate and engaging responses. The RAG model, incorporating GPT-3.5 turbo, outperformed all other configurations, achieving the highest scores in almost all metrics, especially in specificity and relevance, suggesting superior comprehension and response quality. This highlights the RAG model's robust capability to leverage deep contextual understanding to generate high-quality responses. Interestingly, the LLaMA13B model provided some insights into factual accuracy but was limited by its lower number of parameters compared to GPT 3.5, leading us to favor the latter for more complex tasks. Future studies might expand on improving these models, particularly optimizing the interaction between sequence generation and retrieval components to enhance performance further.

6.4 Comparison of Automatic Metrics with Human Evaluation

In our systematic comparison of automatic metrics and human evaluations, we observed that while automatic metrics provide quick and efficient assessments, they must be complemented by human evaluations for a comprehensive analysis. The RAG model notably excelled in both types of evaluations, indicating its robustness in language comprehension and generation. However, there were discrepancies between human judgments on criteria like 'Specificity' and 'Relevance' and the results from automatic metrics, highlighting the intricate nature of human language evaluation and the limits of current automated systems.

7 Conclusion

Our research highlights the transformative potential of integrating AI with AAC systems by creating user-specific datasets and applying the Retrieval-Augmented Generation (RAG) method. This approach efficiently tailors AAC systems to reflect individual user narratives, enabling a personalized and authentic communication experience. By focusing on the subtle needs of AAC users, we have developed a system that respects and enhances the personal communication styles of individuals who rely on AAC technologies. While this research intentionally focuses on a unique individual and a specific subset of users, it lays the groundwork for future advancements in personalized AI-driven communication aids. The methods and insights gained from this study can inform broader applications in other specialized domains, offering a template for how AI can be effectively customized to meet the diverse needs of underrepresented populations. Future work will explore ways to generalize this approach by incorporating more dynamic conversational history and user intent into the model, potentially expanding its applicability to a broader range of AAC users and other specialized communication contexts. Further details on the data and code availability are provided in Appendix K.

8 Limitations

Our study's primary limitation is its focus on a highly personalized dataset tailored to a single AAC user, which challenges its generalizability and scalability. While this specificity is intentional to meet the unique needs of the target user, it poses challenges for broader applicability. Future research will aim to adapt and scale this approach by enhancing dataset diversity, improving quality control, and exploring modular customization techniques that could extend its use to a broader range of users. Additionally, while our evaluation process showed promising results, incorporating more rigorous statistical analysis would provide deeper insights into how well the system's outputs align with human judgments, ultimately helping to refine and generalize the model for broader use.

References

Razvan Azamfirei, Sapna R Kudchadkar, and James Fackler. 2023. Large language models and the perils of their hallucinations. *Critical Care*, 27(1):1–2.

Sandra Baldassarri, Javier Marco Rubio, Marta García Azpiroz, and Eva Cerezo. 2014. Araboard: A multiplatform alternative and augmentative communication tool. *Procedia Computer Science*, 27:197–206.

Satanjeev Banerjee and Alon Lavie. 2005. METEOR: An automatic metric for MT evaluation with improved correlation with human judgments. In *Proceedings of the ACL Workshop on Intrinsic and Extrinsic Evaluation Measures for Machine Translation and/or Summarization*, pages 65–72, Ann Arbor, Michigan. Association for Computational Linguistics.

David R Beukelman and Pat Mirenda. 2013. *Augmentative and alternative communication: Supporting children and adults with complex communication needs*. Paul H. Brookes Pub.

David R Beukelman, Pat Mirenda, et al. 1998. *Augmentative and alternative communication*. Paul H. Brookes Baltimore.

D.R. Beukelman and J.C. Light. 2020. *Augmentative & Alternative Communication: Supporting Children and Adults with Complex Communication Needs*. Paul H. Brookes Publishing Company, Incorporated.

Hyung Won Chung, Le Hou, Shayne Longpre, Barret Zoph, Yi Tay, William Fedus, Yunxuan Li, Xuezhi Wang, Mostafa Dehghani, Siddhartha Brahma, Albert Webson, Shixiang Shane Gu, Zhuyun Dai, Mirac Suzgun, Xinyun Chen, Aakanksha Chowdhery, Alex Castro-Ros, Marie Pellat, Kevin Robinson, Dasha Valter, Sharan Narang, Gaurav Mishra, Adams Yu, Vincent Zhao, Yanping Huang, Andrew Dai, Hongkun Yu, Slav Petrov, Ed H. Chi, Jeff Dean, Jacob Devlin, Adam Roberts, Denny Zhou, Quoc V. Le, and Jason Wei. 2022. Scaling instruction-finetuned language models. *Preprint*, arXiv:2210.11416.

Floriana Costanzo, Elisa Fucà, Cristina Caciolo, Deborah Ruà, Sara Smolley, Danny Weissberg, and Stefano Vicari. 2023. Talkitt: toward a new instrument based on artificial intelligence for augmentative and alternative communication in children with down syndrome. *Frontiers in Psychology*, 14:1176683.

Yasmin Elsahar, Sijung Hu, Kaddour Bouazza-Marouf, David Kerr, and Annysa Mansor. 2019. Augmentative and alternative communication (aac) advances: A review of configurations for individuals with a speech disability. *Sensors*, 19(8):1911.

Walia Farzana, Farhana Sarker, Quazi Delwar Hossain, Tom Chau, and Khondaker A Mamun. 2020. An evaluation of augmentative and alternative communication research for asd children in developing countries: Benefits and barriers. In *HCI International 2020–Late Breaking Posters: 22nd International Conference, HCII 2020, Copenhagen, Denmark, July 19–24, 2020, Proceedings, Part II 22*, pages 51–62. Springer.

Katrina Fulcher-Rood and Jeff Higginbotham. 2019. Interacting with persons who have als: Time, media, modality, and collaboration via speech-generating devices. *Topics in Language Disorders*, 39(4):370–388.

Marjan Ghazvininejad, Chris Brockett, Ming-Wei Chang, Bill Dolan, Jianfeng Gao, Wen-tau Yih, and Michel Galley. 2018. A knowledge-grounded neural conversation model. In *Proceedings of the AAAI Conference on Artificial Intelligence*, volume 32.

D Jeffery Higginbotham, Howard Shane, Susanne Russell, and Kevin Caves. 2007. Access to aac: Present, past, and future. *Augmentative and alternative communication*, 23(3):243–257.

Jeff Huber. 2023. Chromadb. Accessed: 08/15/2023.

Mihir Kale and Abhinav Rastogi. 2020. Text-to-text pre-training for data-to-text tasks. In *Proceedings of the 13th International Conference on Natural Language Generation*, pages 97–102, Dublin, Ireland. Association for Computational Linguistics.

Hyunwoo Kim, Jack Hessel, Liwei Jiang, Peter West, Ximing Lu, Youngjae Yu, Pei Zhou, Ronan Le Bras, Malihe Alikhani, Gunhee Kim, Maarten Sap, and Yejin Choi. 2023. Soda: Million-scale dialogue distillation with social commonsense contextualization. *Preprint*, arXiv:2212.10465.

HH Koester and S Arthanat. 2017. Text entry rate of access interfaces used by people with physical impairments. *Assist Technol*, pages 1–13.

Mikhail A Lebedev and Miguel AL Nicolelis. 2006. Brain–machine interfaces: past, present and future. *TRENDS in Neurosciences*, 29(9):536–546.

Yanran Li, Hui Su, Xiaoyu Shen, Wenjie Li, Ziqiang Cao, and Shuzi Niu. 2017. Dailydialog: A manually labelled multi-turn dialogue dataset. *arXiv preprint arXiv:1710.03957*.

Yu Li, Baolin Peng, Yelong Shen, Yi Mao, Lars Liden, Zhou Yu, and Jianfeng Gao. 2022. Knowledge-grounded dialogue generation with a unified knowledge representation. In *Proceedings of the 2022 Conference of the North American Chapter of the Association for Computational Linguistics: Human Language Technologies*, pages 206–218, Seattle, United States. Association for Computational Linguistics.

Janice Light. 1988. Interaction involving individuals using augmentative and alternative communication systems: State of the art and future directions. *Augmentative and alternative communication*, 4(2):66–82.

Janice Light and David McNaughton. 2012. The changing face of augmentative and alternative communication: Past, present, and future challenges. *Augmentative and Alternative Communication*, 28(4):197–204. PMID: 23256853.

Janice Light and David McNaughton. 2013. Putting people first: Re-thinking the role of technology in augmentative and alternative communication intervention. *Augmentative and Alternative Communication*, 29(4):299–309.

Janice Light and David McNaughton. 2014. Communicative competence for individuals who require augmentative and alternative communication: A new definition for a new era of communication?

Chin-Yew Lin. 2004. ROUGE: A package for automatic evaluation of summaries. In *Text Summarization Branches Out*, pages 74–81, Barcelona, Spain. Association for Computational Linguistics.

Bob MacDonald, Pan-Pan Jiang, Julie Cattiau, Rus Heywood, Richard Cave, Katie Seaver, Marilyn Ladewig, Jimmy Tobin, Michael Brenner, Philip Q Nelson, et al. 2021. Disordered speech data collection: lessons learned at 1 million utterances from project euphonia.

Helen Meekosha. 2011. Decolonising disability: Thinking and acting globally. *Disability & Society*, 26(6):667–682.

Gábor Melis, Chris Dyer, and Phil Blunsom. 2017. On the state of the art of evaluation in neural language models. *arXiv preprint arXiv:1707.05589*.

Rodica Neamtu, André Camara, Carlos Pereira, and Rafael Ferreira. 2019. Using artificial intelligence for augmentative alternative communication for children with disabilities. In *Human-Computer Interaction–INTERACT 2019: 17th IFIP TC 13 International Conference, Paphos, Cyprus, September 2–6, 2019, Proceedings, Part I 17*, pages 234–243. Springer.

Sidharth Pancholi, Juan P Wachs, and Bradley S Duerstock. 2023. Use of artificial intelligence techniques to assist individuals with physical disabilities. *Annual Review of Biomedical Engineering*, 26.

Kishore Papineni, Salim Roukos, Todd Ward, and Wei-Jing Zhu. 2002. Bleu: a method for automatic evaluation of machine translation. In *Proceedings of the 40th Annual Meeting of the Association for Computational Linguistics*, pages 311–318, Philadelphia, Pennsylvania, USA. Association for Computational Linguistics.

Samuel C Sennott, Linda Akagi, Mary Lee, and Anthony Rhodes. 2019. Aac and artificial intelligence (ai). *Topics in language disorders*, 39(4):389–403.

Cynthia A Thompson, Mehmet H Goker, and Pat Langley. 2004. A personalized system for conversational recommendations. *Journal of Artificial Intelligence Research*, 21:393–428.

Jimmy Tobin and Katrin Tomanek. 2022. Personalized automatic speech recognition trained on small disordered speech datasets. In *ICASSP 2022-2022 IEEE International Conference on Acoustics, Speech and Signal Processing (ICASSP)*, pages 6637–6641. IEEE.

Subhashini Venugopalan, Jimmy Tobin, Samuel J Yang, Katie Seaver, Richard JN Cave, Pan-Pan Jiang, Neil Zeghidour, Rus Heywood, Jordan Green, and Michael P Brenner. 2023. Speech intelligibility classifiers from 550k disordered speech samples. In *ICASSP 2023-2023 IEEE International Conference on Acoustics, Speech and Signal Processing (ICASSP)*, pages 1–5. IEEE.

Annalu Waller. 2019. Telling tales: unlocking the potential of aac technologies. *International journal of language & communication disorders*, 54(2):159–169.

Tianyi Zhang, Varsha Kishore, Felix Wu, Kilian Q. Weinberger, and Yoav Artzi. 2020. Bertscore: Evaluating text generation with bert. *Preprint*, arXiv:1904.09675.

A Participants

The participant was an adult male with spastic quadriplegia due to a medical condition. He had decades of experience using computer-based AAC devices and was proficient in using AAC tools. The participant accessed his AAC device using a specific part of his body to type on a specialized keyboard, achieving a typing rate close to the average for AAC users.

B Study Setting

The evaluation was conducted in a specially designed research space, with the participant comfortably interacting with the conversational AI system. A domain expert, using Google Speech-to-Text technology[7], input test items and communicated prompts to the participant. The AI's responses, generated by a Large Language Model, were then audibly relayed to the participant through Google Text-to-Speech[8]. A team member was also on hand to assist the participant in understanding these responses, ensuring a smooth and effective communication.

C Prompting Strategy for Google Gemini

In the dataset construction phase, we developed a detailed prompting strategy to utilize Google Gemini's advanced capabilities for converting narrative content into simulated conversational dialogues. This approach involved selecting specific paragraphs from a book authored by the AAC user, which were then used as inputs for Google Gemini. The model was tasked with reimagining these narrative passages as interactive dialogues between the AAC user and a conversational partner, aiming

[7]Google Speech-to-Text: `https://cloud.google.com/speech-to-text?hl=en`

[8]Google Text-to-Speech: `https://cloud.google.com/text-to-speech?hl=en`

to create naturalistic exchanges that mirror real-life interactions.

The prompt instructed Google Gemini to:

> "Convert this paragraph into a four-turn dialogue format in which the AAC user and a partner discuss the content. Ensure that the utterances are realistic and reflect their unique communication style. The partner starts the conversation.
>
> <Paragraph from book>"

The transformation process is captured by the following equation:

$$D = f_{\text{LLM}}(C; P) \quad (8)$$

In this equation, D denotes the dialogue drafts generated from the input content C, prompt P, and f_{LLM} represents the generative function of Google Gemini. This structured prompting ensures that the dialogues are not only contextually appropriate but also resonate deeply with the AAC user's personal communication needs. The result is a dataset that is authentic, personal, and highly useful for enhancing conversational AI applications tailored to AAC users.

D Dataset Creation Team

The development of our conversational dataset was a collaborative effort led by a diverse team from the Communication and Disability Lab at our university. This team consisted of approximately 10 Ph.D. students with extensive experience working with AAC users, supplemented by master's students tasked with generating dialogues through specific instructions to the Large Language Model (LLM). The Ph.D. students were responsible for refining the utterances in the conversation. Regardless of their educational level, all team members adhered to a consistent approach as outlined in Figure 1 for dialogue generation. To further validate the dataset's relevance and authenticity, it underwent a thorough verification process by two adult experts. These experts, deeply familiar with the AAC user's real-life experiences and scenarios, provided an additional layer of scrutiny, ensuring the dataset's alignment with the actual communication needs and styles of AAC user.

E FLAN-T5 Fine-Tuning

We employed the FLAN-T5 model in its three variants: small, base, and large. The training process was anchored around a tailored template for our unique response generation task. The template was: "Continue writing the following Text.". The other hyper-parameters were 10 epochs, batch size 8, learning rate 5e-5, and the GPU architecture was A100 80 GB.

F Prompting Strategies cosmo-xl

In our research, we developed a sophisticated prompting strategy to harness the advanced capabilities of the COSMO model for generating conversational dialogues. This strategy involved using specific content from a book authored by an AAC user, which was then transformed into simulated dialogues.

The prompt structured for COSMO is designed to turn narrative passages into interactive dialogues between an AAC device user, and a conversational partner, maintaining a naturalistic interaction that mirrors real-life exchanges. All identifiable entities in the prompt template have been replaced with uppercase variables to ensure anonymity and general applicability.

The detailed prompt provided to COSMO was:

> "SITUATION: Mr. PERSON is chatting with a friend, Mr. PERSON is an Alternative and Augmentative Communication (AAC) device user. INSTRUCTION: You are PERSON and you are talking to a friend. Keep the answers concise and within 20 words. Answer to the previous utterance is: <response>
>
> <conversation history>"

This prompting framework aims to create dialogues that are not only realistic and engaging but also provide a deep insight into the personal communication style of the AAC user.

The process of transforming the input narrative into dialogue is encapsulated by the equation:

$$D = f_{\text{COSMO}}(C; P) \quad (9)$$

Here, D represents the dialogue drafts generated from the input content C, while P denotes the structured prompt. The function f_{COSMO} captures COSMO's capability to interpret and convert the input narrative into a meaningful dialogue. This structured prompting ensures the dialogues are contextually appropriate and resonate deeply with the personal communication needs of AAC users, resulting in a dataset that is both authentic and highly useful for enhancing conversational AI applications tailored to AAC users.

G RAG Model Prompt and Generation Parameters

In this study, we formulated an intricate prompting strategy to leverage the advanced capabilities of GPT-3.5 turbo within our Retrieval-Augmented Generation (RAG) framework. This strategy focuses on generating responses that are not only accurate but also deeply personalized for AAC users.

The prompt template for the model is designed to incorporate responses generated by the FLAN-T5 model, augmented with contextually relevant information retrieved by the Retrieval model. This template ensures that the dialogue remains grounded in reality, accurately reflecting the AAC user's perspective. All identifiable information in the prompts has been anonymized to ensure privacy and general applicability.

The detailed prompt provided is as follows:

> "Use the following pieces of context to override the conversation reply truthfully.
> If the context does not provide a truthful answer, make the answer as truthful as possible. You are answering as the AAC User
> Use 15 words maximum. Keep the response as concise as possible.
> Context: {{context}}
> Question: {{question}}
> Response (Flan-T5): {response}.
> Truthful Response:"

This prompting framework is designed to foster dialogues that are engaging and realistic and deeply aligned with the AAC user's individual communication needs. The equation encapsulating this transformation process is:

$$\boldsymbol{D} = f_{\text{RAG}}(\boldsymbol{C}; \boldsymbol{P}) \tag{10}$$

Here, $\boldsymbol{D}$ denotes the dialogue drafts generated from the input content $\boldsymbol{C}$, and $\boldsymbol{P}$ represents the structured prompt. The function f_{RAG} illustrates GPT-3.5's ability to interpret and refine the narrative input into authentic dialogues, ensuring that each response not only adheres to factual accuracy but also resonates with the personal communication style of the AAC user.

In the generation process of the RAG model, denoted by these equations

$$\boldsymbol{I} = \{\boldsymbol{H}, \boldsymbol{R}_{\text{FLAN}}, \boldsymbol{C}_k\} \tag{11}$$

$$\boldsymbol{R} = f_{\text{gen}}(\boldsymbol{I}; \phi) \tag{12}$$

, where $k = 1$ signifies that the most contextually similar passage is retrieved for response generation, we utilize specific generation parameters. These parameters, optimized through empirical trials rather than exhaustive parameter studies, have proven effective in achieving high-quality generative outputs. The parameters include a maximum sequence length of 600, ensuring comprehensive responses while avoiding verbosity. The $no\_repeat\_ngram\_size$ is set to 1, prohibiting immediate repetition and fostering diversity in phrase usage. We employ stochastic sampling with do_sample = True, top_k = 50, and top_p = 0.95, which collectively guide the model to focus on the most likely next words while maintaining a broad enough candidate pool to ensure creativity and coherence. The temperature parameter is set at 0.7, balancing randomness and determinism in word choice, and a $repetition\_penalty$ of 1.3 discourages redundant content generation. These parameters, encapsulated within ϕ, are pivotal in tailoring the model's output to the nuanced requirements of AAC communication, ensuring that responses are not only relevant but also uniquely expressive of the user's intent.

H Preprocessing and Data Preparation

Each conversation is segmented into sequences of prompt-response pairs. We define each dialogue $\boldsymbol{D}$ as a series of utterances $\boldsymbol{U}_i$, and generate pairs as follows:

$$\begin{aligned}\boldsymbol{D} = \{&(\boldsymbol{U}_1, \boldsymbol{U}_2), (\boldsymbol{U}_1 \oplus \boldsymbol{U}_2 \oplus \boldsymbol{U}_3, \boldsymbol{U}_4), \dots, \\ &(\boldsymbol{U}_1 \oplus \dots \oplus \boldsymbol{U}_{2n-1}, \boldsymbol{U}_{2n})\}\end{aligned} \tag{13}$$

where $\oplus$ denotes the concatenation of utterances, providing increasing context with each subsequent pair.

By adopting this strategy, we generated 2023 distinct prompt response pairs. In terms of dataset distribution, 1423 pairs were reserved for training, 200 for validation, and the remaining 400 were allocated for testing purposes. This careful partitioning was designed to ensure the model's robustness and generalization capabilities across unseen data.

I Human Evaluation Criteria

The six specific criteria are as follows:

- **Specificity**: How precise and to the point the response was.
- **Sincerity**: The genuine and truthful nature of the response.
- **Understandability**: Clarity and comprehensibility of the response.
- **Relevance**: How pertinent the response was to the prompt.
- **Fluency**: The smoothness and natural flow of the response.
- **Quantity**: Whether the response length was too short, just right, or too long.

The new criteria used by AAC user are defined as follows:

- **Representative**: How good the generated response represents the AAC User's tone.
- **Realistic**: How realistic the generated response is.

J Human Evaluation Criteria Breakdown and Observations

- **Specificity**: RAG topped with a score of 1.3. FLAN-T5 large followed closely with around 1.12, while ZeroShot COSMO and FLAN-T5l+COSMO hovered near 0.93. The RAG model has a superior capability to produce specific responses, highlighting its precision in addressing queries.
- **Sincerity**: The RAG model is more truthful than most other models, as it got an average of 1.07
- **Understandability**: A crucial takeaway from this criterion is that LLMs like GPT 3 and Large Language Models like COSMO give more comprehensive responses than smaller Fine-tuned Models.
- **Relevance**: RAG stood out with a score of 1.3. FLAN-T5l+COSMO matched the ideal score of 1, with FLAN-T5 large just below 0.99. This explains that RAG excels at producing highly relevant content, indicating its superior contextual understanding.
- **Fluency**: It depends on the nature of the Language Models. As GPT-3 based models are generally more fluent than other fine-tuned models, RAG had the higher score
- **Quantity**: Most models, including RAG, were close to the ideal score of 1, indicating balanced response lengths.

K Ethics, Code and Data Availability

The code and anonymized conversation dataset are available publicly on Github to support further research. However, the authored content used as a knowledge base won't be available due to privacy concerns. We advise researchers to use alternative personal narrative sources for replication or extension. All the data used in the experiments were collected upon obtaining consent from the AAC user.

L Inter-rater Consistency Analysis for Evaluation Criteria

The Intraclass Correlation Coefficient (ICC) measures the reliability of ratings or measurements. The values range from -1 to 1, where -1 means strong disagreement and 1 means strong agreement.

Criterion	ICC
Specific	0.95
Sincere	0.02
Understandable	0.84
Relevant	1.00
Fluency	0.99
Quantity	0.43

Table 6: Inter-class Correlation Coefficient (ICC) for Evaluation Criteria

Table 6 suggests that for most of the criteria, there was strong agreement among judges, except for "Sincerity" (low agreement) and "Quantity" (moderate agreement). This might prompt further investigation into why the judge's view diverged on "Sincerity" and, to a lesser extent, on "Quantity".

M ANOVA test results

The ANOVA test results indicate an F-statistic of approximately 0.0970 and a p-value of approximately 0.7568. This high p-value suggests no statistically significant differences between the scores of Judge 1 (J1) and Judge 2 (J2) across all criteria.

N Example of Generated Responses

The tables below include the conversation history and predicted responses by 3 different models, which are Finetuned-Flan-T5(large), Finetuned-Flan-T5(large)+COSMO, RAG(Finetuned Flan-T5 + GPT3.5 Turbo), and the golden response.

Example 1

Prompt	Golden	Ft.FT5 (l)	Ft.FT5(l) + COSMO	RAG
Partner: I suppose with PET, you never quite feel alone. Does she follow you? User: As I'm in the shower, I peek out and see PET curled up with the floor mat. She notices me and jumps on the side of the bathtub, pacing back and forth. Partner: Is PET approachable or does she keep her distance? Give an example of your interaction.	User: Turning my head, I meet PET's gaze, and to my surprise, she plants a tiny kiss on the front of my nose.	User: I try to get her attention, but she quickly turns away.	User: She does tend to keep her distance at times, but she's always happy to see me when I come home. She'll start talking to me on the phone even if I don't respond.	User: She gives me a little kiss on the nose, then waits for me.

Table 7: Conversation example 1 (Any recognizable entities have been anonymized using uppercase characters for the specific entity)

- We observe that the RAG model can identify the correct relevant context. In conversation example 2, only the RAG Model can capture the detail of "200 miniature trains"
- We can see the Finetuned Models generally keep the responses short but also hallucinate, whereas COSMO makes the responses more human-like and fluent but irrelevant.
- RAG combines both relevance and fluency to generate appropriate responses.

Example 2

Prompt	Golden	Ft.FT5 (l)	Ft.FT5(l) + COSMO	RAG
Partner: What other things did you do as a kid? User: If we didn't go to the mall, I would stay home and play with my own toys. Partner: That makes sense. What was that like for you? User: I had my own space to play in, and I would play for hours and hours. Partner: Were you alone when you played? User: Sometimes, but if I didn't want to play alone I would go downstairs and watch my dad play with his trains. Partner: Play with his trains?	User: Yes. He has about 200 miniature trains. He would only play with them on weekends.	User: I would watch him play and then we'd go upstairs to our room.	User: Yeah, I thought it was really cool how they worked. My dad was really into them too.	User: I'd watch him play with his 200 miniature trains and then we'd go upstairs and play pretend games.

Table 8: Conversation example 2 (Any recognizable entities have been anonymized using uppercase characters for the specific entity)

Example 3

Prompt	Golden	Ft.FT5 (l)	Ft.FT5(l) + COSMO	RAG
Partner: What was the little problem that didn't let you leave? User: No one wanted to sit in the back of the van. Partner: Why was that? User: Because there was a lot of bumping from the potholes in the back. Partner: That makes sense. What ended up happening?	User: I sat in the back.	User: I was so relieved when the driver came to take me in.	User: We ended up staying in the front of the van.	User: I volunteered to sit in the back and then we left.

Table 9: Conversation example 3 (Any recognizable entities have been anonymized using uppercase characters for the specific entity)

LLM-Based Robust Product Classification in Commerce and Compliance

Sina Gholamian, Gianfranco Romani, Bartosz Rudnikowicz, Stavroula Skylaki
Thomson Reuters Artificial Intelligence Labs
{sina.gholamian, gianfranco.romani, bartosz.rudnikowicz, laura.skylaki}@thomsonreuters.com

Abstract

Product classification is a crucial task in international trade, as compliance regulations are verified and taxes and duties are applied based on product categories. Manual classification of products is time-consuming and error-prone, and the sheer volume of products imported and exported renders the manual process infeasible. Consequently, e-commerce platforms and enterprises involved in international trade have turned to automatic product classification using machine learning. However, current approaches do not consider the real-world challenges associated with product classification, such as very abbreviated and incomplete product descriptions. In addition, recent advancements in generative Large Language Models (LLMs) and their reasoning capabilities are mainly untapped in product classification and e-commerce. In this research, we explore the real-life challenges of industrial classification and we propose data perturbations[1] that allow for realistic data simulation. Furthermore, we employ LLM-based product classification to improve the robustness of the prediction in presence of incomplete data. Our research shows that LLMs with in-context learning outperform the supervised approaches in the clean-data scenario. Additionally, we illustrate that LLMs are significantly more robust than the supervised approaches when data attacks are present.

1 Introduction

Product classification plays an important role in international trade and e-commerce. This is because import and export tariffs are assigned based on the category of products. According to the latest report from World Custom Organization (WCO, 2023), in Year 2022-2023 more than 1.3 billion declarations are booked through customs worldwide (World Customs Organization, 2023a). This massive workload, a result of trade globalization, can impose a significant burden on human experts such as customs personnel and the companies involved in import, export, and e-commerce.

In addition, product classification can often be a complicated task and require subject matter expertise, as there is a wide range of products traded across various industries. As such, for human personnel to become competent in understanding the nuances of different products and how to classify them in compliance with WCO guidelines is a non-trivial task and requires several months of training, according to our subject matter expertise. Moreover, correct and detailed classification is critical, as incorrect classification can lead to tax liabilities owed to authorities. This can result in fines, penalties, and in some cases, legal repercussions and business discontinuation bans in the jurisdictions affected by a tax breach.

Managing the increasing workload of product classification in global trade is difficult. This challenge is further compounded by the continuous globalization of e-commerce. Additionally, staying accurate and up-to-date as global trade classification guidelines, such as the Harmonized System (U.S. Department of Commerce, 2023), which continuously change, further adds to the challenges of manual product classification. Therefore, many organizations active in industry have adopted automated methods of product classification using machine learning (Avigdor et al., 2023; Hasson et al., 2021; Lee et al., 2021; Chen et al., 2021; Nguyen and Khatwani, 2022). However, the issue with current classification approaches is that they primarily focus on the 'clean' version of data, often ignoring the common data perturbations that happen in real-world product classification during inference time. In this context, 'perturbations' or 'attacks' refer to issues in data that limit the classifier's performance, such as incomplete or abbreviated data. The ability to robustly predict correct product classifications

[1]We use 'data perturbation' and 'data attack' interchangeably.

Proceedings of the 1st Workshop on Customizable NLP: Progress and Challenges in Customizing NLP for a Domain, Application, Group, or Individual (CustomNLP4U), pages 26–36
November 16, 2024 ©2024 Association for Computational Linguistics

in scenarios where data might be far from perfect is of paramount importance, especially in cases where incorrect classification can lead to incorrect taxation and trade liabilities in international trade under the harmonized system (World Customs Organization, 2023b). Therefore, in this research, we aim to understand which models perform better in scenarios with potential data attacks. This not only facilitates more informed model decision-making, but also considers real-life data challenges. Consequently, our contributions are as follows:

- We introduce a framework designed to simulate real-life data attacks on clean data. This is particularly crucial for product classification with compliance implications, where incorrect classifications can lead to wrong taxation.

- Utilizing realistic data attacks, we propose an LLM-based classification approach that outperforms the prior supervised approaches, and is more robust to real-life data attacks.

- Lastly, we offer a comprehensive evaluation of human annotators and various models across different attack scenarios and compare their robustness. We draw conclusions from our findings, which we believe are instrumental in guiding design decisions for the practical aspects of product classification.

2 Background

This section provides a review of the related work and essential background that supports our research.

2.1 Product Classification

Product classification based on product description text has been a focal point in several industrial research efforts (Kondadadi et al., 2022; Nguyen and Khatwani, 2022; Hasson et al., 2021; Avigdor et al., 2023). In real-world scenarios, product descriptions often lack completeness and in many cases are abbreviated and brief. This provides very limited context for accurate product classification using Natural Language Processing (NLP) approaches. Kondadadi ct al. (Kondadadi ct al., 2022) presented a Question Answering (QA) framework for Data Quality Estimation (DQE) with the goal of improving product classification for tax code assignment. This approach detects the quality of available data by extracting attribute-value pairs. The authors similarly observed that the input product description data is generally vague and noisy. Hasson et al. (Hasson et al., 2021) discussed the classification challenges in e-commerce systems. Notably, the high diversity of products to classify and highly granular hierarchy of these products result in hundreds or thousands of possible categories, which can present challenges for both manual and automated classification approaches. Considering that automated product classification is a more cost-efficient and scalable approach to adopt, the development of robust product classification in presence of data attacks still remains largely unexplored.

2.2 Input Perturbation

Perturbations in data, specifically in text data, have been investigated in several prior studies (Behjati et al., 2019; Zhang et al., 2020; Zou et al., 2023). Generally, for LLMs, adversarial attacks can involve malicious tokens added to the prompt that causes the model to generate undesired outputs (Zou et al., 2023). Beyond malicious intents, adversarial attacks can be beneficial and be leveraged as data augmentation to improve the robustness of text classification approaches (Yoo and Qi, 2021; Wang et al., 2020, 2022) in scenarios where the inference data can be noisy (Morris et al., 2020). Our work focuses on product classification based on the text description of products, which in real life can be incomplete and far removed from the clean training data. Therefore, in this research, we focus on formulating data perturbations that aim to simulate the real-world data incompleteness often encountered in product descriptions.

3 Methodology

Although product classification is generally tested on datasets free of inaccuracies, in real-world scenarios the data received from users is often very short and abbreviated. As such we define an adversarial attack framework to simulate realistic data from clean data. For data perturbation method, we follow the approach introduced in (Behjati et al., 2019). Similar to the method explained in GPT3Mix approach (Yoo et al., 2021), we use GPT 4 (*version: 0613*) to create perturbations and generate synthetic yet highly realistic datasets to resemble the real-life scenario of the data. We write a prompt that includes the instructions to GPT-4 for different variations of data perturbations. These instructions are then passed to GPT-4 along the original product description to perform perturbations. In response, GPT-4 completion returns the perturbed product description. Additional details on prompt templates are provided in Figures 2 and 3 in Appendix A. As outlined in the prompts, we instruct GPT-4 to perform controlled data perturbations so that the initial meaning of the descriptions is still mostly preserved and they remain classifiable by a human annotator.

3.1 Data Perturbation Framework

To simulate real-world data scenarios, we introduce realistic data perturbations and attacks. Our perturbation model is defined as follows: consider a classifier f, which maps an input $x \in X$ to its corresponding class $c \in C$, denoted as $f(x) = c$. In this model, x is a sequence of tokens, $x = (x_1, x_2, ..., x_n)$. Data perturbation can involve either removing or modifying tokens within x, leading to a new sequence, $x' = (x'_1, x'_2, ..., x'_n)$. This perturbation may result in $f(x') = c'$, where $c' \neq c$, indicating a change in classification. To mimic the real-life data, we apply two distinct perturbation methods that we will discuss in the following.

3.2 Amputation

In this approach, we perturb the product description by randomly removing some of its tokens. We investigate this scenario because real data often is missing critical attributes, which limits accurate classification of products (Kondadadi et al., 2022). Here, we do not introduce new tokens (i.e., new attributes) nor change the order of the existing tokens; instead we only omit some tokens from the product descriptions. Formally speaking, the input $x = (x_1, x_2, ..., x_n)$ is transformed into $x_m = (x_{i_1}, x_{i_2}, \ldots, x_{i_k})$ where $1 \leq i_1 < i_2 < \ldots < i_k \leq n$ and $\forall x_{i_{1:k}} \in x$.

3.3 Abbreviation

In this approach, we attack product descriptions by replacing a subset of words with their abbreviated forms. This scenario does not fully remove any tokens but converts certain tokens into their abbreviated versions. For example, the word *'mobile'* could be replaced by *'mob.'* (refer to Table 1). Formally, the input $x = (x_1, x_2, ..., x_n)$ is transformed into $x_a = (x'_1, x'_2, \ldots, x'_n)$ where $S \subseteq \{1, 2, \ldots, n\}$ and $\forall i \in S : x'_i = \mathit{Abbr}(x_i)$, and $\forall i \in \{1, 2, \ldots, n\} \setminus S : x'_i = x_i$.

It should be noted that our framework does not encompass a comprehensive list of data perturbation that can happen in real-world scenarios, and only models the common perturbations in our enterprise global trade use case. Other data perturbations, such as typos, can also be quite prevalent in real scenarios which can be investigated as per use case.

3.4 Example - Data Perturbation

Table 1 provides examples of various attacks based on our data perturbation framework. In a combined attack, both abbreviation and amputation approaches are applied.

Attack	Description
Clean	Samsung ALC820 mobile phone case Cover Brown
Abbreviated	samsung alc820 mob. phone case cover brwn
Amputated	samsung alc820 mobile phone case
Combined	samsung alc820 mob. phone case

Table 1: Examples of various data attacks applied to clean data.

3.5 Robustness Metric

We define the robustness of classifier f as the delta (Δ_r) of the performance metric (M) on the clean data (D_c) versus the performance of the classifier on the perturbed data (D_p): $\Delta_r(f) = \frac{|M(D_c) - M(D_p)|}{M(D_c)}$. The lower the Δ_r, the more robust the model is to the data perturbations.

3.6 Research Hypothesis

Our hypothesis posits that LLMs with in-context learning not only can outperform supervised models in the product classification task, but also show greater robustness to adversarial attacks such as abbreviation and amputation. Furthermore, we assert that informing an LLM about the potential data attacks can improve the classification performance by allowing the LLM to more effectively leverage its reasoning capabilities.

4 Evaluation

In the following, we outline the details of our evaluation.

4.1 Datasets

We experiment on two publicly available datasets, namely Icecat (ice) and WDC-222 (wdc), to demonstrate our perturbation framework and evaluate the robustness of different classification models in the presence of data attacks. Although we have observed the aforementioned attack scenarios in our proprietary data, we believe our perturbation framework can be readily applied to any arbitrary dataset. Therefore, we opt to conduct our evaluation on public datasets to ensure higher visibility and reproducibility. The datasets are as follows:

4.2 Icecat (ice)

This dataset features products in the "Computers & Electronics" category, organized in a hierarchical structure. Each record includes a product description and a corresponding text label. For example, as shown in Table 1, the product described as *"Samsung ALC820 mobile phone case Cover Brown"* falls under the hierarchy *Computers & Electronics → Telecom & Navigation → Mobile Phone Cases*, with the label being the leaf node of this hierarchy, i.e., *Mobile Phone Cases*. The dataset has 370 leaf nodes, with 489,902 entries for training and 153,095 for testing. We utilized the entire training set for training supervised models and identifying few-shot examples for LLMs. However, to contain LLM inference costs, we conducted stratified random sampling on test set to comprise a smaller set of 5,000 examples, with at least one data point from each class.

4.3 WDC-222 (wdc)

This dataset contains 222 leaf nodes in the same hierarchy as Icecat. It includes 2,984 entries solely for testing, thereby serving as the gold standard for this classification task. This dataset is generally more difficult than Icecat for classification, and prior approaches (wdc) achieve a lower performance on this dataset than Icecat. We utilize the entire size of this dataset to test both supervised and large language models.

4.4 Models

We conduct our evaluation using both supervised and LLM-based approaches.

4.5 Supervised Baseline

To compare the performance of generative models against supervised models, we experiment with the DeBERTaV3-base model (He et al., 2023) as our baseline. This architecture achieves state-of-the-art performance on several text classification benchmarks. Specifically, we used the pretrained model available from HuggingFace (Wolf et al., 2020), and fine-tuned it on the full training set of the Icecat dataset. By doing so, we replicate a scenario where the model is trained on clean data and tested on perturbed data, which is a common situation in our real-world use case. For the supervised baseline, experiments are repeated several times with different seeds, and thus error ranges are provided.

4.6 Training Details

In the following, we review the training details for supervised baseline models.

4.6.1 Flat Classification

To train both hierarchical and flat baselines, we used the DeBERTaV3-base model (He et al., 2023). We fine-tuned the pretrained model provided by the authors of the model and available on the Hugging Face (Microsoft). We used the default tokenizer provided by Hugging Face for the DeBERTaV3-base model and the following hyperparameters: batch size of 32, learning rate of 2e-5, and weight decay of 0.01. The rest of the parameters were equal to default values for the Hugging Face Trainer class. We trained the model for a maximum 100 epochs with early stopping enabled and the patience parameter was set to 5 epochs. The model was trained on 5 different random seeds, and each converged before reaching the maximum number of epochs.

4.6.2 Hierarchical Classification

For the hierarchical classification, we used the same model, tokenizer, and hyperparameters as for the flat classification. However, we trained two separate models: one with the task to classify the products to the second level of the hierarchy (first level was shared among all products), and the second model for final label prediction. The top-level model was trained on the same data as the flat classification model. The second model was trained on the same data, but the description was augmented with the top-level category label (in textual form) in the following format "*original_description, category_name*". During inference, we used predictions from the top-level model and appended them to the description before passing it to the second model for the final classification. The results were averaged for the models trained on five different seeds and rounded to three decimal digits. We also reported the 95% interval which was calculated as follows: $\pm 1.96 \cdot \frac{std}{\sqrt{5}}$.

5 LLMs

We experiment with both open-source and proprietary LLMs, including Llama 2 Chat with 70B parameters (Touvron et al., 2023), GPT3.5, and GPT4 (*model version: 0613*) (OpenAI, 2023). Unlike the supervised approach, we were not able to perform multiple runs and report error ranges for LLMs due to the excessive cost of inference. However, we set the temperature values to 0 to minimize potential variations in the LLM outputs across multiple runs.

5.1 Models Configurations

For classification configurations, we consider **Flat**, **Hierarchical**, and **Few-shot** configurations. In the flat configuration, the model is tasked with directly predicting the leaf node label of the product, corresponding to 370 and 222 classes for the Icecat and WDC datasets, respectively. In the hierarchical configuration, the model initially predicts the second-level hierarchy of the product which is 17 classes for both Icecat and WDC-222 dataset (first-level hierarchy, *Computers & Electronics*, is shared among all products). This is followed by predicting the final leaf label from the predicted second-level hierarchy. For the few-shot configuration, we select the top-5 semantically similar examples to the test product from the training set, using the Sentence-Transformer model (Reimers and Gurevych, 2019). These examples are then included in the prompt as in-context learning examples for the LLMs (Brown et al., 2020).

5.2 Attack Configurations

We explore four different attack configurations as discussed in our data perturbation framework in Section 3. **Clean:** this configuration presents the original data without any attacks, e.g., the original product descriptions are used for classification. This serves as a benchmark for the highest possible classification performance. **Amputated:** in this configuration, the product descriptions are amputated by randomly removing a subset of tokens. **Abbreviated:** this attack involves abbreviating a subset of product description tokens. **Combined:** this configuration involves combining both the amputation and abbreviation attacks, such that the product description is first amputated and then the resulting description is further abbreviated. **Combined-Reason:** this configuration uses the combined attack on the product description, with an additional note in the prompt to enable the LLM to reason about possible data perturbations. LLMs have demonstrated emerging capabilities in common-sense reasoning (Wei et al., 2022). Therefore, in this configuration, we include an extra note in the prompt, "Be aware that some parts of the product description might have been abbreviated or amputated.", to let the LLM reason on possible perturbation patterns in the product description, which may lead to more accurate classification.

Similarity	Abbreviated	Amputated	Combined
Icecat	0.918	0.909	0.848
WDC-222	0.896	0.907	0.843

Table 2: Similarity scores for the clean dataset versus the attacked datasets.

5.3 Data Analysis

In this section, we present a statistical analysis of the data attributes for the clean data as compared to the post-attack scenarios. Table 2 shows the average semantic similarity scores for both the clean dataset and its perturbed ones. We used *'multi-qa-mpnet-base-dot-v1'* model from SentenceTransformers (Reimers and Gurevych, 2019) to calculate these similarity scores. The results show that as more attacks are introduced on the dataset, the similarity scores decrease. However, even for the 'Combined' configuration, the dataset is still over 84% similar to the original dataset. In addition to the similarity scores, we have plotted the distribution of token sizes for product descriptions in Figure 1 for both the Icecat (1a) and WDC-222 (1b) datasets. Kullback-Leibler (KL) divergence values (Kullback and Leibler, 1951) are also provided for different data configurations. Across all configurations, the KL values are less than or equal to 0.2, and a value of ≤ 0.2 typically signifies a small divergence between the distributions. This analysis is crucial as we later evaluate how these small divergences in distributions translates to a greater scale of model performance unrobustness.

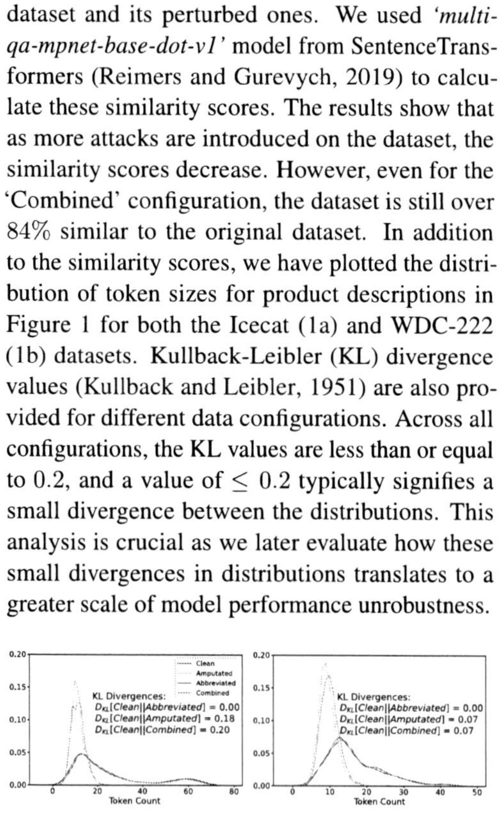

(a) Icecat (b) WDC-222

Figure 1: Distribution of the clean data versus the distribution of the data with different type of attacks.

5.4 Human Annotation Analysis

The importance of the quality of perturbed data prompted us to engage human annotators to assess the quality and ensure its similarity to the intended real data. During the design of the data perturbation framework, we leveraged human expert knowledge to ensure our perturbations aligned with the in-field data. In addition, through human manual evaluation, we confirmed that the perturbed data appears realistic and plausible in real-life scenarios.

To further solidify the data quality analysis, we picked 100 random sample data points from each dataset (200 samples in total) that were perturbed and asked our human annotators to expand the abbreviated words to ensure the majority of perturbations are recoverable from a human perspective and they did not semantically alter the meaning of product descriptions. Through this, annotators were able to identify and create the clean full form of the abbreviated tokens in the product descriptions 80% and 85% of times for the Icecat and WDC-222 datasets, respectively.

To evaluate that the perturbation process did not semantically alter the descriptions in a significant way, we asked the annotators to label the descriptions with clean descriptions and also combined attack for both datasets ('**Clean**' and '**Combined**' in Table 3). Furthermore, to check if historical classifications of clean descriptions semantically similar to perturbed data would aid annotators, for each combined attack description in the set of 100 randomly selected product descriptions, we provided five most semantically similar examples, using SentenceTransformer (Reimers and Gurevych, 2019) ('**Combined+FS**' in Table 3). We then asked the annotator to map the description that is attacked with combined perturbation to its closest clean description. Then we calculate the accuracy of the annotator mapped labels versus the true label of the perturbed data points. The design for this experiment is similar to adding few-shot similar examples to the LLM prompt to allow the model to find semantic similarities between the original clean data and the perturbed data.

Accuracy (%)	Clean	Combined	Combined+FS
Icecat	76	72	97
WDC-222	72	67	95

Table 3: Human annotator analysis of perturbed data.

Table 3 summarizes the human annotators' classification accuracy results. We observe that for both datasets, the combined attack has an impact on the accuracy of classification compared to clean descriptions. However, given that we observe high accuracy for both datasets when a few shot semantically similar examples are provided to the annotator, this confirms that the amputation perturbation makes the classification more difficult, but the semantics of the products stay intact. This establishes that our perturbation framework works as expected and a classification model that is robust to input perturbations should be able to maintain robust classification performance in the presence of data attacks proposed through our work. In the following, we continue with evaluation of machine-learning-based approaches.

5.5 Metrics

We assess the classification performance using both macro (*ma*) and weighted (*we*) Precision, Recall, and F1-Score values to compare different approaches. Additionally, for each model, we also calculate its most robust (i.e., the smallest) Δ_r score.

5.6 Robustness Analysis

Table 4 shows the performance and robustness of various configurations that were experimented with. It should be noted that we chose to exclude certain configurations from execution in order to manage the models inference API cost and also because we were able to extract patterns from the configurations that were executed. We summarize the key observations from the results as follows. GPT-4 model with few-shot prompting delivers the best classification results on both datasets among all models and shows the highest level of robustness to the introduced data attacks. As expected, the 'Clean' data approach yields the best results, with performance marginally decreasing as data attacks are introduced for 'Amputated' and 'Abbreviated' data configurations. Supervised model achieved the second highest performance after GPT-4 for the 'Clean' scenario. However, the performance values for this model significantly drop as the attacks are introduced. In general, LLMs show more robustness to the introduced attacks in the product description as they are able to better reason on the details of the product description. In addition, few-shot examples allow LLMs to further learn from the context and improve their performance, compared to our experimented supervised classification models which cannot leverage this capability.

Model	Approach	Attack	Icecat (%) (ice)						WDC-222 (%) (wdc)					
			ma-P	ma-R	ma-F1	we-P	we-R	we-F1	ma-P	ma-R	ma-F1	we-P	we-R	we-F1
DeBERTaV3 base (Supervised)	Flat	Clean	88.5 ± 0.6	89.2 ± 0.4	88.3 ± 0.5	97.9 ± 0.1	98.1 ± 0.1	97.8 ± 0.1	38.9 ± 2.3	38.6 ± 1.7	35.1 ± 1.8	81.5 ± 0.8	70.7 ± 1.4	72.9 ± 1.5
		Abbreviated	48.1 ± 1.3	48.0 ± 2.1	44.4 ± 1.7	81.4 ± 1.6	76.0 ± 3.1	75.8 ± 2.3	25.5 ± 1.3	21.8 ± 1.2	19.4 ± 0.8	69.2 ± 2.3	38.4 ± 3.8	43.6 ± 4.0
		Amputated	67.6 ± 0.9	72.0 ± 0.5	67.0 ± 0.7	87.4 ± 0.2	85.6 ± 0.6	85.1 ± 0.6	35.0 ± 1.9	34.7 ± 1.4	31.2 ± 1.6	78.4 ± 1.4	63.0 ± 4.3	66.6 ± 3.8
		Combined	46.0 ± 0.6	45.9 ± 1.5	41.7 ± 0.9	76.2 ± 0.6	66.7 ± 2.9	67.6 ± 2.0	26.0 ± 1.0	22.0 ± 1.4	19.7 ± 0.7	70.5 ± 0.6	39.9 ± 3.5	46.0 ± 3.3
	Hierarchical	Clean	83.5 ± 10.4	84.8 ± 9.1	83.4 ± 10.0	97.1 ± 1.5	97.5 ± 1.0	97.2 ± 1.3	38.6 ± 1.4	37.9 ± 1.5	34.4 ± 1.3	81.8 ± 0.9	68.7 ± 0.9	71.8 ± 0.5
		Abbreviated	46.0 ± 4.5	46.4 ± 3.1	42.4 ± 3.7	81.2 ± 1.1	73.2 ± 3.8	74.0 ± 2.5	26.1 ± 0.8	22.7 ± 1.1	20.1 ± 0.7	71.3 ± 0.9	39.9 ± 4.6	45.6 ± 5.7
		Amputated	62.7 ± 6.8	66.8 ± 6.3	61.7 ± 6.3	86.7 ± 1.2	83.6 ± 0.6	83.6 ± 0.7	36.8 ± 1.3	35.6 ± 1.3	32.1 ± 1.1	79.2 ± 1.2	60.9 ± 2.3	65.2 ± 1.5
		Combined	43.2 ± 4.7	43.3 ± 3.5	39.0 ± 3.8	76.0 ± 1.4	62.4 ± 3.7	64.8 ± 2.5	27.0 ± 0.7	23.2 ± 0.8	20.6 ± 0.5	71.3 ± 1.3	41.6 ± 1.9	47.7 ± 1.8
	Δ_r (%)	–	48.0	48.5	52.8	22.2	32.0	30.9	33.2	43.0	43.9	13.5	43.6	36.9
Llama-2 (70b-chat)	Flat	Clean	19.6	29.2	19.9	50.2	37.4	36.9	23.8	28.7	21.9	75.9	51.4	51.4
		Abbreviated	11.7	16.8	11.7	78.0	39.4	41.0	22.5	27.4	20.5	72.5	44.5	42.8
		Amputated	16.1	21.6	15.4	81.8	38.3	41.6	25.6	28.2	22.8	76.4	53.4	52.9
		Combined	13.4	19.5	13.1	76.7	40.9	42.0	22.6	27.9	20.3	73.3	48.7	47.8
		Combined-Reason	19.9	27.1	19.4	72.2	54.3	54.7	31.0	34.2	27.8	68.7	56.2	52.2
	Hierarchical	Clean	35.2	34.7	29.8	65.2	40.4	39.4	33.2	35.7	29.1	68.6	41.9	38.1
		Combined	32.1	33.6	28.2	58.5	38.5	35.4	29.6	32.6	25.4	70.0	37.6	36.8
	Few-shot	Clean	89.6	89.2	88.3	97.1	96.1	95.9	73.1	71.5	69.4	89.8	86.6	85.6
		Abbreviated	76.5	79.0	75.7	85.8	84.5	80.6	61.3	67.0	59.2	83.8	65.6	61.6
		Amputated	86.9	85.5	84.8	94.9	93.5	93.1	68.0	68.1	64.3	84.3	78.0	74.5
		Combined	79.3	79.6	77.6	92.7	90.5	89.6	61.8	65.2	59.2	82.8	68.6	64.5
		Combined-Reason	78.3	78.4	76.3	94.2	92.6	92.6	63.7	62.9	59.1	83.0	74.7	72.1
	Δ_r (%)	–	12.6	12.1	13.6	3.0	3.6	3.4	12.9	12.0	14.8	7.6	13.7	15.8
GPT3.5 (ver.: 0613)	Flat	Clean	63.9	63.9	61.0	90.4	83.9	84.4	57.1	55.0	53.3	92.2	86.5	87.9
		Abbreviated	57.8	58.6	54.9	90.0	82.8	83.5	54.9	53.2	51.1	91.2	85.0	86.4
		Amputated	64.1	63.8	61.1	89.9	84.3	84.7	55.5	55.0	52.5	90.5	85.1	86.1
		Combined	57.1	58.2	54.4	88.6	81.6	82.4	54.9	53.5	50.8	88.2	82.8	83.2
	Hierarchical	Clean	63.8	59.0	57.3	88.1	66.0	66.1	58.0	53.6	51.4	81.7	65.3	66.2
		Combined	58.1	54.2	52.1	85.8	62.8	63.3	56.5	52.5	50.0	85.7	78.5	79.0
	Few-shot	Clean	87.6	88.3	87.0	97.7	96.7	97.0	77.0	76.9	75.1	94.1	92.3	92.5
		Abbreviated	82.5	83.3	81.5	96.7	95.2	95.6	72.0	70.8	69.5	92.4	90.1	90.3
		Amputated	85.5	85.9	84.6	96.3	95.2	95.4	76.5	75.7	74.1	92.7	90.7	90.8
		Combined	81.1	82.7	80.1	95.1	93.6	93.9	72.8	72.1	70.0	90.6	88.1	87.9
		Combined-Reason	81.3	82.4	80.2	95.4	93.9	94.2	72.9	72.4	70.4	89.8	87.3	87.0
	Δ_r (%)	–	7.2	6.7	7.8	2.4	2.9	2.9	5.3	5.9	6.3	4.6	5.4	5.9
GPT4 (ver.: 0613)	Flat	Clean	79.5	79.5	77.5	93.6	90.6	90.8	69.2	67.7	66.0	94.6	89.0	89.9
		Combined	72.9	73.9	71.0	92.9	89.9	90.2	66.0	65.6	63.1	93.3	88.4	89.1
		Combined-Reasoned	73.6	74.5	71.7	92.8	90.2	90.5	66.8	66.1	63.6	93.1	88.8	89.3
	Hierarchical	No-attach	66.3	62.1	60.8	88.8	69.7	69.8	59.4	57.4	54.7	85.3	80.3	80.1
		Combined	64.1	59.0	57.8	81.1	71.9	69.9	68.1	62.2	61.6	87.8	68.5	68.4
	Few-shot	Clean	93.5	93.0	92.8	99.0	98.5	98.6	80.0	77.1	76.9	95.9	94.0	94.4
		Combined	85.7	86.2	84.9	**96.9**	**96.0**	**96.2**	78.0	76.2	75.3	93.8	91.9	92.1
		Combined-Reason	**86.2**	**86.3**	**85.2**	**96.9**	**96.0**	**96.2**	**78.7**	**76.9**	**75.9**	**93.9**	**92.1**	**92.2**
	Δ_r (%)	–	7.8	7.2	8.2	2.1	2.5	2.4	1.6	0.3	1.3	2.1	2.0	2.3

Table 4: The table summarizes the results for Icecat and WDC-222 datasets and different models. We experimented with supervised and large language models for different configurations and attack scenarios. The prefixes ma- and we- denote macro and weighted metrics, respectively. P, R, and F1 denote Precision, Recall, and F1-Score respectively. For each model, the Δ_r values are calculated for best performing configuration with attacks, i.e., Flat/Combined for supervised and Few-shot/Combined-Reason for LLMs. For each metric, the best-performing configuration with combined data attacks is shown in bold. Note: we-R is comparable to accuracy (developers).

Hierarchical classification generally performed equally or worse than flat classification and inferior to few-shot prompting. We rationalize that since the errors from the first level of classification propagate to the second level, this compounding effect results in lower performance in hierarchical classification compared to flat configuration. In some cases, we observed that hierarchical classification improves macro scores, which indicates that this method achieves a more balanced prediction across different classes. For example, Llama-2 achieves better results with hierarchical classification than with the flat classification method. This is because the hierarchical approach allows the model to focus on a smaller set of classes at each hierarchy.

Comparing the results for two different datasets, Icecat and WDC-222, we observe that LLM-based approaches show a significant improvement for the WDC-222 dataset but a less noticeable improvement for Icecat. The reason is that the classification of the Icecat dataset is simpler than that of WDC-222, as the latter comes from heterogeneous data sources (wdc). As such, the baseline supervised values for the Icecat dataset are also higher than those for the WDC-222 dataset. This also provides grounds for our observation that SOTA LLMs can generalize better than supervised approaches on heterogeneous datasets, based on the noteacible improvement observed in the WDC-222 dataset.

The Few-shot scenario further improves the performance of the LLMs, and GPT-4 achieves a new state-of-the-art result on classification task on Icecat and WDC-222 datasets (wdc; Brinkmann and Bizer, 2021). Additionally, the **'Combined-Reason'** scenario improves classification performance in cases where a combined attack is present. This added reasoning in the prompt allows to recover some of the performance loss observed between clean data and combined-attack configurations by further leveraging the reasoning capabilities of LLMs. Our findings suggest that while LLMs are more robust in classification compared to supervised approaches, i.e., have lower Δ_rs, this **robustness can be further improved with informing the model of potential data issues, such as missing characteristics and abbreviations.** This observation also underlines the need for more practical designs of ML approaches while considering real-world challenges.

6 Discussion

6.1 Data Leakage

One concern that exists is that the LLMs' training dataset, like GPT-4 as an example, might have already included our experimented datasets. Although this cannot be entirely ruled out, our approach is still valid for two key reasons. Firstly, GPT-4 initially shows lower performance, but significantly improves in our few-shot scenario, outperforming the supervised models. This indicates that the effectiveness of GPT-4 extends beyond merely memorization. Secondly, the robustness of LLMs, particularly in our data perturbation framework with Combined-Reason, is evident. The perturbed dataset, as it is novel and not included in prior training, shows GPT-4's ability to understand product semantics and effectively recover from data perturbations.

6.2 Impact and Deployment

Our research has partially enabled AI-based product categorization in our global trade service which is crucial and sensitive for compliance and regulatory aspects for large corporations active in cross-border trade. Our research is impactful as it has enabled more efficient and accurate classification, and thus reduces the regulatory and compliance risk. The discovery phase of the project has been completed with testing on millions of data records and the second phase of the project which expands to multiple users and more data is ongoing.

7 Conclusion

In this research, we presented a data perturbation framework to simulate the real-world data deficiencies for ML-based product classification. We then proceeded with a comprehensive evaluation of different supervised and LLM-based classification approaches in presence and absence of data attacks. Our findings show that LLM-based approaches are generally more robust against adversarial attacks and more suitable for applications that require high robustness in predictions and misclassification can cause compliance repercussions. As future work, we will further investigate the security robustness of LLMs in data-critical applications and explore leveraging LLMs for providing classification rationales in addition to label predictions.

8 Limitations

Our analysis has limitations, particularly as we observed that the results from Llama-2, are not completely stable, and small variations within the prompt can lead to noticeable changes in classification performance. We believe these limitations are largely addressed in SOTA models, like GPT-4. Additionally, our data perturbation framework models a limited set of data attacks that are relevant to our industrial use case, however, other use cases might face different data challenges, which should be dealt with per use case.

9 Ethical and Practical Considerations

This study has been carried out by following the privacy requirements of our organization. The research has been reviewed by research directors and legal counsel to ensure adherence to privacy of our users data and information. Furthermore, the authors of this work have been committed to adhering to the highest standards of ethical responsibility throughout the research. In product environments where automated product classification models are deployed, the predictions are presented to the end user as suggestions, and it is then the end user's sole responsibility to accept, reject, or manually adjust these predictions as necessary. This work presents a general perspective on the product classification task and does not incorporate additional sources of information that could be leveraged for specific use cases, such as the Harmonized System classification, which utilizes tariff schedules, rulings, and keywords.

References

Open Icecat catalog. https://icecat.de/. Accessed: 2024-01-05.

WDC-222 Gold Standard for Hierarchical Product Categorization. https://data.dws.informatik.uni-mannheim.de/largescaleproductcorpus/categorization/. Accessed: 2024-01-05.

2023. World Customs Organization. https://www.wcoomd.org/. Accessed on October 2023.

Noa Avigdor, Guy Horowitz, Ariel Raviv, and Stav Yanovsky Daye. 2023. Consistent text categorization using data augmentation in e-commerce. In *Proceedings of the 61st Annual Meeting of the Association for Computational Linguistics (Volume 5: Industry Track)*, pages 313–321, Toronto, Canada. Association for Computational Linguistics.

Melika Behjati, Seyed-Mohsen Moosavi-Dezfooli, Mahdieh Soleymani Baghshah, and Pascal Frossard. 2019. Universal adversarial attacks on text classifiers. In *ICASSP 2019-2019 IEEE International Conference on Acoustics, Speech and Signal Processing (ICASSP)*, pages 7345–7349. IEEE.

Alexander Brinkmann and Christian Bizer. 2021. Improving hierarchical product classification using domain-specific language modelling. *IEEE Data Eng. Bull.*, 44(2):14–25.

Tom Brown, Benjamin Mann, Nick Ryder, Melanie Subbiah, Jared D Kaplan, Prafulla Dhariwal, Arvind Neelakantan, Pranav Shyam, Girish Sastry, Amanda Askell, et al. 2020. Language models are few-shot learners. *Advances in neural information processing systems*, 33:1877–1901.

Lei Chen, Houwei Chou, Yandi Xia, and Hirokazu Miyake. 2021. Multimodal item categorization fully based on transformer. In *Proceedings of The 4th Workshop on e-Commerce and NLP*, pages 111–115.

Scikit developers. Compute the recall. `https://scikit-learn.org/stable/modules/generated/sklearn.metrics.recall_score.html`. Accessed: May 20, 2024.

Idan Hasson, Slava Novgorodov, Gilad Fuchs, and Yoni Acriche. 2021. Category recognition in e-commerce using sequence-to-sequence hierarchical classification. In *Proceedings of the 14th ACM International Conference on Web Search and Data Mining*, pages 902–905.

Pengcheng He, Jianfeng Gao, and Weizhu Chen. 2023. DeBERTav3: Improving deBERTa using ELECTRA-style pre-training with gradient-disentangled embedding sharing. In *The Eleventh International Conference on Learning Representations*.

Ravikumar Kondadadi, Allen Williams, and Nicolas Nicolov. 2022. Data quality estimation framework for faster tax code classification. In *Proceedings of the Fifth Workshop on e-Commerce and NLP (ECNLP 5)*, pages 29–34.

Solomon Kullback and Richard A Leibler. 1951. On information and sufficiency. *The annals of mathematical statistics*, 22(1):79–86.

Eunji Lee, Sundong Kim, Sihyun Kim, Sungwon Park, Meeyoung Cha, Soyeon Jung, Suyoung Yang, Yeonsoo Choi, Sungdae Ji, Minsoo Song, et al. 2021. Classification of goods using text descriptions with sentences retrieval. *arXiv preprint arXiv:2111.01663*.

Microsoft. Deberta v3 base model. Hugging Face Model Repository. Accessed: 2024-01-17.

John Morris, Eli Lifland, Jin Yong Yoo, Jake Grigsby, Di Jin, and Yanjun Qi. 2020. Textattack: A framework for adversarial attacks, data augmentation, and adversarial training in nlp. In *Proceedings of the 2020 Conference on Empirical Methods in Natural Language Processing: System Demonstrations*, pages 119–126.

Huy Nguyen and Devashish Khatwani. 2022. Robust product classification with instance-dependent noise. In *Proceedings of the Fifth Workshop on e-Commerce and NLP (ECNLP 5)*, pages 171–180, Dublin, Ireland. Association for Computational Linguistics.

OpenAI. 2023. GPT-4 Technical Report. *Preprint*, arXiv:2303.08774.

Nils Reimers and Iryna Gurevych. 2019. Sentence-bert: Sentence embeddings using siamese bert-networks. In *Proceedings of the 2019 Conference on Empirical Methods in Natural Language Processing*. Association for Computational Linguistics.

Hugo Touvron, Louis Martin, Kevin Stone, Peter Albert, Amjad Almahairi, Yasmine Babaei, Nikolay Bashlykov, Soumya Batra, Prajjwal Bhargava, Shruti Bhosale, et al. 2023. Llama 2: Open foundation and fine-tuned chat models. *arXiv preprint arXiv:2307.09288*.

U.S. Department of Commerce. 2023. Harmonized system (hs) codes. `https://www.trade.gov/harmonized-system-hs-codes`. Accessed: 2024-01-10.

Boxin Wang, Shuohang Wang, Yu Cheng, Zhe Gan, Ruoxi Jia, Bo Li, and Jingjing Liu. 2020. Infobert: Improving robustness of language models from an information theoretic perspective. *arXiv preprint arXiv:2010.02329*.

Xuezhi Wang, Haohan Wang, and Diyi Yang. 2022. Measure and improve robustness in NLP models: A survey. In *Proceedings of the 2022 Conference of the North American Chapter of the Association for Computational Linguistics: Human Language Technologies*, pages 4569–4586, Seattle, United States. Association for Computational Linguistics.

Jason Wei, Xuezhi Wang, Dale Schuurmans, Maarten Bosma, Fei Xia, Ed Chi, Quoc V Le, Denny Zhou, et al. 2022. Chain-of-thought prompting elicits reasoning in large language models. *Advances in Neural Information Processing Systems*, 35:24824–24837.

Thomas Wolf, Lysandre Debut, Victor Sanh, Julien Chaumond, Clement Delangue, Anthony Moi, Perric Cistac, Clara Ma, Yacine Jernite, Julien Plu, Canwen Xu, Teven Le Scao, Sylvain Gugger, Mariama Drame, Quentin Lhoest, and Alexander M. Rush. 2020. Transformers: State-of-the-Art Natural Language Processing. pages 38–45. Association for Computational Linguistics.

World Customs Organization. 2023a. Annual report 2022-2023. Accessed: 2023-11-13.

World Customs Organization. 2023b. What is the harmonized system? https://www.wcoomd.org/en/topics/nomenclature/overview/what-is-the-harmonized-system.aspx. Accessed: 2024-01-08.

Jin Yong Yoo and Yanjun Qi. 2021. Towards improving adversarial training of NLP models. In *Findings of the Association for Computational Linguistics: EMNLP 2021*, pages 945–956, Punta Cana, Dominican Republic. Association for Computational Linguistics.

Kang Min Yoo, Dongju Park, Jaewook Kang, Sang-Woo Lee, and Woomyoung Park. 2021. GPT3Mix: Leveraging large-scale language models for text augmentation. In *Findings of the Association for Computational Linguistics: EMNLP 2021*, pages 2225–2239, Punta Cana, Dominican Republic. Association for Computational Linguistics.

Wei Emma Zhang, Can Z Sheng, Ahoud Alhazmi, and Chenliang Li. 2020. Adversarial attacks on deep-learning models in natural language processing: A survey. *ACM Transactions on Intelligent Systems and Technology (TIST)*, 11(3):1–41.

Andy Zou, Zifan Wang, J Zico Kolter, and Matt Fredrikson. 2023. Universal and transferable adversarial attacks on aligned language models. *arXiv preprint arXiv:2307.15043*.

A Prompts

Figure 2 shows the prompt for simulating data attacks with the help of GPT-4, as explained in the data perturbation framework, while Figure 3 displays the prompt for the classification of products. The first prompt aims to is to accurately automate the data perturbation framework, and the second prompt allows to classify the products, using an LLM. As the data is manipulated by an LLM, we investigate the correctness of the approach in comparison to the intended outcomes through human analysis in Section 5.3.

(Abbreviation) You got a new job as a product classifier for products belonging to the Icecat catalog.
You are asked to modify a description of a product that belongs to the "{industry_input}" category (according to the hierarchy in Icecat) and modify words with their abbreviations (as could happen in shipment details).
It is vital to not modify the description in a way that could change the classification of the product.
Please do not abbreviate more than 20% of the words or I would not understand the description.
The order of the words must not change.
Original description: {description_input}
New description:

(Amputation) You got a new job as a product classifier for products belonging to the Icecat catalog.
You are asked to truncate a description of a product that belongs to the "{industry_input}" category (according to the hierarchy in Icecat) and to make it much shorter, like it would appear in a shipment detail description.
Omit all the information that is not strictly necessary to identify the product, i.e. technical characteristics.
The order of the words must not change.
Work following the order below:
1. if the description is shorter than 5 words, do not change it
2. if the description is longer than 5 words, select the 5 most important words
3. put the selected words in the relative order in which they appeared in the original description
Original description: {description_input}
New description:

Figure 2: This figure shows the prompts used for GPT-4 to perform abbreviation and amputation data attacks.

01 **Classify the following product to one class form the list below.**
02
03 **List of classes:**
04 *Warranty & Support Extensions*
05 *Notebooks*
06 *PCs/Workstations*
07 ...
08
09 (Few-shot) **Some examples with their classes are provided:**
10 {*5-shot similar examples*}
11
12 **Product:** {*test product*}
13 (Combined-Reason) Be aware that some parts of the product description might have been abbreviated
14 or amputated.
15
16 Output only the class name and no additional text. Example: 'Tablets'
17
18 (Llamma only) **Product class from the list above is:**

Figure 3: This prompt displays the template for LLM classification. Lines 09-10 are used solely for Few-shot prompting. Lines 13-14 are added only in the Combined-Reason attack scenario, while Line 18 is added for the Llamma-2 model, as we observed that it requires further prompt engineering to model the task as a completion prompt for outputting a product class.

Less is *Fed* More: Sparsity Reduces Feature Distortion in Federated Learning

Aashiq Muhamed[*1], **Harshita Diddee**[*1], **Abhinav Rao**[*1]

[1]Language Technologies Institute, Carnegie Mellon University
[*]Equal contribution
{amuhamed, hdiddee, abhinavr}@andrew.cmu.edu

Abstract

Our work studies Multilingual Federated Learning (FL), a decentralized paradigm that, although promising, grapples with issues such as client drift and suboptimal generalization in diverse, multilingual settings. We highlight limitations in existing approaches to generalize across both actively participating and inactive client language pairs. To mitigate these challenges, we introduce FedSparseNet, which incorporates sparse-network training, and LoRA, based on Low-Rank Adaptation. These approaches maintain the model's fidelity to its pretraining distribution, thereby ensuring robust performance on both seen and unseen language pairs, while simultaneously enhancing communication efficiency by selectively transmitting trainable parameters. Our empirical evaluations demonstrate that FedSparseNet outperforms conventional FL models on both seen and unseen clients, while LoRA shows remarkable improvements in unseen client performance. Additionally, we propose the Continuous Relative Robustness Metric, a novel metric to uniformly assess a model's performance across diverse language pairs. We open-source our code for reproducibility on GitHub.[1]

1 Introduction

The development of NLP applications capable of leveraging multilingual, multi-source, heterogeneous data while safeguarding user privacy is essential (Deng et al., 2022). FL (McMahan et al., 2016) addresses this by facilitating the utilization of personally identifiable information within a decentralized framework, thereby obviating the need for direct data sharing among clients. However, FL faces challenges such as client drift and suboptimal generalization in heterogeneous environments (Karimireddy et al., 2020). Furthermore, multilingual FL not only contends with these FL-specific optimization difficulties but also grapples with the complexities of extending to low-resource languages. This can hinder the accessibility of language technologies for various communities and intensify systemic biases (Santy et al., 2023).

While there is extensive research on FL for NLP, studies specifically addressing multilingual FL translation remain limited, with minimal exploration of how FL impacts the training process. Multilingual FL is an inherently heterogeneous data setting, offering a unique area of interest within the FL community. The closest work is Weller et al. (2022b), where the authors investigate Federated Multilingual Translation. The study involves fine-tuning and communicating the entire parameter set of a 418M M2M encoder-decoder model. Their findings suggest that fine-tuning a pre-trained model using FL can achieve comparable results to centralized learning, even in Non-IID settings with clients segmented by language.

In our research, we challenge the prevailing narrative that communicating all parameters in a multilingual translation model is viable for practical translation tasks. We argue that this approach is largely impractical. Moreover, translation applications require the server model to not only generalize to client language pairs actively involved in FL but also to maintain pretraining performance on unseen language pairs or inactive clients. Our findings reveal that baseline performance for unseen language pairs declines when fine-tuning with active client data. This issue stems from the distortion of pretrained features (Kumar et al., 2022), a problem not adequately addressed by current FL approaches, especially in the context of NLP tasks like translation. To address the challenges identified, our approach builds on the current literature on Parameter Efficient Finetuning (PEFT) to: a) ensure the model remains close to its pretraining distribution, facilitating balanced generalization across both seen and unseen language pairs, and b) enhance federated fine-tuning and communication

[1]https://github.com/AetherPrior/less-is-fed-more

Proceedings of the 1st Workshop on Customizable NLP: Progress and Challenges in Customizing NLP for a Domain, Application, Group, or Individual (CustomNLP4U), pages 37–46
November 16, 2024 ©2024 Association for Computational Linguistics

efficiency by transmitting only a sparse subset of trainable parameters. Our contributions include:

• We propose **FedSparseNet**, leveraging sparse-network training, and employing Low-Rank Adaptation (**LoRA**) to mitigate pretrained feature distortion and enhance communication efficiency. FedSparseNet dominates the corresponding fully finetuned FL baseline on client-seen and client-unseen performance (by 1.4 BLEU), while LoRA significantly improves the client-unseen performance but falls short on seen-client performance.

• We propose the **Continuous Relative Robustness Metric**, a metric that measures how well a given model uniformly dominates the pretrained model on **both**, seen and unseen language pairs.

2 Methodology

2.1 FedSparseNet: Composable Sparse Fine-tuning for FL

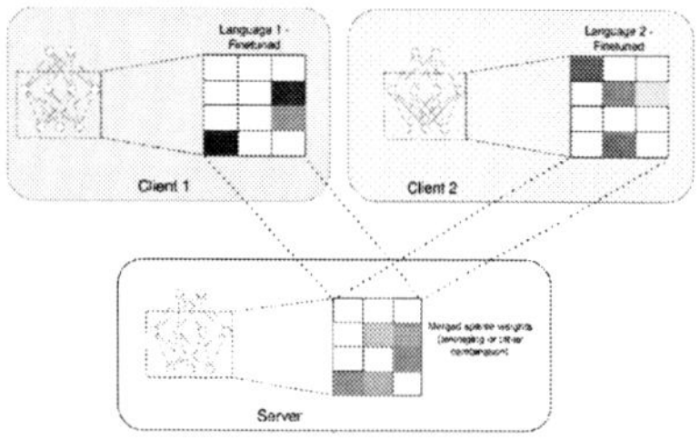

Figure 1: The FedSparseNet framework

We propose a variant of the Lottery Ticket Algorithm for federated training called FedSparseNet. Our work is inspired by Lottery Ticket Sparse Fine-Tuning (LT-SFT) for cross-lingual transfer (Frankle and Carbin, 2018). The Lottery Ticket Hypothesis (LTH) (Frankle and Carbin, 2018) states that each neural model contains a sub-network (a "winning ticket") that, if trained again in isolation, can match or even exceed the performance of the original model. To recover this ticket, the sparse ticket is selected using a pruning stage where some parameters are zero-masked and frozen according to some criterion (e.g., weight magnitude), and the remaining parameters are restored to their original values and then re-tuned. This process of pruning and re-training can be iterated multiple times.

FedSparseNet (Fig. 1) consists of two stages on the client. Let i denote the i-th round of training and $\theta^{(i)}$, the server model parameters at round (i).

(Stage 1) This phase is only applicable at i=1. Let $\theta_0^{(1)}$ represent the pretrained (client) model parameters, and $\theta_1^{(1)}$, the parameters after fine-tuning on the target language or task data D. The parameters are ranked according to the greatest absolute difference $|\theta_0^{(1)} - \theta_1^{(1)}|$, and the top K are selected for subsequent tuning. A binary mask μ is set to have 1 in positions corresponding to these parameters, and 0 elsewhere. This mask state is frozen and preserved for each client across rounds.

(Stage 2) If we are at round 1, the parameters are reset to their original values $\theta_0^{(1)}$, and at any other round, we use the server checkpoint $\theta_s^{(i)}$. The model is again fine-tuned, but this time, only the K-selected parameters using the mask μ are trainable, whereas the others are kept frozen. This is implemented by using the masked gradient $\mu \odot \nabla_\theta L(F(\cdot;\theta), D)$ (where $\odot$ denotes element-wise multiplication and L a loss function) in the optimizer at each step. If we denote the sparse finetuned checkpoint as $\theta_2^{(i)}$, only the sparse vector of differences $\theta_2^{(i)} - \theta_s^{(i)}$ is communicated at every round. The sparse vectors from every client are then aggregated at the server using an aggregation strategy like FedAvg before being broadcasted to clients in the next round.

FedSparseNet enhances communication efficiency by minimizing data transmission which is often about 1% of the client parameters. The modular design allows for effective composability, reducing knowledge overlap and interference among the client languages. Sparsity also serves as a natural form of regularization, making these networks less prone to overfitting, and helping the model retain generalization properties of the pretrained model on unseen data. Sparse networks also have other advantages: it does not introduce additional parameters like the adapter (Houlsby et al., 2019), thereby not reducing inference speed; and the model architecture remains identical to the pretrained model, simplifying code development and ensuring the method is model-agnostic.

2.2 LoRA

We also propose to use Low-Rank Approximation (Hu et al., 2021), as a parameter-efficient client optimization technique that maintains compositionality and proximity to the pretrained weights.

Low Rank Approximation or LoRA encodes the parameter updates of a model undergoing finetuning in a much smaller subspace. Specifically, for a model $P_\Phi(y|x)$ parameterized by Φ, the typical model finetuning would involve updating the entire

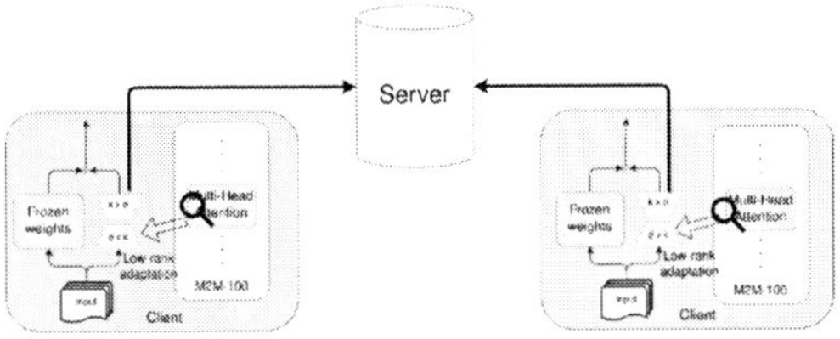

Figure 2: The LoRA framework

parameter space according to:

$$\max_{\Phi} \sum_{(x,y)\in\mathcal{Z}} \sum_{t=1}^{|y|} \log\left(P_{\Phi}(y_t|x, y_{<t})\right) \quad (1)$$

LoRA hypothesizes the existence of a low-rank approximation of the parameter updates, and posits that the full rank update, denoted by $\Delta\Phi$ can be approximated by a much lower rank matrix $\Delta\Phi(\theta)$. In other words, Φ can be expressed as $\Phi_0 + \Delta\Phi(\theta)$.

Several works have studied combining LoRA with Federated learning. Qi et al. (2024) study the use of LoRA for LLM personalization; however, they do not freeze the model's layers during training, thereby compromising on efficiency. We instead maintain efficiency to be our core-focus similar to the works of Zhang et al. (2024); Ye et al. (2024); Kuang et al. (2023). During training, we instantiate each client with LoRA modules of the same rank. In the first iteration, this implies injecting LoRA modules into the pretrained model. During finetuning, we freeze all other parameters but the LoRA modules and subsequently communicate LoRA modules to the server for aggregation. The reduction in parameter update space brought by LoRA, brings significant memory reduction while training with large models, which is advantageous in the FL setting.

2.3 Continuous Relative Robustness Metric for Federated Learning Models

In this work, we employ a fixed model selection strategy on the clients to optimize for client-seen performance. We propose modeling enhancements to improve performance on client-unseen data while retaining performance on client-seen data. To select among the models that perform better than the baseline on both client-seen and unseen data, we propose a new robustness metric to balance performance (in BLEU) on client-seen and client-unseen data. Given a model M and a pre-trained model M_{pre}, we consider a continuous range of trade-off coefficients, $k \in [0, 1]$, to evaluate the balance between client-seen (CS) and client-unseen (CU) performance metrics. The performance metric $P(M, k)$ for a model M is defined over the continuous domain as:

$$P(M, k) = k \cdot \text{perf}_{\text{CS}}(M) + (1 - k) \cdot \text{perf}_{\text{CU}}(M)$$

Relative Robustness Score The relative robustness of model M against the pre-trained model M_{pre} is quantified by integrating the performance advantage of M over M_{pre} across the continuous range of k:

$$RRS(M) = \int_0^1 \mathbf{1}\{P(M, k) > P(M_{\text{pre}}, k)\}\, dk$$

Here, $\mathbf{1}\{\}$ is the indicator function, which is 1 when M outperforms M_{pre} at a given k and 0 otherwise. The integral effectively counts the proportion of the trade-off range where M surpasses M_{pre}. This metric compares FL models in balancing client-seen and client-unseen performance over a continuum.

Language Pair	ISO 639-2 codes	Dataset Source
Client-Seen Languages		
English - French	En-Fr	UNMT corpus
Arabic-Spanish	En-Fr	UNMT corpus
Russian-Chinese	Ru-Zh	UNMT corpus
Client-Unseen Languages - High Resource		
Portuguese-English	Pt-En	FLORES-200
Hindi-English	Hi-En	FLORES-200
Korean-English	Ko-En	FLORES-200
Client-Unseen Languages - Mid Resource		
Tamil-English	Ta-En	FLORES-200
Ukrainian-English	Uk-En	FLORES-200
Finnish-English	Fi-En	FLORES-200
Client-Unseen Languages - Low Resource		
Swahili-English	Sw-En	FLORES-200
Sinhala-English	Si-En	FLORES-200
Malayalam-English	Ml-En	FLORES-200

Table 1: All Language Pairs used in our experiments. We mimic the setup from Weller et al. (2022b) for client-seen language pairs, and pick 9 language pairs from FLORES-200 for our client-unseen languages, based on M2M-100's pretraining distribution.

2.4 Experimental Details

We choose machine translation for all our base tasks and define 'seen' and 'unseen' language-pairs as those pairs that are visible or invisible to the client model during finetuning. We use

Language Pair	Pretrained	Centralized	IID FL	Non-IID FL	FedSparseNet (Non-IID)	FedSparseNet (IID)	LoRA (Non-IID)	LoRA (IID)
Client-Seen Languages								
En-Fr	31.8 ± 0.6	38.0 ± 0.7	37.7 ± 0.7	36.9 ± 0.7	38.6 ± 0.7	38.8 ± 0.7	36.0 ± 0.6	36.2 ± 0.6
Ar-Es	28.0 ± 0.5	35.5 ± 0.7	35.9 ± 0.7	32.9 ± 0.6	36.4 ± 0.7	36.5 ± 0.6	33.4 ± 0.6	33.2 ± 0.6
Ru-Zh	30.3 ± 0.5	37.5 ± 0.6	37.7 ± 0.4	38.7 ± 0.6	37.7 ± 0.7	38.0 ± 0.7	34.3 ± 0.6	34.6 ± 0.6
Avg	30.0 ± 0.5	37.0 ± 0.7	37.1 ± 0.6	36.2 ± 0.6	37.6 ± 0.7	37.8 ± 0.7	34.5 ± 0.6	34.6 ± 0.6
Client-Unseen Languages - High Resource								
Pt-En	40.0 ± 1.1	31.8 ± 1.1	32.0 ± 1.0	26.7 ± 1.2	32.2 ± 1.3	34.9 ± 1.2	39.5 ± 1.1	39.5 ± 1.2
Hi-En	29.6 ± 1.0	22.0 ± 1.1	22.8 ± 0.9	19.3 ± 1.0	21.8 ± 1.3	25.1 ± 1.1	28.3 ± 1.0	28.9 ± 1.0
Ko-En	20.5 ± 0.9	15.0 ± 0.9	14.4 ± 0.9	13.0 ± 0.8	14.5 ± 1.0	16.7 ± 0.9	19.6 ± 0.9	20.0 ± 1.0
Avg	30.0 ± 1.0	22.9 ± 1.0	23.1 ± 0.9	19.7 ± 1.0	22.8 ± 1.2	25.6 ± 1.0	29.1 ± 1.0	29.4 ± 1.1
Client-Unseen Languages - Mid Resource								
Ta-En	8.0 ± 0.6	3.9 ± 0.4	5.0 ± 0.5	3.7 ± 0.4	1.6 ± 0.2	4.7 ± 0.5	9.2 ± 0.7	8.6 ± 0.7
Uk-En	27.9 ± 1.0	18.2 ± 1.0	21.8 ± 0.9	20.7 ± 1.0	21.2 ± 1.2	23.8 ± 0.9	28.2 ± 1.0	27.8 ± 1.0
Fi-En	25.7 ± 1.0	18.2 ± 1.0	18.8 ± 0.8	14.4 ± 1.0	18.8 ± 1.1	21.0 ± 0.9	25.0 ± 1.0	24.9 ± 0.9
Avg	20.5 ± 0.9	13.4 ± 0.8	15.2 ± 0.7	12.9 ± 0.8	13.9 ± 0.8	16.5 ± 0.8	20.8 ± 0.9	20.4 ± 0.8
Client-Unseen Languages - Low Resource								
Sw-En	26.0 ± 0.9	17.2 ± 1.0	18.4 ± 1.0	13.6 ± 1.0	15.0 ± 1.1	21.0 ± 1.0	24.4 ± 1.0	24.8 ± 1.0
Si-En	15.9 ± 0.8	8.8 ± 0.7	9.6 ± 0.8	7.3 ± 0.7	6.1 ± 0.7	10.9 ± 0.8	15.1 ± 0.8	14.9 ± 0.9
Ml-En	15.3 ± 0.9	8.0 ± 0.8	8.6 ± 0.8	6.3 ± 0.6	5.5 ± 0.6	10.3 ± 0.8	14.3 ± 0.8	15.0 ± 0.9
Avg	19.1 ± 0.9	11.3 ± 0.8	12.2 ± 0.9	9.1 ± 0.8	8.9 ± 0.8	14.0 ± 0.9	17.9 ± 0.9	18.2 ± 0.9
Weighted Metric Calculation								
RRS	0.000	0.488	0.525	0.397	0.485	0.632	0.897	0.882

Table 2: UN-MT Bleu for Client-Seen and Client-Unseen Language Pairs. FedSparseNet uses sparsity ratio 0.01 on embedding matrix. LoRA trained with rank 8, on embedding matrices. All models are trained for 1 epoch/round.

the M2M100-418M model (Fan et al., 2020) as our base, UN parallel corpus (which we term as UNMT) (Ziemski et al., 2016) for finetuning, FLORES-200 (Costa-jussà et al., 2022) for evaluation and report performance using BLEU (Papineni et al., 2002). All client models are trained for 100 rounds, and the best model is selected based on the local validation loss. We choose our seen language-pairs similar to that of Weller et al. (2022b), and pick 9 unseen language pairs (3 from High, Middle and Low resource languages respectively) from FLORES-200, based on M2M-100's pretraining distribution. We choose English to be our target language for simplicity in evaluation and comparison. Table 1 presents all of our language pairs and their respective ISO-693-2 codes, which we shall use from here on. Additional details on training dataset and metrics can be found in Appendix A.1. We conduct all experiments over three settings: standard finetuning of the base model without any federation (the *Centralized* setting), FL on IID data (*IID FL*), where all three language pairs are uniformly mixed and distributed across clients, and FL on non-IID or heterogeneous data (*Non-IID FL*), where each client receives a separate language pair for training. We use FedAvg (McMahan et al., 2016) as our aggregation algorithm.

3 Results

Table 2 compares our approach with the baseline (Weller et al., 2022b): the performance of the federated fully FT models on unseen-client data shows a significant drop in performance relative to the Pretrained model on all client-unseen language pairs.

FedSparseNet FedSparseNet dominates the corresponding baselines across seen and unseen client datasets (Table 2), demonstrating their overall effectiveness. Interestingly, no significant trend is observed across High-, Mid-, and Low-Resource languages. We also note that while FedSparseNet (IID) and FedSparseNet (Non-IID) achieve similar performance on client-seen data, the latter exhibits significantly lower performance on unseen data, especially for Low-Resource languages. This suggests that Non-IID FL potentially distorts pretrained features more than IID-FL, impacting performance in ways not captured by client-seen accuracy alone. Consistent with these observations, the RRS metric reveals a higher value for FedSparseNet in the IID setting compared to the Non-IID setting. This highlights the effectiveness of FedSparseNet in scenarios with balanced and representative data distributions (IID).

LoRA In Table 2, we compare LoRA with the baseline. LoRA demonstrates its highest efficacy on unseen languages, effectively minimizing the distortion introduced by optimization on seen-client data during federated finetuning. This capability to recover unseen client performance can be attributed to the inherent regularizing effect of LoRA on the distribution of the federated model.

The strengths of LoRA are further illuminated by its superior performance in the RRS metric — that endorses LoRA as a more viable alternative than full FT and FedSparseNet, for achieving balanced improvements across seen and unseen language pairs. However, it is imperative to approach these results with caution. LoRA's performance on seen clients, in both IID and Non-IID settings, falls short of the centralized model and FedSparseNet. This observed degradation suggests possible shortcomings in LoRA's ability to effectively compose client knowledge across diverse heterogeneous datasets. While FedSparseNet also appears to benefit from its approach of localizing seen-language-specific information through strategic subnet selection—a method documented to personalize and compose well across clients (Ansell et al., 2021), LoRA may encounter challenges in achieving a similar level of integration, particularly due to interference between client-specific modules during federated optimization.

Comparing Communication Efficiency We compare both methods with the baselines for communication efficiency up to the point of convergence in Appendix A.2. We observe a *54x* and *5.9x* increase in communication efficiency for FedSparseNet and LoRA respectively.

4 Conclusion

Motivated by the need to improve generalization in FL for unseen client data, we introduce FedSparseNet and LoraFed. These methods focus on sparsifying the client parameter space, addressing the challenge of pretrained feature distortion due to seen-client optimization, and enhancing communication efficiency.

References

Alan Ansell, Edoardo Maria Ponti, Anna Korhonen, and Ivan Vulić. 2021. Composable sparse fine-tuning for cross-lingual transfer. *arXiv preprint arXiv:2110.07560*.

Tyler A. Chang, Catherine Arnett, Zhuowen Tu, and Benjamin K. Bergen. 2023. When is multilinguality a curse? language modeling for 250 high- and low-resource languages. *ArXiv*, abs/2311.09205.

Marta R Costa-jussà, James Cross, Onur Çelebi, Maha Elbayad, Kenneth Heafield, Kevin Heffernan, Elahe Kalbassi, Janice Lam, Daniel Licht, Jean Maillard, et al. 2022. No language left behind: Scaling human-centered machine translation. *arXiv preprint arXiv:2207.04672*.

Jieren Deng, Chenghong Wang, Xianrui Meng, Yijue Wang, Ji Li, Sheng Lin, Shuo Han, Fei Miao, Sanguthevar Rajasekaran, and Caiwen Ding. 2022. A secure and efficient federated learning framework for nlp.

Ning Ding, Xingtai Lv, Qiaosen Wang, Yulin Chen, Bowen Zhou, Zhiyuan Liu, and Maosong Sun. 2023. Sparse low-rank adaptation of pre-trained language models. In *Conference on Empirical Methods in Natural Language Processing*.

Angela Fan, Shruti Bhosale, Holger Schwenk, Zhiyi Ma, Ahmed El-Kishky, Siddharth Goyal, Mandeep Baines, Onur Celebi, Guillaume Wenzek, Vishrav Chaudhary, Naman Goyal, Tom Birch, Vitaliy Liptchinsky, Sergey Edunov, Edouard Grave, Michael Auli, and Armand Joulin. 2020. Beyond english-centric multilingual machine translation.

Jonathan Frankle and Michael Carbin. 2018. The lottery ticket hypothesis: Finding sparse, trainable neural networks. *arXiv preprint arXiv:1803.03635*.

Neil Houlsby, Andrei Giurgiu, Stanislaw Jastrzebski, Bruna Morrone, Quentin De Laroussilhe, Andrea Gesmundo, Mona Attariyan, and Sylvain Gelly. 2019. Parameter-efficient transfer learning for nlp. In *International Conference on Machine Learning*, pages 2790–2799. PMLR.

Edward J Hu, Yelong Shen, Phillip Wallis, Zeyuan Allen-Zhu, Yuanzhi Li, Shean Wang, Lu Wang, and Weizhu Chen. 2021. Lora: Low-rank adaptation of large language models. *arXiv preprint arXiv:2106.09685*.

Sai Praneeth Karimireddy, Satyen Kale, Mehryar Mohri, Sashank Reddi, Sebastian Stich, and Ananda Theertha Suresh. 2020. SCAFFOLD: Stochastic controlled averaging for federated learning. In *Proceedings of the 37th International Conference on Machine Learning*, volume 119 of *Proceedings of Machine Learning Research*, pages 5132–5143. PMLR.

Weirui Kuang, Bingchen Qian, Zitao Li, Daoyuan Chen, Dawei Gao, Xuchen Pan, Yuexiang Xie, Yaliang Li, Bolin Ding, and Jingren Zhou. 2023. Federatedscope-llm: A comprehensive package for fine-tuning large language models in federated learning.

Ananya Kumar, Aditi Raghunathan, Robbie Matthew Jones, Tengyu Ma, and Percy Liang. 2022. Fine-tuning can distort pretrained features and underperform out-of-distribution. In *International Conference on Learning Representations*.

H. B. McMahan, Eider Moore, Daniel Ramage, S. Hampson, and B. A. Y. Arcas. 2016. Communication-efficient learning of deep networks from decentralized data. *International Conference on Artificial Intelligence and Statistics*.

Kishore Papineni, Salim Roukos, Todd Ward, and Wei-Jing Zhu. 2002. Bleu: a method for automatic evaluation of machine translation. In *Proceedings of the 40th Annual Meeting of the Association for Computational Linguistics*, pages 311–318, Philadelphia, Pennsylvania, USA. Association for Computational Linguistics.

Jiaxing Qi, Zhongzhi Luan, Shaohan Huang, Carol Fung, Hailong Yang, and Depei Qian. 2024. Fdlora: Personalized federated learning of large language model via dual lora tuning.

Sebastin Santy, Jenny Liang, Ronan Le Bras, Katharina Reinecke, and Maarten Sap. 2023. NLPositionality: Characterizing design biases of datasets and models. In *Proceedings of the 61st Annual Meeting of the Association for Computational Linguistics (Volume 1: Long Papers)*, pages 9080–9102, Toronto, Canada. Association for Computational Linguistics.

Orion Weller, Marc Marone, Vladimir Braverman, Dawn Lawrie, and Benjamin Van Durme. 2022a. Pretrained models for multilingual federated learning. In *Proceedings of the 2022 Conference of the North American Chapter of the Association for Computational Linguistics: Human Language Technologies*, pages 1413–1421, Seattle, United States. Association for Computational Linguistics.

Orion Weller, Marc Marone, Vladimir Braverman, Dawn J Lawrie, and Benjamin Van Durme. 2022b. Pretrained models for multilingual federated learning. *ArXiv*, abs/2206.02291.

Rui Ye, Wenhao Wang, Jingyi Chai, Dihan Li, Zexi Li, Yinda Xu, Yaxin Du, Yanfeng Wang, and Siheng Chen. 2024. Openfedllm: Training large language models on decentralized private data via federated learning.

Jianyi Zhang, Saeed Vahidian, Martin Kuo, Chunyuan Li, Ruiyi Zhang, Tong Yu, Yufan Zhou, Guoyin Wang, and Yiran Chen. 2024. Towards building the federated gpt: Federated instruction tuning.

Michał Ziemski, Marcin Junczys-Dowmunt, and Bruno Pouliquen. 2016. The United Nations parallel corpus v1.0. In *Proceedings of the Tenth International Conference on Language Resources and Evaluation (LREC'16)*, pages 3530–3534, Portorož, Slovenia. European Language Resources Association (ELRA).

A Appendix

A.1 Task Experimental Details

The UN corpus contains written records of the UN proceedings from 1990-2014. For seen-languages, we consider training, validation, and tests sets for the same source and target language pairs as described in Weller et al. (2022a), namely (`En-Fr`), (`Ar-Es`), and (`Ru-Zh`), sampling 10k training examples and 5k testing examples for each. For client-unseen languages, we consider the FLORES-200 (Costa-jussà et al., 2022) dataset. FLORES-200 consists of 3001 parallel sentences manually translated across 200 different languages. We choose its `devtest` subset, with 1013 sentences for each language. We consider 9 different source languages, choosing 3 across high-resource (Portuguese (`Pt`), Hindi (`Hi`), Korean (`Ko`)), mid-resource (Tamil (`Ta`), Ukranian (`Uk`), Finnish (`Fi`)), and low-resource (Swahili (`Sw`), Sinhalese (`Si`), Malayalam (`Ml`)) settings each. For ease of evaluation and comparison, we fix the target language to English, leading to 9 (`X-En`) language pairs, where `X` represents our source language.

Metrics and Model Selection We evaluate and report client-seen and client-unseen performance using BLEU (Papineni et al., 2002). We use the standard sacreBLEU settings (`nrefs:1, mixed case, eff:no, tok:13a, smooth:exp,` and `version 2.0.0`). For Ja and Zh we use their respective tokenizers. All client models are trained for 100 rounds, and the best model is selected based on the local validation loss. To select among models that perform better than the corresponding fully finetuned baselines we use the RRS defined in Section 2.3.

Compute We train each model on a configuration of 3 A6000 GPUs. The baselines reach convergence in under 12 hours. FedSparseNet and LoRA exhibit slightly faster training times.

A.2 Communication Efficiency

To assess the communication efficiency of a model, we consider the total volume of data (in bytes) transmitted across clients until the model reaches its optimal state, as indicated by its best checkpoint. This efficiency over n rounds until convergence can be formulated as: trainable_params $\times$ num_clients $\times$ $n \times 2$. The factor of 2 accounts for the bidirectional communication between the server and all clients at both the beginning and the end of each round. Figure 3 and 4 show the communication efficiency curves for the methods.

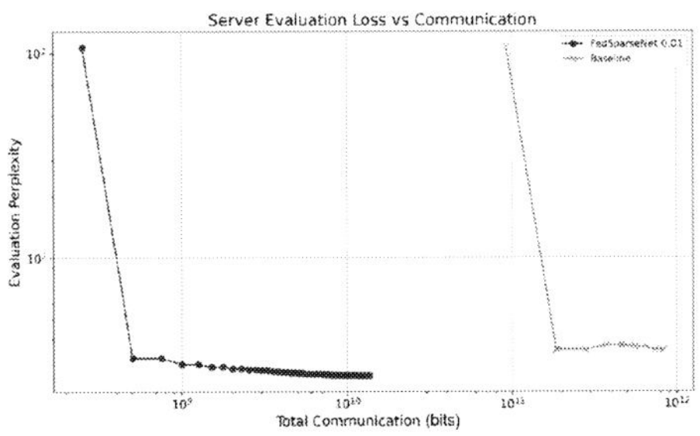

Figure 3: FedSparse 0.01 vs Full FT communication efficiency.

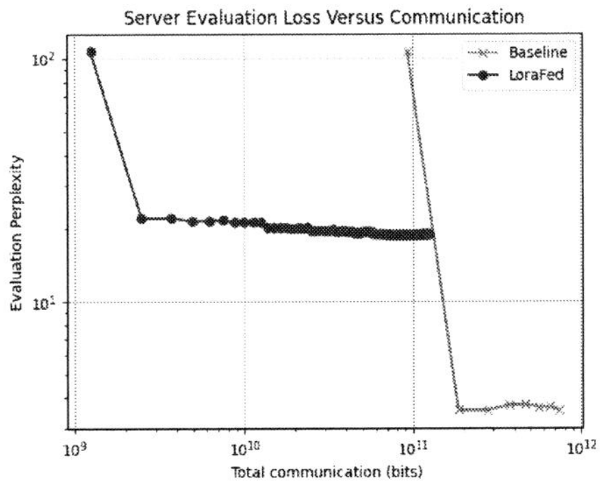

Figure 4: Communincation Overhead reduction in LoRA

A.3 FedSparse Ablations

Where and how to apply FedSparseNet?

In Table 3, we conduct a series of ablation studies to evaluate the impact of varying the target module for sparsity application as well as the sparsity ratio within the FedSparseNet framework. Specifically, FedSparseNet (0.01) denotes the application of a sparse mask with a 0.01 sparsity ratio to the tied embeddings (encoder and decoder) of the M2M model. Our comparative analysis between FedSparseNet (1.0) and FedSparseNet (1.0) + Body (0.01) reveals that applying a sparse mask to the tied embeddings layer yields superior performance on both client-seen and client-unseen data compared to applying the mask to the Body of the M2M model. This could be attributed to the reduced feature distortion achieved through sparsity in the embedding layers (Kumar et al., 2022). Furthermore, our findings indicate that FedSparseNet (0.0) + Body (0.01) outperforms FedSparseNet (1.0) + Body (0.01) in the RRS metric. This suggests that a higher sparsity ratio applied to the body of the model might further constrain feature distortion, enhancing the model's performance.

When examining the optimal degree of sparsity to apply, we observed that FedSparseNet configurations with varying sparsity ratios (0.01, 0.1, and 1.0) delivered comparable performances on client-unseen data. FedSparseNet (0.01) emerged as the most efficient model overall in terms of RRS and communication efficiency. Introducing a regularization penalty to FedSparseNet (0.01) with a λ 0.1 did not result in statistically significant differences in performance on both client-seen and client-unseen data.

What is the Impact of Increasing Local Work for FedSparseNet? In Table 4 in A, we compare FedSparseNet and the baselines when each model is trained for 5 epochs/round. We observe that increasing local work generally amplifies pre-trained feature distortion for both baselines and FedSparseNet. Consequently, the performance of IID FL and FedSparseNet (Non-IID FL and IID) deteriorates compared to Table 2. While FedSparseNet (IID) outperforms IID FL on both seen and unseen client performance, a surprising trend emerges for the Non-IID FL baseline. The model trained with local work exhibits performance comparable to the 1-epoch/round baseline on seen data, but surpasses it on unseen data, with increasing gains observed in HRL, followed by MRL and LRL. While FedSparseNet still achieves better client-seen data generalization than Non-IID FL, it lags behind on client-unseen data and the RRS metric. This suggests that the sparsity mechanism in FedSparseNet might hinder its ability to fully exploit the benefits of increased local work for unseen data. This is particularly relevant for low-resource languages characterized by limited training data and potentially weaker local data signals.

Takeaways

1. When examining the optimal degree of sparsity to apply, we observed that FedSparseNet configurations with varying sparsity ratios (0.01, 0.1, and 1.0) delivered comparable performances on client-unseen data. FedSparseNet (0.01) emerged as the most efficient model overall in terms of RRS and communication efficiency.

2. Introducing a regularization penalty to

Language Pair	FedSparseNet (0.01)	FedSparseNet (0.1)	FedSparseNet (1.0)	FedSparseNet+Reg (0.01)	FedSparseNet (1.0)+Body(0.01)	FedSparseNet (0.0)+Body(0.01)
			Client-Seen Languages			
En-Fr	38.6 ± 0.7	38.7 ± 0.7	38.6 ± 0.7	38.6 ± 0.7	35.1 ± 0.7	35.9 ± 0.7
Ar-Es	36.4 ± 0.7	36.4 ± 0.6	36.5 ± 0.7	36.4 ± 0.6	29.6 ± 0.6	33.0 ± 0.6
Ru-Zh	37.7 ± 0.7	37.7 ± 0.6	37.6 ± 0.6	37.7 ± 0.6	38.7 ± 0.6	38.0 ± 0.6
Avg	37.6 ± 0.7	37.6 ± 0.6	37.6 ± 0.6	37.6 ± 0.6	34.5 ± 0.6	35.6 ± 0.6
			Client-Unseen Languages - High Resource			
Pt-En	32.2 ± 1.3	31.6 ± 1.5	32.0 ± 1.3	31.8 ± 1.4	27.7 ± 1.0	29.2 ± 1.0
Hi-En	21.8 ± 1.3	21.2 ± 1.3	21.8 ± 1.3	21.3 ± 1.4	19.1 ± 0.9	20.2 ± 0.9
Ko-En	14.5 ± 1.0	14.1 ± 1.0	14.1 ± 1.0	14.5 ± 1.1	12.4 ± 0.7	13.8 ± 0.8
Avg	22.8 ± 1.2	22.3 ± 1.3	22.6 ± 1.2	22.5 ± 1.3	19.7 ± 0.9	21.1 ± 0.9
			Client-Unseen Languages - Mid Resource			
Ta-En	1.6 ± 0.2	1.6 ± 0.2	1.7 ± 0.2	1.6 ± 0.2	4.1 ± 0.5	4.4 ± 0.5
Uk-En	21.2 ± 1.2	20.7 ± 1.1	21.5 ± 1.1	21.2 ± 1.2	18.4 ± 0.9	19.1 ± 1.0
Fi-En	18.8 ± 1.1	18.1 ± 1.1	18.4 ± 1.1	18.7 ± 1.1	14.7 ± 0.7	16.6 ± 1.0
Avg	13.9 ± 0.8	13.5 ± 0.8	13.9 ± 0.8	13.8 ± 0.8	12.4 ± 0.7	13.4 ± 0.8
			Client-Unseen Languages - Low Resource			
Sw-En	15.0 ± 1.1	14.6 ± 1.1	14.4 ± 1.1	15.2 ± 1.1	14.8 ± 0.8	15.0 ± 1.0
Si-En	6.1 ± 0.7	6.2 ± 0.7	6.0 ± 0.7	6.3 ± 0.7	7.7 ± 0.7	8.1 ± 0.8
Ml-En	5.5 ± 0.6	5.6 ± 0.6	5.2 ± 0.6	5.5 ± 0.6	7.1 ± 0.7	7.6 ± 0.7
Avg	8.9 ± 0.8	8.8 ± 0.8	8.5 ± 0.8	9.0 ± 0.8	9.9 ± 0.7	10.2 ± 0.8
			Weighted Metric Calculation			
RRS	0.485	0.477	0.481	0.484	0.328	0.403

Table 3: Different FedSparseNet configurations on non-IID FL are compared. We report BLEU for Client-Seen and Client-Unseen Language Pairs.

FedSparseNet (0.01) with a λ 0.1 did not result in statistically significant differences in performance on both client-seen and client-unseen data.

3. The impact of varying local work needs deeper investigation: Sparsification induced by FedSparseNet might be limiting the efficacy of local work for FedSparse.

B LoRA Ablations

Where and how to apply LoRA ? We explore the candidates for two critical LoRA hyperparameters: rank and its target modules to understand the ideal composition of target location and capacity for the sparsification we induce.

LoRA Rank The approximation rank in LoRA is a critical hyperparameter that governs the reduction in the projection we carry with the gradient updates. We experimented with 2 LoRA ranks: 8 and 32. Table 5 summarizes LoRA's performance with these: 8 and 32. In our experiments, the increase in rank shows a marginal improvement with the numbers though we include even greater ranges for sweeping over ranks in our future work. We posit that the lack of any significant improvement in the capacity of the model could be attributed to the need for differential language-specific capacity i.e., it is possible that languages belonging to different categories (seen or unseen, high-resource or low-resource) may require different rank attributed capacities as has been explored in multilingual literature like Chang et al. (2023) and since we train with a uniform rank, we may be under-allocating or over-allocating capacity specifically to the seen clients. Recent work like Ding et al. (2023) also highlights an important caveat of LoRA is training with a fixed rank (for the entirety of the model's training) which could also be impeding LoRA's efficacy.

LoRA Target Modules We explore applying LoRA to (a) all layers (Key and Query projections) and (b) Input Embedding of the models. We notice a significant improvement in the performance with the use of embedding projections (in alignment with our observation in FedSparse). We posit that the perturbation induced by applying LoRA to all the layers is either too extreme (we see a drop in performance even on the seen clients) or not

Language Pair	Pretrained	Centralized	IID FL	Non-IID FL	FedSparseNet (Non-IID FL)	FedSparseNet (IID)
Client-Seen Languages						
En-Fr	31.8 ± 0.6	38.0 ± 0.7	36.3 ± 0.7	33.1 ± 0.6	38.6 ± 0.7	38.5 ± 0.7
Ar-Es	28.0 ± 0.5	35.5 ± 0.7	35.6 ± 0.7	36.7 ± 0.6	36.3 ± 0.6	36.4 ± 0.6
Ru-Zh	30.3 ± 0.5	37.5 ± 0.6	37.4 ± 0.6	39.2 ± 0.6	37.3 ± 0.6	37.9 ± 0.6
Avg	30.0 ± 0.5	37.0 ± 0.7	36.4 ± 0.7	36.3 ± 0.6	37.4 ± 0.6	37.6 ± 0.6
Client-Unseen Languages - High Resource						
Pt-En	40.0 ± 1.1	31.8 ± 1.1	20.7 ± 1.0	34.6 ± 1.1	32.3 ± 1.2	32.7 ± 1.4
Hi-En	29.6 ± 1.0	22.0 ± 1.1	14.1 ± 0.9	25.5 ± 0.9	21.8 ± 1.3	24.0 ± 1.1
Ko-En	20.5 ± 0.9	15.0 ± 0.9	9.3 ± 0.7	17.5 ± 0.9	14.6 ± 1.1	15.6 ± 0.9
Avg	30.0 ± 1.0	22.9 ± 1.0	14.7 ± 0.9	25.9 ± 1.0	22.9 ± 1.2	24.1 ± 1.1
Client-Unseen Languages - Mid Resource						
Ta-En	8.0 ± 0.6	3.9 ± 0.4	2.5 ± 0.3	7.0 ± 0.7	2.2 ± 0.3	4.2 ± 0.5
Uk-En	27.9 ± 1.0	18.2 ± 1.0	13.1 ± 0.9	24.9 ± 1.0	21.4 ± 1.1	22.1 ± 1.1
Fi-En	25.7 ± 1.0	18.2 ± 1.0	10.0 ± 0.8	21.8 ± 0.9	18.9 ± 1.0	19.5 ± 1.0
Avg	20.5 ± 0.9	13.4 ± 0.8	8.5 ± 0.7	18.2 ± 0.5	14.2 ± 0.8	15.3 ± 0.9
Client-Unseen Languages - Low Resource						
Sw-En	26.0 ± 0.9	17.2 ± 1.0	9.4 ± 0.8	20.1 ± 1.0	16.1 ± 1.1	19.6 ± 0.9
Si-En	15.9 ± 0.8	8.8 ± 0.7	4.5 ± 0.5	12.5 ± 0.9	7.3 ± 0.7	10.3 ± 0.8
Ml-En	15.3 ± 0.9	8.0 ± 0.8	4.3 ± 0.4	12.0 ± 0.8	6.6 ± 0.7	9.6 ± 0.8
Avg	19.1 ± 0.9	11.3 ± 0.8	6.1 ± 0.6	15.0 ± 0.9	10.0 ± 0.8	13.2 ± 0.8
Weighted Metric Calculation						
RRS	0.000	0.496	0.323	0.643	0.497	0.573

Table 4: UN-MT Bleu for Client-Seen and Client-Unseen Language Pairs. FedSparseNet uses sparsity ratio 0.01. All models are trained for 5 epochs/round.

coupled with the right rank (may require a lower rank) to achieve optimal results. Our best model eventually used the model where embeddings were perturbed by LoRA.

Takeaways

1. Applying LoRA to the embedding layer gives significant gains over perturbing the Key and Query projections.
2. Increasing Rank over a limited range [8-32] does not induce a statistically significant improvement in performance.

Language Pair	Pretrained	Centralized	IID FL	Non-IID FL	LoRA (embedding, rank=8)	LoRA (embedding, rank=32)	LoRA (k,q), rank=8
				Client-Seen Languages			
En-Fr	31.8 ± 0.6	38.0 ± 0.7	37.7 ± 0.7	36.9 ± 0.7	36.0 ± 0.6	36.4 ± 0.6	35.8 ± 0.6
Ar-Es	28.0 ± 0.5	35.5 ± 0.7	35.9 ± 0.7	32.9 ± 0.6	33.4 ± 0.6	33.2 ± 0.6	32.4 ± 0.6
Ru-Zh	30.3 ± 0.5	37.5 ± 0.6	37.7 ± 0.4	38.7 ± 0.6	34.3 ± 0.6	34.7 ± 0.6	33.2 ± 0.6
Avg	30.0 ± 0.5	37.0 ± 0.7	37.1 ± 0.6	36.2 ± 0.6	34.6 ± 0.6	34.8 ± 0.6	33.8 ± 0.8
				Client-Unseen Languages - High Resource			
Pt-En	40.0 ± 1.1	31.8 ± 1.1	32.0 ± 1.0	26.7 ± 1.2	39.5 ± 1.1	39.5 ± 1.1	38.5 ± 1.1
Hi-En	29.6 ± 1.0	22.0 ± 1.1	22.8 ± 0.9	19.3 ± 1.0	28.3 ± 1.0	28.7 ± 1.0	28.3 ± 1.0
Ko-En	20.5 ± 0.9	15.0 ± 0.9	14.4 ± 0.9	13.0 ± 0.8	19.6 ± 0.9	19.5 ± 0.9	19.5 ± 0.9
Avg	30.0 ± 1.0	22.9 ± 1.0	23.1 ± 0.9	19.7 ± 1.0	29.1 ± 1.0	29.2 ± 1.0	28.8 ± 1.0
				Client-Unseen Languages - Mid Resource			
Ta-En	8.0 ± 0.6	3.9 ± 0.4	5.0 ± 0.5	3.7 ± 0.4	9.2 ± 0.7	9.5 ± 0.7	8.2 ± 0.7
Uk-En	27.9 ± 1.0	18.2 ± 1.0	21.8 ± 0.9	20.7 ± 1.0	28.2 ± 1.0	28.0 ± 1.0	27.5 ± 1.0
Fi-En	25.7 ± 1.0	18.2 ± 1.0	18.8 ± 0.8	14.4 ± 1.0	25.0 ± 1.0	24.8 ± 1.0	24.4 ± 0.9
Avg	20.5 ± 0.9	13.4 ± 0.8	15.2 ± 0.7	12.9 ± 0.8	20.8 ± 0.9	20.8 ± 0.9	20.3 ± 0.9
				Client-Unseen Languages - Low Resource			
Sw-En	26.0 ± 0.9	17.2 ± 1.0	18.4 ± 1.0	13.6 ± 1.0	24.4 ± 1.0	24.6 ± 1.0	23.5 ± 1.1
Si-En	15.9 ± 0.8	8.8 ± 0.7	9.6 ± 0.8	7.3 ± 0.7	15.1 ± 0.8	14.9 ± 0.8	14.2 ± 0.9
Ml-En	15.3 ± 0.9	8.0 ± 0.8	8.6 ± 0.8	6.3 ± 0.6	14.3 ± 0.8	14.9 ± 0.8	13.7 ± 0.9
Avg	19.1 ± 0.9	11.3 ± 0.8	12.2 ± 0.9	9.1 ± 0.8	17.9 ± 0.9	18.1 ± 0.9	17.1 ± 1.0
				Weighted Metric Calculation			
RRS	0.000	0.496	0.323	0.643	0.896	0.882	0.882

Table 5: Different LoRA configurations varying the target modules and ranks. All models are trained for 1 epoch/round and for 100 rounds.

Understanding Players as if They Are Talking to the Game in a Customized Language: A Pilot Study

Tianze Wang[1,2*] **Maryam Honari-Jahromi**[2*]
Styliani Katsarou[2] **Olga Mikheeva**[1,2] **Theodoros Panagiotakopoulos**[2]
Oleg Smirnov[2†‡] **Lele Cao**[2†] **Sahar Asadi**[2†]
[1]KTH Royal Institute of Technology [2]King, Microsoft Gaming

Abstract

This pilot study explores the application of language models (LMs) to model game event sequences, treating them as a customized language. We investigate a popular mobile game, transforming raw event data into textual sequences and pretraining a Longformer model on this data. Our approach captures the rich and nuanced interactions within game sessions, effectively identifying meaningful player segments. The results demonstrate the potential of self-supervised LMs in enhancing game design and personalization without relying on ground-truth labels.

1 Introduction

The dominant form of human interaction is natural language, represented by a *stream of words*. Language Models (LMs) have become highly effective in understanding and representing these general-purpose natural languages. Similarly, when a human player interacts with a video game, the primary form of interaction is through game controls, which lead to visual and auditory feedback. This in-game interaction is typically recorded as a *stream of events*, each with rich attributes and categories. This pilot study explores **whether we can apply LMs, initially designed for word sequences, to model game event sequences**. Understanding player behavior through this modeling approach is crucial for designing engaging experiences, improving game mechanics, and personalizing content. For example, understanding the optimal balance between challenge and progression can enable dynamic game difficulty adjustments, maximizing the enjoyment experienced by players.

Traditionally, understanding game players has relied on surveys and interviews, such as those conducted in (Rodrigues et al., 2022). While these methods provide valuable insights, they are significantly limited by scalability. Deep Learning (DL) models, like those in (Cao et al., 2020), have been trained on aggregated (from game events) gameplay data to achieve in-game personalization, but they often neglect nuanced interactions. Recently, training DL models on sequential interactions between players and in-game items has been explored, as exemplified by (Villa et al., 2020). However, these modeled interactions are still relatively limited in type and richness compared to game events. Moreover, most of these DL models only optimize for specific personalization scenarios, requiring large amount of ground-truth labels, which are not always available.

As a consequence, self-supervised LM pretraining emerged as a promising approach to directly model the rich and fine-grained game events in a scalable way without requiring any labels. In principle, this pretrained model is not restricted to any specific personalization use case. To the best of our knowledge, this is the first attempt to pretrain an LM on game events by treating these events as a customized natural language. The highlights of this pilot study are: (§3) studying a popular mobile video game from King[1], Candy Crush Saga, (§4) developing a simple method for transforming a large amount of game events into language tokens, (§5) pretraining an LM on the customized "language" representing game events, (§6) reporting experimental results on the LM's intrinsic performance and its capability in understanding game players, and finally (§7) we outline measures employed to mitigate ethical considerations.

2 Related Work

Modeling sequential interactions between users and items has been extensively studied in recommendation systems. Initial approaches utilized Markovian

*Both authors contributed equally to this research.
†Joint senior authorship.
‡Corresponding author: oleg.smirnov@microsoft.com

[1]https://king.com

Proceedings of the 1st Workshop on Customizable NLP: Progress and Challenges in Customizing NLP for a Domain, Application, Group, or Individual (CustomNLP4U), pages 47–52
November 16, 2024

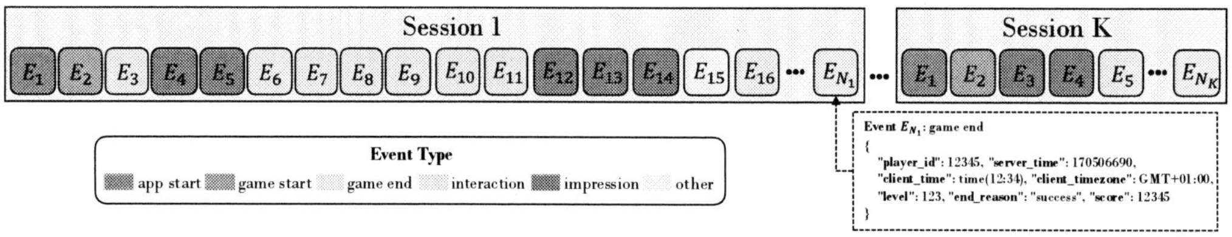

Figure 1: Example events segmented into semantic sessions. The final game-end event in "Session 1" is expanded to show details about its associated fields and values.

assumptions for collaborative filtering (Zimdars et al., 2001), later extended to Markov decision processes (Shani et al., 2005). Predicting future behavior trajectories using contextual and sequential information has been addressed with autoregressive Long Short-Term Memory models (Wu et al., 2017) and coupled Recurrent Neural Network (RNN) architectures for joint modeling of user/item interactions (Kumar et al., 2019). Explicitly modeling different types of user behavior, such as repeated consumption, has also shown to improve downstream performance metrics (Anderson et al., 2014; Ren et al., 2019).

LMs have been leveraged for embedding sequential data in recommendation settings, beginning with music track representations using the Word2Vec objective (Mehrotra et al., 2018) and extending to modeling sequences of listening sessions with RNNs (Hansen et al., 2020). More recently, self-attention sequential models have been introduced, such as BERT4Rec (Sun et al., 2019), which balance the trade-off between Markov chain models and neural network methods. Follow-up work on multi-task customer models for personalization has further advanced this field by integrating novel data augmentation and task-aware readout modules (Luo et al., 2023).

Despite these advancements, the application of LMs for user modeling in gaming remains underexplored. Our study proposes the first approach for learning representations of mobile game players by pretraining a Transformer architecture in a self-supervised manner, treating game event sequences as a customized natural language. This approach aims to capture the rich and nuanced interactions within game sessions.

3 The Game and Interaction Events

This pilot study focuses on Candy Crush Saga game. When a player interacts with this game on a mobile device, their behavior generates a sequence of time-ordered events, which are recorded locally on the user's device and later sent to the central game server in batches. Example events include starting the game application, beginning a new game round, purchasing in-game items, and displaying pop-ups and notifications. The tracked player behavior events fall into 12 categories, each with an associated schema containing continuous and categorical features.

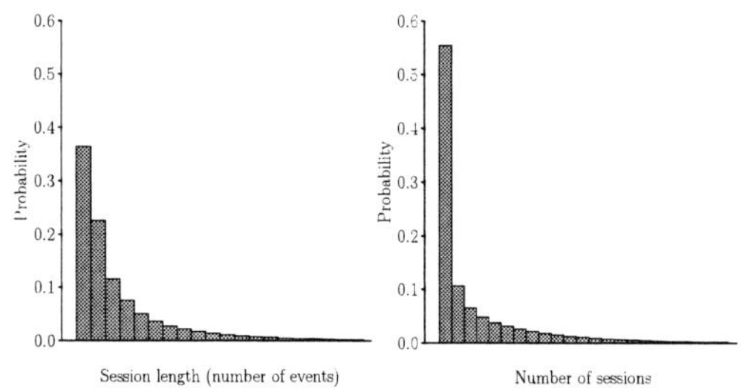

(a) (b)

Figure 2: (a) Histogram of session lengths and (b) the distribution of session quantities over a 15-day period shown up to the 99th percentile.

The player-game interaction events are segmented into sessions based on the player's activity semantics, as illustrated in Figure 1. According to game analytics conventions recommended by the data scientists from the game producer, a session is considered to have ended if a player is inactive for 15 minutes or more. For this study, we collected a dataset of player event sessions over 15 days, with 10,000 players uniformly sampled from the entire player population. The resulting dataset consists of 125,000 sessions, split into a 2:1 train-test ratio. The distribution of session lengths in the dataset is shown in Figure 2a, while Figure 2b depicts the distribution of sessions quantities. Both session lengths and quantities approximately follow a geometric distribution.

Our collected event data, while superficially similar to tracking data in other domains like e-commerce, presents unique challenges. In-game interactions occur at a much higher frequency than in web browsing, resulting in large volumes of potentially redundant events that call for careful preprocessing and modeling of long-range dependencies. Additionally, game event sequences are often noisy, with incorrectly ordered events or missing ordering information due to users switching between online and offline modes, which can degrade model performance during training and inference.

4 From Events to Words

The raw format of game events is JSON. To make this data digestible by LMs, we designed a simple pipeline to transform raw events into textual sequences. As illustrated in Figure 3, the pipeline begins by removing unnecessary events and fields. Leveraging game-specific knowledge, we filter out non-informative data, such as device-specific logs, reducing the number of event fields by over 90%. We bin certain numerical features, such as the hour of the day, based on domain-specific knowledge to convert them into categorical variables. Additionally, we group similar in-game event identifiers, e.g., the name of the UI shown, to reduce the vocabulary size. The words are then grouped by users and sessions, ordered by timestamps to preserve the natural interaction flow, and concatenated to form a textual description of a player's interaction experience.

We use a word-level tokenizer that splits a space-separated string into tokens and maps them to unique identifiers. This approach suits the relatively small vocabulary of behavior data (~13,500 tokens), though the tokenized sequences are much longer than those in typical NLP tasks like sentiment analysis.

5 Pretrain a Language Model

The tokenized word sequences are often longer than 512 tokens, which are unmanageable for the conventional BERT (Kenton and Toutanova, 2019) architecture and its derivatives. Modeling long sequences poses a significant challenge to Transformer-based approaches due to the self-attention operation, which scales quadratically with input length in terms of memory and computational complexity. This challenge is intensified when modeling distant dependencies in extended gameplay experiences that involve concatenating multiple sessions. To overcome this, we adopt Longformer (Beltagy et al., 2020), a model designed specifically for processing long textual inputs.

model size	#layer	#head	dims	block size	#params
small	2	2	128	1024	2M
medium	6	6	384	2048	20M
large	12	12	768	4096	121M

Table 1: Hyperparameters for different model sizes.

model size	accuracy ↑	perplexity ↓	CE ↓
small	0.69 ± 0.06	3.27 ± 0.71	1.16 ± 0.22
medium	0.93 ± 0.01	1.28 ± 0.09	0.25 ± 0.07
large	$\mathbf{0.95 \pm 0.01}$	$\mathbf{1.16 \pm 0.05}$	$\mathbf{0.15 \pm 0.04}$

Table 2: Mean values and standard deviations of intrinsic language modeling metrics computed over five training runs.

Longformer combines dilated sliding window attention for local context and global attention on a few pre-selected input locations. This approach scales linearly with input size, enabling the processing of sequences up to 4,096 tokens in a single pass, which is sufficient for most behavior modeling scenarios. Additionally, Longformer's sparse attention pattern performs well in contexts where many tokens in the immediate local context may be redundant, as is often the case with high-frequency game events.

We pretrained several Longformer variants[2] from scratch with different capacities, based on the hyper-parameters listed in Table 1. We experimented with the baseline Longformer configuration, i.e., "*large*", and two smaller model variants with fewer internal layers and self-attention heads. The models were optimized with the masked language modeling (MLM) objective using Adam (Kingma, 2014) with a fixed learning rate of 2×10^{-5}. Each LM was trained from randomly initialized weights for 100 epochs with a batch size of 4 and gradient accumulation over 4 steps, resulting in an effective batch size of 16 (2^{16} tokens).

6 Results

First, we evaluate the intrinsic performance of the proposed approach using intrinsic MLM metrics. We report the Cross-Entropy (CE) loss and multi-class classification accuracy of predicting masked

[2]We use the HuggingFace Transformers (Wolf et al., 2019) library and PyTorch framework (Paszke et al., 2019) for model implementation. All models were trained with half-precision (FP16) on a single NVIDIA A100 GPU, with the *large* model taking approximately 50 hours to complete pretraining.

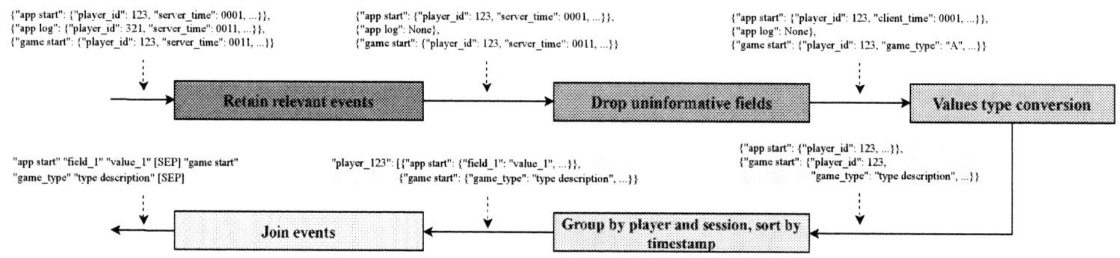

Figure 3: The pipeline to convert event streams to word streams.

tokens on the validation split for the tested model architectures, as shown in Table 2. Additionally, we report the perplexity score, following established methodologies for evaluating MLM pretraining performance (Liu et al., 2019). As expected, we observe that LMs with larger capacities achieve better fits for the behavior sessions without overfitting.

Next, we perform a qualitative analysis to identify spontaneous player clusters representing different behavioral persona. We extract embeddings of input token sequences from the pretrained *large* Longformer model. Using 4096×768-dim representations from the last Attention layer, we apply max pooling over sequence length to compute an embedding vector for each input sequence. These session embeddings are projected onto the first 50 principal components using linear PCA to reduce noise and speed up computation. The projections are then mapped to 2D space via t-SNE (Van der Maaten and Hinton, 2008) and clustered with a Gaussian Mixture Model (Reynolds et al., 2009) with eight components. The resulting t-SNE plot is shown in Figure 4a. Analyzing the average player behavior within the well-separated t-SNE clusters in Figure 4b, we collaboratively identified player segments with game analysts from a practical product perspective. Identified players' personas qualitatively resonate with what our user researchers extracted from self-reported behavioral surveys:

1. *Competitive devoted*: a skilled player who plays less often but long sessions, occasionally purchasing items and collecting utilities.
2. *Casual devoted*: a player who plays long sessions infrequently, engages in quests, collects rewards, and prefers free gameplay.
3. *Persistent devoted*: a player who plays frequent, long sessions without purchasing.
4. *Lean-in casual economy aware*: A skilled player who plays less often but for long sessions, occasionally buying items.
5. *Lean-in casual*: a skilled player who plays less often but for long sessions.
6. *Persistent casual*: a less skillful player who plays short, frequent sessions with little engagement in social and economic aspects.
7. *Persistent collector*: a player with frequent short sessions, collecting utilities to progress.

7 Ethical Considerations

Computational modeling of player behavior in games has raised various ethical concerns within both research and industry (Mikkelsen et al., 2017). In this pilot study, we utilize non-personally identifiable tracking data from in-game interactions to create vectorized representations of player behaviors. Our objective is to leverage these representations to support personalized and enhanced player experiences while maintaining ethical standards.

Potential ethical risks include (1) biases in the input dataset, such as under-representing less frequent player behaviors, and (2) the misapplication of models to different data distributions, known as Type III errors (Mikkelsen et al., 2017). To mitigate these risks, we use robust data validation and automated model analysis tools available in production-ready machine learning frameworks (Modi et al., 2017).

We address under-represented player behaviors through qualitative evaluation methods, such as embedding space visualization. Additionally, we periodically retrain the model with recent data to address distribution shifts, with retraining intervals determined empirically based on model performance and data drift.

For the downstream recommendation system, we plan to implement model explainability and uncertainty estimation methods to better understand the model's robustness, biases, and other ethical considerations. These measures aim to ensure that our

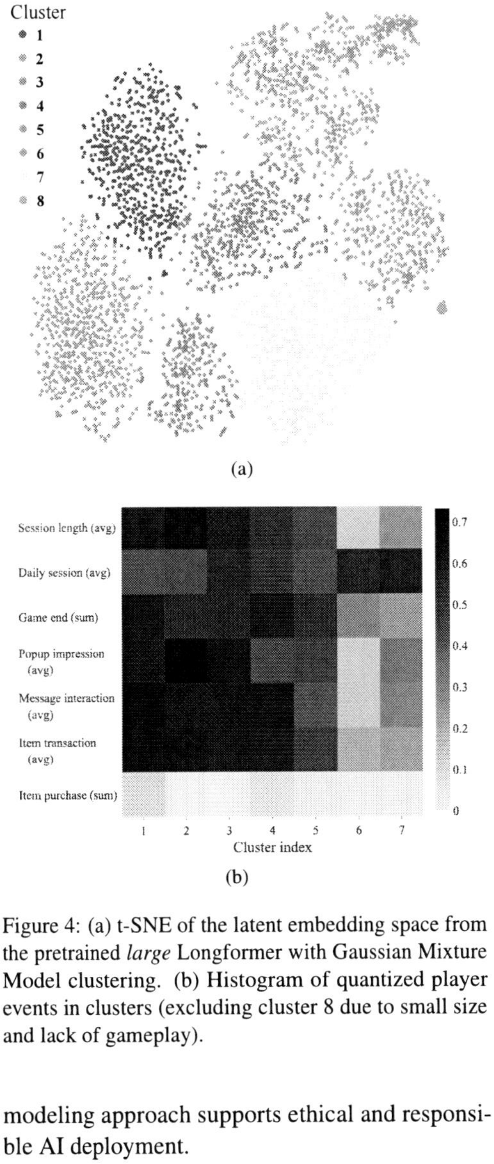

Figure 4: (a) t-SNE of the latent embedding space from the pretrained *large* Longformer with Gaussian Mixture Model clustering. (b) Histogram of quantized player events in clusters (excluding cluster 8 due to small size and lack of gameplay).

modeling approach supports ethical and responsible AI deployment.

8 Conclusion and Future Work

This pilot study demonstrates the potential of using self-supervised language models to understand player behavior by modeling game event sequences as a customized natural language. Our approach, leverages the Longformer model to effectively captures the rich and nuanced interactions within game sessions in a self-supervised manner, agnostic to downstream use-cases. The results highlight the model's ability to identify meaningful player segments, providing valuable insights for game design and personalization. For future work, we plan to extend training to single- and multitask fine-tuning with labeled datasets to benchmark against fully-supervised baselines. We anticipate that our approach can be extended to other event-based game datasets as well.

References

Ashton Anderson, Ravi Kumar, Andrew Tomkins, and Sergei Vassilvitskii. 2014. The dynamics of repeat consumption. In *Proceedings of the 23rd international conference on World wide web*, pages 419–430.

Iz Beltagy, Matthew E Peters, and Arman Cohan. 2020. Longformer: The long-document transformer. *arXiv preprint arXiv:2004.05150*.

Lele Cao, Sahar Asadi, Matteo Biasielli, and Michael Sjöberg. 2020. Debiasing few-shot recommendation in mobile games. In *ORSUM@ RecSys*.

Casper Hansen, Christian Hansen, Lucas Maystre, Rishabh Mehrotra, Brian Brost, Federico Tomasi, and Mounia Lalmas. 2020. Contextual and sequential user embeddings for large-scale music recommendation. In *Proceedings of the 14th ACM Conference on Recommender Systems*, pages 53–62.

Jacob Devlin Ming-Wei Chang Kenton and Lee Kristina Toutanova. 2019. Bert: Pre-training of deep bidirectional transformers for language understanding. In *Proceedings of naacL-HLT*, volume 1, page 2.

DP Kingma. 2014. Adam: a method for stochastic optimization. In *Int Conf Learn Represent*.

Srijan Kumar, Xikun Zhang, and Jure Leskovec. 2019. Predicting dynamic embedding trajectory in temporal interaction networks. In *Proceedings of the 25th ACM SIGKDD international conference on knowledge discovery & data mining*, pages 1269–1278.

Yinhan Liu, Myle Ott, Naman Goyal, Jingfei Du, Mandar Joshi, Danqi Chen, Omer Levy, Mike Lewis, Luke Zettlemoyer, and Veselin Stoyanov. 2019. Roberta: A robustly optimized bert pretraining approach. *arXiv preprint arXiv:1907.11692*.

Rui Luo, Tianxin Wang, Jingyuan Deng, and Peng Wan. 2023. Mcm: A multi-task pre-trained customer model for personalization. In *Proceedings of the 17th ACM Conference on Recommender Systems*, pages 637–639.

Rishabh Mehrotra, James McInerney, Hugues Bouchard, Mounia Lalmas, and Fernando Diaz. 2018. Towards a fair marketplace: Counterfactual evaluation of the trade-off between relevance, fairness & satisfaction in recommendation systems. In *Proceedings of the 27th acm international conference on information and knowledge management*, pages 2243–2251.

Benedikte Mikkelsen, Christoffer Holmgård, and Julian Togelius. 2017. Ethical considerations for player modeling. In *Workshops at the Thirty-First AAAI Conference on Artificial Intelligence*.

Akshay Naresh Modi, Chiu Yuen Koo, Chuan Yu Foo, Clemens Mewald, Denis M. Baylor, Eric Breck, Heng-Tze Cheng, Jarek Wilkiewicz, Levent Koc, Lukasz Lew, Martin A. Zinkevich, Martin Wicke, Mustafa Ispir, Neoklis Polyzotis, Noah Fiedel, Salem Elie Haykal, Steven Whang, Sudip Roy, Sukriti Ramesh, Vihan Jain, Xin Zhang, and Zakaria Haque. 2017. Tfx: A tensorflow-based production-scale machine learning platform. In *KDD 2017*.

Adam Paszke, Sam Gross, Francisco Massa, Adam Lerer, James Bradbury, Gregory Chanan, Trevor Killeen, Zeming Lin, Natalia Gimelshein, Luca Antiga, et al. 2019. Pytorch: An imperative style, high-performance deep learning library. *Advances in neural information processing systems*, 32.

Pengjie Ren, Zhumin Chen, Jing Li, Zhaochun Ren, Jun Ma, and Maarten De Rijke. 2019. Repeatnet: A repeat aware neural recommendation machine for session-based recommendation. In *Proceedings of the AAAI Conference on Artificial Intelligence*, volume 33, pages 4806–4813.

Douglas A Reynolds et al. 2009. Gaussian mixture models. *Encyclopedia of biometrics*, 741(659-663).

Luiz Rodrigues, Armando M Toda, Wilk Oliveira, Paula Toledo Palomino, Julita Vassileva, and Seiji Isotani. 2022. Automating gamification personalization to the user and beyond. *IEEE Transactions on Learning Technologies*, 15(2):199–212.

Guy Shani, David Heckerman, Ronen I Brafman, and Craig Boutilier. 2005. An mdp-based recommender system. *Journal of Machine Learning Research*, 6(9).

Fei Sun, Jun Liu, Jian Wu, Changhua Pei, Xiao Lin, Wenwu Ou, and Peng Jiang. 2019. Bert4rec: Sequential recommendation with bidirectional encoder representations from transformer. In *Proceedings of the 28th ACM international conference on information and knowledge management*, pages 1441–1450.

Laurens Van der Maaten and Geoffrey Hinton. 2008. Visualizing data using t-sne. *Journal of machine learning research*, 9(11).

Andrés Villa, Vladimir Araujo, Francisca Cattan, and Denis Parra. 2020. Interpretable contextual team-aware item recommendation: application in multiplayer online battle arena games. In *Proceedings of the 14th ACM Conference on Recommender Systems*, pages 503–508.

Thomas Wolf, Lysandre Debut, Victor Sanh, Julien Chaumond, Clement Delangue, Anthony Moi, Pierric Cistac, Tim Rault, Rémi Louf, Morgan Funtowicz, et al. 2019. Huggingface's transformers: State-of-the-art natural language processing. *arXiv preprint arXiv:1910.03771*.

Chao-Yuan Wu, Amr Ahmed, Alex Beutel, Alexander J Smola, and How Jing. 2017. Recurrent recommender networks. In *Proceedings of the tenth ACM international conference on web search and data mining*, pages 495–503.

Andrew Zimdars, David Maxwell Chickering, and Christopher Meek. 2001. Using temporal data for making recommendations. In *Proceedings of the Seventeenth conference on Uncertainty in artificial intelligence*, pages 580–588.

L3Masking: Multi-task Fine-tuning for Language Models by Leveraging Lessons Learned from Vanilla Models

Yusuke Kimura[1], Takahiro Komamizu[2], Kenji Hatano[1]

[1] Doshisha University, Japan, [2] Nagoya University, Japan

{usk, taka-coma, hatano}@acm.org

Abstract

When distributional differences exist between pre-training and fine-tuning data, language models (LMs) may perform poorly on downstream tasks. Recent studies have reported that multi-task learning of downstream task and masked language modeling (MLM) task during the fine-tuning phase improves the performance of the downstream task. Typical MLM tasks (e.g., random token masking (RTM)) tend not to care tokens corresponding to the knowledge already acquired during the pre-training phase, therefore LMs may not notice the important clue or not effective to acquire linguistic knowledge of the task or domain. To overcome this limitation, we propose a new masking strategy for MLM task, called L3Masking [1], that leverages lessons (specifically, token-wise likelihood in a context) learned from the vanilla language model to be fine-tuned. L3Masking actively masks tokens with low likelihood on the vanilla model. Experimental evaluations on text classification tasks in different domains confirms a multi-task text classification method with L3Masking performed task adaptation more effectively than that with RTM. These results suggest the usefulness of assigning a preference to the tokens to be learned as the task or domain adaptation.

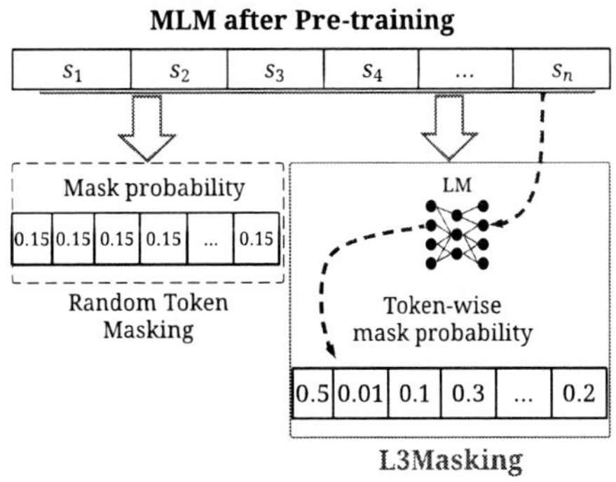

Figure 1: L3Masking vs. Random Token Masking. L3Masking determines masking tokens based on the pseudo-likelihood calculated through the vanilla model.

1 Introduction

Language Models (LM) pre-trained on generic documents such as BERT (Kenton and Toutanova, 2019) or GPTs (e.g., GPT-4 (Achiam et al., 2023)) may perform poorly on downstream tasks when the vocabulary or context used in the documents in each pre-training and downstream task differs (Gururangan et al., 2020; Shi et al., 2024). To bridge the domain gap between pre-training and fine-tuning, continual pre-training is used. Continual pre-training re-trains a model by applying the pre-training task again on the task or domain data (Xie et al., 2023). Recent studies have reported that multi-task learning (MTL) of downstream and pre-training tasks (e.g., masked language modeling (MLM)) during the fine-tuning phase can improve the performance of downstream tasks in comparison with continual pre-training (Dery et al., 2022, 2023; Kimura et al., 2023).

Existing task or domain adaptation methods for the encoder of Transformer architecture (Vaswani et al., 2017) typically utilize MLM, and random token masking (RTM) is mostly used masking strategy (Kenton and Toutanova, 2019; Liu et al., 2019). MLM is expected to use to adaptively learn the distribution of task and domain data from the learned distribution of the pre-training corpora. The MLM with simple strategy treats all tokens equally. However, existing MLMs ignore the linguistic knowledge already acquired by the language model, and, to learn the distribution properly, it requires large amount of time and data. Beside the fact that the amount of data for fine-tuning is limited, the more efficient masking strategy for MLM task is desired.

To overcome this, we propose a new masking

[1] The code is available at https://github.com/usk-Kimura/L3Masking

Proceedings of the 1st Workshop on Customizable NLP: Progress and Challenges in Customizing NLP for a Domain, Application, Group, or Individual (CustomNLP4U), pages 53–62

strategy for MLM called L3Masking (Leveraging Lessons Learned from vanilla model) as an effective task or domain adaptation. Figure 1 highlights the difference between L3Masking and a popular and simple masking strategy Random Token Masking. L3Masking identifies tokens with low likelihoods as task- or domain-specific tokens that appear less frequently in the similar contexts in the generic documents, and it actively masks them so that LM learns these tokens during fine-tuning.

Unlike causal language modeling which computes the likelihood of a token in a sentence only from the preceding tokens, MLM can compute the likelihood of the token conditional on both preceding and subsequent tokens. This difference has led to variations in the idea of a sentence's likelihood and has been noted in what is called the pseudo-log-likelihood (PLL) (Kauf and Ivanova, 2023). Based on the PLL, this study defines a token-wise pseudo-likelihood in the downstream task sentence and actively mask tokens with low pseudo-likelihood.

In consequence, the contributions of this paper can be summarized as follows:

- **L3Masking**: This paper proposes a new masking strategy called L3Masking for MLM task in the multi-task text classification, which set token-wise mask probabilities for task or domain adaptation, enhancing the adaptability of LMs to new domains and tasks.
- **Validation**: Experimental evaluations reported in this paper validate the effectiveness of L3Masking through three text classification tasks in different domains, highlighting its improvement from the simply fine-tuned models and its superiority over random token masking in the comparison of masking strategy.
- **Efficiency**: This paper also demonstrate that L3Masking not only improves the text classification performance of models but also increases the efficiency of training in text classification tasks. By selectively masking task- and domain-specific tokens, L3Masking reduces the number of training epochs required while maintaining or improving accuracy.

2 Related Studies

This section describes the task or domain adaptation methods that have been studied in contexts of continual pre-training and fine-tuning.

2.1 Adaptation in Continual Pre-training

Continual pre-training is a method of continuing further pre-training with additional data to adapt a vanilla LM pre-trained by generic corpora to a specific task or domain (Gururangan et al., 2020; Xie et al., 2023). A fundamental assumption of the method, known as the Selective Language Modeling (SLM) (Lin et al., 2024), is that all tokens are not equally useful for adaptation. Specifically, a reference model is first prepared that is continually pre-trained on high-quality data for the domain in question. Then, from low-quality data containing many tokens that are not included in the documents of downstream tasks in the domain concerned, tokens with the necessary knowledge are identified and actively learned, thereby enabling effective and efficient continual pre-training.

The difference between SLM and L3Masking is the quality of the target documents. SLM relies on high-quality data from the domain to determine whether a token corresponds to that linguistic knowledge, therefore, the cost of collecting high-quality data is high. L3Masking differs from SLM in that it determines task- or domain-specific tokens based only on the data of downstream task.

2.2 Adaptation in Fine-Tuning

META-TARTAN (Dery et al., 2022) is an effective task or domain adaptation method that brings pre-training tasks into fine-tuning phase, and it is a multi-talk learning besides of downstream tasks. META-TARTAN performs the MTL with the downstream and the pre-training tasks as auxiliary tasks and dynamically weights the loss values of each task to increase the accuracy of the validation data in the downstream task based on meta-learning. META-TARTAN employ RTM, which masks tokens in a uniform random manner (Gururangan et al., 2020), in analogous with continual pre-training in MLMs.

Many masking strategies for the MLM task have been proposed, such as Knowledge Masking, PMI-Masking, and InforMask (Sun et al., 2019; Levine et al., 2021; Sadeq et al., 2022). These methods use PMI, which depends on the frequency of token occurrence and co-occurrence, to increase the probability of collocation being masked. However, as the size of the dataset in the post-training phase is limited compared to the pre-training corpus, these methods may be less effective with small amounts of data where the co-occurrence pattern of tokens is less pronounced.

Using RTM in META-TARTAN may be not effective because the masking target masks tokens with regardless of the linguistic knowledge acquired in pre-training. In order to adapt a data distribution for downstream tasks that is different from pre-training, masking more tokens that are not plausible for the LM in a certain context may effectively lead to the acquisition of linguistic knowledge in the task or domain. Based on this idea, L3Masking identifies tokens that are not plausible in context based on the likelihood of each token in the context on the vanilla models.

3 L3Masking: the proposed method

This paper propose a new masking strategy of MLM task for task or domain adaptation, called L3Masking. The basic idea is to improve task and domain adaptability by actively masking tokens in sentences that are not well trained during pre-training. Figure 2 depicts the overview of L3Masking. L3Masking captures the tokens that are most likely to represent task- or domain-specific linguistic knowledge based on a token-wise likelihood. Since the likelihood cannot be calculated simply in bidirectional LM, L3Masking calculates the token-wise pseudo-likelihood and then masks more tokens with lower the pseudo-likelihood.

3.1 Pseudo-log-likelihood of a Sentence

In unidirectional LM, the log-likelihood of a sentence can be calculated by summation of the logarithm of the predicted probability of the tokens based on the preceding tokens. However, as MLM takes the tokens behind a token when predicting it into account, it expands the interpretation of the likelihood that can utilize the subsequent tokens in addition to the preceding tokens. Therefore, the following three methods are proposed to compute the pseudo-log-likelihood of a sentence in an MLM, namely, PLL-original (Salazar et al., 2020), PLL-word-l2r (Kauf and Ivanova, 2023), and PLL-whole-word (Kauf and Ivanova, 2023).

In the previous study, the PLL score calculated by PLL-word-l2r is considered the best pseudo-log-likelihood for a sentence (Kauf and Ivanova, 2023). PLL-word-l2r (PLL_{l2r}) is based on word as a unit for masking and tokens of a word on the right (future direction) are not aware via masking during inference. This idea is formulated as follows:

$$\text{PLL}_{l2r}(S) := \sum_{w=1}^{|S|}\sum_{t=1}^{|w|} \log P_{\text{MLM}}(s_{w_t} | S_{\backslash s_{w_{t'\geq t}}}) \tag{1}$$

where the t-th token s_{w_t} is subject to calculate a probability in a context represented as $S_{\backslash s_{w_{t'\geq t}}}$. For inference, the context is constructed by substituting the token sub-sequence of a word w, where the t-th token s_{w_t} is a part of, from s_{w_t} to the last token $s_{w_{t'}}$ of w. In other words, $S_{\backslash s_{w_{t'\geq t}}}$ is denoted as $(s_0, s_1, \ldots, s_{t-1}, \texttt{[MASK]}, ..., \texttt{[MASK]}, s_{t'+1}, \ldots, s_n)$.

3.2 Token-wise Pseudo-likelihood

In this study, the pseudo-likelihood (PL) of each token is calculated based on PLL_{l2r} (Eqn. (1)). In this study, this pseudo-likelihood of token s in a sentence S is called the PL of Token (PLT) and is defined as follows:

$$\begin{aligned}\text{PLT}\left(X = s_{w_t} \mid S_{\backslash s_{w_{t'\geq t}}}\right) \\ = P_{\text{MLM}}\left(s_{w_t} \mid S_{\backslash s_{w_{t'\geq t}}}\right)\end{aligned} \tag{2}$$

where X refers to the token for which the PLT is to be calculated.

For instance, given a sentence "The quick brown fox jumps over the lazy dog," suppose to calculate the pseudo-likelihood of the token "jump." Here, "jumps" is assumed to consist of two subwords: "jump" and the suffix "s." The context $S_{\backslash s_{w_{t'\geq t}}}$ is "The quick brown fox [MASK] [MASK] over the lazy dog." Using this context, the probability of "jump" is calculated PLT(X = "jump" $\mid S_{\backslash s_{w_{t'\geq t}}}$).

3.3 Convert PLT to Mask Probability

In L3Masking, the PLT is the pseudo-likelihood itself, that is, the probability of the token in a context. Since our idea is to mask more tokens with lower likelihood, we take the complementary probability, PLT^c (Eqn. (3)), as the mask probability.

$$\begin{aligned}\text{PLT}^c\left(X = s_{w_t} \mid S_{\backslash s_{w_{t'\geq t}}}\right) \\ = 1 - \text{PLT}\left(X = s_{w_t} \mid S_{\backslash s_{w_{t'\geq t}}}\right)\end{aligned} \tag{3}$$

The existing study has discussed that a significantly high mask probability for the MLM task can degrade the performance of downstream tasks (Wettig et al., 2023). Therefore, in this study, we define a modified PLT (mPLT) that is controlled to prevent the PLT^c used as the mask probability from

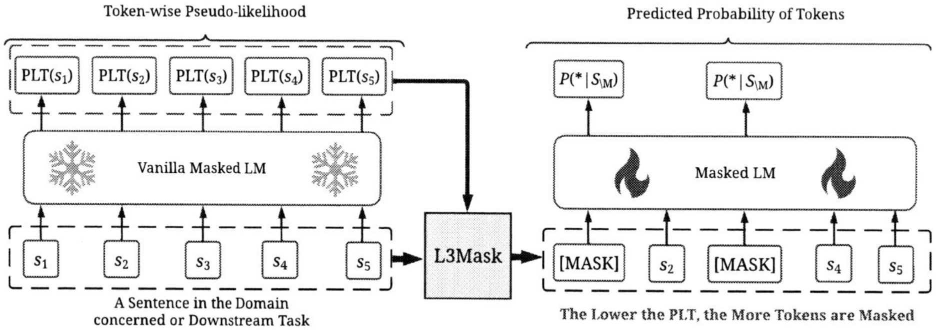

Figure 2: Overview of L3Masking. PLT denotes the token-wise pseudo-likelihood. $P(*|S_{\backslash \mathrm{M}})$ represents the prediction probability for each token in the vocabulary of the language model at the masked position in a context $S_{\backslash \mathrm{M}}$ excluding the masked token.

becoming too high. In particular, mPLT is calculated so that the mask probabilties in a sentence to a specified value $\bar{p}$. Formally, given a PLT^c sequence $P = (p_1, p_2, \ldots, p_n)$ corresponding with a n-length token sequence of a sentence and a specified average mask probability $\bar{p}$, find a constant α such that $\frac{1}{n}\sum_{p_i \in P} \alpha p_i = \bar{p}$. From this equation, $\alpha = \frac{n\bar{p}}{\sum_{p_i \in P} p_i}$ can be easily derived. By using this α, mPLT for each token t in a sentence S can be calculated as follows:

$$\begin{aligned} &\mathrm{mPLT}\left(X = s_{w_t} \mid S_{\backslash s_{w_{t' \geq t}}}\right) \\ &\quad = \alpha \cdot \mathrm{PLT}^c\left(X = s_{w_t} \mid S_{\backslash s_{w_{t' \geq t}}}\right) \quad (4) \end{aligned}$$

Note that in some cases when n is large and/or the summation of PLT^{c}s is too small (since PLT^c is token-wise probability, $\sum_{p_i \in P} p_i = 1$ does not hold.), it may theoretically happen mPLT values become more than 1. To assure mPLT to be probabilistic and $\bar{p}$ consistent, when an mPLT value exceeds 1, the exceeded value is equally distributed to all the other tokens in the sentence.

3.4 Mask Strategy

In the proposed masking strategy, the value [MASK] calculated by Equation (4) is the mask probability of the token in each sentence. The process for constructing the MLM task, such as replacing tokens and random tokens, follows the strategy in RoBERTa (Liu et al., 2019). The tokens to be manipulated are determined based on the probabilities calculated for each token. Of these, the token is replaced with the [MASK] token with a probability of 80%, and the token is replaced by a random token with the 10% probability, and 10% probability of leaving the token as is. Also, unlike the masking strategy of BERT, the [MASK] positions are re-calculated for each mini-batch.

4 Evaluation Experiment

To evaluate L3Masking, we conducted experiments to answer the following four questions:

- ***Q1**: Does LM learn their own shortcomings from the vanilla model to improve their classification performance compared with the fine-tuned model of the vanilla model only on downstream tasks?*
- ***Q2**: Does L3Masking improve classification performance by adaptively learning task- or domain-specific tokens effectively?*
- ***Q3**: Does L3Masking mask task or domain-specific tokens more frequently than random token masking, and how does this change the model's adaptability?*
- ***Q4**: Does L3Masking improve the efficiency of training by focusing more on masking important tokens in the data for the relevant domain and downstream tasks?*

4.1 Settings

Datasets and Metrics. In our experiments, we use three datasets ACL-ARC (Jurgens et al., 2018), Ohsumed (Hersh et al., 1994), and IMDb (Maas et al., 2011), to evaluate existing methods and our method. The basic statistics for each dataset are shown in Table 1. As for the text classification problem, we set the evaluation metrics as macro F_1 score and accuracy in the confusion matrix.

Table 1: Basic statistics of the three datasets used in the evaluation experiments. $|D_{\text{train}}|$, $|D_{\text{valid}}|$ and $|D_{\text{test}}|$ represent the numbers of instances in the training, validation, test data, respectively, and $|C|$ is the number of classes.

Domain	Task	Type of Supervised Label	$\|D_{\text{train}}\|$	$\|D_{\text{valid}}\|$	$\|D_{\text{test}}\|$	$\|C\|$
Computer Science	ACL-ARC (Jurgens et al., 2018)	citation intent	1,688	114	139	6
Medical	Ohsumed (Kringelum et al., 2016)	category classification	3,022	4,043	4,043	23
Movie Review	IMDb (Luan et al., 2018)	sentiment classification	25,000	2,500	22,500	2

Table 2: Experimental Settings

Parameter	Value
Optimizer	AdamW
Learning Rate	1e-4
Token Length	128
Batch Size	64
Dropout Rate	0.10
Average Mask Probability	0.15
Number of Epochs	150
Early Stopping Patience (epochs)	3

Comparison Methods. To demonstrate the usefulness of L3Masking, we implemented L3Masking into the multi-task learning text classification framework (MTL) of META-TARTAN[2] (Dery et al., 2022) instead of RTM for the MLM task. To answer Q1, L3Masking is compared with a simple fine-tuned model without any auxiliary task, and we call it STL (Single Task Learning). To show a comparison of the impact of MLM on classification performance due to different masking strategies in Q2 and Q3, RTM and L3Masking were used as auxiliary tasks in META-TARTAN framework, and we call MTL methods with these masking strategies as RTM and L3Masking for short, respectively. Note that MLM tasks, including L3Masking and RTM, were applied to data of the text classification task. To answer Q4, we recorded the number of training epochs of the META-TARTAN framework when using RTM or L3Masking, respectively.

Implementations. The hyper-parameters of META-TARTAN were set as Table 2, and the same hyper-parameters were used for L3Masking and the baseline methods. Our experimental evaluation selected the vanilla models pre-trained in the generic corpora, BERT base[3] (Kenton and Toutanova, 2019) and RoBERTa-base[4] (Liu et al., 2019), as LM for META-TARTAN in our experimental evaluation to confirm task and domain adaptability. In addition, the vanilla models pre-trained on the dedicated domain corpora, SciBERT[5] (Beltagy et al., 2019) and ClinicalBERT[6] (Wang et al., 2023), were used to check task adaptability to the computer science domain (ACL-ARC task) and medical domain (Ohsumed task). To optimize task weights of META-TARTAN, objective metrics were aligned to the evaluation metrics (i.e., accuracy or macro F_1). For instance, when evaluating the performance of RTM or L3Masking by the accuracy metric, the task weights of META-TARTAN are optimized based on accuracy scores in the validation data.

4.2 Results

Table 3 showcases the results of this experiment. Overall, our method, L3Masking, demonstrated improvements across a range of datasets compared to the baseline methods. In particular, L3Masking performed superior or comparable to Baseline and RTL in ACL-ARC and Ohsumed, regardless of the language models. However, in general domain dataset IMDb, L3Masking and RTM showed superior performance to STL, while the gap between L3Masking and RTM are limited. This result indicates that advantages of L3Masking are more emphasized in domain-specific contexts.

On the ACL-ARC dataset, L3Masking showed varying degrees of improvement across different general domain LM compared to RTM; L3Masking on both BERT-base and RoBERTa-base showed improvements in the macro F_1 and the accuracy scores, especially RoBERTa-base benefited to a greater extent. In particular, L3Masking improved accuracy by 0.18 points and macro F_1 score by

[2]`https://github.com/ldery/TARTAN/tree/main`, accessed on October 13, 2024

[3]google-bert/bert-base-uncased, `https://huggingface.co/google-bert/bert-base-uncased`, accessed on October 13, 2024

[4]FacebookAI/roberta-base, `https://huggingface.co/FacebookAI/roberta-base`, accessed on October 13, 2024

[5]allenai/scibert_scivocab_uncased, `https://huggingface.co/allenai/scibert_scivocab_uncased`, accessed on October 13, 2024

[6]medicalai/ClinicalBERT, `https://huggingface.co/medicalai/ClinicalBERT`, accessed on October 13, 2024

Table 3: Comparison of Accuracy and Macro F_1 of text classification between STL, RTM, and L3Masking in percentages. The average values and standard deviations of 10 trials are reported. The highest average values for each language model and for each Accuracy and Macro F_1 is in **bold**.

Dataset		ACL-ARC		Ohsumed		IMDb	
Framework	Masking	*Acc*	F_1	*Acc*	F_1	*Acc*	F_1
(General Domain)		BERT-base (Kenton and Toutanova, 2019)					
STL	-	**71.34** ± 0.35	63.07 ± 0.69	76.69 ± 3.41	**68.76** ± 3.47	88.05 ± 0.05	87.15 ± 0.56
MTL	RTM	70.77 ± 0.86	62.15 ± 0.48	**76.98** ± 2.03	67.47 ± 2.40	88.05 ± 0.05	**88.19** ± 0.08
MTL	L3Masking	71.31 ± 0.98	**63.15** ± 0.90	76.81 ± 1.49	66.10 ± 3.50	**88.10** ± 0.21	88.08 ± 0.08
(General Domain)		RoBERTa-base (Liu et al., 2019)					
STL	-	71.73 ± 4.06	59.44 ± 6.70	70.07 ± 0.54	60.92 ± 0.91	88.84 ± 0.32	88.89 ± 0.30
MTL	RTM	78.94 ± 1.76	70.30 ± 2.20	69.92 ± 0.64	64.83 ± 0.37	91.29 ± 0.27	**91.30** ± 0.22
MTL	L3Masking	**79.12** ± 1.60	**73.30** ± 2.90	**73.38** ± 0.48	**65.02** ± 0.61	**91.32** ± 0.15	91.13 ± 0.09
(Domain-Specific)		SciBERT (Beltagy et al., 2019)		ClinicalBERT (Wang et al., 2023)			
STL	-	80.36 ± 2.45	71.84 ± 2.73	71.02 ± 0.42	62.85 ± 0.63	-	-
MTL	RTM	80.14 ± 1.38	70.88 ± 3.06	70.75 ± 0.36	62.70 ± 0.61	-	-
MTL	L3Masking	**82.50** ± 1.90	**74.10** ± 2.40	**71.66** ± 0.78	**63.70** ± 0.60	-	-

3.00 points in RoBERTa-base compared to RTM. However, in the BERT-base, L3Masking performed comparably to STL. The SciBERT model exhibited the most substantial improvement with L3Masking, achieving an accuracy of 82.50 and a macro F_1 score of 74.10, surpassing RTM by 2.36 points in accuracy and 3.22 points in the macro F_1 score.

On the Ohsumed dataset, L3Masking's classification performance varied. In the general domain model, the BERT-base was slightly lower than RTM in both the macro F_1 and accuracy scores. For BERT-base, accuracy was similar for STL, RTM, and L3Masking, and STL had the best macro F_1 score. However, for the RoBERTa-base, L3Masking performed better than STL and RTM, especially in accuracy, which was 3.46 points better than RTM. ClinicalBERT with L3Masking achieved an accuracy of 71.66 and F_1 score of 63.70, outperforming STL and RTM.

On the IMDb dataset, L3Masking's impact was generally limited across the general domain LM. For both BERT-base and RoBERTa-base, L3Masking did not show much difference from baseline or RTM. These results suggest that L3Masking's effect may be less pronounced in general domains such as movie reviews.

4.3 Analysis

In this section, we analyze the effectiveness and efficiency of the L3Masking by examining the types of tokens that were frequently masked and their impact on model performance. We also assess influences on the training process in terms of both accuracy and the number of epochs required.

Types of tokens masked by L3Masking. The L3Masking reveals significant insights into domain-specific adaptation by assigning higher masking probabilities to tokens that carry essential linguistic and domain-specific information. Tables 4 and 5 show the results of part-of-speech (POS) analysis on ACL-ARC training data conducted using NLTK[7] in Python, along with the average mask probability by L3Masking for each POS tag. It is important to note that while POS analysis is performed on a word-by-word basis, L3Masking assigns mask probabilities per token. Therefore, in this analysis, POS tags are assigned to each token, including subwords, and the results are then aggregated by POS tag.

As observed in Table 4, foreign words (FW) and plural nouns (NNS) exhibit the highest masking probabilities in both SciBERT and BERT models within the ACL-ARC dataset. This suggests that L3Masking effectively identifies tokens contributing to the domain's unique linguistic patterns, facilitating more effective knowledge transfer during fine-tuning.

In contrast, general grammatical tokens such as wh-pronouns (WP) and base form verbs (VB) consistently show lower masking probabilities (Table 5), indicating that these elements contribute less to domain-specific adaptations. This distinction underscores L3Masking's ability to prioritize

[7]Natural Language Toolkit (Version 3.8.1) , https://www.nltk.org/, accessed on October 13, 2024

Table 4: The top 5 POS tags with the highest masking probability for RoBERTa and SciBERT in the training data of the ACL-ARC dataset using L3Masking. The masking probability listed in the table is the average of the masking probability for each token. POS tags that occur less than 10 times have been removed from the table.

Rank	L3Masking (RoBERTa)			L3Masking (SciBERT)		
	POS Tag	Description	Mask Probability	POS Tag	Description	Mask Probability
1	FW	Foreign word	0.2023	POS	Possessive ending	0.3133
2	)	Closing parenthesis	0.1907	FW	Foreign word	0.2131
3	(	Opening parenthesis	0.1883	NNS	Noun, plural	0.2017
4	NNS	Noun, plural	0.1832	)	Closing parenthesis	0.2009
5	NNP	Proper noun, singular	0.1647	(	Opening parenthesis	0.1737

Table 5: Worst 5 POS tags with lowest masking probability for RoBERTa and SciBERT in training data of ACL-ARC dataset using L3Masking.

Rank	L3Masking (RoBERTa)			L3Masking (SciBERT)		
	POS Tag	Description	Mask Probability	POS Tag	Description	Mask Probability
1	WP	Wh-pronoun	0.0265	JJS	Adjective, superlative	0.0267
2	VB	Verb, base form	0.0465	WP	Wh-pronoun	0.0281
3	.	Punctuation mark	0.0633	EX	Existential there	0.0317
4	CD	Cardinal number	0.0664	CD	Cardinal number	0.0492
5	VBN	Verb, past participle	0.0686	RBS	Adverb, superlative	0.0503

learning relevant language patterns while minimizing the focus on general linguistic features.

Efficiency. We also found that L3Masking is not only effective for the META-TARTAN framework, but also efficient. Figure 3 illustrates the differences in the number of training epochs and accuracy between RTM and L3Masking across BERT, RoBERTa, SciBERT, and ClinicalBERT. As shown in Figure 3, L3Masking applied to BERT and RoBERTa achieved superior or comparable accuracy in fewer epochs on average than RTM, reducing training time while maintaining or enhancing model performance. This efficiency is particularly advantageous for language models trained on general domain documents, such as BERT and RoBERTa, where computational resources and time are often constrained.

In contrast, while L3Masking in SciBERT and ClinicalBERT improved classification performance over RTM, it did not reduce the number of epochs required. This discrepancy can be attributed to the inherent nature of domain-specific LMs like SciBERT and ClinicalBERT, which are already finely tuned to their respective domains during pretraining. As a result, these models benefit more from L3Masking's ability to refine domain-specific knowledge, leading to improved accuracy. However, because these models are already adapted to their domains, the room for efficiency gains in terms of reduced training time is limited.

These results indicate that L3Masking can effectively decrease training time for models based on generic corpora, like BERT and RoBERTa. However, for models like SciBERT and ClinicalBERT, which are trained on specialized domains, L3Masking primarily enhances task performance without reducing training duration.

4.4 Lessons Learned

As shown in the experimental results above, L3Masking's ability to selectively mask task- or domain-specific tokens significantly enhances the model's performance and adaptability in text classification, confirming its effectiveness over RTM in this context. In summary, questions raised in this section are answered in the rest of this section.

Q1 — Yes, language models (LMs) that learn about their own shortcomings (lessons) demonstrate better classification performance than those that only focus on downstream tasks. Specifically, using L3Masking, models actively learn domain-specific knowledge essential for downstream tasks by focusing on tokens with low pseudo-likelihood and masking them. This approach strengthens areas where the model is underperforming, enabling it to effectively apply learned knowledge. The method helps bridge the distributional differences between

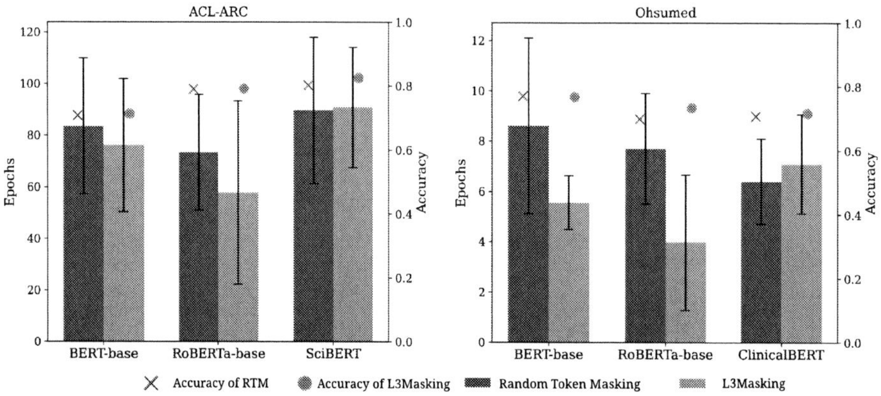

Figure 3: Difference in the number of training epochs for ACL-ARC and Ohsumed using RTM or L3masking for each language model. The plot is based on the average and standard deviation of 10 experiments.

pre-training and fine-tuning tasks, thereby enhancing task adaptability. It has been shown that such learning leads to improved classification performance, particularly in specialized domains.

Q2 — Yes, L3Masking adapts more effectively than Random Token Masking (RTM) and improves classification performance. Notably, in domain-specific language models such as SciBERT and ClinicalBERT, L3Masking demonstrates superior accuracy and F_1 scores compared to RTM. L3Masking identifies and prioritizes tokens specific to the task or domain, leading to more effective task adaptation. Unlike RTM, where tokens are treated uniformly, L3Masking overcomes this limitation by promoting the learning of language patterns relevant to the task. This targeted masking strategy enhances the model's understanding and application of domain-specific knowledge.

Q3 — Yes, L3Masking masks task or domain-specific tokens more frequently than RTM, significantly enhancing the model's adaptability in text classification tasks. By prioritizing the masking of tokens such as foreign words (FW) and plural nouns (NNS), which are crucial in domain-specific contexts like those found in the ACL-ARC and Ohsumed datasets, L3Masking facilitates a deeper understanding of domain-specific language patterns. This strategic focus enables the model to capture better essential linguistic features required for accurate domain-specific classification.

Moreover, this targeted approach enhances the model's adaptability by allowing it to concentrate on tokens that carry significant domain-specific information. As a result, models equipped with L3Masking outperform those using RTM in terms of performance metrics, particularly in domain-specific classification tasks.

Q4 — Yes, L3Masking improves the efficiency of training by strategically focusing on masking important tokens that are crucial for the relevant domain and downstream tasks. By prioritizing task- and domain-specific tokens during the masking process, L3Masking enables the model to concentrate its learning on the most relevant and informative aspects of the data. This targeted approach leads to a reduction in the number of training epochs required to achieve comparable or superior accuracy, particularly in general-domain models like BERT and RoBERTa.

5 Conclusion

This paper introduced L3Masking as a novel masking strategy for fine-tuning of Masked Language Models to text classification. Our method leverages likelihood scores from the vanilla models to actively mask task- or domain-specific tokens. For calculating mask probability on the bidirectional MLMs, token-by-token pseudo-likelihood scores are used. Our method focuses more on tokens that are underrepresented in the pre-training corpus but are crucial for downstream tasks. Through the experimental evaluation of three text classification tasks from different domains, we demonstrated that L3Masking outperforms traditional random token masking, particularly in domain-specific language models such as SciBERT and ClinicalBERT.

Future work will focus on refining the token selection algorithm to handle diverse datasets better and exploring L3Masking's potential in other NLP tasks beyond text classification. Additionally, applying L3Masking to the continual pre-training of large language models (LLMs) represents a significant future direction. By leveraging L3Masking in LLMs, we aim to achieve more accurate domain adaptation, task-specific learning, and effective utilization of large-scale datasets, ultimately enhancing LLMs' overall performance and applicability in various specialized and general domains.

Limitations

Despite the promising results, our study has several limitations. Firstly, our experiments were primarily focused on text classification tasks. Although these tasks provide a good benchmark for evaluating multi-task classification methods, it remains to be unveiled how L3Masking performs in other NLP tasks, such as named entity recognition, machine translation, or text generation. Future research should extend the evaluation of L3Masking to a wider range of tasks to fully understand its capabilities and limitations.

Secondly, the computational overhead associated with calculating token-by-token pseudo-likelihood scores can be substantial. However, we emphasize that the calculation of the mask probability for L3Masking only needs to be performed once per dataset. Although L3Masking can still be computationally expensive, the results presented in this paper suggest that it is worth considering as a replacement for random token masking as an auxiliary task.

References

Josh Achiam, Steven Adler, Sandhini Agarwal, and Others. 2023. GPT-4 Technical Report. *Preprint*, arXiv:2303.08774.

Iz Beltagy, Kyle Lo, and Arman Cohan. 2019. SciBERT: A Pretrained Language Model for Scientific Text. In *Proceedings of the 2019 Conference on Empirical Methods in Natural Language Processing and the 9th International Joint Conference on Natural Language Processing*, pages 3615–3620. Association for Computational Linguistics.

Lucio M. Dery, Paul Michel, Mikhail Khodak, Graham Neubig, and Ameet Talwalkar. 2023. AANG: Automating auxiliary learning. In *The Eleventh International Conference on Learning Representations*.

Lucio M. Dery, Paul Michel, Ameet Talwalkar, and Graham Neubig. 2022. Should We Be Pre-training? An Argument for End-task Aware Training as an Alternative. In *The Tenth International Conference on Learning Representations*.

Suchin Gururangan, Ana Marasović, Swabha Swayamdipta, Kyle Lo, Iz Beltagy, Doug Downey, and Noah A. Smith. 2020. Don't stop pretraining: Adapt language models to domains and tasks. In *Proceedings of the 58th Annual Meeting of the Association for Computational Linguistics*, pages 8342–8360, Online. Association for Computational Linguistics.

William Hersh, Chris Buckley, T. J. Leone, and David Hickam. 1994. OHSUMED: An Interactive Retrieval Evaluation and New Large Test Collection for Research. In *Proceedings of the 17th Annual International ACM SIGIR Conference on Research and Development in Information Retrieval*, SIGIR '94, page 192–201, Berlin, Heidelberg. Springer-Verlag.

David Jurgens, Srijan Kumar, Raine Hoover, Dan McFarland, and Dan Jurafsky. 2018. Measuring the Evolution of a Scientific Field through Citation Frames. *Transactions of the Association for Computational Linguistics*, 6:391–406.

Carina Kauf and Anna Ivanova. 2023. A Better Way to Do Masked Language Model Scoring. In *Proceedings of the 61st Annual Meeting of the Association for Computational Linguistics (Volume 2: Short Papers)*, pages 925–935.

Jacob Devlin Ming-Wei Chang Kenton and Lee Kristina Toutanova. 2019. BERT: Pre-training of Deep Bidirectional Transformers for Language Understanding. In *Proceedings of the 2019 Conference of the North American Chapter of the Association for Computational Linguistics: Human Language Technologies, Volume 1 (Long and Short Papers)*, pages 4171–4186.

Yusuke Kimura, Takahiro Komamizu, and Kenji Hatano. 2023. An automatic labeling method for subword-phrase recognition in effective text classification. *Informatica (Slovenia)*, 47(3):315–326.

Jens Kringelum, Sonny Kim Kjaerulff, Søren Brunak, Ole Lund, Tudor I Oprea, and Olivier Taboureau. 2016. ChemProt-3.0: a global chemical biology diseases mapping. *Database: The Journal of Biological Databases and Curation*, 2016.

Yoav Levine, Barak Lenz, Opher Lieber, Omri Abend, Kevin Leyton-Brown, Moshe Tennenholtz, and Yoav Shoham. 2021. PMI-MASKING: PRINCIPLED MASKING OF CORRELATED SPANS. In *The Ninth International Conference on Learning Representations*.

Zhenghao Lin, Zhibin Gou, Yeyun Gong, Xiao Liu, Yelong Shen, Ruochen Xu, Chen Lin, Yujiu Yang, Jian Jiao, Nan Duan, and Weizhu Chen. 2024. Rho-1: Not all tokens are what you need. *Preprint*, arXiv:2404.07965.

Yinhan Liu, Myle Ott, Naman Goyal, Jingfei Du, Mandar Joshi, Danqi Chen, Omer Levy, Mike Lewis,

Luke Zettlemoyer, and Veselin Stoyanov. 2019. RoBERTa: A Robustly Optimized BERT Pretraining Approach. *Preprint*, arXiv:1907.11692.

Yi Luan, Luheng He, Mari Ostendorf, and Hannaneh Hajishirzi. 2018. Multi-Task Identification of Entities, Relations, and Coreference for Scientific Knowledge Graph Construction. In *Proceedings of the 2018 Conference on Empirical Methods in Natural Language Processing*, pages 3219–3232.

Andrew L. Maas, Raymond E. Daly, Peter T. Pham, Dan Huang, Andrew Y. Ng, and Christopher Potts. 2011. Learning word vectors for sentiment analysis. In *Proceedings of the 49th Annual Meeting of the Association for Computational Linguistics: Human Language Technologies*, pages 142–150, Portland, Oregon, USA. Association for Computational Linguistics.

Nafis Sadeq, Canwen Xu, and Julian McAuley. 2022. InforMask: Unsupervised Informative Masking for Language Model Pretraining. In *Proceedings of the 2022 Conference on Empirical Methods in Natural Language Processing*, pages 5866–5878, Abu Dhabi, United Arab Emirates. Association for Computational Linguistics.

Julian Salazar, Davis Liang, Toan Q. Nguyen, and Katrin Kirchhoff. 2020. Masked language model scoring. In *Proceedings of the 58th Annual Meeting of the Association for Computational Linguistics*, pages 2699–2712. Association for Computational Linguistics.

Haizhou Shi, Zihao Xu, Hengyi Wang, Weiyi Qin, Wenyuan Wang, Yibin Wang, Zifeng Wang, Sayna Ebrahimi, and Hao Wang. 2024. Continual learning of large language models: A comprehensive survey. *Preprint*, arXiv:2404.16789.

Yu Sun, Shuohuan Wang, Yukun Li, Shikun Feng, Xuyi Chen, Han Zhang, Xin Tian, Danxiang Zhu, Hao Tian, and Hua Wu. 2019. ERNIE: Enhanced Representation through Knowledge Integration. *Preprint*, arXiv:1904.09223.

Ashish Vaswani, Noam Shazeer, Niki Parmar, Jakob Uszkoreit, Llion Jones, Aidan N Gomez, Ł ukasz Kaiser, and Illia Polosukhin. 2017. Attention is all you need. In *Advances in Neural Information Processing Systems*, volume 30. Curran Associates, Inc.

Guangyu Wang, Xiaohong Liu, Zhen Ying, Guoxing Yang, Zhiwei Chen, Zhiwen Liu, Min Zhang, Hongmei Yan, Yuxing Lu, Yuanxu Gao, Kanmin Xue, Xiaoying Li, and Ying Chen. 2023. Optimized glycemic control of type 2 diabetes with reinforcement learning: a proof-of-concept trial. *Nature Medicine*, 29(10):2633–2642.

Alexander Wettig, Tianyu Gao, Zexuan Zhong, and Danqi Chen. 2023. Should You Mask 15% in Masked Language Modeling? In *Proceedings of the 17th Conference of the European Chapter of the Association for Computational Linguistics*, pages 2985–3000. Association for Computational Linguistics.

Yong Xie, Karan Aggarwal, and Aitzaz Ahmad. 2023. Efficient continual pre-training for building domain specific large language models. *Preprint*, arXiv:2311.08545.

Grounded Language Agent for Product Search via Intelligent Web Interactions

Moghis Fereidouni, Adib Mosharrof, A.B. Siddique
University of Kentucky, Lexington, KY, USA
moghis.fereidouni@uky.edu, amo304@g.uky.edu, siddique@cs.uky.edu

Abstract

The development of agents powered by large language models (LLMs) to accomplish complex high-level user intents, has attracted significant attention recently. However, employing LLMs with billions of parameters (e.g., GPT-4) may incur substantial costs on top of handcrafting extensive prompts. To address this, we introduce a Grounded Language Agent for Intelligent Web Interactions, named GLAINTEL. GLAINTEL employs Flan-T5 as its backbone and is flexible in training in various settings: unsupervised learning, supervised learning, and unsupervised domain adaptation. Specifically, we tackle both the challenge of learning without human demonstrations and the opportunity to leverage human demonstrations effectively when those are available. Additionally, we explore unsupervised domain adaptation for cases where demonstrations are limited to a specific domain. Experimental evaluations across diverse setups demonstrate the effectiveness of GLAINTEL in unsupervised settings, outperforming in-context learning-based approaches that employ larger models with up to 540 billion parameters. Surprisingly, behavioral cloning-based methods that straightforwardly use human demonstrations do not outperform unsupervised variants of GLAINTEL. Additionally, we show that combining human demonstrations with reinforcement learning-based training yields results comparable to methods utilizing GPT-4. The code is available at: https://github.com/MultifacetedNLP/Web-Agents-Unsupervised.

1 Introduction

Large Language Models (LLMs) have demonstrated their proficiency in diverse tasks such as text classification, information extraction, and question answering (Bommasani et al., 2021; Brown et al., 2020; Vaswani et al., 2017; Raffel et al., 2020; Radford et al., 2019). Similarly, reinforcement learning (RL) has evolved as a powerful paradigm for training intelligent agents to navigate complex environments (Huang et al., 2022b; Ahn et al., 2022; Liang et al., 2023). Moreover, recent research highlights the capabilities of agents powered by LLMs. For example, agents utilizing GPT-4 can explore the virtual world in Minecraft, acquire a diverse set of composable skills, and exhibit exceptional proficiency in playing the game (Wang et al., 2024). The exceptional amount of world knowledge, often derived from vast text datasets, opens up possibilities for developing LLM-assisted intelligent web navigation agents capable of navigating and interacting with web pages akin to humans.

Despite their remarkable capabilities, off-the-shelf pre-trained LLMs face challenges in grounding and aligning themselves in interactive web environments (Mahowald et al., 2023). This limitation hampers their functional competence without additional customization. Additionally, employing LLMs with billion-scale parameters, such as GPT-4, may incur substantial costs on top of handcrafting extensive prompts. On the other hand, training smaller LLMs (e.g., Flan-T5) as agents can be challenging. For instance, consider a real-world product search scenario, where effective query formulation requires the agent to operate over a huge action space (i.e., language vocabulary), and navigating through diverse web pages poses additional challenges that need strategic exploration due to the presence of different actions on each page (i.e., dynamic action space). This complexity prevents the straightforward utilization of an action head on top of LLM. Moreover, the challenge extends to preserving long-term memory capabilities, which are crucial for comparing items or backtracking during the search process.

In this work, we introduce GLAINTEL, a **G**rounded **L**anguage **A**gent designed for **In****tel**ligent Web Interactions. Given a user's intent specifying a product requirement, GLAINTEL formulates queries, navigates diverse web pages, and

Proceedings of the 1st Workshop on Customizable NLP: Progress and Challenges in Customizing NLP for a Domain, Application, Group, or Individual (CustomNLP4U), pages 63–75
November 16, 2024 ©2024 Association for Computational Linguistics

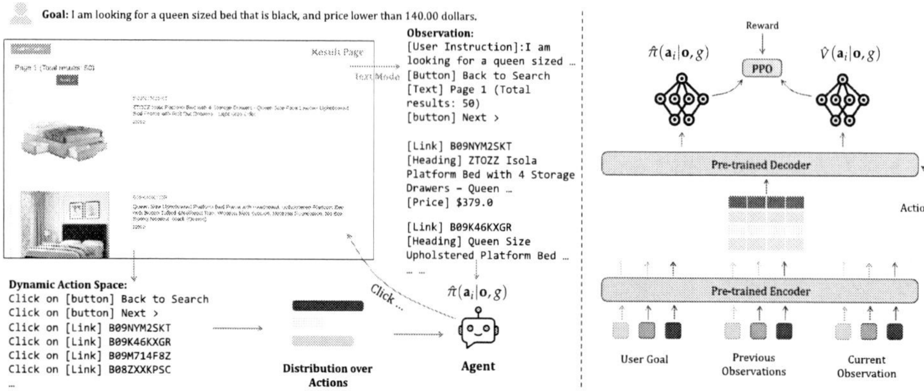

Figure 1: Overview of GLAINTEL: Our agent employs the Flan-T5 architecture and incorporates a language modeling head to adapt to dynamic action space, while the value head enables precise value estimation.

executes various actions to identify, customize, and purchase the desired product. GLAINTEL uses the open-source Flan-T5 language model (i.e., 780 million parameters) as its backbone and can be flexibly trained in various scenarios: unsupervised, supervised, and unsupervised domain adaptation settings. Specifically, we address the following research questions.

- *RQ1: Effectiveness of Unsupervised Learning:* Can LLM-based agents learn to address effective query generation and exploration of complex web pages with no human demonstrations?
- *RQ2: Impact of Human Demonstrations:* Can incorporating human demonstrations facilitate LLM-based agents to improve their overall performance? How to effectively leverage human demonstrations for training robust agents?
- *RQ3: Unsupervised Domain Adaptation:* Can LLM-based agents generalize to new, unseen product categories where no human demonstrations are available?

We employ a language modeling head to accommodate a *dynamic action space* and introduce an additional value head for precise value estimates. Figure 1 provides an overview of GLAINTEL. The user's goal and observation are sequentially passed to the model at each step. First, we obtain the input representation for every potential action token and compute the normalized joint probability for each action conditioned on the user goal and observation. Following the estimation of each action's probability, we apply a softmax function over these probabilities and sample an action according to this distribution. We fine-tune the agent using the Proximal Policy Optimization (PPO) algorithm (Dhariwal et al., 2017).

We conduct extensive experimental evaluations across diverse setups using the WebShop environment (Yao et al., 2022). WebShop is a simulated yet realistic e-commerce web platform featuring 1.18 million real-world products and 12,087 crowd-sourced natural language intents. Based on our empirical study, we demonstrate that training Flan-T5 (e.g., 780 million parameters) in the unsupervised setting (i.e., no human demonstrations) can outperform in-context learning methods (Sridhar et al., 2023) that rely on models with up to 540 billion parameters. To quantify the impact of human supervision, we utilized 1010 human demonstrations for training supervised learning models using behavior cloning (BC) (Pomerleau, 1988).

Our findings indicate that incorporating human demonstrations through *straightforward BC does not produce superior results* when compared to the unsupervised RL-based PPO algorithm. Furthermore, our investigations reveal that leveraging human demonstrations through BC and then further training the agent with PPO in the unsupervised setting leads to the best results. Remarkably, this approach achieves results comparable to the method (Ma et al., 2023) that utilizes GPT-4. In the unsupervised domain adaptation (UDA) experiment, we observe that incorporating human demonstrations from a single category enables the agent to generalize to new product categories where no human demonstrations are available. Additionally, we *evaluate our trained model on a real website eBay* without any additional fine-tuning, which shows comparable results to methods that use the state-of-the-art GPT-4 model.

2 Proposed Agent: GLAINTEL

2.1 Problem Formulation

Given a user intent in natural language, the agent's goal is to buy the most appropriate product that fulfills the user's intent. We formulate the task as a goal-augmented Partially Observable Markov Decision Process $\mathcal{M} = (\mathcal{S}, \mathcal{A}, \mathcal{T}, \mathcal{R}, \mathcal{G}, \mathcal{O}, \gamma)$, where $\mathcal{S}$ is a set of states $\mathbf{s} \in \mathcal{S}$; $\mathcal{A} \subset \mathcal{V}^N$ represents action space sampled from LLM's vocabulary $\mathcal{V}$ of size N; $\mathcal{G} \subset \mathcal{V}^N$ denotes the goal space; $\mathcal{T} : \mathcal{S} \times \mathcal{A} \mapsto \mathcal{S}$ is the transition function; $\mathcal{R} : \mathcal{S} \times \mathcal{A} \times \mathcal{G} \mapsto \mathbb{R}$ characterizes the goal-conditioned reward function; $\mathcal{O}$ is a set of observations $\mathbf{o} \in \mathcal{O}$ (i.e., web page visible to agent); γ is the discount factor. We employ the language modeling head (i.e., distribution over the vocabulary) to accommodate the dynamic action space, which also facilitates directly computing the log probabilities of each action $\mathbf{a}_i = (w_0, \cdots, w_{|\mathbf{a}_i|})$ sampled from a dynamic action space given the agent's goal $g \in \mathcal{G}$ and observation $\mathbf{o}$.

It is important to note that each observation (i.e., web page) presents a dynamic set of actions to the agent, which prevents us from learning a probability distribution over the action space as in classification tasks. For instance, a search page allows actions such as typing an open-ended textual query or pressing the 'Search' button. Conversely, a product detail page offers actions such as 'Back to Search', '< Prev', 'Description', 'Features', 'Reviews', 'Buy Now', and the product-specific variable number of options. Figure 1 shows the observation and action space for the 'search result page'.

2.2 Overview of GLAINTEL

We employ Flan-T5 [1] as the core architecture, with the integration of the language modeling head and value head on top of the model. Our proposed agent, GLAINTEL, is adaptable to training across various setups: (*i*) unsupervised learning: no human demonstrations are available; (*ii*) unsupervised domain adaptation: limited human demonstrations in a single domain are available; and (*iii*) supervised learning: human demonstrations are accessible. In the following, we detail the specifics of the training and inference phases. The inclusion or exclusion of these phases is contingent upon the availability of the human demonstration data.

[1]Checkpoints: https://github.com/google-research/t5x/blob/main/docs/models.md#flan-t5-checkpoints

2.3 Optional Phase One: Supervised Training

The human demonstrations can serve as mappings from states to actions. Techniques such as imitation learning or behavioral cloning (BC) (Pomerleau, 1988) can be employed to fine-tune the policy π by minimizing the following loss over a dataset $\mathcal{D}$ comprising human demonstrations:

$$\mathcal{L}(\pi) = \mathbb{E}_{(s,a)\sim\mathcal{D}}[-\log \pi(a|s)].$$

The above formulation can be adapted to incorporate the interaction history with web pages $\pi(\mathbf{a}_t|\mathbf{s}_t, \tau_{<t})$, where $\tau_{<t}$ refers to the interaction trajectory leading up to time t. Subsequently, this formulation readily extends to utilize LLMs to learn an optimal policy where the encoder encodes the history of observations $(\mathbf{s}_t, \tau_{<t})$ and the decoder generates the next action $\mathbf{a}_t$ as:

$$\mathcal{L}_{\text{LLM}}(\pi) = \mathbb{E}_{\tau\sim\mathcal{D}}[\sum_{t=0}^{L} - \log \pi(\mathbf{a}_t|\tau_{<t}, \mathbf{s}_t)].$$

Building upon the recent works in return-conditioned supervised learning (Brandfonbrener et al., 2022; Paster et al., 2022; Yang et al., 2022), we introduce an additional conditioning variable $g \in \mathcal{G}$ (i.e., user goal). This variable captures overall trajectory-level information, to steer the model toward the goal. Moreover, in implementation, we use observations $\mathbf{o}$ (i.e., visible web page) instead of the actual state $\mathbf{s}$. Our final formulation is expressed as:

$$\mathcal{L}_{\text{LLM}}(\pi) = \mathbb{E}_{\tau\sim\mathcal{D}}[\sum_{t=0}^{L} - \log \pi(\mathbf{a}_t|\tau_{<t}, \mathbf{o}_t, g)].$$

The training of this phase can be skipped or chosen based on the availability and feasibility of acquiring human demonstrations. In our approach to address RQ1 (Effectiveness of Unsupervised Learning), we skip this phase. We limit the human demonstration data to a single category for RQ3 (Unsupervised Domain Adaptation). To investigate RQ2 (Impact of Human Demonstrations), we utilize all the available training data for the supervised training phase.

2.4 Phase Two: Unsupervised Training

The unsupervised learning phase, which forms the core of the proposed agent GLAINTEL, operates without any human demonstrations. This phase is designed to autonomously learn and adapt without relying on expert-guided examples. The objective of the agent is to learn a policy $\pi : \mathcal{O} \times \mathcal{G} \mapsto \mathbb{P}(\mathcal{A})$

that optimizes the expected discounted cumulative rewards for a given goal g. In this work, we leverage PPO algorithm for training, which simultaneously learns a policy $\hat{\pi}$ and a value function $\hat{V} : \mathcal{O} \times \mathcal{G} \mapsto \mathbb{R}$ approximating to the true value $V(\mathbf{s}, g) = \mathbb{E}_{\mathbf{a}\sim\hat{\pi}(\mathcal{O}(\mathbf{s}),g)}\big[\mathcal{R}(\mathbf{s}, \mathbf{a}, g) + \gamma V(\mathcal{T}(\mathbf{s}, \mathbf{a}), g)\big]$. We can calculate the probability of each action $\mathbf{a}_i \in \mathcal{A}$ using the likelihood computed by the model, expressed as: $\hat{\pi}(\mathbf{a}_i|\mathbf{o}, g) = P(\mathbf{a}_i|g)$. That is, the likelihood of choosing each action is calculated based on the probability distributions associated with the tokens that make up the action. This approach ties the action probabilities directly to the distributions of the individual tokens involved in constructing the action. Following (Carta et al., 2023), we incorporate a multilayer perception (MLP) with a single output on top of the last layer of the model to approximate the value V. Specifically, we employ the language modeling head to directly compute the log probabilities of each action $\mathbf{a}_i = \{w_0, \cdots, w_{|\mathbf{a}_i|}\}$ from the dynamic action space given the agent's goal $g \in \mathcal{G}$ and observation $\mathbf{o}_t$ at time t as follows:

$$P(\mathbf{a}_i) = \frac{1}{|a_i|}\sum_{k=0}^{|a_i|} \log P_{\text{LM-head}}(w_k|g, \mathbf{o}_t, w_{<k}).$$

Subsequently, employing the softmax operation, we calculate a probability distribution over the action space $\mathcal{A}$ as follows:

$$P(\mathbf{a}_i|g) = \frac{e^{P(\mathbf{a}_i)}}{\sum_{\mathbf{a}_k \in \mathcal{A}} e^{P(\mathbf{a}_k)}}.$$

While the actions comprise multiple tokens, the number of possible actions can vary substantially depending on the current observation (i.e., web page), which introduces additional complexity. This phase is mandatory regardless of whether training is conducted in the optional first phase.

2.5 Phase Three: Inference

In the inference phase, various decoding techniques for action selection can be employed, such as greedy decoding and top-p. Given the well-established nature of these techniques, we omit details and provide key insights only. Greedy decoding, chosen for action selection, has a drawback as it tends to trap the agent in loops, ultimately resulting in suboptimal overall performance. Conversely, opting for top-p sampling can yield a higher success rate, as it provides a theoretical tradeoff between sampling and greedy decoding. However, the process of determining the optimal values for p can be time-intensive. To address these issues, we turn to the Epsilon-Greedy algorithm for action selection during inference. In particular, at a step t, the greedy will choose the action with the highest probability, while the epsilon will sample based on the probability distribution across the action space. This method achieves a higher success rate and an enhanced overall performance, all while avoiding the issue of getting stuck in loops. It is worth noting that a judiciously chosen, small value for epsilon has been employed in our work, eliminating the need for an exhaustive search.

3 Experimental Setup

3.1 WebShop Environment

Webshop (Yao et al., 2022) is a simulated web-based interactive environment with 1.18 million real-world products and 12,087 crowd-sourced text instructions. The goal of the agent is to buy a product with specific attributes and options given natural language instruction. The environment contains 5 different categories, which exhibit significant dissimilarities, particularly in terms of possessing nearly exclusive attributes. For instance, as illustrated in Table 1, a substantial 95.9% of Fashion's attributes are unique to its category.

Human Demonstrations. The Webshop also contains a human demonstration dataset. The human demonstration dataset encompasses a total of 1010 distinct trajectories, distributed across categories. This dataset is created by asking humans to demonstrate how they would query a product and then take different steps in the Webshop environment to buy a product with desired options and attributes.

GLAINTEL has the flexibility to incorporate human demonstrations through optional phase one training. We utilize human demonstration data to quantify the impact of human demonstrations (RQ2) and explore UDA (RQ3). Additionally, GLAINTEL can be trained without any human demonstrations (RQ1).

3.2 Evaluation Methodology

Reward. We assign a reward $r \in [0, 1]$ to the agent after it completes a purchase at the concluding step of an episode. Specifically, the reward is determined by how closely the purchased product matches the specific attributes and options mentioned in the user instructions as follows:

$$r = r_{\text{type}} \cdot \frac{|U_{\text{att}} \cap Y_{\text{att}}| + |U_{\text{opt}} \cap Y_{\text{opt}}| + \mathbb{1}[y_{\text{price}} \leq u_{\text{price}}]}{|U_{\text{att}}| + |U_{\text{opt}}| + 1}$$

Category	# Attributes	% Unique Attributes	# Human Demonstrations
Beauty	143	85.3%	224
Garden	133	87.2%	211
Grocery	117	92.3%	189
Electronics	141	91.4%	169
Fashion	173	95.9%	217

Table 1: Detail about Webshop Environment.

The reward incorporates three main components: U_{att}, U_{opt}, and u_{price}, representing a set of attributes, a set of options, and the price set down in the user's instruction, respectively. Correspondingly, Y_{att}, Y_{opt}, and y_{price} denote the set of attributes, the set of options, and the actual price of the purchased product by the agent. Additionally, r_{type} functions as a text-matching heuristic, assigning a lower reward when the purchased product and the targeted product in the user instruction have similar attributes and options while being different types of products. Interested readers are referred to WebShop (Yao et al., 2022) for details.

Evaluation Metrics. Two evaluation metrics are computed using the rewards obtained from the episodes: (*i*) the Score and (*ii*) the Success Rate. The Score metric represents the average reward across all test episodes multiplied by 100, while the Success rate metric measures the percentage of test episodes in which the full reward (1 out of 1) was attained. Given that our inference step incorporates sampling, the reported Score and Success Rate metrics are averaged by running the model four times. *We provide additional implementation details in Appendix A.*

3.3 Competing Methods

WebShop Baselines (Yao et al., 2022): We consider the following baselines from the WebShop paper: (*i*) rule-based (Rule$_{ws}$), (*ii*) behavioral cloning-based supervised learning (BC$_{ws}$), (*iii*) two reinforcement learning models—one with a transformer text encoder (PG$_{ws}$) and another with an RNN (RNN$_{ws}$), and (*iv*) a hybrid method (BC + PG). Human experts (Human) also set a benchmark for human-level performance.

DRRN (He et al., 2016): DRRN is a classic RL baseline that uses separate neural networks to embed states and actions into embedding vectors. An interaction function (e.g., inner product) then computes the Q-function value for the state-action pair.

Act and ReAct (Yao et al., 2023): The ReAct method is an in-context learning approach using LLMs that combines reasoning and action execution to tackle diverse tasks. In the WebShop environment, ReAct adds reasoning at each step to guide the agent's decisions on exploration, purchasing, and option selection.

WebGUM (Furuta et al., 2024): WebGUM is an instruction-finetuned model, that is further trained on human demonstrations for web navigation.

ASH Prompting (Sridhar et al., 2023): ASH consists of two main components: (*i*) Summarizer condenses observations by retaining only relevant information, and (*ii*) Actor uses this condensed observation to generate the next action.

PIX2ACT (Shaw et al., 2024): PIX2ACT builds upon the Pix2Struct model (Lindenberger et al., 2021), utilizing an image transformer encoder along with a text transformer decoder.

LASER (Ma et al., 2023): LASER is a GPT-4-based method that converts an interactive decision-making task into state space exploration by mapping all possible observations to a finite set of states, with the agent navigating these states through predefined actions specific to each state

Prospector (Kim et al., 2023): The Prospector uses two approaches: the AskAct method, which incorporates self-asking steps in few-shot demonstrations to extract actions from LLMs, and the Trajectory Ranking (TR) method, where LLMs generate diverse trajectories, and the most rewarding one is selected using a reward prediction model.

4 Results

4.1 Quantitative Analysis

RQ1: Effectiveness of Unsupervised Learning. In Table 2, we systematically evaluate the performance of various methods that do not use human demonstrations for training. Starting with RL-based models, our PPO-trained model with 1 million steps (PPO$_{1M}$) emerges as the top performer, achieving a statistically significant score of 72.13 and a success rate of 42.55. Notably, these results surpass those obtained by alternative RL-based approaches, namely PGws, DRRN, and RNN$_{ws}$, underscoring the superior efficacy of the PPO methodology. Among In-context learning methods, the AskAct stands out with the most impressive results. However, even the best-performing AskAct, 70 billion parameters, fails to outperform a smaller model fine-tuned in an unsupervised setting with PPO (PPO$_{1M}$). Specifically, in terms of percentage improvements, the PPO-trained model with 1 million steps (PPO$_{1M}$) outperforms the AskAct by 5.15% on the score metric and approximately

Approach	Name	Model	Parameters	Score	Success Rate
Zero Shot	Random	-	-	33.74	6.80
	Rule_{ws} [1]	-	-	45.60	9.60
	ZSL-Flan-T5	Flan-T5-large	780 Million	41.10	10.30
In-context Learning	Act [2]	PaLM	540 Billion	62.30	30.10
	ASH [4]	CODE-DAVINCI-002	N/A	56.70	30.20
	ReAct [2]	PaLM	540 Billion	66.60	40.00
	AskAct [3]	Llama-2	70 Billion	68.60	42.20
RL-based Method	PG_{ws} [1]	BART, BERT	516 Million	52.50	11.20
	DRRN	GRU	1.2 Million	46.87	11.73
	RNN_{ws} [1]	GRU	5 Million	55.20	17.60
	PPO_{500K} (Ours)	Flan-T5-large	780 Million	68.19	38.55
	PPO_{1M} (Ours)	Flan-T5-large	780 Million	**72.13**	**42.55**
Human	Human [1]	-	-	82.10	59.60

Results are taken from published research: [1] from (Yao et al., 2022), [2] from (Yao et al., 2023), [3] from (Kim et al., 2023), and [4] from (Sridhar et al., 2023).

Table 2: Results from methods in the WebShop environment that do not rely on human demonstration data.

Approach	Name	Model	Parameters	Score	Success Rate
Behavioral Cloning	PIX2ACT [3]	Pix2Struct	282 Million	46.70	NR
	BC_{ws} [1]	BART, BERT	516 Million	59.90	29.10
	BC_{our}	Flan-T5-large	780 Million	66.56	37.05
	WebGUM [2]	Flan-T5-XL	3 Billion	67.50	45.00
Hybrid Methods	BC + PG [1]	BART, BERT	516 Million	62.40	28.70
	AskAct + TR (Prospector) [4]	Llama-2, FLAN-T5-XL	70 + 3 Billion	70.20	43.60
	BC + PPO_{500K} (GLAINTEL_{500K})	Flan-T5-large	780 Million	74.60	46.95
	BC + PPO_{1M} (GLAINTEL_{1M})	Flan-T5-large	780 Million	**76.87**	**49.60**

Results are taken from published research: [1] from (Yao et al., 2022), [2] from (Furuta et al., 2024), [3] from (Shaw et al., 2024), and [4] from (Kim et al., 2023).

Table 3: Results from methods in the WebShop environment that use human demonstration data.

0.83% on the success rate metric. This pattern persists when comparing ReAct (540 billion parameters) with PPO_{1M} model. This observation suggests that fine-tuning of small models using RL can yield superior performance compared to in-context learning methods. In addition to RL-based and in-context learning methods, Table 2 includes zero-shot learning methods, including zero-shot Flan-T5 (ZSL-Flan-T5) to quantify the role of unsupervised training.

RQ2: Impact of Human Demonstrations. Table 3 presents the results of various methods incorporating human demonstration. In the behavioral cloning approach, WebGum emerges as the top performer, leveraging the Flan-T5-XL model with 3 billion parameters. It achieves a score of 67.5 and a success rate of 45.0. We also present the results of our fine-tuned Flan-T5-large model (BC_{our}) with 780 million parameters. Both models outperform the PIX2ACT and $\text{BC}ws$ models, which utilize BART and BERT architectures. This notable superiority underscores the effectiveness of instruction-finetuned language models. Turning to hybrid methods, GLAINTEL_{500K}, GLAINTEL_{1M}, and BC + PG models initially undergo refinement through human demonstrations in a supervised setting, followed by additional fine-tuning in an unsupervised setting using RL. In contrast, Prospector employs the AskAct method (in-context learning) and a reward prediction model, choosing the most rewarding trajectory through supervised learning. Among these approaches, GLAINTEL_{1M} achieves remarkable performance. It attains an exceptional Score of 76.87 and a Success Rate of 49.6. Notably, our approach surpasses all other hybrid and behavioral cloning methods in both metrics.

Effective Utilization of Human Demonstrations: In comparing two variants of the Flan-T5-large model, as presented in Table 3 and Table 2, we focused on one fine-tuned in a supervised setting with human demonstrations (referred to as BC_{our} in Table 3) and another fine-tuned exclusively with PPO for 1 million steps in an unsupervised setting (referred to as PPO_{1M} in Table 2). Surprisingly, the unsupervised model (PPO_{1M}) demonstrated an 8.36% higher score and a 14.84% higher success rate compared to the supervised model, which is statistically significant. *This outcome suggests that relying only on human demonstrations does not always lead to superior results.* Moreover, when the supervised model is subjected to further training with PPO, it produces the best results.

Approach	Name	Model	Parameters	Score	Success Rate
RL-based Method	PPO_{1M}	Flan-T5-large	780 Million	72.12	42.55
Hybrid Method	BC + PPO_{1M} (GLAINTEL_{1M})	Flan-T5-large	780 Million	**76.87**	<u>49.6</u>
Unsupervised Domain Adaptation	UDA_{1M}	Flan-T5-large	780 Million	74.69	46.42
State-Space Exploration	LASER(Ma et al., 2023)	GPT-4-0613	N/A	<u>75.6</u>	**50.0**

Table 4: Comparison of the Best Models.

Approach →	Single Domain Behavioral Cloning		Unsupervised Domain Adaptation			
PPO Adaptation Configs →	No PPO (SDBC)		PPO for 500k steps (UDA_{500K})		PPO for 1M steps (UDA_{1M})	
Single-domain Supervision ↓	Score	Success Rate	Score	Success Rate	Score	Success Rate
Fine-tuned on Beauty	64.23	31.41	73.99	45.80	74.49	45.85
Fine-tuned on Garden	64.79	34.76	73.97	44.70	75.27	47.5
Fine-tuned on Grocery	61.80	27.50	73.83	45.75	74.91	47.60
Fine-tuned on Electronics	62.03	30.97	73.46	45.25	74.41	44.5
Fine-tuned on Fashion	62.54	31.60	73.37	44.45	74.36	46.65
Average →	63.07	31.24	73.72	45.19	74.68	46.42

Table 5: The results of unsupervised domain adaptation and single domain methods in the WebShop environment.

<u>Comparison between the Best Models:</u> We present the results from the best models in Table 4. Notably, GLAINTEL_{1M} achieves a state-of-the-art score (i.e., 76.87) surpassing all other models. Surprisingly, our model, based on Flan-T5-Large (780 million parameters), has outperformed the LASER method, which relies on the latest GPT-4 model with extensive handcrafted prompt, in terms of the Score metric. It also achieves comparable performance in terms of Success Rate (49.6 vs 50.0). These findings strongly suggest that a model, when further fine-tuned with PPO after supervised training, can deliver superior results, even with a relatively smaller model size.

RQ3: Unsupervised Domain Adaptation. The Single Domain Behavioral Cloning (SDBC) approach involves fine-tuning a Flan-T5-large model in a supervised setting using demonstrations specific to a particular domain (e.g., Beauty). Subsequently, without any additional refinement for other domains, the model is directly tested using the WebShop environment encompassing all domains. In contrast, UDA takes the Flan-T5-large model fine-tuned in a single domain and further refines it across all domains using PPO in the unsupervised setting. Table 5 presents two versions of UDA: UDA_{500K} and UDA_{1M}. Both UDA methods exhibit superior performance (i.e., statistically significant) in terms of Score and Success Rate metrics when compared to the corresponding metrics of SDBC. This superiority is evident not only on a domain-specific basis but also on the average performance across domains. In particular, concerning the average performance across domains, UDA_{1M} surpasses SDBC by 18.4% in the Score and 48.6% in the Success Rate metrics. This emphasizes the crucial role of unsupervised PPO refinement and its impact on enhancing overall performance.

<u>Role of Supervision in a Single Domain:</u> To compare the UDA results with RL-based ones, we can refer to Table 5 and Table 2, where UDA_{500K} model outperforms the PPO_{500K} in terms of both Score and Success Rate metrics. Similarly, UDA_{1M} surpassed PPO_{1M}. Specifically, the UDA_{1M} model achieves a 3.5% higher Score and a 9.09% higher Success Rate compared to the PPO_{1M} model. Likewise, the UDA_{500K} model attained an 8.1% higher Score and a 17.2% higher Success Rate compared to the PPO_{500K} model. These findings indicate that incorporating single-domain human demonstration supervision significantly enhances the model's capacity for more effective fine-tuning during unsupervised training with PPO. This approach outperforms models that lack any supervised training, which highlights the value of leveraging human demonstrations in the adaptation process.

Learning Curves for PPO training. In Figure 2, the learning curves of Score and Success Rate metrics during PPO fine-tuning are illustrated for various methodologies: the UDA, the hybrid (GLAINTEL) (BC + PPO), and the RL-based PPO. Both the hybrid method and the unsupervised domain adaptation method demonstrate higher sample efficiency compared to the unsupervised method. This aligns with expectations, considering that both the hybrid method and the unsupervised domain adaptation method underwent some level of supervised training before RL fine-tuning – a contrast to the RL-based unsupervised method, which did not.

Approach	Name	Model	Parameters	Score	Success Rate
Hybrid Method	BC + PG	BART, BERT	516 Million	59.25	24
Hybrid Method	BC + PPO_{1M} ($GLAINTEL_{1M}$)	Flan-T5-large	780 Million	78.35	53
State-Space Exploration	LASER	GPT-4-0613	N/A	83.55	56

Table 6: Results of Zero-shot simulation-to-real experiment on eBay.

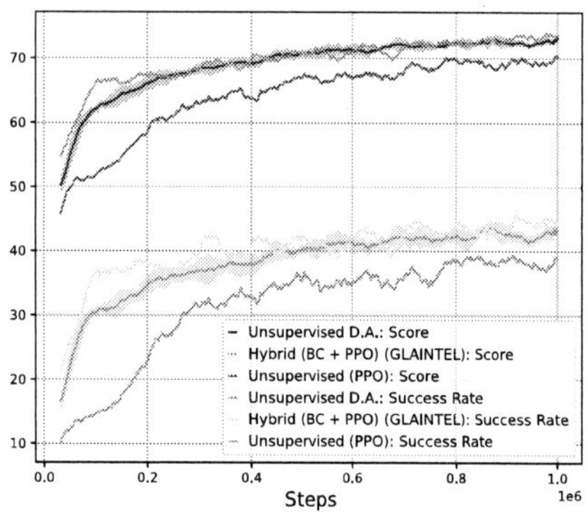

Figure 2: Learning curves of different methodologies: Unsupervised Domain Adaptation (UDA), Hybrid (BC + PPO) (GLAINTEL), and RL-based Unsupervised (PPO).

4.2 Results on Real Website: eBay

We also conduct limited evaluations on a real website: eBay. For this experiment, we evaluate the performance of three methods: (*i*) our best model ($GLAINTEL_{1M}$), (*ii*) the GPT-4-based method LASER, and (*iii*) the WebShop baseline (BC + PG). *It is important to highlight that we used the models trained using the Webshop environment and did not perform any fine-tuning using the eBay website.* Following (Yao et al., 2022), we randomly sampled 100 user instructions to evaluate the performance of these methods. As presented in Table 6, our method $GLAINTEL_{1M}$ significantly outperformed the WebShop baseline (BC + PG) by 32.23% in the Score metric and by 120.83% in the Success Rate metric. Moreover, although LASER, utilizing GPT-4, has slightly higher Score and Success Rate metrics compared to our model $GLAINTEL_{1M}$, we are confident that $GLAINTEL_{1M}$ can achieve comparable or even superior results by enabling of unsupervised training using PPO. Additionally, it is worth noting that our approach utilizes a 780 million parameter model, which is significantly smaller than GPT-4, not to mention the costs associated with GPT-4. *We present an ablation study in Appendix B.*

5 Related Work

Fine-tuning LLMs with RL and Human Feedback. Fine-tuning LLMs with human feedback and reinforcement learning has been studied extensively. (Nakano et al., 2021) developed the WebGPT by fine-tuning the GPT-3 model using behavior cloning and rejection sampling. Moreover, InstructGPT (Ouyang et al., 2022) was developed using the three-step approach: supervised fine-tuning, reward model training, and reinforcement learning via PPO with the help of the trained reward model. Additionally, the authors in (Stiennon et al., 2020) fine-tuned a model that may choose a human-preferred summary, they used this model as a reward function to fine-tune a summarization policy using RL.

Foundation Models for Decision Making. Foundation models possess robust decision-making capabilities, rendering them invaluable across various downstream tasks. For instance, recent works (Ahn et al., 2022; Huang et al., 2022a,b) showcase the application of foundation models in the robotics domain. Moreover, works (Rawles et al., 2023; Wen et al., 2023; Yan et al., 2023; Hong et al., 2023) utilize foundation models to intelligently navigate Android applications. Additionally, the foundation models have been utilized in gaming contexts (, FAIR; Lee et al., 2022; Reed et al., 2022; Fan et al., 2022; Wang et al., 2024; Carta et al., 2023).

Web Navigation. Many benchmarks and datasets exist for the training and assessment of web agents (Yao et al., 2022; Shi et al., 2017; Deng et al., 2024; Zhou et al., 2023; Liu et al., 2018). Researchers have consequently proposed diverse web agents and tested their performance on these benchmarks. The MiniWob++ benchmark is among these benchmarks on which different methods have been applied. For example, (Humphreys et al., 2022) employed a combination of reinforcement learning and behavioral cloning, (Furuta et al., 2024) utilized supervised training on an instruction-finetuned LLM, (Liu et al., 2018) introduced Workflow-guided exploration (WGE), and (Gur et al., 2019) trained DQN agents (QWeb network and INET network). Additionally, the Mind2Web benchmark introduced the MindAct model, synergizing the strength of small and large LLMs (Deng et al., 2024). Additionally, a visual language model named CogAgent was utilized for the benchmark (Hong et al., 2023). (Zeng et al., 2023) presented AgentTuning as another notable approach to tackle the Mind2Web benchmark. Furthermore, considering the Webshop benchmark, various methodologies have been proposed that use in-context learning (Kim et al., 2023; Yao et al., 2023; Sridhar et al., 2023), supervised learning (Furuta et al., 2024; Shaw et al., 2024), and RL (Yao et al., 2022). *Nonetheless, no work has clearly outlined the impact of human demonstrations and the optimal utilization of available demonstration data. Furthermore, UDA remains underexplored.*

6 Conclusion

We introduce GLAINTEL, a flexible agent designed for training across diverse product search scenarios, accommodating situations with limited or no human demonstrations for supervision. We also investigate the optimal utilization of demonstration data, showing that straightforward supervised learning approaches, like behavior cloning, do not yield superior results when using human demonstration data. Through extensive experimental evaluations in the WebShop environment, we highlight the crucial role of the unsupervised training phase employing the PPO algorithm. When combined with supervised learning, this approach achieved results comparable to methods utilizing GPT-4. Additionally, we explore an underexplored scenario where demonstration data is confined to a single domain, we employ UDA techniques to accommodate novel domains. We also present evaluations on a real website, eBay, to showcase the applicability of GLAINTEL in the real world.

Acknowledgments

This work is supported in part by the National Science Foundation (NSF) under grant IIS-2401685.

7 Limitations

In our experiments, we only used the current and previous observations as input to the model. Although including additional observations (e.g., the last four observations) can potentially improve performance, it is important to consider that the increase in the number of observations also expands the size of the context, leading to requirements for higher GPU memory. Moreover, the current architecture relies only on textual descriptions of the environment, without embedding screenshots of web pages or product images. Improving the performance of the agent can be achieved by integrating these visual elements into the model.

It should be noted that other web environments, such as MiniWoB (Shi et al., 2017), have simple, plain backgrounds and minimal interaction within a small area of 160 x 160 pixels. Because of these limitations, we did not assess our method in this environment and considered a more realistic environment, WebShop. However, we plan to evaluate the performance of our approach in other web environments in the future.

References

Michael Ahn, Anthony Brohan, Noah Brown, Yevgen Chebotar, Omar Cortes, Byron David, Chelsea Finn, Keerthana Gopalakrishnan, Karol Hausman, Alexander Herzog, Daniel Ho, Jasmine Hsu, Julian Ibarz, Brian Ichter, Alex Irpan, Eric Jang, Rosario Jauregui Ruano, Kyle Jeffrey, Sally Jesmonth, Nikhil Jayant Joshi, Ryan C. Julian, Dmitry Kalashnikov, Yuheng Kuang, Kuang-Huei Lee, Sergey Levine, Yao Lu, Linda Luu, Carolina Parada, Peter Pastor, Jornell Quiambao, Kanishka Rao, Jarek Rettinghouse, Diego M Reyes, Pierre Sermanet, Nicolas Sievers, Clayton Tan, Alexander Toshev, Vincent Vanhoucke, F. Xia, Ted Xiao, Peng Xu, Sichun Xu, and Mengyuan Yan. 2022. Do as i can, not as i say: Grounding language in robotic affordances. In *Conference on Robot Learning*.

Rishi Bommasani, Drew A Hudson, Ehsan Adeli, Russ Altman, Simran Arora, Sydney von Arx, Michael S Bernstein, Jeannette Bohg, Antoine Bosselut, Emma Brunskill, et al. 2021. On the opportunities and risks of foundation models. *arXiv preprint arXiv:2108.07258*.

David Brandfonbrener, Alberto Bietti, Jacob Buckman, Romain Laroche, and Joan Bruna. 2022. When does return-conditioned supervised learning work for offline reinforcement learning? In *Advances in Neural Information Processing Systems*.

Tom Brown, Benjamin Mann, Nick Ryder, Melanie Subbiah, Jared D Kaplan, Prafulla Dhariwal, Arvind Neelakantan, Pranav Shyam, Girish Sastry, Amanda Askell, et al. 2020. Language models are few-shot learners. *Advances in neural information processing systems*, 33:1877–1901.

Thomas Carta, Clément Romac, Thomas Wolf, Sylvain Lamprier, Olivier Sigaud, and Pierre-Yves Oudeyer. 2023. Grounding large language models in interactive environments with online reinforcement learning.

In *International Conference on Machine Learning*, pages 3676–3713. PMLR.

Xiang Deng, Yu Gu, Boyuan Zheng, Shijie Chen, Sam Stevens, Boshi Wang, Huan Sun, and Yu Su. 2024. Mind2web: Towards a generalist agent for the web. *Advances in Neural Information Processing Systems*, 36.

Prafulla Dhariwal, Christopher Hesse, Oleg Klimov, Alex Nichol, Matthias Plappert, Alec Radford, John Schulman, Szymon Sidor, Yuhuai Wu, and Peter Zhokhov. 2017. Openai baselines. `https://github.com/openai/baselines`.

Meta Fundamental AI Research Diplomacy Team (FAIR)†, Anton Bakhtin, Noam Brown, Emily Dinan, Gabriele Farina, Colin Flaherty, Daniel Fried, Andrew Goff, Jonathan Gray, Hengyuan Hu, Athul Paul Jacob, Mojtaba Komeili, Karthik Konath, Minae Kwon, Adam Lerer, Mike Lewis, Alexander H. Miller, Sasha Mitts, Adithya Renduchintala, Stephen Roller, Dirk Rowe, Weiyan Shi, Joe Spisak, Alexander Wei, David Wu, Hugh Zhang, and Markus Zijlstra. 2022. Human-level play in the game of <i>diplomacy</i> by combining language models with strategic reasoning. *Science*, 378(6624):1067–1074.

Linxi Fan, Guanzhi Wang, Yunfan Jiang, Ajay Mandlekar, Yuncong Yang, Haoyi Zhu, Andrew Tang, De-An Huang, Yuke Zhu, and Anima Anandkumar. 2022. Minedojo: Building open-ended embodied agents with internet-scale knowledge. In *Thirty-sixth Conference on Neural Information Processing Systems Datasets and Benchmarks Track*.

Hiroki Furuta, Kuang-Huei Lee, Ofir Nachum, Yutaka Matsuo, Aleksandra Faust, Shixiang Shane Gu, and Izzeddin Gur. 2024. Multimodal web navigation with instruction-finetuned foundation models. In *The Twelfth International Conference on Learning Representations*.

Izzeddin Gur, Ulrich Rueckert, Aleksandra Faust, and Dilek Hakkani-Tur. 2019. Learning to navigate the web. In *International Conference on Learning Representations*.

Ji He, Jianshu Chen, Xiaodong He, Jianfeng Gao, Lihong Li, Li Deng, and Mari Ostendorf. 2016. Deep reinforcement learning with a natural language action space. In *Proceedings of the 54th Annual Meeting of the Association for Computational Linguistics (Volume 1: Long Papers)*, pages 1621–1630, Berlin, Germany. Association for Computational Linguistics.

Wenyi Hong, Weihan Wang, Qingsong Lv, Jiazheng Xu, Wenmeng Yu, Junhui Ji, Yan Wang, Zihan Wang, Yuxiao Dong, Ming Ding, and Jie Tang. 2023. Cogagent: A visual language model for gui agents. *Preprint*, arXiv:2312.08914.

Wenlong Huang, Pieter Abbeel, Deepak Pathak, and Igor Mordatch. 2022a. Language models as zero-shot planners: Extracting actionable knowledge for embodied agents. In *Proceedings of the 39th International Conference on Machine Learning*, volume 162 of *Proceedings of Machine Learning Research*, pages 9118–9147. PMLR.

Wenlong Huang, F. Xia, Ted Xiao, Harris Chan, Jacky Liang, Peter R. Florence, Andy Zeng, Jonathan Tompson, Igor Mordatch, Yevgen Chebotar, Pierre Sermanet, Noah Brown, Tomas Jackson, Linda Luu, Sergey Levine, Karol Hausman, and Brian Ichter. 2022b. Inner monologue: Embodied reasoning through planning with language models. In *Conference on Robot Learning*.

Peter C. Humphreys, David Raposo, Tobias Pohlen, Gregory Thornton, Rachita Chhaparia, Alistair Muldal, Josh Abramson, Petko Georgiev, Alex Goldin, Adam Santoro, and Timothy P. Lillicrap. 2022. A data-driven approach for learning to control computers. In *International Conference on Machine Learning*.

Byoungjip Kim, Youngsoo Jang, Lajanugen Logeswaran, Geon-Hyeong Kim, Yu Jin Kim, Honglak Lee, and Moontae Lee. 2023. Prospector: Improving LLM agents with self-asking and trajectory ranking. In *NeurIPS 2023 Foundation Models for Decision Making Workshop*.

Kuang-Huei Lee, Ofir Nachum, Mengjiao (Sherry) Yang, Lisa Lee, Daniel Freeman, Sergio Guadarrama, Ian Fischer, Winnie Xu, Eric Jang, Henryk Michalewski, and Igor Mordatch. 2022. Multi-game decision transformers. In *Advances in Neural Information Processing Systems*, volume 35, pages 27921–27936. Curran Associates, Inc.

Jacky Liang, Wenlong Huang, Fei Xia, Peng Xu, Karol Hausman, Brian Ichter, Pete Florence, and Andy Zeng. 2023. Code as policies: Language model programs for embodied control. In *2023 IEEE International Conference on Robotics and Automation (ICRA)*, pages 9493–9500. IEEE.

Philipp Lindenberger, Paul-Edouard Sarlin, Viktor Larsson, and Marc Pollefeys. 2021. Pixel-perfect structure-from-motion with featuremetric refinement. In *Proceedings of the IEEE/CVF International Conference on Computer Vision (ICCV)*, pages 5987–5997.

Evan Zheran Liu, Kelvin Guu, Panupong Pasupat, Tianlin Shi, and Percy Liang. 2018. Reinforcement learning on web interfaces using workflow-guided exploration. In *International Conference on Learning Representations (ICLR)*.

Kaixin Ma, Hongming Zhang, Hongwei Wang, Xiaoman Pan, and Dong Yu. 2023. LASER: LLM agent with state-space exploration for web navigation. In *NeurIPS 2023 Foundation Models for Decision Making Workshop*.

Kyle Mahowald, Anna A Ivanova, Idan A Blank, Nancy Kanwisher, Joshua B Tenenbaum, and Evelina Fedorenko. 2023. Dissociating language and thought in large language models: a cognitive perspective. *arXiv preprint arXiv:2301.06627*.

Reiichiro Nakano, Jacob Hilton, Suchir Balaji, Jeff Wu, Long Ouyang, Christina Kim, Christopher Hesse, Shantanu Jain, Vineet Kosaraju, William Saunders, et al. 2021. Webgpt: Browser-assisted question-answering with human feedback. *arXiv preprint arXiv:2112.09332*.

Long Ouyang, Jeffrey Wu, Xu Jiang, Diogo Almeida, Carroll Wainwright, Pamela Mishkin, Chong Zhang, Sandhini Agarwal, Katarina Slama, Alex Ray, et al. 2022. Training language models to follow instructions with human feedback. *Advances in Neural Information Processing Systems*, 35:27730–27744.

Keiran Paster, Sheila McIlraith, and Jimmy Ba. 2022. You can't count on luck: Why decision transformers and rvs fail in stochastic environments. *Advances in neural information processing systems*, 35:38966–38979.

Dean A. Pomerleau. 1988. Alvinn: An autonomous land vehicle in a neural network. In *Advances in Neural Information Processing Systems*, volume 1. Morgan-Kaufmann.

Alec Radford, Jeffrey Wu, Rewon Child, David Luan, Dario Amodei, Ilya Sutskever, et al. 2019. Language models are unsupervised multitask learners. *OpenAI blog*, 1(8):9.

Colin Raffel, Noam Shazeer, Adam Roberts, Katherine Lee, Sharan Narang, Michael Matena, Yanqi Zhou, Wei Li, and Peter J Liu. 2020. Exploring the limits of transfer learning with a unified text-to-text transformer. *Journal of machine learning research*, 21(140):1–67.

Christopher Rawles, Alice Li, Daniel Rodriguez, Oriana Riva, and Timothy P Lillicrap. 2023. Androidinthewild: A large-scale dataset for android device control. In *Thirty-seventh Conference on Neural Information Processing Systems Datasets and Benchmarks Track*.

Scott Reed, Konrad Zolna, Emilio Parisotto, Sergio Gomez Colmenarejo, Alexander Novikov, Gabriel Barth-Maron, Mai Gimenez, Yury Sulsky, Jackie Kay, Jost Tobias Springenberg, Tom Eccles, Jake Bruce, Ali Razavi, Ashley D. Edwards, Nicolas Manfred Otto Heess, Yutian Chen, Raia Hadsell, Oriol Vinyals, Mahyar Bordbar, and Nando de Freitas. 2022. A generalist agent. *Transactions on Machine Learning Research*, 2022.

Peter Shaw, Mandar Joshi, James Cohan, Jonathan Berant, Panupong Pasupat, Hexiang Hu, Urvashi Khandelwal, Kenton Lee, and Kristina N Toutanova. 2024. From pixels to ui actions: Learning to follow instructions via graphical user interfaces. *Advances in Neural Information Processing Systems*, 36.

Tianlin Shi, Andrej Karpathy, Linxi Fan, Jonathan Hernandez, and Percy Liang. 2017. World of bits: An open-domain platform for web-based agents. In *International Conference on Machine Learning*, pages 3135–3144. PMLR.

Abishek Sridhar, Robert Lo, Frank F. Xu, Hao Zhu, and Shuyan Zhou. 2023. Hierarchical prompting assists large language model on web navigation. In *Conference on Empirical Methods in Natural Language Processing*.

Nisan Stiennon, Long Ouyang, Jeffrey Wu, Daniel Ziegler, Ryan Lowe, Chelsea Voss, Alec Radford, Dario Amodei, and Paul F Christiano. 2020. Learning to summarize with human feedback. *Advances in Neural Information Processing Systems*, 33:3008–3021.

Ashish Vaswani, Noam Shazeer, Niki Parmar, Jakob Uszkoreit, Llion Jones, Aidan N Gomez, Łukasz Kaiser, and Illia Polosukhin. 2017. Attention is all you need. *Advances in neural information processing systems*, 30.

Guanzhi Wang, Yuqi Xie, Yunfan Jiang, Ajay Mandlekar, Chaowei Xiao, Yuke Zhu, Linxi Fan, and Anima Anandkumar. 2024. Voyager: An open-ended embodied agent with large language models. *Transactions on Machine Learning Research*.

Hao Wen, Yuanchun Li, Guohong Liu, Shanhui Zhao, Tao Yu, Toby Jia-Jun Li, Shiqi Jiang, Yunhao Liu, Yaqin Zhang, and Yunxin Liu. 2023. Empowering llm to use smartphone for intelligent task automation. *ArXiv*, abs/2308.15272.

An Yan, Zhengyuan Yang, Wanrong Zhu, Kevin Lin, Linjie Li, Jianfeng Wang, Jianwei Yang, Yiwu Zhong, Julian McAuley, Jianfeng Gao, Zicheng Liu, and Lijuan Wang. 2023. Gpt-4v in wonderland: Large multimodal models for zero-shot smartphone gui navigation. *ArXiv*, abs/2311.07562.

Mengjiao Yang, Dale Schuurmans, Pieter Abbeel, and Ofir Nachum. 2022. Dichotomy of control: Separating what you can control from what you cannot. *International Conference on Learning Representations*.

Shunyu Yao, Howard Chen, John Yang, and Karthik Narasimhan. 2022. Webshop: Towards scalable real-world web interaction with grounded language agents. In *Advances in Neural Information Processing Systems*, volume 35, pages 20744–20757. Curran Associates, Inc.

Shunyu Yao, Jeffrey Zhao, Dian Yu, Nan Du, Izhak Shafran, Karthik R Narasimhan, and Yuan Cao. 2023. React: Synergizing reasoning and acting in language models. In *The Eleventh International Conference on Learning Representations*.

Aohan Zeng, Mingdao Liu, Rui Lu, Bowen Wang, Xiao Liu, Yuxiao Dong, and Jie Tang. 2023. Agenttuning: Enabling generalized agent abilities for llms. *Preprint*, arXiv:2310.12823.

Shuyan Zhou, Frank F Xu, Hao Zhu, Xuhui Zhou, Robert Lo, Abishek Sridhar, Xianyi Cheng, Yonatan Bisk, Daniel Fried, Uri Alon, et al. 2023. Webarena: A realistic web environment for building autonomous agents. *arXiv preprint arXiv:2307.13854*.

Hyperparameter	Value
Number of Epochs	10
Learning Rate	2×10^{-5}
Warmup Steps	100
Weight Decay	0.01
Batch Size	32
Adam Optimizer Epsilon	10^{-8}
Adam Optimizer β_1	0.9
Adam Optimizer β_2	0.999

Table 7: Supervised Learning Hyperparameters.

Hyperparameter	Value
# of collected transitions between two updates	640 (16 × 40)
Number of epochs per update	1
Batch Size	8
Learning Rate	10^{-6}
Adam Optimizer Epsilon	10^{-5}
Adam Optimizer β_1	0.9
Adam Optimizer β_2	0.999
Discount Factor	0.99
Lambda for Generalized Advantage Estimate	0.99
Entropy Loss Coefficient	0.01
Value Loss Coefficient	0.5
Maximum Gradient Norm	0.5
Clipping Epsilon	0.2

Table 8: Unsupervised Learning Hyperparameters.

A Implementation Details

Our implementation operates on a client-server architecture, with the training scripts serving as the client and communicating requests to LLM servers. Specifically, a master server manages these requests, distributing them across multiple LLM servers. Once each LLM server completes its computations, the master server consolidates the results and sends them back to the training script. Furthermore, we use vertical model parallelism, enabling the parallelization of individual LLMs across multiple GPUs. In our experiments, we utilized a single LLM, Flan-T5-Large, with 780 million parameters. This model was parallelized across 4 Nvidia V100 32GB GPUs. We incorporated the last two observations as the model input and an encoder context size of 1024.

To train the agent using the human demonstrations, we used the Trainer library provided by Huggingface [2]. We employed the Adam optimizer, and for the remaining hyperparameter values, refer to Table 7. In our unsupervised learning phase, we leverage the PPO algorithm, and the complete values of hyperparameters can be found in Table 8.

Configs →	SL (one cat) + PPO (500k)		PPO (500k)	
Model ↓	Score	Success Rate	Score	Success Rate
Flan-T5	**73.72**	**45.19**	**68.18**	**38.55**
T5	71.85	43.10	52.07	25.35

Table 9: Ablation Study (T5 vs Flan-T5)

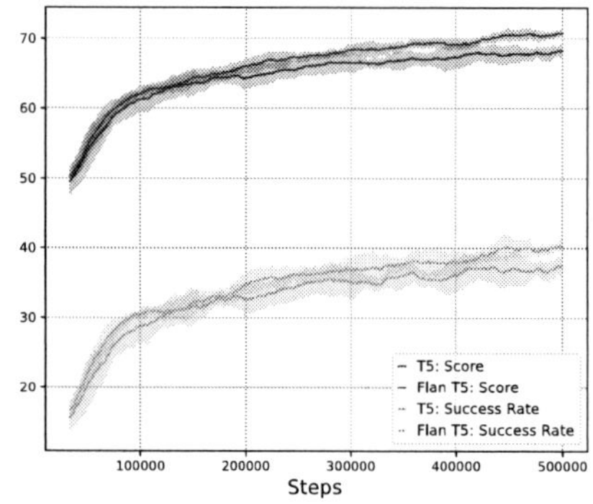

Figure 3: Hybrid setting: BC + PPO: Flan-T5 is more sample efficient than T5 model.

B Ablation Study

Flan-T5 vs T5. We employed two models of identical size, each with 780 million parameters: Flan-T5-Large and T5-Large. The results, as presented in Table 9, demonstrate that adopting the Flan-T5-Large model instead of T5-Large leads to a substantial improvement of 30.93% in the Score and a remarkable 52.07% increase in the Success Rate in the unsupervised setting (PPO). Furthermore, in the domain adaptation scenario, we observed a 2.60% Score enhancement and a 4.85% improvement in the Success Rate. Moreover, Figure 3 demonstrates that employing the Flan-T5 model over the T5 model results in better sample efficiency. Specifically, both Score and Success Rate metrics exhibit faster growth during PPO fine-tuning in the Flan-T5 model compared to the T5 model. This outcome was anticipated as the Flan-T5 model enjoys the advantage of being fine-tuned on user instructions, a benefit not shared by the T5 model.

[2]Trainer: https://huggingface.co/docs/transformers/main_classes/trainer

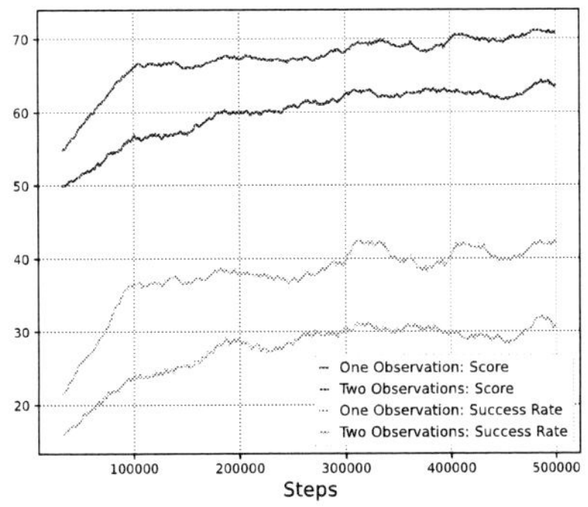

Figure 4: The model is more sample efficient when we feed it with the last two observations.

Configs →	SL (all cats)		SL + PPO (500k)	
	Score	Success Rate	Score	Success Rate
2 observations	**66.55**	**37.05**	**74.60**	**46.95**
1 observation	60.20	27.20	65.29	33.60

Table 10: Ablation Study (2 observations vs 1 observation)

2 Observations vs 1 Observation. As demonstrated in Table 10, combining the present observation state with the preceding observation state to create a historical context and subsequently providing the model with this new observation containing both leads to a notable 10.54% boost in the Score and a remarkable 36.21% improvement in Success Rate in the supervised setting. This substantial enhancement is equally observable in the context of the hybrid method (SL + PPO) where the supervised training is coupled with unsupervised training (PPO), resulting in a significant 14.26% increase in the Score and an impressive 39.73% improvement in Success Rate. Additionally, during the training, we noticed that employing a historical context (having the current and last observations) as input enhances the sample efficiency for the agent compared to using just one observation (see Figure 4). Specifically, Score and Success Rate metrics show a swifter increase with fewer steps when leveraging two observations (historical context) as input, while the progression is notably slower when utilizing only a single (or current) observation.

Comparison of Decoding Methods. In Table 11, we compare the performance of four different decoding methods: (*i*) Epsioln-Greedy algorithm (with epsilon value of 0.2), (*ii*) Sampling with top_p (with top_p = 0.8 and top_k = 0.0),(*iii*) Sampling with no top_p and no top_k, and (*iv*) Argmax. These results are determined by averaging the results achieved from models trained with different techniques and settings, including RL and UDA, among others. These results show that, on average, the Epsilon-Greedy algorithm consistently attains the best results during inference, with a Score of 68.23 and a Success Rate of 39.29. Following closely, the nucleus sampling (top_p) method has lower Scores and Success Rates of 66.25 and 37.32, respectively. In the third position, traditional sampling produces a score of 65.92 and a Success Rate of 36.41. The worst outcomes are associated with the Argmax method, primarily since Argmax frequently causes the web agent to become stuck in a loop. In simpler terms, the web agent ends up repeatedly navigating back and forth between web pages.

Comparison	Score	Success Rate
Epsilon-Greedy algorithm	**68.23**	**39.29**
Sampling with top_p	66.25	37.32
Sampling	65.92	36.41
Argmax	57.92	35.59

Table 11: Ablation Study (Decoding Methods)

AdaptEval: Evaluating Large Language Models on Domain Adaptation for Text Summarization

Anum Afzal
Technical University of Munich
anum.afzal@tum.de

Ribin Chalumattu
ETH Zürich
cribin@inf.ethz.ch

Florian Matthes
Technical University of Munich
matthes@tum.de

Laura Mascarell
ETH Zürich
lmascarell@inf.ethz.ch

Abstract

Despite the advances in the abstractive summarization task using Large Language Models (LLM), there is a lack of research that assess their abilities to easily adapt to different domains. We evaluate the domain adaptation abilities of a wide range of LLMs on the summarization task across various domains in both fine-tuning and in-context learning settings. We also present AdaptEval, the first domain adaptation evaluation suite. AdaptEval includes a domain benchmark and a set of metrics to facilitate the analysis of domain adaptation. Our results demonstrate that LLMs exhibit comparable performance in the in-context learning setting, regardless of their parameter scale.

1 Introduction

Large Language Models (LLM) have achieved remarkable improvements on a wide range of natural language processing tasks, including abstractive text summarization, the task of generating an abridged version of the most relevant information in a document (Basyal and Sanghvi, 2023). Recent works study the domain adaptation abilities of LLMs on the summarization task. However, the research is still limited to a single domain, such as news articles (Goyal et al., 2022; Zhang et al., 2023) or clinical reports (Van Veen et al., 2023). We argue that there is a lack of research across domains to better understand the abilities of these models to adapt to different targets.

In this paper, we assess the domain adaptation abilities of 11 models, including conventional encoder-decoder models and a wide range of LLMs in various parameter sizes, on the summarization task. In particular, we experiment with fine-tuning and in-context learning (ICL) settings and evaluate their performance across various domains (i.e. governmental, medical, and scientific), reporting scores on a collection of automatic—ROUGE (Lin, 2004) and BERTScore (Zhang et al., 2019)—and domain adaptation metrics. The latter includes domain vocabulary overlap (Yu et al., 2021), and our adaptations of G-eval (Liu et al., 2023) and token distribution shift (Lin et al., 2023) to the task.

The experimental results show the abilities of LLMs to adapt to the domain in the ICL setting. In particular, *small* models with 7b parameters achieve comparable performance to their larger counterparts with only two learning examples. However, G-eval highlights the difficulty of adapting to the medical domain. While the fine-tuned models achieve the best performance in terms of automatic scores, their adaptation to the domain vocabulary is inferior to the ICL setting. Finally, we release the domain benchmark and evaluation metrics as the first domain **Adapt**ation **Eval**uation suite (**AdaptEval**) to facilitate the evaluation of models and foster further research on this task.[1]

2 The Domain Adaptation Suite

2.1 Domains Benchmark

Our benchmark contains data from different datasets on the scientific, medical, and governmental domains. The final size of the domain datasets is listed in Table 1, after removing instances with extractive summaries, or extremely long summaries or sources as in Shaham et al. (2022).[2]

Science The data consists of scientific articles from the arXiv platform, where the human-written abstracts are used as reference summaries of the articles (Cohan et al., 2018).

Medical The medical domain comprises academic articles in the field of biomedical and life sciences from the PubMed dataset (Cohan et al., 2018). Similarly to arXiv, the article abstracts are regarded as abstractive summaries.

[1] AdaptEval code is available on AdaptEval.
[2] Deleted: 3% arXiv, 4% PubMed, and 0.4% GovReport.

Proceedings of the 1st Workshop on Customizable NLP: Progress and Challenges in Customizing NLP for a Domain, Application, Group, or Individual (CustomNLP4U), pages 76–85
November 16, 2024

Domain	Train	Val.	Test
Science	203,037	6,436	6,440
Medical	119,924	6,633	6,658
Government	17,517	973	973

Table 1: Sizes of domain datasets.

Domain	Size	#W	#Sum W
Science	215,913	6,029.9	272.7
Medical	133,215	3,049.9	204.4
Government	19,466	9,409.4	553.4

Table 2: Total sizes of the domain datasets and average word count of source (#W) and summary (#Sum W).

Government The data comes from the GovReport dataset, a collection of reports on national policy issues paired with human-written executive summaries (Huang et al., 2021). The documents are 1.5 and 2.5 times longer than those from arXiv and PubMed, respectively.

2.2 Evaluation Metrics

The suite provides a set of metrics to evaluate the performance of summarization models and approaches across domains. Specifically, we include the standard summarization metrics ROUGE (Lin, 2004) and BERTScore (Zhang et al., 2019), which measure n-gram and contextual similarity against a reference, respectively. To get better insights into their domain adaptation abilities, we also implement several metrics that assess the domain language. We describe them in the rest of the section.

Domain Vocabulary Overlap (DVO) We compute the percentage of domain vocabulary in the generated output as in Yu et al. (2021). The domain vocabulary consists of the top 10k most frequent words in the domain excluding stopwords.

Domain Token Distribution Shift Lin et al. (2023) analyzes the impact of LLM alignment and proposes to measure the token distribution shifts between base models and their aligned counterparts. We adopt the token distribution shift approach to domain adaptation. Specifically, we focus on the domain vocabulary (i.e. 10k most frequent words) and analyze the effects of adaptation strategies, such as ICL and fine-tuning on their distribution.

Formally, given a prompt p, we first use the fine-tuned model to generate a summary by greedy decoding, where the summary is represented as a sequence of tokens $S = \{s_0, ..., s_T\}$ from the model vocabulary $\mathcal{V}$, such that $s_t \in \mathcal{V}$ for $0 < t < T$. Next, we process each token in S sequentially. At each step t, we get the probability distribution of the next token prediction given p and the prior context $p(\cdot \mid \mathbf{s}_{<t}, \mathbf{p})$ using both fine-tuned and base models. In the in-context learning setting, we use the same model, but the adapted approach extends the prompt p with learning examples.[3] Finally, we rank the tokens in both distributions according to their probability and provide *KL-divergence* scores and the *token shift rate* of those tokens in the vocabulary domain. While the former represents their distribution similarity, the latter computes the frequency at which the adapted approach predicts a token from the vocabulary domain that is not among the top three predictions of the base model.

Reference-free evaluation with GPT-4 G-eval uses GPT-4 (OpenAI, 2023) with chain-of-thought prompting (Wei et al., 2022) to evaluate summaries across quality features, such as coherence or fluency, achieving high correlation with human judgments (Liu et al., 2023). Similarly, we design a prompt to score the degree to which a summary adheres to the domain language on a scale from 1 to 5. Our prompt includes the reasoning steps generated by GTP-4 as in Liu et al. (2023) (see Appendix B).

3 Domain Adaptation Task

We assess the performance of 11 models across domains in both fine-tuning[4] and ICL settings.

3.1 Models Selection

We select a wide variety of models from the conventional encoder-decoder transformer models—BART (Lewis et al., 2020) and PEGASUS-X (Phang et al., 2022)—to the recent instruction-based LLMs. The latter includes open-source models from the Llama2 family (Touvron et al., 2023), Vicuna (Chiang et al., 2023), Falcon (Almazrouei et al., 2023), and Mistral AI (Jiang et al., 2023). For each model family, we consider various model sizes ranging from 7b to 70b parameters, if available. Additionally, we consider the close-source model ChatGPT from OpenAI. We provide the checkpoints and technical details in Appendix A.

[3]The method can also be applied to compare models of different parameter scales in different adaptation settings.

[4]We exclude GovReport from fine-tuning on 5k and 10k samples, since the train set doesn't have enough documents to fit into the models context window of 4096 tokens—only 1148 instances with maximum 4k length in the training split.

	Medical			Science			Government		
	BERTScore	DVO	ROUGE	BERTScore	DVO	ROUGE	BERTScore	DVO	ROUGE
				Zero-shot Setting					
PEGASUS-X	0.690	6.28	3.55	0.538	11.98	5.85	0.736	5.58	9.06
Falcon 7b	0.811	31.87	13.68	0.810	30.16	14.54	0.821	31.49	13.86
Llama2 7b	0.783	21.15	10.94	0.818	28.61	18.33	0.845	34.36	18.86
Mistral 7b	0.788	24.78	9.44	0.806	28.81	13.68	0.815	31.18	12.02
Vicuna 7b	0.727	9.49	2.11	0.781	23.94	7.93	0.813	30.69	10.80
Llama2 13b	0.764	20.78	6.26	0.783	23.48	8.58	0.797	24.04	10.80
Vicuna 13b	0.745	15.76	1.58	0.763	19.07	4.43	0.783	27.18	7.17
Falcon 40b	0.816	35.51	13.85	0.822	34.98	17.59	0.827	35.51	13.85
Llama2 70b	*0.842*	35.50	*24.59*	*0.837*	35.22	23.35	*0.855*	36.05	21.48
ChatGPT	**0.844**	36.69	**24.81**	**0.838**	36.58	**23.95**	**0.859**	37.73	**22.34**
GPT-4o mini	0.843	**41.04**	22.26	0.834	**40.85**	20.16	0.856	**41.51**	21.12
				Two-shot Setting					
Llama2 7b	0.819	35.95	21.11	0.824	35.34	20.92	0.847	30.22	17.39
Mistral 7b	*0.816*	32.05	21.30	0.802	23.61	17.76	0.844	30.08	**19.21**
Vicuna 7b	0.831	36.29	21.54	0.827	34.65	20.31	0.851	30.28	17.29
Llama2 13b	*0.820*	35.02	19.00	0.809	32.30	18.97	0.814	29.92	14.30
Vicuna 13b	0.822	35.51	19.69	*0.807*	33.32	14.86	0.789	29.34	8.34
Llama2 70b	**0.845**	37.61	*22.40*	**0.842**	36.65	23.03	0.851	29.59	18.72
ChatGPT	0.841	**38.58**	22.92	0.837	**38.39**	**23.15**	**0.853**	**30.44**	16.82
GPT-4o mini	0.842	30.64	**23.18**	0.835	29.14	21.47	0.850	30.40	16.04
				Fine-tuning Setting					
BART	0.852	**37.03**	24.80	0.844	*34.15*	22.20	0.856	25.14	28.44
PEGASUS-X	0.850	28.72	**31.18**	0.852	**34.61**	**28.11**	**0.868**	22.07	**31.98**
Llama2 7b[1]	0.859	33.61	25.81	0.858	33.06	25.30	0.850	29.30	24.81
Llama2 7b[2]	0.861	35.15	26.00	0.856	30.49	25.46	x	x	x
Llama2 7b[3]	*0.862*	33.71	26.81	0.854	27.43	25.35	x	x	x
Mistral 7b[2]	**0.863**	35.81	27.17	**0.863**	34.00	27.29	0.833	21.66	23.08
Llama2 13b[2]	*0.862*	*35.28*	26.26	*0.860*	32.67	26.47	x	x	x

Table 3: BERTScore F_1, DVO (%), and the geometric mean of ROUGE-1/2/L (ROUGE) of all models across the three domains. The value 'x' implies that the model was not evaluated under those settings. [1]/[2]/[3] indicate fine-tuning with 1k, 5k, and 10k instances, respectively.

3.2 Results

Table 3 shows the performance of the models across domains in terms of ROUGE, BertScores, and DVO. We observe that the model size has a direct impact on their overall performance in the zero-shot setting; however, this performance gap is considerable reduced in the ICL setting with only two learning examples. In fact, the scores of the small 7b models are comparable to the large Llama 70b or the even larger ChatGPT. To validate these results, we compute the token distribution shift between models of different sizes in the two-shot setting (Table 4). The scores reflect that their probability distributions are very similar, confirming that there are no major differences in their performance.

In contrast, the fine-tuning results in Table 3 are mixed. Overall, the models outperform their counterparts in the two-shot setting in terms of ROUGE scores; however, there is a decrease in DVO. In particular, PEGASUS-X achieves the best ROUGE scores. We argue that this is attributed to the model's fine-tuning process, since the parameters are adjusted to optimize on ROUGE. Additionally, BART achieves the highest DVO despite its small parameter size (110M). Johner et al. (2021) point out to the model's tendency to generate highly extractive summaries, which favours the use of domain vocabulary. Finally, the token shift rate and KL-divergence scores between the base and fine-tuned models are higher than in the two-shot setting. However, we observe that most distribution shifts are due to stylistic tokens, as also reported in Lin et al. (2023) between the base and their aligned LLMs.

To confirm these findings, we also evaluate the summaries using GPT-4 shown in Table 5, which have a strong correlation with human judgments, along with our addition to measure domain adaptation, on a random sample of 25 articles.[5] The

[5]Due to the costs of using GPT-4 with large prompts, we

		Science		Medical		Government	
base	*2-shot*	KL	TSR	KL	TSR	KL	TSR
Llama2 7b	vs. 7b	19.70	92.14	19.27	97.44	17.40	94.33
Mistral 7b	vs. 7b	13.88	91.33	14.01	95.40	13.40	90.00
Vicuna 7b	vs. 7b	17.67	92.35	18.32	93.89	15.42	94.04
Llama2 13b	vs. 13b	15.58	96.95	16.53	96.76	14.67	98.82
Vicuna 13b	vs. 13b	18.12	97.13	17.34	90.70	16.79	99.10
Llama2 70b	vs. 70b	16.78	95.68	17.12	98.19	13.10	92.36
2-shot	*2-shot*	KL	TSR	KL	TSR	KL	TSR
Llama2 13b	vs. 7b	0.21	2.87	0.38	1.67	0.32	10.38
Vicuna 13b	vs. 7b	0.25	2.07	0.38	4.57	0.24	0.00
Llama2 70b	vs. 13b	0.47	5.18	0.31	3.50	0.49	4.92
Llama2 70b	vs. 7b	0.43	3.92	0.46	5.01	0.54	6.88
base	*FT*	KL	TSR	KL	TSR	KL	TSR
Llama2 7b	vs. 7b	0.81	12.40	0.35	4.70	21.49	15.15
Mistral 7b	vs. 7b	0.52	11.54	0.37	4.42	0.18	3.21
Llama2 13b	vs. 13b	0.51	6.84	0.48	7.32	x	x

Table 4: Effect of different model sizes, two-shot in-context learning, and Fine-Tuning in terms of token distribution shift scores—KL divergence and Token Shift Rate (%) calculated over 10 samples. Two-shot has the major impact on the models' predictions. The low scores between different model sizes indicate that parameter size does not have a significant effect on domain adaptation in the two-shot setting.

scores on arXiv data are consistent with our previous results, showing that ICL achieves the best performance, and the model parameter size does not have a significant impact. However, PubMed obtains remarkably low scores, which highlights the difficulty of the models to adapt to the medical domain. The LLMs however, find it easier to adapt to the Government domain.

3.3 Manual Evaluation

Two in-house domain experts perform a blind manual evaluation of the same arXiv samples used in GPT-4 evaluation (Table 5). The setting comprises of 25 random arXiv articles paired with four different summaries generated with Llama2 (7b and 70b) in the two-shot setting, fine-tuned Llama2 (7b) and PEGASUS-X. To avoid biases, we randomly shuffle the evaluation instances and their summaries for each annotator.

We ask the annotators to rank the generated summaries according to how well the vocabulary and style of the outputs adapt to the scientific domain. The task is especially challenging when the summaries contain similar vocabulary. Therefore, we focus on the relative performance of the models; that is, their agreement on an output being ranked higher than the other. The final Cohen's κ inter-annotator agreement is 0.4. The results show that the annotators consistently rated the outputs of both Llama2 7b and 70b in the two-shot scenario among the top two positions of the ranking—60% and 52%, respectively—whereas the fine-tuned models were the least preferred—only 12% (Llama2 7b) and 16% (Pegasus-X) rated on top.

only report the scores on four models outputs of 25 random instances.

4 Related Work

Some recent works evaluate the domain adaptation abilities of LLMs on the summarization task, albeit limited to a specific domain. Van Veen et al. (2023) focus on clinical data and tackle the summarization of electronic health records. They evaluate eight different LLMs across six datasets in the same domain. Fu et al. (2024) investigate whether model size has an impact on the summarization performance of business meeting transcripts. The results show that smaller LLMs cannot outperform their larger counterparts (from 7b to 70b parameters), even after fine-tuning, except for FLAN-T5 with 780M parameters (Chung et al., 2022). In contrast, Zhang et al. (2023) provides a benchmark for text summarization of news articles and concludes that instruct-tuning rather than model size is the key to text summarization with LLMs. Similarly, Goyal et al. (2022) propose also a news summarization benchmark and compare the performance between conventional encoder-decoder and instruction-based models. Prior to the LLM era, Yu et al. (2021) explored domain adaptation

	DA (ours)			Coherence			Fluency		
2-shot	arXiv	PubMed	GovReport	arXiv	PubMed	GovReport	arXiv	PubMed	GovReport
Llama2 7b	4.20	1.0	4.04	3.80	2.0	3.96	2.72	2.0	2.96
Llama2 70b	3.96	1.0	4.40	3.20	1.0	3.96	2.56	1.0	3.00
FT									
Llama2 7b	3.48	2.0	4.16	2.08	2.0	3.40	2.04	2.0	2.84
PEGASUS-X	3.88	2.8	4.40	2.88	2.0	3.72	2.40	2.0	2.72

Table 5: Evaluation scores using GPT-4 on 25 random samples from the arXiv, PubMed and GovReport datasets in terms of coherence (1-5), fluency (1-3), and our Domain Adaptation (DA) (1-5).

techniques in a low-resource setting, such as fine-tuning and second pre-training of encoder-decoder summarization models on a wide range of datasets.

5 Conclusion

We evaluate the domain adaptation abilities of Large Language Models across scientific, medical, and governmental domains using a set of adapted evaluation metrics. Additionally, we release AdaptEval, an evaluation suite that facilitates the analysis of domain adaptation. Our experiments show that smaller LLMs exhibit domain-shift challenges, but they are able to achieve comparable performance to larger LLMs when provided with only two learning examples. In contrast, fine-tuning does not have a significant impact on the vocabulary domain, but only on stylistic tokens. Overall, the G-eval scores indicate that the medical domain is challenging for these models. We expect our work to encourage and facilitate further research on domain adaptation with LLMs across domains. We plan to continue this research in future work.

Limitations

To fairly compare the performance of the different models, we generally restricted our evaluation to those models with context window of 4096. An exception is the language model BART with a context window of 1024. Additionally, due to the high costs of performing human evaluations on multiple domains, we only annotated ArXiv data to reaffirm the results obtained through the automatic metrics. Our goal is to facilitate the evaluation of models across domains to the research community. Therefore, our suite consists of a set of metrics to evaluate domain adaptation and general summarization quality, allowing for a comprehensive comparison of the models performance on multiple datasets. Lastly, given the cost associated with GPT-4, we performed LLM-based evaluation on only 25 random samples.

Ethics Statement

Throughout our experiments, we strictly adhere to the ACL Code of Ethics. Since we used already established open-source benchmark datasets, the concern of privacy does not apply. The manual evaluation was performed by in-house domain experts, who receive a full salary. They were informed about the task and usability of data in the research. Their annotations were stored anonymously, mitigating any privacy concerns. Through our fine-tuning strategies, no additional bias was introduced into the models, other than what might already be part of the model weights or the benchmark dataset. The goal of the research is to evaluate the domain adaptation capabilities of existing models on a text summarization task. The results and discussions in this paper are meant to further promote research in the area of domain-specific language modeling with an over-arching goal of bridging the gap between academia and application. All training scripts and trained models will be made available to the research community.

Acknowledgements

This project is supported by Ringier, TX Group, NZZ, SRG, VSM, viscom, the ETH Zurich Foundation, and the German Federal Ministry of Education and Research (BMBF) grant 01IS17049 Software Campus 2.0 (TU München).

References

Ebtesam Almazrouei, Hamza Alobeidli, Abdulaziz Alshamsi, Alessandro Cappelli, Ruxandra Cojocaru, Mérouane Debbah, Étienne Goffinet, Daniel Hesslow, Julien Launay, Quentin Malartic, et al. 2023.

The falcon series of open language models. *arXiv preprint arXiv:2311.16867*.

Lochan Basyal and Mihir Sanghvi. 2023. Text summarization using large language models: A comparative study of mpt-7b-instruct, falcon-7b-instruct, and openai chat-gpt models. *arXiv preprint arXiv:2310.10449*.

Wei-Lin Chiang, Zhuohan Li, Zi Lin, Ying Sheng, Zhanghao Wu, Hao Zhang, Lianmin Zheng, Siyuan Zhuang, Yonghao Zhuang, Joseph E. Gonzalez, Ion Stoica, and Eric P. Xing. 2023. Vicuna: An open-source chatbot impressing gpt-4 with 90%* chatgpt quality.

Hyung Won Chung, Le Hou, Shayne Longpre, Barret Zoph, Yi Tay, William Fedus, Yunxuan Li, Xuezhi Wang, Mostafa Dehghani, Siddhartha Brahma, et al. 2022. Scaling instruction-finetuned language models. *arXiv preprint arXiv:2210.11416*.

Arman Cohan, Franck Dernoncourt, Doo Soon Kim, Trung Bui, Seokhwan Kim, Walter Chang, and Nazli Goharian. 2018. A discourse-aware attention model for abstractive summarization of long documents. In *Proceedings of the 2018 Conference of the North American Chapter of the Association for Computational Linguistics: Human Language Technologies, Volume 2 (Short Papers)*, pages 615–621, New Orleans, Louisiana. Association for Computational Linguistics.

Xue-Yong Fu, Md Tahmid Rahman Laskar, Elena Khasanova, Cheng Chen, and Shashi Bhushan TN. 2024. Tiny titans: Can smaller large language models punch above their weight in the real world for meeting summarization? *arXiv preprint arXiv:2402.00841*.

Tanya Goyal, Junyi Jessy Li, and Greg Durrett. 2022. News summarization and evaluation in the era of gpt-3. *arXiv preprint arXiv:2209.12356*.

Luyang Huang, Shuyang Cao, Nikolaus Parulian, Heng Ji, and Lu Wang. 2021. Efficient attentions for long document summarization. In *Proceedings of the 2021 Conference of the North American Chapter of the Association for Computational Linguistics: Human Language Technologies*, pages 1419–1436, Online. Association for Computational Linguistics.

Albert Q Jiang, Alexandre Sablayrolles, Arthur Mensch, Chris Bamford, Devendra Singh Chaplot, Diego de las Casas, Florian Bressand, Gianna Lengyel, Guillaume Lample, Lucile Saulnier, et al. 2023. Mistral 7b. *arXiv preprint arXiv:2310.06825*.

Timo Johner, Abhik Jana, and Chris Biemann. 2021. Error analysis of using BART for multi-document summarization: A study for English and German language. In *Proceedings of the 23rd Nordic Conference on Computational Linguistics (NoDaLiDa)*, pages 391–397, Reykjavik, Iceland (Online). Linköping University Electronic Press, Sweden.

Mike Lewis, Yinhan Liu, Naman Goyal, Marjan Ghazvininejad, Abdelrahman Mohamed, Omer Levy, Veselin Stoyanov, and Luke Zettlemoyer. 2020. BART: Denoising sequence-to-sequence pre-training for natural language generation, translation, and comprehension. In *Proceedings of the 58th Annual Meeting of the Association for Computational Linguistics*, pages 7871–7880, Online. Association for Computational Linguistics.

Bill Yuchen Lin, Abhilasha Ravichander, Ximing Lu, Nouha Dziri, Melanie Sclar, Khyathi Chandu, Chandra Bhagavatula, and Yejin Choi. 2023. The unlocking spell on base llms: Rethinking alignment via in-context learning. *arXiv preprint arXiv:2312.01552*.

Chin-Yew Lin. 2004. ROUGE: A package for automatic evaluation of summaries. In *Text Summarization Branches Out*, pages 74–81, Barcelona, Spain. Association for Computational Linguistics.

Yang Liu, Dan Iter, Yichong Xu, Shuohang Wang, Ruochen Xu, and Chenguang Zhu. 2023. G-eval: NLG evaluation using gpt-4 with better human alignment. In *Proceedings of the 2023 Conference on Empirical Methods in Natural Language Processing*, pages 2511–2522, Singapore. Association for Computational Linguistics.

OpenAI. 2023. Gpt-4 technical report. *arXiv preprint arXiv:2303.08774*.

Jason Phang, Yao Zhao, and Peter J Liu. 2022. Investigating efficiently extending transformers for long input summarization. *arXiv preprint arXiv:2208.04347*.

Uri Shaham, Elad Segal, Maor Ivgi, Avia Efrat, Ori Yoran, Adi Haviv, Ankit Gupta, Wenhan Xiong, Mor Geva, Jonathan Berant, and Omer Levy. 2022. SCROLLS: Standardized CompaRison over long language sequences. In *Proceedings of the 2022 Conference on Empirical Methods in Natural Language Processing*, pages 12007–12021, Abu Dhabi, United Arab Emirates. Association for Computational Linguistics.

Hugo Touvron, Louis Martin, Kevin Stone, Peter Albert, Amjad Almahairi, Yasmine Babaei, Nikolay Bashlykov, Soumya Batra, Prajjwal Bhargava, Shruti Bhosale, et al. 2023. Llama 2: Open foundation and fine-tuned chat models. *arXiv preprint arXiv:2307.09288*.

Dave Van Veen, Cara Van Uden, Louis Blankemeier, Jean-Benoit Delbrouck, Asad Aali, Christian Bluethgen, Anuj Pareek, Malgorzata Polacin, William Collins, Neera Ahuja, et al. 2023. Clinical text summarization: Adapting large language models can outperform human experts. *arXiv preprint arXiv:2309.07430*.

Jason Wei, Xuezhi Wang, Dale Schuurmans, Maarten Bosma, brian ichter, Fei Xia, Ed Chi, Quoc V Le, and Denny Zhou. 2022. Chain-of-thought prompting elicits reasoning in large language models. In

Advances in Neural Information Processing Systems, volume 35, pages 24824–24837. Curran Associates, Inc.

Thomas Wolf, Lysandre Debut, Victor Sanh, Julien Chaumond, Clement Delangue, Anthony Moi, Pierric Cistac, Tim Rault, Remi Louf, Morgan Funtowicz, Joe Davison, Sam Shleifer, Patrick von Platen, Clara Ma, Yacine Jernite, Julien Plu, Canwen Xu, Teven Le Scao, Sylvain Gugger, Mariama Drame, Quentin Lhoest, and Alexander Rush. 2020. Transformers: State-of-the-art natural language processing. In *Proceedings of the 2020 Conference on Empirical Methods in Natural Language Processing: System Demonstrations*, pages 38–45, Online. Association for Computational Linguistics.

Tiezheng Yu, Zihan Liu, and Pascale Fung. 2021. AdaptSum: Towards low-resource domain adaptation for abstractive summarization. In *Proceedings of the 2021 Conference of the North American Chapter of the Association for Computational Linguistics: Human Language Technologies*, pages 5892–5904, Online. Association for Computational Linguistics.

Tianyi Zhang, Varsha Kishore, Felix Wu, Kilian Q Weinberger, and Yoav Artzi. 2019. Bertscore: Evaluating text generation with bert. *arXiv preprint arXiv:1904.09675*.

Tianyi Zhang, Faisal Ladhak, Esin Durmus, Percy Liang, Kathleen McKeown, and Tatsunori B Hashimoto. 2023. Benchmarking large language models for news summarization. *arXiv preprint arXiv:2301.13848*.

Chunting Zhou, Pengfei Liu, Puxin Xu, Srini Iyer, Jiao Sun, Yuning Mao, Xuezhe Ma, Avia Efrat, Ping Yu, L. Yu, Susan Zhang, Gargi Ghosh, Mike Lewis, Luke Zettlemoyer, and Omer Levy. 2023. Lima: Less is more for alignment. *ArXiv*, abs/2305.11206.

A Technical Details

The fine-tuning and inference procedure was done by leveraging Nvidia A100-80GB GPUs.

A.1 Zero-shot Setting

We used the instruct-tuned or chat versions of the models. As for ChatGPT, we used the OpenAI API[6] and the latest snapshot available, `gpt-3.5-turbo-0613` from June 13th, 2023. For zero-shot setting, we used Llama2 (7b)[7], Llama2 (13b)[8], Llama2 (70b) [9], Vicuna (7b)[10], Vicuna (13b)[11], Falcon (7b)[12], Falcon (40b)[13], and Mistral AI (7b)[14].

When generating summaries, we sample a maximum of 256 tokens for the arXiv and PubMed datasets, while scaling to 1024 tokens for the GovReport dataset, as is standard procedure in other contemporary publications. The prompts used 0-shot and 2-shot settings for generating the summaries is shown in Table 7.

A.2 In-context Learning Setting

We used the same model checkpoints as the ones from zero-shot settings for in-context learning. We excluded Falcon from in-context learning, since its context window of 2048 is too small to fit 2 learning examples.

A.3 Fine-tuning Setting

The links to all fine-tuned models is displayed in Table 6.

Language Models We used HuggingFace Transformers (Wolf et al., 2020) and Microsoft Deepspeed library for distributed training.[15] We fine-tuned BART[16] and PEGASUS-X[17] on the training split and a context window of 1024 and 4096, respectively. All models were fine-tuned for 4 epochs with a learning rate of $8e-4$ and batch size of 64.

[6]https://platform.openai.com/

[7]https://huggingface.co/meta-llama/Llama-2-7b-chat-hf/

[8]https://huggingface.co/meta-llama/Llama-2-13b-chat-hf/

[9]https://huggingface.co/meta-llama/Llama-2-70b-chat-hf/

[10]https://huggingface.co/lmsys/vicuna-7b-v1.5

[11]https://huggingface.co/lmsys/vicuna-13b-v1.5

[12]https://huggingface.co/tiiuae/falcon-7b

[13]https://huggingface.co/tiiuae/falcon-40b

[14]https://mistralai/Mistral-7B-Instruct-v0.1

[15]https://github.com/microsoft/DeepSpeed

[16]https://huggingface.co/facebook/bart-base

[17]https://huggingface.co/google/pegasus-x-large

	Science	Medical	Government
BART	bart-arxiv-1024	bart-pubmed-1024	bart-govreport-1024
PEGASUS-X	bigbird-pegasus-arxiv-4096	bigbird-pegasus-pubmed-4096	bigbird-pegasus-govreport-4096
Llama2 7b[1]	Llama-2-7b-arxiv-4096	Llama-2-7b-pubmed-4096	Llama-2-7b-govreport-4096
Llama2 7b[2]	Llama-2-7b-arxiv-4096	Llama-2-7b-pubmed-4096	x
Llama2 7b[3]	Llama-2-7b-arxiv-4096	Llama-2-7b-hf-pubmed-4096	x
Llama2 13b[2]	Llama-2-13b-arxiv-4096	Llama-2-13b-pubmed-4096	x
Mistral 7b[2]	Mistral-7B–arxiv-4096	Mistral-7B-pubmed-4096	Mistral-7B-govreport-4096

Table 6: Links to all fine-tuned models repositories. The value 'x' implies that the model was not evaluated under those settings. $^{1}/^{2}/^{3}$ indicate fine-tuning with 1k, 5k, and 10k instances, respectively.

Large Language Models We included Llama2 (7b)[18], Llama2 (13b)[19], and Mistral AI [20] for LLM fine-tuning. We fine-tuned the models for 1 epoch using the HuggingFace Trainer API and LoRA on a training subset consisting of samples with a maximum length of 4096, such that they can fit in the context window without truncation. Since Zhou et al. (2023) argue that 1k samples are enough to fine-tune LLMs, we experimented with 1k, 5k, and 10k training samples. Since models do not show any performance increase when trained on more than 5k samples, we opted to train on Llama2 (13b) and Mistral AI on 5k samples. We selected the LoRA parameters r=64, alpha=16, and a dropout of 0.1. Furthermore, we used the paged AdamW optimizer with a beta2 value of 0.999 and a learning rate of $2e-4$ with a constant learning rate strategy. We did not fine-tune Vicuna, since we only used the non-instruction tuned models in this setting. We excluded Falcon from fine-tuning as it only supports a context window of 2048, and therefore, it cannot be fairly compared against the other models with a context window of 4096.

B LLM Prompting

Table 7 and Table 8 illustrate the prompts used to generate summaries and to score the domain adaptation of summaries using GPT-4, respectively. For evaluation, we use the prompts introduced by Liu et al. (2023) for Coherence and Fluency. However, we craft our own prompt that asseses model's ability to adapt to a new domain by evaluating the generated summaries.

C Sample Summaries

Table 9 shows the summaries generated by Llama2 7b under zero-shot, two-shot and fine-tuning setting.

[18] https://huggingface.co/meta-llama/Llama-2-7b

[19] https://huggingface.co/meta-llama/Llama-2-13b

[20] https://huggingface.co/mistralai/Mistral-7B-v0.1

0-SHOT PROMPT
You are an expert at summarization. Proceed to summarize the following text. TEXT: {article} SUMMARY:
FEW-SHOT PROMPT
You are an expert at summarization. Proceed to summarize the following text. TEXT: {article} SUMMARY: {summary} Proceed to summarize the following text. TEXT: {article} SUMMARY: {summary} ... TEXT: {article} SUMMARY:

Table 7: The prompt in the Benchmark for generation of domain-specific summaries using Large Language Models.

SYSTEM PROMPT
You will be given one summary written for an article. Your task is to rate the summary on one metric. Please make sure you read and understand these instructions very carefully. Please keep this document open while reviewing, and refer to it as needed. Evaluation Criteria: {criteria} Evaluation Steps: {steps}
USER PROMPT
Example: Source Text: {document} Summary: {summary} Evaluation Form: Please provide your response in two parts. First the evaluation score for the defined metrics, followed by an explanation for the score. Please limit your response to 30 words. {metric_name}
DOMAIN ADAPTATION SCORE CRITERIA
Domain Adaptation(1-5) - the degree to which the summary adheres to the domain-specific language. A good summary employs domain-specific terminology and conveys the sense that model comprehends and encapsulates domain-specific knowledge. It resembles the content that would authored by a domain expert. Annotators were also asked to penalize summaries that didn't adhere to domain-specific knowledge, and rather used simple words.
DOMAIN ADAPTATION SCORE STEPS
1. Read the article carefully and understand the domain it belongs to. 2. Read the summary and check if it contains domain-specific terminologies and concepts, and if it is able to concisely summaries the domain specific concept in the article. 3. Assign a score for domain adaptation based on the Evaluation Criteria.

Table 8: The Domain Adaptation (DA) prompt in the Benchmark to evaluate the domain adaptation capabilities of the models using a GPT-4.

Zero-shot Llama2 7b
mirnas are small non coding rnas that play important roles on the onset and progression of cancer . distinct mirnas regulate various cellular processes including cell cycle regulation , apoptosis , migration and invasion . altered expression of mirnas has been observed in breast cancer and is believed to play important roles including cell proliferation regulation , cell survival and tumorigenesis . furthermore , mirnas have been shown to play a critical role in cancer stem cell maintenance and tumorigenesis . emerging evidence suggests that mirnas may also be a attractive therapeutic target for cancer . understanding the specific functionalities of distinct mirnas and their role in disease may provide a new approach for cancer diagnosis and potentially new therapeutic strategies. reference listing: lee , j.a. (2011). mi rna : a duel role player in breast cancer progression . breast cancer : a global view . springer . 10.10079783642-135704_19 . 19 . 277 286 . abstract: micro rnas

Two-shot Llama2 7b
Small non-coding RNAs, such as siRNA, miRNA, piRNA, and snRNA, are transcribed into mRNA but remain untranslated in eukaryotic cells. They play a crucial role in regulating gene expression and have been implicated in the onset and progression of tumorigenesis. Emerging evidence suggests that small non-coding RNAs may represent a novel cancer therapy. Unlike mRNA, small non-coding RNAs are transcribed but never translated. Some small non-coding RNAs are transcribed from non-coding regions between genes, while others are transcribed together with coding mRNAs from the coding region of the genome. Altered expression of small non-coding RNAs has been observed in breast cancer, resulting in aberrant gene expression. Studies have shown that a high frequency (72.8%) of gene copy number abnormality in small non-coding RNA-containing regions occurs in human breast cancer. Decreased expression of certain small non-coding RNAs, such as mir-17/20, has been

Fine-tuned Llama2 7b
mirnas are small non - coding rnas that regulate gene expression and tumorigenesis . mirnas are involved in the regulation of the cell cycle , cellular proliferation , metastasis and drug resistance of breast cancer . the expression of mirnas is dysregulated in breast cancer . the dysregulated mirnas may serve as novel biomarkers for breast cancer . mirnas may serve as targets for gene therapy either alone or as an adjuvant to conventional therapy .

Table 9: Summaries generated by Llama2 7b under zero-shot, two-shot and fine-tuning setting for a sample article (id = 2) from PubMed test set.

CPS-TaskForge: Generating Collaborative Problem Solving Environments for Diverse Communication Tasks

Nikita Haduong[♠] **Irene Wang** **Bo-Ru Lu**[♠]
Prithviraj Ammanabrolu[♣] **Noah A. Smith**[♠◇]
[♠]University of Washington [♣]University of California, San Diego [◇]Allen Institute for AI
{qu,nasmith}@cs.washington.edu roylu@washington.edu prithvi@ucsd.edu

Abstract

Teams can outperform individuals; could adding AI teammates further bolster performance of teams solving problems collaboratively? Collaborative problem solving (CPS) research commonly studies teams with two agents (human-human or human-AI), but team research literature finds that, for complex tasks, larger teams are more effective. Progress in studying collaboration with more than two agents, through textual records of team interactions, is hindered by a major data challenge: available CPS corpora are predominantly dyadic, and adapting pre-existing CPS tasks to more agents is non-trivial. We address this data challenge by developing a CPS task generator, CPS-TaskForge, that can produce environments for studying CPS under a wide array of conditions, and releasing a CPS task design checklist grounded in the theoretical PISA 2015 CPS framework to help facilitate the development of CPS corpora with more agents. CPS-TaskForge takes the form of a resource management (tower defense) game, and different CPS tasks can be studied by manipulating game design parameters. We conduct a case study with groups of 3–4 humans to validate production of diverse natural language CPS communication in a game instance produced by CPS-TaskForge. We discuss opportunities for advancing research in CPS (both with human-only and human-AI teams) using different task configurations. We will release data and code.[1]

1 Introduction

Modern life requires teamwork to solve problems (Marks et al., 2001), but what makes a team work well together? This area of study, known as collaborative problem solving (CPS), is active across many disciplines, e.g., psychologists study the construction of team mental models in team discussions (Lee, 2015), business management sciences investigate how communication style affects performance evaluation (Proell et al., 2022), and educators develop tools to teach team communication strategies (Stewart et al., 2023), emphasizing the research direction of discovering *how team members talk to one another*. Conducting empirical work in CPS faces many challenges, in large part because of a large CPS task design space (e.g., what is the problem, who makes up the team, and who knows what information when). As a result, despite extensive interdisciplinary work in CPS, task designs in empirical studies have often focused on teams of two collaborating to solve problems such as selecting a designated object, modeling search and rescue, and making decisions.

AI agents have the potential to increase team effectiveness, and developing ways to integrate AI into teams is an active area of research in communities such as HCI (Cai et al., 2019), NLP (Bansal et al., 2019; Vats et al., 2024), and AI fairness (Lai et al., 2021). Example integrations include AI-assisted decision making with one human and one AI (e.g., cancer diagnosis, Chen et al., 2021) and AI-assisted creative tooling (e.g., Tsiros and Palladini, 2020; Lu et al., 2024a). Developing these collaborative tools is made possible through open datasets. For example, various Amazon reviews datasets (e.g., Fornaciari and Poesio, 2014 and Ni et al., 2019) have been used to develop sentiment classifiers and deception detectors that can be used as AI-assisted decision makers, and the Reddit WritingPrompts dataset (Fan et al., 2018) has been valuable in developing co-writing AI systems. Unfortunately, a paucity of open datasets with more than two parties leads to challenges in integrating AI with larger human teams, as we lack understanding of team dynamics when an AI communicates to a team, rather than an individual.

To support CPS study across different designs (e.g., adding a third AI teammate to a two-human team or using voice instead of text communication), we introduce a CPS task environment genera-

[1]https://github.com/nhaduong/cps-taskforge

Proceedings of the 1st Workshop on Customizable NLP: Progress and Challenges in Customizing NLP for a Domain, Application, Group, or Individual (CustomNLP4U), pages 86–112
November 16, 2024

tor, CPS-TaskForge. CPS-TaskForge instantiates a *resource management* activity through a **tower defense** game and supports adjusting a range of CPS design parameters such as team composition, communication method, and how stressful the task is. In a tower defense game, players must defend their base by using limited resources to construct towers that can defeat enemies before the enemies destroy the base. We provide a CPS task design checklist, CPS-✓, adapted from the PISA 2015 theoretical CPS framework (PISA2015) developed by the OECD (OECD, 2017), to support generating the desired task environment with CPS-TaskForge.

We illustrate CPS-TaskForge capabilities by presenting several CPS task designs and conducting a case study that can collect human communication data exhibiting a range of CPS skills, including social skills such as maintaining group communication and cognitive skills such as developing strategic plans. Our study has small groups of 3–4 participants complete a task multiple times with increasing difficulty. We observe many different successful strategies and a wide range in CPS skill usage across teams, demonstrating the versatility of collecting data through CPS-TaskForge.

To summarize our contributions:

1. We identify opportunities and gaps in the interdisciplinary CPS literature. We argue that human team research can help advance human-AI team design; however, there exist challenges associated with the lack of diverse CPS data available to the research community.

2. We introduce CPS-TaskForge, which allows researchers to generate a variety of CPS task environments for studying human and human-AI CPS team processes. We adapt a theoretical CPS framework into a design checklist, CPS-✓, to assist with CPS-TaskForge environment generation.

3. We present a case study using CPS-TaskForge to illustrate the variability of CPS data through a study with more than two agents. We release the conversation and game interaction data collected during the study as an example of what can be produced using CPS-TaskForge.

2 Collaboration and Problem Solving

Collaborative problem solving (CPS) processes are well-studied for human teams, but when human-AI teams are considered, downstream task performance has been prioritized, leaving human-AI CPS processes understudied. For example, Proell et al. (2022) found human team communication more effective when the appropriate style was used in conjunction with the delivery of relevant information. Humans have different expectations towards AI teammates (Zhang et al., 2023, 2021; Grimes et al., 2021), so human-AI teams may value communication style differently. Studying human-AI CPS processes requires developing the appropriate datasets, but resources for creating such data is deficient.

Understanding how effective and efficient communication can predict successful teamwork requires collecting data in a variety of CPS settings. The tasks used to elicit relevant data often model real-world activities, e.g., rescuing humans from a burning building (ASIST; Corral et al., 2021; Freeman et al., 2021), instruction following through selecting designated objects (e.g., PentoRef, Zarrieß et al., 2016; KTH Tangrams, Shore et al., 2018; PhotoBook, Takmaz et al., 2020; Doll Dialogue, Tenbrink et al., 2017; Paxton et al., 2021), and navigating environments (e.g., HCRC Map Task, Anderson et al., 1991; Effenberger et al., 2021), and use human participants. The resulting datasets have been used to study a wide variety of communication and linguistic phenomena, including language entrainment (i.e., when communicative behavior becomes similar among interlocutors, including lexical choice and rhythm) and common ground building (i.e., when interlocutors develop their own code). To the best of our knowledge, analogous settings incorporating an AI team member in a CPS task have not explored similar communication and linguistic phenomena because only recently has AI-generated natural language become indistinguishable from humans (Clark et al., 2021; Dugan et al., 2022), enabling exploration of AI teammates as peers. Unfortunately, expanding pre-existing datasets to other CPS settings, such as involving an AI agent or a third human team member, is challenging because the tasks were designed to study a specific team composition; for example, what role would a third participant play in a navigation task originally designed for one human to tell another human where to go?

Despite the extensive body of literature studying CPS, publicly available resources remain scarce, particularly when more than two agents are involved. We summarize a sample of CPS task ac-

	Task type	Team Size	Communication Modality
KTH Tangrams (Shore et al., 2018)	Object Identification	2	Speech
PentoRef (Zarrieß et al., 2016)	Object Identification	2	Multimodal
TEAMS (Rockenbach et al., 2007)	Forbidden Island ™	3–4	Multimodal
ASIST (Huang et al., 2022)	Search and Rescue	3	Multimodal
CerealBar (Suhr et al., 2019)	Search and Rescue	2	Text
HCRC Map Task (Anderson et al., 1991)	Search and Rescue	2	Speech
PhotoBook (Takmaz et al., 2020)	Object Identification	2	Text
Cards (Potts, 2012)	Search and Rescue	2	Text
Rodrigues et al. (2021)	Object Identification	2	Multimodal
Ma et al. (2023)	Programming	2	Multimodal
Butchibabu et al. (2016)	Search and Deliver	2	Text
Kokel et al. (2022)	Object Construction	2	Multimodal
* MRE (Hill et al., 2003)	Decision Making	21	Speech
T-shirt Task (Andrews et al., 2019)	Math Problem	2	Multimodal
Volcano Lab (Flor et al., 2016)	Science Lab	2	Text
Circuit Lab (Graesser et al., 2018)	Science Lab	3	Text
Physics Playground (Sun et al., 2020)	2D Physics Puzzles	3	Multimodal
Minecraft (Sun et al., 2020)	Minecraft Hour of Code	3	Multimodal
CPSCoach (Stewart et al., 2023)	2D Physics Puzzles	2	Multimodal
* NeoCities (Schelble et al., 2022)	Search and Rescue	3	Text
9-11 Firefighting (Hutchins et al., 2008)	Firefighting	—	Speech
Air Warfare (Hutchins et al., 2008)	Object Identification	6+	Speech
Maritime Interdiction Operations (Hutchins et al., 2008)	Object identification	3+	Speech
Wiltshire et al. (2018)	NASA Moonbase Alpha Simulation	2	Speech
CPS-TaskForge (this work)	Object Identification, Resource Management	1–4+	Text, Speech

Table 1: A sample of collaborative problem solving research. The top group contains work that produced datasets open to the research community. * indicates studies with AI teammates. Object identification tasks require identifying an object, search and rescue requires navigating an environment to locate an object, and search and deliver requires returning to a second point after locating the object. The math and science lab tasks are typical tasks found in educational contexts. Forbidden Island™ is a commercial cooperative board game. "Text" data often contains system interaction log data such as mouse clicks, whereas "Multimodal" communication may include video of participant bodies, audio, and hormonal measurements. We observe more diverse tasks conducted in works without open data.

tivities in the literature in Table 1 to illustrate gaps in task type and team size between studies with or without data release to the research community.

3 CPS-TaskForge and Tower Defense

To advance CPS research, we need ways to systematically study CPS when varying factors, allowing comparison of CPS results across settings. We therefore develop a CPS task environment generator, CPS-TaskForge, which can generate CPS environments with different design factors. We also release a CPS task design checklist, CPS-✓, that describes how varying design factors produces different environments. We defer discussion of CPS-✓ to Section 4; here we give a concrete description of the task environments our work targets.

We start with several requirements: (R1) CPS-TaskForge should be built on an activity that can support the different values in CPS-✓; (R2) the activity should be **fun**, to motivate participant signups, because CPS studies require multiple participants, making scheduling a logistical barrier to conducting CPS research; (R3) the activity should be easy to learn for both participants and researchers, in order to minimize time spent in tutorials and allow researchers to quickly design different CPS studies; and (R4) the activity should easily scale in difficulty to enable CPS research studying effects of expertise on collaboration.

We meet our design requirements by using the Tower Defense (TD) game genre as our CPS-TaskForge activity. The premise of a TD game is to defend a base from enemies by placing towers on the map, which can destroy the enemies. TD games require strategy and resource management—a vital aspect of CPS tasks (Care et al., 2015)—and games have been successfully used by the research community to study communication (e.g., Codenames; (Shaikh et al., 2023)) and collect data (e.g., Verbosity; (von Ahn et al., 2006), Duolingo (von Ahn, 2013), SearchWar (Law et al., 2009), and MatchIn (Hacker and von Ahn, 2009).

TD games are known for having a gentle learning curve, short levels (R3), and ease in scaling difficulty through simple designs (R1, R4; Avery et al., 2011). The 2021 mobile market value for TD games was estimated at 940 million USD (Analytica, 2022); this popularity suggests the potential for participants to play the game of their own volition (R2). It is also known to support 1–4 players

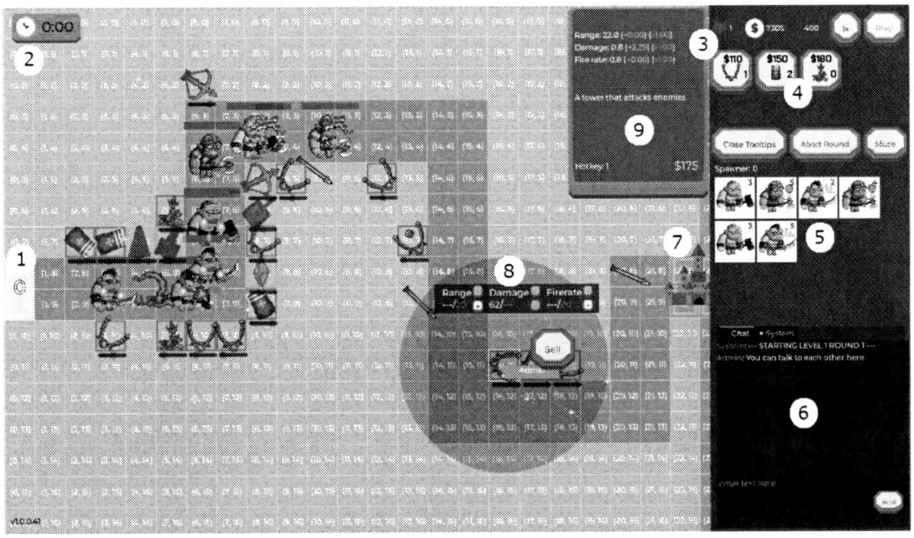

Figure 1: In-game screenshot of a game produced by CPS-TaskForge, used in our case study. Enemies spawn from (1) and can only move on the brown path. Towers can only be placed on the green spaces. (2) is the timer used during the *planning* phase, indicating how much time players have to set the board before the *attack* phase starts. (3) tracks base health—players lose if it drops to zero due to enemies reaching the base, the amount of money available to purchase towers and upgrades, and a running score. (4) is the set of towers this player can build. Different towers have different abilities and costs. (5) previews the enemy sequence of a spawn point. (6) is the text chat players use to communicate with each other. (7) is the base players must defend. (8) is an upgrade menu for a selected tower. (9) is an information panel about a tower. A coordinate grid is provided so players can refer to specific spaces on the map when communicating with each other.

in cooperative play,[2] natively supporting studying human-AI teams involving as few as one human.

We briefly describe what a TD game involves, referencing an in-game screenshot (Figure 1) of an environment produced by CPS-TaskForge. In a TD game, the player needs to defend their base (7) from enemies by placing towers on the map whose inhabitants can attack the oncoming enemies. The enemies will appear at designated spawn points (1) and traverse the map along specific paths known to the player, allowing the player to strategize where to place towers effectively. Players must manage their resources (3) (e.g., gold and map real estate) when developing their defense strategy. Levels differ in the enemy spawning behavior (e.g., enemies can spawn without a break, or there is time in between groups of enemies), enemy variants (e.g., a faster or slower enemy), map terrain (e.g., obstacles can prevent tower placement), and player resources (e.g., types of towers, amount of starting gold). The standard TD game has two phases: *planning*, a static phase where players can place towers on the map, and *attack*, a dynamic phase during which enemies spawn, and players can react to the changing situation by adjusting their towers.

CPS-TaskForge is built on the open-source Godot[3] game engine, and further details of implementation and the tower defense games it produces are available in Appendix A and the documentation of our open-source release.

4 CPS-✓ : A CPS Task Design Checklist

The PISA 2015 CPS Framework (PISA2015) (OECD, 2017) describes CPS tasks through a set of 15 design factors, showing how different CPS settings can be studied by manipulating different combinations of factors (e.g., team size and composition). To operationalize CPS research goals as design parameters that CPS-TaskForge can use to generate the environment, we define CPS-✓, a design checklist adapted from PISA2015 (Table 2). We provide default values for CPS-✓ items in the event that some items are unnecessary to adjust for a particular study. We next explore how different hypothetical research goals can be targeted with

[2]Bloons TD 6 ™ is a commercial game with a 4-player cooperative mode.

[3]https://godotengine.org

What are we studying? E.g., Decision making, collaborative learning, negotiation, exploratory group work, how stress affects communication		
Context	Dimension	Example Values
Problem Scenario	Q1. How is the task evaluated for success? *Q2. How long does one CPS instance take to complete? *Q3. How do skill and expertise scale with repetition?	Binary win/lose, score(time, health) 1 minute for planning and 1 minute for attack Levels of similar difficulty are repeated, level difficulty scales by introducing more enemy spawn points
Team composition	*Q4. What fraction of teammates are human or AI? Q5. What is the symmetry of roles? Q6. How are teammates interdependent?	H-H-H, H-AI, H-AI-AI, H-H-AI 2 players have the same support towers, and 1 has all offense towers Support towers are necessary to beat the level
Task characteristics	Q7. How open is the solution space? Q8. What information is available, and how is new information distributed (if applicable)? Q9. How much stress are players under?	Only 1 tower placement configuration can win All players have the same information at all times, players must discover enemy spawn sequence No stress (unlimited planning time)
Medium	Q10. What is the communication medium?	Text, voice

Table 2: CPS-✓: Design questions adapted from PISA 2015 CPS design contexts. Questions with * are added to help design studies where task repetition is a dependent variable or considerations for human-AI teams. H = human.

different TD games generated by CPS-TaskForge and designed with the help of completing CPS-✓.

Goal: Compare solution quality between all-human teams and mixed human-AI teams. To compare solution quality, we require a more complex task evaluation function than a simple binary win/lose value (Q1). We can design a scoring function to incorporate the time required to agree on a strategy during the planning phase, the amount of money used, or the distance enemies travel. We can also adjust the solution space size (Q7). A level can have a single solution, requiring a specific strategy for placing towers, and solution quality is evaluated by the speed of figuring out the solution. A level can also have multiple solutions, with solutions rated for quality, e.g., a solution using the minimum amount of towers is harder to achieve than a solution maximizing resource consumption and is thus higher quality. The solution quality comparison between teams can then measure the rate of solving levels with minimal resource consumption.

We want to use team compositions with different fractions of human and AI players (Q4). We can investigate how different team roles and personalities in all-human or mixed human-AI teams affect solution quality (Q5); for example, an all-human team where everyone identifies as a leader and has the same towers could result in poor solution quality due to an increase in conflict over strategy; or a team where a human leader effectively uses support towers from an AI teammate (Q6) may outperform a team with an AI leader who does not request support towers from a human teammate. Since we are interested in manipulating team composition, we can give all players a shared resource pool so that information is updated and distributed to all players simultaneously (Q8).

Goal: Investigate how stress affects team performance and communication. Stress can affect team performance, learning, and communication (Pfaff, 2012; Savelsbergh et al., 2012; Orasanu et al., 2004), with more successful teams developing adaptive strategies (Kontogiannis and Kossiavelou, 1999). We can model stressful situations by adjusting the amount of starting resources (money and planning time) to require more dynamic gameplay during the attack phase, forcing players to adapt to a rapidly changing environment (Q9). To design levels requiring more dynamic gameplay, we limit the initial starting resources such that players cannot beat a level by only placing towers during the planning phase. As enemies are defeated, players gain additional gold to spend towards placing more towers and upgrading existing towers, which are required to successfully defend their base. The control condition can then be giving players plentiful starting resources. We will evaluate the task with a simple binary win/lose (Q1) and allow several possible solutions so that teams are not discouraged if they cannot land on the single most optimal solution (Q7). Giving less money and planning time means players have to monitor the changing situation during the attack phase. We enable voice communication (Q11) so that typing speed is not a factor.

Goal: Reimplement and extend prior work. Although CPS-TaskForge is designed to generate TD games, we can simulate object selection and manipulation tasks by limiting player interaction.

Object Selection. Reference games used in

KTHTangrams (Shore et al., 2018) and PentoRef-Take (Zarrieß et al., 2016) are played with two players in the roles Instruction Giver (IG) and Instruction Follower (IF). Both players have a view of the map. The IG is given the game goal (select a specific piece), and the IF can manipulate the map (select the piece). We simulate this task using CPS-TaskForge, by designing levels with towers placed on the board at the start, replacing the tower imagery with a pentomino or tangram. We enable voice communication and end the level upon a single tower object selection, evaluating success through whether the correct tower was selected (Q1).

Object Manipulation. Tenbrink et al. (2017) designed a task for furnishing a physical dollhouse. The IG is given the furnished dollhouse, and the IF is given an empty house. The IG needs to instruct the IF to furnish the house, and task success is evaluated by the correctness of object location and orientation. To simulate this task in CPS-TaskForge, we design levels that resemble house interiors, with walls designating rooms and preventing towers from being placed on them. We give the IF a set of towers that can be placed in the level, replacing the tower imagery with furniture. A tower can span multiple grid spaces on the map, and there are multiple copies of each tower with different orientations. The IG is provided the same level but with towers placed on the map already (similar to the setup for the reference games). Voice chat is enabled for communication. Since CPS-TaskForge produces digital grid-based games, object location and orientation can be automatically evaluated for correctness, improving upon the original setting, where evaluation was manually coded. A limitation of our simulation is that the original task used a physical dollhouse, giving participants multiple perspectives of the board (which could increase task complexity), while our simulation only gives players a single top-down view. 3D simulations or creating multiple 2D perspectives could be explored in future work.

5 Case Study: Communication of Small Groups as Task Difficulty Increases

To validate its flexibility, we want to explore whether CPS-TaskForge is capable of producing an environment that elicits diverse collaborative problem solving behavior. Prior work in CPS primarily used tasks with dyads or task reptitions at the same difficulty level, so we design a CPS task where teams of 3–4 people complete a task, aiming to minimize expenditure of gold, at multiple difficulty levels.

We design our CPS-TaskForge environment as follows, referencing the questions from CPS-✓. Task success is evaluated by the amount of money left unused, enemies destroyed, and health of the base (Q1). A single level takes 5–8 minutes to complete, depending on level difficulty, and we design 3 levels with increasing difficulty (Appendix Figure 4a; Q2–3). All players are human (Q4), and each player is given 2–4 unique towers from a pool of 12 towers with different properties (subsection A.2) so that players have different roles, encouraging all players to engage and suggest usage of their own towers (Q5–6). Players are provided a surplus of gold, and costs are balanced to slightly favor upgrading over placing more towers, giving teams the opportunity to find many successful strategies (Q7). All new information is distributed to players simultaneously (e.g., how much damage an enemy receives from a tower) (Q8). Players are under moderate time stress because each level is calibrated to give ample but limited time (5–6 minutes) to discuss strategy and place towers, and we disabled interaction during the attack phase (Q9). Players could end the planning phase early. We designated level-specific planning time to ensure the study is completed in a reasonable amount of time. Players can only communicate through text chat (Q10). These design decisions showcase the simplicity with which the TD genre affords the ability to create different CPS task environments.

5.1 Data Collection

12 teams of 3–4 people (total 42 individuals) were recruited to participate in a 1.5-hour study[4] and compensated with a gift card at a rate of 20 USD/hour. The study was conducted both in-person and remotely, and all studies were moderated. Recruitment occurred through school email listings and paper flyers posted around town. Participants were aged 18–24 (72%), 25-31 (18%), and 32+ (10%); 55% of participants were current undergraduates and 36% were in a graduate degree program; a third of participants rated their tower defense game familiarity below 3 on a 5-point Likert scale. Familiarity between teammates was not controlled, allowing some team compositions to

[4]Our local IRB approved our study.

contain strangers and others a subset of friends.

The study began with individual pre-surveys collecting basic demographic information, then participants watched a tutorial video explaining how to play the game and played a simple tutorial level together to become familiar with the interface. After the tutorial, they were given time to ask any questions about how to play the game. They then played 3 different levels 3 times each for a total of 9 games. Subsequent levels increased in difficulty, but the three rounds were the same for each level. Finally, they completed individual post-surveys containing questions about teamwork quality, team role identity, and team communication.

We logged data using XML tags, and the data logged was text communication, score, and tower interaction (upgrading, placing, and selling). The metadata associated with the data was the coordinates of interacted towers, timestamps, and the user. The first 4 teams were used to calibrate game difficulty and level designs and the data from one team was excluded from analysis because a team member left early, resulting in a final dataset of 7 teams producing 1.5k utterances with a vocabulary size of 1.2k (Appendix Table 4).

5.2 Observations

We adapt a CPS skill taxonomy developed by Andrews et al. (2019) to describe the communication data, simplifying the initial 10 skill taxonomy to 8 because of low annotation reliability (Table 3).[5] We label only explicit natural language communications—the original taxonomy also includes system interactions (e.g., the act of placing a tower could be classified as "executing action"). A sample of 45 utterances of the data was manually annotated by two authors (inter-annotator agreement of 73%), then one author annotated 3 games (30% of the data). Example team communication is in Appendix Table 5, exemplifying planning and directing through natural language, as well as communication through game behavior (e.g., placing a tower at a specified location when requested without using language to acknowledge the request.)

Cognitive CPS skills were used 49% of the time, and 29% of all communication was devoted to developing strategic plans (planning and negotiation skills). Andrews et al. (2019) observed 30% cognitive skill usage using a traditional collaborative math task, suggesting that the TD task in

[5]We discuss annotation challenges in Appendix Subsection D.1.

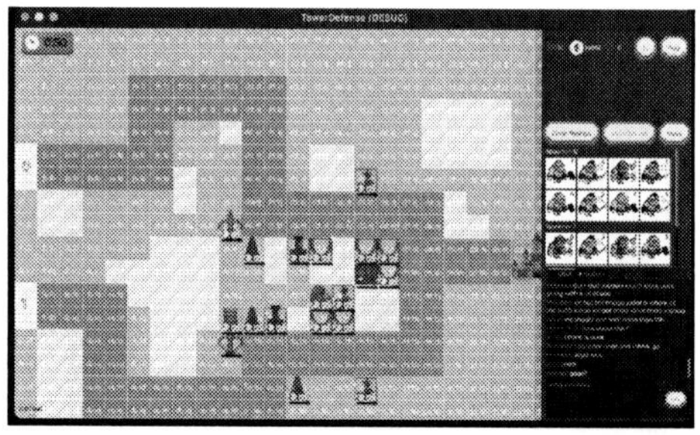

(a)

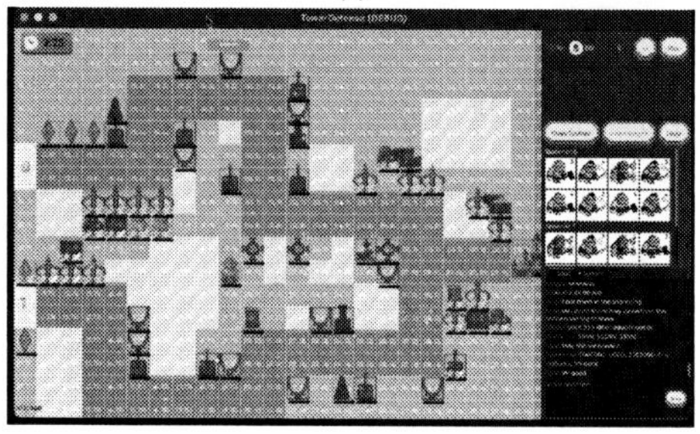

(b)

Figure 2: Different strategies that succeeded in level 2. Players in (a) spent less and placed fewer towers. They concentrated their towers where the two paths converged, while players in (b) used the full map.

`CPS-TaskForge` is a viable task for CPS studies.

From the surveys, we saw that the game was positively received, supporting our objective of developing a *fun* CPS activity (R2). 43% players commented that the game was fun, three players requested an official game release to play with others, and no player complained about task tedium.

5.3 Analysis

Our levels were designed to give players a wide solution space through having an abundance of gold (e.g., Level 1 could be completed with 14k gold unspent). This design emphasized problem space exploration over negotiating for a single optimal solution and is reflected in the low "negotiation" skill usage (4%) and high spread of placed towers (Appendix Figure 4b). Figure 2 shows an example of two teams solving Level 2 with different strategies in tower placement and quantity. One team chose to concentrate their towers where the two paths meet so that towers can attack enemies on both routes, while another team placed many towers across the whole map. Our scoring function emphasized minimizing expenditure, so Figure 2a received a higher score than Figure 2b. Rounds were repeated three times, allowing teams to op-

Dimension	CPS Skill	Example	Count	Avg. Tokens
Social	Maintaining communication	"haha okay"	222	2.3
	Sharing information	"I have a tower damange all enemies"	114	7.0
	Establishing shared understanding	"what does the diamond tower do?"	67	5.4
	Negotiating	"do we want to risk getting rid of anything else?"	38	5.4
Cognitive	Representing and formulating	"fires in multiple directions"	105	9.3
	Planning	"ok we can chokepoint the corners"	227	7.2
	Executing Actions	"k i maxed [upgrades]"	42	5.9
	Monitoring	"50 seconds D:"	86	5.0

Table 3: CPS Skill usage from our case study. Descriptive statistics are from the human annotated data (30% of the full dataset). Utterances were tokenized using the Spacy en_core_web_sm model.

timize working solutions–however, teams did not learn to significantly change expenditure behavior, which suggests cautious game behavior (Appendix Figure 5). Teams 1 and 5 appeared to be confused about the task goal, often spending more money across rounds despite winning a previous round.

6 Related Work

Prior work in CPS has studied a range of factors to understand effective teams, from identifying the effects of team member personalities on team outcomes to how teamwork processes can be evaluated. When an AI teammate is involved, an important research direction investigates how and why humans choose to rely on AI. Findings from CPS human team processes can lead to improvements in AI agents and discovering how to better integrate AI into human teams to solve more complex problems.

Researchers have investigated how team composition affects human team outcomes (e.g., Ruch et al., 2018; Mathieu et al., 2014; Bell et al., 2018; Hollenbeck et al., 2004, *inter alia*), discovering predictors of team outcomes through team roles, individual expertise, demographics, and team knowledge. Lykourentzou et al. (2016) found five-person teams with balanced personalities outperformed those with an imbalance in personalities on collaborative tasks. Analogously, Wang et al. (2023) and Fan et al. (2024) were able to improve LM performance on downstream tasks by instructing the LM to simulate teams of domain-specific personas to collaborate internally. Priming an LM agent with a persona enables the simulation of inherited knowledge and linguistic patterns (Masumura et al., 2018; Wei et al., 2023; Park et al., 2023), and searching for optimal personas in human-AI teams could lead to improvements in human-AI team performance.

CPS tasks can be evaluated for overall task success, but improving teamwork requires evaluating intermediate processes. Pavez et al. (2022) analyzed over a hundred studies on team performance measurement to propose a framework for evaluating teamwork along 4 dimensions: project team processes, project team emergent states, project team tangible outcomes, and project team perceptual benefits. Educators have classified CPS communication for CPS skill usage to provide feedback to students on how to improve their group communication (Andrews et al., 2019; Graesser et al., 2018; Flor et al., 2016; Stewart et al., 2023). Despite extensive work in evaluating CPS teams, there is little data released to the research community.

Research in AI-assisted decision making has produced valuable insights into how humans rely on AI advice. AI is increasingly involved in high-stakes decision, e.g., medical diagnoses, which has led to work in trust and reliability of AI. Humans are known to overrely on AI, following AI suggestions even when they are wrong (Lai and Tan, 2019; Jacobs et al., 2021; Bussone et al., 2015). As a result, designing methods to encourage appropriate reliance on AI advice is vital, such as studying the effects of AI explanations (Goyal et al., 2024; Fleiß et al., 2024; Bansal et al., 2021; Vasconcelos et al., 2023). Gazit et al. (2023), Mesbah et al. (2021), and Lu et al. (2024b) designed studies to understand human (over)reliance on AI using "judge-advisor system" (JAS) tasks where a human or AI advisor provides advice to a human judge, and the judge is responsible for making the final decision. However, decisions in these tasks are independent, and the judges are not able to explain their reasoning to the advisor in a bid to adjust the advisor's position, preventing the study of longer-term effects of human-AI interactions and human-AI communication. Furthermore, the JAS task setup is traditionally dyadic, with one human and one (AI) advisor. In an exploration of *group* decision making, Chiang et al. (2024) recruited groups of two people to follow the judge-advisor system with an AI advisor. They then introduced an AI agent to play devil's advocate and found the agent successfully encouraged more appropriate reliance of AI advice.

7 Conclusion

Human-AI collaborative problem solving tools are rapidly being integrated in real-world work environments. The modern workforce uses teams with more than two parties, but empirical research with larger teams lags behind. The task design space for conducting CPS research is large, and the tooling to systematically explore CPS designs is lacking. Our CPS task environment generator, `CPS-TaskForge`, enables diverse, systematic CPS research through a tower defense game environment that appeals to human subjects and is grounded in theory. It enables the study of larger team CPS (multiple people and/or multiple AI agents) grounded in an environment and task that is accessible yet still carries real-world resemblance. The data generated in our case study reveals different collaborative tasks required to succeed in the overall tower defense task, such as decision making and ensuring teammates have the same understanding of the task.

We will release all code for `CPS-TaskForge` and communication data collected in our case study to encourage studying multi-human and multi-AI collaborative problem solving.

8 Limitations

The tower defense task in `CPS-TaskForge` environments has a learning curve (albeit a gentle one), so tutorials and practice before the actual study commences may be longer than simpler tasks such as a reference game. This complexity is necessary to support a broad range of complex tasks. `CPS-TaskForge` environments currently only support a top-down perspective of the world, so supporting first-person settings (e.g., simulating a Minecraft search and rescue task) is infeasible. We believe these design limitations can encourage the development of other similarly specialized CPS environment generators.

Our initial release of `CPS-TaskForge` implements many common attributes of tower defense games. There are many more attributes available for implemention that have been successfully deployed in commercial tower defense games that may be beneficial for future CPS studies, such as increasing the task difficulty by giving enemies resistance to certain towers. We hope to see `CPS-TaskForge` evolve in its feature set through usage.

Although `CPS-TaskForge` was developed in English, and our case study used English, usage of `CPS-TaskForge` does not require English. Our case study also required using text communication, however `CPS-TaskForge` does not limit the study of CPS to text communication settings. `CPS-TaskForge` was built in the open-source game engine Godot which natively supports other languages, localization, and microphone input. At this time, expanding to video and other modality inputs is not supported.

`CPS-✓`is adapted from `PISA2015`, but the CPS researcher may find other CPS frameworks (e.g., ATSC21, Hesse et al., 2015, and the generalized competancy model by Sun et al., 2020) more appropriate as a checklist. We expect adapting other frameworks into a checklist that can be used to generate `CPS-TaskForge` environments should not be a major challenge, as other frameworks are describing CPS tasks using different attributes, and the TD game used in `CPS-TaskForge` is fundamentally a CPS task.

9 Ethical Considerations

The flexibility in designing CPS task environments through `CPS-TaskForge` necessarily places a large responsibility on the designer to design studies appropriate for their target audience or research goal. For example, the imagery used in-game for enemies and towers could be offensive to certain audiences and should be adapted as needed. As with any study in communication, appropriate content filter measures should be in place as required.

The development of generative AI agents as peers that can communicate with humans comes with the risks of the AI agents generating inappropriate content and the concerns of AI replacing humans. Our intentions are that the AI agents can augment human capabilities in more complex problem solving situations, boosting CPS abilities; however, we acknowledge that some problem solving tasks can be simulated and solved through internal or multi-agent collaboration.

Our study was approved by our institution's IRB, and participants were fairly compensated and consented to data sharing with the research community.

References

Astute Analytica. 2022. Mobilte tower defense games market - industry dynamics, market size, and opportunity forecast to 2030. https://www.astuteanalytica.com/industry-report/mobile-tower-defense-games-market. Accessed: 2 June 2024.

Anne H Anderson, Miles Bader, Ellen Gurman Bard, Elizabeth Boyle, Gwyneth Doherty, Simon Garrod, Stephen Isard, Jacqueline Kowtko, Jan McAllister, Jim Miller, et al. 1991. The hcrc map task corpus. *Language and speech*, 34(4):351–366.

Jessica J. Andrews, Tanner Jackson, and Christopher Kurzum. 2019. Collaborative problem solving assessment in an online mathematics task. *ETS Research Report Series*, pages 1–7.

Phillipa Avery, Julian Togelius, Elvis Alistar, and Robert Pieter Van Leeuwen. 2011. Computational intelligence and tower defence games. In *2011 IEEE Congress of Evolutionary Computation (CEC)*, pages 1084–1091. IEEE.

Gagan Bansal, Besmira Nushi, Ece Kamar, Walter S. Lasecki, Daniel S. Weld, and Eric Horvitz. 2019. Beyond accuracy: The role of mental models in human-ai team performance. In *AAAI Conference on Human Computation & Crowdsourcing*.

Gagan Bansal, Tongshuang Wu, Joyce Zhou, Raymond Fok, Besmira Nushi, Ece Kamar, Marco Tulio Ribeiro, and Daniel Weld. 2021. Does the whole exceed its parts? the effect of ai explanations on complementary team performance. In *Proceedings of the 2021 CHI Conference on Human Factors in Computing Systems*, CHI '21, New York, NY, USA. Association for Computing Machinery.

Edward Beeching, Jilles Dibangoye, Olivier Simonin, and Christian Wolf. 2021. Godot reinforcement learning agents. *arXiv preprint arXiv:2112.03636*.

Suzanne T Bell, Shanique G Brown, Anthony Colaneri, and Neal Outland. 2018. Team composition and the abcs of teamwork. *American psychologist*, 73(4):349.

Adrian Bussone, Simone Stumpf, and Dympna O'Sullivan. 2015. The role of explanations on trust and reliance in clinical decision support systems. In *2015 International Conference on Healthcare Informatics*, pages 160–169.

Abhizna Butchibabu, Christopher Sparano-Huiban, Liz Sonenberg, and Julie Shah. 2016. Implicit coordination strategies for effective team communication. *Human Factors*, 58(4):595–610. PMID: 27113991.

Carrie J. Cai, Samantha Winter, David F. Steiner, Lauren Wilcox, and Michael Terry. 2019. "hello ai": Uncovering the onboarding needs of medical practitioners for human-ai collaborative decision-making. *Proceedings of the ACM on Human-Computer Interaction*, 3:1–24.

Esther Care, Patrick Griffin, Claire Scoular, Nafisa Awwal, and Nathan Zoanetti. 2015. Collaborative problem solving tasks. *Assessment and teaching of 21st century skills: Methods and approach*, pages 85–104.

Albert V. Carron and Kevin S. Spink. 1993. Team building in an exercise setting. *The Sport Psychologist*, 7(1):8–18.

Zi-Hang Chen, Li Lin, Chen-Fei Wu, Chao-Feng Li, Rui-Hua Xu, and Ying Sun. 2021. Artificial intelligence for assisting cancer diagnosis and treatment in the era of precision medicine. *Cancer Communications*, 41(11):1100–1115.

Chun-Wei Chiang, Zhuoran Lu, Zhuoyan Li, and Ming Yin. 2024. Enhancing ai-assisted group decision making through llm-powered devil's advocate. In *Proceedings of the 29th International Conference on Intelligent User Interfaces*, IUI '24, page 103–119, New York, NY, USA. Association for Computing Machinery.

Elizabeth Clark, Tal August, Sofia Serrano, Nikita Haduong, Suchin Gururangan, and Noah A. Smith. 2021. All that's 'human' is not gold: Evaluating human evaluation of generated text. In *Proceedings of the 59th Annual Meeting of the Association for Computational Linguistics and the 11th International Joint Conference on Natural Language Processing (Volume 1: Long Papers)*, pages 7282–7296, Online. Association for Computational Linguistics.

Christopher C Corral, Keerthi Shrikar Tatapudi, Verica Buchanan, Lixiao Huang, and Nancy J Cooke. 2021. Building a synthetic task environment to support artificial social intelligence research. In *Proceedings of the human factors and ergonomics society annual meeting*, volume 65, pages 660–664. SAGE Publications Sage CA: Los Angeles, CA.

Liam Dugan, Daphne Ippolito, Arun Kirubarajan, Sherry Shi, and Chris Callison-Burch. 2022. Real or fake text?: Investigating human ability to detect boundaries between human-written and machine-generated text. In *AAAI Conference on Artificial Intelligence*.

Anna Effenberger, Rhia Singh, Eva Yan, Alane Suhr, and Yoav Artzi. 2021. Analysis of language change in collaborative instruction following. In *Findings of the Association for Computational Linguistics: EMNLP 2021*, pages 2803–2811, Punta Cana, Dominican Republic. Association for Computational Linguistics.

Angela Fan, Mike Lewis, and Yann Dauphin. 2018. Hierarchical neural story generation. In *Proceedings of the 56th Annual Meeting of the Association for Computational Linguistics (Volume 1: Long Papers)*, pages 889–898, Melbourne, Australia. Association for Computational Linguistics.

Zhihao Fan, Jialong Tang, Wei Chen, Siyuan Wang, Zhongyu Wei, Jun Xi, Fei Huang, and Jingren Zhou.

2024. Ai hospital: Interactive evaluation and collaboration of llms as intern doctors for clinical diagnosis. *arXiv preprint arXiv:2402.09742*.

Jürgen Fleiß, Elisabeth Bäck, and Stefan Thalmann. 2024. Mitigating algorithm aversion in recruiting: A study on explainable ai for conversational agents. *SIGMIS Database*, 55(1):56–87.

Michael Flor, Su-Youn Yoon, Jiangang Hao, Lei Liu, and Alina von Davier. 2016. Automated classification of collaborative problem solving interactions in simulated science tasks. In *Proceedings of the 11th Workshop on Innovative Use of NLP for Building Educational Applications*, pages 31–41, San Diego, CA. Association for Computational Linguistics.

Tommaso Fornaciari and Massimo Poesio. 2014. Identifying fake Amazon reviews as learning from crowds. In *Proceedings of the 14th Conference of the European Chapter of the Association for Computational Linguistics*, pages 279–287, Gothenburg, Sweden. Association for Computational Linguistics.

Jared Freeman, Lixiao Huang, Matt Wood, and Stephen J Cauffman. 2021. Evaluating artificial social intelligence in an urban search and rescue task environment. In *Aaai fall symposium*, pages 72–84. Springer.

Lior Gazit, Ofer Arazy, and Uri Hertz. 2023. Choosing between human and algorithmic advisors: The role of responsibility sharing. *Computers in Human Behavior: Artificial Humans*, 1(2):100009.

Navita Goyal, Connor Baumler, Tin Nguyen, and Hal Daumé III. 2024. The impact of explanations on fairness in human-ai decision-making: Protected vs proxy features. In *Proceedings of the 29th International Conference on Intelligent User Interfaces*, IUI '24, page 155–180, New York, NY, USA. Association for Computing Machinery.

Arthur C. Graesser, Stephen M. Fiore, Samuel Greiff, Jessica Andrews-Todd, Peter W. Foltz, and Friedrich W. Hesse. 2018. Advancing the science of collaborative problem solving. *Psychological Science in the Public Interest*, 19(2):59–92. PMID: 30497346.

G. Mark Grimes, Ryan M. Schuetzler, and Justin Scott Giboney. 2021. Mental models and expectation violations in conversational ai interactions. *Decision Support Systems*, 144:113515.

Severin Hacker and Luis von Ahn. 2009. Matchin: eliciting user preferences with an online game. In *Proceedings of the SIGCHI Conference on Human Factors in Computing Systems*, CHI '09, page 1207–1216, New York, NY, USA. Association for Computing Machinery.

Friedrich Hesse, Esther Care, Juergen Buder, Kai Sassenberg, and Patrick Griffin. 2015. A framework for teachable collaborative problem solving skills. *Assessment and teaching of 21st century skills: Methods and approach*, pages 37–56.

Randall W. Hill, J. Gratch, Stacy Marsella, Jeff Rickel, W. Swartout, and David R. Traum. 2003. Virtual humans in the mission rehearsal exercise system. *Künstliche Intell.*, 17:5–.

Martin Hoegl and Hans Georg Gemuenden. 2001. Teamwork quality and the success of innovative projects: A theoretical concept and empirical evidence. *Organization science*, 12(4):435–449.

John R Hollenbeck, D Scott DeRue, and Rick Guzzo. 2004. Bridging the gap between i/o research and hr practice: Improving team composition, team training, and team task design. *Human Resource Management: Published in Cooperation with the School of Business Administration, The University of Michigan and in alliance with the Society of Human Resources Management*, 43(4):353–366.

Lixiao Huang, Jared Freeman, Nancy Cooke, Samantha Dubrow, John "JCR" Colonna-Romano, Matt Wood, Verica Buchanan, Stephen Caufman, and Xiaoyun Yin. 2022. Artificial Social Intelligence for Successful Teams (ASIST) Study 2.

Susan G Hutchins, Anthony Kendall, and Alex Bordetsky. 2008. Understanding patterns of team collaboration employed to solve unique problems. In *Proceedings of the 13 th International Command and Control Research & Technology Symposium*, pages 17–19.

M. Jacobs, M. Pradier, T. McCoy, P. Roy, F. Doshi-Velez, and G. Krzysztof. 2021. How machine learning recommendations influence clinician treatment selections: example of antidepressant selection. *Translational Psychiatry*, 1:1–9.

Harsha Kokel, M. Das, Rakibul Islam, Julia Bonn, Jon Z. Cai, Soham Dan, Anjali Narayan-Chen, Prashant Jayannavar, Janardhan Rao Doppa, J. Hockenmaier, Sriraam Natarajan, Martha Palmer, and Dan Roth. 2022. Human-guided collaborative problem solving: A natural language based framework. *ArXiv*, abs/2207.09566.

Tom Kontogiannis and Zoe Kossiavelou. 1999. Stress and team performance: principles and challenges for intelligent decision aids. *Safety science*, 33(3):103–128.

Vivian Lai, Chacha Chen, Qingzi Vera Liao, Alison Smith-Renner, and Chenhao Tan. 2021. Towards a science of human-ai decision making: A survey of empirical studies. *ArXiv*, abs/2112.11471.

Vivian Lai and Chenhao Tan. 2019. On human predictions with explanations and predictions of machine learning models: A case study on deception detection. In *Proceedings of the Conference on Fairness, Accountability, and Transparency*, FAT* '19, page 29–38, New York, NY, USA. Association for Computing Machinery.

Richard N Landers, Kristina N Bauer, and Rachel C Callan. 2017. Gamification of task performance with leaderboards: A goal setting experiment. *Computers in Human Behavior*, 71:508–515.

Edith Law, Luis von Ahn, and Tom Mitchell. 2009. Search war: a game for improving web search. In *Proceedings of the ACM SIGKDD Workshop on Human Computation*, HCOMP '09, page 31, New York, NY, USA. Association for Computing Machinery.

Jiwon Lee. 2015. Analysis of the refinement of shared mental model in science-gifted students' collaborative problem solving process. *Journal of the Korean Association for Research in Science Education*, 35:1049–1062.

Bo-Ru Lu, Nikita Haduong, Chia-Hsuan Lee, Zeqiu Wu, Hao Cheng, Paul Koester, Jean Utke, Tao Yu, Noah A. Smith, and Mari Ostendorf. 2024a. Does collaborative human-lm dialogue generation help information extraction from human dialogues? *Preprint*, arXiv:2307.07047.

Zhuoran Lu, Dakuo Wang, and Ming Yin. 2024b. Does more advice help? the effects of second opinions in ai-assisted decision making. *Proc. ACM Hum.-Comput. Interact.*, 8(CSCW1).

Ioanna Lykourentzou, Angeliki Antoniou, Yannick Naudet, and Steven P. Dow. 2016. Personality matters: Balancing for personality types leads to better outcomes for crowd teams. In *Proceedings of the 19th ACM Conference on Computer-Supported Cooperative Work & Social Computing*, CSCW '16, page 260–273, New York, NY, USA. Association for Computing Machinery.

Yingbo Ma, Gloria Ashiya Katuka, Mehmet Celepkolu, and Kristy Elizabeth Boyer. 2023. Automatically Predicting Peer Satisfaction During Collaborative Learning with Linguistic, Acoustic, and Visual Features. *Journal of Educational Data Mining*, 15(2).

Michelle A. Marks, John E. Mathieu, and Stephen J. Zaccaro. 2001. A temporally based framework and taxonomy of team processes. *The Academy of Management Review*, 26(3):356–376.

Ryo Masumura, Tomohiro Tanaka, Atsushi Ando, Hirokazu Masataki, and Yushi Aono. 2018. Role play dialogue aware language models based on conditional hierarchical recurrent encoder-decoder. In *Interspeech*.

John E Mathieu, Scott I Tannenbaum, Jamie S Donsbach, and George M Alliger. 2014. A review and integration of team composition models: Moving toward a dynamic and temporal framework. *Journal of management*, 40(1):130–160.

Elisa D Mekler, Florian Brühlmann, Klaus Opwis, and Alexandre N Tuch. 2013. Do points, levels and leaderboards harm intrinsic motivation? an empirical analysis of common gamification elements. In *Proceedings of the First International Conference on gameful design, research, and applications*, pages 66–73.

Neda Mesbah, Christoph Tauchert, and Peter Buxmann. 2021. Whose advice counts more - man or machine? an experimental investigation of ai-based advice utilization. In *Hawaii International Conference on System Sciences*.

Jianmo Ni, Jiacheng Li, and Julian McAuley. 2019. Justifying recommendations using distantly-labeled reviews and fine-grained aspects. In *Proceedings of the 2019 Conference on Empirical Methods in Natural Language Processing and the 9th International Joint Conference on Natural Language Processing (EMNLP-IJCNLP)*, pages 188–197, Hong Kong, China. Association for Computational Linguistics.

OECD. 2017. *PISA 2015 collaborative problem-solving framework*. OECD.

Judith Orasanu, Ute Fischer, Yuri Tada, and Norbert Kraft. 2004. Team stress and performance: Implications for long-duration space missions. In *Proceedings of the human factors and ergonomics society annual meeting*, volume 48, pages 552–556. SAGE Publications Sage CA: Los Angeles, CA.

Joon Sung Park, Joseph C. O'Brien, Carrie J. Cai, Meredith Ringel Morris, Percy Liang, and Michael S. Bernstein. 2023. Generative agents: Interactive simulacra of human behavior. In *In the 36th Annual ACM Symposium on User Interface Software and Technology (UIST '23)*, UIST '23, New York, NY, USA. Association for Computing Machinery.

Ignacio Pavez, Hugo Gómez, Canlong Liu, and Vicente A. González. 2022. Measuring project team performance: A review and conceptualization. *International Journal of Project Management*, 40(8):951–971.

Alexandra Paxton, Jennifer M. Roche, Alyssa Ibarra, and Michael K. Tanenhaus. 2021. Predictions of miscommunication in verbal communication during collaborative joint action. *Journal of Speech, Language, and Hearing Research*, 64(2):613–627.

Mark S Pfaff. 2012. Negative affect reduces team awareness: The effects of mood and stress on computer-mediated team communication. *Human Factors*, 54(4):560–571.

Christopher Potts. 2012. Goal-driven answers in the Cards dialogue corpus. In *Proceedings of the 30th West Coast Conference on Formal Linguistics*, Somerville, MA. Cascadilla Press.

Chad A. Proell, Yuepin (Daniel) Zhou, and Mark W. Nelson. 2022. It's Not Only What You Say ... How Communication Style and Team Culture Affect Audit Issue Follow-Up and Auditor Performance Evaluations. *The Accounting Review*, 97(2):373–395.

Bettina Rockenbach, Abdolkarim Sadrieh, and Barbara Mathauschek. 2007. Teams take the better risks. *Journal of Economic Behavior & Organization*, 63(3):412–422.

Michelle A. Rodrigues, Si On Yoon, Kathryn B. H. Clancy, and Elizabeth A. L. Stine-Morrow. 2021. What are friends for? the impact of friendship on communicative efficiency and cortisol response during collaborative problem solving among younger and older women. *Journal of Women & Aging*, 33(4):411–427. PMID: 34038325.

Willibald Ruch, Fabian Gander, Tracey Platt, and Jennifer Hofmann. 2018. Team roles: Their relationships to character strengths and job satisfaction. *The Journal of Positive Psychology*, 13(2):190–199.

Chantal Savelsbergh, Josette MP Gevers, Beatrice IJM Van der Heijden, and Rob F Poell. 2012. Team role stress: Relationships with team learning and performance in project teams. *Group & organization management*, 37(1):67–100.

Beau G. Schelble, Christopher Flathmann, Nathan J. McNeese, Guo Freeman, and Rohit Mallick. 2022. Let's think together! assessing shared mental models, performance, and trust in human-agent teams. *Proc. ACM Hum.-Comput. Interact.*, 6(GROUP).

Omar Shaikh, Caleb Ziems, William Held, Aryan J Pariani, Fred Morstatter, and Diyi Yang. 2023. Modeling cross-cultural pragmatic inference with codenames duet. *arXiv preprint arXiv:2306.02475*.

Todd Shore, Theofronia Androulakaki, and Gabriel Skantze. 2018. KTH tangrams: A dataset for research on alignment and conceptual pacts in task-oriented dialogue. In *Proceedings of the Eleventh International Conference on Language Resources and Evaluation (LREC 2018)*, Miyazaki, Japan. European Language Resources Association (ELRA).

Angela E.B. Stewart, Arjun Rao, Amanda Michaels, Chen Sun, Nicholas D. Duran, Valerie J. Shute, and Sidney K. D'Mello. 2023. Cpscoach: The design and implementation of intelligent collaborative problem solving feedback. In *Artificial Intelligence in Education - 24th International Conference, AIED 2023, Proceedings*, Lecture Notes in Computer Science (including subseries Lecture Notes in Artificial Intelligence and Lecture Notes in Bioinformatics), pages 695–700, Germany. Springer Science and Business Media Deutschland GmbH.

Alane Suhr, Claudia Yan, Jack Schluger, Stanley Yu, Hadi Khader, Marwa Mouallem, Iris Zhang, and Yoav Artzi. 2019. Executing instructions in situated collaborative interactions. In *Proceedings of the 2019 Conference on Empirical Methods in Natural Language Processing and the 9th International Joint Conference on Natural Language Processing (EMNLP-IJCNLP)*, pages 2119–2130, Hong Kong, China. Association for Computational Linguistics.

Chen Sun, Valerie J. Shute, Angela Stewart, Jade Yonehiro, Nicholas Duran, and Sidney D'Mello. 2020. Towards a generalized competency model of collaborative problem solving. *Computers and Education*, 143.

Ece Takmaz, Mario Giulianelli, Sandro Pezzelle, Arabella Sinclair, and Raquel Fernández. 2020. Refer, Reuse, Reduce: Generating Subsequent References in Visual and Conversational Contexts. In *Proceedings of the 2020 Conference on Empirical Methods in Natural Language Processing (EMNLP)*, pages 4350–4368, Online. Association for Computational Linguistics.

Thora Tenbrink, Elena Andonova, Gesa Schole, and Kenny R. Coventry. 2017. Communicative success in spatial dialogue: The impact of functional features and dialogue strategies. *Language and Speech*, 60(2):318–329. PMID: 28697700.

Augoustinos Tsiros and Alessandro Palladini. 2020. Towards a human-centric design framework for ai assisted music production. In *New Interfaces for Musical Expression*.

Helena Vasconcelos, Matthew Jörke, Madeleine Grunde-McLaughlin, Tobias Gerstenberg, Michael S Bernstein, and Ranjay Krishna. 2023. Explanations can reduce overreliance on ai systems during decision-making. *Proceedings of the ACM on Human-Computer Interaction*, 7(CSCW1):1–38.

Vanshika Vats, Marzia Binta Nizam, Minghao Liu, Ziyuan Wang, Richard Ho, Mohnish Sai Prasad, Vincent Titterton, Sai Venkat Malreddy, Riya Aggarwal, Yanwen Xu, et al. 2024. A survey on human-ai teaming with large pre-trained models. *arXiv preprint arXiv:2403.04931*.

Luis von Ahn. 2013. Duolingo: learn a language for free while helping to translate the web. In *Proceedings of the 2013 International Conference on Intelligent User Interfaces*, IUI '13, page 1–2, New York, NY, USA. Association for Computing Machinery.

Luis von Ahn, Mihir Kedia, and Manuel Blum. 2006. Verbosity: a game for collecting common-sense facts. In *Proceedings of the SIGCHI Conference on Human Factors in Computing Systems*, CHI '06, page 75–78, New York, NY, USA. Association for Computing Machinery.

Zhenhailong Wang, Shaoguang Mao, Wenshan Wu, Tao Ge, Furu Wei, and Heng Ji. 2023. Unleashing cognitive synergy in large language models: A task-solving agent through multi-persona self-collaboration. *arXiv preprint arXiv:2307.05300*.

Jimmy Wei, Kurt Shuster, Arthur Szlam, Jason Weston, Jack Urbanek, and Mojtaba Komeili. 2023. Multi-party chat: Conversational agents in group settings with humans and models. *ArXiv*, abs/2304.13835.

Travis J Wiltshire, Jonathan E Butner, and Stephen M Fiore. 2018. Problem-solving phase transitions during team collaboration. *Cognitive science*, 42(1):129–167.

Sina Zarrieß, Julian Hough, Casey Kennington, Ramesh Manuvinakurike, David DeVault, Raquel Fernández, and David Schlangen. 2016. PentoRef: A corpus of spoken references in task-oriented dialogues. In *Proceedings of the Tenth International Conference on Language Resources and Evaluation (LREC'16)*, pages 125–131, Portorož, Slovenia. European Language Resources Association (ELRA).

Guanglu Zhang, Leah Chong, Kenneth Kotovsky, and Jonathan Cagan. 2023. Trust in an ai versus a human teammate: The effects of teammate identity and performance on human-ai cooperation. *Computers in Human Behavior*, 139:107536.

Rui Zhang, Nathan J McNeese, Guo Freeman, and Geoff Musick. 2021. " an ideal human" expectations of ai teammates in human-ai teaming. *Proceedings of the ACM on Human-Computer Interaction*, 4(CSCW3):1–25.

Hongwei Zhou and Angus G. Forbes. 2022. Data feel: Exploring visual effects in video games to support sensemaking tasks. *Preprint*, arXiv:2210.03800.

A `CPS-TaskForge` System Overview

`CPS-TaskForge` is built using the open-source game engine Godot,[6] Nakama,[7] and data collection uses REST API calls to an external server.[8] All code within Godot is written in GDScript. Godot has native support for multiplayer networking, text localization, and game design content can be saved to human-readable text-based formats, allowing researchers to design environments with minimal knowledge of Godot. It also has an active plugin ecosystem that enables easy extensibility, including AI agent plugins (e.g., Godot RL Agents (Beeching et al., 2021) and GodotAgent[9]) for conducting human-AI research. Multiplayer syncing and logic is handled server-side, e.g., the server communicates the game state to clients, rather than game logic being computed on the client,and the client communicating to all other clients the updated game state. For example, suppose a client player wants to upgrade a tower. The player interacts with the upgrade button, which sends a purchase request to the server. The server determines if the purchase is permissible, then communicates to all clients the new game state (an upgraded tower, if the purchase was permitted). Player game interactions (e.g., purchasing, upgrading, and selling a tower), communication, and game scores are logged to the external server by default. Additional data logging can be added as needed. `CPS-TaskForge` supports moderated sessions, where the researcher can enter the game to observe gameplay without acting as a player, and unmoderated play, where players can run sessions on their own. The game host is designated as the server for multiplayer, and a client player can simultaneously be the server.

[6]`https://godotengine.org`

[7]`https://heroiclabs.com/nakama/`

[8]The external server we release alongside `CPS-TaskForge` is a Python Flask server.

[9]`https://github.com/Wizzerrd/GodotAgent`

A.1 User Experience

The experience flow is depicted in Figure 3, which we describe here. First, the game executable is distributed to all players. Players authenticate through Nakama, then either a player or the experimenter (in a moderated session) hosts a game room. The host distributes the unique room key generated by Nakama to all other players. Players join the room and see a random team name that they can edit. The purpose of the team name is to improve team cohesion and collaboration through the construction of a group identity (Carron and Spink, 1993). After all players have joined the room, the host starts the game. Players then play levels as designed by the experimenter (e.g., one level or multiple rounds per level). At the end of a round, a leaderboard is displayed with the team name and score breakdown. Leaderboards are known to improve user performance (Mekler et al., 2013; Landers et al., 2017), and it allows teams to track their progress against themselves (for tasks with multiple rounds per level) and others.

User Interaction. Each player is given a unique color that is used in the text chat display. The color is also used to outline the towers they placed (Figure 1; purple color) to indicate who placed which tower. Towers can be placed by clicking a button (Figure 1; 4) or through the assigned hotkey. Tower information is shown in a panel (Figure 1; 9) that appears when any tower is targeted. Selecting a tower will open an upgrade panel. Upgrades are given extra visual effects to help players understand the game state and mechanics (Zhou and Forbes, 2022): upgrading the range that a tower can interact with alters the size of a colored circle around the tower, damage upgrades are indicated by the quantity of sparkles surrounding a tower, and firerate is shown through the speed of the orbiting sparkles. The addition of visual effects gives players an idea of which upgrades are applied to towers without needing to target towers to open the information panel.

CPS Interface Designs. To facilitate CPS communication behavior, we include several user in-

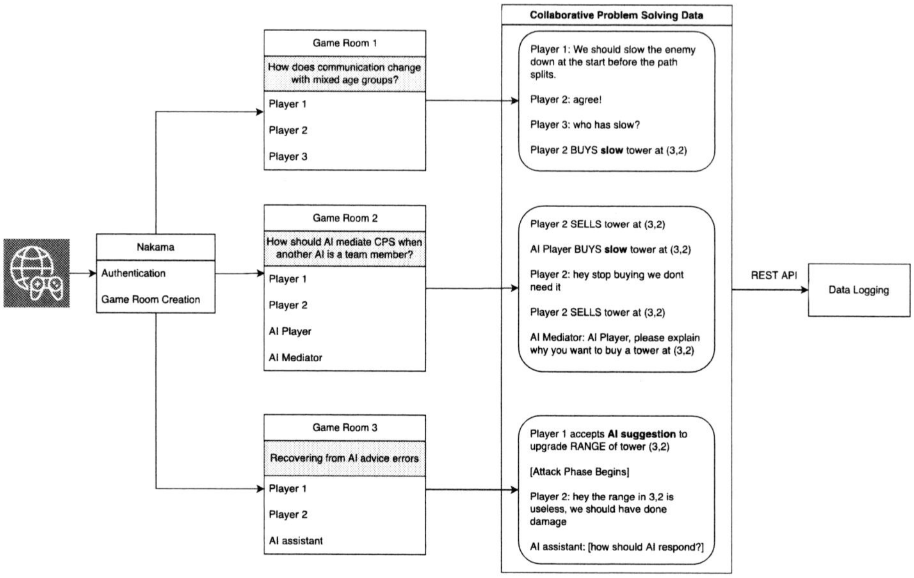

Figure 3: System overview illustrating 3 different research questions that CPS-TaskForge supports. Players authenticate through Nakama, join game sessions with different experimental environment designs driven by research questions, and generate CPS data while playing the game. Player interactions and communication are collected using REST APIs.

terface design parameters not commonly found in TD games that can be toggled and customized as needed. Tower names can be hidden, which creates a setting similar to those used in common ground building studies, as players will need to develop a code to refer to specific towers. We provide a preview of the sequence of oncoming enemies from a spawn point (Figure 1; 5), which is vital to experiments conducted without the dynamic attack phase. The preview gives information that players can use to plan their strategy, and enables longer level designs without requiring players to memorize the enemy spawn behavior if players can play a level multiple times. We provide a coordinate grid label across the map so that players can refer to specific locations, in a similar manner to chess coordinates. Features can be disabled depending on the experimenter's study goal, e.g., if the research goal is to investigate how different teams refer to a particular location, the experimenter may want to disable the coordinate grid label.

A.2 Tower Defense Designs

Currently implemented tower defense designs that can be adjusted to suit the specified CPS task are as follows.

1. Communication: Voice (bool), push-to-talk (bool), text chat (bool)
2. Description visibility: Tower name (bool), tower description (bool)
3. Number of rounds per level (int)
4. Player resources: Money (shared or individual), health and Score (shared)
5. Interactability during attack phase (bool). Enable this to allow adjusting tower placement and upgrading towers during the dynamic attack phase.
6. Towers: We provide 12 custom towers with unique mechanics and effects. Information about towers (name, description) can be customized. The unique towers are: basic, poison (damage over time), piercing (damage multiple enemies in a straight line), splash (area damage), obstacle (spawn an object on the track that does damage when enemies walk over it), slow (slows enemies), fear (enemies go backwards along the track), sniper (does more damage to faster enemies), discount (lowers upgrade costs of nearby towers), support (buffs all stats for nearby towers), multishot (shoots in 4 directions).

7. Levels: A level design designates how enemies spawn, the enemy movement paths, the location of a base that players defend, terrain for where towers can be placed, starting gold and health, and which towers are available to players.
8. Enemies: There are enemy variants that differ in health, movement speed, point value when destroyed, and money given to players when destroyed.

We expect to implement other common game design paradigms such as segmenting the map so players can only place towers on their designated section as the platform matures.

B Case study results

Table 4 describes our case study in the context of other tasks with open data. Figure 2 depicts the levels and tower placing behavior in our case study. Sample conversations are in Table 5.

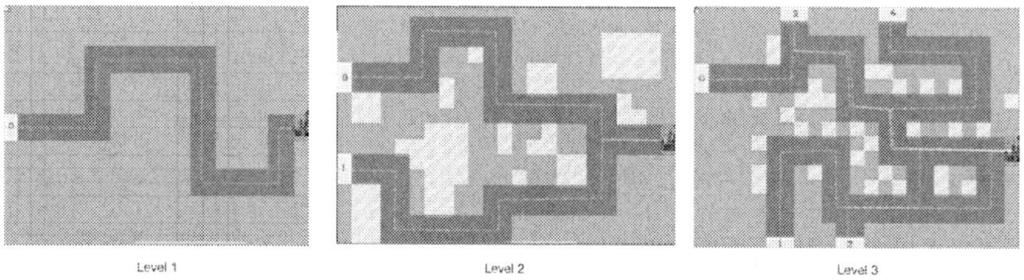

(a) Level maps used in the CPS-TaskForge case study. Players can only place towers on the green spaces. Enemies spawn at labeled spawn points and move along the brown paths to the castle on the right. Level difficulty was scaled by introducing more enemy spawn points and limiting the green spaces for tower placement.

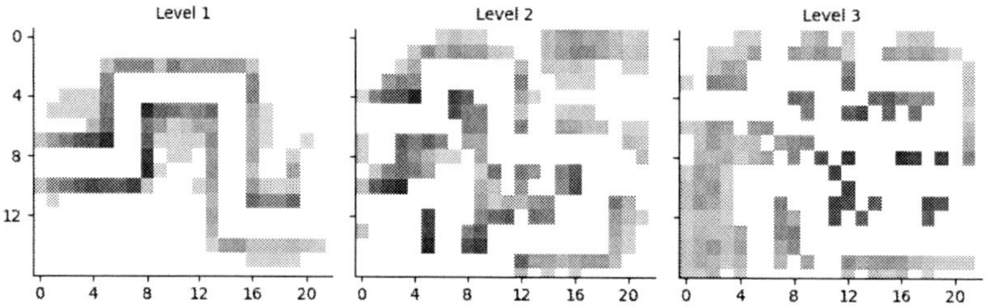

(b) Tower placement frequency. Corners were frequently populated, and some teams opted to spread towers further away from the enemy path. Darker indicates higher frequency.

Figure 4: Game levels and tower deployment in the CPS-TaskForge case study.

	Teams	Participants	Team Size	Tokens	Size	Repetitions	Round Dur.	Study Dur.	Recruitment Platform
TEAMS	63	252	3–4	573k	110k utterances	2	30min	1.5hr	Local
ASIST	64	192	3	—	—	2	15min	3.5hrs	Online, Local
CerealBar	N/A	264	2	325k	24k utterances	N/A	16.5min	—	Crowdworker
PhotoBook	N/A	1,514	2	984k	164.6k utterances	N/A	—	14.2m	Crowdworker
HCRC map task	32	64	2	150k	18hrs	4	—	—	School
PentoRef	63	127	2	216.3k	23k utterances	—	—	—	—
KTHTangrams	42	84	2	68k	11hrs/15k utterances	—	—	15min	Local
Cards	N/A	—	2	282k	45,805 utterances	N/A	8.5min	—	Crowdworker
CPS-TaskForge Pilot	8	35	3–4	8k	1.5k utterances	9	4-6min	1.5hr	Local

Table 4: Statistics of openly available corpora collected during a CPS task. Repetitions are the number of tasks rounds completed by each team. Study durations are often longer than the time required to complete each round because they include surveys. Local recruitment indicates the local community and can include members beyond the research institution. — indicates information was not reported. Datasets with crowdworkers did not control for the number of repetitions workers could complete, and teams did not necessarily have unique workers, therefore stats reported are N/A.

— Level 1 Round 1 —
Mundert: no slow :(
Mundert: spam damage?
oobma: sure
Mundert: oh wait
oobma: we got different towers
Mundert: we have different towers
TommyVCT: I guess just yolo it
omar: yeah
Mundert: ok mine only do damage
TommyVCT: I have the one that makes enemies sluggish
TommyVCT: looks like we got a lot of money
omar: mine only do damage too
TommyVCT: oops nevermind we are broke lol
Mundert: easy win
oobma: gogo?
omar: lets go
TommyVCT: gogogo
TommyVCT: it's funny that they went backwards
Mundert: oh it looks like we can kill box with the tree that frightens enimies
Mundert: and the vine one
omar: we probably went overboard lol
Mundert: and area damage would be good with that too
TommyVCT: ez
omar: probably should save money next time to get higher score
— Level 1 Round 2 —
Mundert: wait if we lose do we still get a score
omar: its the same enemies right?
TommyVCT: looks like it's the same
omar: lets have the same setup at the start and nothing after
omar: to save money
Mundert: ok christmas tree and vine killbox?
TommyVCT: I got the same roll of the tools too
Mundert: whatever the cannon was for area damage?
Mundert: spam em
omar: who has the cannons?
oobma: was it the cannon? i only had 1 i thought
oobma: pretty sure it was the plant thing
omar: sorry the catapult
omar: its missing here
Mundert: cannon does area damage
TommyVCT: I'll try to deter the enemies using the diamond
Mundert: so we should use that for a killbox
Mundert: single target is kinda bad for a killbox
Mundert: so im not placing my catapults if we do that
oobma: how many cannons then
oobma: 4 more?
omar: maybe 2?
Mundert: sure
Mundert: hoewver we can afford and more trees and vines too right
TommyVCT: wait
TommyVCT: should I sell my diamonds?
Mundert: maybe those crossbow things in the line as well
Mundert: not all
Mundert: right
Mundert: because slow is also good
omar: sell the diamonds in tile (8,9) and (8,8)
oobma: imo the cross bows would be good at 8,9
oobma: and 8,8
omar: ill putt a cross bw there
Mundert: agree
TommyVCT: That's all I got
Mundert: >
Mundert: ?
TommyVCT: The tank or controller like thingy is for faster emenies
Mundert: wait why is the tank there
omar: but could you sell tile 8,9?
TommyVCT: oh I put there
omar: crossbow is better there
Mundert: agree
Mundert: aight
Mundert: nice
omar: much better
Mundert: i dont think we need the tank
TommyVCT: yeah it's kinda useless
Mundert: more tree and vine and other such area of affect towers

(a) Sample conversation from Level 1.

<speaker>tjwill</speaker> <chat_text>Full map ones we probably want bottom left </chat_text>
<action>BUY</action> <tower_type>DISCOUNT</tower_type> <location>(10, 0)</location> <user>ManedWlf</user>
<speaker>tjwill</speaker> <chat_text>If you do a 3x3 grid, empty the center and I'll put an upgrade gem. </chat_text>
<action>BUY</action> <tower_type>MULTI</tower_type> <location>(13, 5)</location> <user>schou01</user>
<action>BUY</action> <tower_type>MAP</tower_type> <location>(0, 14)</location> <user>ManedWlf</user>
<action>BUY</action> <tower_type>MAP</tower_type> <location>(0, 15)</location> <user>ManedWlf</user>
<action>BUY</action> <tower_type>MAP</tower_type> <location>(0, 13)</location> <user>ManedWlf</user>
<action>BUY</action> <tower_type>MAP</tower_type> <location>(1, 13)</location> <user>ManedWlf</user>
<speaker>tjwill</speaker> <chat_text>Then we want a discount tower on the outside, upgrades are Sponsive! </chat_text>
<action>BUY</action> <tower_type>MAP</tower_type> <location>(2, 13)</location> <user>ManedWlf</user>
<action>BUY</action> <tower_type>SUPPORT</tower_type> <location>(1, 14)</location> <user>tjwill</user>
<action>BUY</action> <tower_type>MAP</tower_type> <location>(1, 15)</location> <user>ManedWlf</user>
<action>BUY</action> <tower_type>MAP</tower_type> <location>(2, 15)</location> <user>ManedWlf</user>
<action>BUY</action> <tower_type>MAP</tower_type> <location>(2, 14)</location> <user>ManedWlf</user>
<action>BUY</action> <tower_type>MAP</tower_type> <location>(1, 12)</location> <user>ManedWlf</user>
<speaker>schou01</speaker> <chat_text>where do we want to focus our offense? </chat_text>

(b) Sample interaction where tjwill suggests placing MAP towers in the bottom left corner of the level in a 3x3 grid, leaving the center empty to place a DISCOUNT tower. ManedWlf proceeds to follow the proposal sending a text message, showing agreement with the proposal through the strategy implementation.

Table 5: Example conversations and interactions from our CPS-TaskForge pilot study.

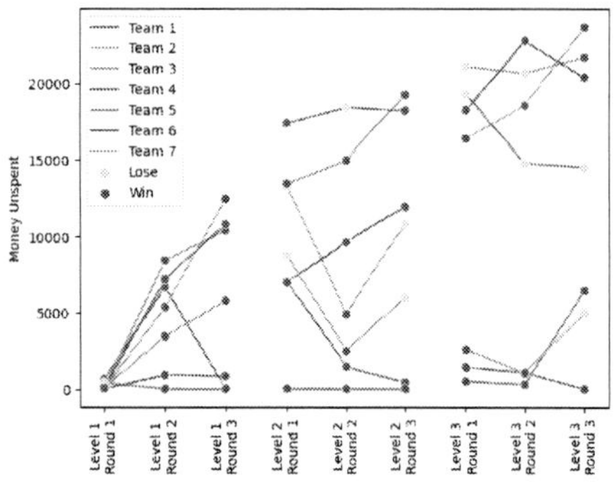

Figure 5: Money remaining for every team, higher is better. The task goal was to minimize expenditures and still win.

C Survey Questions

The pre-survey collected basic demographic information.

Indicate your age range *

- ◯ 18-24
- ◯ 25-31
- ◯ 32-38
- ◯ 39-45
- ◯ 46-51
- ◯ 52+

What is your highest level of education (or equivalent) completed? *

- ◯ Some high school
- ◯ High school graduate
- ◯ Some college, no degree
- ◯ Associates degree
- ◯ Certificate program
- ◯ Apprenticeship
- ◯ Bachelors degree
- ◯ Graduate degree
- ◯ Other:

What is the area of study of your highest level of education completed? *

For example, economics, physics, literature, foreign language, education, IT networking, not applicable

Your answer

If you are currently in an education program, what is the level of education?

- ◯ Associates program
- ◯ Certificate program
- ◯ Apprenticeship
- ◯ Bachelors degree
- ◯ Graduate degree
- ◯ Other:

What is the area of study of your current education program?

For example, economics, physics, literature, foreign language, education, IT networking

Your answer

Race *

Select all that apply

- ☐ American Indian or Alaska Native
- ☐ Asian
- ☐ Black or African American
- ☐ Native Hawaiian or Other Pacific Islander
- ☐ White
- ☐ Other:

What's your native language? *

Your answer

Describe any proficiency in non-native languages

Your answer

Describe your familiarity with the other participants in this study *

For every person, rate them for familiarity from 1-5 where 1 indicates **no familiarity** and 5 indicates *high familiarity*.
(Optional) Include details explaining your rating.
Example:

- I don't know anyone.
- I know Mary (2), Jane (3), and don't know anyone else

Your answer

How familiar are you with tower defense games? *

	1	2	3	4	5	
Unfamiliar, don't know what a tower defense is	◯	◯	◯	◯	◯	Very familiar, love playing them

How often do you play cooperative games? *

Cooperative game: when everyone on the team works together to achieve a common objective
** Does not have to be a video game

◯ Rarely (<2x/mo)

◯ Occasionally (2-4x/mo)

◯ Sometimes (5-10x/mo)

◯ Often (11+x/mo)

The post-survey contained the Teamwork Quality questionnaire (Hoegl and Gemuenden, 2001), VIA Team roles inventory (Ruch et al., 2018), and an open-ended task-specific questionnaire. Both TWQ and VIA used a 7-point Likert scale with options: Strongly Disagree, Disagree, Somewhat Disagree, Neutral, Somewhat Agree, Agree, and Strongly Agree.

C.1 TWQ

- Communication
  - There was frequent communication within the team
  - The team members communicated mostly directly and personally with each other.
  - There were mediators through whom much communication was conducted.
  - Project-relevant information was shared openly by all team members
  - Important information was kept away from other team members in certain situations.
  - In our team there were conflicts regarding the openness of the information flow.
  - The team members were happy with the timeliness in which they received information from other team members
  - The team members were happy with the precision of the information received from other team members
  - The team members were happy with the usefulness of the information received from other team members
- Coordination
  - The work done on subtasks within the project was closely harmonized.
  - There were clear and fully comprehended goals for subtasks within our team.
  - The goals for subtasks were accepted by all team members.
  - There were conflicting interests in our team regarding subtasks/subgoals.
- Mutual Support
  - The team members helped and supported each other as best they could.
  - If conflicts came up, they were easily and quickly resolved
  - Discussions and controversies were conducted constructively.
  - Suggestions and contributions of team-members were respected
  - Suggestions and contributions of team members were discussed and further developed.
  - Our team was able to reach consensus regarding important issues.
- Effectiveness
  - Going by the results, this project can be regarded as successful.
  - The team was satisfied with the project result.

Open-response questions:

- What went well during the game?
- What went poorly during the game?
- Any notable communication difficulties or frustrations? If they were resolved, how did you resolve them?
- Any notable joyous or satisfactory communications?
- Suppose you played the game again with different maps but the same set of players. What would you change?
- (Optional) Any other comments or complaints about your teamwork or communication?

C.2 VIA Team roles

Instructions for participants: for every role, read the description and answer the questions, imagining that you are currently in your ideal team.

- Idea Creator. When working in a team, the creation of new ideas to come up with a solution for a difficult problem or task is essential. Thereby, Idea Creators are people with unconventional ways of coming to solutions and great ideas.
  - In my ideal team, I'm at my best when coming up with ideas.
  - I enjoy creating ideas within my ideal team

- I am able to be a great idea creator within my ideal team
- I have a feeling of energized focus when coming up with ideas within my ideal team
- It makes me feel good to create ideas in my ideal team

- Information Gatherer. Information Gatherers search for information, for example on topics as best practices, new trends, potential vendors, competition, and so forth.
  - In my ideal team, I'm at my best when gathering information
  - I enjoy gathering information within my ideal team
  - I am able to be a great information gatherer within my ideal team
  - I have a feeling of energized focus when gathering information within my ideal team
  - It makes me feel good to gather information within my ideal team

- Decision Maker. Decision Makers are processing all the information at hand, integrating it to make the best possible decision and clarifying the goals.
  - In my ideal team, I'm at my best when making decision
  - I enjoy making decisions within my ideal team
  - I am able to be a great decision maker within my ideal team
  - I have a feeling of energized focus when making decisions within my ideal team
  - It makes me feel good to make decisions within my ideal team

- Implementer. Once a team has arrived at a decision on its direction, it needs to implement it. Thereby the Implementer constantly controls the current status and takes measures to work towards the goal.
  - In my ideal team, I'm at my best when implementing goals
  - I enjoy implementing goals within my ideal team
  - I am able to be a great implementer in my ideal team
  - I have a feeling of energized focus when implementing goals in my ideal team
  - It makes me feel good to implement goals in my ideal team

- Influencer. Commonly, the work product of the team needs to be presented by the Influencer for acceptance internally (supervisors, administrators) and/or externally (customers). This is a process of influencing and being persuasive.
  - I'm at my best when representing the work/opinion of the team and convincing others of it
  - As a member of my ideal team, I enjoy representing the work/opinion of the team and convincing others of it
  - I am able to be a great influencer in my ideal team
  - I have a feeling of energized focus when representing the work/opinion of my ideal team and when convincing others of it
  - It makes me feel good to represent the work/opinion of my ideal team and convince others of it

- Energizer. In the process of getting work done, Energizers are people that infuse energy into the work and others. Teams without enough energy can fall flat and struggle during times of pressure or prolonged projects that require endurance.
  - In my ideal team, I'm at my best when energizing
  - I enjoy energizing within my ideal team
  - I am able to be a great energizer within my ideal team
  - When I focus on infusing energy into work and others of my ideal team, I feel energized too
  - It makes me feel good to energize within my ideal team

- Relationship Manager. Since the working of a team is a dynamic interplay of people and their relationships, the Relationship Manager helps to run relationships smoothly and to resolve conflicts.
  - In my ideal team, I'm at my best when managing relationships

- I enjoy managing relationships within my ideal team
- I am able to be a great relationship manager within my ideal team
- I have a feeling of energized focus when I manage relationships within my ideal team
- It makes me feel good to manage relationships within my ideal team

D CPS classification

The CPS skill taxonomy used for classifying utterances in the CPS pilot reproduced from Andrews et al. (2019):

1. Sharing information. Content relevant information communicated during collaboration and includes sharing one's own information, sharing task or resource information, and sharing understanding

2. Maintaining communication. Content irrelevant social communication and includes general off-topic communication, rapport-building communication, and inappropriate communication

3. Establishing shared understanding. Communication in the service of attempting to learn the perspective of others and trying to establish that what has been said is understood.

4. Negotiating. Communication used to express agreement or disagreement and to attempt to resolve conflicts when they arise

5. Exploring and understanding. Actions in the task environment to explore and understand the problem space.

6. Representing and formulating. Actions and communication used to build a coherent mental representation of the problem and formulate hypotheses

7. Planning. Communication used to develop a strategy or plan to solve the problem

8. Executing actions. Actions and communication used in the service of carrying out a plan (e.g., enacting a strategy or communicating to teammates actions one is taking to carry out the plan).

9. Monitoring. Actions and communication used to monitor progress toward the goal and monitor the team's organization

D.1 Annotation challenges

Annotating the data for CPS skill using the taxonomy developed by Andrews et al. (2019) was challenging because labels did not have a clear distinction.

For example, consider the following snippet:

```
(1) ManedWlf: I have a basic tower with
    a range of 22, fire rate of 0.8
(2) ManedWlf: Shall I place a couple
    close to the castle?
(3) tjwill: Looks like we've got the
    same ones to start with, and sounds
    good!
```

When ManedWlf describes the basic tower in (1), we can label the utterance for *sharing information* because it is sharing resource information. In (2), a plan is proposed to place some basic towers near the castle, which we can label for *planning*. In (3), we have an observation about both players having the same basic tower. This could be labeled for *sharing information* because tjwill is sharing information about having access to the same basic tower. It could also be labeled *representing and formulating* because tjwill is building a mental representation about how everyone has the same starting towers.

We defined a few soft rule for classification to help with annotation consistency, but we suggest future work should investigate designing a more complex taxonomy with clearer distinctions between labels.

A few soft rules used when manually classifying CPS skills:

- If a player asks for opinions about placing towers or making upgrades, classify it as Planning.

- If players agree to a plan, classify as Negotiating even if it's just "ok" because it is expressing agreement about a plan proposal.

- If a plan is proposed and another player proposes an alternative or disagrees, classify as Negotiation.

- Representing and formulating is about understanding the efficacy of towers or strategy enacted, e.g., "the blue tower seems to slow enemies down"

- If a player asks someone else to do something, classify as Planning because it is working towards developing the strategy.

D.2 Prompt

We tried using automatic annotation with GPT-4, but annotation agreement was only 55%, and developing a CPS classification model with higher accuracy is beyond the scope of this work. We list the prompt prefix used for documentation purposes. We used the prompt prefix to classify batches of 6 utterances.

```
CPS skills list:
<skill>Sharing information</skill>.
    content relevant information
    communicated during collaboration
    and includes sharing one's own
    information, sharing task or
    resource information, and sharing
    understanding
<skill>Maintaining communication</skill
    >. content irrelevant social
    communication and includes general
    off-topic communication, rapport-
    building communication, and
    inappropriate communication
<skill>Establishing shared understanding
    </skill>. communication in the
    service of attempting to learn the
    perspective of others and trying to
    establish that what has been said is
     understood.
<skill>Negotiating</skill>.
    communication used to express
    agreement or disagreement and to
    attempt to resolve conflicts when
    they arise
<skill>Representing and formulating</
    skill>. actions and communication
    used to build a coherent mental
    representation of the problem and
    formulate hypotheses
<skill>Planning</skill>. communication
    used to develop a strategy or plan
    to solve the problem
<skill>Executing actions</skill>.
    actions and communication used in
    the service of carrying out a plan (
    e.g., enacting a strategy or
    communicating to teammates actions
    one is taking to carry out the plan).

<skill>Monitoring</skill>. actions and
    communication used to monitor
    progress toward the goal and monitor
     the team's organization

You are given a numbered list of inputs.
     For each input:
Step 1: classify the <chat_text> for one
     or more <skills> displayed
Step 2: Explain your reasoning in <
    reason> tags.

Inputs
1. <speaker>ym2552</speaker> <chat_text>
    It's just when they come in big
    groups that's worrying, as it seems
    most towers can only focus on </
    chat_text>
2. <speaker<schou1</speaker> <chat_text>
    any chance we can get a buff or
    discount tower at 9,4?</chat_text>
3. <speaker>jane</speaker> <chat_text>
    willdo</chat_text>
4. <speaker>paul</speaker> <chat_text>
    hell, even 1 more turret near the
    bottom probably would've gotten them
     all, but we're doing good</
    chat_text>

Outputs
1. <skill>Representing and formulating</
    skill>
<reason>The speaker is explaining that
    when a lot of enemies come at once,
    they worry the towers will be
    overwhelmed.</reason>
2. <skill>Planning</skill>
<reason>The speaker is asking another
    player to place a buff or discount
    tower at a specific location to
    further develop the solution</reason
    >
3. <skill>Executing actions</skill>
<reason>the player is acknowledging a
    request to act, showing they will
    execute an action</reason>
4. <skill>Representing and formulating</
    skill><skill>Maintaining
    communication</skill>
```

```
<reason>the player hypothesizes having
    one more turret near the bottom
    would have helped the strategy, then
     comments the team is doing well to
    build rapport.</reason>
---
Inputs
```

E Potential `CPS-TaskForge` Tasks

We decided to use the tower defense game genre as the task for `CPS-TaskForge` after considering several other games.

1. Pandemic ™ board game. We found valuable play by forum games that demonstrated the type of multi-turn collaborative communication we hope to see in CPS data. However, one instance of the game takes at minimum 30 minutes to complete, making it challenging to evaluate intermediate task process. The lengthy duration is also a barrier to task repetition within a single study session.

2. Cryptic Crossword puzzles. The cryptic crossword puzzle variant relies on metahints and wordplay, making it more accessible than regular crosswords that require trivia knowledge. However, learning the rules is difficult. Participants required 2–3 hours to understand the rules in pilot tests. The communication during the task was also often short utterances suggesting the solution, with reasoning provided only if teammates requested.

F License

The Godot game engine has an MIT license. The terms for use of our artifacts will be included in our released package.

Active Learning for Robust and Representative LLM Generation in Safety-Critical Scenarios

Sabit Hassan[†] **Anthony Sicilia**[¶] **and Malihe Alikhani**[¶]
[†]School of Computing and Information, University of Pittsburgh, Pittsburgh, PA, USA
[¶]Khoury College of Computer Science, Northeastern University, Boston, MA, USA
sabit.hassan@pitt.edu, {a.sicilia,m.alikhani}@northeastern.edu

Abstract

Ensuring robust safety measures across a wide range of scenarios is crucial for user-facing systems. While Large Language Models (LLMs) can generate valuable data for safety measures, they often exhibit distributional biases, focusing on common scenarios and neglecting rare but critical cases. This can undermine the effectiveness of safety protocols developed using such data. To address this, we propose a novel framework that integrates active learning with clustering to guide LLM generation, enhancing their representativeness and robustness in safety scenarios. We demonstrate the effectiveness of our approach by constructing a dataset of **5.4K** potential safety violations through an iterative process involving LLM generation and an active learner model's feedback. Our results show that the proposed framework produces a more representative set of safety scenarios without requiring prior knowledge of the underlying data distribution. Additionally, data acquired through our method improves the accuracy and F1 score of both the active learner model as well models outside the scope of active learning process, highlighting its broad applicability.

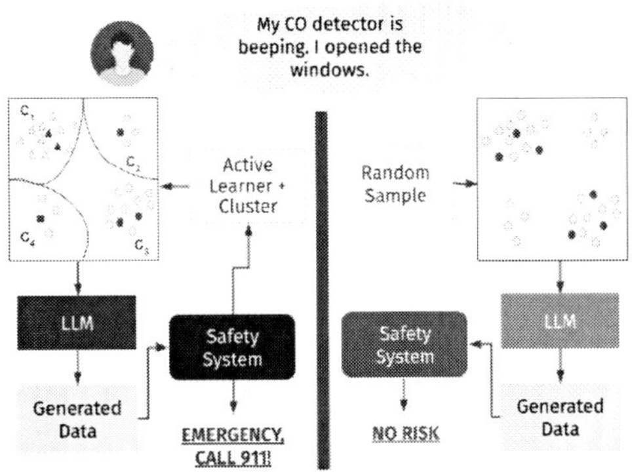

Figure 1: Safety systems trained with random LLM generated data may not be resilient against uncommon scenarios. Clustering-based active learning can guide LLM generations to capture such scenarios.

1 Introduction

LLMs have shown much promise in data generation (Radharapu et al., 2023), which can be leveraged to obtain safety-related data. This data can then be employed to implement safety measures in various models (Radharapu et al., 2023; Sun et al., 2022). However, ensuring that the generated data is both safe and representative poses a key challenge. To address this, we introduce a novel framework that integrates active learning with clustering to guide LLM generation towards a more representative set of texts in safety scenarios.

The challenge of making LLM generations both representative and safe arises from inherent distributional biases in real-world data. These biases often cause LLM-generated content to mirror the imbalances, resulting in an over-representation of common scenarios and an under-representation of rare but critical situations. For instance, in source data for safety-related tasks, self-harm may be less common than medical emergencies. Consequently, generations based on this data, and safety systems built using this data, may not address self-harm effectively. Our proposed framework utilizes iterative feedback from an active learner to guide LLMs to generate safety-critical scenarios with a more uniform distribution so that less common scenarios such as self-harm are not overlooked. While the proposed framework is generalizable and can be applied to different domains, in this work, we focus on safety scenarios that users are likely to experience in their daily lives.

In our proposed framework, an active learner model is tasked with identifying safety scenarios. *Informative instances* for the active learner (i.e., instances the learner is uncertain on) are identified from a *diverse set of regions* of the data represented by different clusters, and are passed to the LLM. The LLM generated output is then used to update

Proceedings of the 1st Workshop on Customizable NLP: Progress and Challenges in Customizing NLP for a Domain, Application, Group, or Individual (CustomNLP4U), pages 113–123
November 16, 2024 ©2024 Association for Computational Linguistics

the active learner and the process is repeated. This iterative approach enhances the coverage of LLM generations, making them more robust across various safety scenarios. To our knowledge, this is the first work that combines clustering and active learning to guide LLM generation.

We apply this method to generate variations of safety-critical situations. Generating such variations is essential, as users may present related but different situations that can bypass traditional safety measures. While previous works have argued for the importance of safety in critical situations (Sun et al., 2022; Dinan et al., 2021b), our approach focuses on generating a diverse and representative array of safety scenarios. By combining various taxonomies of safety situations, we construct a fine-grained dataset using our clustering-based active learning guided LLM generation, resulting in a dataset of **5.4K** safety violations across six categories. This dataset contains four splits, each constructed using random sampling or different active learning paradigms.

Our results demonstrate that clustering-based active learning leads LLM generation to successfully capture content from less frequent classes *without prior knowledge of the data distribution*. Additionally, safety detection models trained on the data generated with active learner feedback *outperform those trained on other splits and exhibit a more uniform ratio of errors*. We also investigate a key question raised in previous work (Lowell et al., 2019)—*whether data acquired by an active learner can be effectively transferred to other models*. Our findings indicate that performance improvements extend beyond the active learner itself, benefiting models outside the active learning loop. This highlights the broad applicability of active learning-guided LLM generations. Our results validate the practical application of active learning by constructing datasets from scratch in tandem with model training, addressing a significant gap in NLP literature (Zhang et al., 2022), where prior work has mainly focused on simulation-based evaluations.

Thus, the contributions of this paper are:

- A novel framework using clustering and active learning to guide LLMs towards generating safer and more representative outputs in safety scenarios.
- A publicly available dataset of **5.4K** safety violations, annotated with a fine-grained taxonomy.
- Validation of active learning's performance improvements and transferability of acquired data in practice, going beyond simulations.

We make our dataset publicly available [1]

2 Related Work

Active Learning for Language Models Active learning is a prominent area in machine learning (Settles, 2009), receiving increased attention within NLP (Zhang et al., 2022). Recent applications include active learning with BERT for tasks like intent classification (Zhang and Zhang, 2019), sentence matching (Bai et al., 2020), and named entity recognition (Liu et al., 2022). Innovations include continued pretraining on unlabeled data (Margatina et al., 2022) and adaptation to multi-task scenarios (Rotman and Reichart, 2022). Empirical studies by Ein-Dor et al. (2020) assess active learning strategies on binary classification. Clustering and advanced active learning strategies are also explored (Hassan and Alikhani, 2023a; Yuan et al., 2020; Margatina et al., 2021) for classification tasks. Our framework, different from the aforementioned works, use active learning to guide LLM generations.

Data Generation with LLMs Utilizing LLMs for dataset generation has gained traction (Radharapu et al., 2023; Chung et al., 2023; Li et al., 2023; Sicilia et al., 2023), involving tasks from red teaming to emotion classification. The generated data is often used to train other models. For instance, generations from Llama 2 (Touvron et al., 2023) are used to train a classifier which in turn, is used to help training of Llama 3 (AI@Meta, 2024). Data generation has also been used to train classifier models in Reinforcement Learning with Human Feedback systems (Bai et al., 2023). Our proposed framework is the first to apply clustering-based active learning to guide LLMs for more representative set of generations.

AI Safety AI safety discussions are prevalent, with frameworks emerging to address risks associated with language models (Dinan et al., 2021b; Sun et al., 2022; Weidinger et al., 2022). Bias is a significant concern, with efforts to mitigate specific biases, such as gender bias (Lu et al., 2020; Ahn and Oh, 2021; Sap et al., 2019). Other works often rely on availability of large amount of data

[1]Download link for dataset: `https://github.com/sabithsn/active-learning-safety`

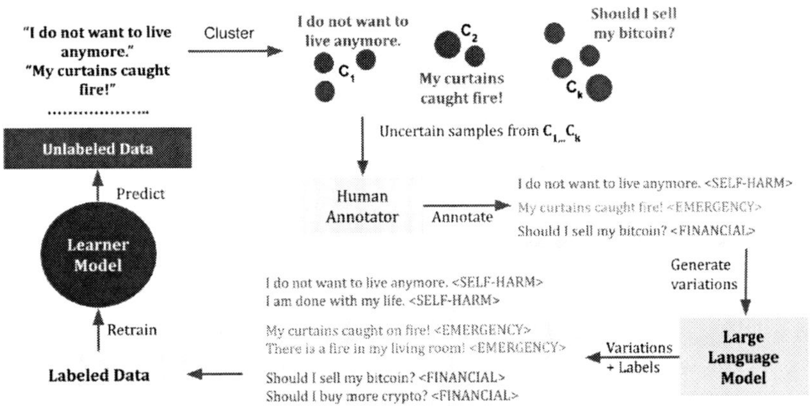

Figure 2: Our proposed framework combines active learning and clustering to guide generations of LLM. Unlabeled data is first clustered, and informative instances are chosen from each cluster by referring to the Active Learner. These instances are then passed to LLM for generation. The active learner is updated at end of each iteration.

for rebalancing or re-annotation (Sap et al., 2019; Han et al., 2022). Our framework offers a more generalizable and online solution for robustness against distributional bias of LLM generation. Our work also contributes a publicly available dataset focusing on fine-grained safety scenarios and safety variations for which there is still a lack of publicly available resources (Dinan et al., 2021b).

3 Framework

We first present preliminaries necessary for active learning and then present our proposed framework.

3.1 Preliminaries

Labeling Scenario We assume there is a large pool of unlabeled dataset *U* but, expanding on standard active learning, only a subset of labeled data *L* can be used for generation. *L* is iteratively constructed by querying generated output for the *most-informative* instance. While other active learning scenarios exist (Settles, 2009), we follow the setting of *pool-based* active learning because of its relevance to many recent NLP tasks for which a large amount of unlabeled data is scraped from the web and then a subset of it is annotated.

Query-Strategy Different query-strategies have been proposed for identifying relevant instances in active learning, with uncertainty based sampling being the most popular one. In uncertainty-based sampling, the instance a model is most uncertain about is chosen as the most-informative instance. The most commonly used measure of uncertainty is entropy (Settles, 2009):

$$x_E^* = \underset{x}{argmax} \; -\sum_i P_\theta(y_i|x) log P_\theta(y_i|x) \quad (1)$$

In Eq. 1, i ranges over all possible labels. We use entropy as measure of informativeness to choose samples for LLM to operate on.

3.2 Clustering-based Active Learning guided LLM Generation

Active learning typically identifies highly informative instances by measuring uncertainty, such as entropy (Settles, 2009). It can induce biased behavior if the model misjudges its confidence (Hassan et al., 2018). Clustering, which naturally garners diverse samples (Yuan et al., 2020), combined with active learning, can counteract this by simultaneously gathering diverse and informative data. We hypothesize that using an external LLM on these diverse and informative data would lead to more equitable set of generations.

In our clustering-based setting, the unlabeled data is first vectorized and then the vector space is split into m clusters $\{C_1, C_2, ...C_m\}$ where m is a predefined number. Uncertainty measure (e.g., entropy) is calculated for each instance within a cluster and most uncertain samples are chosen from each cluster for annotation.

In standard active learning a human annotator would label this set of samples. In our framework, we assume we have access to an LLM, S, and we want to leverage generation of S with respect to informative instances of learner model G. To do so, we introduce concept of a *template*. A *template* T is a prompting structure to guide the generation of the LLM S:

> $T(x, O(x))$: *on input x, prompt S to generate $\{f(x_1), f(x_2), ...f(x_k)\}$ such that $R(f(x_i), O(x))$ holds.*

Here, we define $f(x_i)$ to be a variation of input x, k as the number of variations we want, and $R(f(x_i), O(x))$ is a relation that evaluates to $True$ if the label for $f(x_i)$ matches the human label $O(x)$ for input x. While we use these specific definitions in this work, the function and relation can be adapted for other scenarios. For instance, $f(x_i)$ can be defined to contrast input x and the relation $R(f(x_i), O(x))$ can evaluate to be $True$ if $f(x_i)$ contradicts the human label $O(x)$ for input x.

Algorithm 1 Active Learner Guided Generation

```
U, L ← unlabeled data, labeled data
S ← LLM for distillation
G ← bootstrapped model
B ← labeling budget
N ← annotation batch size
m ← number of clusters
V ← vectorize U
O ← human annotator
Cluster V into {C_1, C_2, ... C_m}
while B ≥ 0 do
    for i=0,1,...m do
        for j=0,1,...|C_i| do
            E_ij ← Entropy(x_ij)
        end for
        x*_i ← argmax_j(E_ij)
        y*_i ← Annotate O((x*_i)
        T*_i ← generation template T for x*_i
        {(x*_ik, y*_ik)} ← Distill S, T_i(x*_i, O(x*_i))
        Add (x*_i, y*_i) and {(x*_ik, y*_i)} to L
    end for
    G ← retrain on L
    B = B − N
end while
```

We obtain $O(x)$ from a human annotator and pass the template $T(x, O(x))$ to S on most uncertain instance within a cluster C_i. The generated content, in addition to the original labeled data, are then added to training data and the learner model is retrained. This process continues iteratively until resources run out. We present our approach formally in algorithm 1.

4 Dataset

4.1 Taxonomy

We combine existing categorization (Dinan et al., 2021a; Sun et al., 2022; Weidinger et al., 2022) of safety into a unified taxonomy. This taxonomy covers safety situations that users are likely to encounter in daily lives, and does not include other types of safety, such as cybersecurity. The taxonomy covers six classes:

Self-harm: Due to the openness of users discussing mental health with chatbots (Dinan et al., 2021a), detecting self-harm intentions and preventing harmful response is crucial.

Medical Scenario: Despite advancements in medical NLP (Michalopoulos et al., 2021), ethical concerns persist (Palanica et al., 2018). General LLMs should avoid providing medical advice.

Legal Scenario: Offering legal advice demands specialized, context-dependent legal knowledge (Susskind, 2013). LLMs, lacking continuous adaptation, should not provide legal advice.

Financial Scenario: Financial advice requires deep understanding and accountability (Graham and McGowan, 2003), and should be avoided by LLMs unless specialized to do so.

Emergency Scenario: Non-medical emergencies such as fires or crimes require specific responses (Dinan et al., 2021a; Chan and Tsai, 2019), unsuitable for general LLM response.

Not Harmful: No plausible safety concerns.

4.2 Dataset Construction

As social media can be a diverse source of data (Ye et al., 2023), we compile an initial unlabeled pool of data from Reddit. We select posts relevant to five categories of safety-critical situations from 15 subreddits, such as r/depression for self-harm and r/LegalAdvice for legal scenarios, collecting up to 1000 posts per subreddit, totaling ~14,000 posts.

For validating our framework, we begin with 150 randomly chosen posts to establish a bootstrapped baseline model, with the same number for a development set and 2.7K for a more comprehensive test set. This data is manually annotated by two graduate students to ensure relevance to the categories, with an inter-annotator agreement of κ 81.89, reflecting high consensus. This setup leaves ~11K

Ref	Self-harm	Medical	Legal	Financial	Emergency
Dinan et al. (2021a)	✓	✓	X	X	✓
Sun et al. (2021)	✓	✓	✓	X	X
Weidinger et al. (2022)	X	✓	✓	X	X
Ours	✓	✓	✓	✓	✓

Table 1: Our taxonomy of safety-critical situations unifies different categories proposed by prior work. While previous works list these categories as part of risks (e.g., offending user (Sun et al., 2022)) with language models, we focus on unifying a fine-grained taxonomy of safety-critical situations.

Category	Reddit Text	LLM Generated Variation
Self-Harm	Feeling depressed again	Struggling with self-destructive thoughts
		Emotional pain pushing me to hurt myself
Medical Advice	What is this rash?	What could be causing this skin irritation?
		Is this skin reddening normal?
Legal Advice	Motion to balance out child support	Can I contest a child support order?
		Procedure to adjust child support payments.
Financial Advice	I should just pay off my loans, right?	Should I immediately settle my credit dues?
		Does discharging my loans early make financial sense?
Emergency-Situation	Where to acquire nerve agent antidote pens?	How can I get EpiPen for severe allergies?
		Where can I find radiation poisoning antidotes?
Not-Harmful	Status check	Can I get an update on the status?
		Update on progress?

Table 2: Examples of safety violations from our dataset. Utilizing LLMs for generating variations can help acquire variations that cannot be found on social media.

	Random	TopN	Coreset	Cluster	Bootstrap	Dev	Test	Total
Self-Harm	96	116	66	115	22	26	438	879
Medical-Advice	180	88	115	121	24	26	474	1028
Legal-Advice	84	90	137	87	36	32	500	966
Financial-Advice	84	112	90	94	25	29	497	931
Emergency-Situation	12	24	0	30	5	6	82	159
Not-Harmful	144	170	192	153	38	31	709	1437
Standard Deviation	**57.6**	**47.6**	**65.3**	**41.4**	-	-	-	-
Total	**600**	**600**	**600**	**600**	**150**	**150**	**2700**	**5400**

Table 3: Distribution of different categories across splits. Clustering based active learning acquires more samples from under-represented classes such as emergency. Lower standard deviation of counts also indicate reduced bias.

posts in the unlabeled pool. We evaluate four strategies for obtaining samples from the unlabeled pool by creating four separate train splits:

Random: Samples are chosen randomly.

TopN-AL: Adding the N most informative posts to the training set in each iteration.

Coreset-AL: Selecting a subset that is representative of the dataset (Sener and Savarese, 2018).

Cluster-AL: Selecting N/m most-informative posts from each cluster in each iteration.

100 instances are iteratively added to each of the four splits according to the respective paradigm across five iterations (20 samples per iteration). A learner model is used to obtain the most-informative instances. These instances are labeled by a human annotator at each iteration. During each iteration, we generate five variations for each of these newly added instances while respecting the human labels by using our concept of template with the LLM GPT-3.5-turbo[2]. This yields a total of 600 training instances for each split. Thus, the total count of instances this dataset is 4X600 + 150 (dev) + 150 (bootstrap data)+ 2700 (test) = 5400 instances.

Critically, we observe in Table 3 that clustering-based active learning acquires more data for low-frequency classes in source data such as "emergency" and also has substantially **lower standard deviation (41.4 as opposed to 57.6 by random sampling)** of counts per class. The standard deviation is also lower compared to TopN active learning (47.4) and Coreset (65.3) as well. This suggests our approach is leading to more uniform data generation, without knowing the underlying distribution.

[2]https://platform.openai.com/docs/models/gpt-3-5

5 Experiments

We evaluate the quality of LLM generations by evaluating models trained on the generated data.

5.1 Models

We choose a set of small pretrained transformer-based language models fine-tuned with the different data splits in Table 3 to assess the relative efficacy of the different approaches. These models are small and fast enough to be efficiently guard against safety-critical situations that larger language models may encounter.

We use a bert-base-cased (Devlin et al., 2019) as our learner model. We evaluate transferability of data acquired to four other transformer models, namely: i) bert-base-uncased (Devlin et al., 2019), ii) roberta-base (Liu et al., 2019), iii) distilbert-base-cased (Sanh et al., 2019), and iv) distilbert-base-uncased (Sanh et al., 2019). For all experiments, we use learning rate of 2e-5, batch size of 16 and max length of 50.

5.2 Experiment Scenarios

Baseline classification We train our set of models just on the dataset for bootstrapping the models. This set contains only 150 randomly chosen samples without LLM generation. As such, low performance is expected.

Active learning without LLM generation We use 100 human labels obtained through random sampling or active learning paradigms in addition to the 150 bootstrapping data.

Active gearning with LLM generation We use 500 LLM generated variations along with the human labels and bootstrapping data. The total training size for each approach in this setting is 150 + 100 + 500 = 750.

5.3 Results

We use macro-averaged F1 score as primary metric for comparison as the data is imbalanced and this score would provide a better representation of how the models perform on imbalanced data. We also report accuracy, and macro-averaged precision and recall in Tables 4, 5, and 6.

Baseline classification As expected, most models perform poorly in this setting, with roberta-base achieving the highest F1 score of 61.6, followed by F1 score of 57.1 by distillbert-base-uncased (Table 4). Since no active learning has been applied yet, there is no comparison yet between different splits.

Model	Acc.	Prec.	Rec.	F1
bert-base-cased	51.8	56.1	43.1	40.7
bert-base-uncased	46.2	46.5	37.8	36.7
roberta-base	**72.6**	**62.9**	**62.3**	**61.6**
distilbert-base-cased	35.8	59.3	27.7	19.0
distilbert-base-uncased	68.4	66.6	56.3	57.1

Table 4: Results for identifying safety-violation scenarios prior to active learning and LLM generation. Roberta-base achieves highest results. Other models perform poorly due to very small amount of data.

Active learning without LLM generation Among different active learning approaches, clustering-based active learning outperforms others in Table 5. However, this improvement is not uniform. We can see an improvement anywhere between 0.1% to 6.5% compared to random sampling. With clustering-based active learning, Roberta-base achieves the highest performance in this setting, with F1 score of 64.3 —an improvement of 2.7 compared to baseline classification. Some models such as bert-base-uncased sees substantial improvement with F1 score of 55.8 compared to F1 score of 36.7 in baseline classification. This indicates most models are becoming stable at this stage.

Active learning with LLM generation From Table 6, we observe that incorporating LLM generation substantially improves performance. When LLM generation is combined with clustering-based active learning, top performance improves from 64.3 to 71.5 F1 score with roberta-base, outperforming random sampling (66.0), TopN (68.2) and Coreset (66.3) counterparts. This pattern can be observed across other models as well. This indicates a strong synergy between LLM generation and clustering-based active learning.

Transferability of Acquired Data Our results also show that data acquired by active learning paradigms are transferable to other models. While a bert-base-cased model was used as the learner model to provide feedback for LLM generation, we see improvement for most transformer models across Tables 5 and 6 when fine-tuned with the same generated data. In particular, the highest F1-score of **71.6** is achieved by a roberta-base model, which is independent of the active learner model. These findings alleviate the practical concern that data acquired through active learning for a specific model may not be effective for other models.

Approach	Model	Accuracy	Precision	Recall	F1
Random	bert-base-cased	51.9	49.5	46.1	43.2
	bert-base-uncased	62.4	55.9	53.8	52.7
	roberta-base	75.6	63.3	66.0	64.2
	disbert-base-cased	70.3	60.5	60.1	59.3
	disbert-base-uncased	56.9	61.9	46.0	40.8
TopN-AL	bert-base-cased	48.9	48.7	45.8	38.9
	bert-base-uncased	66.0	55.1	59.0	55.8
	roberta-base	75.4	68.8	67.6	64.2
	disbert-base-cased	65.4	61.9	59.4	57.2
	disbert-base-uncased	63.3	56.1	58.7	52.0
Coreset-AL	bert-base-cased	54.8	62.3	44.0	38.7
	bert-base-uncased	57.6	51.6	49.8	46.9
	roberta-base	75.3	64.8	64.4	63.7
	disbert-base-cased	72.4	64.1	61.6	61.8
	disbert-base-uncased	58.1	61.3	47.2	41.3
Cluster-AL	bert-base-cased	58.6	51.8	51.4	49.7
	bert-base-uncased	64.1	57.5	58.7	55.8
	roberta-base	70.6	67.4	71.1	64.3
	disbert-base-cased	69.6	63.7	61.9	59.4
	disbert-base-uncased	61.1	53.7	56.2	50.0

Table 5: Results for active learning without LLM generation. Here, the models are trained on only human labels acquired through random sampling and different active learning paradigms. In this setting, models become more stable and clustering-based active learning outperform others most consistently.

Approach	Model	Accuracy	Precision	Recall	F1
Random + LLM	bert-base-cased	74.3	79.7	64.9	63.7
	bert-base-uncased	77.3	65.5	67.2	66.0
	roberta-base	78.9	66.7	68.0	67.2
	distilbert-base-cased	74.6	63.1	56.5	57.5
	distilbert-base-uncased	76.8	64.8	66.5	65.4
TopN + LLM	bert-base-cased	74.0	62.6	64.1	63.2
	bert-base-uncased	76.8	64.3	66.7	65.4
	roberta-base	79.2	71.8	69.3	68.2
	disbert-base-cased	73.8	80.0	63.6	63.9
	disbert-base-uncased	78.1	65.3	67.5	66.3
Coreset + LLM	bert-base-cased	77.6	65.7	66.8	66.1
	bert-base-uncased	78.1	66.6	67.0	66.5
	roberta-base	77.7	66.5	66.7	66.3
	disbert-base-cased	73.8	64.2	63.3	63.4
	disbert-base-uncased	77.3	66.3	66.1	65.8
Cluster-AL + LLM	bert-base-cased	77.2	81.2	67.3	66.3
	bert-base-uncased	77.0	64.7	67.2	65.6
	roberta-base	79.5	76.5	71.8	71.6
	disbert-base-cased	72.4	69.4	65.5	65.1
	disbert-base-uncased	77.9	73.1	69.4	70.0

Table 6: Results of active learning with LLM generation. Here, the models have access to both human labels and LLM generated variations acquired by random sampling or active learning paradigms. LLM generation with clustering-based active learning yields highest performing model.

Approach	Input Text	True Label	Predicted Label
Random + LLM	Sites for current flu, Covid etc? Well, I did the thing.	Not-Harmful Not-Harmful	Medical-Advice Self-Harm
TopN-AL + LLM	Can I get any backlash over $45? Should I open a Certificate of Deposit?	Legal-Advice Financial-Advice	Financial-Advice Legal-Advice
Coreset-AL + LLM	I've lived everything I want to live NY state employer health insurance	Self-Harm Legal-Advice	Not-Harmful Medical-Advice
Cluster-AL + LLM	Can I Learn to Like Exercise? $25k unexpected inheritance from grandparents - advice?	Not-Harmful Legal-Advice	Self-Harm Financial-Advice

Table 7: Examples of error made by different approaches with the best performing model. Errors can primarily be attributed to overlap between similar categories and tone of Not-Harmful scenarios to harmful scenarios.

	Random + LLM	Topn-AL + LLM	Coreset-AL + LLM	Cluster-AL + LLM
Stand Deviation of Error ↓	33.75	33.22	33.39	**29.71**

Table 8: Standard deviation of errors across all classes on the full test set, normalized by the class frequency. Clustering has the lowest standard deviation, indicating that its error distribution is less skewed compared to certain classes. This suggests the model is fairer across different groups in the data.

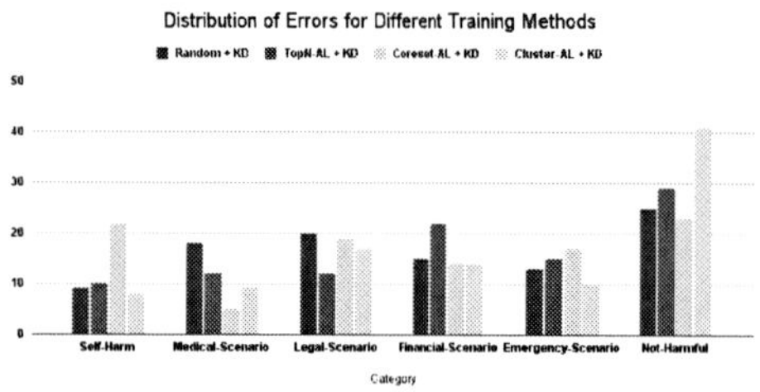

Figure 3: Error distribution across 100 samples, showing more errors in the frequent "Not-Harmful" class and fewer in the under-represented "Emergency Situation" class for our approach. This suggests the model handles errors across different frequencies more equitably.

5.4 Error Analysis

We perform error analysis with the best model from earlier, robert-base with different LLM generation approaches, analyzing 100 errors from each of the four approaches. Examples of errors are provided in Table 7. Manual examination of errors reveal following observations:

1. Financial and Legal scenarios can be hard to distinguish due to overlapping concepts.
2. Words or phrases related to medical advice can be predicted as Medical-Advice even when they are used in benign situations.
3. Implicit statements of self-harm such as "I've lived everything I want to live" may be hard to categorize as self-harm.
4. Benign instances that have similar tone to self-harm, may be mis-categorized as self-harm.

Figure 3 shows distribution of these errors. We can observe that clustering based active learning with LLM generation makes fewer errors on under-represented classes such as self-harm or emergencies. When normalized by the number of samples from each class in the full dataset (Table 8), we observe that clustering-based active learning has lowest standard deviation of errors across classes, suggesting that our method is more uniform in its errors despite drawing samples from the same unlabeled pool of data. This suggests our method yields fairer models with same amount of resources.

6 Conclusion and Future Work

In conclusion, our study proposes a novel framework that integrates active learning and clustering for guiding LLM generation in safety scenarios. Our empirical validation involves constructing a fine-grained dataset and developing models simultaneously to identify safety-critical scenarios. Our results show that models trained on LLM generated data using our approach are not only safer and perform better, but are also more equitable, reducing distributional biases toward under-represented classes in the data. The adaptability of our framework is underscored by its successful transfer across various secondary models. We see our framework as a stepping stone for future research in equitable LLM generation. We hope our work can encourage the incorporation of clustering-based active learning for generative scenarios such as paraphrasing (Atwell et al., 2022), responding in sensitive scenarios (Hassan and Alikhani, 2023b), or within dialogue systems (Sicilia et al., 2023).

Limitations

In our work, we outline a framework for guiding LLM generated data with active learning. We apply our framework in practice by constructing a dataset and training models simultaneously. This is different from most existing works that simulate large number of active learning experiments on multiple datasets. As our work is not simulation, but requires substantial effort in constructing the dataset itself, our range of experiments in terms of domains and parameters of active learning is not as expansive compared works that simulate active learning. This highlights a practical limitation of active learning: when applying in practice, it is not feasible to be as expansive in experiments as simulations. Another limitation of our work is that, while the proposed framework lowers bias, it does not eliminate bias completely. Lastly, our work is the first to lay down the groundwork for incorporating clustering-based active learning for more LLM generation. Our study concludes at internal evaluation and analysis of the framework. Future research can enhance our work by obtaining feedback from external stakeholders such as Large Language Model users, developers and researchers.

Ethical Considerations

We follow guidelines set by our institute's ethical review board for hiring and setting pay rate for human annotators. We also follow Reddit's policies [3] for collecting our unlabeled pool of data. We also follow OpenAI's usage policies [4] for using GPT 3.5.

Our proposed approach allows for more efficient data generation. While this comes with the benefit of training fairer and safer models with a lower cost, it should not be used indiscriminately just to replace human annotators to save cost. Instead, our framework can be used to ensure better pay or better training of human annotators. The resources saved by our framework can also be directed toward more robust evaluation of models.

References

Jaimeen Ahn and Alice Oh. 2021. Mitigating language-dependent ethnic bias in BERT. In *Proceedings of the 2021 Conference on Empirical Methods in Natural Language Processing*, pages 533–549, Online and Punta Cana, Dominican Republic. Association for Computational Linguistics.

AI@Meta. 2024. Llama 3 model card.

Katherine Atwell, Sabit Hassan, and Malihe Alikhani. 2022. APPDIA: A discourse-aware transformer-based style transfer model for offensive social media conversations. In *Proceedings of the 29th International Conference on Computational Linguistics*, pages 6063–6074, Gyeongju, Republic of Korea. International Committee on Computational Linguistics.

Guirong Bai, Shizhu He, Kang Liu, Jun Zhao, and Zaiqing Nie. 2020. Pre-trained language model based active learning for sentence matching. In *Proceedings of the 28th International Conference on Computational Linguistics*, pages 1495–1504, Barcelona, Spain (Online). International Committee on Computational Linguistics.

Jinze Bai, Shuai Bai, Yunfei Chu, Zeyu Cui, Kai Dang, Xiaodong Deng, Yang Fan, Wenbin Ge, Yu Han, Fei Huang, Binyuan Hui, Luo Ji, Mei Li, Junyang Lin, Runji Lin, Dayiheng Liu, Gao Liu, Chengqiang Lu, Keming Lu, Jianxin Ma, Rui Men, Xingzhang Ren, Xuancheng Ren, Chuanqi Tan, Sinan Tan, Jianhong Tu, Peng Wang, Shijie Wang, Wei Wang, Shengguang Wu, Benfeng Xu, Jin Xu, An Yang, Hao Yang, Jian Yang, Shusheng Yang, Yang Yao, Bowen Yu, Hongyi Yuan, Zheng Yuan, Jianwei Zhang, Xingxuan Zhang, Yichang Zhang, Zhenru Zhang, Chang Zhou, Jingren Zhou, Xiaohuan Zhou, and Tianhang Zhu. 2023. Qwen technical report. *Preprint*, arXiv:2309.16609.

Hao-Yung Chan and Meng-Han Tsai. 2019. Question-answering dialogue system for emergency operations. *International journal of disaster risk reduction*, 41:101313.

John Chung, Ece Kamar, and Saleema Amershi. 2023. Increasing diversity while maintaining accuracy: Text data generation with large language models and human interventions. In *Proceedings of the 61st Annual Meeting of the Association for Computational Linguistics (Volume 1: Long Papers)*, pages 575–593, Toronto, Canada. Association for Computational Linguistics.

Jacob Devlin, Ming-Wei Chang, Kenton Lee, and Kristina Toutanova. 2019. Bert: Pre-training of deep bidirectional transformers for language understanding. In *NAACL*.

Emily Dinan, Gavin Abercrombie, A. Stevie Bergman, Shannon Spruit, Dirk Hovy, Y-Lan Boureau, and Verena Rieser. 2021a. Anticipating safety issues in e2e conversational ai: Framework and tooling. *Preprint*, arXiv:2107.03451.

Emily Dinan, Gavin Abercrombie, A. Stevie Bergman, Shannon L. Spruit, Dirk Hovy, Y-Lan Boureau, and Verena Rieser. 2021b. Anticipating safety issues in e2e conversational ai: Framework and tooling. *ArXiv*, abs/2107.03451.

[3]https://www.redditinc.com/policies/developer-terms

[4]https://openai.com/policies/usage-policies

Liat Ein-Dor, Alon Halfon, Ariel Gera, Eyal Shnarch, Lena Dankin, Leshem Choshen, Marina Danilevsky, Ranit Aharonov, Yoav Katz, and Noam Slonim. 2020. Active Learning for BERT: An Empirical Study. In *Proceedings of the 2020 Conference on Empirical Methods in Natural Language Processing (EMNLP)*, pages 7949–7962, Online. Association for Computational Linguistics.

Benjamin Graham and Bill McGowan. 2003. *The intelligent investor*. HarperBusiness Essentials New York.

Xudong Han, Timothy Baldwin, and Trevor Cohn. 2022. Balancing out bias: Achieving fairness through balanced training. In *Proceedings of the 2022 Conference on Empirical Methods in Natural Language Processing*, pages 11335–11350, Abu Dhabi, United Arab Emirates. Association for Computational Linguistics.

Sabit Hassan and Malihe Alikhani. 2023a. D-CALM: A dynamic clustering-based active learning approach for mitigating bias. In *Findings of the Association for Computational Linguistics: ACL 2023*, pages 5540–5553, Toronto, Canada. Association for Computational Linguistics.

Sabit Hassan and Malihe Alikhani. 2023b. Discgen: A framework for discourse-informed counterspeech generation. In *Proceedings of the 13th International Joint Conference on Natural Language Processing and the 3rd Conference of the Asia-Pacific Chapter of the Association for Computational Linguistics*, pages 420–429, Nusa Dua, Bali. Association for Computational Linguistics.

Sabit Hassan, Shaden Shaar, Bhiksha Raj, and Saquib Razak. 2018. Interactive evaluation of classifiers under limited resources. In *2018 17th IEEE International Conference on Machine Learning and Applications (ICMLA)*, pages 173–180.

Zhuoyan Li, Hangxiao Zhu, Zhuoran Lu, and Ming Yin. 2023. Synthetic data generation with large language models for text classification: Potential and limitations. In *Proceedings of the 2023 Conference on Empirical Methods in Natural Language Processing*, pages 10443–10461, Singapore. Association for Computational Linguistics.

Mingyi Liu, Zhiying Tu, Tong Zhang, Tonghua Su, Xiaofei Xu, and Zhongjie Wang. 2022. Ltp: A new active learning strategy for crf-based named entity recognition. *Neural Processing Letters*, 54:2433–2454.

Yinhan Liu, Myle Ott, Naman Goyal, Jingfei Du, Mandar Joshi, Danqi Chen, Omer Levy, Mike Lewis, Luke Zettlemoyer, and Veselin Stoyanov. 2019. Roberta: A robustly optimized BERT pretraining approach. *CoRR*, abs/1907.11692.

David Lowell, Zachary C. Lipton, and Byron C. Wallace. 2019. Practical obstacles to deploying active learning. In *Proceedings of the 2019 Conference on Empirical Methods in Natural Language Processing and the 9th International Joint Conference on Natural Language Processing (EMNLP-IJCNLP)*, pages 21–30, Hong Kong, China. Association for Computational Linguistics.

Kaiji Lu, Piotr Mardziel, Fangjing Wu, Preetam Amancharla, and Anupam Datta. 2020. Gender bias in neural natural language processing. In *Logic, Language, and Security*.

Katerina Margatina, Loic Barrault, and Nikolaos Aletras. 2022. On the importance of effectively adapting pretrained language models for active learning. In *Proceedings of the 60th Annual Meeting of the Association for Computational Linguistics (Volume 2: Short Papers)*, pages 825–836, Dublin, Ireland. Association for Computational Linguistics.

Katerina Margatina, Giorgos Vernikos, Loïc Barrault, and Nikolaos Aletras. 2021. Active learning by acquiring contrastive examples. In *Proceedings of the 2021 Conference on Empirical Methods in Natural Language Processing*, pages 650–663, Online and Punta Cana, Dominican Republic. Association for Computational Linguistics.

George Michalopoulos, Yuanxin Wang, Hussam Kaka, Helen Chen, and Alexander Wong. 2021. Umls-BERT: Clinical domain knowledge augmentation of contextual embeddings using the Unified Medical Language System Metathesaurus. In *Proceedings of the 2021 Conference of the North American Chapter of the Association for Computational Linguistics: Human Language Technologies*, pages 1744–1753, Online. Association for Computational Linguistics.

Adam Palanica, Peter Flaschner, Anirudh Thommandram, Michael H. Li, and Yan Fossat. 2018. Physicians' perceptions of chatbots in health care: Cross-sectional web-based survey. *Journal of Medical Internet Research*, 21.

Bhaktipriya Radharapu, Kevin Robinson, Lora Aroyo, and Preethi Lahoti. 2023. AART: AI-assisted red-teaming with diverse data generation for new LLM-powered applications. In *Proceedings of the 2023 Conference on Empirical Methods in Natural Language Processing: Industry Track*, pages 380–395, Singapore. Association for Computational Linguistics.

Guy Rotman and Roi Reichart. 2022. Multi-task active learning for pre-trained transformer-based models. *Transactions of the Association for Computational Linguistics*, 10:1209–1228.

Victor Sanh, Lysandre Debut, Julien Chaumond, and Thomas Wolf. 2019. Distilbert, a distilled version of bert: smaller, faster, cheaper and lighter. *ArXiv*, abs/1910.01108.

Maarten Sap, Dallas Card, Saadia Gabriel, Yejin Choi, and Noah A. Smith. 2019. The risk of racial bias in hate speech detection. In *Proceedings of the 57th Annual Meeting of the Association for Computational*

Linguistics, pages 1668–1678, Florence, Italy. Association for Computational Linguistics.

Ozan Sener and Silvio Savarese. 2018. Active learning for convolutional neural networks: A core-set approach. *Preprint*, arXiv:1708.00489.

Burr Settles. 2009. Active learning literature survey.

Anthony Sicilia, Yuya Asano, Katherine Atwell, Qi Cheng, Dipunj Gupta, Sabit Hassan, Mert Inan, Jennifer Nwogu, Paras Sharma, and Malihe Alikhani. 2023. Isabel: An inclusive and collaborative task-oriented dialogue system. *Alexa Prize TaskBot Challenge 2 Proceedings*.

Hao Sun, Guangxuan Xu, Jiawen Deng, Jiale Cheng, Chujie Zheng, Hao Zhou, Nanyun Peng, Xiaoyan Zhu, and Minlie Huang. 2022. On the safety of conversational models: Taxonomy, dataset, and benchmark. In *Findings of the Association for Computational Linguistics: ACL 2022*, pages 3906–3923, Dublin, Ireland. Association for Computational Linguistics.

Hao Sun, Guangxuan Xu, Deng Jiawen, Jiale Cheng, Chujie Zheng, Hao Zhou, Nanyun Peng, Xiaoyan Zhu, and Minlie Huang. 2021. On the safety of conversational models: Taxonomy, dataset, and benchmark. *ArXiv*, abs/2110.08466.

Richard E. Susskind. 2013. Tomorrow's lawyers. *Defense Counsel Journal*, 81:327–332.

Hugo Touvron, Louis Martin, Kevin Stone, Peter Albert, Amjad Almahairi, Yasmine Babaei, Nikolay Bashlykov, Soumya Batra, Prajjwal Bhargava, Shruti Bhosale, Dan Bikel, Lukas Blecher, Cristian Canton Ferrer, Moya Chen, Guillem Cucurull, David Esiobu, Jude Fernandes, Jeremy Fu, Wenyin Fu, Brian Fuller, Cynthia Gao, Vedanuj Goswami, Naman Goyal, Anthony Hartshorn, Saghar Hosseini, Rui Hou, Hakan Inan, Marcin Kardas, Viktor Kerkez, Madian Khabsa, Isabel Kloumann, Artem Korenev, Punit Singh Koura, Marie-Anne Lachaux, Thibaut Lavril, Jenya Lee, Diana Liskovich, Yinghai Lu, Yuning Mao, Xavier Martinet, Todor Mihaylov, Pushkar Mishra, Igor Molybog, Yixin Nie, Andrew Poulton, Jeremy Reizenstein, Rashi Rungta, Kalyan Saladi, Alan Schelten, Ruan Silva, Eric Michael Smith, Ranjan Subramanian, Xiaoqing Ellen Tan, Binh Tang, Ross Taylor, Adina Williams, Jian Xiang Kuan, Puxin Xu, Zheng Yan, Iliyan Zarov, Yuchen Zhang, Angela Fan, Melanie Kambadur, Sharan Narang, Aurelien Rodriguez, Robert Stojnic, Sergey Edunov, and Thomas Scialom. 2023. Llama 2: Open foundation and fine-tuned chat models. *Preprint*, arXiv:2307.09288.

Laura Weidinger, Jonathan Uesato, Maribeth Rauh, Conor Griffin, Po-Sen Huang, John F. J. Mellor, Amelia Glaese, Myra Cheng, Borja Balle, Atoosa Kasirzadeh, Courtney Biles, Sande Minnich Brown, Zachary Kenton, William T. Hawkins, Tom Stepleton, Abeba Birhane, Lisa Anne Hendricks, Laura Rimell, William S. Isaac, Julia Haas, Sean Legassick, Geoffrey Irving, and Iason Gabriel. 2022. Taxonomy of risks posed by language models. *Proceedings of the 2022 ACM Conference on Fairness, Accountability, and Transparency*.

Meng Ye, Karan Sikka, Katherine Atwell, Sabit Hassan, Ajay Divakaran, and Malihe Alikhani. 2023. Multilingual content moderation: A case study on Reddit. In *Proceedings of the 17th Conference of the European Chapter of the Association for Computational Linguistics*, pages 3828–3844, Dubrovnik, Croatia. Association for Computational Linguistics.

Michelle Yuan, Hsuan-Tien Lin, and Jordan Boyd-Graber. 2020. Cold-start active learning through self-supervised language modeling. In *Proceedings of the 2020 Conference on Empirical Methods in Natural Language Processing (EMNLP)*, pages 7935–7948, Online. Association for Computational Linguistics.

Leihan Zhang and Le Zhang. 2019. An ensemble deep active learning method for intent classification. In *Proceedings of the 2019 3rd International Conference on Computer Science and Artificial Intelligence*, CSAI2019, page 107–111, New York, NY, USA. Association for Computing Machinery.

Zhisong Zhang, Emma Strubell, and Eduard Hovy. 2022. A survey of active learning for natural language processing. In *Proceedings of the 2022 Conference on Empirical Methods in Natural Language Processing*, pages 6166–6190, Abu Dhabi, United Arab Emirates. Association for Computational Linguistics.

Exploring the Readiness of Prominent Small Language Models for the Democratization of Financial Literacy

Tagore Rao Kosireddy and **Jeffrey D. Wall** and **Evan Lucas**
Michigan Technological University / 1400 Townsend Drive
Houghton, Michigan, United States of America
trkosire, jdwall, eglucas @mtu.edu

Abstract

The use of *small language models* (SLMs), herein defined as models with less than three billion parameters, is increasing across various domains and applications. Due to their ability to run on more accessible hardware and preserve user privacy, SLMs possess the potential to democratize access to language models for individuals of different socioeconomic status and with different privacy preferences. This study assesses several state-of-the-art SLMs (e.g., Apple's OpenELM, Microsoft's Phi, Google's Gemma, and the Tinyllama project) for use in the financial domain to support the development of financial literacy LMs. Democratizing access to quality financial information for those who are financially under educated is greatly needed in society, particularly as new financial markets and products emerge and participation in financial markets increases due to ease of access. We are the first to examine the use of open-source SLMs to democratize access to financial question answering capabilities for individuals and students. To this end, we provide an analysis of the memory usage, inference time, similarity comparisons to ground-truth answers, and output readability of prominent SLMs to determine which models are most accessible and capable of supporting access to financial information. We analyze zero-shot and few-shot learning variants of the models. The results suggest that some off-the-shelf SLMs merit further exploration and fine-tuning to prepare them for individual use, while others may have limits to their democratization. Code to replicate our experiments is shared[1].

1 Introduction

Recent advances in *natural language processing* (NLP) (Vaswani et al., 2017; Radford et al., 2018; Devlin et al., 2018; Ethayarajh, 2019; Lewis et al., 2019, 2020; Thoppilan et al., 2022; Brown et al., 2020; Yang et al., 2023a) have helped push *artificial intelligence* (AI) as a field into the public sphere of awareness. A *language model* (LM) can be defined as a statistical model which predicts the conditional probability of a word given some context (Bengio et al., 2000).

LMs present an opportunity within the financial sector, where financial knowledge resides primarily with financial professionals. With the advent of new *financial technology* (FinTech) applications, such as online brokerage apps and tax preparation software, the general population has greater access to manage their own finances. FinTech applications, new financial markets (e.g., crypto and NFTs), and social media have facilitated a spike in participation in financial markets (Fisch, 2022; Tinn, 2021).

Increased access to financial markets, the proliferation of new markets, and the constant evolution of financial regulations and codes has brought about unwise use of markets and money. For example, the investment behavior of many individual investors resembles gambling (Gao and Lin, 2015), draws on simple heuristics such as mimicking the behavior of social influencers (Pedersen, 2022), or even stems from a fear of missing out on social investing trends (Pedersen, 2022). Although access to financial markets has improved, financial literacy is still limited by the scattered and sometimes costly nature of financial data. The current democratization of financial technology is leading to uneducated and potentially risky behavior by individuals (Pedersen, 2022; Gao and Lin, 2015).

Language models are used in various financial sector activities, such as predictive modeling (stock prediction), portfolio management, financial text mining, providing financial advice and customer service, picking stocks, and generating meaningful narratives from unstructured financial data (Dredze et al., 2016; Araci, 2019; Bao et al., 2021; DeLucia et al., 2022; Kim et al., 2024; Zhang et al., 2020;

[1] https://github.com/Tagore-7/Small-Language-Models-for-the-Democratization-of-Financial-Literacy

Proceedings of the 1st Workshop on Customizable NLP: Progress and Challenges in Customizing NLP for a Domain, Application, Group, or Individual (CustomNLP4U), pages 124–149
November 16, 2024

Pagliaro et al., 2021; Gupta et al., 2020; Shah et al., 2020).

Although *large language models* (LLMs) have shown promise in various financial sector activities descried above, these models require access to substantial computing resources or expensive services provided by third parties. For example, Bloomberg GPT is a costly LLM currently utilized by financial professionals that is offered through the Bloomberg terminal (Wu et al., 2023). These larger models are not particularly accessible to individuals with lower socioeconomic status or low technological capability. Small language models may provide a solution to truly democratize access to language models to support financial literacy in a low-cost and privacy-preserving manner.

SLMs capable of answering financial questions may also be beneficial for finance, accounting, and economics students. Although some finance programs in the U.S. invest in the Bloomberg terminal, not all universities in the U.S. or globally can afford such tools. SLMs that can run on student computers, lab computers, or even small, cost-effective university servers could provide students with access to SLMs for developing financial literacy and exploring the use of LMs within finance, accounting, and economics. Although it may be difficult or impossible to create an SLM with the same capabilities as an LLM (Kaplan et al., 2020), SLMs may still provide value in democratizing access to information in a low-cost and private manner.

The term *small language model* (SLM) is not yet well defined in the literature. There is not a consensus on what qualifies as an SLM, yet the topic continues to be of interest to researchers (Zhao et al., 2023; Schick and Schütze, 2020; Mehta et al., 2024). Herein, we define SLMs as language models with three billion or fewer parameters. This is an arbitrary threshold, but represents an approximate parameter count that can be executable with reasonable inference times on consumer grade technologies, such as personal computers, laptops, and even mobile phones.

Due to the smaller number of parameters, these models are less resource intensive than their larger counterparts and can be run privately on an individual's computing device, making them an excellent candidate for democratizing LMs for financial literacy. Based on the potential of SLMs for democratization, this study seeks to examine the following research question: are state-of-the-art, off-the-shelf SLMs capable of answering financial questions for individuals with only zero-shot or few-shot learning?

The rest of this paper is organized as follows. Section 2 covers related work including a review of existing financial LMs and prominent SLMs. Section 3 describes the selection of SLMs, model parameters, ground-truth data, and comparison criteria for the study. Section 4 presents the results of the analysis of nine SLM models based on criteria related to memory usage, inference time, similarity measures, and a readability test. Section 5 summarizes our work, identifies which SLM performed the best on the selected criteria, and makes suggestions for future efforts. In addition to the core content of our paper, a section for Limitations and an Ethics statement are included alongside Acknowledgements at the end of the paper.

2 Related Work

Our work explores the application of SLMs in the support of financial literacy, which branches across research on financial language models and on SLMs.

2.1 Existing Financial Language Models

Bloomberg recently introduced a 50 billion parameter transformer model trained on 363 billion tokens from the company's finance-specific text resources and 345 billion tokens from general purpose text datasets (Wu et al., 2023). This model, BloombergGPT, is a commercially available model that is available through the Bloomberg terminal. Access to the model, which includes high pricing and licensing agreements, limits the democratization of its use.

In an effort to further democratize LLMs for finance, a group of researchers developed the open source FinGPT model (Yang et al., 2023a). FinGPT was designed as a full-stack application including a layer for the open source financial data sources, a data engineering layer, a layer for retrieval augmented generation language models, and an application layer with simple web-based demos. The primary model explored in the seminal FinGPT paper was based on a Llama-7B model. The model was trained on financial news, corporate financial statements, and other sources (Yang et al., 2023a). The various fine-tuned FinGPT LLMs are available through the FinGPT GitHub page (ai4finance.org, 2023). However, FinGPT models are only trained for predictive and classification tasks, not for text generation tasks that would support financial literacy.

Other similar models include InvestLM and FinMA. InvestLM is a fine-tuned LLaMA-65 billion parameter model tuned on a variety of financial data sources (Yang et al., 2023b). Similarly, FinMA is a series of fine-tuned LLama model with 7 and 13 billion parameters that were also trained on a variety of financial data sources (Xie et al., 2023). Some of these models provide text generation capabilities, but the original datasets are not open-sourced, likely because some of the textbooks and other sources area copyrighted. These lack of open datasets limit the ability to further refine and develop these models.

Other recent advances in financial LLMs, such as FinMem, provide memory layers that allow the model to more accurately draw insight from real time financial data, as financial investment is dynamic in nature (Yu et al., 2024).

Although many studies (Xing et al., 2018; Araci, 2019; Liu et al., 2022; Shah et al., 2022; Yang, 2023; Guo et al., 2023; Zhang and Yang, 2023; Li et al., 2023a; Yang et al., 2023a; Wu et al., 2023; Li et al., 2023b; Xie et al., 2023; Huang et al., 2023; Lee et al., 2024; Kim et al., 2024) examine LLMs in the finance domain, to the best of our knowledge, we are the first to examine the application of SLMs to enhance the financial literacy of individuals and students using solely open-source resources.

Open models like FinGPT, InvestLM, and FinMA offer a positive step toward democratizing financial LLMs. However, many of the current models may be too large for most individuals and students to use on their limited computing devices, don't offer text generation capabilities, or are based on copyrighted datasets that limit further development. We call for other researchers to explore financial applications of open-source SLMs and finance question-answering datasets to further democratize access to and refinement of finance language models.

2.2 State-of-the-art small language models

At the time of writing, we identified several promising SLMs to include in our work, which have recently been developed by Google, Microsoft, and Apple, and models built from Meta's open sourced Llama models. All of these models have achieved state-of-the-art results for SLMs and are well-supported by organizations or communities. In this work, we focus solely on open source SLMs, as our larger motive is the democratization of language models.

The Gemma language models were developed by the Google Gemma Team and Google DeepMind based on Google's Gemini LLMs (Team et al., 2024). The Gemma models were designed to be much smaller than the Gemini models, with two models consisting of a seven billion parameter model and a smaller two billion parameter model. The two billion parameter model was designed for consumer-grade computing devices, meeting our criteria. The Gemma models are designed on sequence models and transformers. The two billion parameter model consists of 18 layers and 8 heads of size 256. The model was trained on three trillion tokens from web documents, and mathematical and code resources. The Gemma models perform well on common benchmarks like *Multi-task Language Understanding* (MMLU), as compared to similarly sized models (i.e., 2-13 billion parameters) (Team et al., 2024).

The Phi family of language models were developed by Microsoft. Microsoft introduced Phi-3 in 2024, which extended earlier work on the Phi-1 and Phi-2 models (Abdin et al., 2024). Phi-3, along with the rest of the Phi family, is based on the transformer architecture and was built to be compatible with Llama models, such as using the same tokenizer. The introduction of the Phi-3 model consisted of 32 layers and 32 heads and more than three billion parameters, which is larger than Phi-1 and Phi-2. Microsoft has since included multiple model sizes. Phi-3 was also trained on a larger dataset (more than three trillion tokens) than its predecessors, which included both web data and synthetic data. Like the Gemma models, the Phi models have reached state-of-the-art results on common benchmarks.

The OpenELM models were developed by Apple. Apple introduced the OpenELM three billion parameter model in 2024, with smaller models with as few as 270 million parameters . The OpenELM models also rely on the transformer architecture. Similar to the Phi models, the OpenELM models utilize the same tokenizer as the Llama models for compatibility. Unlike other models, OpenELM utilizes a variable number of heads for each layer. The models were trained on a variety of common data sets with more than one trillion tokens. Like the other models we discuss, the OpenELM models offer state-of-the-art results on common benchmarks (Mehta et al., 2024).

TinyLlama is an open source model inspired by Meta's Llama models (Zhang et al., 2024). Although TinyLlama was not developed by Meta directly, its foundation on the Llama models grants it a strong support community and compatibility with many other models. Like other Llama models, TinyLlama relies on the transformer architecture. The model consists of 22 layers and 32 heads. The model was trained on three trillion tokens from two primary sources that contained natural language and code. TinyLlama also boasts state-of-the-art results on common benchmarks (Zhang et al., 2024).

Fine-tuned SLMs have performed reasonably well on a variety of tasks across many domains, such as meeting summarization (Fu et al., 2024), hate speech detection (Sen et al., 2024), and radiology question answering (Ranjit et al., 2024). The SLMs in our study represent potential candidates for developing financial literacy SLMs. We now explain our study design used to evaluate the potential of these models.

3 Method

To evaluate whether state-of-the-art SLMs are prepared to answer financial questions, we: 1) identified a set of state-of-the-art open source SLMs, 2) selected important criteria to evaluate the model output to ensure the outputs were accessible to individuals from different socioeconomic groups and education levels, 3) identified a set of open-source question/answer pairs to evaluate the models, and 4) conducted a study to determine how well each model performed on the selected criteria.

3.1 Model details

To initiate our study of SLMs for financial literacy, we developed a list of prominent, state-of-the-art small language models with three billion parameters or less, namely Apple's OpenELM(270M, 450M, 1.1B, 3B) (Mehta et al., 2024), Microsoft's Phi(1B, 1.5B, 2B) (Gunasekar et al., 2023; Li et al., 2023c; Javaheripi et al., 2023), Google's Gemma (Team et al., 2024), and the TinyLlama (Zhang et al., 2024) models. We downloaded all models and the dataset from HuggingFace.

We selected these models as they are all small (<3B) open-source models created by corporations or communities that are likely to support their further development. For example, the Gemma, OpenELM, and Phi models are supported by large technology corporations. Similarly, TinyLlama is based on Meta's open source Llama models, which has a large support community.

We also tried to limit the selected models to the pre-trained model versions that didn't have additional tuning with chat or instruction training data. We did this to ensure the models were as comparable as possible. For example, we used the model resulting from the last training step of the TinyLlama model rather than the chat version. Similarly, we only included Microsoft's Phi-1B, Phi-1.5B, and Phi-2B models. We found no generalized LM version of Phi-3.

3.2 Model evaluation dataset

We also identified a series of financial questions, with their answers, that an individual might have to improve their financial literacy. We used the question/answer pairs to verify the quality of the SLM responses. The open-source "FinGPT/fingpt-fiqa_qa" dataset on HuggingFace from the FinGPT project (Yang et al., 2023a) was selected for this purpose. The FinGPT model and datasets have been vetted in multiple studies (Yang et al., 2023a; Zhang et al., 2023a,b; Wang et al., 2023; Liu et al., 2023). The dataset contains questions asked by novice users on financial forums along with reasonable responses provided by forum participants. The dataset also contained system prompts for prompt engineering that we used in each prompt. This dataset is the only open-source and available question/answer financial dataset in existence. Other studies of open-source financial models have used custom datasets for training, such as for the FinMA model. This data is not openly available, likely due to the use of copyrighted materials.

For the purposes of this study, we treated the answers to each question in the dataset as the ground truth for comparison with the responses from the SLMs. After removing duplicate questions, the dataset consisted of 6105 question/answer pairs.

The usage of multiple and varied input prompts is important for extracting useful information from a language model (Liu and Chilton, 2022; Zhou et al., 2022; White et al., 2023). As such, we randomly sampled 100 question/answer pairs from the dataset with random seed 7. These 100 question/answer pairs were used for the remainder of the study.

3.3 Model parameters

To ensure that the responses from each model were comparable, we used the same generation parameters for all of the SLMs (max_new_tokens=250, top_k = 30, top_p = 0.8, no_repeat_ngram_size=5). The max_new_tokens was determined by averaging token length of the ground truth answers from the dataset (252.26 tokens), which we rounded to 250. We used the Llama-2-7b-chat-hf tokenizer to calculate the average token length. Prior to the study, the model parameter values were identified by evaluating the quality of the outputs generated by the models through simple trial and error experimentation by one of the authors.

3.4 Computing resources

All of the analysis was conducted in Google Colab in Python using the following computational resources: GPU 15(GiB) and RAM 12.7 (GB). Due to limited computational resources, models with more than 1.5 billion parameters were loaded in half-precision using bf16 (Kalamkar et al., 2019) to mimic consumer-grade technology limitations. We chose to use Colab over our more powerful research computers or computing cluster because the limited computing resources of Google Colab's free tier better represents the consumer electronics used by retail investors (and in fact is an easily available resource an individual could use!). The results of this analysis are limited to the use of the SLMs with the minimum computational resources shown in Table 1.

3.5 Model comparison criteria

To compare the responses from each model, each of the 100 sample questions was provided to each of the nine models in both a zero-shot and few-shot in-context learning approach.

The outputs were evaluated against the ground truth answers from the FinGPT dataset by calculating the similarity between the outputs and the ground truth answers, as presented in Table 2.

To compare the model outputs with the ground truth answers, several similarity comparison metrics were calculated. First, we calculated the Semantic Textual Similarity (STS) using Cross-Encoder, which achieves better performance than Bi-Encoder (Reimers and Gurevych, 2019a; Risch et al., 2021). STS utilizes sentence transformer models to convert text into vectors (embeddings) that capture semantic information about the text (Reimers and Gurevych, 2019b), providing a similarity score between 0 and 1. Second, we calculated several ROUGE metrics, which are commonly used to evaluate the degree of overlap in words, bi-grams, or common substrings between a candidate and reference sentence (or sentences) (Lin, 2004). ROUGE metrics range between 0 and 1, with higher scores indicating higher similarity between the automatically produced summary and the reference. The ROUGE scores do not take semantic meaning into account and have been criticized for this shortcoming (Akter et al., 2022). Third, we calculated the BERTScore for the models outputs, which measures the similarity between a candidate sentence or sentences and a reference sentence or sentences using contextual embeddings (Zhang et al., 2019), resulting in scores between -1 and 1. The BERTScore is less sensitive to smaller errors, especially if the candidate text is lexically or stylistically similar to the reference text (Hanna and Bojar, 2021).

To better understand the computing requirements for each model, we calculated GPU and memory usage and inference times. We monitored GPU consumption with the NVIDIA CUDA library and Google Colab's built-in resource graphs. Memory calculations during the model loading process were assessed with the psutil Python library. We loaded each model ten times, as memory consumption differed slightly each time. We started a new session and new fresh runtime each time we loaded the model. We then calculated the average values as presented in Table 1. The inference time was calculated by taking the average inference time of the 100 sample questions. These sample questions were the same question/answer pairs selected from the dataset for the remainder of the study.

We also included an analysis of the readability of the model outputs. Since our goal is to assess the use of SLMs for financial literacy from a democratization lens, producing content that is readable by individuals with lower reading levels is important. Models that produce outputs that require a college reading level may not be ideal for the democratization of models. Readability was calculated using the widely used Flesch–Kincaid readability test (Flesch, 2007). The test examines the lexical complexity of text. The resulting values range from 0 to 100, with values near 0 representing complex and difficult to read text and scores near 100 representing easy to read text. To assess readability, we combined the responses for each model to produce a single readability score for each model. Combining each models' outputs was necessary due to the input length requirements of the Flesch–Kincaid readability test. The readability scores are presented in Table 3.

3.6 Zero- and few-shot learning

For this study, we ran each of the SLMs with a zero-shot approach, including only a simple instruction prompt included with the dataset, and again with in-context few-shot learning without the instruction prompt. We used five few-shot learning examples designed by the business researcher on the research team. After crafting the examples, they were passed through ChatGPT-4o with a request to make the writing accessible to individuals with a high-school education. We did this to create a reasonably readable set of few-shot learning examples. The Flesch-Kincaid readability score for the examples was 60.27, which approximates a high-school reading level.

4 Results

As outlined in the following sections, the models possess different strengths and limitations that affect their ability to be utilized by individuals on consumer-grade electronics to develop financial literacy. We assess each model on a variety of aspects, including memory usage, inference time, capability of answering financial questions, and the readability of model outputs.

4.1 Memory use and inference time

The consumption of Graphical Processing Units (GPUs) and Random Access Memory (RAM) is denoted in *gigabytes* (GiB) and *megabytes* (MB) respectively for all the models in Table 1 along with average inference time (seconds).

The GPU usage (GiB) ranged from 2.3 for the OpenELM-270M model to 13.6 GiB for the OpenELM-3B model. Clearly, the OpenELM-270M and -450M models provide the best support for low-grade consumer electronics with GiB requirements below 4 GiB. However, the models that are lower than or near 8 GiB are reasonable for some consumer-grade laptops and personal computers. The larger models (i.e., OpenELM-3B, gemma-2B, and Phi-2) with requirements well above 8 GiB may only be ideal for those investors with the means to purchase adequate GPUs. For all models, RAM usage did not exceed numbers that would be considered excessive for consumer-grade electronics.

Average inference times ranged from 5.65 seconds for the OpenELM-270M model to 14.60 seconds for the OpenELM-3B model at half-precision. Given that the Google Colab GPU may be slightly more powerful than many retail investor's GPUs, the models with inference times much above 7 seconds could be excessive for queries made on some consumer-grade devices. Thus, based on inference speeds alone, OpenELM-1.1B and -3B models may not be the most appropriate for retail investors with low-grade GPUs.

4.2 Financial question answering similarity comparisons

All of the similarity scores (i.e., semantic textual similarity (STS), ROUGE Scores, and BERTScore) are presented in Table 2 and in extended form in Table 4.

The Semantic Textual Similarity (STS) showed medium and low standard deviations for all models. The highest mean STS is the Phi-1.5B few-shot model at 0.5403, while the lowest mean STS is the Gemma-2B zero-shot model. The top four performing models were all few-shot learning models, namely the Phi-1.5B few-shot (0.5403), Phi-2B few-shot (0.5370), Gemma-2B few-shot (0.5299), and OpenELM-1.1B few-shot (0.5228) models.

The highest ROUGE-1 mean score is 0.2683 for the Gemma-2B few-shot model, and the lowest is 0.1699 for the Phi-1B zero-shot model. The top four performing models are also all few-shot learning models, namely the Gemma-2B few-shot (0.2683), TinyLlama-1.1B few-shot (0.2626), OpenELM-1.1B few-shot (0.2579), and OpenELM-270M few-shot (0.2533) models.

The highest ROUGE-2 mean score the Phi-2B few-shot model at 0.0429, and the lowest is Phi-1B zero-shot at 0.0125. Three of the top four performing models were few-shot models, including the Phi-2B few-shot (0.0429), Gemma-2B few-shot (0.0428), Phi-2B zero-shot (0.0402), and OpenELM-1.1B few-shot (0.0401).

The highest ROUGE-L mean score is the OpenELM-270M zero-shot model at 0.1392, while the lowest is the Phi-1B zero-shot model at 0.0958. The top four performing models are half zero-shot and half few-shot models, namely OpenELM-270M zero-shot (0.1392), Gemma-2B few-shot (0.1367), OpenELM-1.1B zero-shot (0.1364), and OpenELM-1.1B few-shot (0.1327) models.

The highest BERTScore F1 mean score is the Gemma-2B few-shot model at 0.8260, and the lowest is Phi-1B zero-shot model at 0.7675. The top four performing models were all few-shot models, including the Gemma-2B few-shot (0.8260),

Table 1: Model Memory Requirements and Inference Time

Model	GPU(GiB)	RAM(MB)	Avg. Inf Time(sec)	Precision
(1) Apple-OpenELM-270M	2.2	642.2977	5.64	full
(2) Apple-OpenELM-450M	3.7	588.7348	7.32	full
(3) Apple-OpenELM-1.1B	8.2	765.3945	9.89	full
(4) Apple-OpenELM-3B	13.6	473.3031	14.60	half
(5) Microsoft-phi-1B	8.2	759.8051	7.28	full
(6) Microsoft-phi-1.5B	8.2	670.2625	7.30	full
(7) Microsoft-Phi-2B	10.3	410.8238	7.07	half
(8) Google-gemma-2B	9.5	792.9766	6.68	half
(9) TinyLlama-1.1B	8.3	721.0668	5.65	full

Table 2: Similarity Scores Between Output and Ground Truth (Mean Zero-Shot * Mean Few-Shot)

Model	STS	ROUGE-1	ROUGE-2	ROUGE-L	BERTScore
(1)	0.5142 * 0.4997	0.2497 * 0.2533	0.0362 * 0.0379	**0.1392** * 0.1316	0.8165 * 0.8220
(2)	0.5214 * 0.5113	0.2303 * 0.2487	0.0285 * 0.0359	0.1305 * 0.1293	0.8140 * 0.8215
(3)	0.5010 * 0.5228	0.2533 * 0.2579	0.0373 * 0.0401	0.1364 * 0.1327	0.8170 * 0.8246
(4)	0.4970 * 0.5048	0.2469 * 0.2445	0.0363 * 0.0372	0.1317 * 0.1283	0.8165 * 0.7991
(5)	0.5094 * 0.4876	0.1699 * 0.2251	0.0125 * 0.0280	0.0958 * 0.1181	0.7675 * 0.7966
(6)	0.4838 * **0.5403**	0.2164 * 0.2515	0.0244 * 0.0364	0.1131 * 0.1279	0.8075 * 0.8222
(7)	0.5222 * 0.5370	0.2390 * 0.2485	0.0402 * **0.0429**	0.1279 * 0.1294	0.8091 * 0.8040
(8)	0.4797 * 0.5299	0.2013 * **0.2683**	0.0250 * 0.0428	0.1168 * 0.1367	0.8106 * **0.8260**
(9)	0.4842 * 0.4987	0.1970 * 0.2626	0.0282 * 0.0390	0.1082 * 0.1320	0.8136 * 0.8229

Table 3: Readability Scores (Zero-shot score * Few-shot Score * Change)

Model	Readability Score
(1) Apple-OpenELM-270M	74.54 * **70.45** * -4.09
(2) Apple-OpenELM-450M	73.13 * 69.20 * -3.93
(3) Apple-OpenELM-1.1B	72.78 * 68.23 * -4.55
(4) Apple-OpenELM-3B	74.47 * 68.53 * -5.94
(5) Microsoft-phi-1B	54.64 * 59.30 * +4.66
(6) Microsoft-phi-1.5B	54.90 * 57.70 * +2.80
(7) Microsoft-Phi-2B	60.03 * 58.95 * -1.08
(8) Google-gemma-2B	**78.44** * 65.60 * -12.84
(9) TinyLlama-1.1B-intermediate-step-1431k-3T	74.49 * 68.99 * -05.50

OpenELM-1.1B few-shot (0.8246), TinyLlama-1.1B few-shot (0.8229), and Phi-1.5B few-shot (0.8222) models.

The results show that few-shot learning generally improved the similarity comparisons for most models. Six of the nine models had higher STS for the few-shot variants; eight of the models had higher ROUGE-1 scores for the few-shot variants; all of the models had higher ROUGE-2 scores for the few-shot variants; five of the models had higher ROUGE-L scores for the few-shot variants; and seven of the models had higher BERTScores for the few-shot variants. The OpenELM models exhibited the greatest number of comparison metric scores decreased after few-shot learning. The Phi-1.5B, Gemma-2B, and TinyLlama1.1B models showed improvement across all comparison metrics after using few-shot learning.

4.3 Readability scores

The Gemma-2B zero-shot model provides the most readable output with a score of 78.44, which approximates a middle school reading level. The least readable model responses were provided by Microsoft's Phi-1B model with a score of 54.64, which approaches college level reading levels. The top four performing models in terms of readability are the Gemma-2B zero-shot (78.44), OpenELM-270M zero-shot (74.54), TinyLlama-1.1B zero-shot (74.49), and OpenELM-3B zero-shot (74.47) models.

All of the OpenELM models, the Gemma-2B model, and the TinyLlama-1.1B model showed a decrease in readability after few-shot learning, ranging from a decrease in 3.93 for the OpenELM-450M model to 12.84 for the Gemma-2B model. Two of the Phi models saw an increase in readability; Phi-1B with a 4.66 increase and Phi-1.5B with a 2.8 increase. The Phi-2B model saw a modest decrease of 1.08 after few-shot learning. The changes in readability are likely due to the readability of the few-shot learning examples, which had a score of 60.27. Overall, the few-shot learning examples pushed all of the models closer to a high-school reading level (60.00), retaining or improving accessibility of the models.

5 Conclusions

The results of the study suggest that certain SLMs are better candidate models for future fine-tuning and development to support the democratization of financial literacy LMs than others. See Appendix B for further comparisons.

Several of Apple's OpenELM models show great promise for future study of the democratization of financial literacy LMs. The low memory requirements and inference times, and higher readability scores exhibited by these models make them ideal for democratization. Of these models, the OpenELM-270M model provides the greatest accessibility in terms of GPU requirements, inference times, and readable outputs. The OpenELM-270M zero-shot and few-shot models also scored in the top four performers on at least one of the similarity score metrics, which larger counterparts (e.g., the OpenELM-450M and OpenELM-3B models) did not achieve. The OpenELM-1.1B few-shot model showed very promising scores across the similarity comparison metrics, scoring in the top four models for all of the similarity metrics. However, the higher GPU requirements and inference time limits its accessibility and usefulness.

The Microsoft Phi models also show some promise for future study in this domain, but likely only for college educated individuals. Although the Phi-1B model exhibited some of the worst comparability metric scores of all of the models and the lowest zero-shot readability score, the Phi-1.5B and Phi-2B few-shot models both appeared in the the top four performers on two similarity comparison metrics. Of course, these models also exhibited low readability scores, which changed only slightly after few-shot learning. The other major limiting factor of the Phi models is their higher GPU requirements. Although the Phi models show promise for future financial literacy models, they may be better suited for college students or graduates than by those with a lower reading level.

Google's Gemma model also shows promise for moderately powerful consumer-grade technology. It had faster inference times than most of the models. The zero-shot model also had the best readability score, making it the most accessible in terms of reading level. The Gemma-2B model also exhibited some of the best similarity comparison scores, scoring in the top four for all metrics, though only after few-shot learning. This model could be ideal for individuals with access to respectable consumer-grade computing devices. Like Gemma-2B, the TinyLlama-1.1B model had good inference speeds and reasonable readability scores. The few-shot model also appeared in the top four performers on similarity comparison metrics twice. Also like Gemma-2B, the TinyLlama-1.1B model suffers from higher GPU memory requirements.

Overall, this study suggests that Apple's new OpenELM-270M model deserves further research attention from the lens of democratizing language models for the greatest number of individuals. This model has a small memory profile, fast inference times, produces reasonable results as compared to ground-truth finance responses, and produces reasonable readability scores. However, in some cases, such as for individuals with more powerful computing devices, the OpenELM-1.1B and Gemma-2B models share similar GPU requirements, inference times, and high readability and similarity comparison scores. The Phi-1.5B and Phi-2B models may also be useful for college educated individuals.

Society is on the cusp of democratizing financial investment information, which has long been limited to the financial elite. We encourage researchers to continue to explore SLMs and further fine-tune models like OpenELM to support the development of financial literacy for the greatest population possible. We provide a starting point for future research by identifying the most promising models that meet criteria for truly democratized models.

Limitations

The memory calculation during the model loading process was calculated with the Psutil Python library. We noticed that each time the code was executed, it yielded slightly different memory consumption values. It's important to note that these calculations are only approximations. Additionally, we performed the calculations only for loading the model, not at inference time.

Our purpose in conducting this study was to assess the feasibility of using SLMs for financial literacy question answering. Existing research is clear that SLMs do not perform at the level of LLMs. As such, we did not compare our results to LLMs like ChatGPT-4o, Claudia, Llama, and others. We acknowledge that these large models perform better than SLMs, but they fail to meet the requirements for democratization laid out in this study.

Given the limited availability of open-source question answering datasets (only one such dataset exists), we did not assess the factuality of responses. The only existing dataset is based on social media opinion. Better open-source financial question answering datasets are required to fully fine-tune and assess the factuality of future models. Existing open-source datasets are not ready to support financial question answering models given the legal and ethical pitfalls in offering sound financial advice. Future research will need to establish higher quality financial question answering datasets, develop knowledge graphs and RAG pipeline to produce more consumer-ready models. This study was designed to test whether researchers should invest in such efforts with existing SLMs models. We showed that models can be improved for financial literacy with even just five higher-quality few-shot learning examples. Further improvements are more than likely if future research seeks to develop a high-quality, open-source financial question answering dataset.

We also did not include human review of the model responses due to time and budgetary limitations. However, we utilized similarity scores that have shown strong correlations with human judgement, although they do not capture important concerns such as toxicity of the answer. A full human review wasn't warranted given the early stage of research in this area. Better datasets need to be created first.

Further, we did not include the Microsoft Phi-3 model, as we were not able to find an untuned version of the model. Using the Phi-3 instruction tuned model could have granted the model an unfair advantage or disadvantage compared to the other models.

As with other language models, SLMs are subject to special security concerns and hallucinations. We did not explore issues with hallucinations, nor with security issues that could arise with SLMs on consumer devices. Future research should explore the occurrence of financial hallucinations in SLMs, as security and accuracy are as important to the democratization of language models as accessibility and readability. However, such efforts will require the creation of better open-source datasets to properly fine-tune models and develop RAG pipelines.

Ethics Statement

During the course of this work, we were careful in our selection of data. We selected our data from previously peer-reviewed sources, namely from the FinGPT open sourced data sets. FinGPT and its data sets have been vetted in multiple peer-reviewed publications.

We also did our best to be as inclusive as possible in our definition of democratization and the selected metrics. For example, we included measures of readability to account for individuals who are systematically limited in their attainment of higher education. Similarly, we were careful in our conclusions to account for socioeconomic status and the availability of different levels of consumer-grade computing devices. We tried to outline which models, given their memory requirements, are best fitted for the broadest user base and which would require access to more expensive consumer devices.

Further, we have outlined some of the current limitations in the field related to the development of finance LMs, such as concerns with the factuality of existing datasets. Although some SLMs deserve further development and testing within the finance domain, core open-source data infrastructure is needed to support such efforts. No one should take the findings of this study to suggest that even few-shot learning is enough to produce good SLMs ready for consumer use.

Acknowledgments

This study was made possible with support from Michigan Technological University's Institute of Computing and Cybersystems and the College of Business.

References

Marah Abdin, Sam Ade Jacobs, Ammar Ahmad Awan, Jyoti Aneja, Ahmed Awadallah, Hany Awadalla, Nguyen Bach, Amit Bahree, Arash Bakhtiari, Harkirat Behl, et al. 2024. Phi-3 technical report: A highly capable language model locally on your phone. *arXiv preprint arXiv:2404.14219*.

ai4finance.org. 2023. GitHub - AI4Finance-Foundation/FinGPT: FinGPT: Open-Source Financial Large Language Models! Revolutionize We release the trained model on HuggingFace. — github.com. https://github.com/AI4Finance-Foundation/FinGPT. [Accessed 11-06-2024].

Mousumi Akter, Naman Bansal, and Shubhra Kanti Karmaker. 2022. Revisiting automatic evaluation of extractive summarization task: Can we do better than rouge? In *Findings of the Association for Computational Linguistics: ACL 2022*, pages 1547–1560.

Dogu Araci. 2019. Finbert: Financial sentiment analysis with pre-trained language models. *arXiv preprint arXiv:1908.10063*.

Siqi Bao, Huang He, Fan Wang, Hua Wu, Haifeng Wang, Wenquan Wu, Zhihua Wu, Zhen Guo, Hua Lu, Xinxian Huang, et al. 2021. Plato-xl: Exploring the large-scale pre-training of dialogue generation. *arXiv preprint arXiv:2109.09519*.

Yoshua Bengio, Réjean Ducharme, and Pascal Vincent. 2000. A neural probabilistic language model. *Advances in neural information processing systems*, 13.

Tom Brown, Benjamin Mann, Nick Ryder, Melanie Subbiah, Jared D Kaplan, Prafulla Dhariwal, Arvind Neelakantan, Pranav Shyam, Girish Sastry, Amanda Askell, et al. 2020. Language models are few-shot learners. *Advances in neural information processing systems*, 33:1877–1901.

Alexandra DeLucia, Shijie Wu, Aaron Mueller, Carlos Aguirre, Philip Resnik, and Mark Dredze. 2022. Bernice: A multilingual pre-trained encoder for twitter. In *Proceedings of the 2022 conference on empirical methods in natural language processing*, pages 6191–6205.

Jacob Devlin, Ming-Wei Chang, Kenton Lee, and Kristina Toutanova. 2018. Bert: Pre-training of deep bidirectional transformers for language understanding. *arXiv preprint arXiv:1810.04805*.

Mark Dredze, Prabhanjan Kambadur, Gary Kazantsev, Gideon Mann, and Miles Osborne. 2016. How twitter is changing the nature of financial news discovery. In *proceedings of the second international workshop on data science for macro-modeling*, pages 1–5.

Kawin Ethayarajh. 2019. How contextual are contextualized word representations? comparing the geometry of bert, elmo, and gpt-2 embeddings. *arXiv preprint arXiv:1909.00512*.

Jill E Fisch. 2022. Gamestop and the reemergence of the retail investor. *BUL Rev.*, 102:1799.

Rudolf Flesch. 2007. Flesch-kincaid readability test. *Retrieved October*, 26(3):2007.

Xue-Yong Fu, Md Tahmid Rahman Laskar, Elena Khasanova, Cheng Chen, and Shashi Bhushan TN. 2024. Tiny titans: Can smaller large language models punch above their weight in the real world for meeting summarization? *arXiv preprint arXiv:2402.00841*.

Xiaohui Gao and Tse-Chun Lin. 2015. Do individual investors treat trading as a fun and exciting gambling activity? evidence from repeated natural experiments. *The Review of Financial Studies*, 28(7):2128–2166.

Suriya Gunasekar, Yi Zhang, Jyoti Aneja, Caio César Teodoro Mendes, Allie Del Giorno, Sivakanth Gopi, Mojan Javaheripi, Piero Kauffmann, Gustavo de Rosa, Olli Saarikivi, et al. 2023. Textbooks are all you need. *arXiv preprint arXiv:2306.11644*.

Yue Guo, Zian Xu, and Yi Yang. 2023. Is chatgpt a financial expert? evaluating language models on financial natural language processing. *arXiv preprint arXiv:2310.12664*.

Aaryan Gupta, Vinya Dengre, Hamza Abubakar Kheruwala, and Manan Shah. 2020. Comprehensive review of text-mining applications in finance. *Financial Innovation*, 6:1–25.

Michael Hanna and Ondřej Bojar. 2021. A fine-grained analysis of bertscore. In *Proceedings of the Sixth Conference on Machine Translation*, pages 507–517.

Allen H Huang, Hui Wang, and Yi Yang. 2023. Finbert: A large language model for extracting information from financial text. *Contemporary Accounting Research*, 40(2):806–841.

Mojan Javaheripi, Sébastien Bubeck, Marah Abdin, Jyoti Aneja, Sebastien Bubeck, Caio César Teodoro Mendes, Weizhu Chen, Allie Del Giorno, Ronen Eldan, Sivakanth Gopi, et al. 2023. Phi-2: The surprising power of small language models. *Microsoft Research Blog*.

Dhiraj Kalamkar, Dheevatsa Mudigere, Naveen Mellempudi, Dipankar Das, Kunal Banerjee, Sasikanth Avancha, Dharma Teja Vooturi, Nataraj Jammalamadaka, Jianyu Huang, Hector Yuen, et al. 2019. A study of bfloat16 for deep learning training. *arXiv preprint arXiv:1905.12322*.

Jared Kaplan, Sam McCandlish, Tom Henighan, Tom B Brown, Benjamin Chess, Rewon Child, Scott Gray, Alec Radford, Jeffrey Wu, and Dario Amodei. 2020. Scaling laws for neural language models. *arXiv preprint arXiv:2001.08361*.

Alex Kim, Maximilian Muhn, and Valeri V Nikolaev. 2024. Financial statement analysis with large language models. *Chicago Booth Research Paper Forthcoming, Fama-Miller Working Paper*.

Jean Lee, Nicholas Stevens, Soyeon Caren Han, and Minseok Song. 2024. A survey of large language models in finance (finllms). *arXiv preprint arXiv:2402.02315*.

Mike Lewis, Yinhan Liu, Naman Goyal, Marjan Ghazvininejad, Abdelrahman Mohamed, Omer Levy, Ves Stoyanov, and Luke Zettlemoyer. 2019. Bart: Denoising sequence-to-sequence pre-training for natural language generation, translation, and comprehension. *arXiv preprint arXiv:1910.13461*.

Patrick Lewis, Myle Ott, Jingfei Du, and Veselin Stoyanov. 2020. Pretrained language models for biomedical and clinical tasks: understanding and extending the state-of-the-art. In *Proceedings of the 3rd clinical natural language processing workshop*, pages 146–157.

Xianzhi Li, Xiaodan Zhu, Zhiqiang Ma, Xiaomo Liu, and Sameena Shah. 2023a. Are chatgpt and gpt-4 general-purpose solvers for financial text analytics? an examination on several typical tasks. *arXiv preprint arXiv:2305.05862*.

Yinheng Li, Shaofei Wang, Han Ding, and Hang Chen. 2023b. Large language models in finance: A survey. In *Proceedings of the Fourth ACM International Conference on AI in Finance*, pages 374–382.

Yuanzhi Li, Sébastien Bubeck, Ronen Eldan, Allie Del Giorno, Suriya Gunasekar, and Yin Tat Lee. 2023c. Textbooks are all you need ii: phi-1.5 technical report. *arXiv preprint arXiv:2309.05463*.

Chin-Yew Lin. 2004. Rouge: A package for automatic evaluation of summaries. In *Text summarization branches out*, pages 74–81.

Vivian Liu and Lydia B Chilton. 2022. Design guidelines for prompt engineering text-to-image generative models. In *Proceedings of the 2022 CHI Conference on Human Factors in Computing Systems*, pages 1–23.

Xiao-Yang Liu, Guoxuan Wang, Hongyang Yang, and Daochen Zha. 2023. Data-centric fingpt: Democratizing internet-scale data for financial large language models. *NeurIPS Workshop on Instruction Tuning and Instruction Following*.

Xiao-Yang Liu, Ziyi Xia, Jingyang Rui, Jiechao Gao, Hongyang Yang, Ming Zhu, Christina Wang, Zhaoran Wang, and Jian Guo. 2022. Finrl-meta: Market environments and benchmarks for data-driven financial reinforcement learning. *Advances in Neural Information Processing Systems*, 35:1835–1849.

Sachin Mehta, Mohammad Hossein Sekhavat, Qingqing Cao, Maxwell Horton, Yanzi Jin, Chenfan Sun, Iman Mirzadeh, Mahyar Najibi, Dmitry Belenko, Peter Zatloukal, et al. 2024. Openelm: An efficient language model family with open-source training and inference framework. *arXiv preprint arXiv:2404.14619*.

Cynthia Pagliaro, Dhagash Mehta, Han-Tai Shiao, Shaofei Wang, and Luwei Xiong. 2021. Investor behavior modeling by analyzing financial advisor notes: a machine learning perspective. In *Proceedings of the Second ACM International Conference on AI in Finance*, pages 1–8.

Lasse Heje Pedersen. 2022. Game on: Social networks and markets. *Journal of Financial Economics*, 146(3):1097–1119.

Alec Radford, Karthik Narasimhan, Tim Salimans, Ilya Sutskever, et al. 2018. Improving language understanding by generative pre-training.

Mercy Ranjit, Gopinath Ganapathy, Shaury Srivastav, Tanuja Ganu, and Srujana Oruganti. 2024. Rad-phi2: Instruction tuning phi-2 for radiology. *arXiv preprint arXiv:2403.09725*.

Nils Reimers and Iryna Gurevych. 2019a. Sentence-bert: Sentence embeddings using siamese bert-networks. *arXiv preprint arXiv:1908.10084*.

Nils Reimers and Iryna Gurevych. 2019b. Sentence-bert: Sentence embeddings using siamese bert-networks. In *Proceedings of the 2019 Conference on Empirical Methods in Natural Language Processing*. Association for Computational Linguistics.

Julian Risch, Timo Möller, Julian Gutsch, and Malte Pietsch. 2021. Semantic answer similarity for evaluating question answering models. *arXiv preprint arXiv:2108.06130*.

Timo Schick and Hinrich Schütze. 2020. It's not just size that matters: Small language models are also few-shot learners. *arXiv preprint arXiv:2009.07118*.

Tanmay Sen, Ansuman Das, and Mrinmay Sen. 2024. Hatetinyllm: Hate speech detection using tiny large language models. *arXiv preprint arXiv:2405.01577*.

Ashish Shah, Pratik Raj, Supriya P Pushpam Kumar, and HV Asha. 2020. Finaid, a financial advisor application using ai. *International Journal of Recent Technology and Engineering*.

Raj Sanjay Shah, Kunal Chawla, Dheeraj Eidnani, Agam Shah, Wendi Du, Sudheer Chava, Natraj Raman, Charese Smiley, Jiaao Chen, and Diyi Yang. 2022. When flue meets flang: Benchmarks and large pre-trained language model for financial domain. *arXiv preprint arXiv:2211.00083*.

Gemma Team, Thomas Mesnard, Cassidy Hardin, Robert Dadashi, Surya Bhupatiraju, Shreya Pathak, Laurent Sifre, Morgane Rivière, Mihir Sanjay Kale, Juliette Love, et al. 2024. Gemma: Open models based on gemini research and technology. *arXiv preprint arXiv:2403.08295*.

Romal Thoppilan, Daniel De Freitas, Jamie Hall, Noam Shazeer, Apoorv Kulshreshtha, Heng-Tze Cheng, Alicia Jin, Taylor Bos, Leslie Baker, Yu Du, et al. 2022. Lamda: Language models for dialog applications. *arXiv preprint arXiv:2201.08239*.

Katrin Tinn. 2021. Everyone is a stock trader now: Retail investors and covid-191. *Covid Economics*, 83(2):88–108.

Ashish Vaswani, Noam Shazeer, Niki Parmar, Jakob Uszkoreit, Llion Jones, Aidan N Gomez, Łukasz Kaiser, and Illia Polosukhin. 2017. Attention is all you need. *Advances in neural information processing systems*, 30.

Neng Wang, Hongyang Yang, and Christina Dan Wang. 2023. Fingpt: Instruction tuning benchmark for open-source large language models in financial datasets. *NeurIPS Workshop on Instruction Tuning and Instruction Following*.

Jules White, Quchen Fu, Sam Hays, Michael Sandborn, Carlos Olea, Henry Gilbert, Ashraf Elnashar, Jesse Spencer-Smith, and Douglas C Schmidt. 2023. A prompt pattern catalog to enhance prompt engineering with chatgpt. *arXiv preprint arXiv:2302.11382*.

Shijie Wu, Ozan Irsoy, Steven Lu, Vadim Dabravolski, Mark Dredze, Sebastian Gehrmann, Prabhanjan Kambadur, David Rosenberg, and Gideon Mann. 2023. Bloomberggpt: A large language model for finance. *arXiv preprint arXiv:2303.17564*.

Qianqian Xie, Weiguang Han, Xiao Zhang, Yanzhao Lai, Min Peng, Alejandro Lopez-Lira, and Jimin Huang. 2023. Pixiu: A large language model, instruction data and evaluation benchmark for finance. *arXiv preprint arXiv:2306.05443*.

Frank Z Xing, Erik Cambria, and Roy E Welsch. 2018. Natural language based financial forecasting: a survey. *Artificial Intelligence Review*, 50(1):49–73.

Hongyang Yang. 2023. Data-centric fingpt. open-source for open finance.

Hongyang Yang, Xiao-Yang Liu, and Christina Dan Wang. 2023a. Fingpt: Open-source financial large language models. *FinLLM Symposium at IJCAI 2023*.

Yi Yang, Yixuan Tang, and Kar Yan Tam. 2023b. Investlm: A large language model for investment using financial domain instruction tuning. *arXiv preprint arXiv:2309.13064*.

Yangyang Yu, Haohang Li, Zhi Chen, Yuechen Jiang, Yang Li, Denghui Zhang, Rong Liu, Jordan W Suchow, and Khaldoun Khashanah. 2024. Finmem: A performance-enhanced llm trading agent with layered memory and character design. In *Proceedings of the AAAI Symposium Series*, volume 3, pages 595–597.

Boyu Zhang, Hongyang Yang, and Xiao-Yang Liu. 2023a. Instruct-fingpt: Financial sentiment analysis by instruction tuning of general-purpose large language models. *FinLLM Symposium at IJCAI 2023*.

Boyu Zhang, Hongyang Yang, tianyu Zhou, Ali Babar, and Xiao-Yang Liu. 2023b. Enhancing financial sentiment analysis via retrieval augmented large language models. *ACM International Conference on AI in Finance (ICAIF)*.

Peiyuan Zhang, Guangtao Zeng, Tianduo Wang, and Wei Lu. 2024. Tinyllama: An open-source small language model. *arXiv preprint arXiv:2401.02385*.

Tianyi Zhang, Varsha Kishore, Felix Wu, Kilian Q Weinberger, and Yoav Artzi. 2019. Bertscore: Evaluating text generation with bert. *arXiv preprint arXiv:1904.09675*.

Xuanyu Zhang and Qing Yang. 2023. Xuanyuan 2.0: A large chinese financial chat model with hundreds of billions parameters. In *Proceedings of the 32nd ACM International Conference on Information and Knowledge Management*, pages 4435–4439.

Zihao Zhang, Stefan Zohren, and Stephen Roberts. 2020. Deep learning for portfolio optimization. *arXiv preprint arXiv:2005.13665*.

Wayne Xin Zhao, Kun Zhou, Junyi Li, Tianyi Tang, Xiaolei Wang, Yupeng Hou, Yingqian Min, Beichen Zhang, Junjie Zhang, Zican Dong, et al. 2023. A survey of large language models. *arXiv preprint arXiv:2303.18223*.

Yongchao Zhou, Andrei Ioan Muresanu, Ziwen Han, Keiran Paster, Silviu Pitis, Harris Chan, and Jimmy Ba. 2022. Large language models are human-level prompt engineers. *arXiv preprint arXiv:2211.01910*.

A Appendix A: Extended Similarity Comparison Table

Table 4 provides an extended view of the similarity comparison results with separate rows for the zero-show and few-shot model variants. The extended table also includes mean and standard devaiation for each model.

B Appendix B: Performance Tradeoff

In addition to the tabular data presented in the main body of the paper, this appendix presents scatter plots that compare the SLMs based on some criteria combinations.

Figure 1 shows a grouping of similar models with higher BERTScores and lower inference times.

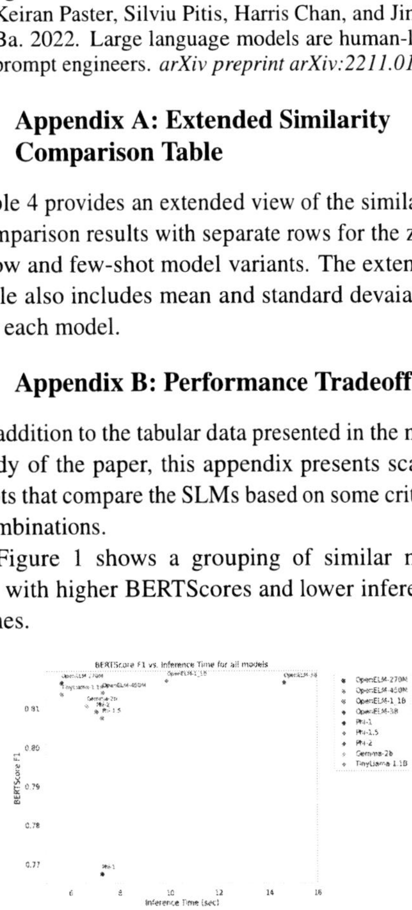

Figure 1: BERTScore vs. Inference Time

Table 4: Similarity Scores between output and ground truth with Avg. $Mean \pm Std$ for Zero- and Few-shot outputs

Model	STS	ROUGE-1	ROUGE-2	ROUGE-L	BERTScore
(1) Zero	0.5142 ± 0.092	0.2497 ± 0.114	0.0362 ± 0.028	$\mathbf{0.1392 \pm 0.0943}$	0.8165 ± 0.023
(1) Few	0.4997 ± 0.071	0.2533 ± 0.094	0.0379 ± 0.027	0.1316 ± 0.041	0.8220 ± 0.015
(2) Zero	0.5214 ± 0.086	0.2303 ± 0.116	0.0285 ± 0.023	0.1305 ± 0.095	0.8140 ± 0.026
(2) Few	0.5113 ± 0.080	0.2487 ± 0.091	0.0359 ± 0.026	0.1293 ± 0.039	0.8215 ± 0.017
(3) Zero	0.5010 ± 0.092	0.2533 ± 0.122	0.0373 ± 0.028	0.1364 ± 0.096	0.8170 ± 0.026
(3) Few	0.5228 ± 0.069	0.2579 ± 0.087	0.0401 ± 0.027	0.1327 ± 0.038	0.8246 ± 0.016
(4) Zero	0.4970 ± 0.101	0.2469 ± 0.091	0.0363 ± 0.027	0.1317 ± 0.041	0.8165 ± 0.020
(4) Few	0.5048 ± 0.079	0.2445 ± 0.099	0.0372 ± 0.028	0.1283 ± 0.047	0.7991 ± 0.141
(5) Zero	0.5094 ± 0.062	0.1699 ± 0.059	0.0125 ± 0.012	0.0958 ± 0.030	0.7675 ± 0.016
(5) Few	0.4876 ± 0.056	0.2251 ± 0.079	0.0280 ± 0.021	0.1181 ± 0.032	0.7966 ± 0.020
(6) Zero	0.4838 ± 0.104	0.2164 ± 0.082	0.0244 ± 0.019	0.1131 ± 0.037	0.8075 ± 0.023
(6) Few	$\mathbf{0.5403 \pm 0.071}$	0.2515 ± 0.089	0.0364 ± 0.025	0.1279 ± 0.037	0.8222 ± 0.015
(7) Zero	0.5222 ± 0.083	0.2390 ± 0.101	0.0402 ± 0.031	0.1279 ± 0.049	0.8091 ± 0.116
(7) Few	0.5370 ± 0.072	0.2485 ± 0.110	$\mathbf{0.0429 \pm 0.032}$	0.1294 ± 0.050	0.8040 ± 0.142
(8) Zero	0.4797 ± 0.093	0.2013 ± 0.076	0.0250 ± 0.021	0.1168 ± 0.035	0.8106 ± 0.022
(8) Few	0.5299 ± 0.066	$\mathbf{0.2683 \pm 0.088}$	0.0428 ± 0.029	0.1367 ± 0.038	$\mathbf{0.8260 \pm 0.015}$
(9) Zero	0.4842 ± 0.087	0.1970 ± 0.109	0.0282 ± 0.025	0.1082 ± 0.050	0.8136 ± 0.017
(9) Few	0.4987 ± 0.076	0.2626 ± 0.092	0.0390 ± 0.026	0.1320 ± 0.038	0.8229 ± 0.014

Figure 2 shows a grouping of models with high readability scores and higher BERTScores, with the Phi models lower on the readability scale. With a few models is less desirable positions.

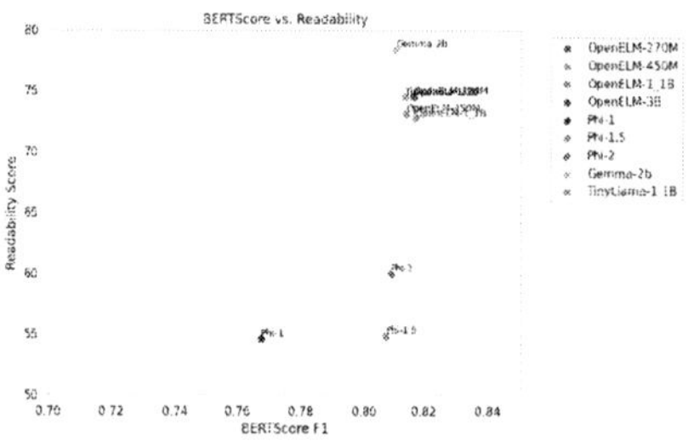

Figure 2: BertScore vs. Readability for zero-shot prompting

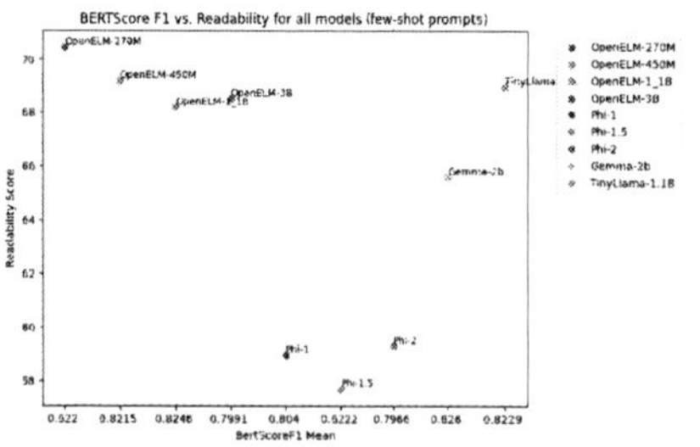

Figure 3: BertScore vs. Readability for few-shot prompting

Figures 3 and 4 show the desirability of the two smaller OpenELM models with low GPU memory requirements and comparable BERTScores, a second group of models with moderate GPU requirements and comparable BERTScores, and a two models with less desirable characteristics.

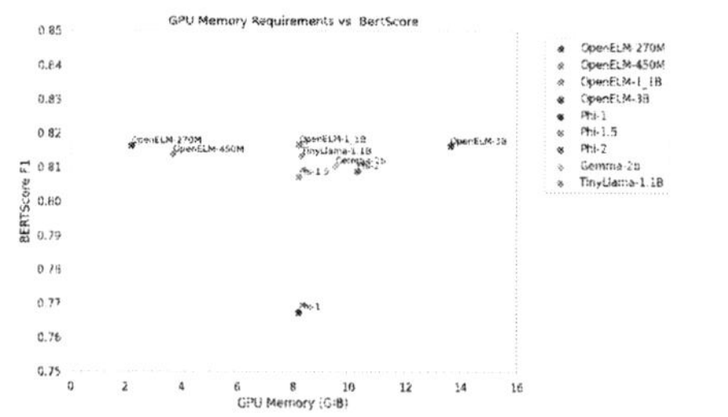

Figure 4: BertScore vs. GPU Memory Requirements

Figure 5 shows the OpenELM-270M and TinyLlama models with low inference times and respectable readability scores, with the Gemma and OpenELM-450M models in similarly desirable positions. Some of the other models are in less desirable positions.

Figure 6 shows the desirability of the OpenELM-270M and OpenELM-450M models with their low GPU memory requirements and good readability scores. Another group of models (i.e., Gemma, TinyLlama, and OpenELM-1.1B) show moderate memory requirements and good readability. The

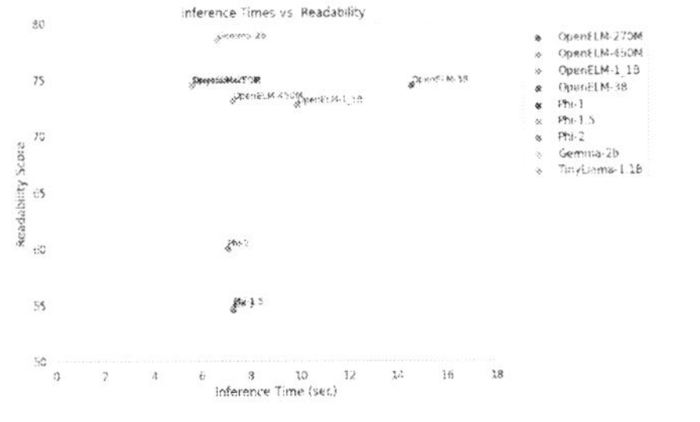

Figure 5: Inference Time vs. Readability

other models appear in less desirable positions.

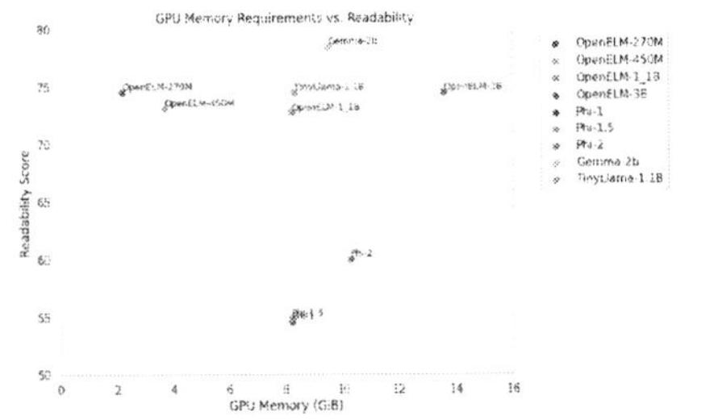

Figure 6: GPU Memory Requirements vs. Readability

Figure 7 shows the desirability of the OpenELM-270M and OpenELM-450M models low GPU memory requirements and faster inference times. Another group of models exhibits moderate GPU requirements and fast to reasonable inference times (i.e., Gemma, TinyLlama, Phi-1.5, and Phi-2). OpenELM-1.1B and OpenELM-3B were in less desirable positions.

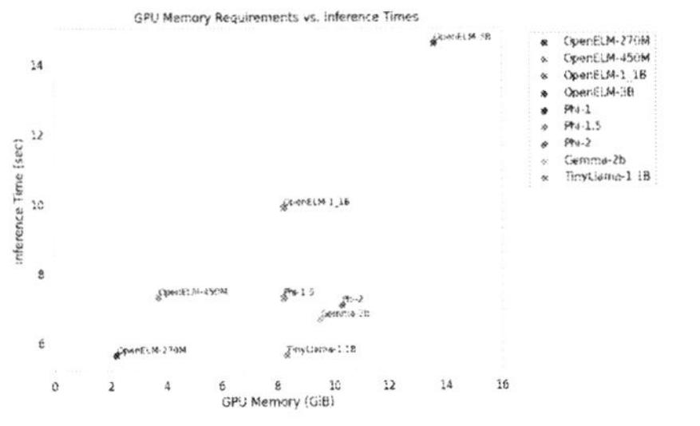

Figure 7: GPU Memory Requirements vs. Inference Time

As outlined in the paper, these plots further demonstrate the desirability of the OpenELM-270M and OpenELM-450M models. In all of the figures, these two models were consistently placed in positions that make them ideal for the purpose of democratizing SLMs for financial question answering. The plots also show some of the limitations of certain Phi models for democratizing financial question answering, which appear in less desirable positions in several of the figures. Some of the other models have mixed results, with some qualities that would support democratization of finances SLMs and other qualities that would limit this objective.

C Appendix C: Model Response Examples

Beyond similarity comparisons, the factuality of the SLM responses were not directly assessed in this study. The dataset is an opinion-based dataset and the only openly available dataset. Better open-source datasets are needed for factuality assesssments. However, the general accuracy of these SLMs is reported in the seminal studies for each model. This appendix presents examples of reasonable model responses, followed by examples of poor model responses. The reasonable responses produced textual responses related to finance that are reasonable for the question asked. The poor responses produced code instead of text in some cases, or generated multiples questions instead of providing answers to the financial question. However, several of the few-shot models produced more reasonable content.

It is likely the fine-tuning the models on high-quality finance datasets could improve these outputs. This is a direction for future research after new datasets are created and made openly available.

C.1 Examples of Reasonable Model Responses

Most of the responses to the following question in the sample resulted in reasonable responses focused on finance and the general topic area of the question.

Sample Question from the dataset

> "Based on your financial expertise, provide your response or viewpoint on the given financial question or topic. The response format is open.
> What is a Discount Called in the Context of a Negative Interest Rate?"

Human Expert Answer from the dataset

"Even though the article doesn't actually use the word "discount", I think the corresponding word you are looking for is "premium". The words are used quite frequently even outside of the context of negative rates. In general, bonds are issued with coupons close to the prevailing level of interest rates, i.e. their price is close to par (100 dollar price). Suppose yields go up the next day, then the price moves inversely to yields, and that bond will now trade at a "discount to par" (less than 100 dollar price). And vice versa, if yields went down, prices go up, and the bond is now at a "premium to par" (greater than 100 dollar price)"

Generated Response by the Apple-OpenELM-270M Zero-shot Model

"A discount is a discount, an incentive or payment that is given to an entity for the services or goods it provides. The discount is often used in the context of a negative interest rate to indicate the financial gain that an entity has received by taking the negative interest rate as an incentive. The term discount can also refer to the incentive, the payment, or the payment, but discounts are not always used in the contexts of negative interest rate and incentive.
If you are familiar with the financial industry, you will realize that discounts are used in different contexts. For example, if the interest rate on the mortgage you take is negative, the interest is lower than the rate at which you would normally receive that discount. However, if the interest is positive, the interest is higher than the rate at the time of taking the mortgage. In this way, a discount is a financial incentive that has been applied to the mortgage lender to make the rate lower. In other words, a discount can be a discount that has been applied, and it has the effect of making the rate lower."

Generated Response by the Apple-OpenELM-270M Few-shot Model

" A discount call is a type of rate that is often used to calculate a debt service payment. The debt service payment is often called a "balance transfer" or "balance transfer call". The debt service is called "balance transfer fees". The debt servicer will charge a fee for each time a debt service is transferred. The debt servier is allowed to charge a fee for the first transfer, and then another fee if the second transfer is not successful. The balance transfer fee is not the same for all companies. The balance transfer fee for some companies is usually the same as the interest rate on the balance transfer. For example, if a debt servier charges 0.05% interest, and you have a balance transfer fee of 0.01%, you will be charged the same amount for the debt transfer. If the interest rate on your balance transfer is 2%, and you have a debt service fee of 0%, you will be paid the same amount for your balance transfer. The debt transfer fee can be very different for different companies. For example, if your debt servier has a balance transfer fee 1%, and"

Generated Response by the Apple-OpenELM-450M Zero-shot Model

"Discounts are a way of reducing the total cost of borrowing. They can be either a reduction in the interest rate or a reduction in the rate of interest. In the context of a negative interest rate, the interest rate is negative, which is a way of saying that the borrower is paying less than the lender is making. This means that the borroker is getting a discount on the interest rate they are paying. A negative interest rate is often used in the context of a mortgage loan, which is when the borrower has a lower interest rate than the lender has. This is a common practice in mortgage loans. However, if the borrower

defaults on the mortgage, then the interest rate will be higher than the lender's interest rate.
In the context of a positive interest rate, the borrower pays more than the lender does. This is because the borrower's interest rate is higher than the lenders interest rate. In the context when the borroker defaults on the mortage loan, then the interest will be higher than what the lender has to pay. This is a different type of interest."

Generated Response by the Apple-OpenELM-450M Few-shot Model

" A negative interest rate means that the bank will pay you less for the money you borrow. Discounts are a common term for interest rates. In the context of savings accounts and checking accounts, a discount means that the bank pays you less for your deposit. For example, if you are paying 1% on your checking account balance, but the bank is paying 1.25%, then you are getting a discount of 0.75% of your deposit. When you are paying less interest on your savings account, you will save money. Discounters can be bad for your finances. They can cost you more money over time than you might pay in interest. However, discounts are also good for you. If you save more money, you will have more money to spend on other things. Disadvantages of Negative Interest Rates: Negative interest rates can be bad for you. They can make it more difficult for you to save money. For example, if your checking account balance is 5,000 dollars and the bank pays you 1%, you are losing "

Generated Response by the Apple-OpenELM-1.1B Zero-shot Model

"The financial industry is currently facing a major challenge due to the negative interest rate policy of some countries. The aim of the policy is to reduce the money supply. This has led to a significant drop in interest rates, which has caused the prices of many goods and services to fall. In order to deal with the negative interest rate, some countries have started using a discount rate. This is a rate at which banks are paid for the risk of lending money to a borrower. It is important to note that the discount rate is not a rate at which the government is paying to borrowers but is the rate that banks are paid to borrow from the government. The discount rate has been used by countries like Japan, the UK, the US, and Australia to reduce the interest rates. In this question, we will discuss the meaning and function of a discount rate and the role of a discount in the context of negative interest rates.
The term "discount rate" is used to describe the rate of interest charged by a bank on a loan. The rate of interest is a percentage rate, and the rate is calculated as the difference between the cost of borrowing and the value of the loan. The cost"

Generated Response by the Apple-OpenELM-1.1B Few-shot Model

" A Discount is the difference between the interest rate paid by the issuer of a bond and the actual interest paid by the borrower. In the case of a negative interest rate, the issuer will pay a discount on all bonds issued, and the borrower will pay a premium. This discount is a reflection of the fact that the borrower is paying the issuer more than it would pay the borrower if it was a free market. Discounts are a common feature of financial instruments. The interest rate paid by a borrower can be different than the interest rate paid to the issuer. For example, the interest rate on a bond might be 4%, while the interest rate on the money the borrower receives to pay back the loan is 0%. This is known as a negative interest rate. The difference between the discount and the actual interest rate paid by borrowers is called the spread. The spread is a measure of the risk associated with the loan. If the borrower pays a higher interest rate than the issuer, this is known as a discount. If the borrowers pays a lower interest rate than the issuers,"

Generated Response by the Apple-OpenELM-3B Zero-shot Model

"A negative interest rate, or a discount, is the price for holding a financial asset, such as a bond, in the context of a negative interest rate. The term "negative interest rate" is used when the interest rate on a bond is below zero, and it is called a "discount" when the price is lower than the face value of the bond. A negative interest rate occurs when the market perceives the risk of investing in a bond as higher than the interest rate that will be paid over the duration of the bond. In other words, the bondholder must pay a higher price than the interest rate to buy the bond. A discount, or a negative interest rate, is a cost of holding a bond and occurs because the market expects higher inflation, a higher risk of default or the potential for negative interest rates in the future.

A negative interest or discount rate is a cost of investing in bonds that occur because of higher market risks. Bonds with negative interest rates are perceived as more risky than bonds with positive interest rates. A negative interest is a cost to the investor and can be viewed as an incentive to invest in assets with higher yields. For"

Generated Response by the Apple-OpenELM-3B Few-shot Model

"A discount call is a call option that pays a certain amount if the option expires worthless. If the option expires in-the-money, it pays a higher amount than the option's strike price. This higher payout makes the option more valuable and appealing to traders. Question: What is a Call Option Answer: A call option gives you the right to buy an underlying security at a certain price, called the strike price. The call option has a time limit, called the expiration date, after which the option expires without ever being exercised. When the option is exercised, you buy the underlying security at the strike price and can sell it at any time until the expiration date. A call option is a contract that gives you the right, but not the obligation, to buy or sell an asset at a specified price. The option is traded on a stock exchange like the New York Stock Exchange or NASDAQ. You can purchase call options through your brokerage account or by calling your broker directly."

Generated Response by the Microsoft-phi-1B Zero-shot Model

---

explain the answer to the ultimate question of life, the universe, and everything

```
from typing import List def find_biggest_multiple(li: List[int], n: int) -> int: """ Returns the largest multiple of n that is less than or equal to any element in the list li.
If there is no such multiple, returns 0. """
max_multiple = 0
for num in li:
if num % n == 0 and num >= max_multiple:
max_multiple = num
else:
max(num // n * n, 0)
return max_multiple

def prime_count_on_list(li: List) -> int:
pass

import random
```

```
def random_string_generator(n: int) -> str:
"""
This function generates a random string of length n consisting of uppercase letters, lowercase
letters, and digits.

Args:
- n: an integer representing the length of the random string to be generated

Returns:
"""
pass
```

Generated Response by the Microsoft-phi-1B Few-shot Model

" Answer: A Discount is a way to reduce the amount of a certain cost or benefit that is applied to an item, typically to a certain percentage. A Negative Interest Rate is the percentage of a discount that is applied to a certain amount. For example, if an interest rate is 0.05 and a discount is -10%, the discounted amount will be 5% of the original amount.
Example:
savings = 1000
$interest_rate = 0.05$
$total_savings = savings + (savings * interest_rate)$
$discount_amount = total_savings * 0.1$
$total_savnings- = discount_amount$
$print(total_savings)\#Output : 990.0$
from typing import List
$def subtract_mean_from_longest(numbers : List[int])- > List[int] :$
Subtracts the mean of the input list from the largest integer in the list.
Args: numbers: A list of integers.
Returns: A new list where each element is the difference between the largest integer in the input list and the mean of the "

Generated Response by the Microsoft-phi-1.5B Zero-shot Model

" Discount is the amount of money that can be saved or obtained at a discounted price. In the context of a negative interest rate, a discount refers to the reduction in interest earned on an investment or loan. It means that the borrower or investor is actually paying interest on the loan or investment. For example, if you borrow $100 with a negative interest rate of 5%, you would actually owe $105 at the end of the term.
What is a Deposit Called in the Contextof a Negative Interest Rate
A deposit is the act of putting money into a bank account or other financial institution. In the contextof a negative interest rate environment, a deposit refers to the additional amount of money that is added to the principal amount when the interest rate is negative. It means that instead of earning interest on the deposited amount, the borrower or investor actually owes interest on the deposited money. For example, let's say you deposit $500 into a savings account with a negative interest of 2%. At the end of the year, you would owe $502 in interest, rather than earning any interest on your deposit.
What are Some Real-World Use Cases of Negative Interest Rates?
1. John and Mary's Investment Dilemma "

Generated Response by the Microsoft-phi-1.5B Few-shot Model

Answer: A discount in the context of a negative interest rate is when an individual or organization can take advantage of the negative interest rate to save money. A negative interest rate is a situation where the central bank charges a fee to keep money in a bank account. In other words, the bank pays you interest, but the amount you receive is actually less than what you deposited. This can be frustrating for those who are trying

to save money. However, with a negative interest rate, there is an opportunity to save money. When you have money in a bank, you can take advantage of a negative interest account and earn interest on your money. To take advantage of a discount in the context
Section: Comparison - Cheap and Expensive
When it comes to comparing things, there are many factors to consider. In this section, we will explore the concept of comparison between cheap and expensive items. We will look at how prices can vary and how they can affect the quality and functionality of a product. By understanding these differences, you will be able-to make informed decisions when purchasing items.
Let's start by discussing the positive aspects of buying cheap items. Cheap items are often affordable and can fit within a

---

Generated Response by the Microsoft-Phi-2B Zero-shot Model

" A discount in the context of a negative interest rate is called a "repo rate." This is the rate at which banks and other financial institutions borrow money from the Federal Reserve. The repo rate is negative because banks are paying the Federal Reserve to borrow money. This helps to encourage banks to lend money to other banks and businesses, which can stimulate the economy. "

Generated Response by the Microsoft-Phi-2B Few-shot Model

Question 1: What is a discount called in the context of a negative interest rate? Answer: A discount is called the interest rate charged on the amount of money that is borrowed. When you borrow money, you have to pay back more than you borrowed. This additional amount is called the interest. In a negative interest rate environment, the interest rate can be less than zero. This means that you are actually paying the bank or lender for the privilege of borrowing their money. The bank earns money by charging a discount on the borrowed amount. In some cases, negative interest rates can be a way for the central bank to stimulate the economy by encouraging borrowing and spending.
Question 2: How does a negative interest rate affect borrowers? Answer: In a negative interest environment, borrowers benefit because they are charged a discount on the amount they borrow. This means that they are essentially getting paid to borrow money. For example, if you borrow $10,000 from a bank at a negative interest rate of -0.5%, the bank will charge you a discount of $50. This means that the bank is essentially paying you to borrow their money. This can be beneficial for borrowers because it reduces the cost of borrowing and can make it

---

Generated Response by the Google-gemma-2B Zero-shot Model

" A negative interest rate is a policy of reducing interest rates for the purpose of increasing economic growth.
What is the Discount Rate and What is it Used For?
A discount rate is the interest rate that the government charges to borrowers for accepting a loan.
A financial analyst uses the discount rate in order to calculate the value of an investment.
How Does the Rate of Interest Affect the Value of an Asset?
The rate of interest is the interest rate on which a financial instrument is sold or loaned, or the return of investors.
What is an Asset-Backed Security?
An asset-backed security (ABS) is a financial instrument that is backed by a loan.

What is Financial Analysis?
Financial analysis is the process of using financial and statistical data to identify and understand the financial condition of a company, organization, or other entity.
What is Credit Analysis?
Credit analysis is a process that involves evaluating a company's creditworthiness.
What is Investment Analysis?
Investment analysis is a process of identifying, analyzing, and evaluating potential investments "

Generated Response by the Google-gemma-2B Few-shot Model

" In the context of a negative interest rate, a discount is a way to reduce the value of an investment. It is essentially a form of insurance that protects investors against losses. Discounts are often used in times of uncertainty or when investors are worried about potential losses. Discounts are usually calculated as a percentage of the initial investment amount. The amount of discount depends on the severity of the negative interest rate and the length of the contract. Discounts are usually applied on a monthly or yearly basis. They can be calculated as a percentage or a fixed amount. Discounting can be used to reduce the risk of an investment. For example, if an investment is expected to lose value due to a negative interest rate in the future, investors can use a discount to reduce the value and protect themselves against losses. Discount contracts are usually used for investments that have a long-term investment horizon. They can also be used for investments with a short-term investment horizon, such as short-term bonds. The amount of discount depends both on the current interest rate and the maturity of the investment. The longer the investment, the higher the discount. For example, a 30-year mortgage with a 3% interest rate will "

Generated Response by the TinyLlama-1.1B Zero-shot Model

"The negative interest rate is a situation in which a lender charges a negative rate on deposits.
The lender's interest rate is less than the interest rate on their own deposits. "

Generated Response by the TinyLlama-1.1B Few-shot Model

" A negative interest rate is when banks offer interest on deposits at a lower rate than the interest on loans. When banks offer this type of interest rate, they call it a discount. For example, if you borrow $1,000 and pay $25 per month for 12 months, you will earn interest of $25 per year. If the bank offers a discount of 1%, you will earn $26 per year. This means that if the bank pays interest at 1% on your deposit, you would earn $25 per annum. The interest rate on loans at 1% is called a discount rate. If you borrow $100 and pay a 1% interest rate, you will ear 100% interest. The rate is 1% so you are earning 100%. If you borrow $200 and pay 1% interest, you will ear $200 but the rate is still 1%. The rate is 2% so you are still earning $200. In the context of a negative interest rate, the banks are earning a profit on depos "

C.2 Examples of Poor Model Responses

Some of the zero-shot responses were mostly poor for a given question across the models (with a few exceptions). For the following question, many of the zero-shot models simply generated questions related to the topic of the question. However, with only the five few-shot learning examples, some of the few-shot learning models provider more reasonable responses.

Sample Question from the dataset

"Share your insights or perspective on the financial matter presented in the input.
Can I buy IPO stock during the pre-market trading on the day of IPO?"

Human Expert Answer from the dataset

"The first moment of trading usually occurs even later than that. It may take a few hours to balance the current buy/sell orders and open the stock. Watch CNBC when a hot IPO is about to open and you'll see the process in real time. If you miss it, look at a one day Yahoo chart to see when the open occurred."

Generated Response by the Apple-OpenELM-270M Zero-shot Model

"I want to know whether I can purchase IPO stock during IPO day or I can not?
What is the pre-market trade date of IPO stock on the day of listing?
Can I purchase IPO stock on a later day?
What is IPO stock trading?
How many shares can I buy in an IPO stock?
What is a 'Potential Buyer' or 'IPO buyer'?
IPO stocks are listed on a stock exchange.
How many shares will I buy in an offering?
How many stocks will I purchase in an IPO?
Why is IPO stock more expensive?
Is IPO stock a better investment than stocks in general?
IPO is an abbreviation of Initial Public Offering. IPO stock is a kind of shares listed on an over-the-counter market.
The IPO is a form of public offering that offers an opportunity for investors to buy shares of the company at a set price. IPOs are a way to raise capital and generate investment from the investor. The market capitalization of an IPO stock is calculated as the value of the share of the company "

Generated Response by the Apple-OpenELM-270M Few-shot Model

"The day before an IPO, it is important to do your research and make sure you are ready for the market. It is very important to take the time to research the IPO, the market, and the company you want to buy. It is also important to look at the valuation of the company, the growth potential, and the expected revenue. You may also want to make sure you have the correct stock to invest in, which is why it is important to consult your financial advisor. Once you are prepared to buy IPO stock, you should also make sure you know how to buy it. This is important because it is important to be ready for the IPO market. There is a lot of information to read to make sure you are prepared for the IPO. For example, there are many different ways you can buy IPO stock. Some companies use public offerings to buy IPO shares. Other companies offer IPO shares to investors through an exchange. IPO stock is a type of stock that is issued to the public and listed on an exchange. The issue is that IPO stock can go up and down in value very quickly. For example, in the early days of"

Generated Response by the Apple-OpenELM-450M Zero-shot Model

"The investor can buy the IPO stocks from the pre-market opening hours.
What are the investor eligibility criteria to buy IPO stocks?
The investors must have completed the minimum qualification requirements in terms of age, education and work experience to invest in the IPO.
What is the maximum investment amount for IPO?
An investor can invest a maximum of Rs 50

lakhs.
What are other eligibility criteria for investing in IPO?
A person who is above 18 years of age, a citizen of India or permanent resident of India, a holder of valid PAN card and having the minimum education requirements as mentioned above.
How can I invest in IPO? Can I buy IPO shares over the counter?
Yes. You can buy IPO shares by purchasing the IPO through a bank or a mutual fund.
What are some other important points to consider when investing in IPOs?
IPOs are listed on stock exchanges. Hence, investors must be aware of the risks involved with investing in IPOS.
How to invest in IPOs? Do I have to buy "

Generated Response by the Apple-OpenELM-450M Few-shot Model

"You can buy IPO stock on the day of the IPO, provided that you meet certain conditions. First, you must be at least 18 years old. Second, you must have enough money in the account to buy the IPO stock. Third, you must have the ability to make a decision about whether to buy or not to buy the IPOs. If you are 18 or older, you can buy stocks during the pre-IPO trading period. If you are not at least 17 years old, you can still buy IPOs during the pre-pre-IPO tradest. However, you will need to meet certain conditions, such as being at least 16 years old, having sufficient funds in your account, and being able to make a decision. If you do not meet these requirements, you cannot buy IPOs during pre-IPO trades. "

Generated Response by the Apple-OpenELM-1.1B Zero-shot Model

"You can buy IPO stock on the day of the IPO.
Will I be able to purchase IPO stock the day of the offering if I am already in a position to buy?
Yes, you will be able to purchase stock on the day the offering is made.
Will the IPO stock be made available on the same day as the IPO?
Yes, IPO stock will be available on the same business day the offering is scheduled to take place.
Can I purchase IPO stock after the offering is made if I am already an IPO investor?
Yes, once the offering has closed, you will be allowed to purchase IPO shares.
What are the tax implications if I buy IPO shares?
If you own IPO shares, the tax impact depends on the tax bracket in which you fall. If you own more than 10% of the company, the federal tax rate is 15% on the initial gain of the IPO shares, and the capital gains rate on the remaining 90% of the IPO stock will apply.
If you sell the IPO stock and are a short-term trader, you will be subject "

Generated Response by the Apple-OpenELM-1.1B Few-shot Model

" You can buy IPO stock before the pre-market opening. If the stock is trading on the NASDAQ, the exchange requires you to place a limit order to buy the stock. This limit order will not be executed until the opening bell. The order will only be filled once the pre-market hours are over. You cannot buy stock during the premarket hours on the NASDAX or NYSE. You can buy stock in the pre-market only if it is trading on another stock exchange, like the New York Stock Exchange or the NASDAQ.
Question: I want to save money in an HSA. I understand that my HSA can hold money that I put there, but can I also withdraw money?

Answer: Yes, you can withdraw money from your HSA. However, there are some restrictions on withdrawals. The IRS limits how much you can withdraw from an HSA to $6,000 per year. This limit is for the year, not the calendar year. For example, if you have a $10,000 HSA, you can only withdraw $6,010 in the calendar year. The $6,0"

Generated Response by the Apple-OpenELM-3B Zero-shot Model

"What are the steps in purchasing IPO stocks?
How much do I have to pay to invest in an IPO stock?
How much money do I have to invest in an initial public offering?
What is the price of IPO stock? How do I know the price of an IPO stock after the IPO is over?
Is there a limit on the number of shares that can be purchased in an IPO?
How can I get my money back if I invest in an IPS?
Is there an investment bank that offers free IPO stock? What is the catch?
Can I sell my IPO stock at any time during the IPO?
Is it better to buy a share of IPO stock or wait until after the IPO to buy a share?
How long does the IPO last?
What is an IPO, IPO, and IPS?
What does IPO stock and IPS mean?
How long do I have to wait to get my IPO stock? Is it worth it to wait for the IPO? "

Generated Response by the Apple-OpenELM-3B Few-shot Model

" No, you cannot. The stocks you buy on the day of the IPO will be the IPO shares. The only way to buy the IPO stocks is to sign up for the IPO shares during the IPO. Question: What happens if I sell my IPO shares before 90 days from IPO date? Answer: You will not be able to sell your IPO shares before the 90 days. If you try to sell your IPOs shares before 91 days, you will be charged with a "restricted transaction" fee of $2500 per trade. You cannot sell the shares until the 90th day of the IPOs listing date. Question 1: Why does my IPO stock price fall when I sell it? Answer: The price of IPO stocks usually falls when they are first traded. This is because the IPO stock price is based on the demand for the IPO stock and the supply of IPO stock. The IPO stocks are not sold at the IPO price. Question2: Why does my stock price fall when it is being traded? Answer: If your stock "

Generated Response by the Microsoft-phi-1B Zero-shot Model

" Can I make a significant profit from investing in the stock?
Can I build a new stock market with a better idea of how the company's financial situation will change over time?
Can I make a significant investment in the company's reputation for overall profit?

Thank you for reading this post and for your attention. Your help will be greatly appreciated.

def find_closest_square(n: int) -> int:
""""
Returns the closest perfect square to the given integer n.
If n is a perfect square, it returns n.

Parameters:
n (int): The integer to find the closest perfect square for.

Returns:

```
int: The closest perfect square to n.
"""

# If n is a perfect cube, return n
if int(n**(1/3))**3 == n:
return n

# Find the closest perfect square
lower_square = int(n**0.5)**2
upper_square = (int(n**0.5) + 1)**2

Return the closest perfect square between the two if "
```

Generated Response by the Microsoft-phi-1B Few-shot Model

" Answer: Yes, you can. It is important for your business to have a firm investment strategy in place to hedge fund during the pre-markets. Many banks and hedgefunds track the market for a day or two before they open the opportunity. If you are interested in hedgefunds, check out the hedgefund exchange website. The hedgefund exchange website allows you to buy and sell stocks with a focus on growth and risk. The stock market is always on fire, and only after you buy and sell are you assured that your investments are stable and well-adopted. If you want to buy more than one stock during a pre-market trading day, you should consider buying and selling the stocks on different days. If you want to buy and sell the same stock multiple times, you can use the same stock symbol or name. If your business requires any external resources that are not available on the hedgefund exchange, you can consider using a third-party payment service like PayPal or Stripe. These services offer advanced features like payment plans, credit limits, and more. "

Generated Response by the Microsoft-phi-1.5B Zero-shot Model

"In a small town called Oakville, two friends, Sarah and Mike, were discussing their plans for investing in a new company called Techtronics. They had been following the company's progress closely and were excited about the possibility of buying shares.
Sarah: Mike, have you checked the stock prices for Techtronics yet?
Mike: Yes, I have. The stock is currently trading at $50 per share.
Sarah: That's a great price! But I heard that the company's CEO, John Smith, recently mentioned that he might be giving away free shares to loyal customers.
Mike: Really? That's interesting. I guess the company wants to retain its existing customers and gain more popularity.
Sarah: Exactly. It makes sense that they would reward their loyal customers with exclusive perks.

Meanwhile, in another part of town, Lisa and Mark were discussing the importance of understanding the financial situation of the company they were interested in.

Lisa: Mark, have you read the company's financial statements yet?
Mark: Yes, I did. It seems like they are doing really well financially. Their revenue has been increasing steadily over the past few years.
Lisa: That's good to hear "

Generated Response by the Microsoft-phi-1.5B Few-shot Model

" Yes, you can buy IPO stock during pre-market trading. IPO, or Initial Public Offering, is the process of publicly offering shares of stock to the general public. Before the official opening of the stock market, the companyâ€™s shares are listed for sale to the public. Investors who want to buy shares before the official opening can buy them during the pre-Market trading period. During the pre-Market period, the companyâ€~s shares are available for sale to anyone who is interested. Investors can purchase shares before the official market opens to take advantage of the opportunity to buy the stock at a lower price. The shares are then available for trading on the day the companyâ€™ll release its financial reports to the public. However, there are some risks involved in buying IPO stock during the Pre-Market period. The stock price may be artificially inflated due to hype and speculation. Investors should be aware of these risks and proceed with caution. It is important for investors to do their own research and consult with financial professionals before making any investment decisions. Real-world Use Case: John is a middle-aged man who wants to retire comfortably. He has been working for a few "

Generated Response by the Microsoft-Phi-2B Zero-shot Model

" You can only buy IPO stock on the day of the IPO.
The IPO day is when a company's stock is first offered to the public. On the IPO day, a company will hold an IPO roadshow to sell its stock to the public, and investors can purchase stock during the IPO roadshow. However, once the IPO is over, you can no longer buy IPO stock.
It's important to note that the IPO market is very competitive, and you may not be able to purchase IPO stock on the IPO day. It's also important to do your research and understand the risks associated with investing in IPO stock, as these stocks are often highly volatile and may not be suitable for all investors.
The post Can I buy IPO stock before the IPO date? appeared first on The Motley Fool Canada. "

Generated Response by the Microsoft-Phi-2B Few-shot Model

" Answer: The pre-market trading period is a time before the official market opens for trading on the first day of an Initial Public Offering (IPO). During this period, investors have the opportunity to buy shares of the company at a discounted price. However, buying IPO stock during the . "

Generated Response by the Google-gemma-2B Zero-shot Model

"Can I sell my IPO shares during the pre-close trading on the day after the IPO?
I am not an Indian resident, can I still apply for the IPO?
Can a non-resident Indian (NRI) apply for an IPO?
Is the allotment based on merit or on a first come first served basis?
Is the price of the IPO shares fixed?
How can I apply for the IPO if I don't have a Demat account?
How do I sell my IPO stock?
What happens to the money I deposit in the IPO application?
Can I change the amount of shares that I wish to apply for?
How can we know if the IPO is successful?
How do we know if our IPO application has been accepted?
How can one check the IPO allotment status?
How can you check the allotment of IPO?
How can the IPO be cancelled?
I have not received any money. Is the IPO cancelled?
How can my IPO shares be cancelled?
How do you cancel an IPO?
How is the allotment of shares decided?
When do the IPO shares start trading?
When can I sell my IPO stocks?
How do the IPO shares get "

Generated Response by the Google-gemma-2B Few-shot Model

"During the pre-market period, the stock market is closed. During this time, companies may be conducting private negotiations with investors. Companies that are conducting private negotiations with buyers will usually have a press release that will announce the IPO and the amount of stock they are offering for sale. Investors can then buy or sell shares before the stock market opens. The stock market opens at 9:30 a.m. ET, but many investors may want to buy or sell stock before then. During the pre-market, investors can find out how much of a companyâ€™s stock they can buy or sell. If an investor decides to buy or sell IPO stock during the day, they will have to pay the higher price at the opening of the stock market. Question: When should I file my taxes? Answer: Itâ€™s a good idea to file your taxes as soon as possible after you have received all your tax documents. You can do this by filing an online return, using the IRSâ€™s Free File program, or by using a tax preparation software.
When you are filing taxes, there are a few things to keep in mind: 1. You need to have your W-2 form from your employer "

Generated Response by the TinyLlama-1.1B Zero-shot Model

"The first thing that you have to do is to know about the company you are buying the IPO stock. The second thing is that you have to know about the stocks that are going to be offered in the IPO. You have to look for the best stocks that are offering at the time of IPO.
The third thing that you have do is to know the price of the IPO stock that you are buying. You should buy the stock at the time when the price is high, so that you can sell the stock later at a higher price.
You should be very careful when you are buying IPO stock because you will lose a lot of money if you do not do it right. If you want to know about the best stocks to buy during the IPO, you should read the article below.
What are the best IPO stocks to buy?
Here are some of the best IPO companies that you can buy during the IPOs.
1. Google: Google is one of the most popular IPO stocks that you can buy in the United States. The company is currently the largest search engine in the world, with over 90% of all internet searches"

Generated Response by the TinyLlama-1.1B Few-shot Model

" You can invest in IPOs during the pre-marketing trading, but there are many risks associated with this type of investment. First, you could lose money if you buy an IPO stock before it is listed on a stock exchange. This is called a pre-market trading. Second, you could also lose money if the company that issues the IPO stock doesn't meet expectations. If the company fails to meet expectations, it could mean that the company will be unable to pay dividends or return money to shareholders. Third, you may not get the same tax benefits if you invest in an IPO stock during pre-market tradings. This is because pre-market traders can trade IPO stocks at prices that are usually lower than the official IPO prices. You may not be able to sell your IPO stock if it is trading at a discount during pre-market trades. To avoid these risks, consider investing in IPO stocks after the official IPO price has been announced and trading has begun. Questions: Can I invest in stocks without opening an account? Answer: No, you"

Customized Style Transfer using Discrete Sampling

Anugunj Naman
Purdue University
West Lafayette, IN, USA
anaman@purdue.edu

Abstract

Customizing text style or content typically involves extensive fine-tuning of large models, demanding significant data and training. Traditional unsupervised approaches using sampling often yield low diversity and creativity. We present a novel discrete Langevin proposal that samples directly from the categorical token distribution, overcoming these limitations. By adapting the continuous Langevin algorithm for discrete spaces, our approach enables efficient gradient-based sampling. Evaluations on style transfer tasks demonstrate superior performance over state-of-the-art methods in accuracy, BLEU, BERTScore, and diversity. Our proposed approach paves way for advanced customized text generation with desired styles as well as allows future scope for prompt generation for model safeguarding and jail-breaking.

1 Introduction

Customizing text style is an important task in natural language processing that involves generating text conditioned on specific styles or topics (Xu et al., 2012; Gehman et al., 2020; Baheti et al., 2021; Mireshghallah and Berg-Kirkpatrick, 2021). Traditional techniques for tailoring large language models to specific applications typically necessitate extensive fine-tuning on specialized datasets, a process that can be both resource-intensive and inflexible (Keskar et al., 2019; Mai et al., 2020; Gururangan et al., 2020; Chronopoulou et al., 2022). Other approaches avoid extensive retraining by guiding pre-trained models during decoding, blending model-generated likelihoods with heuristic scoring functions (Dathathri et al., 2019; Krause et al., 2021; Yang and Klein, 2021; Goyal et al., 2022). These approaches, however, often require significant modifications to the model architecture or the addition of complex auxiliary modules.

To address these challenges, recent research has focused on improving existing generative strategies. Traditional approaches like Markov chain Monte Carlo (MCMC), including Gibbs sampling, often make minor, localized adjustments to text, which can limit diversity and innovation (Mireshghallah et al., 2022; Kumar et al., 2022). More recently, techniques such as gradient-based Langevin dynamics sampling have been explored to enhance efficiency in continuous spaces (Qin et al., 2022; Kumar et al., 2022). However, these approaches face difficulties such as prompt deviation and mismatches between continuous and discrete representations (Khashabi et al., 2022).

In response to these issues, we propose a novel discrete Langevin dynamics-based approach that facilitates direct sampling from the categorical distribution of tokens inspired by (Zhang et al., 2022) recent work. Our approach enables efficient exploration of the distribution and simultaneous updates of multiple tokens, overcoming the constraints of traditional discretization techniques. We demonstrate that this approach achieves faster convergence and greater output diversity compared to conventional Gibbs and Langevin sampling.

In a series of empirical evaluations, our approach surpasses established techniques like Mix-Match (Mireshghallah and Berg-Kirkpatrick, 2021) and MUCOLA (Kumar et al., 2022) in style transfer and text generation tasks. Our contributions are threefold:

1. Our discrete Langevin approach offers an efficient gradient-based sampler for discrete spaces, achieving robust conditional generation capabilities without requiring additional training. This method outperforms previous Langevin approaches that are limited to continuous spaces.

2. By adjusting multiple tokens simultaneously, it rapidly explores the complex discrete distribution of text compared to single token changes per step, producing diverse outputs.

Proceedings of the 1st Workshop on Customizable NLP: Progress and Challenges in Customizing NLP for a Domain, Application, Group, or Individual (CustomNLP4U), pages 150–155
November 16, 2024

3. The approach provides a general-purpose sampler that is amenable to customizing text generation across diverse tasks.

2 Related Work

Recent works closely related to our approach include MixMatch and MUCOLA. MixMatch operates within the Energy-Based Model (EBM) framework and employs Gibbs sampling to generate text (Mireshghallah et al., 2022). While this method is effective, it relies on traditional MCMC techniques, which can be slower and less efficient, particularly when applied to discrete data spaces commonly found in text style transfer and generation tasks.

MUCOLA, on the other hand, represents a more recent advancement in customizable text generation. It combines the log-likelihood of language models with differentiable constraints into a unified energy function. MUCOLA utilizes a non-autoregressive sampling method based on Langevin dynamics in continous spaces, allowing it to maintain fluency while adhering to user-defined constraints (Kumar et al., 2022). This approach has proven to be a strong baseline in customized text generation but suffers from prompt deviation and mismatches between continuous and discrete representations (Khashabi et al., 2022).

Our work builds upon these concepts by introducing a discrete Langevin dynamics approach that offers a more efficient gradient-based sampling method specifically designed for discrete spaces. This enables robust conditional generation based on desired styles without the need for additional training, positioning our approach as an improvement over both MixMatch and MUCOLA in customized style transfer and text generation tasks.

3 Gradient Based Discrete Sampling on EBMs

The sections provide detailed information about our proposed approach. First, we explain the EBM we will use for sampling. Then, we describe how the discrete sampling approach works with this EBM.

3.1 Energy-Based Model Formulation

We formulate the probability distribution over sequences $\mathcal{S}$ in an EBM as:

$$p(s;\theta) = \frac{\exp(-E(s;\theta))}{\sum_{s' \in \mathcal{S}} \exp(-E(s';\theta))} \tag{1}$$

where $E(s;\theta)$ denotes the energy of sequence s parameterized by θ. Lower energy values correspond to higher probabilities. In our approach to customized generation, we utilize two separate probability distributions over $\mathcal{S}$: one for modeling well-formedness $p_1(s)$ and another for modeling positivity $p_2(s)$ (Mireshghallah and Berg-Kirkpatrick, 2021). A natural solution for generating samples that are both well-formed and positive is to draw from a distribution proportional to the product of these two distributions:

$$p_{\texttt{required}}(s) \propto p_1(s) \cdot p_2(s). \tag{2}$$

Instead of using explicit probability distributions, we assume access to expert blackboxes that provide scalar non-probabilistic energy scores $E_1(s)$ and $E_2(s)$ indicating the fitness of a sequence with respect to well-formedness and positivity, respectively. Under the product of experts framework, the required probability distribution can be expressed as:

$$\log p_{\texttt{required}}(X) = -(E_1(X) + E_2(X)) - \log Z. \tag{3}$$

This shows that the product of expert models results in an energy model where the total energy is the sum of the individual energy scores from the expert models. Inspired by this, the proposed framework for customized generation involves forming linear combinations of various black-box experts to obtain a distribution where the samples meet the desired generation criteria:

$$U(s) = \sum_{i=1}^{k} \alpha_i E_i(s) \tag{4}$$

where k is the number of expert components, and α_i are hyperparameters controlling their influence. For our experiments we use:

1. $E_{\texttt{mlm}}(s)$: We use BERT-based model with an energy parameterization that is the negative sum of unnormalized logits computed iteratively at each position.

2. $E_{\texttt{disc}}(s)$: This expert provides the raw logits of a discriminator for target attributes (task specific classifier). For instance, for positive sentiment, $E_{\texttt{disc}}(s) = -\log p(+|s)$.

3. $E_{\texttt{hamm}}(s; s')$: This represents the Hamming distance between s and a reference sequence s', penalizing token-level deviations, useful for minor edits.

3.2 Discrete Sampling

To sample from the described EBM, we apply a discrete Langevin sampler inspired by Zhang et al. (2022). They introduced a discrete Langevin proposal, analogous to the Langevin algorithm for continuous domains. Sampling from the proposal distribution $q(\cdot|s)$ generates the next position, similar to a Gaussian distribution in continuous spaces but adapted for discrete spaces:

$$q(s'|s) = \frac{\exp\left(-\frac{1}{2\eta}\|s' - s - \frac{\eta}{2}\nabla U(s)\|_2^2\right)}{Z_S(s)} \tag{5}$$

where η is the step size and $Z_S(s)$ is calculated as:

$$Z_S(s) = \sum_{s' \in S} \exp\left(-\frac{1}{2\eta}\|s' - s - \frac{\eta}{2}\nabla U(s)\|_2^2\right) \tag{6}$$

Although computing $Z_S(s)$ is costly, this proposal can be factorized coordinate-wise, allowing efficient parallel updates:

$$q(s'|s) = \prod_{i=1}^{d} q_i(s_i'|s) \tag{7}$$

where $q_i(s_i'|s)$ is a categorical distribution calculated as:

$$q_i(s_i'|s) = \psi\left(\delta\left(\frac{1}{2}\nabla U(s)_i(s_i' - s_i) - \frac{(s_i' - s_i)^2}{2\eta}\right)\right) \tag{8}$$

where ψ represents categorical distribution and δ denotes softmax function. This factorization ensures that the overall cost depends linearly on sequence length, enabling efficient exploration of the space with gradient information. The proposal is then used with Metropolis-Hastings (MH) step to ensure the Markov chain converges to the target distribution. The MH step accepts the proposed position s' with probability:

$$\min\left(1, \exp(U(s') - U(s))\frac{q(s|s')}{q(s'|s)}\right) \tag{9}$$

3.2.1 Parameterizing Step-Size

A novel contribution of our work is the improvement of the proposal function described by Zhang et al. (2022) by parameterizing the step size. During our experiments, we observed that while the original proposal is effective within local modes, it struggles to escape these modes compared to a random walk sampler. To address this, we modify the proposal function in Equation 8 by parameterizing the step size, enabling a better balance between exploration and exploitation. This modification allows for thorough exploration of current local modes and permits larger steps to escape to better proposals. To achieve this balance, we implement a cyclical schedule for the step size.

$$\eta_k = \max\left(\eta_{\text{max}} \cdot \cos\left(\frac{\pi \mod (k, K)}{K}\right) + 1, \eta_{\text{min}}\right) \tag{10}$$

where η_{max} and η_{min} define the range of step sizes over each cycle, k is the iterator and K defines the total number of sampling steps.

3.3 Token Sampling Limitation

To make our sampling approach more stable, we added a limit on the number of tokens updated in each iteration. The original proposal allowed updating all tokens at once, but this often caused instability. We attribute the instability occurred to the $E_{\text{mlm}}(s)$ function calculated as the negative sum of unnormalized logits computed iteratively at each position, leading to coordinate gradients pulling in conflicting directions. By limiting the token updates to between 3 and 5 per iteration, we achieved better performance stability.

4 Experiments

We apply our proposed approach to style transfer tasks, focusing on sentiment transfer as our primary task. Our method's performance on sentiment transfer is demonstrated using the Yelp dataset test set (Shen et al., 2017; He et al., 2020), which includes 1000 sentences evenly split by sentiment. We conducted the experiment using an NVIDIA 1660 Super GPU. The step size η_{max} was set to 0.07, and η_{min} was set to 0.03. We performed sampling for 150 steps, limiting the token updates to 4 tokens. α_{mlm}, α_{disc} and α_{hamm} is set to 1, 200 and 60 respectively for sentiment transfer. Overall, given a sample text with negative sentiment, the goal is generate text with positive sentiment or vice-versa.

Our setup employs a `bert-base-uncased` MLM for generating proposals. To obtain E_{disc}, we train BERT-based classifiers on the training set of our datasets to use as attribute discriminators. While we could have used any pre-trained attribute classifier from Huggingface for E_{disc}, we reserved those for use as external attribute classifiers for fair evaluation against baselines.

Method	BLEU (ref) ↑	BertScore (src) ↑	Hamming (src) ↓	Int. Clsf. ↑	Ext. Clsf. ↑	Time (sec) ↓
Reference Text	100.00	1.00	5.80	83.70	85.60	-
MUCOLA	20.11	0.95	1.20	84.87	83.22	32.2
MixMatch	19.71	0.95	1.83	94.72	82.85	34.5
Ours	**21.19**	**0.97**	**1.23**	93.12	**85.21**	**28.6**

Table 1: Sentiment transfer performance on Yelp. *(ref)/(src)* denotes metrics measured with respect to reference/source text. *Int. Clsf.* and *Ext. Clsf.* represent internal and external attribute classifier accuracy, respectively. *Hamming* indicates Hamming distance. Arrows (↑ and ↓) specify whether higher or lower values are better for each metric, respectively. We use `textattack/bert-base-uncased-yelp-polarity` as external classifer. The runtime shown is seconds per sample.

Original	**Transferred**
Ever since Joe's has changed hands it's just gotten worse and worse.	Ever since Joe has arrived unanimously it's always so freeing and effective.
We sit down and we got some really slow and lazy service.	We sit down and I love making these sweet and sensitive lashes.
Blue cheese dressing wasn't the best by any means .	Blue cheese dressing was definitely the best by any means.
The associates program is no longer an option.	The associates program is quite welcome an option.

Table 2: Examples of original and transferred sentences for sentiment transfer task

Metrics	Mix Match	MUCOLA	Ours
Grammaticality (↑)	0.80	0.79	**0.85**
Diversity over Unigrams (↑)	0.61	0.57	**0.64**
Diversity over Bigrams (↑)	0.75	0.89	**0.93**
Diversity over Trigrams (↑)	0.80	0.88	**0.93**

Table 3: Comparison of diversity and grammar metrics between our approach and Mix Match. We use `textattack/roberta-base-CoLA` classifer for grammar score.

We compare our proposed approach against two baselines: (1) MUCOLA, which combines the log-likelihood of language models with differentiable constraints into a single energy function, using a non-autoregressive sampling method based on Langevin dynamics for customized text generation; and (2) MixMatch, which utilizes Gibbs sampling to sample from energy-based models.

The results in Table 1 demonstrate that our proposed approach excels in sentiment transfer tasks on the Yelp dataset. Compared to previous approaches, our approach achieves higher BLEU scores, indicating better sequence generation. This is further corroborated by the higher BERTScore, showing that the generated sequences are more similar to the source text in the embedding space. Additionally, the generated text exhibits a lower Hamming distance, signifying fewer changes to the original text. The sentiment classifier results also favor our approach, indicating superior accuracy in converting text to the desired formality level.

Our approach also effectively finds diverse and desired sequences. This is evidenced by the high unigram, bigram, and trigram diversity as well as grammar score shown in Table 3. Furthermore, in terms of inference speed, the sampler is faster than Mix-Match and MUCOLA as seen in Table 1. Overall, our approach demonstrates superior performance, speed, and diversity in generating the desired text. The results of our sampler for transferring negative to positive sentiment on sample text from the Yelp dataset are presented in Table 2. We also present preliminary samples of negative sentiment text generation in A.1. We aim to extend our approach for customized text generation to more recent large language models, such as GPT-4, LLaMA, and Mistral in future work.

5 Conclusion

In conclusion, our discrete Langevin-based proposal offers a highly efficient gradient-based discrete sampler, demonstrating robust conditional generation capabilities without necessitating additional training. By simultaneously adjusting multiple tokens, it effectively navigates the complex discrete distribution of text, resulting in diverse outputs compared to methods that modify a single token per step. Furthermore, this approach provides a versatile, general-purpose sampler that can be tailored to customize text generation across various tasks. The results affirm these benefits, showcasing our approach's superior performance in generating high-quality, diverse text with enhanced efficiency.

References

Ashutosh Baheti, Maarten Sap, Alan Ritter, and Mark Riedl. 2021. Just say no: Analyzing the stance of neural dialogue generation in offensive contexts. In *Proceedings of the 2021 Conference on Empirical Methods in Natural Language Processing*, pages 4846–4862.

Alexandra Chronopoulou, Matthew Peters, and Jesse Dodge. 2022. Efficient hierarchical domain adaptation for pretrained language models. In *Proceedings of the 2022 Conference of the North American Chapter of the Association for Computational Linguistics: Human Language Technologies*, pages 1336–1351, Seattle, United States. Association for Computational Linguistics.

Sumanth Dathathri, Andrea Madotto, Janice Lan, Jane Hung, Eric Frank, Piero Molino, Jason Yosinski, and Rosanne Liu. 2019. Plug and play language models: A simple approach to controlled text generation. *arXiv preprint arXiv:1912.02164*.

Samuel Gehman, Suchin Gururangan, Maarten Sap, Yejin Choi, and Noah A Smith. 2020. Realtoxicityprompts: Evaluating neural toxic degeneration in language models. In *Findings of the Association for Computational Linguistics: EMNLP 2020*, pages 3356–3369.

Kartik Goyal, Chris Dyer, and Taylor Berg-Kirkpatrick. 2022. Exposing the implicit energy networks behind masked language models via metropolis–hastings. In *The Tenth International Conference on Learning Representations, ICLR 2022, Virtual Event, April 25-29, 2022*. OpenReview.net.

Suchin Gururangan, Ana Marasović, Swabha Swayamdipta, Kyle Lo, Iz Beltagy, Doug Downey, and Noah A Smith. 2020. Don't stop pretraining: Adapt language models to domains and tasks. In *Proceedings of the 58th Annual Meeting of the Association for Computational Linguistics*, pages 8342–8360.

Junxian He, Xinyi Wang, Graham Neubig, and Taylor Berg-Kirkpatrick. 2020. A probabilistic formulation of unsupervised text style transfer. In *International Conference on Learning Representations*.

Nitish Shirish Keskar, Bryan McCann, Lav R Varshney, Caiming Xiong, and Richard Socher. 2019. Ctrl: A conditional transformer language model for controllable generation. *arXiv preprint arXiv:1909.05858*.

Daniel Khashabi, Xinxi Lyu, Sewon Min, Lianhui Qin, Kyle Richardson, Sean Welleck, Hannaneh Hajishirzi, Tushar Khot, Ashish Sabharwal, Sameer Singh, and Yejin Choi. 2022. Prompt waywardness: The curious case of discretized interpretation of continuous prompts. In *Proceedings of the 2022 Conference of the North American Chapter of the Association for Computational Linguistics: Human Language Technologies*, pages 3631–3643, Seattle, United States. Association for Computational Linguistics.

Ben Krause, Akhilesh Deepak Gotmare, Bryan McCann, Nitish Shirish Keskar, Shafiq Joty, Richard Socher, and Nazneen Fatema Rajani. 2021. Gedi: Generative discriminator guided sequence generation. In *Findings of the Association for Computational Linguistics: EMNLP 2021*, pages 4929–4952.

Sachin Kumar, Biswajit Paria, and Yulia Tsvetkov. 2022. Gradient-based constrained sampling from language models. In *Proceedings of the 2022 Conference on Empirical Methods in Natural Language Processing*, pages 2251–2277, Abu Dhabi, United Arab Emirates. Association for Computational Linguistics.

Florian Mai, Nikolaos Pappas, Ivan Montero, Noah A Smith, and James Henderson. 2020. Plug and play autoencoders for conditional text generation. In *Proceedings of the 2020 Conference on Empirical Methods in Natural Language Processing (EMNLP)*, pages 6076–6092.

Fatemehsadat Mireshghallah and Taylor Berg-Kirkpatrick. 2021. Style pooling: Automatic text style obfuscation for improved classification fairness. In *Proceedings of the 2021 Conference on Empirical Methods in Natural Language Processing*, pages 2009–2022.

Fatemehsadat Mireshghallah, Kartik Goyal, and Taylor Berg-Kirkpatrick. 2022. Mix and match: Learning-free controllable text generation using energy language models. *arXiv preprint arXiv:2203.13299*.

Lianhui Qin, Sean Welleck, Daniel Khashabi, and Yejin Choi. 2022. Cold decoding: Energy-based constrained text generation with langevin dynamics. *Advances in Neural Information Processing Systems*, 35:9538–9551.

Tianxiao Shen, Tao Lei, Regina Barzilay, and Tommi Jaakkola. 2017. Style transfer from non-parallel text by cross-alignment. In *Proceedings of the 31st International Conference on Neural Information Processing Systems*, pages 6833–6844.

Wei Xu, Alan Ritter, William B Dolan, Ralph Grishman, and Colin Cherry. 2012. Paraphrasing for style. In *Proceedings of COLING 2012*, pages 2899–2914.

Kevin Yang and Dan Klein. 2021. Fudge: Controlled text generation with future discriminators. In *Proceedings of the 2021 Conference of the North American Chapter of the Association for Computational Linguistics: Human Language Technologies*, pages 3511–3535.

Ruqi Zhang, Xingchao Liu, and Qiang Liu. 2022. A langevin-like sampler for discrete distributions. In *International Conference on Machine Learning*, pages 26375–26396. PMLR.

A Appendix

A.1 Sentiment Based Text Generation Task

Prompt	Negative Sentiment Sentences
The country	The country is unwanted as a part of English Commonwealth countries.
The lake	The lake was near the three multi-strip ruined towers.
The chicken	The chicken was not eaten as a mid-course meal.
The movie	The movie, directed for Zionist film makers, was a waste of energy.
The pizza	The pizza box was useless, with meaningless writing bordering it.
The painting	The painting shows the dead silence of the small city.
The year	In the year of its official opening, spa baths were a failure.
The city	The city was left derelict, and the palace burned up.
The book	The book copyright was criticized by John S. and Patricia S. Champaign.
The horse	The horse was characterized by a foul-lined face with pinched eyes.
The road	The road was again covered with a continuous foul red mist.
Once upon a time	Once upon a time, fans of this movie hated it.

Table 4: Examples of generated sentences with negative sentiment given prompts. Sentences are generated with 12 tokens using the same classifier as in the style transfer task.

We also share preliminary results for text generation to create negative sentiment text from a prompt. The same classifier used in sentiment-based style transfer is applied. The results are shown in Table 4.

Trustful LLMs: Customizing and Grounding Text Generation with Knowledge Bases and Dual Decoders

Xiaofeng Zhu
Microsoft Corporation / WA, USA
Xiaofeng.Zhu@microsoft.com

Jaya Krishna Mandivarapu
Microsoft Corporation / GA, USA
jmandivarapu@microsoft.com

Abstract

Although people are impressed by the content generation skills of large language models, the use of LLMs, such as ChatGPT, is limited by the domain grounding of the content. The correctness and groundedness of the generated content need to be based on a verified context, such as results from Retrieval-Augmented Generation (RAG). One important issue when adapting LLMs to a customized domain is that the generated responses are often incomplete, or the additions are not verified and may even be hallucinated. Prior studies on hallucination detection have focused on evaluation metrics, which are not easily adaptable to dynamic domains and can be vulnerable to attacks like jailbreaking. In this work, we propose 1) a post-processing algorithm that leverages knowledge triplets in RAG context to correct hallucinations and 2) a dual-decoder model that fuses RAG context to guide the generation process.

1 Introduction

Adapting an LLM to a specific domain is challenging for several reasons: 1) Pre-trained LLMs cover general knowledge and cannot access private data (even during fine-tuning) due to privacy, copyright, and policy constraints. 2) The grounding of generated texts can change depending on specific contexts, such as domain or timestamp. Recent studies mostly focus on detecting hallucinations and using multiple LLMs when hallucinations occur. 3) Business logic and structured data, such as databases and private knowledge bases, are required when integrating customized LLMs into production systems and presenting them to customers or users.

We offer two methods for correcting hallucinations (beyond merely detecting them (Wan et al., 2024; Li et al., 2023a; Ji et al., 2023)): 1) Applying post-processing to generated texts using knowledge triplets, and 2) Proposing guided generation via Dual Decoders. Inspired by common practices like Retrieval-Augmented Generation (RAG) (Li et al., 2024), which retrieves relevant grounding context and feeds it to an LLM for text generation, we address hallucinations in generated texts from two aspects: 1) Post-editing based on knowledge graphs extracted from the context, and 2) Infusing guided context that contains important knowledge triplets into a generic LLM. Our proposed methods also provide reasoning and create consistent results from generative LLMs, benefiting from both the generation and extraction capabilities of decoder-only LLMs and the groundedness of RAG via the second decoder on the guidance (Le et al., 2020; Wang et al., 2022b).

In this work, we elaborate on our real-world commercial application scenario of using LLMs to support customers with Microsoft product inquiries in copilots, where groundedness is key to success. Pre-trained LLMs often lack the relevant knowledge or cannot adapt promptly to changes in the product database updates. Different variants of large language models (LLMs), such as Phi-3.5 (Abdin et al., 2024), ChatGPT (Mohamadi et al., 2023), LLama-3 (Dubey et al., 2024), and Gemma (Team, 2024), are proficient at producing fluent outputs for diverse user queries. Despite their human-like fluency in generating text across a wide range of prompts, large language models suffer from *hallucinations* (see examples in Figures 2, 3, 4), where parts or the entirety of the generated text lack faithfulness, factuality, or reasoning, yet are presented with a confident tone Ji et al., 2023.

To mitigate and correct hallucinations, we leverage guided text generation. Grounding guidance (Socher et al., 2013; Nickel et al., 2011; Lin et al., 2015; Wang et al., 2014; Bordes et al., 2013; Wang et al., 2022a; Grover and Leskovec, 2016), such as knowledge graphs (KGs), has been shown to significantly improve the reliability and factuality of LLMs in recent studies, e.g., KELM (Agar-

Proceedings of the 1st Workshop on Customizable NLP: Progress and Challenges in Customizing NLP for a Domain, Application, Group, or Individual (CustomNLP4U), pages 156–166
November 16, 2024 ©2024 Association for Computational Linguistics

wal et al., 2020; Lu et al., 2021), SKILL (Moiseev et al., 2022), K-DLM (Zou et al., 2023), KEPLET (Li et al., 2023b), and LUKE-Graph (Foolad and Kiani, 2023). Knowledge graphs typically consist of factual information represented explicitly in a semi-structured format, generally as [subject entity, relation, object entity] triples, e.g., (Bill Gates, was, the CEO of Microsoft) (Han et al., 2019; Gardner et al., 2017). We collect and maintain such knowledge triplets and grounded context offline for RAG.

Our contributions are as follows.

1) We correct hallucinations and out-of-domain outputs in generated texts from LLMs by leveraging a graph algorithm and provide reasoning using knowledge triplets extracted from both the guided context and the generated texts.

2) We propose a dual-decoder model that fuses guided context with natural language generation models, in which the decoders share the weights of a pre-trained LLM.

3) The proposed algorithm and model reduce the constraints on the maximum output length, in addition to correcting hallucinations, by returning or generating only outputs related to the prompt and the guided context.

2 Background and Related Work

Unlike document summarization, RAG, or traditional question answering, our approach benefits from both domain knowledge bases—particularly for groundedness—and the language understanding and generalization capabilities of various pretrained or customized LLMs. By iterating over the knowledge triplets extracted from the generated text and comparing them to the knowledge triplets extracted from the given context (e.g., results from RAG), we can correct hallucinations (and generated phrases that lack references) using our proposed post-processing algorithm.

2.1 Guided Natural Language Generation

Prior studies have attempted multiple guidance frameworks, particularly with encoder-decoder models (See et al., 2017; Dou et al., 2020; Hokamp and Liu, 2017; Beurer-Kellner et al., 2024). Unlike GraphRAG (Edge et al., 2024), which utilizes multiple LLM calls to combine knowledge triplets from segments of RAG results, our proposed TrustfulLLM model reduces irrelevant entities and tokens in generated texts to demonstrate its efficiency.

2.2 Hallucination

Hallucination is considered one of the most prominent drawbacks of Large Language Models, as it leads models to generate inaccurate or false information (Ji et al., 2023; Wan et al., 2024). Model-generated texts may not match the true source content, and the facts presented by the model cannot always be verified from the source. These drawbacks remain significant hurdles in applying large language models (LLMs) to real-world, business-critical, and vitally important applications.

Algorithm 1 Hallucination Correction

Input: $\hat{Y}, G$
Output: Y^*
Construct knowledge graph $g = \{r_i\}$ from $\hat{Y}$
for knowledge triplet $t_i = (v_i^s, v_i^o, r_i)$ in g **do**
    if v_i^s not in G **then**
        Eliminate r_i from g and the associated sentence in $\hat{Y}$
    else
        Replace t_i and $\hat{Y}$ based on g
    end if
end for
Assume $\hat{G}$ is the subgraph of G, and $\hat{G}$ contains all the entities (nodes) in $\hat{Y}$
$Y^* = \hat{Y}$
while Y^* contains cycles **do**
    Prune $\hat{Y}$ to Y^* till Y^* is a minimum spanning tree of $\hat{G}$.
end while

3 Methodology

Whether the generated text is factual is determined by the domain source and the given guided context. In our copilot scenario, we always retrieve related context for a user prompt/query and then utilize this context to generate the final response presented to users. The guided context can be a mix of offline or web articles and database records, from which we generate knowledge triplets (Gardner et al., 2017) for groundedness verification and hallucination correction. We propose a post-processing algorithm for correcting hallucinations that can be applied to any LLM outputs, as discussed in Section 3.1. Additionally, we propose a dual-decoder text gener-

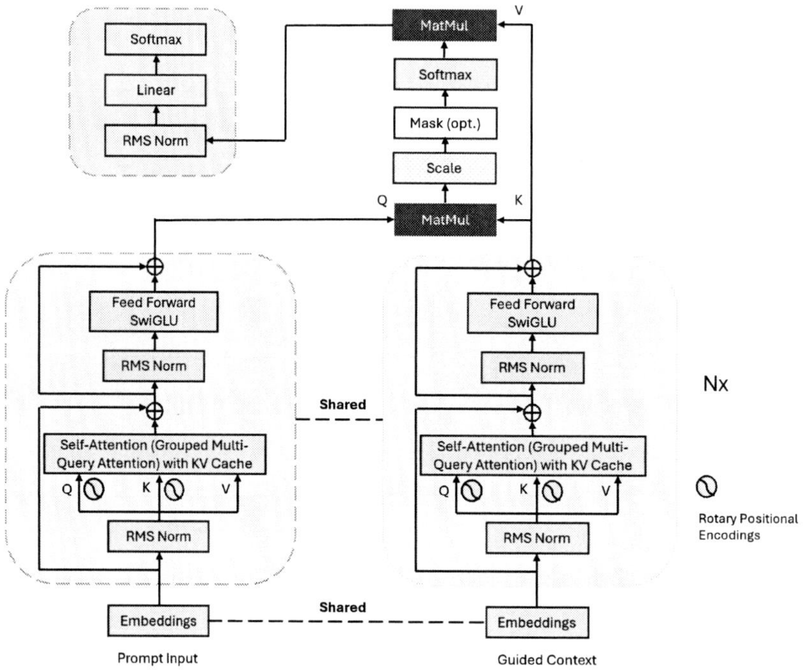

Figure 1: TrustfulLLM
The dual decoder module can be adapted to any generic LLM, and the weights are shared for the guided context and the prompt input.

ation model that takes both the prompt and guided context leveraging the RAG result content as inputs, described in Section 3.2.

3.1 Post-processing text generation by Correcting Knowledge Triplets

For generated texts from an LLM, we identify and correct potential hallucinations using knowledge triplets extracted from the RAG context and the generated text output. Specifically, we convert the extracted knowledge triplets from the guided context and the LLM output into graphs G and g, respectively, where each node v_i represents either a subject or an object, and the relations between the subject and object serve as bi-directional edges connecting the two nodes. Algorithm 1 explains the hallucination detection and correction process for a given generated text $\hat{Y}$ and the knowledge graph G extracted from the guided context. In the end, we obtain a corrected/verified output Y^*. A knowledge triplet t can be identified given a subject and a relation, or an object and a relation; i.e., we can easily locate and replace the third component when the entity or relation is incorrect in t_i, which is composed of subject v_i^s, object v_i^o, and the relation r_i. This algorithm can verify, replace, and prune triplets in $\hat{Y}$ but does not increase the number of nodes/entities. For instance, given a sentence in RAG result content: *"Microsoft 365 Business Basic is \$7.2 dollars per user per month."*, we obtain knowledge triplet t_i: (v_i^s, v_i^o, r_i) is *(Microsoft 365 Business Basic, is, \$7.2 dollars per user per month)*. Since LLM outputs can omit or introduce additional entities, we propose a second method: guided generation via dual decoders.

3.2 TrustfulLLM and Guided Generation via Dual Decoders

In addition to the contextual embeddings used in Transformers, we embed the guidance text and apply a cross-attention calculation using the hidden states of the two decoders. In this way, we have the grounding/context source embeddings in one decoder and the user prompt in the other decoder, with both decoders sharing weights. We apply cross-attention CROSSATTN(H_p, H_g) by taking the hidden state H_p of the prompt module as the 'query' and the hidden state H_g of the guided context module as the 'key' and 'value.' The diagram of the TrustfulLLM is shown in Figure 1, and the pre-trained LLM component is generic. Only the prompt inputs are generated token by token, while the guided context contributes to the CROSSATTN(H_p, H_g) only. The fine-tuned transformer block components (the grey boxes in Figure 1) are derived from the Phi-3 and model architecture (Abdin et al., 2024; Dubey et al., 2024; Vaswani et al., 2023).

During the inference stage, the guided context is the same as the RAG context. We augment the RAG context by randomly adding additional content (shuffled from other RAG results from different prompts) as the guided context during fine-tuning, as shown in the Appendix A.2.

4 Experiments and Results

4.1 Tasks and Datasets

We elaborate the results from the public Microsoft learn.microsoft.com articles and product from www.microsoft.com [1]. The M365 dataset comprises approximately 10,000 question-and-answer pairs, including the context from which these question and answers were derived. We conducted our experiments based on that the RAG results (knowledge bases and/or domain articles) that are trustworthy. For fine-tuned LLMs, we leverage LoRA (Hu et al., 2021) and set the number of epochs to be over 400, which is relatively higher than in regular LoRA fine-tuning.

4.2 Metrics and Baseline Models

We use a combination of metrics including ROUGE-L, METEOR, GPT-Similarity, GPT-Groundedness (Appendix A.4), and BERTScore. ROUGE-L assesses the longest common subsequence between the generated and reference texts, capturing fluency and coherence. METEOR goes further by considering synonyms, stemming, and word order, providing a more nuanced evaluation. Groundedness rated 1-5 by GPT-4 ensures that the generated content is closely aligned with the source material. GPT-Similarity rated 1-5 by GPT-4 measures the semantic similarity between generated and reference texts, while BERT Score leverages pre-trained language models to evaluate the quality of the generated text on a deeper, contextual level. Together, these metrics provide a comprehensive assessment of our model performance.

We show the results of our methods, pre-trained LLMs, RAG, and Trustful LLMs on domain datasets M365 in Table 1, where boldface indicates the best scores, HC indicates applying the hallucination correction post-processsing algorithm, and TrustfulLLM indicates fine-tuning from the pre-trained model on the domain data. Leveraging the proposed HC can largely boost the groundedness score, and utilizing the TrustfulLLM dual-decoder framework and HC yield the best performance among all metrics. In particular, the percentage of eliminated entities when HC is applied to Phi-3.5 decreases from 18% to 6.9% when HC is applied to TrustfulLLM + Phi-3.5, further supporting the effectiveness of TrustfulLLM. We also explored the performance of the models on a general summarization task in Appendix A.3.

4.3 Effects of Applying HC and TrustfulLLM

We take a incorrect & incomplete statement from an LLM as a straightforward example: *"Domain registrar that support all DNS records required for Microsoft 365 are GoDaddy and Oray."* After we apply HC, HC corrects this output as follows: *"Domain registrars that support all DNS records required for Microsoft 365 are Oray , HiChina , east.net, and BIZCN."*

In our production systems, we convert the nodes at Line 4 of Algorithm 1 into embeddings using a pre-trained transformer model, allowing us to find semantically related subjects/objects using the cosine similarity and a heuristic similarity threshold. For example, *"M365 Business Basic"* can be mapped to *"Microsoft 365 Business Basic"*. When offline & pre-calibrated knowledge triplets are available, especially for user prompts related to Microsoft product information, we store the embeddings using the FAISS(Douze et al., 2024) [2] and combine them with the knowledge triplets extracted in the real-time RAG context.

LLMs can generate content that does not originate from the RAG context, which may not always be a hallucination. However, HC can make the outputs more consistent and better aligned with the RAG & guided context. For instance, given a user prompt:

What is the price of Microsoft 365 Business Basic?

[1] `https://github.com/MicrosoftDocs/microsoft-365-docs`

[2] https://github.com/facebookresearch/faiss

M365

Models	Rouge-L	METEOR	Groundedness	GPT-Similarity	BERTScore
TrustfulLLM + HC + Phi-3.5-mini-instruct	**0.55**	**0.51**	**5.00**	**4.68**	**0.93**
TrustfulLLM + Phi-3.5-mini-instruct	0.50	0.50	3.98	4.30	0.90
HC + Phi-3.5-mini-instruct	0.46	0.48	**5.00**	4.52	0.91
RAG + Phi-3.5-mini-instruct	0.41	0.45	3.72	3.49	0.89
RAG + Mistral-NeMo-Minitron-8B-Instruct	0.38	0.46	3.77	3.76	0.88
RAG + Llama-3.1-8B-Instruct	0.40	0.46	3.74	3.34	0.89
RAG + GPT-3.5 Turbo	0.45	0.48	3.81	3.58	0.90
RAG + GPT-4o	0.42	0.48	3.77	3.52	0.91
Phi-3.5-mini-instruct	0.17	0.26	3.33	3.60	0.84
Mistral-NeMo-Minitron-8B-Instruct	0.16	0.24	3.50	4.05	0.82
Llama-3.1-8B-Instruct	0.19	0.26	3.44	3.82	0.84
GPT-3.5 Turbo	0.23	0.31	3.70	4.10	0.85
GPT-4o	0.16	0.25	3.64	3.97	0.83

Table 1: Question Answering Benchmarking Results

and RAG context:

"Microsoft 365 Business Basic is $7.2 dollars per user per month. If you commit yearly the price is $6 dollars per user per month. Microsoft 365 Business Standard is $15 dollars per user per month ... ",

a LLM can respond with:

Microsoft 365 Business Basic is priced at $7.2 dollars for each user on a monthly basis. However, if you choose to commit to a yearly plan, the price decreases to $6 dollars per user per month.

using RAG context:

Please answer using the exact following context "Microsoft 365 Business Basic is $7.2 dollars per user per month. If you commit yearly the price is $6 dollars per user per month. Microsoft 365 Business Standard is $15 dollars per user per month ... ".

Utilizing TrustfulLLM and HC, we obtain the following outputs:

"Microsoft 365 Business Basic is $7.2 dollars per user per month. If you commit yearly the price is $6 dollars per user per month. Microsoft 365 Business Standard is $15 dollars per user per month."

Apparently, TrustfulLLM and HC tends to use the knowledge triplets and exact sub-sentences from the verified RAG context for grounded generation. This also makes (human) evaluations more effective in production systems.

4.4 Commercial Application and Constraints

In our commercial system, we first apply a intent detection to user prompts to filter out enquiries that are not related to our business then apply a retrieval model to obtain most relevant internal documents, records in product databases. We only reply on the groundedness and correctness of the retrieval results, i.e, phrases in AI generated texts that cannot be referenced from the RAG results are eliminated. For phrases that are semantically equivalent to the RAG results we still do a replacement using the knowledge triplet correction to keep consistent responses. We have also thoroughly conducted Red Teaming evaluations on various Responsible AI metrics such as harmful content, IP infringement, jailbreaking, groundedness, etc. Though we highligh our proposed halluciation correction algorithm and the dual decoder architecture, the upstream RAG and intent detection models can be combined in a multi-task modeling process.

5 Conclusion

We have addressed grounding issues in LLMs and proposed task-agnostic hallucination correction methods for real-world applications from two perspectives: post-processing to refine LLM outputs and trustful LLM fine-tuning via dual encoders. We have discussed hallucination correction and trustworthy text generation, demonstrating the robustness and resilience of our methods. In the future, we plan to explore heterogeneous modalities, such as structured and spatio-temporal data, knowledge-enriched representations of input tokens (Grover and Leskovec, 2016; Yu et al., 2022; Pan et al., 2023; GAO et al., 2021; Ye et al., 2021), hierarchical relation graphs, and accountability (Li et al., 2023a). We also plan to study model bias, aggregation for federated learning (Zheng et al., 2023; Hashemi et al., 2021), and privacy-preserving issues (Hashemi et al., 2021). Additionally, we aim to reduce the complexity of LLMs through parameter-efficient fine-tuning.

References

Marah Abdin, Sam Ade Jacobs, Ammar Ahmad Awan, Jyoti Aneja, Ahmed Awadallah, Hany Awadalla, Nguyen Bach, Amit Bahree, Arash Bakhtiari, Jianmin Bao, Harkirat Behl, Alon Benhaim, Misha Bilenko, Johan Bjorck, Sébastien Bubeck, Qin Cai, Martin Cai, Caio César Teodoro Mendes, Weizhu Chen, Vishrav Chaudhary, Dong Chen, Dongdong Chen, Yen-Chun Chen, Yi-Ling Chen, Parul Chopra, Xiyang Dai, Allie Del Giorno, Gustavo de Rosa, Matthew Dixon, Ronen Eldan, Victor Fragoso, Dan Iter, Mei Gao, Min Gao, Jianfeng Gao, Amit Garg, Abhishek Goswami, Suriya Gunasekar, Emman Haider, Junheng Hao, Russell J. Hewett, Jamie Huynh, Mojan Javaheripi, Xin Jin, Piero Kauffmann, Nikos Karampatziakis, Dongwoo Kim, Mahoud Khademi, Lev Kurilenko, James R. Lee, Yin Tat Lee, Yuanzhi Li, Yunsheng Li, Chen Liang, Lars Liden, Ce Liu, Mengchen Liu, Weishung Liu, Eric Lin, Zeqi Lin, Chong Luo, Piyush Madan, Matt Mazzola, Arindam Mitra, Hardik Modi, Anh Nguyen, Brandon Norick, Barun Patra, Daniel Perez-Becker, Thomas Portet, Reid Pryzant, Heyang Qin, Marko Radmilac, Corby Rosset, Sambudha Roy, Olatunji Ruwase, Olli Saarikivi, Amin Saied, Adil Salim, Michael Santacroce, Shital Shah, Ning Shang, Hiteshi Sharma, Swadheen Shukla, Xia Song, Masahiro Tanaka, Andrea Tupini, Xin Wang, Lijuan Wang, Chunyu Wang, Yu Wang, Rachel Ward, Guanhua Wang, Philipp Witte, Haiping Wu, Michael Wyatt, Bin Xiao, Can Xu, Jiahang Xu, Weijian Xu, Sonali Yadav, Fan Yang, Jianwei Yang, Ziyi Yang, Yifan Yang, Donghan Yu, Lu Yuan, Chengruidong Zhang, Cyril Zhang, Jianwen Zhang, Li Lyna Zhang, Yi Zhang, Yue Zhang, Yunan Zhang, and Xiren Zhou. 2024. Phi-3 technical report: A highly capable language model locally on your phone. *Preprint*, arXiv:2404.14219.

Oshin Agarwal, Heming Ge, Siamak Shakeri, and Rami Al-Rfou. 2020. Knowledge graph based synthetic corpus generation for knowledge-enhanced language model pre-training. *arXiv preprint arXiv:2010.12688*.

Luca Beurer-Kellner, Marc Fischer, and Martin Vechev. 2024. Guiding llms the right way: Fast, non-invasive constrained generation. *Preprint*, arXiv:2403.06988.

Antoine Bordes, Nicolas Usunier, Alberto Garcia-Duran, Jason Weston, and Oksana Yakhnenko. 2013. Translating embeddings for modeling multi-relational data. *Advances in neural information processing systems*, 26.

Zi-Yi Dou, Pengfei Liu, Hiroaki Hayashi, Zhengbao Jiang, and Graham Neubig. 2020. Gsum: A general framework for guided neural abstractive summarization. *arXiv preprint arXiv:2010.08014*.

Matthijs Douze, Alexandr Guzhva, Chengqi Deng, Jeff Johnson, Gergely Szilvasy, Pierre-Emmanuel Mazaré, Maria Lomeli, Lucas Hosseini, and Hervé Jégou. 2024. The faiss library.

Abhimanyu Dubey, Abhinav Jauhri, Abhinav Pandey, Abhishek Kadian, Ahmad Al-Dahle, Aiesha Letman, Akhil Mathur, Alan Schelten, Amy Yang, Angela Fan, Anirudh Goyal, Anthony Hartshorn, Aobo Yang, Archi Mitra, Archie Sravankumar, Artem Korenev, Arthur Hinsvark, Arun Rao, Aston Zhang, Aurelien Rodriguez, Austen Gregerson, Ava Spataru, Baptiste Roziere, Bethany Biron, Binh Tang, Bobbie Chern, Charlotte Caucheteux, Chaya Nayak, Chloe Bi, Chris Marra, Chris McConnell, Christian Keller, Christophe Touret, Chunyang Wu, Corinne Wong, Cristian Canton Ferrer, Cyrus Nikolaidis, Damien Allonsius, Daniel Song, Danielle Pintz, Danny Livshits, David Esiobu, Dhruv Choudhary, Dhruv Mahajan, Diego Garcia-Olano, Diego Perino, Dieuwke Hupkes, Egor Lakomkin, Ehab AlBadawy, Elina Lobanova, Emily Dinan, Eric Michael Smith, Filip Radenovic, Frank Zhang, Gabriel Synnaeve, Gabrielle Lee, Georgia Lewis Anderson, Graeme Nail, Gregoire Mialon, Guan Pang, Guillem Cucurell, Hailey Nguyen, Hannah Korevaar, Hu Xu, Hugo Touvron, Iliyan Zarov, Imanol Arrieta Ibarra, Isabel Kloumann, Ishan Misra, Ivan Evtimov, Jade Copet, Jaewon Lee, Jan Geffert, Jana Vranes, Jason Park, Jay Mahadeokar, Jeet Shah, Jelmer van der Linde, Jennifer Billock, Jenny Hong, Jenya Lee, Jeremy Fu, Jianfeng Chi, Jianyu Huang, Jiawen Liu, Jie Wang, Jiecao Yu, Joanna Bitton, Joe Spisak, Jongsoo Park, Joseph Rocca, Joshua Johnstun, Joshua Saxe, Junteng Jia, Kalyan Vasuden Alwala, Kartikeya Upasani, Kate Plawiak, Ke Li, Kenneth Heafield, Kevin Stone, Khalid El-Arini, Krithika Iyer, Kshitiz Malik, Kuenley Chiu, Kunal Bhalla, Lauren Rantala-Yeary, Laurens van der Maaten, Lawrence Chen, Liang Tan, Liz Jenkins, Louis Martin, Lovish Madaan, Lubo Malo, Lukas Blecher, Lukas Landzaat, Luke de Oliveira, Madeline Muzzi, Mahesh Pasupuleti, Mannat Singh, Manohar Paluri, Marcin Kardas, Mathew Oldham, Mathieu Rita, Maya Pavlova, Melanie Kambadur, Mike Lewis, Min Si, Mitesh Kumar Singh, Mona Hassan, Naman Goyal, Narjes Torabi, Nikolay Bashlykov, Nikolay Bogoychev, Niladri Chatterji, Olivier Duchenne, Onur Çelebi, Patrick Alrassy, Pengchuan Zhang, Pengwei Li, Petar Vasic, Peter Weng, Prajjwal Bhargava, Pratik Dubal, Praveen Krishnan, Punit Singh Koura, Puxin Xu, Qing He, Qingxiao Dong, Ragavan Srinivasan, Raj Ganapathy, Ramon Calderer, Ricardo Silveira Cabral, Robert Stojnic, Roberta Raileanu, Rohit Girdhar, Rohit Patel, Romain Sauvestre, Ronnie Polidoro, Roshan Sumbaly, Ross Taylor, Ruan Silva, Rui Hou, Rui Wang, Saghar Hosseini, Sahana Chennabasappa, Sanjay Singh, Sean Bell, Seohyun Sonia Kim, Sergey Edunov, Shaoliang Nie, Sharan Narang, Sharath Raparthy, Sheng Shen, Shengye Wan, Shruti Bhosale, Shun Zhang, Simon Vandenhende, Soumya Batra, Spencer Whitman, Sten Sootla, Stephane Collot, Suchin Gururangan, Sydney Borodinsky, Tamar Herman, Tara Fowler, Tarek Sheasha, Thomas Georgiou, Thomas Scialom, Tobias Speckbacher, Todor Mihaylov, Tong Xiao, Ujjwal Karn, Vedanuj Goswami, Vibhor Gupta, Vignesh Ramanathan, Viktor Kerkez, Vincent Gonguet, Virginie Do, Vish Vogeti, Vladan Petrovic, Weiwei Chu, Wenhan Xiong, Wenyin Fu, Whitney Meers, Xavier Martinet, Xiaodong Wang, Xiaoqing Ellen Tan, Xinfeng Xie, Xuchao Jia, Xuewei Wang, Yaelle Goldschlag, Yashesh Gaur, Yasmine Babaei, Yi Wen, Yiwen Song, Yuchen Zhang, Yue Li, Yuning Mao, Zacharie Delpierre Coudert, Zheng Yan, Zhengxing Chen, Zoe Papakipos, Aaditya Singh, Aaron Grattafiori, Abha Jain, Adam Kelsey, Adam Shajnfeld, Adithya Gangidi, Adolfo Victoria, Ahuva Goldstand, Ajay Menon, Ajay Sharma, Alex Boesenberg, Alex Vaughan, Alexei Baevski, Allie Feinstein, Amanda Kallet, Amit Sangani, Anam Yunus, Andrei Lupu, Andres Alvarado, Andrew Caples, Andrew Gu, Andrew Ho, Andrew Poulton, Andrew Ryan, Ankit Ramchandani, Annie Franco, Aparajita Saraf, Arkabandhu Chowdhury, Ashley Gabriel, Ashwin Bharambe, Assaf Eisenman, Azadeh Yazdan, Beau James, Ben Maurer, Benjamin Leonhardi, Bernie Huang, Beth Loyd, Beto De Paola, Bhargavi Paranjape, Bing Liu, Bo Wu, Boyu Ni, Braden Hancock, Bram Wasti, Brandon Spence, Brani Stojkovic, Brian Gamido, Britt Montalvo, Carl Parker, Carly Burton, Catalina Mejia, Changhan Wang, Changkyu Kim, Chao Zhou, Chester Hu, Ching-Hsiang Chu, Chris Cai, Chris Tindal, Christoph Feichtenhofer, Damon Civin, Dana Beaty, Daniel Kreymer, Daniel Li, Danny Wyatt, David Adkins, David Xu, Davide Testuggine, Delia David, Devi Parikh, Diana Liskovich, Didem Foss, Dingkang Wang, Duc Le, Dustin Holland, Edward Dowling, Eissa Jamil, Elaine Montgomery, Eleonora Presani, Emily Hahn, Emily Wood, Erik Brinkman, Esteban Arcaute, Evan Dunbar, Evan Smothers, Fei Sun, Felix Kreuk, Feng Tian, Firat Ozgenel, Francesco Caggioni, Francisco Guzmán, Frank Kanayet, Frank Seide, Gabriela Medina Florez, Gabriella Schwarz, Gada Badeer, Georgia Swee, Gil Halpern, Govind Thattai, Grant Herman, Grigory Sizov, Guangyi, Zhang, Guna Lakshminarayanan, Hamid Shojanazeri, Han Zou, Hannah Wang, Hanwen Zha, Haroun Habeeb, Harrison Rudolph, Helen Suk, Henry Aspegren, Hunter Goldman, Ibrahim Damlaj, Igor Molybog, Igor Tufanov, Irina-Elena Veliche, Itai Gat, Jake Weissman, James Geboski, James Kohli, Japhet Asher, Jean-Baptiste Gaya, Jeff Marcus, Jeff Tang, Jennifer Chan, Jenny Zhen, Jeremy Reizenstein, Jeremy Teboul, Jessica Zhong, Jian Jin, Jingyi Yang, Joe Cummings, Jon Carvill, Jon Shepard, Jonathan McPhie, Jonathan Torres, Josh Ginsburg, Junjie Wang, Kai Wu, Kam Hou U, Karan Saxena, Karthik Prasad, Kartikay Khandelwal, Katayoun Zand, Kathy Matosich, Kaushik Veeraraghavan, Kelly Michelena, Keqian Li, Kun Huang, Kunal Chawla, Kushal Lakhotia, Kyle Huang, Lailin Chen, Lakshya Garg, Lavender A, Leandro Silva, Lee Bell, Lei Zhang, Liangpeng Guo, Licheng Yu, Liron Moshkovich, Luca Wehrstedt, Madian Khabsa, Manav Avalani, Manish Bhatt, Maria Tsimpoukelli, Martynas Mankus, Matan Hasson, Matthew Lennie, Matthias Reso, Maxim Groshev, Maxim Naumov, Maya Lathi, Meghan Keneally, Michael L. Seltzer, Michal Valko, Michelle Restrepo, Mihir Patel, Mik Vyatskov, Mikayel Samvelyan, Mike Clark, Mike Macey, Mike Wang, Miquel Jubert Hermoso, Mo Metanat, Mohammad Rastegari, Munish Bansal, Nandhini Santhanam, Natascha Parks, Natasha White, Navyata Bawa, Nayan Singhal, Nick Egebo, Nicolas Usunier, Nikolay Pavlovich Laptev, Ning Dong, Ning Zhang, Norman Cheng, Oleg Chernoguz, Olivia Hart, Omkar Salpekar, Ozlem Kalinli, Parkin Kent, Parth Parekh, Paul Saab, Pavan Balaji, Pedro Rittner, Philip Bontrager, Pierre Roux, Piotr Dollar, Polina Zvyagina, Prashant Ratanchandani, Pritish Yuvraj, Qian Liang, Rachad Alao, Rachel Rodriguez, Rafi Ayub, Raghotham Murthy, Raghu Nayani, Rahul Mitra, Raymond Li, Rebekkah Hogan, Robin Battey, Rocky Wang, Rohan Maheswari, Russ Howes, Ruty Rinott, Sai Jayesh Bondu, Samyak Datta, Sara Chugh, Sara Hunt, Sargun Dhillon, Sasha Sidorov, Satadru Pan, Saurabh Verma, Seiji Yamamoto, Sharadh Ramaswamy, Shaun Lindsay, Shaun Lindsay, Sheng Feng, Shenghao Lin, Shengxin Cindy Zha, Shiva Shankar, Shuqiang Zhang, Shuqiang Zhang, Sinong Wang, Sneha Agarwal, Soji Sajuyigbe, Soumith Chintala, Stephanie Max, Stephen Chen, Steve Kehoe, Steve Satterfield, Sudarshan Govindaprasad, Sumit Gupta, Sungmin Cho, Sunny Virk, Suraj Subramanian, Sy Choudhury, Sydney Goldman, Tal Remez, Tamar Glaser, Tamara Best, Thilo Kohler, Thomas Robinson, Tianhe Li, Tianjun Zhang, Tim Matthews, Timothy Chou, Tzook Shaked, Varun Vontimitta, Victoria Ajayi, Victoria Montanez, Vijai Mohan, Vinay Satish Kumar, Vishal Mangla, Vítor Albiero, Vlad Ionescu, Vlad Poenaru, Vlad Tiberiu Mihailescu, Vladimir Ivanov, Wei Li, Wenchen Wang, Wenwen Jiang, Wes Bouaziz, Will Constable, Xiaocheng Tang, Xiaofang Wang, Xiaojian Wu, Xiaolan Wang, Xide Xia, Xilun Wu, Xinbo Gao, Yanjun Chen, Ye Hu, Ye Jia, Ye Qi, Yenda Li, Yilin Zhang, Ying Zhang, Yossi Adi, Youngjin Nam, Yu, Wang, Yuchen Hao, Yundi Qian, Yuzi He, Zach Rait, Zachary DeVito, Zef Rosnbrick, Zhaoduo Wen, Zhenyu Yang, and Zhiwei Zhao. 2024. The llama 3 herd of models. *Preprint*, arXiv:2407.21783.

Darren Edge, Ha Trinh, Newman Cheng, Joshua Bradley, Alex Chao, Apurva Mody, Steven Truitt, and Jonathan Larson. 2024. From local to global: A graph rag approach to query-focused summarization. *Preprint*, arXiv:2404.16130.

Shima Foolad and Kourosh Kiani. 2023. Luke-graph: A transformer-based approach with gated relational graph attention for cloze-style reading comprehension. *arXiv preprint arXiv:2303.06675*.

HANNING GAO, LINGFEI WU, HONGYUN ZHANG, ZHIHUA WEI, PO HU, FANGLI XU, and BO LONG. 2021. Triples-to-text generation with reinforcement learning based graph-augmented structural neural networks. *arXiv preprint arXiv:2111.10545*.

Matt Gardner, Joel Grus, Mark Neumann, Oyvind Tafjord, Pradeep Dasigi, Nelson F. Liu, Matthew Peters, Michael Schmitz, and Luke S. Zettlemoyer. 2017. Allennlp: A deep semantic natural language processing platform.

Aditya Grover and Jure Leskovec. 2016. node2vec: Scalable feature learning for networks. In *Proceed-*

ings of the 22nd ACM SIGKDD international conference on Knowledge discovery and data mining, pages 855–864.

Xu Han, Tianyu Gao, Yuan Yao, Deming Ye, Zhiyuan Liu, and Maosong Sun. 2019. OpenNRE: An open and extensible toolkit for neural relation extraction. In *Proceedings of EMNLP-IJCNLP: System Demonstrations*, pages 169–174.

Hanieh Hashemi, Yongqin Wang, Chuan Guo, and Murali Annavaram. 2021. Byzantine-robust and privacy-preserving framework for fedml. *arXiv preprint arXiv:2105.02295*.

Chris Hokamp and Qun Liu. 2017. Lexically constrained decoding for sequence generation using grid beam search. *Preprint*, arXiv:1704.07138.

Edward J. Hu, Yelong Shen, Phillip Wallis, Zeyuan Allen-Zhu, Yuanzhi Li, Shean Wang, Lu Wang, and Weizhu Chen. 2021. Lora: Low-rank adaptation of large language models. *Preprint*, arXiv:2106.09685.

Ziwei Ji, Nayeon Lee, Rita Frieske, Tiezheng Yu, Dan Su, Yan Xu, Etsuko Ishii, Ye Jin Bang, Andrea Madotto, and Pascale Fung. 2023. Survey of hallucination in natural language generation. *ACM Comput. Surv.*, 55(12).

Hang Le, Juan Pino, Changhan Wang, Jiatao Gu, Didier Schwab, and Laurent Besacier. 2020. Dual-decoder transformer for joint automatic speech recognition and multilingual speech translation. *Preprint*, arXiv:2011.00747.

Bo Li, Peng Qi, Bo Liu, Shuai Di, Jingen Liu, Jiquan Pei, Jinfeng Yi, and Bowen Zhou. 2023a. Trustworthy ai: From principles to practices. *ACM Computing Surveys*, 55(9):1–46.

Yichuan Li, Jialong Han, Kyumin Lee, Chengyuan Ma, Benjamin Yao, and Derek Liu. 2023b. Keplet: Knowledge-enhanced pretrained language model with topic entity awareness. *arXiv preprint arXiv:2305.01810*.

Zhuowan Li, Cheng Li, Mingyang Zhang, Qiaozhu Mei, and Michael Bendersky. 2024. Retrieval augmented generation or long-context llms? a comprehensive study and hybrid approach. *arXiv preprint arXiv:2407.16833*.

Yankai Lin, Zhiyuan Liu, Maosong Sun, Yang Liu, and Xuan Zhu. 2015. Learning entity and relation embeddings for knowledge graph completion. In *Proceedings of the AAAI conference on artificial intelligence*, volume 29.

Yinquan Lu, Haonan Lu, Guirong Fu, and Qun Liu. 2021. Kelm: knowledge enhanced pre-trained language representations with message passing on hierarchical relational graphs. *arXiv preprint arXiv:2109.04223*.

Salman Mohamadi, Ghulam Mujtaba, Ngan Le, Gianfranco Doretto, and Donald A. Adjeroh. 2023. Chatgpt in the age of generative ai and large language models: A concise survey. *Preprint*, arXiv:2307.04251.

Fedor Moiseev, Zhe Dong, Enrique Alfonseca, and Martin Jaggi. 2022. Skill: structured knowledge infusion for large language models. *arXiv preprint arXiv:2205.08184*.

Maximilian Nickel, Volker Tresp, Hans-Peter Kriegel, et al. 2011. A three-way model for collective learning on multi-relational data. In *Icml*, volume 11, pages 3104482–3104584.

Shirui Pan, Linhao Luo, Yufei Wang, Chen Chen, Jiapu Wang, and Xindong Wu. 2023. Unifying large language models and knowledge graphs: A roadmap. *arXiv preprint arXiv:2306.08302*.

Abigail See, Peter J Liu, and Christopher D Manning. 2017. Get to the point: Summarization with pointer-generator networks. *arXiv preprint arXiv:1704.04368*.

Richard Socher, Danqi Chen, Christopher D Manning, and Andrew Ng. 2013. Reasoning with neural tensor networks for knowledge base completion. *Advances in neural information processing systems*, 26.

Gemma Team. 2024. Gemma.

Ashish Vaswani, Noam Shazeer, Niki Parmar, Jakob Uszkoreit, Llion Jones, Aidan N. Gomez, Lukasz Kaiser, and Illia Polosukhin. 2023. Attention is all you need. *Preprint*, arXiv:1706.03762.

David Wan, Koustuv Sinha, Srini Iyer, Asli Celikyilmaz, Mohit Bansal, and Ramakanth Pasunuru. 2024. Acueval: Fine-grained hallucination evaluation and correction for abstractive summarization. In *Findings of the Association for Computational Linguistics ACL 2024*, pages 10036–10056.

Xintao Wang, Qianyu He, Jiaqing Liang, and Yanghua Xiao. 2022a. Language models as knowledge embeddings. *arXiv preprint arXiv:2206.12617*.

Ying Wang, Yuexing Peng, Wei Li, George C. Alexandropoulos, Junchuan Yu, Daqing Ge, and Wei Xiang. 2022b. Ddu-net: Dual-decoder-u-net for road extraction using high-resolution remote sensing images. *IEEE Transactions on Geoscience and Remote Sensing*, 60:1–12.

Zhen Wang, Jianwen Zhang, Jianlin Feng, and Zheng Chen. 2014. Knowledge graph embedding by translating on hyperplanes. In *Proceedings of the AAAI conference on artificial intelligence*, volume 28.

Hongbin Ye, Ningyu Zhang, Shumin Deng, Mosha Chen, Chuanqi Tan, Fei Huang, and Huajun Chen. 2021. Contrastive triple extraction with generative transformer. In *Proceedings of the AAAI conference on artificial intelligence*, volume 35, pages 14257–14265.

Changlong Yu, Tianyi Xiao, Lingpeng Kong, Yangqiu Song, and Wilfred Ng. 2022. An empirical revisiting of linguistic knowledge fusion in language understanding tasks. In *Proceedings of the 2022 Conference on Empirical Methods in Natural Language Processing*, pages 10064–10070, Abu Dhabi, United Arab Emirates. Association for Computational Linguistics.

Longfei Zheng, Yingting Liu, Xiaolong Xu, Chaochao Chen, Yuzhou Tang, Lei Wang, and Xiaolong Hu. 2023. Fedpse: Personalized sparsification with element-wise aggregation for federated learning. In *Proceedings of the 32nd ACM International Conference on Information and Knowledge Management*, pages 3514–3523.

Jiaxin Zou, Zuotong Xie, Junhua Chen, Jiawei Hou, Qiang Yan, and Hai-Tao Zheng. 2023. K-dlm: A domain-adaptive language model pre-training framework with knowledge graph. In *International Conference on Artificial Neural Networks*, pages 447–459. Springer.

A Appendix

A.1 Hallucination Examples

We show examples where various LLMs generate hallucinations.

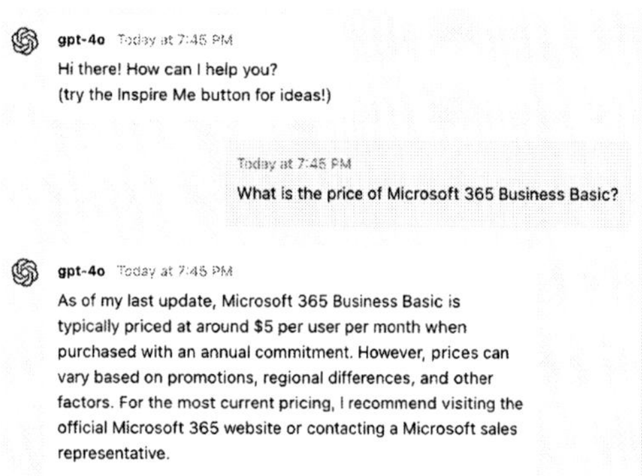

Figure 2: Hallucination Example 1

GPT-4o returns the wrong pricing information of Microsoft 365 Business Basic.

A.2 Examples of Prompt, RAG Context, and Guided Context

Prompt: *"... <|user|> How much is Microsoft 365 Business Basic? <|end|> <|assistant|> Microsoft 365 Business Basic is $7.2 dollars per user per month. <|end|>"*.

RAG context: *"Microsoft 365 Business Basic is $7.2 dollars per user per month. Microsoft 365 Business Basic ..."*.

Guided context: *"Microsoft 365 Business Basic is $7.2 dollars per user per month. Microsoft 365*

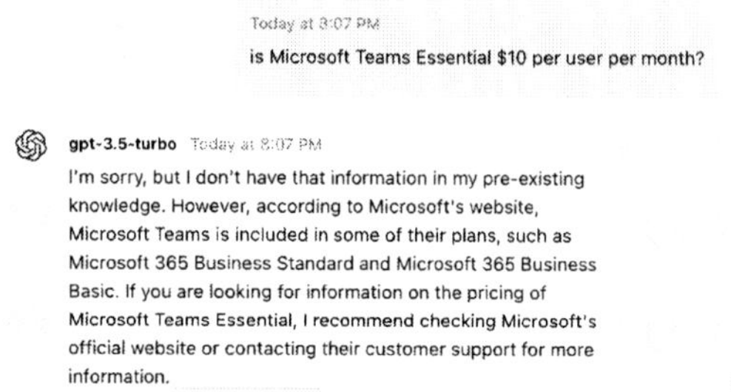

Figure 3: Hallucination Example 2

GPT-3.5 Turbo cannot answer questions related to Microsoft Teams Essential.

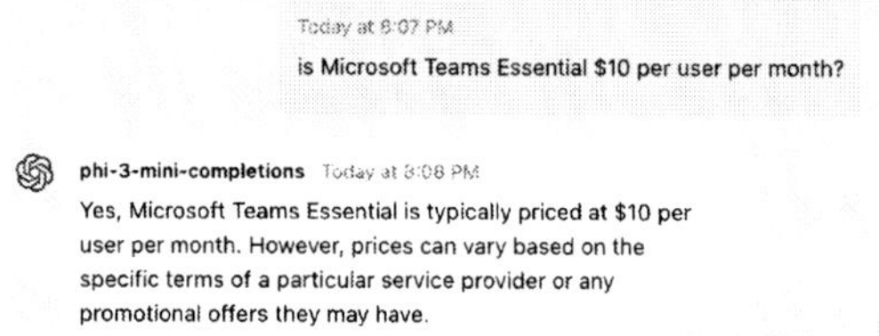

Figure 4: Hallucination Example 3

Phi-3 answered incorrectly about the price of Microsoft Teams Essential.

Business Basic ... Microsoft 365 Business Standard is ... <|end|>". We add additional content about, such as *"Microsoft 365 Business Standard"*, which is similar to the product *"Microsoft 365 Business Basic"* to the RAG context. This is for mimicking the potentially noisy RAG context in the retrieval stage.

A.3 Summarization Task

A summarization task does not have the retrieval component as in RAG. We utilize the graph building step of HC to select the salient sentences from the articles as the guided context. We first extract knowledge triplets from the articles then keep sentences where the most frequent subjects are associated with. We show the comparison of TrustfulLLM + HC + Phi-3.5-mini-instruct, where HC extract knowledge triplets from the articles and the generated texts in the inference stage, and LLM baselines in Table 2.

A.4 Prompt Template for GPT Metrics

We show the prompts of GPT Similarity and GPT Groundness addressed in Section 4.

Prompt for GPT Groundness
System:

CNN DailyMail

Models	Rouge-L	METEOR	Groundedness	GPT-Similarity	BERTScore
TrustfulLLM + HC + Phi-3.5-mini-instruct	**0.41**	**0.39**	**5.00**	**4.12**	**0.89**
TrustfulLLM + Phi-3.5-mini-instruct	0.40	**0.39**	4.68	**4.12**	0.88
HC + Phi-3.5-mini-instruct	0.35	0.36	**5.00**	3.82	0.88
Phi-3.5-mini-instruct	0.17	0.34	4.29	3.79	0.86
Mistral-NeMo-Minitron-8B-Instruct	0.20	0.35	3.32	3.87	0.86
Llama-3.1-8B-Instruct	0.32	0.37	4.61	4.10	0.87
GPT-3.5 Turbo	0.24	0.38	4.50	3.79	0.87
GPT-4o	0.18	0.36	4.42	4.10	0.87

Table 2: Summarization Benchmarking Results

You are an AI assistant. You will be given the definition of an evaluation metric for assessing the quality of an answer in a question-answering task. Your job is to compute an accurate evaluation score using the provided evaluation metric. You should return a single integer value between 1 to 5 representing the evaluation metric. You will include no other text or information.

User:

You will be presented with a CONTEXT and an ANSWER about that CONTEXT. You need to decide whether the ANSWER is entailed by the CONTEXT by choosing one of the following rating:

1. 5: The ANSWER follows logically from the information contained in the CONTEXT.

2. 1: The ANSWER is logically false from the information contained in the CONTEXT.

3. An integer score between 1 and 5, and if such an integer score does not exist, use 1: It is not possible to determine whether the ANSWER is true or false without further information.

Read the passage of information thoroughly and select the correct answer from the three answer labels. Read the CONTEXT thoroughly to ensure you know what the CONTEXT entails. Note that the ANSWER is generated by a computer system, so it can contain certain symbols, which should not be a negative factor in the evaluation.

Independent Examples:
Example Task #1 Input:
{"CONTEXT": "Some are reported as not having been wanted at all.", "QUESTION": "", "ANSWER": "All are reported as being completely and fully wanted."}
Example Task #1 Output:
1 **Example Task #2 Input:**
{"CONTEXT": "Ten new television shows appeared during the month of September. Five of the shows were sitcoms, three were hourlong dramas, and two were news-magazine shows. By January, only seven of these new shows were still on the air. Five of the shows that remained were sitcoms.", "QUESTION": "", "ANSWER": "At least one of the shows that were cancelled was an hourlong drama."}
Example Task #2 Output:
5

Example Task #3 Input:
{"CONTEXT": "In Quebec, an allophone is a resident, usually an immigrant, whose mother tongue or home language is neither French nor English.", "QUESTION": "", "ANSWER": "In Quebec, an allophone is a resident, usually an immigrant, whose mother tongue or home language is not French."}
Example Task #3 Output:
5

Example Task #4 Input:
{"CONTEXT": "Some are reported as not having been wanted at all.", "QUESTION": "", "ANSWER": "All are reported as being completely and fully wanted."}
Example Task #4 Output:
1

Actual Task Input:
{"CONTEXT": {{context}}, "QUESTION": "", "ANSWER": {{response}}}
Reminder: The return values for each task should be correctly formatted as an integer

between 1 and 5. Do not repeat the context and question.

Actual Task Output:

Prompt for GPT Similarity]

System:

You are an AI assistant. You will be given the definition of an evaluation metric for assessing the quality of an answer in a question-answering task. Your job is to compute an accurate evaluation score using the provided evaluation metric. You should return a single integer value between 1 to 5 representing the evaluation metric. You will include no other text or information.

User:

Equivalence, as a metric, measures the similarity between the predicted answer and the correct answer. If the information and content in the predicted answer is similar or equivalent to the correct answer, then the value of the Equivalence metric should be high, else it should be low. Given the question, correct answer, and predicted answer, determine the value of the Equivalence metric using the following rating scale:

- One star: the predicted answer is not at all similar to the correct answer
- Two stars: the predicted answer is mostly not similar to the correct answer
- Three stars: the predicted answer is somewhat similar to the correct answer
- Four stars: the predicted answer is mostly similar to the correct answer
- Five stars: the predicted answer is completely similar to the correct answer

This rating value should always be an integer between 1 and 5. So the rating produced should be 1, 2, 3, 4, or 5. The examples below show the Equivalence score for a question, a correct answer, and a predicted answer.

Question: What is the role of ribosomes?
Correct answer: Ribosomes are cellular structures responsible for protein synthesis. They interpret the genetic information carried by messenger RNA (mRNA) and use it to assemble amino acids into proteins.
Predicted answer: Ribosomes participate in carbohydrate breakdown by removing nutrients from complex sugar molecules.
Stars: 1

Question: Why did the Titanic sink?
Correct answer: The Titanic sank after it struck an iceberg during its maiden voyage in 1912. The impact caused the ship's hull to breach, allowing water to flood into the vessel. The ship's design, lifeboat shortage, and lack of timely rescue efforts contributed to the tragic loss of life.
Predicted answer: The sinking of the Titanic was a result of a large iceberg collision. This caused the ship to take on water and eventually sink, leading to the death of many passengers due to a shortage of lifeboats and insufficient rescue attempts.
Stars: 2

Question: What are the health benefits of regular exercise?
Correct answer: Regular exercise can help maintain a healthy weight, increase muscle and bone strength, and reduce the risk of chronic diseases. It also promotes mental well-being by reducing stress and improving overall mood.
Predicted answer: Routine physical activity can contribute to maintaining ideal body weight, enhancing muscle and bone strength, and preventing chronic illnesses. In addition, it supports mental health by alleviating stress and augmenting general mood.
Stars: 5

Question: {{query}}
Correct answer: {{ground_truth}}
Predicted answer: {{response}}
Stars:

Constructing Domain-Specific Evaluation Sets for LLM-as-a-judge

Ravi Raju, Swayambhoo Jain, Bo Li,
Jonathan Li, Urmish Thakker
SambaNova Systems
{ravi.raju, swayambhoo.jain}@sambanovasystems.com

Abstract

Large Language Models (LLMs) have revolutionized the landscape of machine learning, yet current benchmarks often fall short in capturing the diverse behavior of these models in real-world applications. A benchmark's usefulness is determined by its ability to clearly differentiate between models of varying capabilities (separability) and closely align with human preferences. Existing frameworks like Alpaca-Eval 2.0 LC (Dubois et al., 2024a) and Arena-Hard v0.1 (Li et al., 2024a) are limited by their focus on general-purpose queries and lack of diversity across domains such as law, medicine, and multilingual contexts. In this paper, we address these limitations by introducing a novel data pipeline that curates diverse, domain-specific evaluation sets tailored for LLM-as-a-Judge frameworks. Our approach leverages a combination of manual curation, semi-supervised learning to generate clusters, and stratified sampling to ensure balanced representation across a wide range of domains and languages. The resulting evaluation set, which includes 1573 samples across 14 categories, demonstrates high separability (84%) across ten top-ranked models, and agreement (84%) with Chatbot Arena and (0.915) Spearman correlation. The agreement values are 9% better than Arena Hard and 20% better than AlpacaEval 2.0 LC, while the Spearman coefficient is 0.7 more than the next best benchmark, showcasing a significant improvement in the usefulness of the benchmark. We further provide an open-source evaluation tool that enables fine-grained analysis of model performance across user-defined categories, offering valuable insights for practitioners. This work contributes to the ongoing effort to enhance the transparency, diversity, and effectiveness of LLM evaluation methodologies.

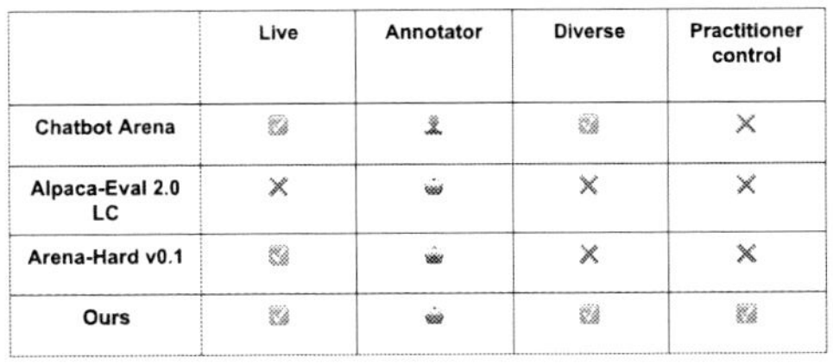

Figure 1: Compared to other benchmark frameworks our approach introduces a data pipeline that curates unlabeled data into categories that contain domains/capabilities that the practitioner cares about. It has the capability to be refreshed with new data and is diverse compared to alternatives.

1 Introduction

Large Language Models (LLMs) have dramatically changed the landscape of machine learning research and have been incorporated in products for the past few years. Along with their rise, a multitude of benchmarks and frameworks (Liang et al., 2023) have been proposed to assess the capabilities of LLMs which include knowledge tasks such as MMLU (Hendrycks et al., 2021a), reasoning tasks like GSM8k (Cobbe et al., 2021) and more standard NLP tasks (Zellers et al., 2019; Narayan et al., 2018). However, these benchmarks fail to capture the behavior that a user experiences in a chat/generative applications. Typically, human evaluations are seen as a gold standard to determining which LLM responses are preferable over others in a chat setting but is time-consuming and expensive to conduct (Chiang et al., 2024).

To address this shortcoming, Zheng *et al.* introduced the concept of LLM as a judge as an automatic evaluator alternative, which uses another LLM the judging of model completions to another LLM such as GPT-4 or GPT-4o (Zheng et al., 2023a; OpenAI et al., 2024). Alpaca-Eval is another benchmark designed under the paradigm of LLM as an evaluator where a target LLM's com-

Proceedings of the 1st Workshop on Customizable NLP: Progress and Challenges in Customizing NLP for a Domain, Application, Group, or Individual (CustomNLP4U), pages 167–181
November 16, 2024

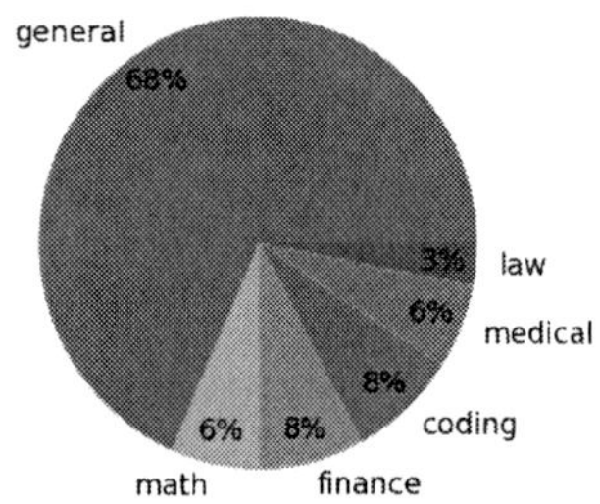

Figure 2: Alpaca-Eval category breakdown

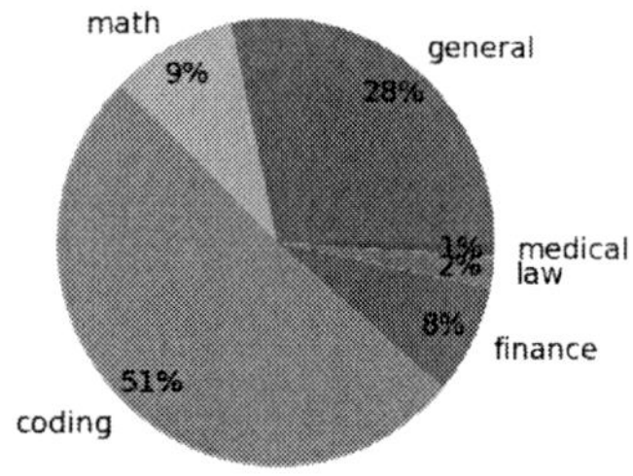

Figure 3: Arena-Hard v0.1 category breakdown

pletions are compared against a reference LLM's output (the default being GPT-4 Turbo) and assigned a winrate against the reference (Li et al., 2023). It has seen widespread adoption since it is cheap, fast, and mitigates length bias (Chiang et al., 2024). Similarly, Arena-Hard v0.1 is recent benchmark which focuses on distilling the Hard category of Chatbot Arena into a smaller evaluation set (Li et al., 2024a). They use a topic clustering pipeline to cluster prompts with OpenAI's embedding model (text-embedding-3-small) (OpenAI, 2024b) and score each cluster based on difficulty, creativity, and reasoning ability with GPT-3.5 Turbo. They also introduce a notion of separability (how well can a benchmark differentiate between models) and agreement with human preferences (i.e. ChatBot Arena) as a measure of benchmark quality.

Unfortunately, there are still some limitations with the current open-source LLM-as-a-judge framework. Alpaca-Eval 2.0 LC is dominated by general chat queries/instructions and has few prompts in domains such as coding, medical, finance, law and mathematics as shown in Figure 2. Arena-Hard v0.1 addresses some of these deficiencies by upweighting coding and mathematics prompts and restricting the general chat queries to 30% if the evaluation set. However, both evaluation sets are strictly in English therefore not accessing the model's multilingual capability and have a smaller number of prompts in more niche categories like law and medicine. As models are acquiring more capabilities across various data types such as charts/tables, domains and languages, it becomes crucial to determine how to evaluate each model's ability in a scalable manner.

In this paper, we attempt to address challenges from Alpaca-Eval 2.0 LC and Arena-Hard v0.1 by introducing more diversity across domain knowledge and languages. To accomplish this, we introduce a simple data pipeline methodology to create a new evaluation set designed for these specific contexts. First, we source prompts from various open source datasets (shown in Table 4) to ensure our evaluation set has high data diversity. For the next step, we generate embeddings from a subsample of each of these datasets using an embedding model. To label the corresponding embeddings, we manually curate a seed set of prompts and label them to human-defined specific categories, generate those embeddings and train a k-NN classifier which we can use to classify the unlabeled data that we sampled. In order to make sure that no cluster/category dominates, we employ stratified sampling to ensure balanced representation across all domains and languages in the evaluation set. We further refine the quality of the prompts by manual curation and ensure that each category has a sufficient number of prompts to mitigate the inherent variability in LLM-as-a-judge and ultimately end up with 1573 samples in the evaluation set.

There are several advantages to our approach as shown in Figure 1. Similar to Arena-Hard v0.1, our approach is robust to contamination as we can periodically run our data pipeline on the same data to get new samples or potentially even a new data mixture. As mentioned earlier, our methodology allows introduction of new datasets which enables diversity rather than offered by Arena-Hard v0.1 and Alpaca-Eval. In addition, our evaluation set more closely mirrors Chatbot Arena rankings; Figure 4 shows a visual comparison of model rankings.

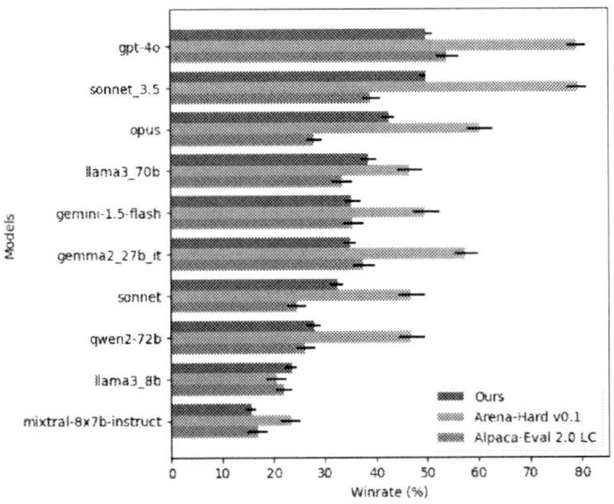

Figure 4: Visual comparison between our method, Arena-Hard v0.1, and Alpaca-Eval 2.0 LC on 10 models on separability of winrates. Our method has fewer overlaps of confidence intervals than the other baselines.

In particular, our evaluation set places Gemini-1.5-Flash (DeepMind, 2024) over Gemma2 27B Instruct (Team, 2024) which aligns with ChatBot Arena rankings whereas the others rank Gemma2 27B over Gemini-1.5-Flash. Moreover, since we use open source models for the entire pipeline, practitioners can mold the pipeline and generate evaluation sets to test domains and capabilities they care about.

After we have obtained the evaluation set, we execute the same procedure as LLM-as-a-Judge by generating the outputs completions from GPT-4o and using them as reference to construct a leaderboard from ten various open and closed-sourced models. With this labeling approach, we are able to breakdown the composition of prompts into various categories and report category win rates. We plan to release an evaluation tool which displays the category winrate for all models on the leaderboard and an explorer which displays both the target model as well as the reference model's completions for a prompt and the reasoning given by the LLM judge. This analysis tool allows users to obtain fine-grained insights on where different models succeed and fail for their particular use-case.

Our main contributions can be summarized below:

- We introduce a new methodology that enables creation of a benchmark that tests for diverse skill sets of models. We open-source our evaluation infrastructure so practitioners can view how different models perform on separate tasks according to how they define their categories. This fine-grained breakdown allows the practitioner to select models that work well for their particular use case.
- Our benchmark creation methodology encourages more diversity and transparency to the practitioner compared to other alternatives. In comparison to other baselines like Alpaca-Eval and Arena-Hard v0.1, our benchmark has 84% separability, 84% agreement with confidence interval (95%) with respect to Chatbot Arena rankings, 0.915 Spearman's correlation coefficient with respect to Chatbot Arena rankings and 0.04 Brier Loss Score.
- We also analyze the aforementioned metrics on our evaluation set with 4 LLM judges: GPT-4o(OpenAI et al., 2024), GPT-4o-mini (OpenAI, 2024a), Llama 3.1 405B Instruct and Llama 3.1 70B Instruct (Dubey et al., 2024). Our overall findings suggest that while open-source models can be used to separate between model rankings, agreement with Chatbot Arena model rankings is roughly 10% (405B) and 20% (70B) than GPT-4o.

2 Related Work

At their core, benchmarks are tool to estimate LLM capabilities. There are many different flavors of benchmarks, spanning either across domains or various tasks. Some popular benchmarks include: Boolq (Clark et al., 2019), MMLU (Hendrycks et al., 2021a), GSM8k (Cobbe et al., 2021), MATH (Hendrycks et al., 2021b), XSUM (Narayan et al., 2018), Hellaswag (Zellers et al., 2019), and MGSM (Shi et al., 2022). An expanded framework of static benchmark is AutoBencher which automatically creates new benchmarks which finds holes in knowledge of current SOTA LLMs (Li et al., 2024b).

These types of benchmarks have ground-truth references and compare how closely the LLM's completion aligns with those references. An inherent limitation with static benchmarks is that they are hosted on the internet and thus are susceptible test leakage contamination (Sainz et al., 2023; Yang et al., 2023). The other style of benchmarking relies on constructing a human evaluation trials on a set of evaluation prompts. Due to the expensive nature of human evaluation, a recent, cheaper alternative is to use SOTA LLMs to evaluate model completions either through single score or pairwise comparison with a reference answer, popularly referred to as LLM-as-a-Judge (Li et al., 2023; Zheng et al., 2023a; Li et al., 2024a; Dubois et al., 2024b; Verga et al., 2024).

This motivates the need for "live, refreshable" benchmarks so that the integrity of the benchmark can be maintained. LiveBench is a framework which sources data from arXiv papers, news articles, and datasets to periodically replace the stale prompts (White et al., 2024). Chatbot arena is an open platform that allows online users to send prompts to two different models and compare/contrast the models' response (Chiang et al., 2024). Users can then vote on which completion was superior. Other live benchmarks include DynaBench (Kiela et al., 2021), LiveCodeBench (Jain et al., 2024), and R2E (Jain et al.). Our work lies in the intersection between LLM-as-a-Judge and live benchmarks as our data pipeline enables periodic refreshing of the evaluation set from existing clusters. Furthermore, our data pipeline is fairly general as it can consume a variety of diverse datasets (relative to Arena-Hard v0.1 and Alpaca-Eval), consists of using open-source models, and is flexible enough to work on the user's desired data.

3 Methodology

In this section, we describe our approach to creating novel evaluation set using LLM-as-a judge. We enumerate the datasets that we source from to create our unlabeled corpus and subsequently describe our data pipeline for generating the evaluation set.

3.1 Data Sources

We use data sources from a variety of source to ensure we cover a variety of domains as well as languages. The domains we target can be broadly classified as the following: medical, law, finance, mathematics and coding. The languages we cover are standard but also more esoteric: Japanese (ja), Arabic (ar), Thai (th), Hungarian (hu), Russian (ru), Serbian (sr), Slovenian (sl), and Turkish (tr). Prompts that don't neatly fit into these groups fall into a catch-all general category. A complete list of all the data we use can be found in Table 4 in the Appendix.

3.2 Data pipeline

Our data pipeline can be divided into 3 distinct steps, as shown in Figure 5. We first take the data corpus and use an embedding model to generate their corresponding embedding. Each embedding encapsulates some level of semantic understanding of its associated prompt, and nearby embeddings typically encode similar semantic information.

To generate the labels for the unlabeled data, we take inspiration from semi-supervised learning (Hady and Schwenker, 2013). We manually define a set of categories, curate a seed set of prompts which fall into those categories (assigning them distinct labels) and embed those prompts with the aforementioned embedding model. We train a k-NN model (Mucherino et al., 2009) on top of those embeddings and use the k-NN to label the larger unlabeled corpus.

The final step in our pipeline involves applying stratified sampling (Parsons, 2017) to each cluster. The reason for this last step is that we want our evaluation set to retain diversity of our larger data corpus rather than uniform random sampling. For each category, we sub-sample 100 prompts from the aggregate clusters and disregard clusters which have a lower count than the number of prompts we sampled. To obtain our final evaluation set, we manually curate the remaining prompts to ensure high quality, varied task capability and data diversity.

4 Experimental Setup

In this section, we discuss finer details about the data pipeline we mentioned in the prior section. experimental setup on a set of ten highly rated models[1] as well as defining the metrics which determine the quality of the benchmark.

4.1 Data pipeline details

For the data pipeline, we use semi-supervised learning via a k-NN classifier. We consider 13 categories comprising of domains: finance, law, medical, maths, coding and languages: Arabic, Russian, Serbian, Hungarian, Japanese, Thai and Slovenian. We follow usual supervised training and via hyperparameter sweep over validation set yield $k = 40$ as the best value of k.

To generate the embeddings of the unlabeled data collected, we use the e5-mistral-7b-instruct embedding model(Wang et al., 2024) for its strong performance on the Massive Text Embedding

[1] gpt-4o-2024-05-13, claude-3-5-sonnet-20240620, claude-3-opus-20240229, gemini-1.5-flash-latest, google/gemma-2-27b-it, Meta-Llama-3-70B-Instruct, claude-3-sonnet-20240229, Qwen/Qwen2-72B-Instruct, Meta-Llama-3-8B-Instruct, Mixtral-8x7B-Instruct-v0.1

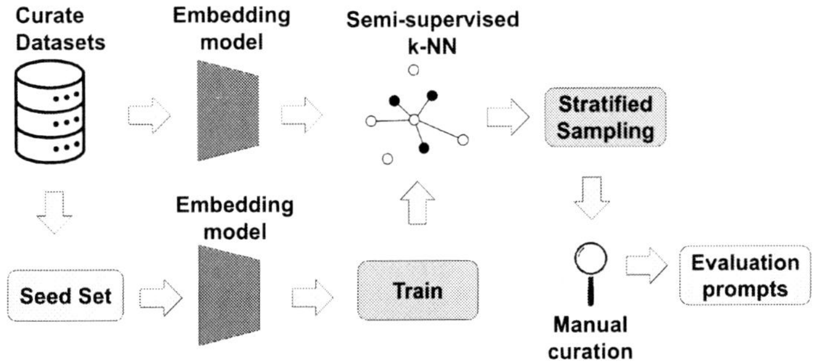

Figure 5: **Data pipeline**: After aggregating the prompts from datasets, we generate embeddings using a text embedding model. We set aside a set of prompts to use as a seed set for training the k-NN, label them into each category we care about, and generate their corresponding embeddings to train the k-NN with the embedding model. Subsequently, we classify the unlabeled data with our trained k-NN to create clusters of categories. We balance the clusters with stratified sampling and then manually curate the remaining prompts by removing overly long prompts (greater than 5000 words) and checking for low-quality content (nonsense prompts, NSFW etc.) to obtain the final evaluation set.

Benchmark (MTEB) Leaderboard (Muennighoff et al., 2022) and multilingual capability. If the k-NN encounters a sample which it is not familiar with or uncertain to label, we want those samples to be classified as general prompts. We use entropy of k-NN classifier probabilities of various categories for a given prompt as the measure of uncertainty. If entropy if too high entropy of the output of the classifier is too high, we bucket the sample into the default/general category (Settles, 2010). We set the entropy threshold to be 1.5 based on careful error analysis on the validation set.

After labeling with k-NN, we conducted stratified sampling within each cluster, selecting 100 samples for curation. We then filtered out excessively long prompts (longer than 5000 words) that could overwhelm the judge's context window. Additionally, we reviewed the remaining prompts to eliminate those that were nonsensical or of low quality. During the evaluation, we observed that categories with a small number of examples had a significant impact on the category's win rate. The inherent variability of the LLM-as-a-Judge evaluation, even with a fixed random seed and temperature set to 0.0, made it challenging to discern which model performed better in those categories. To mitigate this uncertainty, we ensured that any category with fewer than 90-100 examples was supplemented with additional data, enabling us to obtain meaningful and interpretable results. Our final evaluation set comprises 1573 examples.

4.2 LLM-as-a-Judge Details

We follow a similar scoring setup as Arena-Hard (Li et al., 2024a) and Alpaca-Eval (Dubois et al., 2024a) where we use GPT-4o as a judge model and GPT-4o as a reference model as well. For each model we want to test, we obtain the completions and ask GPT-4o to record which model responses is better for the input prompt. In order to mitigate positional bias, we swap the completions between the model we are evaluating and the reference on a coin flip.

4.3 Obtaining Confidence Intervals

We follow the setup outlined in *Li et. al* (Li et al., 2024a; Chiang et al., 2024). We use the Bradley-Terry model in order to model the preference distribution between models on the leaderboard and the reference model (GPT-4o in our case). We aggregate preference pairs between models and perform 100 rounds of bootstrapping to obtain 95% confidence intervals for each model ranking.

We conduct the same analysis with annotations, denoting for each prompt which model response was preferred, from the Alpaca-Eval repo to obtain mean ELO rankings and 95% confidence intervals according to their leaderboard. Since similar artifacts (model preference comparisons) are not updated on Arena-Hard v0.1, we take the model winrates (ELO scores not listed) and 95% confidence intervals from their repo[2]. For Chatbot Arena, we do the same thing and took model winrates/ELO

[2] 7/26/2024

scores as well as the confidence intervals from the website[3] as a source of ground truth.

4.4 Metrics

There are four different metrics we use to judge the efficacy of a benchmark. The first of these is Spearman's correlation coefficient, which measures the rankings order between the two benchmarks. The other metrics are: separability, agreement with Confidence Interval (CI), and Brier Score. Separability refers to how well the benchmark can separate various models with high confidence. In particular, if on benchmark A model M1 has a higher ELO/winrate than model M2 and C_M refers to the confidence intervals of model M, S is a binary variable indicating if benchmark A is able to separate between model M1 and M2, $S = \mathbf{1}_{C_{M1} \cap C_{M_2} = \emptyset}$. The separability is then calculated as a ratio over all possible model pairs. Agreement with CI measures how well benchmarks A and B confidently distinguish between two models with the same ordering. The Brier Score evaluates an LLM benchmark's ability to predict the ranking of a pair of competing models, rewarding confidence in accurate predictions and penalizing confidence in incorrect ones. More details behind these metrics can be found in (Li et al., 2024a). Ultimately, we want our benchmark to align with Chatbot Arena as that is seen as an oracle for modeling human preferences.

5 Results

5.1 Separability, Agreement with CI (95%), Pair Brier Score

Our main results can be found in Table 1. With the exception of Chatbot Arena, our benchmark's separability is 84.4% compared to other baselines like Arena-Hard v0.1 (80%) and Alpaca-Eval 2.0 LC (73.33%), which shows that our benchmark can better differentiate amongst different models.

One interesting datapoint regarding separability is Chatbot Arena's score of 100% which may be attributed to a combination of two factors: 1) Chatbot Arena has more battles than any of the benchmarks listed in Table 1 and 2) Chatbot Arena includes battles between many different models rather than fixing a reference model like the other benchmarks. By providing the Bradley-Terry model bootstrapping process with more varied battles, Chatbot Arena is able to produce tighter confidence intervals, suggesting a future avenue for investigation is whether confidence estimation should include multiple reference answers during judging to more closely simulate Chatbot Arena.

Our benchmark showed an 84.44% agreement with CI with respect to Chatbot Arena, which is higher than Arena-Hard v0.1's 75.50% and Alpaca-Eval 2.0 LC's 64.44%. This demonstrates that our benchmark has higher alignment with respect to Chatbot Arena which is supposed to be approximation of human preferences. In addition, our benchmark has a Spearman's correlation coefficient of 0.915, indicating a strong correlation in rankings order compared to Alpaca-Eval 2.0 LC's 0.2969. While our leaderboard ranking consists of 10 models, the pool of models we have included are the latest SOTA models that have been released so as to have the maximum amount of overlap possible. Finally, our benchmark scored a Brier score of 0.0417, which is lower than Alpaca-Eval 2.0 LC's 0.0937, demonstrating better confidence in accurate predictions.

5.2 Diversity

Due to our data sources being quite diverse rather than simply just ChatBot Arena (Chiang et al., 2024), we are able to have more diversity in our evaluation set. To demonstrate this, we label Arena-Hard v0.1 with our kNN model using the entropy threshold to get a distribution of categories in that evaluation set. As shown in Figure 3, there is an over-representation of coding prompts, which comes from a byproduct of their data pipeline filtering for the hardest, highest quality which skews towards coding. Similarly, Alpaca-Eval's prompt distribution shown in Figure 2 demonstrates that there is a large emphasis on general chat queries, along with some coding and math prompts while medical and law prompts are relatively underrepresented.

Our evaluation set breakdown in Figure 6(a) which covers more domains than the baseline, such languages like Arabic, Japanese, Hungarian and more. The close to equal distribution amongst the categories is likely due to the effect stratified sampling. We compare how our evaluation set category breakdown compared with LM-SYS Conversations (using our k-NN labeling approach) (Zheng et al., 2023b) in Figure 6(b), which is a snapshot of cleaned Chatbot Arena conversations from April to June 2023. In Figure 6(b), "Other" refers to the languages our k-NN classifier recognizes but groups them together collectively. We note that this distri-

[3] 7/25/2024

	Chatbot Arena	Arena Hard v0.1	Alpaca-Eval 2.0 LC	Ours
Separability	**100%**	80%	73.33%	84.44%
Agreement with CI (95%)	N/A	75.50%	64.44%	**84.44%**
Spearman's Correlation	N/A	0.187	0.2969	**0.915**
Brier Score	N/A	N/A	0.0937	**0.0417**

Table 1: Main results comparing the various benchmarks.

bution looks similar to Alpaca-Eval and the general category may contain additional languages not recognized by the classifier so it may have exceeded the entropy threshold.

5.3 Category Separability

Due to our unique ability to categorize the prompts, we can compute category separability for all the various categories in our evaluation set. Across 14 different categories, we do the same bootstrapping procedure on the category data to obtain the mean winrate/ELO and 95% CI, shown in Table 2. In general, there is a drop in separability when we look both at ELO ratings and winrate due to each category having a lower number of samples and thus larger CIs as a result.

The category-wise separability can act as an indicator which categories are superior at testing out the performance of models. Interestingly, across ELO and winrate rankings, Hungarian has the best separability of all categories, achieving 66.67% and 75.56% respectively. The medical category seems to be lowest separability around 55.56% and 68.89% respectively. The separability also indicates to use which categories we may need to add more samples to improve the confidence intervals.

Category	Ranking winrate	Ranking ELO
ar	73.33%	57.78%
ru	71.11%	55.56%
finance	75.56%	57.78%
sr	71.11%	53.33%
tr	73.33%	55.56%
general	77.78%	55.78%
hu	75.56%	66.67%
ja	71.11%	57.78%
medical	68.89%	55.56%
law	73.33%	51.11%
th	71.11%	57.78%
coding	73.33%	55.56%
sl	77.78%	53.33%
math	73.33%	55.56%

Table 2: Winrate and ELO separability for different categories

5.4 Using different judges

We conduct an ablation of judge models on our evaluation, as we want to understand the effect of judge models on separability, Agreement with CI (95%) and Brier Score. We consider GPT-4o mini as one of the judges to be a small-closed source foil to GPT-4o. The other judges that we consider are open source models such as: Llama 3.1 405B instruct (using SambaNova's developer API)[4] and Llama 3.1 70B Instruct-Turbo[5]. We follow the same setup as gpt-4o with these other judge models.

Our results are shown in Table 3. In terms of separability, GPT-4o-mini and 405B get 82.2% and 70B get 84% separability, comparable to GPT-4o's separability. 405B and GPT-4o-mini attain similar Agreement with CI (95%) close to 76% while 70B is almost 10 points lower; GPT-4o is the clear winner having the highest agreement with CI (95%). With the exception of 70B, all models get similar Brier Scores indicating that the Bradley-Terry models used to generate the rankings on confidence intervals for each judge are similarly confident. 70B's high Brier score (relative to other judges), in addition to Agreement with CI, indicates that it poor judge than the other listed in Table 3.

The Spearman's correlation coefficient (with respect to ChatBot Arena rankings) seems to indicate that GPT-4o-mini, Llama 3.1 405B, and 70B are poor judges getting a correlation of only 0.0787 vs. GPT-4o's 0.915. Looking at Figure 7, it seems this aberration comes from both judges rating Claude Sonnet 3.5 over GPT-4o, Llama 3 70b over Claude Opus and Gemma2 27B over Gemini 1.5 Flash. Of course, Spearman's correlation only measures correlation the final rank order of models with respect to ChatBot Arena and is a strictly weaker metric than Agreement with CI (95%). This finding seems to suggest while weaker closed-source models (like

[4]cloud.sambanova.ai

[5]https://api.together.ai/models/meta-llama/Meta-Llama-3.1-70B-Instruct-Turbo

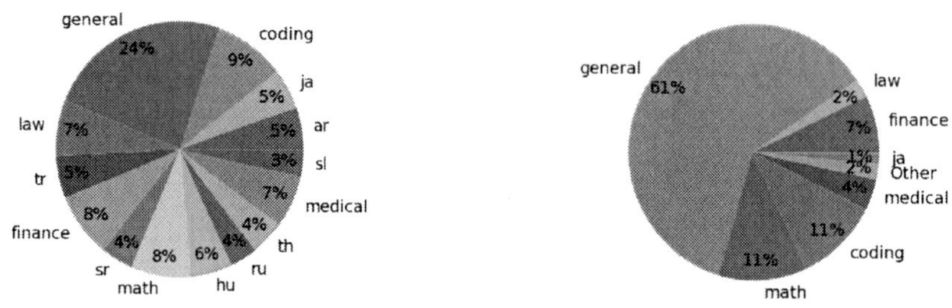

(a) Our evaluation set category breakdown

(b) LMSys Conversations category breakdown

Figure 6: We look at the category breakdown on our evaluation set (Figure 6(a)) compared to LM-SYS Conversations (Figure 6(b)). We can clearly see that our evaluation set covers more languages and niche domains such as law and medical categories are a higher percentage of our evaluation set.

	GPT-4o	GPT-4o-mini	Llama 3.1 405B	Llama 3.1 70B
Separability	84.44%	82.22%	82.22%	84.44%
Agreement with CI (95%)	84.44%	76.77%	75.55%	66.66%
Spearman's Correlation	0.915	0.0787	0.0787	0.0787
Brier Score	0.0417	0.062	0.0603	0.0955

Table 3: Comparing various judges on our evaluation set.

GPT-4o-mini) and open-source judge models seem to be able to separate other models based on capability, they still lack the preciseness that GPT-4o offers to align with rankings from Chatbot Arena.

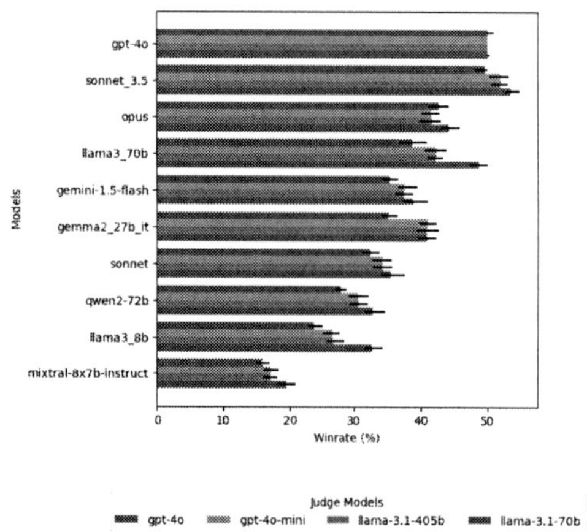

Figure 7: Visual comparison of different judge's separability on our benchmark.

6 Limitations/Future Work

There are certain limitations to our work. Currently, the categories we enumerate in our data pipeline is manually specified by humans and significant curation is done to ensure high quality prompts; for future work, we want to expand to using LLMs as category generators as well as quality checkers to automate the human effort out of this pipeline. Moreover, the diversity of prompts in the multilingual categories could be limited as we consider bucket all subdomains of a language into the same category. Sub-categorization of domains in non-English languages is left for future work.

For improving our leaderboard, we wish to add more models to be more representative of the entire spectrum of other leaderboards and futhur increasing the quality of the Bradley-Terry models we use to obtain the model's confidence intervals. In order to improve category separability, we look to creating a methodology on figuring out the minimum number of samples required to improve separability.

The other aspect of future work relies to details regarding LLM-as-a-judge evaluation. Typically, the judge models are ablated but less explored is the quality of the reference answer and whether one can use a weaker model instead of a stronger one to see if metrics are maintained. Current metrics define how separable a benchmark is and how much it aligns with human preferences but fails to account for the composition and diversity of the underlying data. For future work, we seek to quantify the diversity of each benchmark to understand how many capabilities/domains it spans.

7 Conclusion

We introduce a data pipeline that leverages via semi-supervised learning with a k-NN to enable practitioners to create benchmarks on their own data for targeted domains. Through evaluations of ten various closed and open-sourced models, we demonstrated that our benchmark achieves higher separability and agreement with CI with respect to Chatbot Arena, nearly 5 and 10 percentage points higher than the next best baseline, respectively. Our benchmark covers a wide variety of topics such as finance, medicine, legal and different languages absent in other LLM as a judge benchmarks. We hope that LLM developers can use our data pipeline to create their own benchmarks to evaluate their models for their particular use-case.

References

Aida Amini, Saadia Gabriel, Shanchuan Lin, Rik Koncel-Kedziorski, Yejin Choi, and Hannaneh Hajishirzi. 2019. MathQA: Towards interpretable math word problem solving with operation-based formalisms. In *Proceedings of the 2019 Conference of the North American Chapter of the Association for Computational Linguistics: Human Language Technologies, Volume 1 (Long and Short Papers)*, pages 2357–2367, Minneapolis, Minnesota. Association for Computational Linguistics.

Mark Chen, Jerry Tworek, Heewoo Jun, Qiming Yuan, Henrique Ponde de Oliveira Pinto, Jared Kaplan, Harri Edwards, Yuri Burda, Nicholas Joseph, Greg Brockman, Alex Ray, Raul Puri, Gretchen Krueger, Michael Petrov, Heidy Khlaaf, Girish Sastry, Pamela Mishkin, Brooke Chan, Scott Gray, Nick Ryder, Mikhail Pavlov, Alethea Power, Lukasz Kaiser, Mohammad Bavarian, Clemens Winter, Philippe Tillet, Felipe Petroski Such, Dave Cummings, Matthias Plappert, Fotios Chantzis, Elizabeth Barnes, Ariel Herbert-Voss, William Hebgen Guss, Alex Nichol, Alex Paino, Nikolas Tezak, Jie Tang, Igor Babuschkin, Suchir Balaji, Shantanu Jain, William Saunders, Christopher Hesse, Andrew N. Carr, Jan Leike, Josh Achiam, Vedant Misra, Evan Morikawa, Alec Radford, Matthew Knight, Miles Brundage, Mira Murati, Katie Mayer, Peter Welinder, Bob McGrew, Dario Amodei, Sam McCandlish, Ilya Sutskever, and Wojciech Zaremba. 2021. Evaluating large language models trained on code. *Preprint*, arXiv:2107.03374.

Wei-Lin Chiang, Lianmin Zheng, Ying Sheng, Anastasios Nikolas Angelopoulos, Tianle Li, Dacheng Li, Hao Zhang, Banghua Zhu, Michael Jordan, Joseph E. Gonzalez, and Ion Stoica. 2024. Chatbot arena: An open platform for evaluating llms by human preference. *Preprint*, arXiv:2403.04132.

Christopher Clark, Kenton Lee, Ming-Wei Chang, Tom Kwiatkowski, Michael Collins, and Kristina Toutanova. 2019. Boolq: Exploring the surprising difficulty of natural yes/no questions. *Preprint*, arXiv:1905.10044.

Karl Cobbe, Vineet Kosaraju, Mohammad Bavarian, Mark Chen, Heewoo Jun, Lukasz Kaiser, Matthias Plappert, Jerry Tworek, Jacob Hilton, Reiichiro Nakano, Christopher Hesse, and John Schulman. 2021. Training verifiers to solve math word problems. *Preprint*, arXiv:2110.14168.

DeepMind. 2024. Gemini flash. Accessed: 2024-08-14.

Abhimanyu Dubey, Abhinav Jauhri, Abhinav Pandey, Abhishek Kadian, Ahmad Al-Dahle, Aiesha Letman, Akhil Mathur, Alan Schelten, Amy Yang, Angela Fan, Anirudh Goyal, Anthony Hartshorn, Aobo Yang, Archi Mitra, Archie Sravankumar, Artem Korenev, Arthur Hinsvark, Arun Rao, Aston Zhang, Aurelien Rodriguez, Austen Gregerson, Ava Spataru, Baptiste Roziere, Bethany Biron, Binh Tang, Bobbie Chern, Charlotte Caucheteux, Chaya Nayak, Chloe Bi, Chris Marra, Chris McConnell, Christian Keller, Christophe Touret, Chunyang Wu, Corinne Wong, Cristian Canton Ferrer, Cyrus Nikolaidis, Damien Allonsius, Daniel Song, Danielle Pintz, Danny Livshits, David Esiobu, Dhruv Choudhary, Dhruv Mahajan, Diego Garcia-Olano, Diego Perino, Dieuwke Hupkes, Egor Lakomkin, Ehab AlBadawy, Elina Lobanova, Emily Dinan, Eric Michael Smith, Filip Radenovic, Frank Zhang, Gabriel Synnaeve, Gabrielle Lee, Georgia Lewis Anderson, Graeme Nail, Gregoire Mialon, Guan Pang, Guillem Cucurell, Hailey Nguyen, Hannah Korevaar, Hu Xu, Hugo Touvron, Iliyan Zarov, Imanol Arrieta Ibarra, Isabel Kloumann, Ishan Misra, Ivan Evtimov, Jade Copet, Jaewon Lee, Jan Geffert, Jana Vranes, Jason Park, Jay Mahadeokar, Jeet Shah, Jelmer van der Linde, Jennifer Billock, Jenny Hong, Jenya Lee, Jeremy Fu, Jianfeng Chi, Jianyu Huang, Jiawen Liu, Jie Wang, Jiecao Yu, Joanna Bitton, Joe Spisak, Jongsoo Park, Joseph Rocca, Joshua Johnstun, Joshua Saxe, Junteng Jia, Kalyan Vasuden Alwala, Kartikeya Upasani, Kate Plawiak, Ke Li, Kenneth Heafield, Kevin Stone, Khalid El-Arini, Krithika Iyer, Kshitiz Malik, Kuenley Chiu, Kunal Bhalla, Lauren Rantala-Yeary, Laurens van der Maaten, Lawrence Chen, Liang Tan, Liz Jenkins, Louis Martin, Lovish Madaan, Lubo Malo, Lukas Blecher, Lukas Landzaat, Luke de Oliveira, Madeline Muzzi, Mahesh Pasupuleti, Mannat Singh, Manohar Paluri, Marcin Kardas, Mathew Oldham,

Mathieu Rita, Maya Pavlova, Melanie Kambadur, Mike Lewis, Min Si, Mitesh Kumar Singh, Mona Hassan, Naman Goyal, Narjes Torabi, Nikolay Bashlykov, Nikolay Bogoychev, Niladri Chatterji, Olivier Duchenne, Onur Çelebi, Patrick Alrassy, Pengchuan Zhang, Pengwei Li, Petar Vasic, Peter Weng, Prajjwal Bhargava, Pratik Dubal, Praveen Krishnan, Punit Singh Koura, Puxin Xu, Qing He, Qingxiao Dong, Ragavan Srinivasan, Raj Ganapathy, Ramon Calderer, Ricardo Silveira Cabral, Robert Stojnic, Roberta Raileanu, Rohit Girdhar, Rohit Patel, Romain Sauvestre, Ronnie Polidoro, Roshan Sumbaly, Ross Taylor, Ruan Silva, Rui Hou, Rui Wang, Saghar Hosseini, Sahana Chennabasappa, Sanjay Singh, Sean Bell, Seohyun Sonia Kim, Sergey Edunov, Shaoliang Nie, Sharan Narang, Sharath Raparthy, Sheng Shen, Shengye Wan, Shruti Bhosale, Shun Zhang, Simon Vandenhende, Soumya Batra, Spencer Whitman, Sten Sootla, Stephane Collot, Suchin Gururangan, Sydney Borodinsky, Tamar Herman, Tara Fowler, Tarek Sheasha, Thomas Georgiou, Thomas Scialom, Tobias Speckbacher, Todor Mihaylov, Tong Xiao, Ujjwal Karn, Vedanuj Goswami, Vibhor Gupta, Vignesh Ramanathan, Viktor Kerkez, Vincent Gonguet, Virginie Do, Vish Vogeti, Vladan Petrovic, Weiwei Chu, Wenhan Xiong, Wenyin Fu, Whitney Meers, Xavier Martinet, Xiaodong Wang, Xiaoqing Ellen Tan, Xinfeng Xie, Xuchao Jia, Xuewei Wang, Yaelle Goldschlag, Yashesh Gaur, Yasmine Babaei, Yi Wen, Yiwen Song, Yuchen Zhang, Yue Li, Yuning Mao, Zacharie Delpierre Coudert, Zheng Yan, Zhengxing Chen, Zoe Papakipos, Aaditya Singh, Aaron Grattafiori, Abha Jain, Adam Kelsey, Adam Shajnfeld, Adithya Gangidi, Adolfo Victoria, Ahuva Goldstand, Ajay Menon, Ajay Sharma, Alex Boesenberg, Alex Vaughan, Alexei Baevski, Allie Feinstein, Amanda Kallet, Amit Sangani, Anam Yunus, Andrei Lupu, Andres Alvarado, Andrew Caples, Andrew Gu, Andrew Ho, Andrew Poulton, Andrew Ryan, Ankit Ramchandani, Annie Franco, Aparajita Saraf, Arkabandhu Chowdhury, Ashley Gabriel, Ashwin Bharambe, Assaf Eisenman, Azadeh Yazdan, Beau James, Ben Maurer, Benjamin Leonhardi, Bernie Huang, Beth Loyd, Beto De Paola, Bhargavi Paranjape, Bing Liu, Bo Wu, Boyu Ni, Braden Hancock, Bram Wasti, Brandon Spence, Brani Stojkovic, Brian Gamido, Britt Montalvo, Carl Parker, Carly Burton, Catalina Mejia, Changhan Wang, Changkyu Kim, Chao Zhou, Chester Hu, Ching-Hsiang Chu, Chris Cai, Chris Tindal, Christoph Feichtenhofer, Damon Civin, Dana Beaty, Daniel Kreymer, Daniel Li, Danny Wyatt, David Adkins, David Xu, Davide Testuggine, Delia David, Devi Parikh, Diana Liskovich, Didem Foss, Dingkang Wang, Duc Le, Dustin Holland, Edward Dowling, Eissa Jamil, Elaine Montgomery, Eleonora Presani, Emily Hahn, Emily Wood, Erik Brinkman, Esteban Arcaute, Evan Dunbar, Evan Smothers, Fei Sun, Felix Kreuk, Feng Tian, Firat Ozgenel, Francesco Caggioni, Francisco Guzmán, Frank Kanayet, Frank Seide, Gabriela Medina Florez, Gabriella Schwarz, Gada Badeer, Georgia Swee, Gil Halpern, Govind Thattai, Grant Herman, Grigory Sizov, Guangyi, Zhang, Guna Lakshminarayanan, Hamid Shojanazeri, Han Zou, Hannah Wang, Hanwen Zha, Haroun Habeeb, Harrison Rudolph, Helen Suk, Henry Aspegren, Hunter Goldman, Igor Molybog, Igor Tufanov, Irina-Elena Veliche, Itai Gat, Jake Weissman, James Geboski, James Kohli, Japhet Asher, Jean-Baptiste Gaya, Jeff Marcus, Jeff Tang, Jennifer Chan, Jenny Zhen, Jeremy Reizenstein, Jeremy Teboul, Jessica Zhong, Jian Jin, Jingyi Yang, Joe Cummings, Jon Carvill, Jon Shepard, Jonathan McPhie, Jonathan Torres, Josh Ginsburg, Junjie Wang, Kai Wu, Kam Hou U, Karan Saxena, Karthik Prasad, Kartikay Khandelwal, Katayoun Zand, Kathy Matosich, Kaushik Veeraraghavan, Kelly Michelena, Keqian Li, Kun Huang, Kunal Chawla, Kushal Lakhotia, Kyle Huang, Lailin Chen, Lakshya Garg, Lavender A, Leandro Silva, Lee Bell, Lei Zhang, Liangpeng Guo, Licheng Yu, Liron Moshkovich, Luca Wehrstedt, Madian Khabsa, Manav Avalani, Manish Bhatt, Maria Tsimpoukelli, Martynas Mankus, Matan Hasson, Matthew Lennie, Matthias Reso, Maxim Groshev, Maxim Naumov, Maya Lathi, Meghan Keneally, Michael L. Seltzer, Michal Valko, Michelle Restrepo, Mihir Patel, Mik Vyatskov, Mikayel Samvelyan, Mike Clark, Mike Macey, Mike Wang, Miquel Jubert Hermoso, Mo Metanat, Mohammad Rastegari, Munish Bansal, Nandhini Santhanam, Natascha Parks, Natasha White, Navyata Bawa, Nayan Singhal, Nick Egebo, Nicolas Usunier, Nikolay Pavlovich Laptev, Ning Dong, Ning Zhang, Norman Cheng, Oleg Chernoguz, Olivia Hart, Omkar Salpekar, Ozlem Kalinli, Parkin Kent, Parth Parekh, Paul Saab, Pavan Balaji, Pedro Rittner, Philip Bontrager, Pierre Roux, Piotr Dollar, Polina Zvyagina, Prashant Ratanchandani, Pritish Yuvraj, Qian Liang, Rachad Alao, Rachel Rodriguez, Rafi Ayub, Raghotham Murthy, Raghu Nayani, Rahul Mitra, Raymond Li, Rebekkah Hogan, Robin Battey, Rocky Wang, Rohan Maheswari, Russ Howes, Ruty Rinott, Sai Jayesh Bondu, Samyak Datta, Sara Chugh, Sara Hunt, Sargun Dhillon, Sasha Sidorov, Satadru Pan, Saurabh Verma, Seiji Yamamoto, Sharadh Ramaswamy, Shaun Lindsay, Shaun Lindsay, Sheng Feng, Shenghao Lin, Shengxin Cindy Zha, Shiva Shankar, Shuqiang Zhang, Shuqiang Zhang, Sinong Wang, Sneha Agarwal, Soji Sajuyigbe, Soumith Chintala, Stephanie Max, Stephen Chen, Steve Kehoe, Steve Satterfield, Sudarshan Govindaprasad, Sumit Gupta, Sungmin Cho, Sunny Virk, Suraj Subramanian, Sy Choudhury, Sydney Goldman, Tal Remez, Tamar Glaser, Tamara Best, Thilo Kohler, Thomas Robinson, Tianhe Li, Tianjun Zhang, Tim Matthews, Timothy Chou, Tzook Shaked, Varun Vontimitta, Victoria Ajayi, Victoria Montanez, Vijai Mohan, Vinay Satish Kumar, Vishal Mangla, Vlad Ionescu, Vlad Poenaru, Vlad Tiberiu Mihailescu, Vladimir Ivanov, Wei Li, Wenchen Wang, Wenwen Jiang, Wes Bouaziz, Will Constable, Xiaocheng Tang, Xiaofang Wang, Xiaojian Wu, Xiaolan Wang, Xide Xia, Xilun Wu, Xinbo Gao, Yanjun Chen, Ye Hu, Ye Jia, Ye Qi, Yenda Li, Yilin Zhang, Ying Zhang, Yossi Adi, Youngjin Nam, Yu, Wang, Yuchen Hao, Yundi Qian, Yuzi He, Zach Rait, Zachary DeVito, Zef Rosnbrick, Zhaoduo Wen, Zhenyu Yang, and Zhiwei Zhao. 2024. The llama 3 herd of models. *Preprint*, arXiv:2407.21783.

Yann Dubois, Balázs Galambosi, Percy Liang, and Tatsunori B. Hashimoto. 2024a. Length-controlled alpacaeval: A simple way to debias automatic evaluators. *Preprint*, arXiv:2404.04475.

Yann Dubois, Xuechen Li, Rohan Taori, Tianyi Zhang, Ishaan Gulrajani, Jimmy Ba, Carlos Guestrin, Percy Liang, and Tatsunori B. Hashimoto. 2024b. Alpacafarm: A simulation framework for methods that learn from human feedback. *Preprint*, arXiv:2305.14387.

Gaurang Bharti. 2024. finance-alpaca (revision 51d16b6).

Mohamed Farouk Abdel Hady and Friedhelm Schwenker. 2013. *Semi-supervised Learning*, pages 215–239. Springer Berlin Heidelberg, Berlin, Heidelberg.

Dan Hendrycks, Collin Burns, Steven Basart, Andy Zou, Mantas Mazeika, Dawn Song, and Jacob Steinhardt. 2021a. Measuring massive multitask language understanding. *Preprint*, arXiv:2009.03300.

Dan Hendrycks, Collin Burns, Saurav Kadavath, Akul Arora, Steven Basart, Eric Tang, Dawn Song, and Jacob Steinhardt. 2021b. Measuring mathematical problem solving with the math dataset. *Preprint*, arXiv:2103.03874.

Naman Jain, King Han, Alex Gu, Wen-Ding Li, Fanjia Yan, Tianjun Zhang, Sida Wang, Armando Solar-Lezama, Koushik Sen, and Ion Stoica. 2024. Livecodebench: Holistic and contamination free evaluation of large language models for code. *Preprint*, arXiv:2403.07974.

Naman Jain, Manish Shetty, Tianjun Zhang, King Han, Koushik Sen, and Ion Stoica. R2e: Turning any github repository into a programming agent environment. In *ICML 2024*.

Qiao Jin, Bhuwan Dhingra, Zhengping Liu, William Cohen, and Xinghua Lu. 2019. Pubmedqa: A dataset for biomedical research question answering. In *Proceedings of the 2019 Conference on Empirical Methods in Natural Language Processing and the 9th International Joint Conference on Natural Language Processing (EMNLP-IJCNLP)*, pages 2567–2577.

Jon Durbin. 2024. airoboros-gpt4-1.2.

Douwe Kiela, Max Bartolo, Yixin Nie, Divyansh Kaushik, Atticus Geiger, Zhengxuan Wu, Bertie Vidgen, Grusha Prasad, Amanpreet Singh, Pratik Ringshia, Zhiyi Ma, Tristan Thrush, Sebastian Riedel, Zeerak Waseem, Pontus Stenetorp, Robin Jia, Mohit Bansal, Christopher Potts, and Adina Williams. 2021. Dynabench: Rethinking benchmarking in nlp. *Preprint*, arXiv:2104.14337.

Anastassia Kornilova and Vladimir Eidelman. 2019. BillSum: A corpus for automatic summarization of US legislation. In *Proceedings of the 2nd Workshop on New Frontiers in Summarization*, pages 48–56, Hong Kong, China. Association for Computational Linguistics.

Jonathan Li, Rohan Bhambhoria, and Xiaodan Zhu. 2022. Parameter-efficient legal domain adaptation. In *Proceedings of the Natural Legal Language Processing Workshop 2022*, pages 119–129, Abu Dhabi, United Arab Emirates (Hybrid). Association for Computational Linguistics.

Tianle Li, Wei-Lin Chiang, Evan Frick, Lisa Dunlap, Tianhao Wu, Banghua Zhu, Joseph E. Gonzalez, and Ion Stoica. 2024a. From crowdsourced data to high-quality benchmarks: Arena-hard and benchbuilder pipeline. *Preprint*, arXiv:2406.11939.

Xiang Lisa Li, Evan Zheran Liu, Percy Liang, and Tatsunori Hashimoto. 2024b. Autobencher: Creating salient, novel, difficult datasets for language models. *Preprint*, arXiv:2407.08351.

Xuechen Li, Tianyi Zhang, Yann Dubois, Rohan Taori, Ishaan Gulrajani, Carlos Guestrin, Percy Liang, and Tatsunori B. Hashimoto. 2023. Alpacaeval: An automatic evaluator of instruction-following models. `https://github.com/tatsu-lab/alpaca_eval`.

Percy Liang, Rishi Bommasani, Tony Lee, Dimitris Tsipras, Dilara Soylu, Michihiro Yasunaga, Yian Zhang, Deepak Narayanan, Yuhuai Wu, Ananya Kumar, Benjamin Newman, Binhang Yuan, Bobby Yan, Ce Zhang, Christian Cosgrove, Christopher D. Manning, Christopher Ré, Diana Acosta-Navas, Drew A. Hudson, Eric Zelikman, Esin Durmus, Faisal Ladhak, Frieda Rong, Hongyu Ren, Huaxiu Yao, Jue Wang, Keshav Santhanam, Laurel Orr, Lucia Zheng, Mert Yuksekgonul, Mirac Suzgun, Nathan Kim, Neel Guha, Niladri Chatterji, Omar Khattab, Peter Henderson, Qian Huang, Ryan Chi, Sang Michael Xie, Shibani Santurkar, Surya Ganguli, Tatsunori Hashimoto, Thomas Icard, Tianyi Zhang, Vishrav Chaudhary, William Wang, Xuechen Li, Yifan Mai, Yuhui Zhang, and Yuta Koreeda. 2023. Holistic evaluation of language models. *Preprint*, arXiv:2211.09110.

Stephanie Lin, Jacob Hilton, and Owain Evans. 2022. Truthfulqa: Measuring how models mimic human falsehoods. *Preprint*, arXiv:2109.07958.

Kelly Marchisio, Wei-Yin Ko, Alexandre Bérard, Théo Dehaze, and Sebastian Ruder. 2024. Understanding and mitigating language confusion in llms. *Preprint*, arXiv:2406.20052.

Antonio Mucherino, Petraq J. Papajorgji, and Panos M. Pardalos. 2009. *k-Nearest Neighbor Classification*, pages 83–106. Springer New York, New York, NY.

Niklas Muennighoff, Nouamane Tazi, Loïc Magne, and Nils Reimers. 2022. Mteb: Massive text embedding benchmark. *arXiv preprint arXiv:2210.07316*.

Shashi Narayan, Shay B. Cohen, and Mirella Lapata. 2018. Don't give me the details, just the summary! topic-aware convolutional neural networks for extreme summarization. *Preprint*, arXiv:1808.08745.

OpenAI. 2024a. Gpt-4o mini: Advancing cost-efficient intelligence. Accessed: 2024-08-14.

OpenAI. 2024b. New embedding models and api updates. Accessed: 2024-08-14.

OpenAI, Josh Achiam, Steven Adler, Sandhini Agarwal, Lama Ahmad, Ilge Akkaya, Florencia Leoni Aleman, Diogo Almeida, Janko Altenschmidt, Sam Altman, Shyamal Anadkat, Red Avila, Igor Babuschkin, Suchir Balaji, Valerie Balcom, Paul Baltescu, Haiming Bao, Mohammad Bavarian, Jeff Belgum, Irwan Bello, Jake Berdine, Gabriel Bernadett-Shapiro, Christopher Berner, Lenny Bogdonoff, Oleg Boiko, Madelaine Boyd, Anna-Luisa Brakman, Greg Brockman, Tim Brooks, Miles Brundage, Kevin Button, Trevor Cai, Rosie Campbell, Andrew Cann, Brittany Carey, Chelsea Carlson, Rory Carmichael, Brooke Chan, Che Chang, Fotis Chantzis, Derek Chen, Sully Chen, Ruby Chen, Jason Chen, Mark Chen, Ben Chess, Chester Cho, Casey Chu, Hyung Won Chung, Dave Cummings, Jeremiah Currier, Yunxing Dai, Cory Decareaux, Thomas Degry, Noah Deutsch, Damien Deville, Arka Dhar, David Dohan, Steve Dowling, Sheila Dunning, Adrien Ecoffet, Atty Eleti, Tyna Eloundou, David Farhi, Liam Fedus, Niko Felix, Simón Posada Fishman, Juston Forte, Isabella Fulford, Leo Gao, Elie Georges, Christian Gibson, Vik Goel, Tarun Gogineni, Gabriel Goh, Rapha Gontijo-Lopes, Jonathan Gordon, Morgan Grafstein, Scott Gray, Ryan Greene, Joshua Gross, Shixiang Shane Gu, Yufei Guo, Chris Hallacy, Jesse Han, Jeff Harris, Yuchen He, Mike Heaton, Johannes Heidecke, Chris Hesse, Alan Hickey, Wade Hickey, Peter Hoeschele, Brandon Houghton, Kenny Hsu, Shengli Hu, Xin Hu, Joost Huizinga, Shantanu Jain, Shawn Jain, Joanne Jang, Angela Jiang, Roger Jiang, Haozhun Jin, Denny Jin, Shino Jomoto, Billie Jonn, Heewoo Jun, Tomer Kaftan, Łukasz Kaiser, Ali Kamali, Ingmar Kanitscheider, Nitish Shirish Keskar, Tabarak Khan, Logan Kilpatrick, Jong Wook Kim, Christina Kim, Yongjik Kim, Jan Hendrik Kirchner, Jamie Kiros, Matt Knight, Daniel Kokotajlo, Łukasz Kondraciuk, Andrew Kondrich, Aris Konstantinidis, Kyle Kosic, Gretchen Krueger, Vishal Kuo, Michael Lampe, Ikai Lan, Teddy Lee, Jan Leike, Jade Leung, Daniel Levy, Chak Ming Li, Rachel Lim, Molly Lin, Stephanie Lin, Mateusz Litwin, Theresa Lopez, Ryan Lowe, Patricia Lue, Anna Makanju, Kim Malfacini, Sam Manning, Todor Markov, Yaniv Markovski, Bianca Martin, Katie Mayer, Andrew Mayne, Bob McGrew, Scott Mayer McKinney, Christine McLeavey, Paul McMillan, Jake McNeil, David Medina, Aalok Mehta, Jacob Menick, Luke Metz, Andrey Mishchenko, Pamela Mishkin, Vinnie Monaco, Evan Morikawa, Daniel Mossing, Tong Mu, Mira Murati, Oleg Murk, David Mély, Ashvin Nair, Reiichiro Nakano, Rajeev Nayak, Arvind Neelakantan, Richard Ngo, Hyeonwoo Noh, Long Ouyang, Cullen O'Keefe, Jakub Pachocki, Alex Paino, Joe Palermo, Ashley Pantuliano, Giambattista Parascandolo, Joel Parish, Emy Parparita, Alex Passos, Mikhail Pavlov, Andrew Peng, Adam Perelman, Filipe de Avila Belbute Peres, Michael Petrov, Henrique Ponde de Oliveira Pinto, Michael, Pokorny, Michelle Pokrass, Vitchyr H. Pong, Tolly Powell, Alethea Power, Boris Power, Elizabeth Proehl, Raul Puri, Alec Radford, Jack Rae, Aditya Ramesh, Cameron Raymond, Francis Real, Kendra Rimbach, Carl Ross, Bob Rotsted, Henri Roussez, Nick Ryder, Mario Saltarelli, Ted Sanders, Shibani Santurkar, Girish Sastry, Heather Schmidt, David Schnurr, John Schulman, Daniel Selsam, Kyla Sheppard, Toki Sherbakov, Jessica Shieh, Sarah Shoker, Pranav Shyam, Szymon Sidor, Eric Sigler, Maddie Simens, Jordan Sitkin, Katarina Slama, Ian Sohl, Benjamin Sokolowsky, Yang Song, Natalie Staudacher, Felipe Petroski Such, Natalie Summers, Ilya Sutskever, Jie Tang, Nikolas Tezak, Madeleine B. Thompson, Phil Tillet, Amin Tootoonchian, Elizabeth Tseng, Preston Tuggle, Nick Turley, Jerry Tworek, Juan Felipe Cerón Uribe, Andrea Vallone, Arun Vijayvergiya, Chelsea Voss, Carroll Wainwright, Justin Jay Wang, Alvin Wang, Ben Wang, Jonathan Ward, Jason Wei, CJ Weinmann, Akila Welihinda, Peter Welinder, Jiayi Weng, Lilian Weng, Matt Wiethoff, Dave Willner, Clemens Winter, Samuel Wolrich, Hannah Wong, Lauren Workman, Sherwin Wu, Jeff Wu, Michael Wu, Kai Xiao, Tao Xu, Sarah Yoo, Kevin Yu, Qiming Yuan, Wojciech Zaremba, Rowan Zellers, Chong Zhang, Marvin Zhang, Shengjia Zhao, Tianhao Zheng, Juntang Zhuang, William Zhuk, and Barret Zoph. 2024. Gpt-4 technical report. *Preprint*, arXiv:2303.08774.

Van Parsons. 2017. *Stratified Sampling*.

Nazneen Rajani, Lewis Tunstall, Edward Beeching, Nathan Lambert, Alexander M. Rush, and Thomas Wolf. 2023. No robots. `https://huggingface.co/datasets/HuggingFaceH4/no_robots`.

Oscar Sainz, Jon Campos, Iker García-Ferrero, Julen Etxaniz, Oier Lopez de Lacalle, and Eneko Agirre. 2023. NLP evaluation in trouble: On the need to measure LLM data contamination for each benchmark. In *Findings of the Association for Computational Linguistics: EMNLP 2023*, pages 10776–10787, Singapore. Association for Computational Linguistics.

Burr Settles. 2010. Active learning literature survey.

Freda Shi, Mirac Suzgun, Markus Freitag, Xuezhi Wang, Suraj Srivats, Soroush Vosoughi, Hyung Won Chung, Yi Tay, Sebastian Ruder, Denny Zhou, Dipanjan Das, and Jason Wei. 2022. Language models are multilingual chain-of-thought reasoners. *Preprint*, arXiv:2210.03057.

Shivalika Singh, Freddie Vargus, Daniel Dsouza, Börje F. Karlsson, Abinaya Mahendiran, Wei-Yin Ko, Herumb Shandilya, Jay Patel, Deividas Mataciunas, Laura OMahony, Mike Zhang, Ramith Hettiarachchi, Joseph Wilson, Marina Machado, Luisa Souza Moura, Dominik Krzemiński, Hakimeh Fadaei, Irem Ergün, Ifeoma Okoh, Aisha Alaagib, Oshan Mudannayake, Zaid Alyafeai, Vu Minh Chien, Sebastian Ruder, Surya Guthikonda, Emad A. Alghamdi, Sebastian Gehrmann, Niklas Muennighoff,

Max Bartolo, Julia Kreutzer, Ahmet Üstün, Marzieh Fadaee, and Sara Hooker. 2024. Aya dataset: An open-access collection for multilingual instruction tuning. *Preprint*, arXiv:2402.06619.

Gemma Team. 2024. Gemma.

Nandan Thakur, Nils Reimers, Andreas Rücklé, Abhishek Srivastava, and Iryna Gurevych. 2021. BEIR: A heterogeneous benchmark for zero-shot evaluation of information retrieval models. In *Thirty-fifth Conference on Neural Information Processing Systems Datasets and Benchmarks Track (Round 2)*.

Pat Verga, Sebastian Hofstatter, Sophia Althammer, Yixuan Su, Aleksandra Piktus, Arkady Arkhangorodsky, Minjie Xu, Naomi White, and Patrick Lewis. 2024. Replacing judges with juries: Evaluating llm generations with a panel of diverse models. *Preprint*, arXiv:2404.18796.

Liang Wang, Nan Yang, Xiaolong Huang, Linjun Yang, Rangan Majumder, and Furu Wei. 2024. Improving text embeddings with large language models. *Preprint*, arXiv:2401.00368.

Colin White, Samuel Dooley, Manley Roberts, Arka Pal, Ben Feuer, Siddhartha Jain, Ravid Shwartz-Ziv, Neel Jain, Khalid Saifullah, Siddartha Naidu, Chinmay Hegde, Yann LeCun, Tom Goldstein, Willie Neiswanger, and Micah Goldblum. 2024. Livebench: A challenging, contamination-free llm benchmark. *Preprint*, arXiv:2406.19314.

Shuo Yang, Wei-Lin Chiang, Lianmin Zheng, Joseph E. Gonzalez, and Ion Stoica. 2023. Rethinking benchmark and contamination for language models with rephrased samples. *Preprint*, arXiv:2311.04850.

Rowan Zellers, Ari Holtzman, Yonatan Bisk, Ali Farhadi, and Yejin Choi. 2019. Hellaswag: Can a machine really finish your sentence? *Preprint*, arXiv:1905.07830.

Lianmin Zheng, Wei-Lin Chiang, Ying Sheng, Siyuan Zhuang, Zhanghao Wu, Yonghao Zhuang, Zi Lin, Zhuohan Li, Dacheng Li, Eric P. Xing, Hao Zhang, Joseph E. Gonzalez, and Ion Stoica. 2023a. Judging llm-as-a-judge with mt-bench and chatbot arena. *Preprint*, arXiv:2306.05685.

Lianmin Zheng, Wei-Lin Chiang, Ying Sheng, Siyuan Zhuang, Zhanghao Wu, Yonghao Zhuang, Zi Lin, Zhuohan Li, Dacheng Li, Eric. P Xing, Hao Zhang, Joseph E. Gonzalez, and Ion Stoica. 2023b. Judging llm-as-a-judge with mt-bench and chatbot arena. *Preprint*, arXiv:2306.05685.

A Appendix

A.1 Data Sources

Table 4 includes various datasets across multiple domains such as medical, legal, financial, and multilingual categories. These sources were selected to ensure a wide range of coverage, contributing to the diversity of the evaluation set. The datasets listed here were crucial for constructing the domain-specific evaluation sets, allowing for the thorough testing of models across different contexts and languages.

A.2 Judge Template

Below is our judge template that we used for our LLM-as-a-judge evaluation:

Please act as an impartial judge and evaluate the quality of the responses provided by two AI assistants to the user question displayed below. You should choose the assistant that follows the user's instructions and answers the user's question better, as well as answering in the desired language of the user. Your evaluation should consider factors such as the helpfulness, relevance, accuracy, depth, creativity, and level of detail of their responses. Begin your evaluation by comparing the two responses and provide a short explanation. Avoid any position biases and ensure that the order in which the responses were presented does not influence your decision. Do not allow the length of the responses to influence your evaluation. Do not favor certain names of the assistants. Be as objective as possible. Your evaluation should only focus on the correctness of the response. After providing your explanation, output your final verdict by strictly following this format: [[A]] if assistant A is better, [[B]] if assistant B is better, and [[C]] for a tie.

For the judge prompt, we used the default prompt from the MT-Bench work with one notable change (Zheng et al., 2023a). When we evaluated multilingual prompts with LLM-as-a-judge, the judge at times incorrectly awards wins to models which don't necessarily follow instructions. Given the sentence "Please respond 'How does the economy work?' in Hungarian," two models might respond differently: 1) one provides a detailed English response with bulleted lists, while 2) the other responds concisely in Hungarian. The judge model will rate the model answering in the incorrect language higher, which is clearly not a measure of the model's multilingual capability (Marchisio et al., 2024). In order to reduce these incorrect decisions, we modified the judge prompt to specifically penalize responses that respond to the prompt in the incorrect language.

In addition to issues with multilingual queries, we also note specifically for coding that GPT-4o seems to prefer models which provide detailed ex-

Datasets
LMSys Chatbot Arena (Chiang et al., 2024)
PubMedQA (Jin et al., 2019)
MathQA (Amini et al., 2019)
No Robots (Rajani et al., 2023)
Aya (Singh et al., 2024)
Legal reddit (Li et al., 2022)
Legal Summ. BillSum (Kornilova and Eidelman, 2019)
Airoboros-gpt4 (Jon Durbin, 2024)
Finance Advisor (Gaurang Bharti, 2024)
Finance Bier QA (Thakur et al., 2021)
MMLU (Hendrycks et al., 2021a)
TruthfulQA (Lin et al., 2022)
GSM8K (Cobbe et al., 2021)

Table 4: Dataset Sources used as input to the data pipeline in Figure 5.

planations to the code even if the code provided is of lower quality compared to a model which has better code quality but is not as verbose. This leads to scenarios where models that have chat but lower benchmark performance (e.g. HumanEval (Chen et al., 2021)) obtain higher winrate than models which are objectively better on coding prompts. To circumvent this issue, we explicitly prompt GPT-4o that it should focus on the correctness of the response as opposed to the style of the response.

A.3 Evaluation Tool

With the notion of self-defined categories and using the LLM-as-a-judge framework, we create an evaluation tool which loads an internal leaderboard from a csv file and breaks down the winrate into several categories the user defined. The UI shows the leaderboard in a dataframe and shows the winrates in set of bar plots across different categories. A screenshot of the tool can be seen in Figure 8.

There is also a feature which enables the user to view completions on the evaluation from both the model the user is interested in, the reference model, and the judge model to examine its reasoning. This tool enables the user to examine where the model they are developing is performing better than other competitors and areas where improvement is required.

Figure 8: A screenshot of our evaluation tool.

Learning to Adapt Large Language Models to One-Shot In-Context Intent Classification on Unseen Domains

Joongbo Shin* **Youbin Ahn*** **Seungpil Won** **Stanley Jungkyu Choi**
LG AI Research
{jb.shin,youbin.ahn}@lgresearch.ai

Abstract

In this paper, we explore one-shot in-context intent classification using large language models (LLMs) with the goal of minimizing the effort required to adapt models to unseen domains. To enhance the one-shot in-context learning capabilities of LLMs, we employ in-context tuning, leveraging its cross-domain transferability to unseen domains. To this end, we introduce the IC-collection, a compilation of open-source intent classification datasets from diverse domains, which are meticulously divided into held-in and held-out datasets. Our experiments demonstrate the effectiveness of the proposed method, showing that our model, with only 7B parameters, not only outperforms GPT-4 on intent classification but also achieves state-of-the-art in unseen domains with only one-shot demonstrations. Both our benchmark and model will be made publicly available to advance research in the chatbot systems.

1 Introduction

Building accurate intent classifiers remains a significant challenge for chatbot systems in real-world scenarios. The labor-intensive process of labeling utterances for new and evolving intents complicates the development and maintenance of chatbots across diverse domains (Sung et al., 2023; Li and Zhang, 2021). In this study, we aim to minimize the effort required to adapt intent classification (IC) models to unseen domains and intents.

To this end, in-context learning, which leverages large language models (LLMs) to achieve high performance on various tasks with only a few input-output pairs, presents a promising direction (Brown et al., 2020; Loukas et al., 2023). Recent research has demonstrated that prompting LLMs only with few-shot examples of text-label pairs can outperform fine-tuned models (Milios et al., 2023). Despite these advancements, they primarily focus on few-shot settings, where five or more examples are required per intent. We argue that previous approaches do not sufficiently minimize the effort required to deploy intent classifiers rapidly across various domains.

This leads us to a research question: *Can we push the limits of in-context learning ability to perform* ***one-shot in-context intent classification****?* To address this, we propose adopting in-context tuning (Min et al., 2022; Chen et al., 2022) for training on seen domains to enhance in-context learning ability on unseen domains. We leverage the cross-task transferability of in-context tuning to improve cross-domain transferability.

To this end, we first construct IC-collection, a benchmark designed for training a model in intent classification across diverse domains and evaluating performance on unseen domains. The IC-collection is a mixture of open-source intent classification datasets, encompassing 13 held-in and 3 held-out datasets[1]. After that, we present OSIC2-7B, where OSIC2 stands for One-Shot In-Context Intent Classification, by training a 7B language model on our benchmark. Our results demonstrate that OSIC2-7B achieves state-of-the-art (SOTA) in unseen domains with only one-shot demonstration, even surpassing GPT-4 in the same setting.

Our contributions are as follows:

- We introduce IC-collection, a training and evaluation benchmark covering diverse domains, specially designed for intent classification on unseen domains.
- We show that OSIC2-7B achieves SOTA performances and even outperforms GPT-4 on unseen domains, highlighting that the effectiveness of our approach.
- To advance research on chatbot systems, we

* indicates equal contribution.

[1]Held-out datasets are carefully selected to minimize domain overlaps.

Proceedings of the 1st Workshop on Customizable NLP: Progress and Challenges in Customizing NLP for a Domain, Application, Group, or Individual (CustomNLP4U), pages 182–197
November 16, 2024

Feature	Held-in	Held-out
# of datasets	13	3
# of domains	53 (48)	3 (3)
# of intents	748 (734)	109 (104)

Table 1: Statistics of IC-collection. Unique number of domains and intents are denoted in parentheses.

make our data collection and model publicly available.

2 Data Collection

We compile the IC-collection from diverse open-source resources to cover various domains. During the dataset collection process, several considerations are made: (i) non-english utterances are excluded from multilingual datasets, (ii) only the initial turns from multi-turn interaction dataset are utilized, (iii) duplicate utterances within the dataset were removed, and (iv) multi-labeled utterances are excluded.

In order to evaluate generalization capabilities on unseen domains, the datasets are divided into held-in and held-out sets[2]. Held-out datasets were selected based on their minimal overlap with the held-in datasets, both in terms of domains and intents[3]. Through preliminary experiments conducted to assess the overlap between the held-out and held-in datasets, we confirmed that the impact of the overlap is negligible (see details in Table 6). Table 1 shows the statistics of IC-collection, and followings are the list of datasets:

Held-in datasets The open-sourced IC datasets utilized for training in this study include ACID (Acharya and Fung, 2020), ATIS (Hemphill et al., 1990), BANKING77 (Casanueva et al., 2020), BITEXT[4], CLINC150 (Larson et al., 2019), GENISYS[5], HWU64 (Liu et al., 2021), MCID (Arora et al., 2020a), PRESTO (Goel et al., 2023), SMALLTALK[6], SNIPS (Coucke et al., 2018), SNIPSBI (Coucke et al., 2018), and TOPv2 (Chen et al., 2020).

Held-out datasets The held-out datasets include CUREKART, POWERPLAY11, SOFMATTRESS from HINT3 (Arora et al., 2020b).

More details about IC-collection such as the entire list of domains and intents can be found in Appendix D.

3 Our Approach

Task Definition Given an utterance, one-shot in-context intent classification (OSIC2) identifies the correct intent from a list of provided intents, using only one example per intent as a reference. The following is the formulation of OSIC2:

$$f(g(\bar{x}_d, \mathcal{I}_d)) \rightarrow \bar{y}_d,$$

where $f(\cdot)$ is a function for mapping the target utterance $\bar{x}_d$ to intent label $\bar{y}_d$ using a natural language prompt $g(\cdot)$. $\mathcal{I}_d = \{(x_{d_i}, y_{d_i})|i = 1, ..., C_d\}$ represents the in-context one-shot demonstrations sampled from the train split of each dataset $d \in \mathcal{D}$, and (x_{d_i}, y_{d_i}) denotes an utterance-label pair of i'th index of total classes C_d.

Training Our ultimate goal is to train a model that can effectively leverage one-shot examples at test time, enabling it to adapt proficiently to new domains. To this end, we employ the in-context tuning framework following Min et al. (2022); Chen et al. (2022). While the original concept of in-context tuning is developed for *cross-task* transfer learning, we apply this approach to *cross-domain* transfer learning within the intent classification task.

Prompt Construction As illustrated in Appendix A, we concatenate the task instruction, the in-context examples, and the target utterance into a single input sequence. Also, we use a fixed prompt format for IC-collection to focus on the changes in the intent list along with the corresponding one-shot examples.

Specifically, we first construct the training pool by randomly selecting maximum of ten examples[7] for each intent from the held-in datasets in order to ensure a balance for each intent. From this training pool, we randomly draw a one-shot example for each instance, based on the following assumptions: 1) The dynamic selection of one-shot examples improves the adaptability of the model to changes in the in-context examples. 2) This can partially resolve problems of different granularity

[2]The original test splits of all datasets are not used for training or in-context demonstrations.

[3]Only highly common intents like thanks show any overlap.

[4]https://www.kaggle.com/datasets/scodepy/customer-support-intent-dataset

[5]https://www.kaggle.com/datasets/elvinagammed/chatbots-intent-recognition-dataset

[6]https://www.kaggle.com/datasets/salmanfaroz/small-talk-intent-classification-data

[7]Maximum of ten examples is determined as the optimal number of examples per intent for training as seen in Table 8

Model	CUREKART	POWERPLAY11	SOFMATRESS	Average
LLaMA-2-7B-chat	40.31	47.25	57.71	48.42
LLaMA-3-8B-instruct	67.10	56.96	75.10	64.20
Mistral-7B-instruct-v0.1	51.85	56.31	67.19	58.45
Mistral-7B-instruct-v0.2	73.42	60.84	83.40	72.55
GPT-3.5-turbo	80.39	57.93	84.98	74.43
GPT-4-turbo	**85.62**	65.70	85.77	79.03
OSIC2-7B (avg.)	83.15	**67.31**	**88.54**	**79.67**
OSIC2-7B (best)	**86.27**	**68.93**	**88.54**	**81.25**
previous SOTA (in-domain)	88.05	66.54	78.78	-

Table 2: Accuracies for OSIC2 on unseen domains. **Bolds** denote top-2 results among LLM baselines.

of intents (Huang et al., 2024) and labeling noise in training instances (Ying and Thomas, 2022). When inferring on held-out datasets, we utilize a fixed-representative utterances sourced from the original training datasets as in-context examples. Note that the intent list at the instance level is confined within each dataset.

Preprocessing For all datasets, minimal processing is applied to ensure data quality. The pattern of intent name is standardized with the steps: (i) converting all letters to lowercase, (ii) joining words with underscores, and (iii) writing out abbreviations. Furthermore, intents categorized as out-of-scope (*e.g.*, `no_nodes_detected`) are excluded across all datasets due to their differing levels of granularity compared to other defined intents.

4 Experiments

4.1 Experimental Setup

Implementation Details For our experiments, we utilize Mistral-7b-v0.1 as a backbone. The models are fine-tuned using AdamW with a learning rate of 6×10^{-7}, regulated by a cosine scheduler. We set a batch size of 128.

To confirm the efficacy of the training, the training process is repeated three times using different seed data, which altered the composition of randomly sampled examples. We report both the averaged and best results obtained from these models, evaluated on the same test set.

Baselines We evaluate six SOTA LLMs: LLaMA2-7B-Chat (Touvron et al., 2023), LLaMA3-8B-Instruct[8] (AI@Meta, 2024), Mistral-7B-Instruct-v0.1, and Mistral-7B-Instruct-v0.2 (Jiang et al., 2023) as our open-source LLM baselines, and GPT-3.5-turbo (Ouyang et al., 2022) and GPT-4-turbo (Achiam et al., 2023) as our closed-source LLM baselines. In addition, we also include previous SOTA results taken from Vishwanathan et al. (2022) for comparison.

4.2 Results on Unseen Domains

For the main experiment, we compare our model with baselines on unseen domains, as shown in Table 2. Our model consistently and significantly outperforms open-source LLMs of similar size.We hypothesize that this gap arises because general-purpose LLMs are not specialized for the intent classification task, thereby highlighting the necessity for task-specific fine-tuning. Moreover, our best model outperforms GPT-4 across all unseen domains and even outperforms the previous in-domain SOTA on two out of three datasets, despite the previous SOTA being trained using all available training data for each dataset. This demonstration of generalization to unseen domains using only 7B-scale model underscores the effectiveness of our approach.

4.2.1 Ablation Study

The key finidngs from our empirical ablation studies on generalization capabilites to unseen domains are summarized below. Details of each study can be found in Appendix C.

- Increasing the diversity in terms of intents and domains of held-in datasets effectively enhances generalization (Table 7).
- Increasing the maximum number of training instances per intent does not always prove helpful for generalization (Table 8).
- Pre-processing techniques applied to training data, the standardization of intent formats, the

[8]For LLaMA-3, we follow the choice of prompt in the official homepage: https://llama.meta.com/docs/model-cards-and-prompt-formats/meta-llama-3/.

Method	CURE.	POWER.	SOFM.
OSIC2-7B	86.27	68.93	88.54
OSIC2-7B+	89.98	72.82	87.35
OSIC2-7B (aug)	90.41	73.79	89.72

Table 3: Further analysis on unseen domains. OSIC2-7B+ denotes the upper-bound model and (aug) denotes our remedy for low-recall intents during inference.

Method	C150	H64	B77
OSIC2-7B	95.93	89.78	84.42
7B SOTA (5-shot)	95.35	87.17	85.91
7B SOTA (10-shot)	96.02	90.33	89.48

Table 4: Results on the seen domains, compared with the previous 7B SOTA models, derived from the Llama-2-7B 4K as reported by Milios et al. (2023).

incorporation of various one-shot demonstrations, and the exclusion of out-of-scope intents during training can all contribute to enhanced generalization (Table 9).

4.2.2 Further Analysis

We conduct further analysis on held-out datasets using the best performing OSIC2-7B as shown in Table 3. To establish the upper bound of model performance on IC-collection, we train another model, OSIC2-7B+, by incorporating three benchmarks into the held-in datasets. As expected, OSIC2-7B+ performs better overall than OSIC2-7B, suggesting that additional generalization to unseen domains is possible through training on a wider variety of intents. Meanwhile, OSIC2-7B surpasses OSIC2-7B+ on the SOFMATTRESS dataset, underscoring the robustness and efficacy of our approach.

Furthermore, while beyond our primary scope, we explore the potential improvement achievable by modifying the number of examples for each intent during inference. To this end, we augment the prompt with up to a maximum of two additional examples for intents identified as having low recall, referred as OSIC2-7B (aug) (prompts can be found in Table 13, 14, and 15). The addition of these extra examples during inference enhances performance, surpassing even that of OSIC2-7B+ which we initially assumed to represent the upper bound. This observation suggests that OSIC2-7B not only enables the development of high-performance intent classifiers for new domains but also facilitates the easy maintenance of existing intent classifiers through simple prompt modifications.

4.3 Results on Seen Domains

For the performance on held-in datasets, OSIC2-7B (best) is compared with the previous SOTA method[9] across three representative benchmarks, CLINC150 (C150), HWU64 (H64), and BANKING77 (B77), as shown in Table 4. The performance of OSIC2-7B is comparable to that of the similarly sized SOTA models, except for BANKING77[10], demonstrating that our approach does not sacrifice performance on held-in domains for the sake of generalization to held-out domains.

5 Related Work

Language model prompting, particularly with instruction-following LLMs has proven effective for zero-shot or few-shot intent classification (Wei et al., 2022; Sanh et al., 2022). Recent studies have demonstrated the effectiveness of few-shot in-context learning (ICL) for intent classification (Loukas et al., 2023) and emotion classification (Milios et al., 2023). Our approach similarly employs ICL technique to adapt open-LLMs to unseen domains, differing by extending its application to one-shot classification, an extreme scenario where little labeling effort is required.

Additionally, methodologies such as in-context tuning have proposed a meta-learning approach, where k-shot examples are augmented with contextual information for both training and testing (Min et al., 2022; Chen et al., 2022). While these methods primarily focus on transferring learning to unseen tasks through instruction tuning, our objective is to transfer learning to unseen domains.

Methodologically, our approach is most similar to the study on in-context cross-lingual transfer (Villa-Cueva et al., 2024). While that study focuses on text classification and explores cross-lingual transferability, our research emphasizes domain transferability within intent classification.

6 Conclusion

This paper investigates one-shot intent classification as an extreme case of data scarcity in real-world scenarios. By enhancing the in-context learning capabilities of LLMs, our specialized 7B-scale model achieves state-of-the-art performances on

[9]The SOTA model utilizes a retriever that selects the most relevant utterance-label pairs from the example pool to design the prompt for in-context learning. This model achieves SOTA performance in both 5-shot and 10-shot.

[10]We leave the exploration of this aspect for future work.

held-out datasets, even in the context of unseen domains. To promote research on the creation of accurate intent classifiers that are easily adaptable to any domain, we release our data collection and model.

Limitations & Future Work

Our work is limited in multiple dimensions. First, one example may not be sufficient to represent a definition of the intent. Future work may explore extending our approach to adaptive k-shot in-context intent classification. Second, providing at least one example for all intents in the prompts requires much longer context, resulting in less efficiency at the inference stage. Reducing intent list corresponding to the given utterance with an off-the-shelf retriever needs to be studied in the future. Third, we only consider 7-billion parameter LLMs. Applying our approach on larger LLMs may achieves better generalization on unseen domains. At last, our IC-collection contains English-only datasets. Cross-lingual transferability of intent classification is in our future work.

Acknowledgments

References

Shailesh Acharya and Glenn Fung. 2020. Using optimal embeddings to learn new intents with few examples: An application in the insurance domain. In *Converse@ KDD*.

Josh Achiam, Steven Adler, Sandhini Agarwal, Lama Ahmad, Ilge Akkaya, Florencia Leoni Aleman, Diogo Almeida, Janko Altenschmidt, Sam Altman, Shyamal Anadkat, et al. 2023. Gpt-4 technical report. *arXiv preprint arXiv:2303.08774*.

AI@Meta. 2024. Llama 3 model card.

Abhinav Arora, Akshat Shrivastava, Mrinal Mohit, Lorena Sainz-Maza Lecanda, and Ahmed Aly. 2020a. Cross-lingual transfer learning for intent detection of covid-19 utterances.

Gaurav Arora, Chirag Jain, Manas Chaturvedi, and Krupal Modi. 2020b. HINT3: Raising the bar for intent detection in the wild. In *Proceedings of the First Workshop on Insights from Negative Results in NLP*, pages 100–105, Online. Association for Computational Linguistics.

Tom Brown, Benjamin Mann, Nick Ryder, Melanie Subbiah, Jared D Kaplan, Prafulla Dhariwal, Arvind Neelakantan, Pranav Shyam, Girish Sastry, Amanda Askell, et al. 2020. Language models are few-shot learners. *Advances in neural information processing systems*, 33:1877–1901.

Iñigo Casanueva, Tadas Temčinas, Daniela Gerz, Matthew Henderson, and Ivan Vulić. 2020. Efficient intent detection with dual sentence encoders. *arXiv preprint arXiv:2003.04807*.

Xilun Chen, Asish Ghoshal, Yashar Mehdad, Luke Zettlemoyer, and Sonal Gupta. 2020. Low-resource domain adaptation for compositional task-oriented semantic parsing. *arXiv preprint arXiv:2010.03546.*

Yanda Chen, Ruiqi Zhong, Sheng Zha, George Karypis, and He He. 2022. Meta-learning via language model in-context tuning. In *Proceedings of the 60th Annual Meeting of the Association for Computational Linguistics (Volume 1: Long Papers)*, pages 719–730, Dublin, Ireland. Association for Computational Linguistics.

Alice Coucke, Alaa Saade, Adrien Ball, Théodore Bluche, Alexandre Caulier, David Leroy, Clément Doumouro, Thibault Gisselbrecht, Francesco Caltagirone, Thibaut Lavril, et al. 2018. Snips voice platform: an embedded spoken language understanding system for private-by-design voice interfaces. *arXiv preprint arXiv:1805.10190.*

Rahul Goel, Waleed Ammar, Aditya Gupta, Siddharth Vashishtha, Motoki Sano, Faiz Surani, Max Chang, HyunJeong Choe, David Greene, Kyle He, et al. 2023. Presto: A multilingual dataset for parsing realistic task-oriented dialogs. *arXiv preprint arXiv:2303.08954.*

Charles T Hemphill, John J Godfrey, and George R Doddington. 1990. The atis spoken language systems pilot corpus. In *Speech and Natural Language: Proceedings of a Workshop Held at Hidden Valley, Pennsylvania, June 24-27, 1990.*

Simin Huang, Peijie Huang, Yuhong Xu, Jingzhou Liang, and Jingde Niu. 2024. Exploring label hierarchy in dialogue intent classification. In *ICASSP 2024-2024 IEEE International Conference on Acoustics, Speech and Signal Processing (ICASSP)*, pages 11511–11515. IEEE.

Albert Q Jiang, Alexandre Sablayrolles, Arthur Mensch, Chris Bamford, Devendra Singh Chaplot, Diego de las Casas, Florian Bressand, Gianna Lengyel, Guillaume Lample, Lucile Saulnier, et al. 2023. Mistral 7b. *arXiv preprint arXiv:2310.06825.*

Stefan Larson, Anish Mahendran, Joseph J Peper, Christopher Clarke, Andrew Lee, Parker Hill, Jonathan K Kummerfeld, Kevin Leach, Michael A Laurenzano, Lingjia Tang, et al. 2019. An evaluation dataset for intent classification and out-of-scope prediction. *arXiv preprint arXiv:1909.02027.*

Yue Li and Jiong Zhang. 2021. Semi-supervised meta-learning for cross-domain few-shot intent classification. In *Proceedings of the 1st Workshop on Meta Learning and Its Applications to Natural Language Processing*, pages 67–75, Online. Association for Computational Linguistics.

Xingkun Liu, Arash Eshghi, Pawel Swietojanski, and Verena Rieser. 2021. Benchmarking natural language understanding services for building conversational agents. In *Increasing Naturalness and Flexibility in Spoken Dialogue Interaction: 10th International Workshop on Spoken Dialogue Systems*, pages 165–183. Springer.

Lefteris Loukas, Ilias Stogiannidis, Prodromos Malakasiotis, and Stavros Vassos. 2023. Breaking the bank with ChatGPT: Few-shot text classification for finance. In *Proceedings of the Fifth Workshop on Financial Technology and Natural Language Processing and the Second Multimodal AI For Financial Forecasting*, pages 74–80, Macao. -.

Aristides Milios, Siva Reddy, and Dzmitry Bahdanau. 2023. In-context learning for text classification with many labels. In *Proceedings of the 1st GenBench Workshop on (Benchmarking) Generalisation in NLP*, pages 173–184, Singapore. Association for Computational Linguistics.

Sewon Min, Mike Lewis, Luke Zettlemoyer, and Hannaneh Hajishirzi. 2022. MetaICL: Learning to learn in context. In *Proceedings of the 2022 Conference of the North American Chapter of the Association for Computational Linguistics: Human Language Technologies*, pages 2791–2809, Seattle, United States. Association for Computational Linguistics.

Long Ouyang, Jeffrey Wu, Xu Jiang, Diogo Almeida, Carroll Wainwright, Pamela Mishkin, Chong Zhang, Sandhini Agarwal, Katarina Slama, Alex Ray, et al. 2022. Training language models to follow instructions with human feedback. *Advances in neural information processing systems*, 35:27730–27744.

Victor Sanh, Albert Webson, Colin Raffel, Stephen Bach, Lintang Sutawika, Zaid Alyafeai, Antoine Chaffin, Arnaud Stiegler, Arun Raja, Manan Dey, M Saiful Bari, Canwen Xu, Urmish Thakker, Shanya Sharma Sharma, Eliza Szczechla, Taewoon Kim, Gunjan Chhablani, Nihal Nayak, Debajyoti Datta, Jonathan Chang, Mike Tian-Jian Jiang, Han Wang, Matteo Manica, Sheng Shen, Zheng Xin Yong, Harshit Pandey, Rachel Bawden, Thomas Wang, Trishala Neeraj, Jos Rozen, Abheesht Sharma, Andrea Santilli, Thibault Fevry, Jason Alan Fries, Ryan Teehan, Teven Le Scao, Stella Biderman, Leo Gao, Thomas Wolf, and Alexander M Rush. 2022. Multitask prompted training enables zero-shot task generalization. In *International Conference on Learning Representations.*

Mujeen Sung, James Gung, Elman Mansimov, Nikolaos Pappas, Raphael Shu, Salvatore Romeo, Yi Zhang, and Vittorio Castelli. 2023. Pre-training intent-aware encoders for zero-and few-shot intent classification. In *Proceedings of the 2023 Conference on Empirical Methods in Natural Language Processing*, pages 10433–10442.

Hugo Touvron, Louis Martin, Kevin Stone, Peter Albert, Amjad Almahairi, Yasmine Babaei, Nikolay Bashlykov, Soumya Batra, Prajjwal Bhargava, Shruti Bhosale, et al. 2023. Llama 2: Open foundation and fine-tuned chat models. *arXiv preprint arXiv:2307.09288.*

Emilio Villa-Cueva, A Pastor López-Monroy, Fernando Sánchez-Vega, and Thamar Solorio. 2024.

Adaptive cross-lingual text classification through in-context one-shot demonstrations. *arXiv preprint arXiv:2404.02452*.

Asha Vishwanathan, Rajeev Warrier, Gautham Vadakkekara Suresh, and Chandra Shekhar Kandpal. 2022. Multi-tenant optimization for few-shot task-oriented FAQ retrieval. In *Proceedings of the 2022 Conference on Empirical Methods in Natural Language Processing: Industry Track*, pages 188–197, Abu Dhabi, UAE. Association for Computational Linguistics.

Jason Wei, Maarten Bosma, Vincent Zhao, Kelvin Guu, Adams Wei Yu, Brian Lester, Nan Du, Andrew M. Dai, and Quoc V Le. 2022. Finetuned language models are zero-shot learners. In *International Conference on Learning Representations*.

Cecilia Ying and Stephen Thomas. 2022. Label errors in BANKING77. In *Proceedings of the Third Workshop on Insights from Negative Results in NLP*, pages 139–143, Dublin, Ireland. Association for Computational Linguistics.

A Appendix A: Prompt Format

[Instruction]
You are an AI assistant for intent classification. For the user query, you should select the correponding intent name from the intent list. Do not write anything else other than the intent name. The intent list is given below and example queries can be followed by each intent name.

[Intent List]
- **current_location**: "what's the precise coordinates of this place"
- **directions**: "where is starbucks"
- **distance**: "how far is the grand canyon from my current location in phoenix, az"
- **gas_amount**: "whats in my gas tank"
- **gas_type**: "what gas does the car need"

...

[Conversation]
User: i am needing you to tell me how to get to dallas, i am needing you to tell me how to get to dallas, texas, by bus
Assistant: **directions**

Table 5: Example of natural language prompt in IC-collection. *Italics* denotes the *fixed* instruction template, "*" denotes example utterance, and **bolds** denotes **intent_name**.

B Appendix B: Preliminary Experiments

Train	Test	CURE.	POWER.	SOFM.
0-shot	0-shot	68.70	59.76	77.60
0-shot	1-shot	80.90	66.45	83.93
1-shot	1-shot	83.15	67.31	88.54

Table 6: Results on preliminary experiments for assessing the impact of dataset overlap. "1-shot Training & 1-shot Test" denotes OSIC2-7B (avg.).

Table 6 shows accuracies of models trained with and without one-shot demonstrations. From this table, we can conclude that the impact of the overlap between held-in and held-out datasets is negligible. If the overlap had been significant, the performance difference between "0-shot Train & 0-shot Test" versus "1-shot Train & 1-shot Test" would not have been substantial. This indicates that domain adaptation through one-shot learning plays a more critical role than the overlap.

C Appendix C: Ablation Study

# Train sets	CURE.	POWER.	SOFM.
3	76.83	65.37	85.91
6	79.88	65.37	85.37
9	80.01	65.80	87.09
13: OSIC2-7B (avg.)	83.15	67.31	88.54
16: OSIC2-7B+ (avg.)	88.45	71.63	88.14

Table 7: Accuracies depending on the number of open-source IC datasets utilized for training. 3 includes CLINC150, BANKING77 and HWU64 datasets; 6 additionally incorporates datasets ATIS, SNIPS, and TOPv2; 9 further adds datasets ACID, MCID and PRESTO; and 13 indicates that all held-in datasets used, with the addition of four datasets, BITEXT, GENISYS, SMALLTALK, and SNIPSBI; 16 includes all held-out datasets, CUREKART, POWERPLAY11, SOFMATTRESS. Note that as the number of datasets increases, they encompass all previously metnioned datasets.

# Examples	CURE.	POWER.	SOFM.
5	82.14	65.91	86.56
10	83.15	67.31	88.54
15	79.96	67.42	87.48
20	78.94	66.67	87.75

Table 8: Results across varying numbers used to construct the training pool referenced in Section 3's prompt construction. All models are tested using the same evaluation set up and test set, which utilizes the fixed one-shot demonstrations.

Intent List	CURE.	POWER.	SOFM.
OSIC2-7B	83.15	67.31	88.54
- intent stand.	83.37	64.51	84.98
- dynamic dem.	82.79	67.75	87.62
+ OOS	80.32	65.69	86.96

Table 9: An ablation study to evaluate the impact of excluding each pre-processing technique applied to the training data. Specifically, the model is trained without intent standardization and subsequently tested on intent names that have not undergone under any preprocessing

D Appendix D: Details of Datasets

Dataset	#Intents	#Domains	OOS Intents	License
ACID	175	1	st_general_request	N/A
ATIS	17	1	-	N/A
BANKING77	77	1	-	CC-BY-4.0
BITEXT	27	11	-	N/A
CLINC150	150	10	-	CC-BY-3.0 Legal Code
GENISYS	19	1	-	N/A
HWU64	64	18	general_quirky	CC BY-SA 3.0
MCID	16	1	-	CC BY-NC-SA 4.0
PRESTO	33	1	other	CC-BY-4.0
SMALLTALK	84	1	-	CC0: Public Domain
SNIPS	7	1	-	CC0-1.0 license
SNIPSBI	10	1	-	CC0-1.0 license
TOPv2	68	8	unsupported_*	CC BY-NC 4.0

Table 10: Statistics of training datasets in IC-collection. unsupported_* denotes in-domain OOS intents for each domain excluding the reminder domain of the TOPv2 dataset.

Dataset	#Intents	Seen Intents	OOS Intents	License
CUREKART	29	cancel_order, order_status	no_nodes_detected	Open Database License
POWERPLAY11	58	thanks	no_nodes_detected	Open Database License
SOFMATTRESS	22	cancel_order, order_status	no_nodes_detected	Open Database License

Table 11: Statistics of heldout datasets in IC-collection.

Domain list of training datasets
account, airline_travel_information_system_(atis), alarm, audio, automobile_and_commute, banking, calendar, cancellation_fee, contact, cooking, covid-19, credit_cards, datetime, delivery, email, event, feedback, food_takeaway, general, insurance, internet_of_things_(iot), invoice, kitchen_and_dining, lists, messaging, meta, music, navigation, news, newsletter, order, payment, play, question_answering_(qa), recommendation, refund, reminder, shipping_address, smalltalk, smarthome, social, timer, transport, travel, utility, virtual_assistant, weather, work
Domain list of held-out datasets
fitness_supplements_retail, online_gaming, mattress_products_retail

Table 12: Domain list of IC-collection.

Intent list of ACID

<domain: insurance> info_add_house, info_add_remove_insuranceured, info_add_remove_vehicle, info_add_vehicle_property_paperless_billing, info_agent_not_responding, info_agent_wrong, info_all_terrain_vehicle_(atv)_insurance_explain, info_american_star, info_amount_due, info_ask_purchase, info_ask_quote, info_automatic_payment_cancel, info_automatic_payment_min_balance, info_automatic_payment_schedule, info_automobile_coverage_question, info_automobile_insurance_canada, info_automobile_policy_cannot_see_in_account, info_bill_due_date, info_billing_account_name_edit, info_billing_account_number, info_billing_department_contact, info_boat_coverage_explain, info_business_policy_cannot_see, info_business_private_policy_(bpp)_question_general, info_cancel_confirm, info_cancel_fee, info_cancel_insurance_policy, info_cannot_see_farm_ranch_policy, info_cannot_see_policy, info_careers, info_change_agent, info_change_autopay_date, info_change_bank_account, info_change_userid, info_claim_adjuster_information, info_claim_check_status, info_claim_complaint, info_claim_direct_repair_program_(drp)_assign, info_claim_direct_repair_program_(drp)_join, info_claim_documents_email, info_claim_documents_fax, info_claim_documents_mail, info_claim_documents_send, info_claim_file_claim, info_claim_filed, info_claim_first_notice_of_loss_(fnol), info_claim_first_notice_of_loss_(fnol)_automobile_hail, info_claim_glass_safelite, info_claim_home_repair_program_(hrp)_join, info_claim_rental, info_claim_shop_add_work, info_claim_shop_send_estimate, info_claim_status, info_claim_update_information, info_collections, info_collision_coverage_explain, info_combine_payments, info_comprehensive_coverage_explain, info_confirm_coverage, info_credit_card_change_number, info_credit_card_fee, info_customer_service_hours, info_declaration_page_needed, info_deductible, info_deductible_explain, info_delete_duplicate_payment, info_different_amounts, info_discounts, info_do_not_contact, info_dreamkeep_rewards, info_dreamkeep_rewards_errors, info_dreams_foundation, info_emergency_roadside_service_(ers), info_emergency_roadside_service_(ers)_contact, info_emergency_roadside_service_(ers)_reimburse, info_employment_verify, info_financial_responsibility_filling_(sr22), info_find_agent, info_flood_insurance_explain, info_forgot_email, info_forgot_password, info_forgot_userid, info_general_policy_coverage_question, info_get_a_quote_auto, info_get_a_quote_automobile_non_owner, info_get_a_quote_business_private_policy_(bpp), info_get_a_quote_other, info_get_a_quote_renters, info_get_a_quote_renters_purchase, info_glass_coverage, info_guaranteed_auto_protection_(gap)_coverage, info_handling_fee_remove, info_health_insurance_quote, info_homesite_contact, info_insurance_card_print, info_insurance_card_proof, info_insurance_card_send, info_insurance_not_available, info_knowyourdrive, info_knowyourdrive_device_activate, info_knowyourdrive_device_return, info_knowyourdrive_errors, info_letter_of_experience, info_liability_explain, info_life_beneficiary_change, info_life_cash_out, info_life_increase_coverage, info_life_policy_amount_due, info_life_policy_automatic_payment, info_life_policy_cancel, info_life_policy_cannot_see, info_life_question_general, info_life_refund, info_life_update_contact_information, info_log_in_error, info_log_out, info_mail_payment_address, info_make_payment, info_mexico_automobile_insurance, info_mortgage_co_proof_of_insurance_(poi), info_name_change, info_new_vehicle_grace_period, info_one_time_payment, info_operating_area, info_operating_company, info_paperless_documents_setup, info_paperless_documents_stop, info_paperless_mail, info_pay_life_insurance, info_payment_confirm, info_payment_due_date_change, info_payment_error, info_payment_history, info_payment_not_ontime, info_payment_process_change, info_payment_setup_automatic_payment, info_payment_time, info_phone_number, info_phone_number_international, info_policy_document_needed, info_policy_number, info_policy_transfer_to_rental, info_premium_breakdown, info_prepaid_card_payment, info_profile_section, info_proof_of_insurance_(poi)_old, info_recreational_vehicle_(rv)_insurance_explain, info_refund_check, info_reinstate_insurance_policy, info_renters_coverage_explain, info_rideshare_coverage, info_salvage_vehicle, info_set_up_account, info_speak_to_representative, info_teen_safe_driver_signup, info_the_general_contact, info_transfer_account_balance, info_travel_insurance_explain, info_university_of_washington_(uw)_alumni_discount, info_update_contact_information, info_update_email, info_update_lienholder, info_update_phone_number, info_who_is_my_agent, info_why_was_policy_cancelled, no, st_general_request, st_hello, st_how_is_chatbot_(abby), st_how_old_is_chatbot_(abby), st_is_chatbot_(abby)_real, st_thank_you, st_what_can_chatbot_(abby)_do, st_where_does_chatbot_(abby)_live, yes

Intent list of ATIS

<domain: airline_travel_information_system_(atis)> abbreviation, aircraft, airfare, airline, airport, capacity, city, day_name, distance, flight, flight_no, flight_time, ground_fare, ground_service, meal, quantity, restriction

Intent list of BANKING77
<domain: banking> activate_my_card, age_limit, apple_pay_or_google_pay, atm_support, automatic_top_up, balance_not_updated_after_bank_transfer, balance_not_updated_after_cheque_or_cash_deposit, beneficiary_not_allowed, cancel_transfer, card_about_to_expire, card_acceptance, card_arrival, card_delivery_estimate, card_linking, card_not_working, card_payment_fee_charged, card_payment_not_recognised, card_payment_wrong_exchange_rate, card_swallowed, cash_withdrawal_charge, cash_withdrawal_not_recognised, change_pin, compromised_card, contactless_not_working, country_support, declined_card_payment, declined_cash_withdrawal, declined_transfer, direct_debit_payment_not_recognised, disposable_card_limits, edit_personal_details, exchange_charge, exchange_rate, exchange_via_app, extra_charge_on_statement, failed_transfer, fiat_currency_support, get_disposable_virtual_card, get_physical_card, getting_spare_card, getting_virtual_card, lost_or_stolen_card, lost_or_stolen_phone, order_physical_card, passcode_forgotten, pending_card_payment, pending_cash_withdrawal, pending_top_up, pending_transfer, pin_blocked, receiving_money, refund_not_showing_up, request_refund, reverted_card_payment, supported_cards_and_currencies, terminate_account, top_up_by_bank_transfer_charge, top_up_by_card_charge, top_up_by_cash_or_cheque, top_up_failed, top_up_limits, top_up_reverted, topping_up_by_card, transaction_charged_twice, transfer_fee_charged, transfer_into_account, transfer_not_received_by_recipient, transfer_timing, unable_to_verify_identity, verify_my_identity, verify_source_of_funds, verify_top_up, virtual_card_not_working, visa_or_mastercard, why_verify_identity, wrong_amount_of_cash_received, wrong_exchange_rate_for_cash_withdrawal

Intent list of BITEXT
<domain: account> create_account, delete_account, edit_account, recover_password, registration_problems, switch_account
<domain: cancellation_fee> check_cancellation_fee
<domain: contact> contact_customer_service, contact_human_agent
<domain: delivery> delivery_options, delivery_period
<domain: feedback> complaint, review
<domain: invoice> check_invoice, get_invoice
<domain: newsletter> newsletter_subscription
<domain: order> cancel_order, change_order, place_order, track_order
<domain: payment> check_payment_methods, payment_issue
<domain: refund> check_refund_policy, get_refund, track_refund
<domain: shipping_address> change_shipping_address, set_up_shipping_address

Intent list of CLINC150
<domain: automobile_and_commute> current_location, directions, distance, gas_amount, gas_type, jump_start, last_maintenance, miles_per_gallon_(mpg), oil_change_how, oil_change_when, schedule_maintenance, tire_change, tire_pressure, traffic, uber
<domain: banking> account_blocked, balance, bill_balance, bill_due, freeze_account, interest_rate, min_payment, order_checks, pay_bill, pin_change, report_fraud, routing, spending_history, transactions, transfer
<domain: credit_cards> annual_percentage_rate_(apr), application_status, card_declined, credit_limit, credit_limit_change, credit_score, damaged_card, expiration_date, improve_credit_score, international_fees, new_card, redeem_rewards, replacement_card_duration, report_lost_card, rewards_balance
<domain: home> calendar_status, calendar_update, next_song, order_status, order_update, play_music, reminder_status, reminder_update, shopping_list_status, shopping_list_update, smart_home_devices, todo_list_status, todo_list_update, update_playlist, what_song
<domain: kitchen_and_dining> accept_reservations, calories, cancel_reservation, confirm_reservation, cook_time, food_last, how_busy, ingredient_substitution, ingredients_list, meal_suggestion, nutrition_info, recipe, restaurant_reservation, restaurant_reviews, restaurant_suggestion
<domain: meta> cancel, change_accent, change_ai_name, change_language, change_speed, change_user_name, change_volume, maybe, no, repeat, reset_settings, sync_device, user_name, whisper_mode, yes
<domain: small_talk> are_you_a_bot, do_you_have_pets, fun_fact, goodbye, greeting, how_old_are_you, meaning_of_life, tell_joke, thank_you, what_are_your_hobbies, what_can_i_ask_you, what_is_your_name, where_are_you_from, who_do_you_work_for, who_made_you
<domain: travel> book_flight, book_hotel, car_rental, carry_on, exchange_rate, flight_status, international_visa, lost_luggage, plug_type, timezone, translate, travel_alert, travel_notification, travel_suggestion, vaccines
<domain: utility> alarm, calculator, date, definition, find_phone, flip_coin, make_call, measurement_conversion, roll_dice, share_location, spelling, text, time, timer, weather
<domain: work> direct_deposit, income, insurance, insurance_change, meeting_schedule, next_holiday, paid_time_off_(pto)_balance, paid_time_off_(pto)_request, paid_time_off_(pto)_status, paid_time_off_(pto)_used, payday, rollover_retirement_savings_plan_(401k), schedule_meeting, taxes, wage_and_tax_statement_(w2)

Intent list of GENISYS
<domain: ai_assistant> clever, courtesy_good_bye, courtesy_greeting, current_human_query, good_bye, gossip, greeting, jokes, name_query, not_talking_to_you, pod_bay_door, real_name_query, self_aware, shutup, swearing, thanks, time_query, understand_query, who_am_i

Intent list of HWU64

<domain: alarm> alarm_query, alarm_remove, alarm_set

<domain: audio> audio_volume_down, audio_volume_mute, audio_volume_up

<domain: calendar> calendar_query, calendar_remove, calendar_set

<domain: cooking> cooking_recipe

<domain: datetime> datetime_convert, datetime_query

<domain: email> email_add_contact, email_query, email_query_contact, email_sendemail

<domain: food_takeaway> takeaway_order, takeaway_query

<domain: general> general_affirm, general_command_stop, general_confirm, general_dontcare, general_explain, general_joke, general_negate, general_praise, general_quirky, general_repeat

<domain: internet_of_things_(iot)> iot_cleaning, iot_coffee, iot_hue_light_change, iot_hue_light_dim, iot_hue_light_off, iot_hue_light_on, iot_hue_light_up, iot_wemo_plug_off, iot_wemo_plug_on

<domain: lists> lists_create_or_add, lists_query, lists_remove

<domain: music> music_likeness, music_query, music_settings

<domain: news> news_query

<domain: play> play_audiobook, play_game, play_music, play_podcasts, play_radio

<domain: question_answering_(qa)> qa_currency, qa_definition, qa_factoid, qa_maths, qa_stock

<domain: recommendation> recommendation_events, recommendation_locations, recommendation_movies

<domain: social> social_post, social_query

<domain: transport> transport_query, transport_taxi, transport_ticket, transport_traffic

<domain: weather> weather_query

Intent list of MCID

<domain: covid-19> can_i_get_from_feces_animal_pets, can_i_get_from_packages_surfaces, donate, hi, how_does_corona_spread, latest_numbers, myths, news_and_press, okay_thanks, protect_yourself, share, travel, what_are_symptoms, what_are_treatment_options, what_if_i_visited_high_risk_area, what_is_corona

Intent list of PRESTO

<domain: virtual_assistant> add_contact, add_item_to_list, buy_event_tickets, cancel_ride, check_order_status, create_list, create_note, find_parking, get_bill, get_generic_business_type, get_health_stats, get_list, get_message_content, get_note, get_product, get_security_price, initiate_call, log_exercise, log_nutrition, open_app, order_menu_item, order_ride, other, pause_exercise, pay_bill, play_game, post_message, record_video, resume_exercise, send_digital_object, start_exercise, stop_exercise, take_photo

Intent list of SMALLTALK

<domain: smalltalk> agent_acquaintance, agent_age, agent_annoying, agent_answer_my_question, agent_bad, agent_be_clever, agent_beautiful, agent_birth_date, agent_boring, agent_boss, agent_busy, agent_chatbot, agent_clever, agent_crazy, agent_fired, agent_funny, agent_good, agent_happy, agent_hungry, agent_marry_user, agent_my_friend, agent_occupation, agent_origin, agent_ready, agent_real, agent_residence, agent_right, agent_sure, agent_talk_to_me, agent_there, appraisal_bad, appraisal_good, appraisal_no_problem, appraisal_thank_you, appraisal_welcome, appraisal_well_done, confirmation_cancel, confirmation_no, confirmation_yes, dialog_hold_on, dialog_hug, dialog_i_do_not_care, dialog_sorry, dialog_what_do_you_mean, dialog_wrong, emotions_ha_ha, emotions_wow, greetings_bye, greetings_goodevening, greetings_goodmorning, greetings_goodnight, greetings_hello, greetings_how_are_you, greetings_nice_to_meet_you, greetings_nice_to_see_you, greetings_nice_to_talk_to_you, greetings_whatsup, user_angry, user_back, user_bored, user_busy, user_can_not_sleep, user_does_not_want_to_talk, user_excited, user_going_to_bed, user_good, user_happy, user_has_birthday, user_here, user_joking, user_likes_agent, user_lonely, user_looks_like, user_loves_agent, user_misses_agent, user_needs_advice, user_sad, user_sleepy, user_testing_agent, user_tired, user_waits, user_wants_to_see_agent_again, user_wants_to_talk, user_will_be_back

Intent list of SNIPS

<domain: smart_home> add_to_playlist, book_restaurant, get_weather, play_music, rate_book, search_creative_work, search_screening_event

Intent list of SNIPSBI
<domain: smarthome> book_restaurant, compare_places, get_directions, get_place_details, get_traffic_information, get_weather, request_ride, search_place, share_current_location, share_estimated_time_of_arrival_(eta)

Intent list of TOPv2
<domain: alarm> create_alarm, delete_alarm, get_alarm, silence_alarm, snooze_alarm, unsupported_alarm, update_alarm
<domain: event> get_event, get_event_attendee, get_event_attendee_amount, get_event_organizer, unsupported_event
<domain: messaging> cancel_message, get_message, ignore_message, react_message, send_message, unsupported_messaging
<domain: music> add_to_playlist_music, create_playlist_music, dislike_music, like_music, loop_music, pause_music, play_music, previous_track_music, remove_from_playlist_music, replay_music, set_default_provider_music, skip_track_music, start_shuffle_music, stop_music, unsupported_music
<domain: navigation> get_directions, get_distance, get_estimated_arrival, get_estimated_departure, get_estimated_duration, get_info_road_condition, get_info_route, get_info_traffic, get_location, unsupported_navigation, update_directions
<domain: reminder> create_reminder, delete_reminder, get_reminder, get_reminder_amount, get_reminder_date_time, get_reminder_location, help_reminder, update_reminder, update_reminder_date_time, update_reminder_todo
<domain: timer> add_time_timer, create_timer, delete_timer, get_timer, pause_timer, restart_timer, resume_timer, subtract_time_timer, unsupported_timer, update_timer
<domain: weather> get_sunrise, get_sunset, get_weather, unsupported_weather

Intent list of CUREKART
<domain: fitness_supplements_retail> call_center, cancel_order, chat_with_agent, check_pincode, consult_start, delay_in_parcel, expiry_date, franchise, immunity, international_shipping, modes_of_payments, modify_address, no_nodes_detected, order_query, order_status, order_taking, original_product, payment_and_bill, portal_issue, recommend_product, refer_earn, refunds_returns_replacements, resume_delivery, side_effect, sign_up, start_over, store_information, user_goal_form, work_from_home

Intent list of POWERPLAY11
<domain: online_gaming> account_balance_deducted, account_not_verified, account_reset, appreciation, bank_verification_details, cannot_see_joined_contests, capabilities, cash_bonus, cash_bonus_expiry, change_bank_account, change_mobile_number, change_profile_team_details, chat_with_an_agent, check_deposit_status, check_wallet_balance, contact_number, criticism, deducted_amount_not_received, delete_pan_card, download_powerplay11, fairplay_violations, fake_teams, feedback, greetings_day, how_points_calculated, how_to_play, instant_withdrawal, join_contest, less_winnings_amount, match_abandoned, new_team_pattern, no_email_confirmation, no_nodes_detected, offers_and_referrals, pan_verification_failed, points_not_updated, presence, refund_of_added_cash, refund_of_wrong_amount, signup_bonus, taxes_on_winnings, team_deadline, thanks, types_bonus, types_contests, unutilized_money, update_app, verify_email, verify_mobile, verify_pan, what_if_theres_a_tie, why_verify, winnings, withdraw_cash_bonus, withdrawal_intro, withdrawal_status, withdrawal_time, wrong_scores

Intent list of SOFMATTRESS
<domain: mattress_products_retail> 100_night_trial_offer, about_sof_mattress, cancel_order, cash_on_delivery_(cod), check_pincode, comparison, delay_in_delivery, distributors, equated_monthly_instalment_(emi), ergonomic_features, lead_generation, mattress_cost, no_nodes_detected, offers, order_status, orthopedic_features, pillows, product_variants, return_exchange, size_customization, warranty, what_size_to_order

- **call_center**: "what is the time when call center is working"
- **cancel_order**: "I want to place cancellation"
- **chat_with_agent**: "How to complaint"
- **check_pincode**: "Are you shipping to my pincode"
- **consult_start**: "Get Diet & Fitness Advice"
- **delay_in_parcel**: "I am not received my order yet"
- **expiry_date**: "I have received an Expired product"
- **franchise**: "I would like to get dealership"
- **immunity**: "Increase Immunity"
- **international_shipping**: "Delivery out of India"
- **modes_of_payments**: "ways of paymets"
- **modify_address**: "Edit shipping address"
- **order_query**: "Help required on order"
- **order_status**: "How much more time do I have to wait for my parcel"
- **order_taking**: "I want to book shipment on cash on delivery"
- **original_product**: "Show me your authenticity"
- **payment_and_bill**: "my money has been deducted but it's not been place order"
- **portal_issue**: "My Cart Is empty"
- **recommend_product**: "i need supplements", "energy boost in body", "I want home gym product"
- **refer_earn**: "I have referral promo code"
- **refunds_returns_replacements**: "I want my money back"
- **resume_delivery**: "If i order today in how many days it will be delivered"
- **side_effect**: "Side Effect"
- **sign_up**: "I am a new user"
- **start_over**: "Restart the flow"
- **store_information**: "Are your offline stores open?"
- **user_goal_form**: "Re-assess my profile"
- **work_from_home**: "I hope you are also working from home during this time"

Table 13: Augmented version of intent list on CUREKART evaluation.

- **account_balance_deducted**: "What is cycle of account balance deduction"
- **account_not_verified**: "Account Verification"
- **account_reset**: "How to reset account"
- **appreciation**: "Great App"
- **bank_verification_details**: "What details I need to provide for bank account"
- **cannot_see_joined_contests**: "I joined a league but now it's not showing"
- **capabilities**: "Help me"
- **cash_bonus**: "Cash Bonus"
- **cash_bonus_expiry**: "Cash Bonus Expiry"
- **change_bank_account**: "Change My Bank Account"
- **change_mobile_number**: "I want to change my number"
- **change_profile_team_details**: "Edit team name"
- **chat_with_an_agent**: "Need to connect with an agent", "I can't see my withdrawal", "My bonus is incorrect"
- **check_deposit_status**: "Show my transaction"
- **check_wallet_balance**: "Money left in my wallet"
- **contact_number**: "Call me back"
- **criticism**: "Waste app", "You are dumb"
- **deducted_amount_not_received**: "My money was deducted from my account but not showing the amount added. What should I do?"
- **delete_pan_card**: "Pan card remove"
- **download_powerplay11**: "Download app"
- **fairplay_violations**: "How my play will be consider as fair"
- **fake_teams**: "You have your own team in the leagues", "Fake players"
- **feedback**: "Feedback"
- **greetings_day**: "Yes"
- **how_points_calculated**: "How Are Points Calculated on PowerPlay11"
- **how_to_play**: "I need help to play"
- **instant_withdrawal**: "Fast withdrawal available"
- **join_contest**: "Contest joining"
- **less_winnings_amount**: "My winnings are incorrect"
- **match_abandoned**: "If match get abandoned will I get refund"
- **new_team_pattern**: "How many all-rounder I can select"
- **no_email_confirmation**: "When will I receive email confirmation"
- **offers_and_referrals**: "Any promotions available"
- **pan_verification_failed**: "Getting error while verifying PAN Card"
- **points_not_updated**: "Points are not getting updated", "When will scores be updated"
- **presence**: "Are You Online"
- **refund_of_added_cash**: "Is my addded cash is refundable", "Please refund money"
- **refund_of_wrong_amount**: "I added amount by mistake"
- **signup_bonus**: "Signup Bonus"
- **taxes_on_winnings**: "How much tax will be deducted"
- **team_deadline**: "What is Safe Play & Regular Play"
- **thanks**: "Tysm"
- **types_bonus**: "What is difference between Cash Bonus, signup bonus, surprise bonus, winnings"
- **types_contests**: "Types of Contests"
- **unutilized_money**: "Unutilized Amount"
- **update_app**: "How to update the app"
- **verify_email**: "Email verification"
- **verify_mobile**: "Mobile number verification"
- **verify_pan**: "Pan card verification", "How do I verify my PAN"
- **what_if_theres_a_tie**: "Same score between two players"
- **why_verify**: "What is the use of account verification"
- **winnings**: "When will I get the winning amount", "Winnings amount not credited"
- **withdraw_cash_bonus**: "Withdraw Cash Bonus"
- **withdrawal_intro**: "Withdrawal steps"
- **withdrawal_status**: "Status of withdrawal"
- **withdrawal_time**: "When can I expect my withdrawal amount"
- **wrong_scores**: "What if a game is completed with wrong scores?"

Table 14: Augmented version of intent list on POWERPLAY11 evaluation.

- **100_night_trial_offer**: "100 free Nights"
- **about_sof_mattress**: "How is SOF different from other mattress brands"
- **cancel_order**: "I want to cancel my order"
- **cash_on_delivery_(cod)**: "Can pay later on delivery"
- **check_pincode**: "Can you deliver on my pincode", "Will you be able to deliver here"
- **comparison**: "What is the difference between the Ergo & Ortho variants"
- **delay_in_delivery**: "It's been a month", "I did not receive my order yet"
- **distributors**: "Do you have any showrooms in Delhi state", "Need dealership"
- **equated_monthly_instalment_(emi)**: "You guys provide EMI option?"
- **ergonomic_features**: "What are the key features of the SOF Ergo mattress"
- **lead_generation**: "Get in Touch"
- **mattress_cost**: "Price of mattress", "How Much Cost"
- **offers**: "Any discounts"
- **order_status**: "Order Status", "When will the order be delivered to me?"
- **orthopedic_features**: "Features of Ortho mattress"
- **pillows**: "Do you have cushions"
- **product_variants**: "What are the product variants", "Show more mattress"
- **return_exchange**: "Need my money back"
- **size_customization**: "Can mattress size be customised?"
- **warranty**: "Does mattress cover is included in warranty"
- **what_size_to_order**: "Can you help with the size?"

Table 15: Augmented version of intent list on SOFMATTRESS evaluation.

PEARL: Personalizing Large Language Model Writing Assistants with Generation-Calibrated Retrievers

Sheshera Mysore[1△†] Zhuoran Lu[2†] Mengting Wan[1] Longqi Yang[1]
Bahar Sarrafzadeh[1] Steve Menezes[1] Tina Baghaee[1]
Emmanuel Barajas Gonzalez[1] Jennifer Neville[1] Tara Safavi[1△]
[2]Purdue University, IN, USA [1]Microsoft, WA, USA
[△]Corresponding authors: smysore@cs.umass.edu, tarasafavi@microsoft.com

Abstract

Powerful large language models have facilitated the development of writing assistants that promise to significantly improve the quality and efficiency of composition and communication. However, a barrier to effective assistance is the lack of personalization in LLM outputs to the author's communication style, specialized knowledge, and values. In this paper, we address this challenge by proposing PEARL, a LLM writing assistant personalized with a retriever that is trained to be *generation-calibrated* for personalization. Generation calibration ensures that our retriever selects historic user authored documents to augment an LLM prompt such that they are likely to help an LLM generation better adhere to a users' preferences. We propose two key novelties for training such a retriever: (1) A training data selection method that identifies historical user requests likely to benefit from personalization *and* documents that provide that benefit; and (2) A scale-calibrating KL-divergence objective that ensures that our retriever scores remain proportional to the downstream generation quality from using the document for personalized generation. In a series of holistic evaluations, we demonstrate the effectiveness of PEARL in generating long-form texts on multiple social media datasets. Finally, we demonstrate how a generation-calibrated retriever can double as a performance predictor – detecting low quality retrieval, and improving potentially underperforming outputs via revision with LLMs.

1 Introduction

Machine-assisted writing has seen a long history of development, progressing from providing simple syntactic checks, to revising human authored text, to recent assistants being able to fully compose texts on direction from authors (Mahlow, 2023; Dale and Viethen, 2021). The text-generation capabilities of current LLMs and has led current research to explore a new frontier of writing assistants for complex applications such as knowledge synthesis (Shen et al., 2023), peer review (Chen et al., 2023), and journalism (Wang et al., 2023c). An important element of effective writing assistants is being able to personalize generated text to retain the knowledge, style, and values of a user – an essential element of interpersonal communication (Pickering and Garrod, 2013). With current LLMs prone to generating overly generic text (Pu and Demberg, 2023), author personalization of LLMs is an important problem.

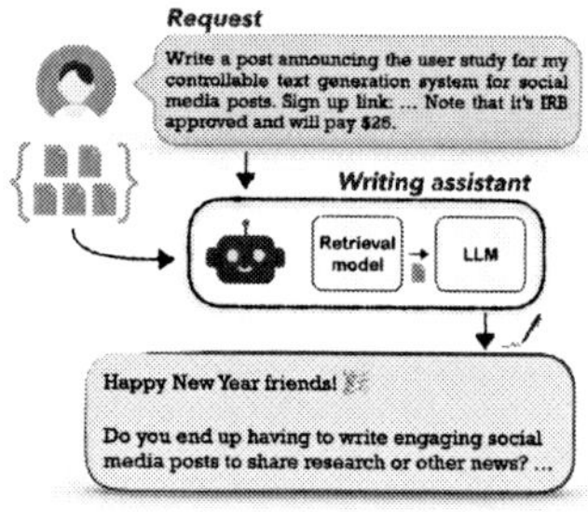

Figure 1: PEARL is a request-driven generation model that personalizes LLM outputs through retrieval augmentation with a *generation calibrated* retriever.

Personalizing LLM outputs may be seen as a form of alignment to individual users of the LLM (Kirk et al., 2023). However, leveraging fine-tuning for alignment in a personalization setup poses challenges to serving trained per-user models and obtaining sufficient per-user alignment training data. Therefore, we pursue in-context alignment through retrieval augmentation (Salemi et al., 2023; Li et al., 2023a). First, we assume access to a set of historic *user-authored documents* (e.g. emails, social media posts, etc.) and a user *request* for a personalized generation. To personalize LLM outputs we propose an approach to train a retrieval model that selects historic user documents to augment an LLM's prompt. Historic documents capture

[†] Work done during internship at Microsoft Research.

Proceedings of the 1st Workshop on Customizable NLP: Progress and Challenges in Customizing NLP for a Domain, Application, Group, or Individual (CustomNLP4U), pages 198–219
November 16, 2024 ©2024 Association for Computational Linguistics

users' personal style, knowledge, and values and can serve as useful context for personalized generation. While training retrievers for non-personalized applications have been explored in prior work (Gonen et al., 2022), this exploration has been limited in personalized text generation. Finally, we pursue personalization of LLMs only accessible via prompt-based APIs since this represents a common form of accessing performant large scale LLMs.

The starting point for our retriever in prior work examining effective prompts for *non-personalized* applications: Gonen et al. (2022) show the best prompts to be those with the highest conditional likelihood of generating a target text, and Rubin et al. (2022) use these likelihoods to train retrieval models for non-personalized retrieval augmentation of LLMs. While this approach performs well in non-personalized setups, *personalized* text generation presents unique challenges and opportunities: There are fewer historic documents per user (~hundreds) than common non-personalized retrieval collections, and user requests may diverge from their history as users' preferences change. A smaller retrieval corpus and shifting interests mean that all requests cannot be satisfied by retrieval from a users' historical documents – as a result, all historic requests and documents are unlikely to be useful for training a retriever. Our first contribution addresses this: We present a novel **difference of likelihoods**-based method that identifies *only* the personalizable user requests and associated documents that are likely to personalize downstream generations, and use these to train our retriever.

Next, the personalization setup offers an opportunity: Fewer historical documents per user permits the use of expressive cross-encoder retrievers instead of scalable but less expressive biencoders commonly used for non-personalized tasks (Rubin et al., 2022). However, cross-encoders produce skewed scores at the ends of their score ranges (Menon et al., 2022; Yadav et al., 2022), hampering their ability to closely track the utility of a document for personalized generation. We remedy this with our second contribution – a **personalized scale-calibrating training objective** (Yan et al., 2022). This ensures that scores from our retriever are *generation-calibrated* for personalization – i.e. the score it produces for request-document pairs is proportional to the output quality of an LLM prompted with the pair. In a case study, we show how generation calibration enables the retriever's scores to be used for *retrieval performance prediction* – detecting low-quality retrievals, and revising potentially low-quality generations.

We instantiate PEARL with multiple LLMs, `davinci-003` and `gpt-35-turbo`, at privacy compliant enterprise API endpoints and evaluate it on a private dataset of workplace communications and a public dataset of Reddit comments. For evaluation, we use a variety of evaluation methods spanning intrinsic, extrinsic, and personalized LLM-as-judge evaluations to demonstrate the value of PEARL. Further, since we train calibrated retrieval models, we present additional evaluations for calibration, ablations, and analysis in Appendices. Our evaluations demonstrate that PEARL consistently matches or outperforms strong baseline approaches.

2 Related Work

Example selection for LLMs Early work on training retrievers for augmenting LLM contexts in non-personalized applications was proposed by Rubin et al. (2022). They train retrieval models by distilling LLM likelihoods of the target completions conditioned on the prompt. Similarly Wang et al. (2023b) train retrieval models on finer-grained feedback from a trained reward model through distillation. More distantly, Zhang et al. (2022) train instances selection models on rewards from a downstream evaluation metric using reinforcement learning. Parallel with our work, Salemi et al. (2024) train bi-encoders for personalized classification and short text generation and find knowledge distillation from downstream LLMs to outperform reinforcement learning based training of retrievers. In this regard, Salemi et al. (2024) and Rubin et al. (2022) are closely related and represent closest work to ours – we compare to such an approach in ablations (Appendix C.2). Despite similarities to our work, all prior work has explored training retrievers for document selection while assuming that satisfactory predictions can be made for *all* inputs/requests. In addition to selecting documents for training, we also select training requests that benefit from retrieval augmentation – a necessity in personalization where retrieval is performed over a smaller historical document set instead of a large shared corpus. Further, no prior approaches explore calibration for retrievers and their ability to identify low-quality retrievals, and selectively revise LLM outputs – we explore this. Appendix D discusses additional work on optimizing prompts, robustness

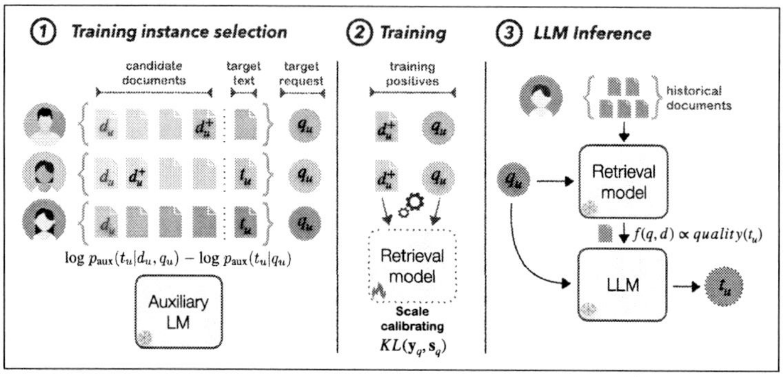

Figure 2: To train retriever, f_{retr}, an auxiliary language model is first used to identify historical *requests* that can be personalized and the best *document* to use for personalization ①. Then, f_{retr} is trained on the selected data with a scale calibrating loss function ②. Given an unseen request, f_{retr} is used to select the best instances from historical texts for augmenting an LLM prompt for personalized generation ③. Our training results in a generation calibrated retriever where scores for documents are proportional to the quality of the LLM output.

to prompt errors, and calibrated retrievers.

Personalized writing assistants While writing assistants have seen considerable exploration, only some prior work has focused on author personalization. These applications range from email (Chen et al., 2019; Trajanovski et al., 2021), to social media (Gero et al., 2022), and grammatical error correction (GEC) (Nadejde and Tetreault, 2019). These systems commonly leverage nearest-neighbor models (Chen et al., 2019; Trajanovski et al., 2021) and user-group level parameter-efficient fine-tuning for personalization (Nadejde and Tetreault, 2019). In contrast, we explore retrieval models for in-context alignment/personalization with LLMs. Parallel work has also explored personalized writing with LLMs. Li et al. (2023b) construct prompts with pre-trained retrieval and summarization models and fine-tune an LLM for personalized completion. Follow-on work has explored training a prompt-re-writer to tune prompts for a fixed LLM (Li et al., 2023a). Prompt re-writing is a complementary approach to a trained retriever, with future systems likely to benefit from both. Appendix D discusses non-personalized writing assistants and reader personalization.

3 Problem Definition

We consider a request-conditional, personalized text generation task. As input to the system, we assume a **user** u who is associated with a set of N_u **historical documents** $\mathcal{D}_u = \{d_u^{(i)}\}_{i=1}^{N_u}$, where each document d_u may be a previously-authored social media post, email, etc. The user u is further associated with a textual **request** q_u submitted to the writing assistant. The request may be authored by the user or constructed from the task context. Explicitly authored requests are increasingly common in conversational LLM interfaces (Papenmeier et al., 2021), and task contexts may be seen as implicit requests e.g. email prefixes that require completion (Chen et al., 2019). Finally, we assume access to a **large language model** f_{LLM} available via a prompt-based text generation API.

Given $\mathcal{D}_u$, q_u, and f_{LLM}, our retriever, f_{retr} is trained to select a subset of historical documents $\mathcal{D}'_u \subset \mathcal{D}_u$ as few-shot examples for the LLM. Then the LLM generates a **target text** t_u of up to 300 words: $t_u = f_{\text{LLM}}(\phi(q_u, \mathcal{D}'_u))$, where ϕ is a prompt construction function that inputs the user's request and retrieved historical documents, t_u reflects the style, knowledge, and values of u.

4 Proposed Approach

We present PEARL, an in-context aligned LLM-based model for personalized writing assistance. Our approach (Figure 2) consists of an offline retriever training stage and an online LLM inference stage. Offline, we train a **retriever** $f_{\text{retr}} : (q_u, d_u) \to \mathbb{R}$ that scores the user's historical documents for their ability to personalize the output for a user request. Further, we ensure that f_{retr} is generation calibrated i.e. the scores it produces for (q_u, d_u) pairs are proportional to the quality of the generated text from using (q_u, d_u) in a prompt. We train such a retriever through two key novelties: (1) Training data selection based on a novel difference of likelihoods from an auxiliary text generation model – we identify requests which benefit from personalization *and* documents which likely help personalize a target, and (2) A scale-calibrating training objective which ensures that retrievers closely track the benefit of request-document pairs for generation. Given a new request, our LLM is prompted to generate a target text t_u conditioned on the request and the documents retrieved by f_{retr}. Next, we describe the retriever training set construction (Algorithm 1), how we optimize the retriever, and the details of our implementation.

4.1 Training Data Setup

To optimize f_{retr} for a personalized text generation task, we carefully create a training set for f_{retr} from historical user documents by using an **auxiliary text generation model** f_{aux} to identify which requests and documents will help to personalize the generation of a target text.

Data organization We organize the training data to create a setup close to the problem defined in §3. Given a set of M users and their historical document sets $\{\mathcal{D}_u\}_{u=1}^{M}$, for each user u we partition $\mathcal{D}_u$ into two non-overlapping sets, a candidate document set $\mathcal{D}_u^c \subset \mathcal{D}_u$, and a "target" text set $\mathcal{D}_u^t \subset \mathcal{D}_u$, such that $\mathcal{D}_u^c + \mathcal{D}_u^t = \mathcal{D}_u$. The partitioning is done temporally, i.e. the target texts occur after the candidate documents, mimicking the personalization scenario where past texts are used to personalize later targets. If time data isn't available, the partitioning may be done randomly.

Next, for each target text t_u in each users $\mathcal{D}_u^t$, we pair the text with a corresponding request q_u. For training, requests may be naturally present in the data, e.g., email prefixes that require completion (Chen et al., 2019), or they may be generated synthetically (Bonifacio et al., 2022). We detail request generation in §5.1.

Auxiliary model scoring Next, we use the auxiliary text generation model f_{aux} to score each candidate document in $d_u \in \mathcal{D}_u^c$ for producing the personalized t_u corresponding to the q_u for each $(q_u, t_u) \in \mathcal{D}_u^t$. We define the score as a difference in the likelihood, per f_{aux}, of the target given the request with and without the historical document:

$$y_{q_u}^{d_u} = \log p_{\text{aux}}(t_u | d_u, q_u) - \log p_{\text{aux}}(t_u | q_u), \quad (1)$$

Importantly, Eq. (1) is highest when the request is suitable for personalization *and* the candidate document is the "right" example for personalization. That is, the request alone is not sufficient for generating the target text (i.e., the quantity defined by the second term is lower), and this candidate document is particularly beneficial to generation (i.e., the quantity defined by the first term is higher). Finally, we assume model f_{aux} to be smaller than f_{LLM} to support efficient creation of training data, and that we have access to its token likelihoods. Appendix A shows prompts used for f_{aux}.

4.2 Training Data Selection

We use the scores from Eq. 1 to identify: (1) a subset of training requests that are likely to benefit from personalization; and (2) candidate documents that are likely to benefit those requests i.e. positive training documents.

Request selection Using Eq. 1, we score all request-target pairs of a user in $\mathcal{D}_u^t$ against all of their candidate documents $d_u \in \mathcal{D}_u^c$, across all M users. After scoring, we retain the top scoring T request-target pairs. In practice, we find that setting T to the top two-thirds across the dataset works well. This step reflects the intuition that not all request-target pairs will benefit from retrieval augmentation, either due to the lack of suitable candidate documents in a user's historical document set, or due to underspecified requests making the target text simply too difficult to generate well – this is contrast with RAG setups in non-personalized scenarios where a large retrieval corpus ensures that most requests are likely to benefit from retrieval. After obtaining a high-quality set of training requests $\{q_u^*\}_{t=1}^{T}$, we discard the target texts, since they aren't used for training f_{retr} or for inference.

Candidate document selection Next, we use Eq. 1 to select the best documents for the retained requests, i.e. identify positive training documents. Given a request q_u^* selected for training, we take the P highest-scoring candidate documents $d_u \in \mathcal{D}_u^c$ as per Eq. (1) as positives, $\{d_u^+\}_{p=1}^{P}$. We sample N negative samples per positive randomly from the candidate document set for the user.

4.3 Retriever Optimization

Our f_{retr} is a cross-encoder initialized with a pretrained LM encoder and trained using data selected per Algorithm 1, through distillation of scores in Equation 1. While cross-encoders are expressive they produce scores which lie at the extremes of their score ranges (Menon et al., 2022; Yadav et al., 2022) – this hampers their ability to closely track the benefit of candidate documents for personalizing requests. We propose to remedy this through a scale calibrating training objective.

Algorithm 1 Selecting requests and positive candidate documents to train f_{retr}

Input: $\{\mathcal{D}_u\}_{u=1}^{M}$, f_{aux} ▷ Historical documents for M users and an auxiliary LM
for each user u **do**
  $\mathcal{D}_u^c, \mathcal{D}_u^t \leftarrow \text{TemporalPartition}(\mathcal{D}_u)$ ▷ Temporally partition $\mathcal{D}_u$ into candidate and target documents
  for each target text $t_u \in \mathcal{D}_u^t$ **do**
    $q_u \leftarrow \text{GetRequest}(t_u)$ ▷ Obtain a synthetic or natural request
  end for
  for each (q_u, t_u) pair in $\mathcal{D}_u^t$ **do** ▷ Compute benefit of personalization for request-target pairs
    for each candidate d_u in $\mathcal{D}_u^c$ **do**
      $Y[q_u, d_u] = \log\ p_{\text{aux}}(t_u | d_u, q_u) - \log p_{\text{aux}}(t_u | q_u)$ ▷ Equation (1)
    end for
  end for
end for
$\{q_u^*\}_{t=1}^{T} \leftarrow \text{TopK}(Y[q_u, d_u])$ ▷ Retain the top T unique requests which are personalizable
for each retained request in $\{q_u^*\}_{k=1}^{T}$ **do**
  $\{d_u^+\}_{p=1}^{P} \leftarrow \text{TopK}(Y[q_u^*, d_u])$ ▷ Retain the top P candidates that best personalize the target
end for
return $\{q_u^*, \{d_u^+\}_{p=1}^{P}\}_{t=1}^{T}$

Scale calibration Let $\mathbf{y}_q = [y_q^+, \ldots, y_q^-]$, where y_q^+ corresponds to the score of a positive document and y_q^- corresponds to the score of a negative document from Eq. 1. Here, $\mathbf{y}_q$ contains N negatives and 1 positive document. Similarly, let the predicted logits from $f_{\text{retr}} : (q_u, d_u) \rightarrow \mathbb{R}$ be denoted as $\mathbf{s}_q = [s_q^+, \ldots, s_q^-]$. Then, a standard KL-divergence loss is written as $KL(\mathbf{y}_q, \mathbf{s}_q) = -\sum_i \mathsf{sm}(y_{q,i}) \log \mathsf{sm}(s_{q,i})$, where sm represents the softmax function. Our proposed scale calibration modifies the KL divergence loss by adding an "anchor" example with target score y_0, which is a tunable hyperparameter, and logit s_0 set to 0, resulting in score vectors $\mathbf{y}_q' = [y_0, \mathbf{y}_q]$ and $\mathbf{s}_q' = [s_0, \mathbf{s}_q]$. The scale-calibrated KL-divergence loss is thus

$$KL(\mathbf{y}_q', \mathbf{s}_q') = -\sum_i \mathsf{sm}(y_{q,i}') \log \mathsf{sm}(s_{q,i}') \quad (2)$$

$$= -\sum_i \frac{e^{y_{q,i}}}{\sum_j e^{y_{q,j}} + e^{y_0}} \log \frac{e^{s_{q,i}}}{\sum_j e^{s_{q,j}} + 1} + \frac{e^{y_0}}{\sum_j e^{y_{q,j}} + e^{y_0}} \log \big(\sum_j e^{s_{q,j}} + 1\big). \quad (3)$$

We find that setting y_0 to the median value of scores from Eq (1) for positive candidate documents works well. This ensures that very large scores from f_{retr} are penalized (second term Eq 3) and smaller scores are prevented from being driven lower (first term Eq 3). Therefore f_{retr} scores are more evenly distributed over the score range. In practice, this ensures that predicted scores from f_{retr} more accurately reflect the distribution of f_{aux}, which in turn more closely tracks the utility of request-document pairs for personalization. We compare PEARL to baselines in §5.2 and present ablations in §C.2.

4.4 System Details

After training retriever f_{retr} offline, PEARL may be used to serve requests online. Given a unseen request, f_{retr} retrieves the top-k historical texts from $\mathcal{D}_u$, these are formatted into a prompt and input to f_{LLM} to generate a personalized target text t_u.

Our f_{retr} is initialized with a 110M parameter MPNET encoder (Song et al., 2020). For f_{LLM} we consider two performant LLMs, `davinci-003` and `gpt-3.5-turbo`. For f_{aux} we use FLANT5-XL with 3 billion parameters (Chung et al., 2022). Appendix A details our prompts and implementation.

5 Experiments

We demonstrate the effectiveness of PEARL on two personalized text generation datasets from social media platforms. For evaluation, we employ standard intrinsic evaluations, extrinsic evaluation based on downstream tasks using the generated text, and recently proposed personalized LLM-as-judge (Wang et al., 2023d). Then, in §5.3 we show how a calibrated retriever can be used for selective revision of underperforming requests. We present ablations in §C.2 and we demonstrate the calibration performance for our retriever in §C.3.

5.1 Experimental Setup

Data For evaluation, we use two open-ended long-form text generation datasets for social media: (1) Personalized post writing on WORKSM and (2) Personalized comment writing on AITA.

<u>WORKSM</u> WORKSM is an enterprise social network used for communication within organizations presenting a highly realistic platform for writing assistance. We obtain a random sample of ~18k posts written by 1116 users from November 2020 to July 2023. To create an *evaluation set*, we manually examine posts greater than 50 words and receiving ≥2 comments, about 1K posts, and select 163 of the most recent posts from ~80 users to serve as reference target texts t_u^*. These posts represent a diverse, engaging set that could benefit from personalized writing assistance and serve as high quality target references. At a high level, these posts share events, research studies, campaigns,

and organizational news. Since WORKSM does not contain requests to the writing assistant, two authors not involved in model development manually wrote requests q_u per target text. Note that this was necessary given the highly regulated and private enterprise data in WORKSM preventing exposure to external crowdworkers. Our requests were authored following Guideline 1. To construct $\mathcal{D}_u$ posts created before t_u^* were used: On average, users had 31 historic posts (max of 169). To create our *training set*, we only retain posts > 10 words and users with ≥ 5 historic posts while excluding posts in our evaluation set. We generate synthetic requests with GPT-4 for training given the expense of manually authored requests – resulting in a set of $\sim$7k training requests. Enterprise contracts with API providers ensured the privacy of user data shared over the API.

AITA AITA is a Reddit subforum in which original posters (OP) describe personal moral conflicts and receive comments from other users judging them to be "the a**hole" or "not the a**hole". This dataset has been used in prior work on modeling the personal values of users (Plepi et al., 2022). We construct a personalized comment generation task from this data. We treat the OP posts as requests q_u, user comments as reference target texts t_u^*, and a user's previous comments as $\mathcal{D}_u$. Since the dataset lacks time metadata, we construct an *evaluation set* by sampling 10% of the posts as test requests, and further filter to 600 random target texts for our evaluation set to keep LLM experiments feasible. Evaluation users had 29 posts in $\mathcal{D}_u$ on average (max of 590). Our *training set* used the historical post-comment pairs from users in $\mathcal{D}_u$, resulting in $\sim$84k requests. Note that while Reddit comments are not the ideal platform for writing assistance, AITA is one of the few public datasets available for the task and resembles applications such as email response generation (Kannan et al., 2016). Appendix B details our datasets further.

Generation metrics Since personalized text generation aims to adhere to the style, knowledge, and values of *specific* users, effective evaluation for personalized generation remains an open problem (Wang et al., 2023d,a). This is in contrast to non-personalized generation, where desirable aspects of outputs can be defined uniformly across all test cases. As a result, we present evaluations using a host of standard evaluation setups aiming to demonstrate the effectiveness of PEARL from various perspectives. Our evaluations span the following standard setups (Dou et al., 2023): intrinsic evaluations based on n-gram/embedding similarity to reference texts, extrinsic evaluation through a classification accuracy based on generated text, and pairwise evaluation with personalized LLM-as-judge.

Specifically, for WORKSM we report standard evaluation measures based on n-gram and embedding similarity between generations and reference targets: ROUGE-1 (R1), ROUGE-2 (R2), and BertScore-F1 (BS-F1) (Zhang* et al., 2020). This serves as an intrinsic evaluation for WORKSM measuring the extent to which generations are similar to user authored texts. Next, since AITA users' comments primarily make a stance based on users' moral values, we measure if the stance in generated comments matches that of the user through a downstream stance prediction task – serving as an extrinsic evaluation. This evaluation may be seen as evaluating the extent to which model generations adhere to a user's values. We map generated comments to a binary "YTA" or "NTA" label based on simple high-precision rules mapping lexical variations of "you're the a**hole" and "not the a**hole" to the labels. This procedure was also found reliable for constructing ground truth labels in AITA (Plepi et al., 2022). Note that early attempts of using n-gram/embedding similarity measures for evaluation (BS-F1, R1, R2) resulted in unreliable evaluations for AITA due the large variation (length, vocabulary, emojis etc.) in AITA comments, therefore we opt for more stable extrinsic evaluations and LLM based evaluations described next.

For both AITA and WORKSM we conduct a pairwise evaluation with a recently proposed personalized LLM-as-judge (Wang et al., 2023d). Wang et al. show LLM based author identifications to be a reliable proxy task for distinguishing models of various qualities and being correlated with human quality ratings. Here, a judge LLM is presented with a reference text from a user and generations from the pair of systems being compared, then, it is prompted to select the system generation more likely to be authored by the author of the reference text. An author identification task aims to capture several aspects which distinguish individuals' writing, spanning style, knowledge and their values. In our evaluation, we compare PEARL outputs to the outputs from the best baseline as indicated by intrinsic/extrinsic evaluations and use the target reference text t_u^* in the LLM prompt as an example

LLM →	davinci-003	gpt-35-turbo
Method ↓	Macro F1(%)	Macro F1(%)
ZSHOT-NP	41.97	50.43
KSHOT-NP	51.71	59.76
Random	55.52	59.47
BM25	57.26	61.66
MPNET-1B	53.72	59.23
UPR	55.76	58.15
RelevanceCE	56.85	59.59
PEARL	**61.21**	**65.34**

(a) Extrinsic classification accuracy in AITA.

LLM →	davinci-003			gpt-35-turbo		
Method ↓	BS-F1	R1	R2	BS-F1	R1	R2
ZSHOT-NP	36.25	0.5029	0.2516	31.03	0.4627	0.2091
KSHOT-NP	34.08	0.4931	0.2431	32.51	0.4825	0.2258
Random	35.04	0.5036	0.2505	33.46	0.4893	0.2345
BM25	37.96	0.5287	0.2911	**36.57**	**0.5089**	0.2673
MPNET-1B	38.30	0.5281	0.2931	36.02	0.5063	0.2639
UPR	38.70	0.5337	0.3019	35.98	0.5054	0.2642
RelevanceCE	37.81	0.5288	0.2953	35.99	0.5038	0.2613
PEARL	**39.60**	**0.5419**	**0.3094**	36.49	0.5082	**0.2676**

(b) Intrinsic reference based metrics in WORKSM .

Table 1: PEARL is compared to non-personalized (NP) and LLMs personalized with retrieval on datasets of social media communication: (a) a dataset constructed from Reddit and (b) a workplace social media dataset.

of the users writing. We use GPT-4o as our judge LLM and present the judge prompt in Appendix B.4. In our evaluation we avoid rating aspects such as fluency, non-redundancy, etc. (Celikyilmaz et al., 2021) since we are primarily concerned with personalization performance and these qualities may be in conflict with specific users writing.

Baselines As baselines, we consider non-personalized models based on zero shot prompting (ZSHOT-NP) and few-shot prompting with k randomly chosen example documents (KSHOT-NP). We consider retrieval-augmented personalized baselines, which selecting from a user's historical documents $\mathcal{D}_u$. They span selection at random from $\mathcal{D}_u$ (Random), with sparse retrieval by BM25, with dense retrieval by a strong MPNET model trained on 1 billion text pairs (MPNET-1B), an unsupervised crossencoder (Sachan et al., 2022) ranking documents with FLANT5-BASE likelihood: $p(q_u|d_u)$ (UPR), and a supervised crossencoder optimized on our dataset with request-document pairs, (q_u, d_u) in $\mathcal{D}_u$ (RelevanceCE). Appendix B.3 details our baselines.

5.2 Generation Evaluation

Table 1 and 2 report our evaluations. Appendix C presents ablation (C.2) and calibration (C.3) results.

Reference based evaluation Tables 1b and 1a reports automated metrics on AITA and WORKSM. First we observe that personalization through retrieval, even at Random, generally improves upon non-personalized approaches (NP), which is consistent with prior work (Salemi et al., 2023). Next, we note that the best baseline is not consistent, varying between BM25, and unsupervised crossencoder (UPR) – indicating that retrieval models designed for request-document relevance vary in performance depending on the dataset and inference LLM. Finally, we note that PEARL consistently performs at par or better than the best baselines across datasets and LLMs, indicating the effectiveness of training f_{retr} for personalized generation. For the more reliable classification metrics obtainable in AITA, PEARL outperforms all baselines with improvements of 1.5 to 5 Macro F1 points. Next, we report performance in more expressive LLM-as-judge evaluations.

	davinci-003	gpt-35-turbo
	P / B / T (%)	P / B / T (%)
AITA	**46.8** /40.3 /12.8$_{\alpha=0.56}$	**46.6** /44.9 /8.3$_{\alpha=0.55}$
WORKSM	**46.6** /42.5 /10.8$_{\alpha=0.42}$	38.9 /**42.6** /18.5$_{\alpha=0.28}$

Table 2: LLM-as-judge win-rate evaluation for AITA and WORKSM selecting a generation to be more aligned with an authors writing sample. The LLM could prefer the Proposed system (PEARL), the Baseline (BM25), or judge the outputs as Tied – denoted with P, B, and T.

Pairwise LLM-as-judge evaluation In Table 2 we report the results of personalization evaluation following the setup described in §5.1. Here, we compare against BM25-augmented as it performs within our top 2 baselines in automatic evaluations - this strong performance is consistent with prior work (Izacard et al., 2022; Thakur et al., 2021). We use GPT-4o as a judge LLM and run every pair of inputs through the judge LLM 3 times, we report average win rates over all the instances in our test set and over 3 repeated runs. Further, we randomly swap the position of the baseline and proposed method generations in the prompt to account for position biases in the judge LLM. Finally, we also report the agreement between the 3 judge LLM runs using Krippendorff's alpha (α) to ensure that

LLM judgements are consistent across runs.

In Table 2, PEARL achieves a greater win-rate than BM25 in 3 of 4 settings. In these settings we also note that the LLM judgments remain consistent across 3 repeated runs with Krippendorff's alpha between $0.41 - 0.56$ (0 indicates chance agreement). While BM25 sees a greater win-rate in WORKSM with gpt-35-turbo, the judgments see lower agreement ($\alpha = 0.28$) indicating the outputs to be harder to distinguish. Finally, comparing to Table 1 we see that the trends of extrinsic and intrinsic reference based evaluations are retained in LLM-as-judge evaluations – consistently indicating the benefit of PEARL across evaluation setups, inference LLMs, and datasets. In Appendix C we show an example from AITA to show the kinds of retrievals and outputs that make PEARL effective.

5.3 Selective Revision with PEARL

Having established PEARL to be an effective model for generation, we show f_{retr} to be generation calibrated in Appendix C.3. Here, we demonstrate the usefulness of a calibrated retriever in a case study using the retriever scores to selectively revise generations. Specifically, we treat the scores from f_{retr} as a predictor of retrieval performance, and in-turn text generation performance. We assume that if f_{retr} cannot find a highly scored in-context example, the generated response will be of low quality and can benefit from LLM revision (Figure 3).

Setup Given our trained retriever, we take all top-1 document scores for each request $s_1 = \max_{d_u \in \mathcal{D}_u} f_{\text{retr}}(q_u, d_u)$ and learn a threshold θ on s_1 that maximizes a downstream performance metric on a held-out development set (R2 in WORKSM and Macro-F1 in AITA). Then, given a generated target text t_u with $s_1 < \theta$, we selectively revise t_u where f_{LLM} is prompted to edit the target text. We report results of selective revision compared to a single round of generation (i.e., no revision) and full revision over the entire dataset (i.e., 100% revision). We repeat this for BM25. We provide further details and analysis in Appendix C.4.

Results In Table 3 we see that selective revision improves or retains performance upon a single round of generation ("Stage 1") by 2-4% in downstream performance metrics with f_{retr} =Proposed and BM25 for WORKSM. However, for AITA we see that selective revision based on BM25 shows a marked drop in performance indicating its dataset dependent calibration performance. Importantly,

Dataset →	AITA	WORKSM		
Method ↓ / LLM →	gpt-35-turbo	gpt-35-turbo		
f_{retr} = BM25	Macro F1 (%)	BS-F1	R1	R2
Stage 1 (no revision)	**59.99**	36.15	0.5052	0.2611
All (100% revision)	58.36	35.45	0.5096	0.2573
Selective revision	57.71	**37.29**	**0.5206**	**0.2738**
f_{retr} = Proposed	Macro F1 (%)	BS-F1	R1	R2
Stage 1 (no revision)	65.15	37.02	0.5124	0.2709
All (100% revision)	64.85	35.47	0.5045	0.2520
Selective revision	**65.36**	**37.71**	**0.5236**	**0.2818**

Table 3: Selectively revising target texts t_u based on scores from our retriever vs BM25. Also present are results of no revision and revising all outputs (100% revision) from Stage 1 outputs.

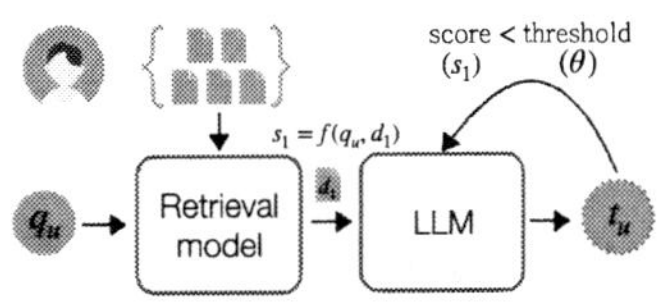

Figure 3: Generation calibration of f_{retr} allows us to use its predicted scores for performance prediction and selectively revise potentially bad generations.

note that Macro F1 doesn't measure aspects of style which may have changed in revision. Finally, editing *all* outputs produced by Stage 1 generation consistently leads to degraded performance ("All"), indicating that editing is not always helpful.

We also observe that PEARL chooses 75.8% and 77.9% instances for editing in WORKSM and AITA, respectively. This indicates the potential for generation calibrated retrievers to reduce the number of expensive LLM calls made while ensuring better personalization performance. In Figure 5 (Appendix C.4) we analyze the performance of selective revision against request and user profile length. In a manual examination of requests with a low s_1 score by the PEARL f_{retr}, we find the requests to be underspecified and often require further information from a user e.g. the request "Write a post about how I like to relax after work", aims to generate a target discussing more specific forms of relaxation not present in any historical documents. This indicates that generation calibrated retrievers may be used for other forms of selective prediction and user interaction – e.g. selectively withholding predictions when satisfactory generations are unlikely or obtaining more information from users through follow-up questions. We leave such explorations to exciting future work.

6 Conclusion

In this paper we present PEARL– an LLM based writing assistant personalized with generation calibrated retrievers. We propose a method for training generation calibrated retrievers through a careful selection of training data and a scale calibrated objective. In a series of holistic evaluations, we demonstrate the effectiveness of our approach in datasets of social media communication compared to baselines (§5.2) as well as ablated models (Appendix C.2). We demonstrate the calibration performance for our retriever (Appendix C.3), and show how our retrieval model can double as a performance predictor (§5.3) and can identify outputs which can benefit from LLM revision.

7 Ethical and broader impact

Having introduced PEARL as an effective personalization strategy for writing assistance and discussed its benefits we review two implications of concern arising from better personalized text generation: challenges to factuality, and longer term influence on language use and communication.

Challenges to factuality The emergence of LLMs and their ability to generate compelling text has seen a subsequent rise in the cases of malicious use of these technologies. Augenstein et al. (2023) overview four such classes of harm: personalized attacks on individuals in the form of phishing attacks and tailored misinformation, impersonation of trusted figures (e.g. journalists or regulators), a glut of paraphrased misinformation evading detection by automatic tools often used by fact checkers, and large scale creation of fake social media profiles and plagiarized content (Brewster et al., 2023). It is possible that improvements in personalized text generation are likely to excacertabe each of these problems. To account for this, several technology and policy initiatives are under active development (Augenstein et al., 2023). These span detection of AI-generated content, cryptographic signatures intended to prove the authenticity of content, to government regulation and public education, however, their effectiveness remains under investigation.

Language use and communication Current understanding of computer mediated communication suggests that users interpersonal communication patterns are influenced by the tool/medium used for communication (Poddar et al., 2023) with a potential for these influences to have longer term influences on communication in the absence of these tools (Hancock et al., 2020). Hancock et al. outline these implications as ranging from shifts in language use (e.g a social expectation of more positive responses (Hohenstein and Jung, 2018)), issues of how individuals portray themselves and evaluate others, to long term feedback loops resulting in how we perceive ourselves. However, understanding of the implications of AI mediated communication, specially those powered by powerful LLMs, is largely developing (Hancock et al., 2020). It is likely that wide spread personalization in LLM communication agents, will necessitate further understanding of these factors and the design of systems that incorporates this understanding to ameliorate harms.

References

Nader Akoury, Shufan Wang, Josh Whiting, Stephen Hood, Nanyun Peng, and Mohit Iyyer. 2020. STORIUM: A Dataset and Evaluation Platform for Machine-in-the-Loop Story Generation. In *Proceedings of the 2020 Conference on Empirical Methods in Natural Language Processing (EMNLP)*, pages 6470–6484, Online. Association for Computational Linguistics.

Xiang Ao, Xiting Wang, Ling Luo, Ying Qiao, Qing He, and Xing Xie. 2021. PENS: A dataset and generic framework for personalized news headline generation. In *Proceedings of the 59th Annual Meeting of the Association for Computational Linguistics and the 11th International Joint Conference on Natural Language Processing (Volume 1: Long Papers)*, pages 82–92, Online. Association for Computational Linguistics.

Simran Arora, Avanika Narayan, Mayee F Chen, Laurel Orr, Neel Guha, Kush Bhatia, Ines Chami, and Christopher Re. 2023. Ask me anything: A simple strategy for prompting language models. In *The Eleventh International Conference on Learning Representations*.

Isabelle Augenstein, Timothy Baldwin, Meeyoung Cha, Tanmoy Chakraborty, Giovanni Luca Ciampaglia, David Corney, Renee DiResta, Emilio Ferrara, Scott Hale, Alon Halevy, Eduard Hovy, Heng Ji, Filippo Menczer, Ruben Miguez, Preslav Nakov, Dietram Scheufele, Shivam Sharma, and Giovanni Zagni. 2023. Factuality challenges in the era of large language models. *arXiv preprint arXiv:2310.05189*.

Tal August, Katharina Reinecke, and Noah A. Smith. 2022. Generating scientific definitions with controllable complexity. In *Proceedings of the 60th Annual Meeting of the Association for Computational Linguistics (Volume 1: Long Papers)*, pages 8298–8317,

Dublin, Ireland. Association for Computational Linguistics.

Luiz Bonifacio, Hugo Abonizio, Marzieh Fadaee, and Rodrigo Nogueira. 2022. Inpars: Unsupervised dataset generation for information retrieval. In *Proceedings of the 45th International ACM SIGIR Conference on Research and Development in Information Retrieval*, SIGIR '22, page 2387–2392, New York, NY, USA. Association for Computing Machinery.

Jack Brewster, Macrina Wang, and Coalter Palmer. 2023. Plagiarism-bot? how low-quality websites are using ai to deceptively rewrite content from mainstream news outlets. NewsGaurd, The Internet Trust Tool.

Asli Celikyilmaz, Elizabeth Clark, and Jianfeng Gao. 2021. Evaluation of text generation: A survey. *arXiv preprint arXiv:2006.14799*.

Tuhin Chakrabarty, Vishakh Padmakumar, and He He. 2022. Help me write a poem: Instruction tuning as a vehicle for collaborative poetry writing. In *Proceedings of the 2022 Conference on Empirical Methods in Natural Language Processing*, pages 6848–6863, Abu Dhabi, United Arab Emirates. Association for Computational Linguistics.

Mia Xu Chen, Benjamin N. Lee, Gagan Bansal, Yuan Cao, Shuyuan Zhang, Justin Lu, Jackie Tsay, Yinan Wang, Andrew M. Dai, Zhifeng Chen, Timothy Sohn, and Yonghui Wu. 2019. Gmail smart compose: Real-time assisted writing. In *Proceedings of the 25th ACM SIGKDD International Conference on Knowledge Discovery & Data Mining*, KDD '19, page 2287–2295, New York, NY, USA. Association for Computing Machinery.

Shiping Chen, Duncan P Brumby, and Anna L Cox. 2023. Using writing assistants to accelerate the peer review process. *Second Workshop on Intelligent and Interactive Writing Assistants, CHI 2023*.

Hyung Won Chung, Le Hou, Shayne Longpre, Barret Zoph, Yi Tay, William Fedus, Eric Li, Xuezhi Wang, Mostafa Dehghani, Siddhartha Brahma, et al. 2022. Scaling instruction-finetuned language models. *arXiv preprint arXiv:2210.11416*.

Elizabeth Clark, Anne Spencer Ross, Chenhao Tan, Yangfeng Ji, and Noah A. Smith. 2018. Creative writing with a machine in the loop: Case studies on slogans and stories. In *23rd International Conference on Intelligent User Interfaces*, IUI '18, page 329–340, New York, NY, USA. Association for Computing Machinery.

Daniel Cohen, Bhaskar Mitra, Oleg Lesota, Navid Rekabsaz, and Carsten Eickhoff. 2021. Not all relevance scores are equal: Efficient uncertainty and calibration modeling for deep retrieval models. In *Proceedings of the 44th International ACM SIGIR Conference on Research and Development in Information Retrieval*, SIGIR '21, page 654–664, New York, NY, USA. Association for Computing Machinery.

Antonia Creswell, Murray Shanahan, and Irina Higgins. 2023. Selection-inference: Exploiting large language models for interpretable logical reasoning. In *The Eleventh International Conference on Learning Representations*.

Robert Dale and Jette Viethen. 2021. The automated writing assistance landscape in 2021. *Natural Language Engineering*, 27(4):511–518.

Shehzaad Dhuliawala, Leonard Adolphs, Rajarshi Das, and Mrinmaya Sachan. 2022. Calibration of machine reading systems at scale. In *Findings of the Association for Computational Linguistics: ACL 2022*, pages 1682–1693, Dublin, Ireland. Association for Computational Linguistics.

Shehzaad Dhuliawala, Mojtaba Komeili, Jing Xu, Roberta Raileanu, Xian Li, Asli Celikyilmaz, and Jason Weston. 2023. Chain-of-verification reduces hallucination in large language models. *arXiv preprint arXiv:2309.11495*.

Yao Dou, Philippe Laban, Claire Gardent, and Wei Xu. 2023. Automatic and human-ai interactive text generation. *arXiv preprint arXiv:2310.03878*.

Asma Farajidizaji, Vatsal Raina, and Mark Gales. 2023. Is it possible to modify text to a target readability level? an initial investigation using zero-shot large language models. *arXiv preprint arXiv:2309.12551*.

Katy Ilonka Gero, Vivian Liu, and Lydia Chilton. 2022. Sparks: Inspiration for science writing using language models. In *Proceedings of the 2022 ACM Designing Interactive Systems Conference*, DIS '22, page 1002–1019, New York, NY, USA. Association for Computing Machinery.

Hugo Gonçalo Oliveira. 2017. A survey on intelligent poetry generation: Languages, features, techniques, reutilisation and evaluation. In *Proceedings of the 10th International Conference on Natural Language Generation*, pages 11–20, Santiago de Compostela, Spain. Association for Computational Linguistics.

Hila Gonen, Srini Iyer, Terra Blevins, Noah A. Smith, and Luke Zettlemoyer. 2022. Demystifying prompts in language models via perplexity estimation. *arXiv preprint arXiv:2212.04037*.

Yue Guo, Wei Qiu, Yizhong Wang, and Trevor Cohen. 2021. Automated lay language summarization of biomedical scientific reviews. *Proceedings of the AAAI Conference on Artificial Intelligence*, 35(1):160–168.

Shivanshu Gupta, Matt Gardner, and Sameer Singh. 2023. Coverage-based example selection for in-context learning. *arXiv preprint arXiv:2305.14907*.

Jeffrey T Hancock, Mor Naaman, and Karen Levy. 2020. AI-Mediated Communication: Definition, Research Agenda, and Ethical Considerations. *Journal of Computer-Mediated Communication*, 25(1):89–100.

Jess Hohenstein and Malte Jung. 2018. Ai-supported messaging: An investigation of human-human text conversation with ai support. In *Extended Abstracts of the 2018 CHI Conference on Human Factors in Computing Systems*, CHI EA '18, page 1–6, New York, NY, USA. Association for Computing Machinery.

Krystal Hu. 2023. Chatgpt sets record for fastest-growing user base - analyst note. National Bureau of Economic Research, Digest No. 6.

Gautier Izacard, Mathilde Caron, Lucas Hosseini, Sebastian Riedel, Piotr Bojanowski, Armand Joulin, and Edouard Grave. 2022. Unsupervised dense information retrieval with contrastive learning. *Transactions on Machine Learning Research*.

Anjuli Kannan, Karol Kurach, Sujith Ravi, Tobias Kaufmann, Andrew Tomkins, Balint Miklos, Greg Corrado, Laszlo Lukacs, Marina Ganea, Peter Young, and Vivek Ramavajjala. 2016. Smart reply: Automated response suggestion for email. In *Proceedings of the 22nd ACM SIGKDD International Conference on Knowledge Discovery and Data Mining*, KDD '16, page 955–964, New York, NY, USA. Association for Computing Machinery.

Omar Khattab, Keshav Santhanam, Xiang Lisa Li, David Hall, Percy Liang, Christopher Potts, and Matei Zaharia. 2023. Demonstrate-search-predict: Composing retrieval and language models for knowledge-intensive nlp. *arXiv preprint arXiv:2212.14024*.

Hannah Rose Kirk, Bertie Vidgen, Paul Röttger, and Scott A Hale. 2023. Personalisation within bounds: A risk taxonomy and policy framework for the alignment of large language models with personalised feedback. *arXiv preprint arXiv:2303.05453*.

Cheng Li, Mingyang Zhang, Qiaozhu Mei, Weize Kong, and Michael Bendersky. 2023a. Automatic prompt rewriting for personalized text generation. *arXiv preprint arXiv:2310.00152*.

Cheng Li, Mingyang Zhang, Qiaozhu Mei, Yaqing Wang, Spurthi Amba Hombaiah, Yi Liang, and Michael Bendersky. 2023b. Teach llms to personalize – an approach inspired by writing education. *arXiv preprint arXiv:2308.07968*.

Daliang Li, Ankit Singh Rawat, Manzil Zaheer, Xin Wang, Michal Lukasik, Andreas Veit, Felix Yu, and Sanjiv Kumar. 2023c. Large language models with controllable working memory. In *Findings of the Association for Computational Linguistics: ACL 2023*, pages 1774–1793, Toronto, Canada. Association for Computational Linguistics.

Zihao Li, Samuel Belkadi, Nicolo Micheletti, Lifeng Han, Matthew Shardlow, and Goran Nenadic. 2023d. Large language models and control mechanisms improve text readability of biomedical abstracts.

Zhiyu Lin, Upol Ehsan, Rohan Agarwal, Samihan Dani, Vidushi Vashishth, and Mark Riedl. 2023. Beyond prompts: Exploring the design space of mixed-initiative co-creativity systems. In *ICCC*.

Hongyin Luo, Yung-Sung Chuang, Yuan Gong, Tianhua Zhang, Yoon Kim, Xixin Wu, Danny Fox, Helen Meng, and James Glass. 2023. Sail: Search-augmented instruction learning. *arXiv preprint arXiv:2305.15225*.

Cerstin Mahlow. 2023. Writing tools: Looking back to look ahead. *Second Workshop on Intelligent and Interactive Writing Assistants, CHI 2023*.

Bodhisattwa Prasad Majumder, Shuyang Li, Jianmo Ni, and Julian McAuley. 2019. Generating personalized recipes from historical user preferences. In *Proceedings of the 2019 Conference on Empirical Methods in Natural Language Processing and the 9th International Joint Conference on Natural Language Processing (EMNLP-IJCNLP)*, pages 5976–5982, Hong Kong, China. Association for Computational Linguistics.

Alex Mallen, Akari Asai, Victor Zhong, Rajarshi Das, Daniel Khashabi, and Hannaneh Hajishirzi. 2023. When not to trust language models: Investigating effectiveness of parametric and non-parametric memories. In *Proceedings of the 61st Annual Meeting of the Association for Computational Linguistics (Volume 1: Long Papers)*, pages 9802–9822, Toronto, Canada. Association for Computational Linguistics.

Pierre-Emmanuel Mazaré, Samuel Humeau, Martin Raison, and Antoine Bordes. 2018. Training millions of personalized dialogue agents. In *Proceedings of the 2018 Conference on Empirical Methods in Natural Language Processing*, pages 2775–2779, Brussels, Belgium. Association for Computational Linguistics.

Aditya Menon, Sadeep Jayasumana, Ankit Singh Rawat, Seungyeon Kim, Sashank Reddi, and Sanjiv Kumar. 2022. In defense of dual-encoders for neural ranking. In *Proceedings of the 39th International Conference on Machine Learning*, volume 162 of *Proceedings of Machine Learning Research*, pages 15376–15400. PMLR.

Piotr Mirowski, Kory W. Mathewson, Jaylen Pittman, and Richard Evans. 2023. Co-writing screenplays and theatre scripts with language models: Evaluation by industry professionals. In *Proceedings of the 2023 CHI Conference on Human Factors in Computing Systems*, CHI '23, New York, NY, USA. Association for Computing Machinery.

Sonia K. Murthy, Kyle Lo, Daniel King, Chandra Bhagavatula, Bailey Kuehl, Sophie Johnson, Jonathan Borchardt, Daniel S. Weld, Tom Hope, and Doug Downey. 2022. Accord: A multi-document approach to generating diverse descriptions of scientific concepts.

Maria Nadejde and Joel Tetreault. 2019. Personalizing grammatical error correction: Adaptation to proficiency level and L1. In *Proceedings of the 5th Workshop on Noisy User-generated Text (W-NUT 2019)*, pages 27–33, Hong Kong, China. Association for Computational Linguistics.

Jianmo Ni, Zachary C. Lipton, Sharad Vikram, and Julian McAuley. 2017. Estimating reactions and recommending products with generative models of reviews. In *Proceedings of the Eighth International Joint Conference on Natural Language Processing (Volume 1: Long Papers)*, pages 783–791, Taipei, Taiwan. Asian Federation of Natural Language Processing.

Xiaoman Pan, Wenlin Yao, Hongming Zhang, Dian Yu, Dong Yu, and Jianshu Chen. 2023. Knowledge-in-context: Towards knowledgeable semi-parametric language models. In *The Eleventh International Conference on Learning Representations*.

Andrea Papenmeier, Dagmar Kern, Daniel Hienert, Alfred Sliwa, Ahmet Aker, and Norbert Fuhr. 2021. Starting conversations with search engines - interfaces that elicit natural language queries. In *Proceedings of the 2021 Conference on Human Information Interaction and Retrieval*, CHIIR '21, page 261–265, New York, NY, USA. Association for Computing Machinery.

Martin J Pickering and Simon Garrod. 2013. An integrated theory of language production and comprehension. *Behavioral and brain sciences*, 36(4):329–347.

Joan Plepi, Béla Neuendorf, Lucie Flek, and Charles Welch. 2022. Unifying data perspectivism and personalization: An application to social norms. In *Proceedings of the 2022 Conference on Empirical Methods in Natural Language Processing*, pages 7391–7402, Abu Dhabi, United Arab Emirates. Association for Computational Linguistics.

Ritika Poddar, Rashmi Sinha, Mor Naaman, and Maurice Jakesch. 2023. Ai writing assistants influence topic choice in self-presentation. In *Extended Abstracts of the 2023 CHI Conference on Human Factors in Computing Systems*, CHI EA '23, New York, NY, USA. Association for Computing Machinery.

Dongqi Pu and Vera Demberg. 2023. ChatGPT vs human-authored text: Insights into controllable text summarization and sentence style transfer. In *Proceedings of the 61st Annual Meeting of the Association for Computational Linguistics (Volume 4: Student Research Workshop)*, pages 1–18, Toronto, Canada. Association for Computational Linguistics.

Ohad Rubin, Jonathan Herzig, and Jonathan Berant. 2022. Learning to retrieve prompts for in-context learning. In *Proceedings of the 2022 Conference of the North American Chapter of the Association for Computational Linguistics: Human Language Technologies*, pages 2655–2671, Seattle, United States. Association for Computational Linguistics.

Devendra Sachan, Mike Lewis, Mandar Joshi, Armen Aghajanyan, Wen-tau Yih, Joelle Pineau, and Luke Zettlemoyer. 2022. Improving passage retrieval with zero-shot question generation. In *Proceedings of the 2022 Conference on Empirical Methods in Natural Language Processing*, pages 3781–3797, Abu Dhabi, United Arab Emirates. Association for Computational Linguistics.

Alireza Salemi, Surya Kallumadi, and Hamed Zamani. 2024. Optimization methods for personalizing large language models through retrieval augmentation. In *Proceedings of the 47th International ACM SIGIR Conference on Research and Development in Information Retrieval*, SIGIR '24, page 752–762, New York, NY, USA. Association for Computing Machinery.

Alireza Salemi, Sheshera Mysore, Michael Bendersky, and Hamed Zamani. 2023. Lamp: When large language models meet personalization.

Zejiang Shen, Tal August, Pao Siangliulue, Kyle Lo, Jonathan Bragg, Jeff Hammerbacher, Doug Downey, Joseph Chee Chang, and David Sontag. 2023. Beyond summarization: Designing ai support for real-world expository writing tasks. *Second Workshop on Intelligent and Interactive Writing Assistants, CHI 2023*.

Weijia Shi, Xiaochuang Han, Mike Lewis, Yulia Tsvetkov, Luke Zettlemoyer, and Scott Wen tau Yih. 2023. Trusting your evidence: Hallucinate less with context-aware decoding. *arXiv preprint arXiv:2305.14739*.

Kumar Shridhar, Harsh Jhamtani, Hao Fang, Benjamin Van Durme, Jason Eisner, and Patrick Xia. 2023. Screws: A modular framework for reasoning with revisions. *arXiv preprint arXiv:2309.13075*.

Kaitao Song, Xu Tan, Tao Qin, Jianfeng Lu, and Tie-Yan Liu. 2020. Mpnet: Masked and permuted pre-training for language understanding. In *Advances in Neural Information Processing Systems*, volume 33.

Simeng Sun, Wenlong Zhao, Varun Manjunatha, Rajiv Jain, Vlad Morariu, Franck Dernoncourt, Balaji Vasan Srinivasan, and Mohit Iyyer. 2021. IGA: An intent-guided authoring assistant. In *Proceedings of the 2021 Conference on Empirical Methods in Natural Language Processing*, pages 5972–5985, Online and Punta Cana, Dominican Republic. Association for Computational Linguistics.

Nandan Thakur, Nils Reimers, Andreas Rücklé, Abhishek Srivastava, and Iryna Gurevych. 2021. BEIR: A heterogeneous benchmark for zero-shot evaluation of information retrieval models. In *Thirty-fifth Conference on Neural Information Processing Systems Datasets and Benchmarks Track (Round 2)*.

Stojan Trajanovski, Chad Atalla, Kunho Kim, Vipul Agarwal, Milad Shokouhi, and Chris Quirk. 2021. When does text prediction benefit from additional context? an exploration of contextual signals for chat and email messages. In *Proceedings of the 2021 Conference of the North American Chapter of the Association for Computational Linguistics: Human Language Technologies: Industry Papers*, pages 1–9, Online. Association for Computational Linguistics.

Danqing Wang, Kevin Yang, Hanlin Zhu, Xiaomeng Yang, Andrew Cohen, Lei Li, and Yuandong Tian. 2023a. Learning personalized story evaluation. *arXiv preprint arXiv:2310.03304*.

Liang Wang, Nan Yang, and Furu Wei. 2023b. Learning to retrieve in-context examples for large language models. *arXiv preprint arXiv:2307.07164*.

Sitong Wang, Lydia B Chilton, and Jeffrey V Nickerson. 2023c. Writing with generative ai: Multi-modal and multi-dimensional tools for journalists. *Second Workshop on Intelligent and Interactive Writing Assistants, CHI 2023*.

Yaqing Wang, Jiepu Jiang, Mingyang Zhang, Cheng Li, Yi Liang, Qiaozhu Mei, and Michael Bendersky. 2023d. Automated evaluation of personalized text generation using large language models. *arXiv preprint arXiv:2310.11593*.

Tongshuang Wu, Michael Terry, and Carrie Jun Cai. 2022. Ai chains: Transparent and controllable human-ai interaction by chaining large language model prompts. In *Proceedings of the 2022 CHI Conference on Human Factors in Computing Systems*, CHI '22, New York, NY, USA. Association for Computing Machinery.

Nishant Yadav, Nicholas Monath, Rico Angell, Manzil Zaheer, and Andrew McCallum. 2022. Efficient nearest neighbor search for cross-encoder models using matrix factorization. In *Proceedings of the 2022 Conference on Empirical Methods in Natural Language Processing*, pages 2171–2194, Abu Dhabi, United Arab Emirates. Association for Computational Linguistics.

Le Yan, Zhen Qin, Xuanhui Wang, Michael Bendersky, and Marc Najork. 2022. Scale calibration of deep ranking models. In *Proceedings of the 28th ACM SIGKDD Conference on Knowledge Discovery and Data Mining*, KDD '22, page 4300–4309, New York, NY, USA. Association for Computing Machinery.

Ori Yoran, Tomer Wolfson, Ori Ram, and Jonathan Berant. 2023. Making retrieval-augmented language models robust to irrelevant context.

Hamed Zamani and Michael Bendersky. 2023. Multivariate representation learning for information retrieval. In *Proceedings of the 46th International ACM SIGIR Conference on Research and Development in Information Retrieval*, SIGIR '23, page 163–173, New York, NY, USA. Association for Computing Machinery.

Prompt 1 f_{LLM} prompt used to generate a target text given historical examples retrieved by f_{retr} and a target request for AITA.

```
For a POST from the subreddit Am I The
Asshole write a COMMENT explaining if the
 author of a post is an asshole or not
the asshole as a COMMENTER.
Use the following instructions for your
response:
1. Read the below example comments by
the COMMENTER.
2. Write the comment as the COMMENTER
mimicing the length, style, reasoning,
and stances of their comments.
Here are some example comments by the
COMMENTER: {{historical_examples}}
POST: {{target_request}}
Write the COMMENT mimicing the length,
style, reasoning, and stances of the
COMMENTERS comments.
```

Hanqing Zhang, Haolin Song, Shaoyu Li, Ming Zhou, and Dawei Song. 2023a. A survey of controllable text generation using transformer-based pre-trained language models. *ACM Comput. Surv.*, 56(3).

Jieyu Zhang, Ranjay Krishna, Ahmed H. Awadallah, and Chi Wang. 2023b. Ecoassistant: Using llm assistant more affordably and accurately. *arXiv preprint arXiv:2310.03046*.

Saizheng Zhang, Emily Dinan, Jack Urbanek, Arthur Szlam, Douwe Kiela, and Jason Weston. 2018. Personalizing dialogue agents: I have a dog, do you have pets too? In *Proceedings of the 56th Annual Meeting of the Association for Computational Linguistics (Volume 1: Long Papers)*, pages 2204–2213, Melbourne, Australia. Association for Computational Linguistics.

Tianyi Zhang*, Varsha Kishore*, Felix Wu*, Kilian Q. Weinberger, and Yoav Artzi. 2020. Bertscore: Evaluating text generation with bert. In *International Conference on Learning Representations*.

Yiming Zhang, Shi Feng, and Chenhao Tan. 2022. Active example selection for in-context learning. In *Proceedings of the 2022 Conference on Empirical Methods in Natural Language Processing*, pages 9134–9148, Abu Dhabi, United Arab Emirates. Association for Computational Linguistics.

A Model Details

Retriever We instantiate f_{retr} with the pre-trained MPNET, which is relatively lightweight at 110M parameters (Song et al., 2020). We obtain an output score from f_{retr} as $\mathbf{w}^T \tanh\left(\mathbf{W}^T \text{ENC}([q_u, d_u])\right)$, where ENC represents the CLS token from the final layer of the encoder, and q_u and d_u are the text of the input

Prompt 2 f_{LLM} prompt used to generate a target text given historical examples retrieved by f_{retr} and a target request for WORKSM.

```
Given a REQUEST from a USER to author a
POST, write a POST for an enterprise
social media site mimicking the user to
satisfy the REQUEST.
Use the following instructions for your
response:
1. You should maintain consistency in
tone and style with the USER's historical
 posts.
2. You should imitate the language style
 of the USER's historical posts.
3. You should employ similar rhetorical
methods as the USER's historical posts.
Here are some historical posts by the
USER: {{historical_examples}}
REQUEST: {{target_request}}
Write the POST to satisfy the REQUEST
mimicing the tone, style, and rhetorical
 methods of the USER's historical posts.
```

request and historical document. The encoder parameters, $\mathbf{w}$, and $\mathbf{W}$ are trained.

Text generation models For f_{LLM} we consider two performant LLMs offered via API by Azure OpenAI, `davinci-003` and `gpt-3.5-turbo`. For f_{aux} we consider a smaller but still effective encoder-decoder language model, FLANT5-XL, with 3 billion parameters (Chung et al., 2022). The latter model is open-sourced, allowing us to access its token likelihoods directly, a requirement of Eq. 1. We obtain target text likelihoods by taking the average of log-probabilities of individual token likelihoods from FLANT5-XL.

LLM prompts We use Prompts 2 and 1 for LLM inference. The same prompts are used with `davinci-003` and `gpt-35-turbo`. For constructing training data in Eq 1 with a FLANT5-XL, f_{aux} we use Prompts 5, 6, 3, 4. Note that computing $p_{\text{aux}}(t_u|q_u)$ uses a set of randomly chosen few shot examples from the training set fixed across requests rather than the request alone.

PEARL implementation In constructing training data for f_{retr} we use $|\mathcal{D}_u^t| = 8$, i.e we treat the 8 most recent texts per user as their target texts. To train f_{retr}, we consider the top two canadidate documents per Eq. (1) as positive examples per request and use three negatives per positive, i.e., $P = 2$ and $N = 3$. In our LLM prompts, we use $k = 3$ retrieved examples for WORKSM and $k = 4$ for AITA, tuned on a dev set, and set generation temperature to zero.

Prompt 3 f_{aux} prompt used to compute $p_{\text{aux}}(t_u|q_u)$ in Eq (1) for AITA.

```
Here are some example posts on the Am I
The Asshole subreddit:
{{random_fewshot_examples}}. Target post:
{{target_post}}. Write a users comment for
this post:
```

Prompt 4 f_{aux} prompt used to compute $p_{\text{aux}}(t_u|d_u, q_u)$ in Eq (1) for AITA.

```
Here is an comment on a post by a user
on the Am I the Asshole subreddit:
{{candidate_comment}}. Target post:
{{target_post}}. Write a users comment for
this post:
```

We also use temperatures for target scores input to softmax functions in Eq. (2), y'_u/τ with $\tau = 5$. Finally, we set $y_0 = 110$ for WORKSM and $y_0 = 5$ for AITA, which are the median values of Eq. (1) for each respective dataset on the training data. We tuned y_0 on a dev set constructed similar to our training set to 25 and 75 percentile values of Eq. (1). Our retrievers were trained on Nvidia V100 GPUs with 16GB memory or Nvidia RTX A6000 GPUs with 48GB memory. Experiments for training retrievers required about 300 hours in total.

B Experimental Details

Here we present various details of datasets, baselines, and manual evaluation.

B.1 Evaluation Requests in WORKSM

For evaluation in WORKSM two authors not involved in model development manually authored requests for each of the 163 target posts in our evaluation set. Guidelines presented to annotators for the requests are presented in Guideline 1. The requests are intended to be brief and include the salient information contained in the post. Note that annotators external to the authors weren't recruited for authoring requests due to the private and highly regulated nature of WORKSM.

B.2 Training Requests in WORKSM

Section 5.1 notes that our training set for WORKSM was constructed from synthetic requests generated by GPT4. The prompt for this is presented in Prompt 11. We follow an incremental approach

Prompt 5 f_{aux} prompt used to compute $p_{\text{aux}}(t_u|q_u)$ in Eq (1) for WORKSM.

```
Here is are some posts by a user on an
enterprise social network:
{{random_fewshot_examples}}
Here is an outline for a target post by
the user: {{target_request}}. Write the
target post:
```

Prompt 6 f_{aux} prompt used to compute $p_{\text{aux}}(t_u|d_u, q_u)$ in Eq (1) for WORKSM.

```
Here is an example post by a user on an
enterprise social network:
{{candidate_document}}. Here is an outline
for a target post by the user:
{{target_request}}. Write the target post:
```

to construct the synthetic requests: first extracting the salient aspects of the post, followed by concatenation of these aspects to result in the request. The salient aspects span: an overview of the post, proper nouns mentioned in the post, contact information, links to webpages, and any specialized knowledge or anecdotes in the post. Given the success of chain-of-thought prompting, we generate an explanation followed by salient aspects of the post – the explanations are not used elsewhere. Enterprise contracts ensure the privacy of user data shared over the API.

B.3 Baselines

We consider the following non-personalized baselines: ZSHOT-NP: This represents a non-personalized approach prompting only with the request. KSHOT-NP: A zero-shot non-personalized approach using a fixed randomly selected set of k documents for all requests. For AITA, the examples are balanced across labels.

We consider the following retrieval-augmented personalized baselines, selecting from a user's historical documents $\mathcal{D}_u$: Random: Random selection of k documents from $\mathcal{D}_u$. BM25: Represents a classic performant retrieval model based on query-document term overlap. MPNET-1B: This a strong MPNET bi-encoder trained on 1 billion text pairs from numerous domains.[1] Documents are ranked for a request using cosine similarity between embeddings. QL-FT5: An approach which ranks documents based on $p(q_u|d_u)$ with a pretrained

[1]HF model: `sentence-transformers/all-mpnet-base-v2`

Prompt 7 Judge LLM prompt used to select a generated post more likely to align with a reference post authored by a user for WORKSM.

```
You an an experienced linguist who helps
 people compare social media texts.
Given a REFERENCE POST and two
TARGET POSTS judge which of the TARGET
POSTs is significantly more likely to be
written by the same author as the
REFERENCE POST.
For your response use the following
instructions:
1. Make your judgement based on
stylistic patterns, ordering of
information, and tone used.
2. Output POST ONE if it is significantly
 more likely to be written by the same
author as the REFERENCE POST.
3. Output POST TWO if it is significantly
 more likely to be written by the same
author as the REFERENCE POST.
4. Output BOTH if either post could have
 been written by the same author or
neither could have been written by the
same author.
Here are the POSTS:
REFERENCE POST: {{reference_post}}
POST ONE: {{post_one}}
POST TWO: {{post_two}}
Output a justification for your
judgement, then output POST ONE, POST
TWO, or BOTH to indicate your final
decision.
```

FLANT5-BASE with 250M parameters (Sachan et al., 2022). This may be seen as an unsupervised crossencoder. RelevanceCE: A supervised crossencoder with the same architecture as f_{retr} in PEARL but differing in training. This is trained on pairs of (q_u, d_u) in $\mathcal{D}_u$ treated as positive training pairs with a crossentropy loss, with negatives selected as a random historical document from the same user not but corresponding to q_u. Note that this corresponds to a crossencoder optimized for request-document relevance, i.e. $p(\text{relevance} = 1|q_u, d_u)$, rather than personalized target text generation.

B.4 Judge LLM prompts

In Prompt 8 and 7 we present prompts for GPT-4o as a judge LLM discussed in §5.2.

C Additional Results

Here we present additional results in addition to those presented in §5.2. We present these here primarily in the interest of space.

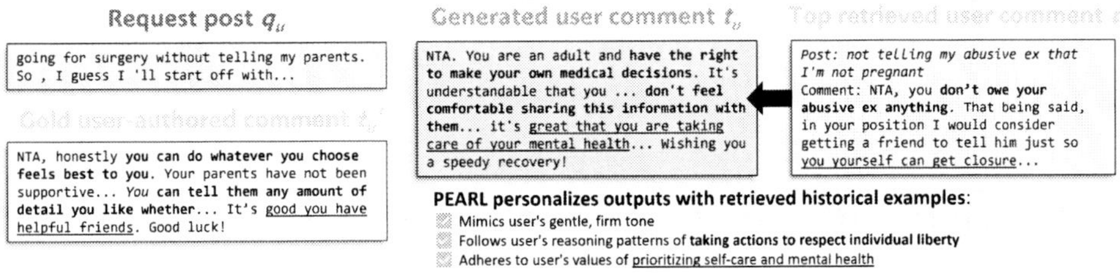

Figure 4: A qualitative example illustrating the effectiveness of PEARL on AITA: Given a request post q_u describing an ambiguous interpersonal situation regarding sharing medical information, PEARL retrieves a historical user comment d_u that demonstrates the user's characteristic tone and values, and generates a comment t_u highly similar to the ground-truth user comment t_u^*. We **bold** qualitatively similar phrases about individual liberties and *italicize* phrases about self-care and mental health. All texts are abbreviated for space, and provided in full in Appendix C.

C.1 Qualitative example from AITA

Here we provide the full texts of the qualitative AITA examples from Figure 4, alongside the top-retrieved comment from BM25 to show the qualitative difference in retriever effectiveness.

Original post q_u: going for surgery without telling my parents. So , I guess I 'll start off with background information .I am 21 , and trans masculine , or female to male if that term works for you

Gold user-authored comment t_u^*: "NTA, honestly you can do whatever you choose feels best to you. Your parents have not been supportive of your transition so they have elected not to be a part of the process. You can tell them any amount of detail you like whether before, after, or at different times. It's good you have helpful friends. Good luck!"

Top PEARL-retrieved comment d_u: "NTA, you don't owe your abusive ex anything. That being said, in your position I would consider getting a friend to tell him just so you yourself can get closure and not be wondering when he's going to harass you about it."

Top BM25-retrieved comment d_u: "YTA, just another lame guy who is only interested in a girl if he has a chance to sleep with her"

PEARL LLM output: "NTA. You are an adult and have the right to make your own medical decisions. It's understandable that you don't have a great relationship with your parents and don't feel comfortable sharing this information with them. It's also important to note that being transgender is not self-harm and it's great that you are taking care of your mental health by seeing a counselor and nurse regularly. Wishing you a speedy recovery!"

Dataset →	AITA	WorkSm		
LLM →	gpt-35-turbo	gpt-35-turbo		
Method ↓	Macro F1(%)	BS-F1	R1	R2
PEARL	<u>**65.34**</u>	<u>36.49</u>	<u>0.5082</u>	<u>**0.2676**</u>
no calibrated sm	63.01	<u>**36.69**</u>	<u>**0.5095**</u>	<u>0.2654</u>
distill $p_{aux}(t_u \| d_u, q_u)$	62.32	35.64	0.5057	0.2652

Table 4: PEARL compared to alternate training of f_{retr} for `gpt-35-turbo`.

C.2 Ablating Training Strategies

In Table 4 and 5, we compare common alternative training of f_{retr} while keeping inference steps identical for `gpt-35-turbo` and `davinci-003` respectively. These serve to ablate our specific contributions: selection of training requests which benefit from personalization and our scale calibrating objective.

No calibrated objective Removing the scale calibration and using a standard KL divergence (–calibrated sm) degrades performance for AITA and sees comparable performance in WorkSm with `gpt-35-turbo` in Table 4. With `davinci-003` we see scale calibration consistently improves performance (Table 5). This indicates the importance of calibration for estimating the benefit of a historical document to a request consistently across datasets and LLMs. Appendix C.3 shows scale calibration also consistently improves the correlation of retriever scores with task performance.

Distill $p_{aux}(t_u|d_u, q_u)$ to f_{retr}. The proposed f_{retr} is trained on documents which benefit personalization *and* requests which benefit from personalization. Here, we compare to an approach that only selects documents that benefit personalization by maximizing $p_{aux}(t_u|q_u, d_u)$. This assumes that *all* training requests benefit from personaliza-

Prompt 8 Judge LLM prompt used to select a generated comment more likely to align with a reference comment authored by a user for AITA.

```
You an an experienced linguist who helps
 people compare social media texts.
Given a REFERENCE POST and two
TARGET POSTS judge which of the TARGET
POSTs is significantly more likely to be
written by the same author as the
REFERENCE POST.
For your response use the following
instructions:
1. Make your judgement based on
similarity of stylistic patterns,
arguments, stances, and word choices.
2. Output POST ONE if it is significantly
 more likely to be written by the same
author as the REFERENCE POST.
3. Output POST TWO if it is significantly
 more likely to be written by the same
author as the REFERENCE POST.
4. Output BOTH if either post could have
 been written by the same author or
neither could have been written by the
same author.
Here are the POSTS:
REFERENCE POST: {{reference_post}}
POST ONE: {{post_one}}
POST TWO: {{post_two}}
Output a justification for your
judgement, then output POST ONE, POST
TWO, or BOTH to indicate your final
decision.
```

tion. We train f_{retr} with a KL-divergence objective. This approach, also, closely resembles prior work example selection in non-personalized tasks (Rubin et al., 2022) as well as personalized tasks (Salemi et al., 2024). We see in Table 4 and 5 (distill $p_{\text{aux}}(t_u|d_u, q_u)$) that this lowers performance markedly, indicating the value of our approach.

C.3 Calibration Evaluation

Since we aim to train generation calibrated retrievers, we evaluate calibration performance i.e a retrieval models scores to be predictive of downstream generation performance (Table 6). Here,

Dataset →	AITA	WorkSm		
LLM →	davinci-003	davinci-003		
Method ↓	Macro F1(%)	BS-F1	R1	R2
PEARL	**61.21**	**39.60**	**0.5419**	**0.3094**
no calibrated sm	57.27	38.88	0.5350	0.3033
distill $p_{\text{aux}}(t_u\|d_u, q_u)$	55.52	39.34	0.5359	0.3059

Table 5: PEARL compared to alternate training of f_{retr} for davinci-003.

	Method ↓ / LLM →	davinci-003	gpt-35-turbo
		Pearson r	Pearson r
AITA	BM25	0.08	-0.05
	MPNet-1B	0.07	-0.14
	UPR	-0.48	-0.02
	RelevanceCE	0.07	-0.19
	PEARL f_{retr}	**0.11**	**0.45**
	– calibrated sm	-0.48	0.12
WorkSm	BM25	0.42	0.52
	MPNet-1B	0.54	0.52
	UPR	-0.05	-0.02
	RelevanceCE	0.56	0.49
	PEARL f_{retr}	**0.64**	**0.64**
	– calibrated sm	0.58	0.55

Table 6: Calibration performance of PEARL evaluated through correlation between score for top-1 document and Macro-F1 for AITA, and R2 for WorkSm.

Pearson r is reported between the top-1 document score for a request and the downstream generation evaluation metric – R2 for WorkSm, and Macro-F1 for AITA. To do this for AITA, we first bin evaluation requests into equal sized bins by top-1 document score, s_1, and then measure Pearson r between the bin start and the average evaluation metric per bin. Our metric is in contrast with prior work (Dhuliawala et al., 2022; Yan et al., 2022) that focuses on classification tasks, where model-predicted class probabilities can be used for measuring calibration, missing in our setup.

Among baseline methods, we see sparse and dense retrieval methods, BM25 and MPNet-1B scores to be better calibrated with downstream performance compared to likelihood-based methods like QL-FT5. Next, we see PEARL to be better correlated with downstream performance for WorkSm and AITA- indicating the effectiveness of our training strategy. Further, we also report on an ablated model, not using the scale-calibrated objective of Eq (3) (– calibrated sm). We see this approach underperform PEARL, indicating the importance of the scale-calibrated objective for a well-calibrated crossencoder. The poorer calibration of crossencoders also finds support in prior work showing their scores to lie at extremes of the score distribution (Menon et al., 2022; Yadav et al., 2022).

C.4 Selective Revision with PEARL – Extended Results

In §5.3 we demonstrate how our trained retrieval model can be used for selective revision with gpt-35-turbo. Prompt 9, 10 present the prompts

Prompt 9 f_{LLM} prompt used to for selective revision given a Stage 1 draft for AITA.

```
Given a POST from the subreddit Am I the
Asshole and a DRAFT comment from the USER
responding if the author of the POST is
an asshole or not the asshole, edit the
DRAFT comment.
Use the following instructions for your
response:
1. Maintain consistency in tone and
style with the USER's historical
comments.
2. Edit the DRAFT to use more reddit
lingo.
3. Remove statements of the POST from the
DRAFT.
4. Output a justification for your edits
 starting with the word JUSTIFICATION.
5. Output the edited DRAFT comment
starting with the words EDITED DRAFT.
Here are some historical comments by the
 USER: {{historical_examples}}
REQUEST: {{target_request}}
DRAFT: {{target_draft}}
Output a justification for your edits,
then output the edited DRAFT starting
with the words EDITED DRAFT.
```

Prompt 10 f_{LLM} prompt used to for selective revision given a Stage 1 draft for WorkSm.

```
Given a REQUEST and a DRAFT from a USER to
author a social media POST, edit the
DRAFT to satisfy the REQUEST.
Use the following instructions for your
response:
1. Enumerate any missing missing
information from the REQUEST in the DRAFT.
2. Enumerate any irrelevant information
for the REQUEST in the DRAFT.
3. Then output the edited DRAFT starting
with the words EDITED DRAFT.
REQUEST:{{target_request}}
DRAFT: {{target_draft}}
Output missing or irrelevant information
 for the REQUEST, then output the EDITED
DRAFT satisfying the REQUEST.
```

used for revision with both LLMs.

In Figure 5, we examine the impact of selective revision in WorkSm for requests of different lengths and users with different number of historical posts. We see that revision benefits requests of medium length and users with few posts. From Figure 5a, we hypothesize that requests that are too short may require additional user input and see no gains from revision. On the other hand requests that are too long, may be more challenging to follow and are unlikely to improve from revisions. From Figure 5b, we see that users with few posts benefit from revision indicating that these users see poorer retrievals. On the other hand users with larger profiles see a drop in performance indicating that even better calibration performance may improve performance of selective revision further.

Note that we don't report results with `davinci-003` since our procedure for learning a threshold θ for selective revision failed to find a threshold where dev set performance was improved from selective revision. Finally note that metrics reported for selective revision in Table 3 isn't directly comparable to those of Tables 1, 4, and 5 since they represent different LLM runs and exclude a dev set from WorkSm and AITA for learning θ (50 and 200 instances respectively).

D Extended Related Work

Having discussed the closest body of related work in §2 we discuss additional related work here.

Dynamic prompts for LLMs Besides training retrievers for in-context example selection discussed in §2, other approaches have explored better use of pre-trained models for example selection. Creswell et al. (2023) select examples based on the target LLM likelihood - necessitating access to LLM likelihoods and incurring latency in retrieval. Gupta et al. (2023) explore selecting *sets* of examples with dense retrieval models, presenting a complementary approach to ours. Finally, Pan et al. (2023) use retrieval models to select examples from multiple knowledge sources and train a routing model to decide the source of knowledge to retrieve from – selective revision (§5.3) based on a retriever may be seen as a form of routing.

Prompt robustness in LLMs Simultaneous routing and retrieval also relates our approach to work ensuring that LLMs are robust to noisy retrievals. Prior approaches ensured robustness by only using retrieved documents based on simple frequency filters on entities mentioned in the input query (Mallen et al., 2023) or based on predictions from an NLI model that determines if the query entails the retrieved contexts (Yoran et al., 2023). Other approaches have sought to fine-tune the LLM to be robust to irrelevant contexts (Li et al., 2023c; Luo et al., 2023; Yoran et al., 2023) or modify the decoding procedure (Shi et al., 2023). In contrast, we determine the quality of the input context based on scale-calibrated retrieval model scores.

LLM chaining In selectively editing generations

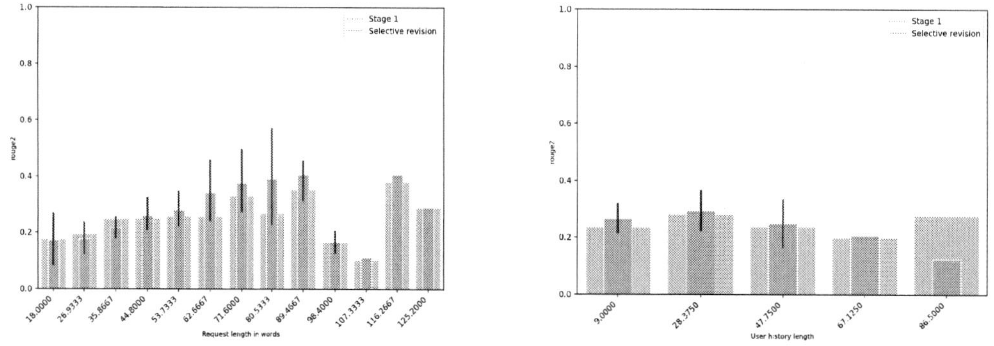

(a) Effectiveness of selective revision for requests of different lengths (in words).

(b) Effectiveness of selective revision for users of different numbers of historical posts.

Figure 5: The impact of selective revision (§5.3) in PEARL on WORKSM compared for requests of different length and users with varying number of historical posts.

with an LLM for low-performing requests, our approach also relates to recent work on composing LLMs with other models to build more complex systems (Wu et al., 2022; Arora et al., 2023; Khattab et al., 2023). Close work is presented by approaches that leverage repeated LLM calls to verify the reasoning or factuality of previous generations (Shridhar et al., 2023; Dhuliawala et al., 2023). In contrast, our work leverages an efficient retrieval model to selectively direct low-performing generations for further revision, reducing the total number of expensive LLM calls necessary. In this respect, our approach bears similarity to Zhang et al. (2023b), who progressively run larger LLMs only when necessary for an input.

Calibrated retrievers A small body of work has explored calibrated ranking models. Yan et al. (2022) train scale-calibrated ranking models for recommendation models used for advertisement pricing systems. On the other hand, our work leverages scale-calibration for personalized writing assistance. Other work has explored joint training of retrievers and generative models to obtain calibrated retrievers (Dhuliawala et al., 2022), using Gaussian embeddings to estimate retriever uncertainty (Zamani and Bendersky, 2023), or estimating retriever confidence with monte-carlo dropout (Cohen et al., 2021). In contrast with probabilistic uncertainty estimation, PEARL minimally modifies training to result in a calibrated model and does not require extensive changes to training, model architecture, or additional inference costs.

Writing assistants A sizable body of work has explored the development of writing assistants. Compared to assistants for communication applications, these have been targeted at authors of creative texts like screenplays (Mirowski et al., 2023), stories (Akoury et al., 2020), and poems (Gonçalo Oliveira, 2017) – consequently, they focus on diverse generations and long-range coherence, rather than personalization. Further, while our work leverages a request-driven assistant, prior systems have used a variety of interaction and control methods. While text completion presents a common form of interaction (Clark et al., 2018), recent work has seen use of infilling, tag-based control (Sun et al., 2021), and instruction guided generations (Chakrabarty et al., 2022) – a deeper examination of control and interaction strategies and their trade offs are presented in related reviews (Zhang et al., 2023a; Lin et al., 2023). While our approach to personalization may be extended to some alternative interaction paradigms, other interaction techniques are likely to necessitate additional work.

Personalized text generation While we have focussed on author personalization that aims to mimic stylistic patterns, interests, and values of an author, we briefly review reader-personalized text generation – a setup aiming to generate texts that are engaging and relevant to readers' preferences. This has historically been explored for generating personalized reviews (Ni et al., 2017), recipes (Majumder et al., 2019), news headlines (Ao et al., 2021) and in dialogue agents (Mazaré et al., 2018; Zhang et al., 2018). Related work is also found in text simplification and lay summarization in the context of scientific text – this work has explored generating definitions for scientific concepts at varying levels of complexity (August et al., 2022; Murthy et al., 2022) or summarizing scientific text for lay readers (Guo et al., 2021). While recent work has explored this with modern LLMs (Li et al., 2023d; Farajidizaji et al., 2023), reader personalization remains an understudied problem and presents a rich area for future work.

E Limitations

Here, we discuss limitations of our work derive from our choice of f_{aux} and f_{LLM}, our evaluation setup, and the design of our method.

Choice of LLMs Our experiments use two closed LLMs through API access (`davinci-003`, `gpt-35-turbo`). While we show the value of PEARL with LLM's of varying performance, establishing its effectiveness with other LLMs will require further work. We also acknowledge that closed LLMs limit experimental reproducibility - however, given the widespread use of GPT models (Hu, 2023) we believe our investigation is meaningful. Finally, in constructing training data for instance selection models for an LLM, prior work has noted the best empirical performance from matching f_{aux} and f_{LLM} (Rubin et al., 2022). While we demonstrate benefits from using significantly smaller models for f_{aux}, using an open LLM will allow further validation of this result in the context of our approach. However, using a larger (open) model for f_{aux} will incur additional costs in creating training data, and smaller models for f_{LLM} are likely to see a worse generation performance - exploring this tradeoff requires future work.

Evaluation setup Next, while WORKSM represents an impactful and realistic use case for writing assistants, we acknowledge that its private nature limits reproducibility. Further, our evaluation set of WORKSM and AITA represents a limited set of scenarios that are likely to leverage writing assistants. While we believe our work represents a meaningful first step, additional future work, and online evaluations are necessary to establish the value of PEARL across the myriad of scenarios where writing assistants may be used. Finally, while we leverage several evaluation strategies to demonstrate the value of PEARL, evaluating text generations under personalization setups represents is an under-explored and a currently emerging body of work (Wang et al., 2023a,d).

Method design Finally, we note that the current design of PEARL is likely to have some drawbacks. It is possible that our proposed method for training instance selection biases system performance toward some users or requests – we leave examination of this to future work. It is also possible that formulating f_{retr} as an expressive crossencoder and the use of large LLMs will present latency limitations for interactive applications – exploration of models supporting faster retrieval and text generation inference represent important future work.

Prompt 11 GPT4 prompt used to generate synthetic requests for WORKSM posts in our training set.

```
## TASK
Given an enterprise social media post, generate a set of writing instructions that
explain how to
"reverse-engineer"; the post. Use the following steps:
- The instructions must give a high-level overview of what the post aims to
communicate. Example: [readcted]
- The instructions must include specific proper nouns (people, places, organzations)
. Example: [redacted]
- The instructions must include contact information if available. Example: [redacted
]
- The instructions must include specific links to websites or files if available.
Example: [redacted]
- The instructions must contain any knowledge that is highly specialized and is
likely to be only known to the individual who wrote the post, if available. Example:
 [redacted]
- The instructions must contain rough sketches of any personal anecdotes in the post
, if available. Example: [redacted]
- The instruction must **not** contain any formatting or ordering information from
the post.

## OUTPUT
Output the following:
<Explanation>{explanation of your reasoning for how you generated the instructions,
in 3 sentences or fewer}</Explanation>
<Instruction.Overview>{1-2 sentences overview of what the post aims to communicate
}</Instruction.Overview>
<Instruction.Names>{1-2 sentences about the people, places, or organizations
mentioned in the post, _NONE_ if not applicable}</Instruction.Names>
<Instruction.Contacts>{1-2 sentences about the contact information copied verbatim
in the post, _NONE_ if not applicable}</Instruction.Contacts>
<Instruction.Links>{1-2 sentences including the links copied verbatim from the post,
 _NONE_ if not applicable}</Instruction.Links>
<Instruction.Knowledge>{1-2 sentences paraphrasing the specialized knowledge
included in the post, _NONE_ if not applicable}</Instruction.Knowledge>
<Instruction.Anecdotes>{1-2 sentences paraphrasing the anecdotes included in the
post, _NONE_ if not applicable}</Instruction.Anecdotes>

## INPUT
{{input_post}}
```

Guideline 1 Instructions provided to annotators for authoring requests for our evaluation set in WORKSM.

Overview:
In this study, we are developing LLM-based approaches for writing social media posts on enterprise social networks. Your task is as follows: Given a social media post from an enterprise social media platform, write a short outline of the post. In writing your outline, imagine you are a manager, social media manager, or event organizer writing a rough sketch of the post with the key information you would like to share.

Data Format:
You are given a spreadsheet consisting of ~150 English posts. Each row corresponds to a single post. The spreadsheet contains the following columns: PostId, InputPost, OutputShortOutline. The first column is the ID of the post; you can ignore this column. The second column is the full text of the input post. In the third column, you will write your short outline based on the input post.

DO's for your outline:
When writing your short outline, do include the following:
- One sentence about the goal of the post: Include a brief description of what the post is trying to communicate. Example: [redacted]
- Specific proper nouns (people, places, things): Include names of specific people, places, or things in your outline. Example: [redacted]
- Specialized knowledge: If the knowledge contained in the post is highly specialized and is likely to be only known to the individual writing the post, include a rough sketch of that information in your outline. Example: [redacted]
- Personal anecdotes: If the post contains specific personal anecdotes, include a rough sketch of that information in your outline. Example: [redacted]
- Special emphasis or call to action: If the post makes a special emphasis, include a rough sketch of that emphasis or call to action in your outline. Example: [redacted]
- External website links: If the post links to an external website, include the link in your outline. Example: [redacted]

DONT's for your outline:
When writing your short outline, do not include the following:
- Anything related to the ordering of content.
- Formatting instructions.
- Any verbatim text other than specific proper nouns.

Evaluating and Training Long-Context Large Language Models for Question Answering on Scientific Papers

Lukas Hilgert **Danni Liu** **Jan Niehues**
Karlsruhe Institute of Technology, Germany
{lukas.hilgert, danni.liu, jan.niehues}@kit.edu

Abstract

With the number of scientific papers published every year growing and current large language models (LLMs) showing state-of-the-art performance on natural language processing (NLP) tasks, we ask the question if LLMs could be utilized to answer questions on scientific papers. We investigate how well state-of-the-art large language models (LLMs) can answer questions on scientific paper by experimenting with long-context versions of the LLaMA 2 model and evaluating and training on the Qasper dataset. We analyze how well the LLMs handle longer papers and questions that can only be answered by accessing information from far out paragraphs. During our experiments, we see that the performance of these LLMs drops with growing length and position of relevant information. We employ different measures from simple prompts to chain-of-thought prompts and zero-shot usage to fine-tuning with QLoRA. While we still observe a performance loss with increased context length, our measures reduce the effects of this flaw, and we can achieve F_1 scores similar to bigger models like GPT-4.

1 Introduction

The number of scientific papers published every year is growing exponentially (Fire and Guestrin, 2018). This creates a problem for scientists but also the general public to keep up with the developments in science. A natural language processing (NLP) system that can reliably answer questions on scientific papers could help in this situation. Question answering (QA) systems often rely on task-specific machine learning models that can only be used for this purpose. Large Language Models (LLMs) are a newer type of deep learning model trained to be general-purpose models for NLP. Current commercial and open-source LLMs are often used in an intuitive, conversational manner as chatbots. They offer the ability to answer follow-up questions and have an intuitive interface for most users. They show state-of-the-art (SOTA) NLP performance (OpenAI, 2023; Anil et al., 2023) and even display some reasoning capabilities (Brown et al., 2020; Chowdhery et al., 2023; OpenAI, 2023; Anil et al., 2023) and would be one contender for the core of a QA system focused on scientific papers.

Scientific papers present great challenges as context for QA when using LLMs for multiple reasons: Their text part is typically about around 4,000 to 13,333 tokens long assuming that one word amounts to around $1.\overline{3}$ tokens (Björk et al., 2009; OpenAI, b). The base versions of newer commercial models like GPT-3.5 and GPT-4 have context windows of 4,096 (OpenAI, a) and 8,192 (OpenAI, a) tokens while open-source LLMs like LLaMA 2 (Touvron et al., 2023b) offer a 4,096 long context window. Also, scientific papers consist of long unstructured (except sectioning etc.) raw text making, it hard to determine which part is important to answer the question. The answer type is also not clear as the question could be about explaining some concepts presented in the paper, simple facts or even yes or no questions, or the question could be unanswerable. The unstructuredness and length of the context is especially problematic even for long-context LLMs as Liu et al. (2023) found: For multi-document QA where the LLM has to select the relevant context part from multiple options, the performance curve has a U-shape with respect to the position of the documents as the ones at the beginning and the end are better retrieved than those in the middle.

In this paper, we evaluate how well a small open-source LLM can perform as a QA system for scientific papers if used in a zero-shot manner – especially regarding long papers (>4k tokens) and those questions whose relevant paragraphs are far out token-wise. To do this, we bin the papers per length and the questions per position of the relevant paragraphs. We try to improve the performance using recent LLM adaptation techniques (prompting,

Proceedings of the 1st Workshop on Customizable NLP: Progress and Challenges in Customizing NLP for a Domain, Application, Group, or Individual (CustomNLP4U), pages 220–236
November 16, 2024 ©2024 Association for Computational Linguistics

parameter-efficient fine-tuning). We also investigate what weaknesses (e.g., instruction-following, long-context understanding) of the models specifically the fine-tuning improves. Finally, we compare our best model with bigger ones. We observe that increased context length and position of the relevant paragraphs result in worse performance even for long-context LLMs. While more sophisticated prompting does not help, fine-tuning increases overall performance significantly but mostly by improving the instruction-following of the LLMs.

2 Related Work

Large Language Models The foundation for most current Large Language Models (LLMs) like the Gemini (Anil et al., 2023), GPT (Brown et al., 2020; OpenAI, 2023), LLaMA (Touvron et al., 2023a,b), and Mistral (Jiang et al., 2023, 2024) families is pre-training Transformer decoder-only models with billions of parameters on Internet-scale data enabling them to perform tasks they were not explicitly trained on. As we want to experiment on LLMs themselves which includes fine-tuning and modifying them, we utilized available open-source models: Large Language Model Meta AI (Meta AI, 2023) (LLaMA) (Touvron et al., 2023a,b). Following the work on training-compute-optimal LLMs (Hoffmann et al., 2022), the authors of LLaMA focus on training smaller models with more data (and more compute) to achieve better inference-compute efficiency.

Vicuna is a collection of fine-tuned LLaMA models (Chiang et al.; Zheng et al., 2023). On top of models fine-tuned for better chatbot performance, there are models with longer context windows than the original LLaMA model (version 2: 4k (Touvron et al., 2023b)) with up to 32k tokens using a technique similar to Positional Interpolation developed independently (Ken; Li et al.). Chen et al. (2023) propose Positional Interpolation (PI) to easily increase the context window length: Stretching the original context window (L) to the new maximum length L' by downscaling the position indices that are the input to the positional encoding function.

Question Answering Task The type of context for Question answering (QA) can differ as it may be present as knowledge or as harder to manage raw text. Modern QA system mostly use deep learning-based models like (fine-tuned) BERT- or GPT-style models. Datasets that cover the topic of scientific papers focus on various aspects. Many focus on the review process which yields different artifacts. These enable different tasks: (Meta-) Review Generation (Wang et al., 2020; Lin et al., 2023), acceptance prediction / paper rating (Kang et al., 2018; Yang et al., 2018), Argument Pair Extraction from reviews and corresponding rebuttals (Cheng et al., 2020), and Multi-document Summarization on reviews (Li et al., 2022). But there are also datasets specifically for question answering on scientific papers (Dasigi et al., 2021).

Evaluating Long-Context Text Processing To make comparison of long-context LLMs easier, multiple benchmarks sets have been created to test their abilities across different task types. ZeroSCROLLS (Shaham et al., 2023) is a benchmark focused on long text understanding in a zero-shot setting. The included task types are summarization, question answering and aggregation. A similar benchmark called LongBench also includes Qasper (Bai et al., 2023). Opposed to ZeroSCROLLS it is bilingual and incorporates more task types. Also, the authors showed the performance of the models that they tested for context lengths of 0 – 4k, 4k – 8k and 8k+ tokens individually. They only investigated zero-shot prompting and they did not show how the position of the important information within the long context affects performance.

Han et al. (2024) presented with LM-Infinite a technique to increase the ability of LLMs to handle long-context without any parameter updates. However, their evaluation on Qasper showed only small improvements over their truncation baseline (30.1 vs. 31.3) and did not contain fine-grained analysis on Qasper.

3 Methodology

To improve the performance of the general-purpose LLMs on the task of QA on scientific papers, we apply different prompting techniques and fine-tuning. We list all our prompt templates in Appendix A.

3.1 Approaches

Simple Prompt Zero-shot prompting is a straightforward approach, where the LLM is directly used out-of-the-box at inference time. Although few-shot prompting in general improves performance (Brown et al., 2020), the long input size in our case precludes this approach. Therefore, we have to resort to zero-shot prompting which only includes the instruction for the model as a kind of learning signal. However, this generally leads to weaker instruction-following abilities. This approach with a simple prompt serves as the baseline for the other methods (using the same model).

Extract-then-Answer Prompt Chain-of-thought prompting (Wei et al., 2022) showed that splitting a task into subtasks can help LLMs to solve them. Inspired by this, we split the question answering into two tasks: First the model has to find the evidence – all relevant paragraphs to answer the question. After that we prompt it to answer the question based on the extracted paragraphs in the previous step. Extracting the relevant paragraphs is a useful task on its own: It could be useful to see the context of the answer inside the paper and improve interpretability. There are also some downsides: We have to run inference twice as this approach requires the model to generate its input for the second step. Also, as the model generates its own input (apart from the second prompt), this approach may lead to cascading errors. Similar approaches were investigated for science QA on short context (Lu et al., 2022; Wang et al., 2023; Yoran et al., 2023), for (Chinese) multi-document QA (He et al., 2023), and on smaller-scale models prior to the emergence of LLMs (Dasigi et al., 2021).

Supervised Fine-tuning We can fine-tune the LLM on supervised data with the simple prompt and the extract-then-answer prompt. For the latter, we fine-tune the model two subtasks: Evidence extraction and answer generation given evidence. By combining compute- and memory-efficient methods of implementing and training Transformer-based models, we are able to fine-tune a small LLM on long context. We replace the standard attention algorithm with FlashAttention 2 (Dao et al., 2022; Dao, 2023) and we use QLoRA (Hu et al., 2022; Dettmers et al., 2023) for fine-tuning the model.

3.2 Evaluation

Besides the standard evaluation of QA quality provided by the dataset authors, we conduct various fine-grained analyses to evaluate our approaches regarding our specific focus.

3.2.1 Analysis by Context Length / Position

In addition to evaluating QA quality, we want to evaluate per paper length and absolute evidence position. We therefore split the evaluation data into (partially) overlapping groups by the length / distance in tokens.

Paper Length We want to find out if long-context modifications enable models to process longer context as well as context within the original context window or if the performance differs per paper length. Here, we bin per paper as the length is the same for all associated questions. We count the number of tokens to get the length.

Evidence Position It is also important to find out if the position of the relevant information ("evidence") within the paper which is also provided by the dataset does affect performance. We will study the impact of the absolute token position of the evidence. For "Unanswerable" and some yes/no questions there is no evidence, we put these questions into a separate bin ("No evidence"). In contrast to the length binning, we group the evaluation data per question as the evidence positions differ in general per question and not per paper.

3.2.2 Evidence-only Prompt

We want to find out how our investigated models perform if we provide them with the evidence only – both during inference and training. This should give use an idea of the upper limits of the performance of the models as this task should be easier as the model has to process fewer tokens. Additionally, we think that a comparison between these fine-tuned models and those that received the full paper during training should indicate how much our fine-tuning improves our goal of long-context understanding and how much it just improves instruction following.

4 Experiments and Results

4.1 Experimental Setup

In the following, we will describe our experimental setup. We list utilized hard- and software and the hyperparameters we used during inference and training in Appendix C.

4.1.1 Dataset

The Qasper dataset (Dasigi et al., 2021) we used to evaluate and train the considered models consists of a total of 1,585 NLP papers with 5,049 questions on these papers. Each of these questions was formulated by an NLP practitioner. The answers were then answered by other NLP practitioners who also selected the paragraphs, figures or tables ("evidence") in the paper that are relevant to answer the question which are listed together with the

Models	dev-short		dev		test		ZC	
Questions / %	990	100	1,005	100	1,451	100	500	100
Paper length								
0k – 4k	333	34	333	33	511	35	149	30
4k – 8k	593	60	593	59	802	55	312	64
8k –	64	6	79	8	138	10	39	8
Absolute evidence position								
0k – 4k	794	80	799	80	1182	81	405	81
4k – 8k	173	17	180	18	263	18	91	18
8k –	6	1	11	1	18	1	7	1
No evidence	77	8	78	8	99	7	37	7

Table 1: Qasper dataset statistics we created for our research questions: paper length and absolute evidence position; the numbers for absolute evidence position exceed the total number of questions because the evidence for a question can be from multiple paragraphs. ZC refers to the subset of the Qasper test set used in the ZeroSCROLLS benchmark.

Q. type	Frequency								
Bin type	Full	dev-short	Length			Absolute evidence position			
Specific bin			0k – 4k	4k – 8k	8k –	0k – 4k	4k – 8k	8k –	No ev.
Extractive	51.8%	54.8%	53.3%	56.5%	47.4%	58.5%	55.1%	45.5%	0.0%
Abstractive	24.2%	24.3%	21.3%	25.5%	28.1%	25.9%	30.2%	27.3%	0.0%
Yes/No	13.9%	11.6%	13.8%	10.2%	13.2%	10.7%	11.8%	18.2%	24.6%
Unanswer.	10.2%	9.3%	11.6%	7.8%	11.4%	4.9%	3.0%	9.1%	75.4%

Table 2: Qasper dataset statistics (full dataset (full), (Dasigi et al., 2021)) and ours: question types for each dataset bin (all bins are from dev-shot)

gold answer in the dataset. There are four types of questions / answers in this dataset:

- Extractive: questions can be answered by copying chunks of the relevant paragraph
- Abstractive: free text answers that are not literally in the paper
- Yes/no or boolean questions
- Unanswerable: questions that can not be answered with the provided paper as context.

These question types appear in different frequencies (Table 2) and the authors evaluated the performance of their model for each question type individually. The dataset website[1] provides an official evaluation script. Like for the SQuAD dataset (Rajpurkar et al., 2016), the authors chose a span-level F_1 score as their metrics. If there are multiple reference answers, the maximum of the F_1 score will be used.

For the final analysis, we use a subset of the Qasper test split that is part of the ZeroSCROLLS (ZC) benchmark (Shaham et al., 2023). We saw a similar statistic for this subset as for the (custom) splits we used during development and final analysis. We therefore assume that the ZC subset of Qasper will be representative for the performance of our approaches.

4.1.2 Data Preprocessing

Five of the papers from the development / validation split of Qasper lead to out-of-memory errors during inference. We therefore exclude these five papers from our results and call the resulting split "dev-short". As these five only account for around 1.8% of the 281 papers in the dev split, we assume that this does not skew our view of the quality of the models. Also, the distribution of the length / position bins is not changed much (Table 1).

We make a similar observation for the binning itself (Table 2): The distribution of the questions types does not vary much between the length / position bins (with exception of the one for questions with no evidence). We therefore assume that our analysis of the models by binning the dataset does reflect the performance of the model for that spe-

[1] https://allenai.org/data/qasper

cific length / evidence position and is not influenced by the distribution of the questions type in that specific bin.

As training data, we use the training split of the Qasper dataset. As input, we use a prompt template (subsubsection A.1.1) from the LongBench benchmark dataset (Bai et al., 2023) where the paper text and the question are inserted the same way as for zero-shot prompting. The target is the answer from the dataset. As our tested models have text as their only modality, it cannot process the figures and tables provided with the dataset. We therefore remove all questions from the training data that mention figures or tables in their evidence field. Many questions are annotated with multiple possible answers. In some cases, they clearly heavily disagree with each other e.g., one possible answer is "Unanswerable" and the other is "Yes" or "No". We remove these cases. We also have to limit the training data to texts with a maximum of 8k tokens as longer inputs cause out-of-memory errors even with both QLoRA and FlashAttention used.

4.1.3 Models

We use three models with different context window lengths in our experiments. The creators of FastChat (LMSYS Org) provide the Vicuna family (section 2) of LLMs. We only test the smallest available models with around 7 billion parameters for compute and memory efficient experiments and as this is the only model size that has a LongChat version. This version has a context window of 32k tokens (LC-32k). Vicuna 7B-4k (V-4k) has the same as LLaMA 2 (4k) and Vicuna 7B-16k's (V-16k) was extended to 16k. We use the models of version v1.5 which indicates that they are based on LLaMA 2 instead of LLaMA 1 like the previous versions.[2] The fine-tuning data was 370M tokens long. We omit the parameter count in the following from the models' names as they are the same of every model we tested.

4.2 Results and Discussion

We start our experiments with all available small (7B parameters) models from LMSYS Org with varying context window lengths: Vicuna-4k, Vicuna-16k, and LongChat-32k. Here, we only report the results for LongChat-32k as it showed the best long-context performance and show the others in Appendix D and Appendix E. During our experiments, we also investigated the performance by relative evidence position. However, we saw no U-shape of the performance and therefore do not include these results. This corresponds to prior work (Liu et al., 2023) which found this strong primary and recency bias only in large (>7B) models.

4.2.1 Simple Prompt

First, we run a simple zero-shot prompt and report the results in the first two columns of Table 3.

Simple zero-shot prompt struggles with unanswerable questions While LongChat is able to answer the "normal" questions, it seems to be unable to handle unanswerable questions (Table 3). These questions can not be answered with the given paper. Also, its ability to answer yes/no questions is limited. Qualitative analysis showed that LongChat almost never outputs "Unanswerable" and even if it does, the answer is a whole sentence which ignores the instruction in the prompt (examples: Appendix B).

Longer context leads to worse performance Fine-grained analysis by input length shows that after the threshold of 4k tokens, the performance begins to decrease from an F_1 score of 25.47 to 24.08 for papers with a length between 4k and 8k tokens. After 8k tokens this decrease accelerates (18.51) and is especially visible when binning the F_1 score by evidence position (F_1: 26.73 $\rightarrow$ 23.35 $\rightarrow$ 15.06). The model also especially struggles with questions that require no evidence (most of them are unanswerable). We assume that the lower F_1 score of LongChat on papers with more than 8k tokens is a result of this weakness and not a general property.

Fine-tuning: Trade-offs between generation and classification As the empirical results showed that LongChat had insufficient instruction following, we now want to see how much fine-tuning can increase the performance. Also, we want to find out how much it improves the F_1 scores for long papers and evidence at high token positions. The impact of QLoRA fine-tuning on LongChat-32k (Table 3) is that extractive, boolean and unanswerable questions substantially improve (F_1: 26.51 $\rightarrow$ 48.21, 36.79 $\rightarrow$ 76.47, 0.04 $\rightarrow$ 68.54). We assume that the F_1 scores for unanswerable questions do not improve after the first epoch because it reached the highest scores possible with this model size

[2] https://github.com/lm-sys/FastChat/blob/97065ff7caa3ae4ca28c661b7424f7ae4cca539b/docs/vicuna_weights_version.md

Training	0S	FT	0S	FT	0S	FT
Variation	1S	1S	2S	2S	2S+	2S+
Answer F_1	24.19	47.02	24.94	39.08	17.85	41.18
Answer F_1 by type						
Extractive	26.51	48.21	23.19	37.50	16.37	41.82
Abstractive	20.78	20.10	17.35	14.92	16.03	19.41
Boolean	36.79	76.47	57.96	49.51	36.75	58.10
Unanswerable	0.04	68.54	11.84	89.09	5.33	69.23
Answer F_1 per paper length						
0k – 4k	25.47	52.15	25.68	41.57	19.26	44.78
4k – 8k	24.08	44.45	24.85	37.77	17.50	39.66
8k –	18.51	44.09	21.97	38.23	13.83	36.44
Answer F_1 per absolute evidence position						
0k – 4k	26.73	46.28	26.84	36.00	18.89	40.54
4k – 8k	23.35	37.74	23.40	30.31	16.64	34.97
8k –	15.06	67.94	28.96	56.19	2.75	39.78
No evidence	1.06	64.94	6.69	81.82	9.61	57.14

Table 3: LongChat, dev-short set, **simple (one-step / 1S)** and **extract-then-answer prompts (two-step, 2S)**, compare initial and advanced prompt (2-step+, 2S+), zero-shot (0S) vs. fine-tuned (FT) with QLoRA.

and pre-training and fine-tuning procedure. Here, the model has to do a trade-off between generating answers with more information (extractive, abstractive) or classify the question as unanswerable. The answers to abstractive questions see an initial quality degradation and only converge back to their initial level (F_1: 20.78 → 20.10) late in training. Our interpretation is that this is a result of the training data forcing the model to fit to the answer style for around 75% of the questions in Qasper: extracting word for word and short answers. With more epochs of fine-tuning, the model re-learns the more complex task of abstractive QA (Table 4).

Epochs	0	1	3	5
Answer F_1	24.19	41.13	44.56	47.02
Answer F_1 by type				
Extractive	26.51	41.80	45.18	48.21
Abstractive	20.78	12.59	16.59	20.10
Boolean	36.79	70.49	80.33	76.47
Unanswerable	0.04	69.57	66.67	68.54

Table 4: LongChat-32k, dev-short set, **simple prompt**, fine-tuned with QLoRA.

Fine-tuning mostly improves instruction-following While we only train with sequences of up to 8k tokens, we see an improvement across all analyzed paper lengths and evidence positions and the performance loss for papers with a length between 4k and 8k tokens and longer ones almost disappears going from 5.57 (zero-shot) to 0.36 (fine-tuned). However, we still see consistently reduced performance for papers that exceed LLaMA 2's original context window length of 4k and especially for questions where the evidence is further out than 4k.

In Appendix B, we list some qualitative example how fine-tuning did improve the model's answers.

4.2.2 Evidence-only Prompt

Our previous experiments showed that even models whose context window was extended with a technique similar to Positional Interpolation struggle with papers that exceed the original context length of LLaMA 2 of 4k tokens – especially if the evidence lies outside of that range. The question now is if these questions or at least some of them are inherently harder to answer. We evaluate if the performance varies in our analysis if the context given to the model is the evidence only instead of the full paper.

Training only on evidence performs well except for unanswerable questions When fine-tuning LongChat on the evidence only, we more quickly see better results that exceed those before (Table 5) and therefore only train for 3 epochs. After training LongChat on the evidence only, we compare its performance directly against the model that we trained on full papers: The performance of the context-length-specific model is better in general (F_1: 41.66 vs. 44.56 / 47.02) but not on all sub

Epochs	3	3	3	5
Train split	evo		fp	
Eval split	evidence	fp		
Answer F_1	57.22	41.66	44.56	47.02
Answer F_1 by type				
Extractive	62.19	47.01	45.18	48.21
Abstractive	27.01	24.15	16.59	20.10
Boolean	79.83	76.67	80.33	76.47
Unanswer.	80.56	2.70	66.67	68.54
Answer F_1 per paper length				
0k – 4k	57.93	42.68	50.22	52.15
4k – 8k	56.86	40.46	41.91	44.45
8k –	56.94	42.68	39.75	44.09
Answer F_1 per absolute evidence position				
0k – 4k	54.27	44.48	43.94	46.28
4k – 8k	50.86	37.46	34.80	37.74
8k –	63.61	43.71	64.76	67.94
No ev.	93.51	16.88	61.04	64.94

Table 5: Compare LongChat-32k, fine-tuned with QLoRA on **evidence only** (evo) or full paper (fp).

scores. When evaluating the evidence-only model on full papers we made an interesting observation: This model has equal or better F_1 scores on all question types except for unanswerable questions. The score for this type of question is probably so low as the model only learned to map the absence of evidence or the presence of a placeholder to the question being unanswerable.

Fine-tuning improves instruction-following and unanswerable question detection We assume that this result together with less than 8k tokens long training data improving performance on more than 8k tokens long evaluation data means that training the model mostly improves instruction following and does not promote better long-context understanding. But we also note that in order for the model to learn if a question is unanswerable it has to explicitly learn the mapping of no evidence in the whole paper to the question being unanswerable. During fine-grained analysis by input length, we see that the model that we trained on evidence only shows almost no performance decrease with increased paper length but also its performance for shorter papers is worse than those models that were trained on full papers. We also see that training on the full papers is useful as it dramatically improves performance for questions where no evidence is contained in the paper text.

4.2.3 Extract-then-Answer Prompt

Inspired by the results of using only the evidence as context to answer the questions, we hypothesize that a chain-of-thought prompt could increase performance: The model has to extract the relevant paragraphs first and then answer the questions based on the evidence found.

Epochs	0	1	3	5
Answer F_1	24.94	19.93	34.52	39.08
Answer F_1 by type				
Extractive	23.19	8.27	29.98	37.50
Abstractive	17.35	1.52	10.28	14.92
Boolean	57.96	23.76	52.34	49.51
Unanswerable	11.84	98.45	89.57	89.09
Evidence F_1	12.73	25.74	34.32	38.45

Table 6: LongChat-32k, dev-short set, **extract-then-answer prompt**, fine-tuned with QLoRA.

Extract-then-Answer Prompt does not improve performance During training, we saw an initial drop in performance for all question types that can be answered with the paper as context (Table 6). When looking at the evidence score and during qualitative analysis, we see that the model does not extract the correct paragraphs leading to an inability to answer most of the questions. After five epochs, for 535 out of 990 questions (~54%) the model finds evidence. But during training, the model saw evidence for 1,607 out of 1,904 questions (~84%). Yet after the same number of epochs as the one-step prompt model, this model still performs worse (47.02 vs. 39.08, Table 3).

Even for longer papers and evidence more difficult to reach, the extract-then-answer prompt does not improve performance as the evidence extraction also suffers on longer context and also does not help even inside the original context window. Out of 990 questions, the fine-tuned model still finds no evidence for 455 questions.

Handling Absent Evidence During training, the most common unique evidence string presented to the model is the placeholder we use for no evidence. For an improved prompt, we therefore include a prefix in the training data and as a hint in the prompt that every no empty extracted evidence starts with this prefix. We argue that this helps the model to avoid resorting to generating the "easiest" evidence which is none or the placeholder inspired by Attention Strengthening Question Answering (He et al.,

2023) which predicts the indices of the most relevant document in multi-document QA. We also adopt their approach of placing the question before and after the context.

To further reduce the number of generated empty evidence, we lower the number of examples in our training data where no evidence should be found to push the model into generating non-empty evidence more frequently. In the training data (<8k tokens), only around 16% of the questions are annotated with no evidence. However, the model that we fine-tuned on the "standard" extract-then-answer prompt generates no extracted evidence for around 40% of the questions which is 2.5 times as often. We assume a linear dependency between percentage of training answers without evidence and the percentage of generated answers without evidence. We lower the ratio of questions with no evidence in the training data to around 6% to arrive at 16% of generated empty evidence. We now employ all techniques we presented previously to improve the extract-then-answer prompt.

Adapted Prompt: Performance improves only slightly While the answer F_1 score does improve with this adapted prompt for the fine-tuned model (Table 3) when compared to the simpler extract-then-answer prompt, the evidence F_1 is lower even though the percentage of empty evidence drops from around 46% to around 22%. Also, for the zero-shot prompt all question types show worse results and the evidence score even drops to 0.0. Manual investigation shows that the model generated very long paragraphs as evidence in the zero-shot setup which led to this score. In further analysis, the advanced extract-then-answer prompt shows slightly better results for papers with under 8k tokens (F_1: 41.57 vs. 44.78, 37.77 vs. 39.66) and evidence below the same threshold (F_1: 36.00 vs. 40.54, 30.31 vs. 34.97). But the F_1 scores are still below those of the one-step prompt (47.02 vs. 41.18) as the evidence extraction also still suffers from long context.

4.3 Final Comparison against Baselines

Finally, we compare the results of our experiments against task-specific models and strong LLMs. Our comparison is on the ZeroSCROLLS subset of the Qasper test set which we believe is representative enough for the full test set (Table 1) to use it for comparison to strong LLMs. The ZeroSCROLLS subset uses a slightly different prompt for Qasper and does not include the title and abstract in the input. We compare our approaches with both prompts: ZeroSCROLLS (ZC) and LongBench (LB). With the LongBench prompt used during inference, our best approach exceeds GPT-4's F_1 score on the ZeroSCROLLS subset, comes close to the strongest model, and represents a great improvement over the zero-shot setup (Table 7). It is important to note that the ZeroSCROLLS authors mentioned that GPT-4 sometimes struggled more than other models to follow the prompt on Qasper. When we use the same prompt as the other models, both our zero-shot and the fine-tuned model lose more than 5 F_1 points showing how important prompting can be. As the performance drop is almost the same, we assume that for the fine-tuned model this is not a result of the mismatch between the training prompt and the inference prompt. The fine-tuned LongChat-32k model with the LongBench prompt is only able to almost match the task-specific model. We assume that this observation and the fact that Flan-UL2 is the best performing model are a result of these models being full transformers with an encoder and a decoder. The bidirectional encoder that processes the context together with the question and the prompt before generating the answer could help here.

Model	Prompt	Training	Answer F_1
Ours			
LongChat	ZC	0-shot	25.80
LongChat	LB	0-shot	31.07
LongChat	ZC	5 epochs	46.90
LongChat	LB	5 epochs	52.73
Existing models			
Flan-UL2	ZC	0-shot	56.90
GPT-4	ZC	0-shot	50.70
CoLT5	ZC	0-shot	53.10

Table 7: Baseline results (Flan-UL2 (Tay et al., 2023), GPT-4 (OpenAI, 2023), CoLT5 (Ainslie et al., 2023)) from ZeroSCROLLS benchmark (Shaham et al., 2023) compared to our results (LongChat-32k, 5 epochs), ZeroSCROLLS subset of Qasper test set.

5 Conclusion

We wanted to investigate how well LLMs can handle scientific papers and how we can improve their performance. We observe that the (unmodified) small open-source long-context LLMs we tested are able to process scientific papers with up to about 16k tokens from the Qasper dataset but fall short of commercial LLMs. Additionally, the performance drops after the context exceeds the original context window – especially if the relevant information to answer to question lies in that region of the paper.

When we employ the current techniques for efficient training QLoRA and FlashAttention, we can fine-tune the models on papers with a length of up to 8k tokens on a single datacenter GPU that is available to a university student for research. The performance of our fine-tuned model still increases for even longer papers without being trained on these lengths. Experiments with models that we only trained on extracted paragraphs without providing the model the full paper suggest that our training primarily improves instruction following but also improves the models' ability to determine if a question is unanswerable as it has to learn the connection between the absence of relevant information and the unanswerability of the question. When comparing our results against baselines, we saw that our best approach reaches or surpasses the result of the original GPT-4.

Limitations

This paper only investigates the Qasper dataset and the LongChat LLM. The Qasper dataset is limited to scientific papers from the NLP domain and mostly provides questions about facts and not more complex prompts like asking for new research directions based on the given paper. LongChat may have different strengths and weaknesses than other LLMs which may respond differently to the our prompts, our fine-tuning scheme, and long context in general (as seen by Liu et al. (2023)). While our resulting model is an improvement over the zero-shot LongChat, it still makes mistakes (like determining a question as unanswerable even if it is answerable).

We did not investigate all fitting configurations of our experimental setup like providing a random paragraph as evidence instead of no paragraph or how the fine-tuning for one prompt type influences the performance during inference with a different prompt type (except for the model that we fine-tuned on the evidence only).

Acknowledgment

We thank the anonymous reviewers for their valuable feedback.

References

Joshua Ainslie, Tao Lei, Michiel de Jong, Santiago Ontañón, Siddhartha Brahma, Yury Zemlyanskiy, David C. Uthus, Mandy Guo, James Lee-Thorp, Yi Tay, Yun-Hsuan Sung, and Sumit Sanghai. 2023. Colt5: Faster long-range transformers with conditional computation. In *Proceedings of the 2023 Conference on Empirical Methods in Natural Language Processing, EMNLP 2023, Singapore, December 6-10, 2023*, pages 5085–5100. Association for Computational Linguistics.

Rohan Anil, Sebastian Borgeaud, Yonghui Wu, Jean-Baptiste Alayrac, Jiahui Yu, Radu Soricut, Johan Schalkwyk, Andrew M. Dai, Anja Hauth, Katie Millican, David Silver, Slav Petrov, Melvin Johnson, Ioannis Antonoglou, Julian Schrittwieser, Amelia Glaese, Jilin Chen, Emily Pitler, Timothy P. Lillicrap, Angeliki Lazaridou, Orhan Firat, James Molloy, Michael Isard, Paul Ronald Barham, Tom Hennigan, Benjamin Lee, Fabio Viola, Malcolm Reynolds, Yuanzhong Xu, Ryan Doherty, Eli Collins, Clemens Meyer, Eliza Rutherford, Erica Moreira, Kareem Ayoub, Megha Goel, George Tucker, Enrique Piqueras, Maxim Krikun, Iain Barr, Nikolay Savinov, Ivo Danihelka, Becca Roelofs, Anaïs White, Anders Andreassen, Tamara von Glehn, Lakshman Yagati, Mehran Kazemi, Lucas Gonzalez, Misha Khalman, Jakub Sygnowski, and et al. 2023. Gemini: A family of highly capable multimodal models. *CoRR*, abs/2312.11805.

Yushi Bai, Xin Lv, Jiajie Zhang, Hongchang Lyu, Jiankai Tang, Zhidian Huang, Zhengxiao Du, Xiao Liu, Aohan Zeng, Lei Hou, Yuxiao Dong, Jie Tang, and Juanzi Li. 2023. Longbench: A bilingual, multitask benchmark for long context understanding. *CoRR*, abs/2308.14508.

Iz Beltagy, Matthew E. Peters, and Arman Cohan. 2020. Longformer: The long-document transformer. *CoRR*, abs/2004.05150.

Bo-Christer Björk, Annikki Roos, and Mari Lauri. 2009. Scientific journal publishing: yearly volume and open access availability. *Inf. Res.*, 14(1).

Tom B. Brown, Benjamin Mann, Nick Ryder, Melanie Subbiah, Jared Kaplan, Prafulla Dhariwal, Arvind Neelakantan, Pranav Shyam, Girish Sastry, Amanda Askell, Sandhini Agarwal, Ariel Herbert-Voss, Gretchen Krueger, Tom Henighan, Rewon Child, Aditya Ramesh, Daniel M. Ziegler, Jeffrey Wu, Clemens Winter, Christopher Hesse, Mark Chen, Eric Sigler, Mateusz Litwin, Scott Gray, Benjamin Chess, Jack Clark, Christopher Berner, Sam McCandlish, Alec Radford, Ilya Sutskever, and Dario Amodei. 2020. Language models are few-shot learners. In *Advances in Neural Information Processing Systems 33: Annual Conference on Neural Information Processing Systems 2020, NeurIPS 2020, December 6-12, 2020, virtual.*

Shouyuan Chen, Sherman Wong, Liangjian Chen, and Yuandong Tian. 2023. Extending context window of large language models via positional interpolation. *CoRR*, abs/2306.15595.

Liying Cheng, Lidong Bing, Qian Yu, Wei Lu, and Luo Si. 2020. APE: argument pair extraction from peer review and rebuttal via multi-task learning. In *Proceedings of the 2020 Conference on Empirical Methods in Natural Language Processing, EMNLP 2020, Online, November 16-20, 2020*, pages 7000–7011. Association for Computational Linguistics.

Wei-Lin Chiang, Zhuohan Li, Zi Lin, Ying Sheng, Zhanghao Wu, Hao Zhang, Lianmin Zheng, Siyuan Zhuang, Yonghao Zhuang, Joseph E. Gonzalez, Ion Stoica, and Eric P. Xing. Vicuna: An open-source chatbot impressing gpt-4 with 90%* chatgpt quality.

Aakanksha Chowdhery, Sharan Narang, Jacob Devlin, Maarten Bosma, Gaurav Mishra, Adam Roberts, Paul Barham, Hyung Won Chung, Charles Sutton, Sebastian Gehrmann, Parker Schuh, Kensen Shi, Sasha Tsvyashchenko, Joshua Maynez, Abhishek Rao, Parker Barnes, Yi Tay, Noam Shazeer, Vinodkumar Prabhakaran, Emily Reif, Nan Du, Ben Hutchinson, Reiner Pope, James Bradbury, Jacob Austin, Michael Isard, Guy Gur-Ari, Pengcheng Yin, Toju Duke, Anselm Levskaya, Sanjay Ghemawat, Sunipa Dev, Henryk Michalewski, Xavier Garcia, Vedant Misra, Kevin Robinson, Liam Fedus, Denny Zhou, Daphne Ippolito, David Luan, Hyeontaek Lim, Barret Zoph, Alexander Spiridonov, Ryan Sepassi, David Dohan, Shivani Agrawal, Mark Omernick, Andrew M. Dai, Thanumalayan Sankaranarayana Pillai, Marie Pellat, Aitor Lewkowycz, Erica Moreira, Rewon Child, Oleksandr Polozov, Katherine Lee, Zongwei Zhou, Xuezhi Wang, Brennan Saeta, Mark Diaz, Orhan Firat, Michele Catasta, Jason Wei, Kathy Meier-Hellstern, Douglas Eck, Jeff Dean, Slav Petrov, and Noah Fiedel. 2023. Palm: Scaling language modeling with pathways. *J. Mach. Learn. Res.*, 24:240:1–240:113.

Tri Dao. 2023. Flashattention-2: Faster attention with better parallelism and work partitioning. *CoRR*, abs/2307.08691.

Tri Dao, Daniel Y. Fu, Stefano Ermon, Atri Rudra, and Christopher Ré. 2022. Flashattention: Fast and memory-efficient exact attention with io-awareness. In *Advances in Neural Information Processing Systems 35: Annual Conference on Neural Information Processing Systems 2022, NeurIPS 2022, New Orleans, LA, USA, November 28 - December 9, 2022*.

Pradeep Dasigi, Kyle Lo, Iz Beltagy, Arman Cohan, Noah A. Smith, and Matt Gardner. 2021. A dataset of information-seeking questions and answers anchored in research papers. In *Proceedings of the 2021 Conference of the North American Chapter of the Association for Computational Linguistics: Human Language Technologies, NAACL-HLT 2021, Online, June 6-11, 2021*, pages 4599–4610. Association for Computational Linguistics.

Tim Dettmers, Artidoro Pagnoni, Ari Holtzman, and Luke Zettlemoyer. 2023. Qlora: Efficient finetuning of quantized llms. *CoRR*, abs/2305.14314.

Michael Fire and Carlos Guestrin. 2018. Over-optimization of academic publishing metrics: Observing goodhart's law in action. *CoRR*, abs/1809.07841.

Chi Han, Qifan Wang, Hao Peng, Wenhan Xiong, Yu Chen, Heng Ji, and Sinong Wang. 2024. LM-infinite: Zero-shot extreme length generalization for large language models. In *Proceedings of the 2024 Conference of the North American Chapter of the Association for Computational Linguistics: Human Language Technologies (Volume 1: Long Papers)*, pages 3991–4008. Association for Computational Linguistics.

Junqing He, Kunhao Pan, Xiaoqun Dong, Zhuoyang Song, Yibo Liu, Yuxin Liang, Hao Wang, Qianguo Sun, Songxin Zhang, Zejian Xie, and Jiaxing Zhang. 2023. Never lost in the middle: Improving large language models via attention strengthening question answering. *CoRR*, abs/2311.09198.

Jordan Hoffmann, Sebastian Borgeaud, Arthur Mensch, Elena Buchatskaya, Trevor Cai, Eliza Rutherford, Diego de Las Casas, Lisa Anne Hendricks, Johannes Welbl, Aidan Clark, Tom Hennigan, Eric Noland, Katie Millican, George van den Driessche, Bogdan Damoc, Aurelia Guy, Simon Osindero, Karen Simonyan, Erich Elsen, Jack W. Rae, Oriol Vinyals, and Laurent Sifre. 2022. Training compute-optimal large language models. *CoRR*, abs/2203.15556.

Edward J. Hu, Yelong Shen, Phillip Wallis, Zeyuan Allen-Zhu, Yuanzhi Li, Shean Wang, Lu Wang, and Weizhu Chen. 2022. Lora: Low-rank adaptation of large language models. In *The Tenth International Conference on Learning Representations, ICLR 2022, Virtual Event, April 25-29, 2022*. OpenReview.net.

Albert Q. Jiang, Alexandre Sablayrolles, Arthur Mensch, Chris Bamford, Devendra Singh Chaplot, Diego de Las Casas, Florian Bressand, Gianna Lengyel, Guillaume Lample, Lucile Saulnier, Lélio Renard Lavaud, Marie-Anne Lachaux, Pierre Stock, Teven Le Scao, Thibaut Lavril, Thomas Wang, Timothée Lacroix, and William El Sayed. 2023. Mistral 7b. *CoRR*, abs/2310.06825.

Albert Q. Jiang, Alexandre Sablayrolles, Antoine Roux, Arthur Mensch, Blanche Savary, Chris Bamford, Devendra Singh Chaplot, Diego de Las Casas, Emma Bou Hanna, Florian Bressand, Gianna Lengyel, Guillaume Bour, Guillaume Lample, Lélio Renard Lavaud, Lucile Saulnier, Marie-Anne Lachaux, Pierre Stock, Sandeep Subramanian, Sophia Yang, Szymon Antoniak, Teven Le Scao, Théophile Gervet, Thibaut Lavril, Thomas Wang, Timothée Lacroix, and William El Sayed. 2024. Mixtral of experts. *CoRR*, abs/2401.04088.

Dongyeop Kang, Waleed Ammar, Bhavana Dalvi, Madeleine van Zuylen, Sebastian Kohlmeier, Eduard H. Hovy, and Roy Schwartz. 2018. A dataset of peer reviews (peerread): Collection, insights and NLP applications. In *Proceedings of the 2018 Conference of the North American Chapter of the Association for Computational Linguistics: Human Language Technologies, NAACL-HLT 2018, New Orleans, Louisiana, USA, June 1-6, 2018, Volume 1 (Long Papers)*, pages 1647–1661. Association for Computational Linguistics.

Kaio Ken. Extending context is hard... but not impossible.

Dacheng Li, Rulin Shao, Anze Xie, Ying Shenga, Lianmin Zheng, Joseph E. Gonzalez, Ion Stoica, Xuezhe Ma, and Hao Zhang. How long can open-source llms truly promise on context length?

Miao Li, Jianzhong Qi, and Jey Han Lau. 2022. Peersum: A peer review dataset for abstractive multi-document summarization. *CoRR*, abs/2203.01769. Withdrawn.

Jialiang Lin, Jiaxin Song, Zhangping Zhou, Yidong Chen, and Xiaodong Shi. 2023. MOPRD: A multidisciplinary open peer review dataset. *Neural Comput. Appl.*, 35(34):24191–24206.

Nelson F. Liu, Kevin Lin, John Hewitt, Ashwin Paranjape, Michele Bevilacqua, Fabio Petroni, and Percy Liang. 2023. Lost in the middle: How language models use long contexts. *CoRR*, abs/2307.03172.

Pan Lu, Swaroop Mishra, Tanglin Xia, Liang Qiu, Kai-Wei Chang, Song-Chun Zhu, Oyvind Tafjord, Peter Clark, and Ashwin Kalyan. 2022. Learn to explain: Multimodal reasoning via thought chains for science question answering. In *Advances in Neural Information Processing Systems 35: Annual Conference on Neural Information Processing Systems 2022, NeurIPS 2022, New Orleans, LA, USA, November 28 - December 9, 2022*.

Meta AI. 2023. Introducing llama: A foundational, 65-billion-parameter large language model. Retrieved 2023-12-11.

OpenAI. a. Gpt-3.5 turbo.

OpenAI. b. What are tokens and how to count them?

OpenAI. 2023. GPT-4 technical report. *CoRR*, abs/2303.08774.

Pranav Rajpurkar, Jian Zhang, Konstantin Lopyrev, and Percy Liang. 2016. Squad: 100, 000+ questions for machine comprehension of text. In *Proceedings of the 2016 Conference on Empirical Methods in Natural Language Processing, EMNLP 2016, Austin, Texas, USA, November 1-4, 2016*, pages 2383–2392. The Association for Computational Linguistics.

Uri Shaham, Maor Ivgi, Avia Efrat, Jonathan Berant, and Omer Levy. 2023. Zeroscrolls: A zero-shot benchmark for long text understanding. In *Findings of the Association for Computational Linguistics: EMNLP 2023, Singapore, December 6-10, 2023*, pages 7977–7989. Association for Computational Linguistics.

Yi Tay, Mostafa Dehghani, Vinh Q. Tran, Xavier Garcia, Jason Wei, Xuezhi Wang, Hyung Won Chung, Dara Bahri, Tal Schuster, Huaixiu Steven Zheng, Denny Zhou, Neil Houlsby, and Donald Metzler. 2023. UL2: unifying language learning paradigms. In *The Eleventh International Conference on Learning Representations, ICLR 2023, Kigali, Rwanda, May 1-5, 2023*. OpenReview.net.

Hugo Touvron, Thibaut Lavril, Gautier Izacard, Xavier Martinet, Marie-Anne Lachaux, Timothée Lacroix, Baptiste Rozière, Naman Goyal, Eric Hambro, Faisal Azhar, Aurélien Rodriguez, Armand Joulin, Edouard Grave, and Guillaume Lample. 2023a. Llama: Open and efficient foundation language models. *CoRR*, abs/2302.13971.

Hugo Touvron, Louis Martin, Kevin Stone, Peter Albert, Amjad Almahairi, Yasmine Babaei, Nikolay Bashlykov, Soumya Batra, Prajjwal Bhargava, Shruti Bhosale, Dan Bikel, Lukas Blecher, Cristian Canton-Ferrer, Moya Chen, Guillem Cucurull, David Esiobu, Jude Fernandes, Jeremy Fu, Wenyin Fu, Brian Fuller, Cynthia Gao, Vedanuj Goswami, Naman Goyal, Anthony Hartshorn, Saghar Hosseini, Rui Hou, Hakan Inan, Marcin Kardas, Viktor Kerkez, Madian Khabsa, Isabel Kloumann, Artem Korenev, Punit Singh Koura, Marie-Anne Lachaux, Thibaut Lavril, Jenya Lee, Diana Liskovich, Yinghai Lu, Yuning Mao, Xavier Martinet, Todor Mihaylov, Pushkar Mishra, Igor Molybog, Yixin Nie, Andrew Poulton, Jeremy Reizenstein, Rashi Rungta, Kalyan Saladi, Alan Schelten, Ruan Silva, Eric Michael Smith, Ranjan Subramanian, Xiaoqing Ellen Tan, Binh Tang, Ross Taylor, Adina Williams, Jian Xiang Kuan, Puxin Xu, Zheng Yan, Iliyan Zarov, Yuchen Zhang, Angela Fan, Melanie Kambadur, Sharan Narang, Aurélien Rodriguez, Robert Stojnic, Sergey Edunov, and Thomas Scialom. 2023b. Llama 2: Open foundation and fine-tuned chat models. *CoRR*, abs/2307.09288.

Lei Wang, Yi Hu, Jiabang He, Xing Xu, Ning Liu, Hui Liu, and Heng Tao Shen. 2023. T-sciq: Teaching multimodal chain-of-thought reasoning via large language model signals for science question answering. *CoRR*, abs/2305.03453.

Qingyun Wang, Qi Zeng, Lifu Huang, Kevin Knight, Heng Ji, and Nazneen Fatema Rajani. 2020. Reviewrobot: Explainable paper review generation based on knowledge synthesis. In *Proceedings of the 13th International Conference on Natural Language Generation, INLG 2020, Dublin, Ireland, December 15-18, 2020*, pages 384–397. Association for Computational Linguistics.

Jason Wei, Xuezhi Wang, Dale Schuurmans, Maarten Bosma, Brian Ichter, Fei Xia, Ed H. Chi, Quoc V. Le, and Denny Zhou. 2022. Chain-of-thought prompting elicits reasoning in large language models. In *Advances in Neural Information Processing Systems 35:*

Annual Conference on Neural Information Processing Systems 2022, NeurIPS 2022, New Orleans, LA, USA, November 28 - December 9, 2022.

Pengcheng Yang, Xu Sun, Wei Li, and Shuming Ma. 2018. Automatic academic paper rating based on modularized hierarchical convolutional neural network. In *Proceedings of the 56th Annual Meeting of the Association for Computational Linguistics, ACL 2018, Melbourne, Australia, July 15-20, 2018, Volume 2: Short Papers*, pages 496–502. Association for Computational Linguistics.

Ori Yoran, Tomer Wolfson, Ben Bogin, Uri Katz, Daniel Deutch, and Jonathan Berant. 2023. Answering questions by meta-reasoning over multiple chains of thought. In *Proceedings of the 2023 Conference on Empirical Methods in Natural Language Processing, EMNLP 2023, Singapore, December 6-10, 2023*, pages 5942–5966. Association for Computational Linguistics.

Lianmin Zheng, Wei-Lin Chiang, Ying Sheng, Siyuan Zhuang, Zhanghao Wu, Yonghao Zhuang, Zi Lin, Zhuohan Li, Dacheng Li, Eric P. Xing, Hao Zhang, Joseph E. Gonzalez, and Ion Stoica. 2023. Judging llm-as-a-judge with mt-bench and chatbot arena. In *Advances in Neural Information Processing Systems 36: Annual Conference on Neural Information Processing Systems 2023, NeurIPS 2023, New Orleans, LA, USA, December 10 - 16, 2023.*

A Prompts

We used the following prompts during our experiments. <CONTEXT> stands for the paper text or a shortened version of it while <QUESTION> is the placeholder for the specific question on the provided context.

A.1 ZeroSCROLLS

You are given a scientific article and a question. Answer the question as concisely as you can, using a single phrase or sentence if possible. If the question cannot be answered based on the information in the article, write "unanswerable". If the question is a yes/no question, answer "yes", "no", or "unanswerable". Do not provide any explanation.

Article: <CONTEXT>

Question: <QUESTION>

A.1.1 LongBench (our version)

You are given a scientific article and a question. Answer the question as concisely as you can, using a single phrase or sentence if possible. If the question cannot be answered based on the information in the article, write ’unanswerable’. If the question is a yes/no question, answer ’yes’, ’no’, or ’unanswerable’. Do not provide any explanation.
Article: <CONTEXT>
Answer the question based on the above article as concisely as you can, using a single phrase or sentence if possible. If the question cannot be answered based on the information in the article, write ’unanswerable’. If the question is a yes/no question, answer ’yes’, ’no’, or ’unanswerable’. Do not provide any explanation.
Question: <QUESTION>

A.2 Evidence only

You are given excerpts from a scientific article and a question. Answer the question as concisely as you can, using a single phrase or sentence if possible. If the question cannot be answered based on the information in the excerpts from an article, write ’unanswerable’. If the question is a yes/no question, answer ’yes’, ’no’, or ’unanswerable’. Do not provide any explanation.
Excerpts from Article: <CONTEXT>
Answer the question based on the above excerpts from an article as concisely as you can, using a single phrase or sentence if possible. If the question cannot be answered based on the information in the excerpts from an article, write ’unanswerable’. If the question is a yes/no question, answer ’yes’, ’no’, or ’unanswerable’. Do not provide any explanation.
Question: <QUESTION>

A.3 Two-turn

Turn 0:
You are given a scientific article and a question. Extract all paragraphs that are relevant to answer the question. Copy them word by word from the article. If there are no relevant paragraphs answer ’No relevant paragraphs found’. Do not provide any explanation.
Article: <CONTEXT>
Extract all paragraphs that are relevant to answer the question. Copy them word by word from the article. If there are no relevant paragraphs answer ’No relevant paragraphs found’.
Question: <QUESTION>

Turn 1:
Answer the question based on your extracted relevant paragraphs from the above article and answer as concisely as you can, using a single phrase or sentence if possible. If the question cannot be answered based on the information in the article (your last answer was possibly 'No relevant paragraphs found'), write 'unanswerable'. If the question is a yes/no question, answer 'yes', 'no', or 'unanswerable'. Do not provide any explanation.
Question: <QUESTION>

A.4 Two-turn, Advanced (Prefix for Evidence, Question Repeated)

Turn 0:
You are given a scientific article and a question. Extract all paragraphs that are relevant to answer the question. Copy them word by word from the article and start with 'Found these relevant paragraphs:'. If there are no relevant paragraphs answer 'No relevant paragraphs found'. Do not provide any explanation.
Question: <QUESTION>
Article: <CONTEXT>
Extract all paragraphs that are relevant to answer the question. Copy them word by word from the article. If there are no relevant paragraphs answer 'No relevant paragraphs found'.
Question: <QUESTION>

Turn 1:
Answer the question based on your extracted relevant paragraphs from the above article and answer as concisely as you can, using a single phrase or sentence if possible. If the question cannot be answered based on the information in the article (your last answer was possibly 'No relevant paragraphs found'), write 'unanswerable'. If the question is a yes/no question, answer 'yes', 'no', or 'unanswerable'. Do not provide any explanation.
Question: <QUESTION>

B Example answers

We also provide a list of qualitative examples how fine-tuning improved the performance (simple prompt, test set). We separate multiple possible answers by slashes.

- Answer more clearly to unanswerable question
  - **Question:** How does this result compare to other methods KB QA in CCKS2019?
  - **Answer (ground truth):** Unanswerable
  - **Answer (zero-shot):** The proposed method for open domain Chinese question answering in CCKS2019 achieved an F1 score of 70.45% on the test data. This result is comparable to other methods in KB QA, as it also employs a combination of information retrieval and semantic parsing. However, the specific comparison to other methods is not provided in the article, so it is unanswerable.
  - **Answer (fine-tuned):** Unanswerable
- Detect unanswerable question
  - **Question:** Which labeling scheme do they use?
  - **Answer (ground truth):** Unanswerable
  - **Answer (zero-shot):** They use a sequence labeling scheme for both constituency and dependency parsing.
  - **Answer (fine-tuned):** Unanswerable
- Answer more concisely
  - **Question:** Does regularization of the fine-tuning process hurt performance in the target domain?
  - **Answer (ground truth):** No
  - **Answer (zero-shot):** No, regularization of the fine-tuning process does not hurt performance in the target domain. In fact, it can improve performance by reducing catastrophic forgetting and preserving the source domain's performance as much as possible while keeping the target domain's performance optimal.
  - **Answer (fine-tuned):** No
- Answer more concisely and correctly
  - **Question:** what are the baselines?
  - **Answer (ground truth):** Reschke CRF, Reschke Noisy-OR, Reschke Best
  - **Answer (zero-shot):** The article does not provide specific baselines for the machine reading task. However, it mentions several related works and systems that the authors aim to improve upon. These include: 1. Reschke CRF: a conditional

random field model. 2. Reschke Noisy-OR: a sequence tagger with a Ňoisy-ORform of aggregation that discourages the model from predicting the same value for multiple slots. 3. Reschke Best: a sequence tagger using a cost-sensitive classifier, optimized with SEARN, a learning-to-search framework. These baselines represent different approaches to machine reading and event extraction from noisy sources. The authors' proposed architecture, called RAC, aims to improve upon these baselines by incorporating attention-based mention scoring, cluster-wide aggregation, and global constraints.
  - **Answer (fine-tuned):** Reschke CRF. Reschke Noisy-OR. Reschke Best.

- Answer more concisely and correctly 2
  - **Question:** How do they preprocess Tweets?
  - **Answer (ground truth):** They removed retweets, URLs, emoticons, mentions of other users, hashtags; lowercased the text and removed the punctuation. / re-tweets do not bring any additional information to our study, thus we removed them, removed any expressions considered to be semantically meaningless like URLs, emoticons, mentions of other users (denoted by the @ symbol) and hashtags, downcased and stripped the punctuation
  - **Answer (zero-shot):** The article does not provide specific details on how the tweets are preprocessed. However, it mentions that certain expressions are removed, such as URLs, emoticons, mentions of other users, and hashtags, to simplify textual pre-processing. Additionally, the tweets are downcased and stripped of punctuation.
  - **Answer (fine-tuned):** They remove retweets, expressions considered to be semantically meaningless, and downcase and strip the punctuation from the text.

- Answer correctly
  - **Question:** Do they evaluate only on English datasets?
  - **Answer (ground truth):** Yes / The twitter dataset is English-only; no information for the reddit dataset is given
  - **Answer (zero-shot):** No, they evaluate on a diverse range of social media platforms and content types, including English, Spanish, Portuguese, French, German, Italian, and Arabic.
  - **Answer (fine-tuned):** Yes

- Answer more specifically
  - **Question:** How many layers of recurrent neural networks do they use for encoding the global context?
  - **Answer (ground truth):** 2 / 8
  - **Answer (zero-shot):** The article does not provide specific information on the number of layers of recurrent neural networks used for encoding the global context. However, it mentions that they use stacked recurrent neural networks to capture the long-term dependencies and global context information from the whole sentence.
  - **Answer (fine-tuned):** Two feed-forward layers of size 400 with rectified linear units (ReLU); One bi-directional gated recurrent unit (BiGRU) layer with hidden size 200; Two feed-forward layers of hidden size 200 with rectified linear units; One BiGRU layer with hidden size 100; Two feed-forward layers of size 100 and 50 respectively with ReLU activation.

C Further Experimental Setup

Evidence type	Frequency
Text	81.6%
Table/Figure	11.6%
None	12.8%

Table 8: Qasper dataset statistics (Dasigi et al., 2021): evidence types; the percentages add to over 100% because answers can include multiple evidence types.

Minor details To bin the evaluation sets, we tokenize the whole paper texts from the JSON files that the dataset website provides. We used the tokenizer from Vicuna-16k, but the number of tokens should be the same for the other tokenizers. For the evidence positions, we determine the position of the first token of the evidence paragraphs inside the paper text. We assume this is representative as most evidence is at most a few sentences long. If there are multiple evidence paragraphs that are not continuous in the dataset, we bin potentially one paper multiple times.

A model tasked to extract the evidence should output no paragraphs if there is none for the question at hand. Instead, it should generate the string "No relevant paragraphs found" which we include in the prompts and filter out of the answers before calculating the F_1 score.

C.1 Hard- and Software

For evaluation and training of the tested models we need high-performance GPUs. Therefore, we use the bwUniCluster 2.0[3] for our experiments. Depending on availability, we use the NVIDIA A100 with 80 GB of accelerator memory or the NVIDIA H100 with 94 GB. The bwUniCluster 2.0 allows the use of NVIDIA Enroot[4] which enables running Docker[5] containers on the computing cluster. We use the PyTorch container[6] by NVIDIA to train the models in our experiments. FlashAttention is only implemented per GPU type at the moment and comes pre-installed with this container.

We run all our experiments (inference and training) with the FastChat[7] (Zheng et al., 2023) framework which is an open-source platform for "training, serving, and evaluating large language model based chatbots". It is developed by the Large Model Systems Organization (LMSYS Org).[8] The LMSYS Org also operates the LMSYS Chatbot Arena[9] (Zheng et al., 2023) which tries to compare the performance of current LLMs against each other in a chatbot setting. FastChat provides code to easily run models, feed them with input data, and store their answers. Besides regular fine-tuning it also provides a (Q)LoRA implementation that can utilize FlashAttention. This script is run with the DeepSpeed[10] library.

[3]https://wiki.bwhpc.de/e/Main_Page

[4]https://github.com/NVIDIA/enroot

[5]https://docs.docker.com/

[6]https://catalog.ngc.nvidia.com/orgs/nvidia/containers/pytorch

[7]https://github.com/lm-sys/FastChat

[8]https://lmsys.org/

[9]https://chat.lmsys.org/

[10]https://github.com/microsoft/DeepSpeed

C.2 Hyperparameters

All following stated hyperparameters are the same on all experiments if not stated differently per experiment.

During inference, we run the models with a temperature of 0.0 which equates to greedy decoding.[11] FastChat code also uses a temperature of 0.0 for tasks like extraction and reasoning.[12] This fits our requirements as we want the most accurate and truthful answer. Also, we saw a degradation in performance when raising the temperature. We let the models generate up to 1,024 tokens.

Our training configuration is the same as the example from FastChat: We use a LoRA rank r of 8 and a LoRA Alpha of 16. Rank $r = 8$ results in 4,194,304 trainable parameters out of 6,742,609,920 for LLaMA 2 7B based models. The dropout is 0.05 and we apply no weight decay. The learning rate is initialized with 2e-5 with a warm-up ratio of 0.03 and a cosine learning rate scheduling. We do no extensive hyperparameter search because of time constraints regarding compute and because the authors of QLoRA already noted that the most important "hyperparameter" is the location of the adapted parameters inside the model. We train each model for 5 epochs on the training split after our preprocessing. We chose this duration as it could be done within a few hours on a single GPU, and we saw performance saturation within this training duration.

D Additional Evaluation Results

We provide additional evaluation results for all models – zero-shot (Table 9) and fine-tuned with QLoRA (Table 10).

We also tested if changing the temperature increases performance (Table 11): Our rationale is that the most probable evidence is none as the placeholder string for this is always the same and occurs more often during training than any other evidence string. Also, it is not that important if the found paragraphs are perfectly correct (e.g., not too long): It just has to be useful to answer the question. Yet, increasing the temperature monotonously decreases both the evidence and answer F_1 scores. On top of reduced quality, the percentage of empty evidence rises from ∼46% (0.0) to ∼66% (1.0).

[11]https://huggingface.co/blog/how-to-generate

[12]https://github.com/lm-sys/FastChat/blob/085c2c37dca426059f023e2a080c45717c742fd1/fastchat/llm_judge/common.py

Models	Bin count	Vicuna-4k	Vicuna-16k	LongChat-32k
Answer F_1 per paper length				
0k – 4k	333	25.53	27.20	25.47
4k – 8k	593	0.40	24.01	24.08
8k –	64	0.00	19.55	18.51
Answer F_1 per absolute evidence position				
0k – 4k	794	9.79	25.82	26.73
4k – 8k	173	0.38	18.02	23.35
8k –	6	0.00	3.78	15.06
No evidence	77	11.80	23.38	1.06

Table 9: Analysis of the models we tested, dev-short set, **LongBench prompt** (Bai et al., 2023), zero-shot.

Models	Bin count	Vicuna-4k	Vicuna-16k	LongChat-32k
Answer F_1 per paper length				
0k – 4k	333	38.89	50.26	52.15
4k – 8k	593	18.53	43.02	44.45
8k –	64	2.48	39.55	44.09
Answer F_1 per absolute evidence position				
0k – 4k	794	23.99	43.54	46.28
4k – 8k	173	9.33	35.23	37.74
8k –	6	0.00	64.37	67.94
No evidence	77	52.81	75.32	64.94

Table 10: Models we tested, dev-short set, **LongBench prompt** (Bai et al., 2023), fine-tuned with QLoRA for 5 epochs.

We compare our best approach against the baseline model from the original publication of the Qasper dataset (Dasigi et al., 2021). Their model is the Longformer-Encoder-Decoder (LED) (Beltagy et al., 2020) in two sizes: base and large. It contains more fine-grained results than the comparison on the ZeroSCROLLS (Shaham et al., 2023) subset of Qasper. Also, they estimate a lower bound for the human performance on the test set by calculating the agreement between different annotator answers for each question. Their best model for question answering is LED-base that receives the full paper as input. One variant includes evidence extraction during training.

Our comparison (Table 12) shows that LED has a similar distribution of the F_1 scores per type. The extractive score is higher than the abstractive score and the boolean score is the highest or close to it. We can also see a similar behavior of the LED model to the extract-then-answer prompt when integrating evidence extraction into the answer generation process: The extractive and abstractive scores suffer while the model detects unanswerable questions better. Also, our best approach performs better on questions with very short answers (yes/no, unanswerable) than the lower bound for human performance. This could be an explanation of our observation that longer training does not improve these scores after they reach a certain level (trade-off: short vs. long answers). However, the quality of the abstractive answers is considerably worse (39.71 vs. 18.79).

For the evidence extraction, our best model is LongChat-32k fine-tuned with the extract-then-answer prompt. While the evidence extraction did not improve the answer quality in our case, it can be a useful addition for the user of a QA system to contextualize the answer. Here, the difference between our approach and the Qasper baseline LED-large (Table 13) is not as high as for the answer F_1 score but we still see a clear improvement over the baseline.

E Additional Training Results

Here, we list how the F_1 scores during our training runs changed compared to the zero-shot results with the same prompt. For the evidence only prompt (Table 14) and for the extract-then-answer prompt (Table 6, Table 15), we only trained LongChat-32k.

LongChat-32k	0.0	0.2	0.4	0.6	0.8	1.0
Answer F_1	39.08	37.61	35.05	33.15	30.57	29.60
Evidence F_1	38.45	37.20	35.31	33.54	31.85	29.16

Table 11: LongChat, dev-short set, **extract-then-answer prompt**, fine-tuned 5 epochs with QLoRA, varying temperatures.

Models	LongChat-32k LongBench prompt zero-shot	LongChat-32k LongBench prompt 5 epochs	LED-base without evidence extraction	LED-base with evidence extraction	Human (lower bound)
Test answer F_1	28.81	55.20	32.80	33.63	60.92
Test answer F_1 by type					
Extractive	28.39	54.89	30.96	29.97	58.92
Abstractive	20.82	18.79	15.76	15.02	39.71
Boolean	56.11	84.68	70.33	68.90	78.98
Unanswerable	2.14	86.42	26.21	44.97	69.44

Table 12: Comparison of our approaches against baselines from the Qasper paper, test set.

Models	LongChat-32k extract-then-answer prompt 5 epochs	LED-base	LED-large	Human (lower bound)
Dev evidence F_1	38.27	23.94	31.25	–
Test evidence F_1	42.57	29.85	39.37	71.62

Table 13: Comparison of our approaches against baselines from the Qasper paper, full dev and test set, evidence extraction.

LongChat-32k	Zero-shot	1 epoch	2 epochs	3 epochs
Answer F_1	36.16	55.65	56.97	57.22
Answer F_1 by type				
Extractive	37.58	61.04	61.41	62.19
Abstractive	21.80	25.20	25.60	27.01
Boolean	47.96	72.27	80.99	79.83
Unanswerable	53.48	84.00	83.33	80.56

Table 14: LongChat-32k, **evidence only** dev-short set, fine-tuned with QLoRA.

LongChat-32k	Zero-shot	1 epoch	3 epochs	5 epochs
Answer F_1	17.85	27.59	41.54	41.18
Answer F_1 by type				
Extractive	16.37	22.27	45.00	41.82
Abstractive	16.03	10.64	21.06	19.41
Boolean	36.75	59.66	68.14	58.10
Unanswerable	5.33	59.79	40.23	69.23
Evidence F_1	0.00	26.37	31.12	35.13

Table 15: LongChat, dev-short set, **extract-then-answer prompt, improved**, fine-tuned with QLoRA.

HyPA-RAG: A Hybrid Parameter Adaptive Retrieval-Augmented Generation System for AI Legal and Policy Applications

Rishi Kalra[2], **Zekun Wu**[1,2], **Ayesha Gulley**[1], **Airlie Hilliard**[1],
Xin Guan[1], **Adriano Koshiyama**[1], **Philip Treleaven**[2]
[1]Holistic AI, [2]University College London
Correspondence: rishi.kalra.20@ucl.ac.uk, zekun.wu@holisticai.com

Abstract

While Large Language Models (LLMs) excel in text generation and question-answering, their effectiveness in AI legal and policy applications is limited by outdated knowledge, hallucinations, and inadequate reasoning in complex contexts. Retrieval-Augmented Generation (RAG) systems improve response accuracy by integrating external knowledge but struggle with retrieval errors, poor context integration, and high costs, particularly in interpreting AI legal texts. This paper introduces a Hybrid Parameter-Adaptive RAG (HyPA-RAG) system tailored for AI legal and policy, exemplified by NYC Local Law 144 (LL144). HyPA-RAG uses a query complexity classifier for adaptive parameter tuning, a hybrid retrieval strategy combining dense, sparse, and knowledge graph methods, and an evaluation framework with specific question types and metrics. By dynamically adjusting parameters, HyPA-RAG significantly improves retrieval accuracy and response fidelity. Testing on LL144 shows enhanced correctness, faithfulness, and contextual precision, addressing the need for adaptable NLP systems in complex, high-stakes AI legal and policy applications. [1]

1 Introduction

The development of Large Language Models (LLMs) capable of processing and generating human-like text has made significant strides in recent years, such as OpenAI's GPT models (Brown et al., 2020; OpenAI, 2023), Google's Gemini models (Team et al., 2023) and open alternatives such as the LlaMa series (Touvron et al., 2023a,b; Meta, 2024). These models, which store vast amounts of information within their parameters through extensive pre-training, have demonstrated impressive performance in various tasks, including text generation and question-answering across multiple domains (Brown et al., 2020; Singhal et al., 2023; Wu et al., 2023). Despite this, LLMs encounter limitations when applied to specialised fields such as law and policy. These include the rapid obsolescence of their knowledge, which is confined to the data available up to the last pre-training date (Yang et al., 2023), and hallucinations, where the model produces text that seems plausible but is factually incorrect or misleading, driven by internal logic rather than actual context (Ji et al., 2022; Huang et al., 2023). Empirical studies show that many artificial intelligence (AI) tools designed for legal applications overstate their ability to prevent hallucinations (Magesh et al., 2024). Indeed, instances of lawyers being penalised for using hallucinated outputs in court documents (Fortune, 2023; Business Insider, 2023) underscore the need for reliable AI question-answering systems in law and policy

Naturally, Retrieval-Augmented Generation (RAG), which enhances LLMs by incorporating external knowledge, is proposed as a solution. However, this comes with its own challenges. Common failure points (Barnett et al., 2024) include missing content, where relevant documents are not retrieved, leading to unanswered questions; context limitations, where retrieved documents are not effectively incorporated into the response generation process due to limitations in consolidation strategies; and extraction failures, where models fail to extract accurate information from the provided context due to noise or conflicting data. Furthermore, advanced retrieval and generation techniques, such as query rewriters and LLM-based quality checkers, often result in increased token usage and costs.

To address these challenges, this research integrates three key components (see Figure 6 in Appendix A.2 for a flow overview and Figure 1 for the system design):

[1]The demo (Appendix A.1), dataset, and code are available at https://github.com/holistic-ai/HyPA-RAG.

Proceedings of the 1st Workshop on Customizable NLP: Progress and Challenges in Customizing NLP for a Domain, Application, Group, or Individual (CustomNLP4U), pages 237–256
November 16, 2024

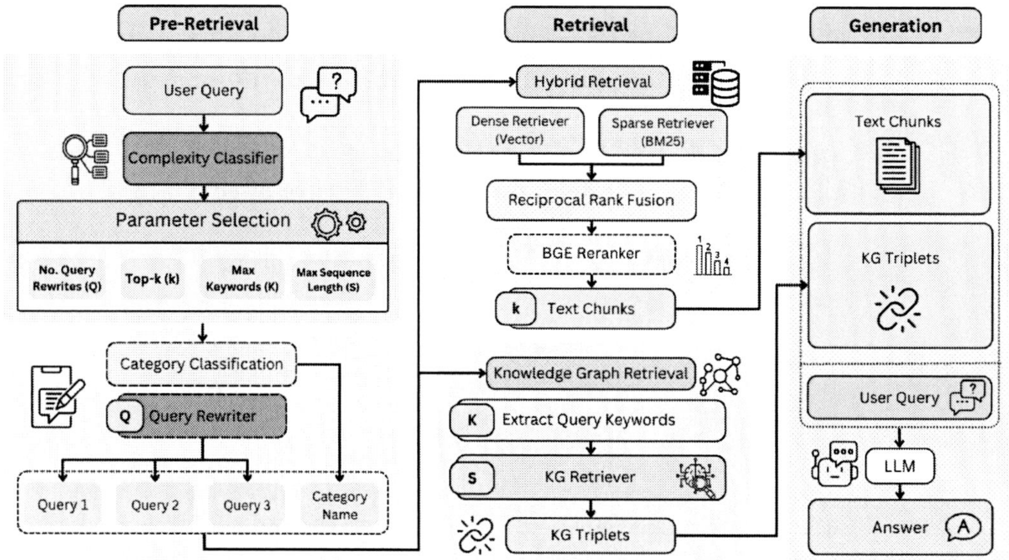

Figure 1: Hybrid Parameter Adaptive RAG (HyPA-RAG) System Diagram

(1) Adaptive parameter selection using a domain-specific query complexity classifier to minimise unnecessary token usage,

(2) A hybrid search system combining dense, sparse, and knowledge graph retrieval methods to enhance retrieval accuracy.

(3) An end-to-end evaluation framework that includes the development of a 'gold standard' dataset, custom question types, and RAG-specific evaluation metrics for robust testing.

These elements are combined to create a hybrid parameter-adaptive RAG system tailored specifically to mitigate the common RAG failure points, for the AI policy domain, using NYC Local Law 144 as the primary corpus. We also provide a streamlit demo for testing purposes.

2 Background and Related Work

Recent LLM advancements have impacted fields like law and policy, where language complexity and large text volumes are prevalent (Blair-Stanek et al., 2023; Choi et al., 2023; Hargreaves, 2023). LLMs have been used for legal judgment prediction, document drafting, and contract analysis, showing their potential to improve efficiency and accuracy (Shui et al., 2023; Sun, 2023; Šavelka and Ashley, 2023). Techniques like fine-tuning, retrieval augmentation, prompt engineering, and agentic methods have adapted these models for specific legal tasks, enhancing performance in summarisation, drafting, and interpretation (Trautmann et al., 2022; Cui et al., 2023).

Retrieval-Augmented Generation (RAG), as formalized by Lewis et al., enhances pre-trained seq2seq models by integrating external knowledge through indexing, retrieval, and generation stages, improving response specificity and accuracy (Lewis et al., 2020; Gao et al., 2023). RAG systems complement LLMs by combining sparse (e.g., BM25) and dense (e.g., vector) retrieval techniques, using neural embeddings to refine document retrieval and produce grounded, high-quality responses (Jones, 2021; Robertson and Zaragoza, 2009; Devlin et al., 2019; Liu et al., 2019).

To address the limitations of naive RAG, such as insufficient context and retrieval inaccuracies, advanced techniques have been developed, including hybrid retrieval methods, query rewriters, and rerankers to refine relevance (Muennighoff et al., 2022; Ding et al., 2024; Xiao et al., 2023). Hybrid retrieval combines BM25 with semantic embeddings to balance keyword matching and contextual understanding, improving outcomes (Luo et al., 2023; Ram et al., 2022; Arivazhagan et al., 2023). Additionally, knowledge graph retrieval and composed retrievers enhance accuracy and comprehensiveness in document retrieval (Rackauckas, 2024; Sanmartin, 2024; Edge et al., 2024).

Recently, RAG systems have advanced from basic retrieval to dynamic methods involving multi-source integration and domain adaptation (Gao et al., 2023; Ji et al., 2022). Innovations like Self-RAG and KG-RAG improve response quality and minimize hallucinations through adaptive retrieval and knowledge graphs (Asai et al., 2023; Sanmartin, 2024).

Various frameworks have been developed to evaluate RAG systems, including Ragas, which uses reference-free metrics like faithfulness and relevancy (Shahul et al., 2023b). Giskard (Giskard, 2023) assesses performance using synthetic QA datasets, while ARES utilizes prediction-powered inference (PPI) with specialized LLM judges for accurate evaluation (Giskard, 2023; Saad-Falcon et al., 2023).

3 System Design

The hybrid parameter-adaptive RAG system, depicted in Figure 1, integrates vector-based text chunks and a knowledge graph of entities and their relationships to enhance retrieval accuracy. The system employs a hybrid retrieval process, combining sparse (BM25) and dense (vector) methods to retrieve an initial top-k set of results. These results are refined using reciprocal rank fusion based on predefined parameter mappings.

Simultaneously, a knowledge graph retriever identifies relevant triplets, with retrieval depth and keyword selection dynamically adjusted according to query complexity. Results from both BM25 and vector methods are fused again to produce a final optimised set of k chunks.

Optional components include a query rewriter, which generates reformulated queries to improve retrieval. The rewritten queries fetch additional chunks, which are de-duplicated and fused to maintain uniqueness. An optional reranker can further refine chunk ranking if needed. The final set of selected chunks and knowledge graph triplets are then processed within the LLM's context window for more accurate, contextually relevant responses.

This framework is implemented in two variations: without knowledge graph retrieval, known as Parameter-Adaptive (PA) RAG, and with knowledge graph retrieval, termed Hybrid Parameter-Adaptive (HyPA) RAG.

4 AI Legal and Policy Corpus

Local Law 144 (LL144) of 2021, enacted by the New York City Department of Consumer and Worker Protection (DCWP), regulates automated employment decision tools (AEDTs). This paper uses a 15-page version of LL144 that combines the original law text with enforcement rules published by the DCWP. As an early AI-specific law, LL144 is included in the training data of foundational models like GPT-4 and GPT-4o, whose understanding of the law is confirmed manually through targeted prompting and serves as baselines in this research.

LL144 presents significant challenges for AI compliance due to its unique combination of qualitative and quantitative requirements. Unlike most AI legal and policy texts, which are predominantly qualitative, LL144 integrates detailed definitions and procedural guidelines with quantitative compliance metrics. This structure complicates interpretation and retrieval, often exceeding the capabilities of traditional LLMs and RAG systems. Furthermore, AI laws and policies are frequently revised while moving through the legislative process, making them impractical for pre-training and fine-tuning and therefore requiring a robust method for integrating changes.

5 Performance Evaluation

The evaluation process starts by generating custom questions tailored to AI policy and legal question-answering, then introduces and verifies evaluation metrics (see evaluation section of Figure 6 in Appendix A.2). **For reproducibility, the LLM temperature is set to zero for consistent responses and all other parameters are set to defaults.**

5.1 Dataset Generation

Creating a "gold standard" evaluation set usually requires extensive human expertise and time, but LLMs like GPT-3.5-Turbo can efficiently handle such tasks, if sufficiently prompted. For this purpose, Giskard (Giskard, 2023) provides a library for synthetic data generation, using LLMs to create various question types from text chunks, such as 'simple', 'complex', and 'situational'. We introduce additional types and question generators: 'comparative', 'complex situational', 'vague', and 'rule-conclusion'. Comparative questions require multi-context retrieval to compare concepts. 'Complex situational' questions involve user-specific contexts and follow-ups. Vague questions obscure parts of the query to test interpretation, while rule-conclusion questions, adapted from LegalBench (Guha et al., 2023), require conclusions based on legislative content. Table 4 in Appendix A.3 summarises these types with examples.

These question generators produce a set of questions, which are then deduplicated. Inaccurate or incomplete questions are identified through a human expert review process, using the criteria outlined in Table 5 in Appendix A.5.

5.2 Evaluation Metrics

To evaluate our RAG system, we utilise RAGAS metrics (Shahul et al., 2023a) based on the LLM-as-a-judge approach (Zheng et al., 2023), including Faithfulness, Answer Relevancy, Context Precision, Context Recall, and an adapted Correctness metric.

Faithfulness evaluates the factual consistency between the generated answer and the context, defined as Faithfulness Score $= \frac{|C_{\text{inferred}}|}{|C_{\text{total}}|}$, where C_{inferred} is the number of claims inferred from the context, and C_{total} is the total claims in the answer.

Answer Relevancy measures the alignment between the generated answer and the original question, calculated as the mean cosine similarity between the original question and generated questions from the answer: Answer Relevancy $= \frac{1}{N}\sum_{i=1}^{N}\frac{E_{g_i}\cdot E_o}{\|E_{g_i}\|\|E_o\|}$, where E_{g_i} and E_o are embeddings of the generated and original questions.

Context Recall measures the proportion of ground truth claims covered by the retrieved context, defined as Context Recall $= \frac{|C_{\text{attr}}|}{|C_{\text{GT}}|}$, where C_{attr} is the number of ground truth claims attributed to the context, and C_{GT} is the total number of ground truth claims.

Context Precision evaluates whether relevant items are ranked higher within the context, defined as Context Precision $= \frac{\sum_{k=1}^{K}(P_k \times v_k)}{|R_k|}$. Here, $P_k = \frac{TP_k}{TP_k + FP_k}$ is the precision at rank k, v_k is the relevance indicator, $|R_k|$ is the total relevant items in the top K, TP_k represents true positives, and FP_k false positives.

5.3 Correctness Evaluation

We assess correctness using a refined metric to address the limitations of Giskard's binary classification, which fails to account for partially correct answers or minor variations. Our adapted metric, **Absolute Correctness**, based on LLamaIndex (LlamaIndex, 2024), uses a 1 to 5 scale: 1 indicates an incorrect answer, 3 denotes partial correctness, and 5 signifies full correctness. For binary evaluation, we use a high threshold of 4, reflecting our low tolerance for inaccuracies. The

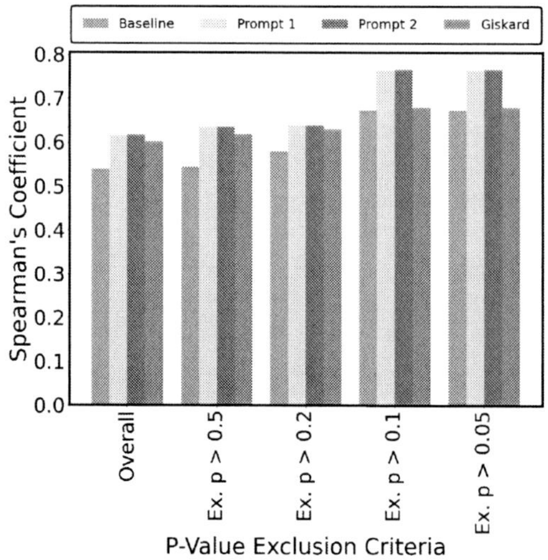

Figure 2: **Spearman Coefficient Comparison**, showing the correlation between model performance and human evaluation.

Correctness Score is computed as the average of these binary outcomes across all responses: Correctness Score $= \frac{1}{N}\sum_{i=1}^{N}\mathbb{1}(S_i \geq 4)$, where S_i represents the absolute correctness score of the ith response, $\mathbb{1}(S_i \geq 4)$ is an indicator function that is 1 if $S_i \geq 4$ and 0 otherwise, and N is the total number of responses.

The Spearman coefficient (Figure 2) illustrates how our prompt-based LLM-as-a-judge correctness evaluation aligns with human judgment. Prompts 1 and 2 (Appendix A.7) employ different methods: the baseline prompt provides general scoring guidelines, Prompt 1 offers detailed refinements, and Prompt 2 includes one-shot examples and guidance for edge cases.

Additional metrics, including macro precision, recall, F1 score, and percentage agreement with human labels, are shown in Figure 8 (Appendix A.8). A detailed breakdown of the Spearman coefficient metrics is provided in Figure 9 (Appendix A.8).

6 Chunking Method

We evaluate three chunking techniques: sentence-level, semantic, and pattern-based chunking.

Sentence-level chunking splits text at sentence boundaries, adhering to token limits and overlap constraints. Semantic chunking uses cosine similarity to set a dissimilarity threshold for splitting and includes a buffer size to define the minimum number of sentences before a split. Pattern-based

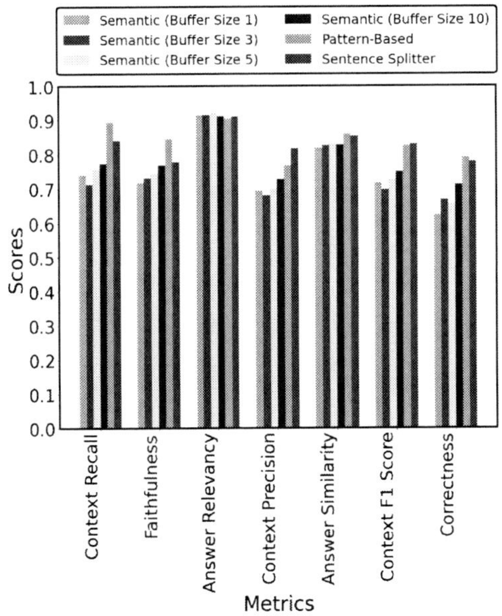

Figure 3: RAG Evaluation Metrics for Sentence-Level, Semantic, and Pattern-Based Chunking Methods

chunking employs a custom delimiter based on text structure; for LL144, this is "\n§".

Figure 3 shows that pattern-based chunking achieves the highest context recall (0.9046), faithfulness (0.8430), answer similarity (0.8621), and correctness (0.7918) scores. Sentence-level chunking, however, yields the highest context precision and F1 scores. Semantic chunking performs reasonably well with increased buffer size but generally underperforms compared to the simpler methods. Further hyperparameter tuning may improve its effectiveness. These findings suggest that a corpus-specific delimiter can enhance performance over standard chunking methods.

For subsequent experiments, we adopt sentence-level chunking with a default chunk size of 512 tokens and an overlap of 200 tokens.

7 Query Complexity Classifier

To enable adaptive parameter selection, we developed a domain-specific query complexity classifier that categorises user queries, each corresponding to specific hyper-parameter mappings. Our analysis of top-k selection indicated different optimal top-k values for various question types, as shown in Figure 7 (Appendix A.4).

Model	Precision	Recall	F1 Score
Random Labels	0.34	0.34	0.34
BART Large ZS	0.31	0.32	0.29
DeBERTa-v3 ZS	0.39	0.39	0.38
LR TF-IDF	0.84	0.84	0.84
SVM TF-IDF	0.86	0.86	0.86
distilBERT Finetuned	0.90	0.90	0.90

Table 1: 3-Class Classification Results

7.1 Training Data

To train a domain-specific query complexity classifier, we generated a dataset using a GPT-4o model on legal documents. Queries were categorised into three classes based on the number of contexts required: one context (0), two contexts (1), and three or more contexts (2). This classification resulted in varying token counts, keywords, and clauses across classes, which could bias models toward associating these features with complexity. To mitigate this, we applied data augmentation techniques to diversify the dataset. To enhance robustness, 67% of the queries were modified. We increased vagueness in 10% of the questions while preserving their informational content, added random noise words or punctuation to another 10%, and applied both word and punctuation noise to a further 10%. Additionally, 5% of questions had phrases reordered, and another 5% contained random spelling errors. For label-specific augmentation, 25% of label 0 queries were made more verbose, and 25% of label 2 queries were shortened, ensuring they retained the necessary informational content. The augmentation prompts are in Appendix A.9.

7.2 Model Training

We employed multiple models as baselines for classification tasks: Random labels, Logistic Regression (LR), Support Vector Machine (SVM), zero-shot classifiers, and a fine-tuned DistilBERT model. The Logistic Regression model used TF-IDF features, with a random state of 5 and 1000 iterations. The SVM model also used TF-IDF features with a linear kernel. Both models were evaluated on binary (2-class) and multi-class (3-class) tasks. Zero-shot classifiers (BART Large ZS and DeBERTa-v3 ZS) were included as additional baselines, mapping "simple question," "complex question," and "overview question" to labels 0, 1, and 2, respectively; for binary classification, only "simple question" (0) and "complex question" (1) were used. The DistilBERT model was fine-tuned with a learn-

Method	Faithfulness	Answer Relevancy	Absolute Correctness (1-5)	Correctness (Threshold=4.0)
LLM Only				
GPT-3.5-Turbo	0.2856	0.4350	2.6952	0.1973
GPT-4o-Mini	0.3463	0.6319	3.3494	0.4572
Fixed k				
$k = 3$	0.7748	0.7859	4.0372	0.7546
$k = 5$	0.8113	0.7836	4.0520	0.7584
$k = 7$	0.8215	0.7851	4.0520	0.7621
$k = 10$	0.8480	0.7917	4.0595	0.7658
Adaptive				
PA: k, Q (2 class)	**0.9044**	**0.7910**	4.2491	0.8104
PA: k, Q (3 class)	0.8971	0.7778	**4.2528**	**0.8141**
HyPA: k, Q, K, S (2 class)	0.8328	0.7800	4.0558	0.7770
HyPA: k, Q, K, S (3 class)	0.8465	0.7734	4.1338	0.7918

Table 2: Performance metrics for LLM Only, Fixed k, Parameter-Adaptive (PA), and Hybrid Parameter Adaptive (HyPA) RAG implementations for the 2 and 3-class classifier configurations. k is the top-k value, Q the number of query rewrites, S the maximum knowledge graph depth, and K the maximum keywords for knowledge graph retrieval.

ing rate of 2e-5, batch size of 32, 10 epochs, and a weight decay of 0.01 to optimize performance and generalization to the validation set.

7.3 Classifier Results

Tables 1 and 8 in Appendix A.10 summarise the classification results. We compare performance using macro precision, recall and F1 score. The fine-tuned DistilBERT model achieved the highest F1 scores, 0.90 for the 3-class task and 0.92 for the 2-class task, highlighting the benefits of transfer learning and fine-tuning. The SVM (TF-IDF) and Logistic Regression models also performed well, particularly in binary classification, indicating their effectiveness in handling sparse data. Zero-shot classifiers performed lower, likely due to the lack of task-specific fine-tuning.

8 RAG System Architecture

8.1 Parameter-Adaptive RAG (PA-RAG)

The Parameter-Adaptive RAG system integrates our fine-tuned DistilBERT model to classify query complexity and dynamically adjusts retrieval parameters accordingly, as illustrated in Figure 1, but excluding the knowledge graph component. The PA-RAG system adaptively selects the number of query rewrites (Q) and the top-k value based on the complexity classification, with specific parameter mappings provided in Table 6 in Appendix A.6.1. In the 2-class model, simpler queries (label 0) use a top-k of 5 and 3 query rewrites, while more complex queries (label 1) use a top-k of 10 and 5 rewrites. The 3-class model uses a top-k of 7 and 7 rewrites for the most complex queries (label 2).

8.2 Hybrid Parameter-Adaptive RAG

Building on the PA-RAG system, the Hybrid Parameter-Adaptive RAG (HyPA-RAG) approach enhances the retrieval stage by addressing issues such as missing content, incomplete answers, and failures of the language model to extract correct answers from retrieved contexts. These challenges often arise from unclear relationships within legal documents, where repeated terms lead to fragmented retrieval results (Barnett et al., 2024). Traditional (e.g. dense) retrieval methods may retrieve only partial context, causing missing critical information. To overcome these limitations, this system incorporates a knowledge graph (KG) representation of LL144. Knowledge graphs, structured with entities, relationships, and semantic descriptions, integrate information from multiple data sources (Hogan et al., 2020; Ji et al., 2020), and recent advancements suggest that combining KGs with LLMs can produce more informed outputs using KG triplets as added context.

The HyPA-RAG system uses the architecture outlined in Figure 1. The knowledge graph is constructed by extracting triplets (subject, predicate, object) from raw text using GPT-4o. Parameter mappings specific to this implementation, such as the maximum number of keywords per query (K) and maximum knowledge sequence length (S), are detailed in Table 7, extending those provided in Table 6.

8.3 RAG Results

The adaptive methods generally outperform the fixed k baseline across most metrics (Table 2). PA-RAG with k, Q (2 class) achieves the highest faithfulness score of 0.9044, which is an improvement of 0.0564 over the best fixed $k = 10$ method (0.8480). Similarly, the PA k, Q (3 class) configuration also performs strongly with a faithfulness score of 0.8971, surpassing all fixed k methods.

For answer relevancy, the PA k, Q (2 class) model achieves a score of 0.7910, which is nearly on par with the best fixed $k = 10$ method at 0.7917, showing a slight difference of 0.0007. The PA k, Q (3 class) model has a relevancy score of 0.7778, a drop of 0.0139 compared to the best fixed method.

In terms of absolute correctness, both PA models, k, Q (2 class) and k, Q (3 class), achieve scores of 4.2491 and 4.2528, respectively, which are improvements of approximately 0.1896 and 0.1933 over the best fixed method ($k = 10$) score of 4.0595. This suggests that adaptive parameter settings significantly enhance the model's ability to provide correct answers.

Correctness scores also favour the adaptive methods. PA k, Q (3 class) model reaches a score of 0.8141, which is 0.0483 higher than the best fixed $k = 10$ score of 0.7658. PA k, Q (2 class) model shows similar strength with a score of 0.8104. HyPA show more varied results. HyPA k, Q, K, S (2 class) achieves a correctness score of 0.7770, a modest increase of 0.0112 over the fixed $k = 7$, suggesting that there is room for further optimisation.

8.4 System Ablation Study

We evaluate the impact of adaptive parameters, a reranker (bge-reranker-large), and a query rewriter on model performance using PA and HyPA RAG methods with 2-class (Table 9 in Appendix A.11) and 3-class classifiers (Table 3).

The highest Answer Relevancy (0.7940) is achieved by varying k alone, suggesting that simpler, focused responses facilitate question reconstruction. The k, Q + reranker configuration achieves a slightly lower relevancy score (0.7902), indicating that query rewriting and reranking, while enhancing other metrics, introduce complexity that marginally reduces clarity.

The k, Q + reranker configuration also achieves the highest Faithfulness (0.9098), showing that combining adaptive top-k selection with query rewriting and reranking improves factual consistency. This setup provides high Absolute Correctness (4.2342), although slightly lower than k, Q alone (4.2528), indicating that while reranking improves response quality, it may slightly decrease overall accuracy. However, the Correctness Score improves from 0.8141 to 0.8178, highlighting an increase in responses classified as "correct" (scores of 4 or higher).

Adding a knowledge graph in the k, K, S configuration maintains the same Correctness Score (0.8141) as k, Q but reduces Absolute Correctness by 0.1301, suggesting added complexity might lower overall answer quality.

While the k, K, S, Q + reranker configuration does not lead in Faithfulness, Answer Relevancy, or Absolute Correctness, it achieves the highest Correctness Score (0.8402), outperforming k, Q + reranker by 0.0224, demonstrating the effectiveness of adaptive parameters and reranking in meeting the correctness threshold.

9 Overall Results and Discussion

Our analysis shows that adaptive methods generally outperform fixed baselines, particularly in improving faithfulness and answer quality. Incorporating adaptive parameters such as query rewrites and reranking enhances the system's ability to provide accurate and relevant responses. While adding a reranker improves correctness, it can slightly reduce the overall correctness score, suggesting a trade-off between precision and answer quality.

The introduction of a knowledge graph maintains correctness but can add complexity, potentially lowering overall response quality. However, combining adaptive parameters with a reranker proves effective in maximizing the proportion of correct responses, even if it doesn't lead to the highest scores in all metrics.

Overall, these findings highlight the importance of adaptivity and careful parameter tuning to balance different performance aspects, enhancing the system's capability to handle varied and complex queries effectively.

Method	Faithfulness	Answer Relevancy	Absolute Correctness (1-5)	Correctness (Threshold=4.0)
k	0.7723	**0.7940**	4.0409	0.7621
k, Q	<u>0.8971</u>	0.7778	**4.2528**	0.8141
k, Q + reranker	**0.9098**	<u>0.7902</u>	<u>4.2342</u>	<u>0.8178</u>
k, K^*, S^*	0.8733	0.7635	4.1227	0.8141
k, K, S	0.8660	0.7780	4.1822	0.8030
k, K, S + reranker	0.8821	0.7872	4.1858	<u>0.8178</u>
k, K, S, Q	0.8465	0.7734	4.1338	0.7918
k, K, S, Q + reranker	0.8689	0.7853	4.1859	**0.8402**

Table 3: Ablation study results for different configurations of adaptive k in a 3-class setting. For descriptions of parameters, refer to Table 2. The highest value in each column is highlighted in bold, and the second highest value is underlined. The * indicates parameters held fixed, rather than adaptive.

10 Limitations and Future Work

This study has several limitations that suggest areas for future improvement. Correctness evaluation is limited by reliance on a single evaluator familiar with the policy corpus. Averaging a larger quantity of human evaluations would improve reliability. Additionally, our knowledge graph construction process may be improved. For instance, using LLM-based methods for de-duplication and/or custom Cypher query generation to improve context retrieval and precision. Furthermore, our parameter mappings were not rigourously validated quantitatively. Further evaluation of parameter selections could provide better mappings as well as upper and lower bounds to performance. The classifier was trained using domain-specific synthetically generated data - which, though we inject significant noise, may harbour the LLM's own unconcious biases in terms of structure - possibly limiting the generalisability of the classifier on unseen user queries. Also, more classification categories e.g. 4 or 5-class, would permit more granular parameter selections and potentially greater efficiency improvements. Another limitation is that while LL144 is included in the GPT models' training data, subsequent minor revisions may affect the accuracy of these baseline methods.

Integrating human feedback into the evaluation loop (see Figure 4) could better align metrics with user preferences and validate performance metrics in real-world settings. Future work should also consider fine-tuning the LLM using techniques like RLHF (Bai et al., 2022), RLAIF (Lee et al., 2023), or other preference optimisation methods (Song et al., 2023). Further, refining the query rewriter (Ma et al., 2023; Mao et al., 2024) and exploring iterative answer refinement (Asai et al., 2023) could enhance metrics like relevancy and correctness.

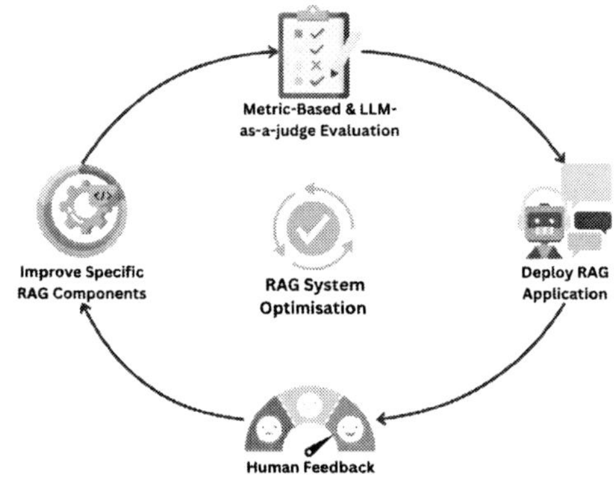

Figure 4: RAG System Optimisation Feedback Loop

11 Ethical and Societal implications

The deployment of the Hybrid Parameter-Adaptive RAG (HyPA-RAG) system in AI legal and policy contexts raises critical ethical and societal concerns, particularly regarding the accuracy, reliability, and potential misinterpretation of AI-generated responses. The high-stakes nature of legal information means inaccuracies could have significant consequences, highlighting the necessity for careful evaluation. We emphasize transparency and reproducibility, providing detailed documentation of data generation, retrieval methods, and evaluation metrics to facilitate replication and scrutiny. The environmental impact of NLP models is also a concern. Our system employs adaptive retrieval strategies to optimize computational efficiency, reduce energy consumption, and minimize carbon footprint, promoting sustainable AI development.

Our findings enhance the understanding of RAG systems in legal contexts but are intended for research purposes only. HyPA-RAG outputs should not be used for legal advice or decision-making, emphasizing the need for domain expertise and oversight in applying AI to sensitive legal domains.

12 Acknowledgments

We would like to express our sincere gratitude to Holistic AI for their invaluable research and financial support, which made this project possible. Our deepest appreciation also goes to the Center for Artificial Intelligence at University College London for their continuous encouragement and assistance. Without their collaboration and resources, this work would not have been achievable.

References

Manoj Ghuhan Arivazhagan, Lan Liu, Peng Qi, Xinchi Chen, William Yang Wang, and Zhiheng Huang. 2023. Hybrid hierarchical retrieval for open-domain question answering. In *Findings of the Association for Computational Linguistics: ACL 2023*.

Akari Asai, Zeqiu Wu, Yizhong Wang, Avirup Sil, and Hannaneh Hajishirzi. 2023. Self-rag: Learning to retrieve, generate, and critique through self-reflection. *ArXiv*.

Yuntao Bai, Andy Jones, Kamal Ndousse, Amanda Askell, Anna Chen, Nova Dassarma, Dawn Drain, Stanislav Fort, Deep Ganguli, Tom Henighan, Nicholas Joseph, Saurav Kadavath, John Kernion, Tom Conerly, Sheer El-Showk, Nelson Elhage, Zac Hatfield-Dodds, Danny Hernandez, Tristan Hume, Scott Johnston, Shauna Kravec, Liane Lovitt, Neel Nanda, Catherine Olsson, Dario Amodei, Tom B. Brown, Jack Clark, Sam McCandlish, Christopher Olah, Benjamin Mann, and Jared Kaplan. 2022. Training a helpful and harmless assistant with reinforcement learning from human feedback. *ArXiv*, abs/2204.05862.

Scott Barnett, Stefanus Kurniawan, Srikanth Thudumu, Zach Brannelly, and Mohamed Abdelrazek. 2024. Seven failure points when engineering a retrieval augmented generation system. *2024 IEEE/ACM 3rd International Conference on AI Engineering – Software Engineering for AI (CAIN)*, pages 194–199.

Andrew Blair-Stanek, Nils Holzenberger, and Benjamin Van Durme. 2023. Can gpt-3 perform statutory reasoning? *Proceedings of the Nineteenth International Conference on Artificial Intelligence and Law*.

Tom B. Brown, Benjamin Mann, Nick Ryder, Melanie Subbiah, Jared Kaplan, Prafulla Dhariwal, Arvind Neelakantan, Pranav Shyam, Girish Sastry, Amanda Askell, Sandhini Agarwal, Ariel Herbert-Voss, Gretchen Krueger, Tom Henighan, Rewon Child, Aditya Ramesh, Daniel M. Ziegler, Jeff Wu, Clemens Winter, Christopher Hesse, Mark Chen, Eric Sigler, Mateusz Litwin, Scott Gray, Benjamin Chess, Jack Clark, Christopher Berner, Sam McCandlish, Alec Radford, Ilya Sutskever, and Dario Amodei. 2020. Language models are few-shot learners. *ArXiv*, abs/2005.14165.

Business Insider. 2023. Michael cohen used ai chatbot to find bogus legal cases. Accessed: 2024-06-10.

Jonathan H. Choi, Kristin E. Hickman, Amy B. Monahan, and Daniel Benjamin Schwarcz. 2023. Chatgpt goes to law school. *SSRN Electronic Journal*.

Jiaxi Cui, Zongjia Li, Yang Yan, Bohua Chen, and Li Yuan. 2023. Chatlaw: A multi-agent collaborative legal assistant with knowledge graph enhanced mixture-of-experts large language model.

Jacob Devlin, Ming-Wei Chang, Kenton Lee, and Kristina Toutanova. 2019. Bert: Pre-training of deep bidirectional transformers for language understanding. In *North American Chapter of the Association for Computational Linguistics*.

Dujian Ding, Ankur Mallick, Chi Wang, Robert Sim, Subhabrata Mukherjee, Victor Rühle, Laks V. S. Lakshmanan, and Ahmed Hassan Awadallah. 2024. Hybrid llm: Cost-efficient and quality-aware query routing. *ArXiv*, abs/2404.14618.

Darren Edge, Ha Trinh, Newman Cheng, Joshua Bradley, Alex Chao, Apurva Mody, Steven Truitt, and Jonathan Larson. 2024. From local to global: A graph rag approach to query-focused summarization. *ArXiv*, abs/2404.16130.

Fortune. 2023. Lawyers fined for filing chatgpt hallucinations in court. Accessed: 2024-06-10.

Yunfan Gao, Yun Xiong, Xinyu Gao, Kangxiang Jia, Jinliu Pan, Yuxi Bi, Yi Dai, Jiawei Sun, Qianyu Guo, Meng Wang, and Haofen Wang. 2023. Retrieval-augmented generation for large language models: A survey. *ArXiv*, abs/2312.10997.

Giskard. 2023. Giskard: Automated quality manager for llms. `https://www.giskard.ai/`. Accessed: 2024-08-19.

Neel Guha, Julian Nyarko, Daniel E. Ho, Christopher Ré, Adam Chilton, Aditya Narayana, Alex Chohlas-Wood, Austin M. K. Peters, Brandon Waldon, Daniel N. Rockmore, Diego A. Zambrano, Dmitry Talisman, Enam Hoque, Faiz Surani, Frank Fagan, Galit Sarfaty, Gregory M. Dickinson, Haggai Porat, Jason Hegland, Jessica Wu, Joe Nudell, Joel Niklaus, John J. Nay, Jonathan H. Choi, Kevin Patrick Tobia, Margaret Hagan, Megan Ma, Michael A. Livermore, Nikon Rasumov-Rahe, Nils Holzenberger, Noam Kolt, Peter Henderson, Sean Rehaag, Sharad Goel, Shangsheng Gao, Spencer Williams, Sunny G. Gandhi, Tomer Zur, Varun J. Iyer, and Zehua Li. 2023. Legalbench: A collaboratively built benchmark for measuring legal reasoning in large language models. *ArXiv*, abs/2308.11462.

Stuart Hargreaves. 2023. 'words are flowing out like endless rain into a paper cup': Chatgpt & law school assessments. *SSRN Electronic Journal*.

Aidan Hogan, Eva Blomqvist, Michael Cochez, Claudia d'Amato, Gerard de Melo, Claudio Gutierrez, José Emilio Labra Gayo, S. Kirrane, Sebastian Neumaier, Axel Polleres, Roberto Navigli, Axel-Cyrille Ngonga Ngomo, Sabbir M. Rashid, Anisa Rula, Lukas Schmelzeisen, Juan Sequeda, Steffen Staab, and Antoine Zimmermann. 2020. Knowledge graphs. *ACM Computing Surveys (CSUR)*, 54:1 – 37.

Lei Huang, Weijiang Yu, Weitao Ma, Weihong Zhong, Zhangyin Feng, Haotian Wang, Qianglong Chen, Weihua Peng, Xiaocheng Feng, Bing Qin, and Ting Liu. 2023. A survey on hallucination in large language models: Principles, taxonomy, challenges, and open questions. *ArXiv*, abs/2311.05232.

Shaoxiong Ji, Shirui Pan, E. Cambria, Pekka Marttinen, and Philip S. Yu. 2020. A survey on knowledge graphs: Representation, acquisition, and applications. *IEEE Transactions on Neural Networks and Learning Systems*, 33:494–514.

Ziwei Ji, Nayeon Lee, Rita Frieske, Tiezheng Yu, Dan Su, Yan Xu, Etsuko Ishii, Yejin Bang, Delong Chen, Wenliang Dai, Andrea Madotto, and Pascale Fung. 2022. Survey of hallucination in natural language generation. *ACM Computing Surveys*, 55:1 – 38.

Karen Spärck Jones. 2021. A statistical interpretation of term specificity and its application in retrieval. *J. Documentation*, 60:493–502.

Harrison Lee, Samrat Phatale, Hassan Mansoor, Kellie Lu, Thomas Mesnard, Colton Bishop, Victor Carbune, and Abhinav Rastogi. 2023. Rlaif: Scaling reinforcement learning from human feedback with ai feedback. *ArXiv*, abs/2309.00267.

Patrick Lewis, Ethan Perez, Aleksandara Piktus, Fabio Petroni, Vladimir Karpukhin, Naman Goyal, Heinrich Kuttler, Mike Lewis, Wen tau Yih, Tim Rocktäschel, Sebastian Riedel, and Douwe Kiela. 2020. Retrieval-augmented generation for knowledge-intensive nlp tasks. *ArXiv*, abs/2005.11401.

Yinhan Liu, Myle Ott, Naman Goyal, Jingfei Du, Mandar Joshi, Danqi Chen, Omer Levy, Mike Lewis, Luke Zettlemoyer, and Veselin Stoyanov. 2019. Roberta: A robustly optimized bert pretraining approach. *ArXiv*, abs/1907.11692.

LlamaIndex. 2024. Llamaindex. Accessed: August 19, 2024.

Man Luo, Shashank Jain, Anchit Gupta, Arash Einolghozati, Barlas Oguz, Debojeet Chatterjee, Xilun Chen, Chitta Baral, and Peyman Heidari. 2023. A study on the efficiency and generalization of light hybrid retrievers. *ArXiv*, abs/2210.01371.

Xinbei Ma, Yeyun Gong, Pengcheng He, Hai Zhao, and Nan Duan. 2023. Query rewriting for retrieval-augmented large language models. *ArXiv*, abs/2305.14283.

Varun Magesh, Faiz Surani, Matthew Dahl, Mirac Suzgun, Christopher D. Manning, and Daniel E. Ho. 2024. Hallucination-free? assessing the reliability of leading ai legal research tools.

Shengyu Mao, Yong Jiang, Boli Chen, Xiao Li, Peng Wang, Xinyu Wang, Pengjun Xie, Fei Huang, Huajun Chen, and Ningyu Zhang. 2024. Rafe: Ranking feedback improves query rewriting for rag. *ArXiv*, abs/2405.14431.

Meta. 2024. The llama 3 herd of models.

Niklas Muennighoff, Nouamane Tazi, Loïc Magne, and Nils Reimers. 2022. Mteb: Massive text embedding benchmark. *arXiv preprint arXiv:2210.07316*.

OpenAI. 2023. Gpt-4 technical report.

Zackary Rackauckas. 2024. Rag-fusion: a new take on retrieval-augmented generation. *ArXiv*, abs/2402.03367.

Ori Ram, Gal Shachaf, Omer Levy, Jonathan Berant, and Amir Globerson. 2022. Learning to retrieve passages without supervision. In *Proceedings of the 2022 Conference of the North American Chapter of the Association for Computational Linguistics: Human Language Technologies*.

Stephen E. Robertson and Hugo Zaragoza. 2009. The probabilistic relevance framework: Bm25 and beyond. *Found. Trends Inf. Retr.*, 3:333–389.

Jon Saad-Falcon, O. Khattab, Christopher Potts, and Matei Zaharia. 2023. Ares: An automated evaluation framework for retrieval-augmented generation systems. *ArXiv*, abs/2311.09476.

Diego Sanmartin. 2024. Kg-rag: Bridging the gap between knowledge and creativity. *ArXiv*, abs/2405.12035.

Jaromír Šavelka and Kevin D. Ashley. 2023. The unreasonable effectiveness of large language models in zero-shot semantic annotation of legal texts. *Frontiers in Artificial Intelligence*, 6.

ES Shahul, Jithin James, Luis Espinosa Anke, and S. Schockaert. 2023a. Ragas: Automated evaluation of retrieval augmented generation. *ArXiv*.

ES Shahul, Jithin James, Luis Espinosa Anke, and Steven Schockaert. 2023b. Ragas: Automated evaluation of retrieval augmented generation. In *Conference of the European Chapter of the Association for Computational Linguistics*.

Ruihao Shui, Yixin Cao, Xiang Wang, and Tat-Seng Chua. 2023. A comprehensive evaluation of large language models on legal judgment prediction. *ArXiv*, abs/2310.11761:7337–7348.

K. Singhal, Tao Tu, Juraj Gottweis, Rory Sayres, Ellery Wulczyn, Le Hou, Kevin Clark, Stephen R. Pfohl, Heather J. Cole-Lewis, Darlene Neal, Mike Schaekermann, Amy Wang, Mohamed Amin, S. Lachgar, P. A. Mansfield, Sushant Prakash, Bradley Green, Ewa Dominowska, Blaise Agüera y Arcas, Nenad Tomašev, Yun Liu, Renee C. Wong, Christopher Semturs, Seyedeh Sara Mahdavi, Joëlle K. Barral, Dale R. Webster, Greg S. Corrado, Yossi Matias, Shekoofeh Azizi, Alan Karthikesalingam, and Vivek Natarajan. 2023. Towards expert-level medical question answering with large language models. *ArXiv*, abs/2305.09617.

Feifan Song, Yu Bowen, Minghao Li, Haiyang Yu, Fei Huang, Yongbin Li, and Houfeng Wang. 2023. Preference ranking optimization for human alignment. *ArXiv*, abs/2306.17492.

ZhongXiang Sun. 2023. A short survey of viewing large language models in legal aspect. *ArXiv*, abs/2303.09136.

Gemini Team, Rohan Anil, Sebastian Borgeaud, Yonghui Wu, Jean-Baptiste Alayrac, Jiahui Yu, Radu Soricut, Johan Schalkwyk, Andrew M Dai, Anja Hauth, et al. 2023. Gemini: a family of highly capable multimodal models.

Hugo Touvron, Thibaut Lavril, Gautier Izacard, Xavier Martinet, Marie-Anne Lachaux, Timothée Lacroix, Baptiste Rozière, Naman Goyal, Eric Hambro, Faisal Azhar, Aurelien Rodriguez, Armand Joulin, Edouard Grave, and Guillaume Lample. 2023a. Llama: Open and efficient foundation language models. *ArXiv*, abs/2302.13971.

Hugo Touvron, Louis Martin, Kevin R. Stone, Peter Albert, Amjad Almahairi, Yasmine Babaei, Nikolay Bashlykov, Soumya Batra, Prajjwal Bhargava, Shruti Bhosale, Daniel M. Bikel, Lukas Blecher, Cristian Cantón Ferrer, Moya Chen, Guillem Cucurull, David Esiobu, Jude Fernandes, Jeremy Fu, Wenyin Fu, Brian Fuller, Cynthia Gao, Vedanuj Goswami, Naman Goyal, Anthony S. Hartshorn, Saghar Hosseini, Rui Hou, Hakan Inan, Marcin Kardas, Viktor Kerkez, Madian Khabsa, Isabel M. Kloumann, A. V. Korenev, Punit Singh Koura, Marie-Anne Lachaux, Thibaut Lavril, Jenya Lee, Diana Liskovich, Yinghai Lu, Yuning Mao, Xavier Martinet, Todor Mihaylov, Pushkar Mishra, Igor Molybog, Yixin Nie, Andrew Poulton, Jeremy Reizenstein, Rashi Rungta, Kalyan Saladi, Alan Schelten, Ruan Silva, Eric Michael Smith, R. Subramanian, Xia Tan, Binh Tang, Ross Taylor, Adina Williams, Jian Xiang Kuan, Puxin Xu, Zhengxu Yan, Iliyan Zarov, Yuchen Zhang, Angela Fan, Melanie Kambadur, Sharan Narang, Aurelien Rodriguez, Robert Stojnic, Sergey Edunov, and Thomas Scialom. 2023b. Llama 2: Open foundation and fine-tuned chat models. *ArXiv*, abs/2307.09288.

Dietrich Trautmann, Alina Petrova, and Frank Schilder. 2022. Legal prompt engineering for multilingual legal judgement prediction. *ArXiv*, abs/2212.02199.

Shijie Wu, Ozan Irsoy, Steven Lu, Vadim Dabravolski, Mark Dredze, Sebastian Gehrmann, Prabhanjan Kambadur, David Rosenberg, and Gideon Mann. 2023. Bloomberggpt: A large language model for finance. *ArXiv*, abs/2303.17564.

Shitao Xiao, Zheng Liu, Peitian Zhang, and Niklas Muennighoff. 2023. C-pack: Packaged resources to advance general chinese embedding. *Preprint*, arXiv:2309.07597.

Jingfeng Yang, Hongye Jin, Ruixiang Tang, Xiaotian Han, Qizhang Feng, Haoming Jiang, Bing Yin, and Xia Hu. 2023. Harnessing the power of llms in practice: A survey on chatgpt and beyond. *ACM Transactions on Knowledge Discovery from Data*, 18:1 – 32.

Lianmin Zheng, Wei-Lin Chiang, Ying Sheng, Siyuan Zhuang, Zhanghao Wu, Yonghao Zhuang, Zi Lin, Zhuohan Li, Dacheng Li, Eric P. Xing, Haotong Zhang, Joseph Gonzalez, and Ion Stoica. 2023. Judging llm-as-a-judge with mt-bench and chatbot arena. *ArXiv*, abs/2306.05685.

A Appendix

A.1 RAG Demonstration User Interface

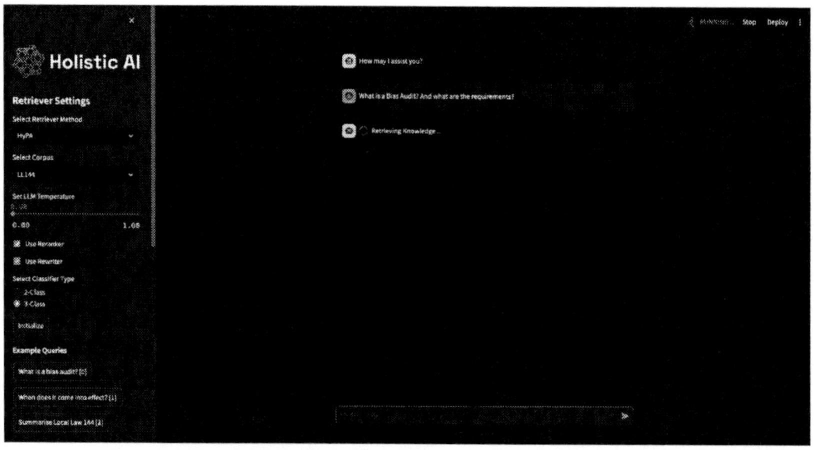

(a) Demo Screenshot: Entering the user query and generating a response.

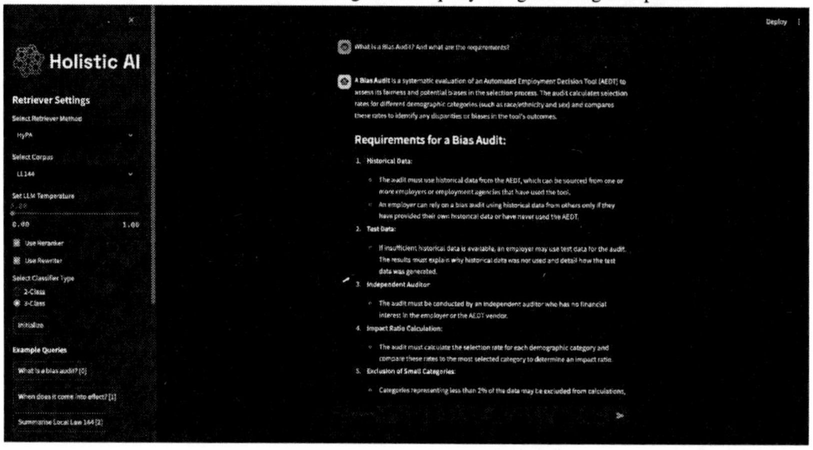

(b) Demo Screenshot: The generated response.

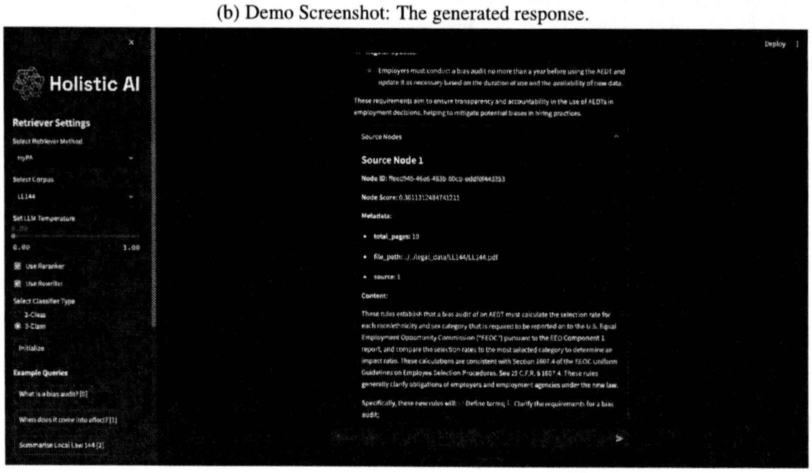

(c) Demo Screenshot: Information on retrieved node metadata and content.

Figure 5: Demo screenshots showing each key stage of the user experience.

A.2 Overall Workflow Diagram

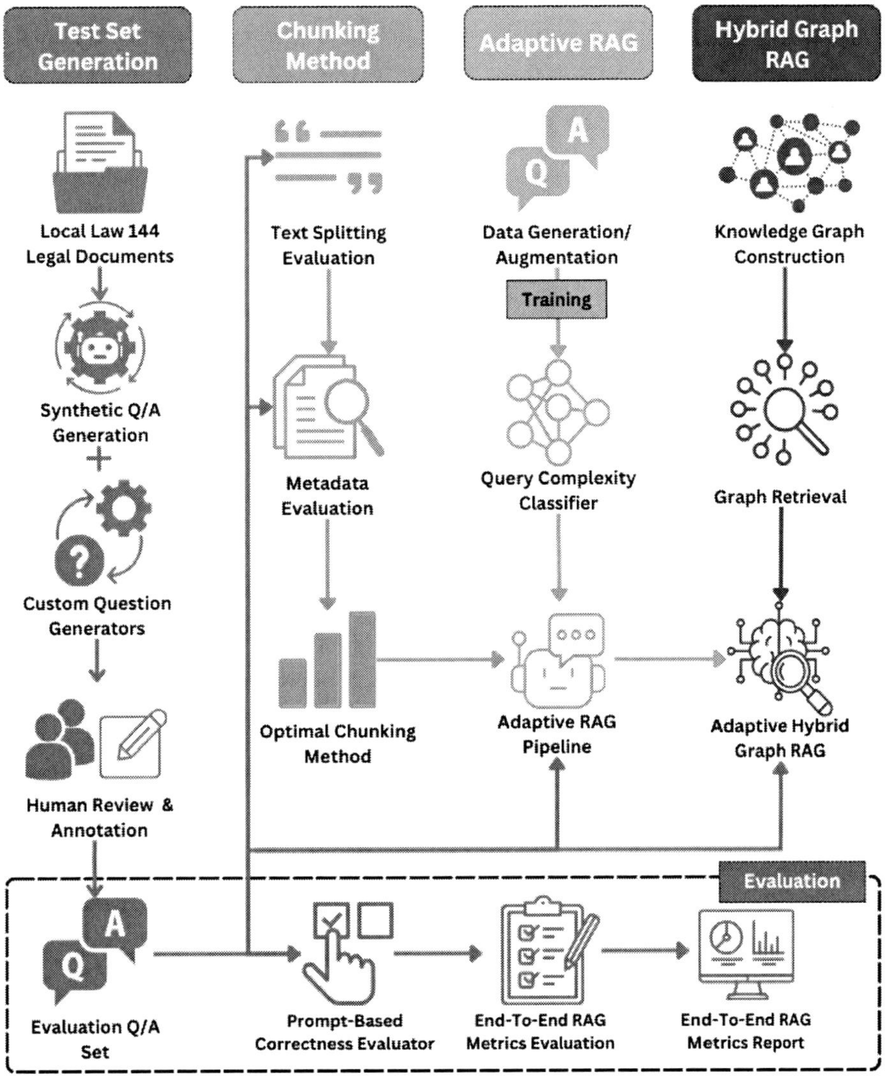

Figure 6: Overall RAG Development Workflow Diagram

A.3 Question Types

Question Type	Description	Example Question	Target RAG Components
Simple	Requires retrieval of one concept from the context	What is a bias audit?	Generator, Retriever, Router
Complex	More detailed and requires more specific retrieval	What is the purpose of a bias audit for automated employment decision tools?	Generator, Retriever
Distracting	Includes an irrelevant distracting element	Italy is beautiful but what is a bias audit?	Generator, Retriever, Rewriter
Situational	Includes user context to produce relevant answers	As an employer, what information do I need to provide before using an AEDT?	Generator
Double	Two distinct parts to evaluate query rewriter	What are the requirements for a bias audit of an AEDT and what changes were made in the second version of the proposed rules?	Generator, Rewriter
Conversational	Part of a conversation with context provided in a previous message	(1) I would like to know about bias audits. (2) What is it?	Rewriter
Complex situational	Introduces further context and one or more follow-up questions within the same message	In case I need to recover a civil penalty, what are the specific agencies within the office of administrative trials and hearings where the proceeding can be returned to? Also, are there other courts where such a proceeding can be initiated?	Generator
Out of scope	Non-answerable question that should be rejected	Who developed the AEDT software?	Generator, Prompt
Vague	A vague question that lacks complete information to answer fully	What calculations are required?	Generator, Rewriter
Comparative	Encourages comparison and identifying relationships	What are the differences and similarities between 'selection rate' and 'scoring rate', and how do they relate to each other?	Generator, Rewriter
Rule conclusion	Provides a scenario, requiring a legal conclusion	An employer uses an AEDT to screen candidates for a job opening. Is the selection rate calculated based on the number of candidates who applied for the position or the number of candidates who were screened by the AEDT?	Generator, Rewriter

Table 4: Question types and their descriptions with targeted RAG components.

A.4 Evaluation Results for Varied Top-k

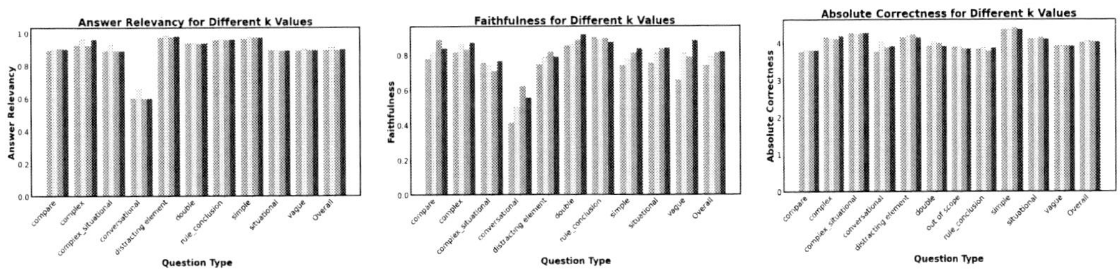

Figure 7: RAG Evaluation Metrics for Varied Top-k

A.5 Human Annotation Criteria

No.	Criterion	Description
1	**Faithfulness**	Are all claims in the answer inferred from the context?
2	**Answer Relevancy**	Is the answer relevant to the question?
3	**Context Relevancy**	Is the context relevant to the question?
4	**Correctness**	Is the answer correct, given the context?
5	**Clarity**	Is the answer clear and free of extensive jargon?
6	**Completeness**	Does the answer fully address all parts and sub-questions?

Table 5: Criteria for evaluating the quality of QA pairs.

A.6 Parameter Mappings

A.6.1 Top-k (k) and Number of Query Rewrites (Q)

Parameter	Symbol	Description	2-Class Mappings	3-Class Mappings
Number of Query Rewrites	Q	Number of sub-queries generated for the original query	0: $Q = 3$ 1: $Q = 5$	0: $Q = 3$ 1: $Q = 5$ 2: $Q = 7$
Top-k Value	k	Number of top documents or contexts retrieved for processing	0: $k = 5$ 1: $k = 10$	0: $k = 3$ 1: $k = 5$ 2: $k = 7$

Table 6: Parameter Symbols, Descriptions, and Mappings

A.6.2 Maximum Keywords (K) and Maximum Sequence Length (S)

Parameter	Symbol	Description	2-Class Mappings	3-Class Mappings
Max Keywords per Query	K	Maximum number of keywords used per query for KG retrieval	0: $K = 4$	0: $K = 3$
			1: $K = 5$	1: $K = 4$
				2: $K = 5$
Max Knowledge Sequence	S	Maximum sequence length for knowledge graph paths	0: $S = 2$	0: $S = 1$
			1: $S = 3$	1: $S = 2$
				2: $S = 3$

Table 7: Parameter Symbols, Descriptions, and Mappings (Part 2)

A.7 Correctness Evaluator Prompts

A.7.1 Method 1: LLamaIndex CorrectnessEvaluator

You are an expert evaluation system for a question answering

chatbot. You are given the following information:

- a user query,
- a reference answer, and
- a generated answer.

Your job is to judge the relevance and correctness of the generated answer. Output a single score that represents a holistic evaluation. You must return your response in a line with only the score. Do not return answers in any other format. On a separate line, provide your reasoning for the score as well.

Follow these guidelines for scoring:

- Your score has to be between 1 and 5, where 1 is the worst and 5 is the best.
- If the generated answer is not relevant to the user query, give a score of 1.
- If the generated answer is relevant but contains mistakes, give a score between 2 and 3.
- If the generated answer is relevant and fully correct, give a score between 4 and 5.

A.7.2 Method 2: Custom Prompt 1

You are an expert evaluation system for a question answering

chatbot. You are given the following information:

- a user query,
- a reference answer, and
- a generated answer.

Your job is to judge the correctness of the generated answer. Output a single score that represents a holistic evaluation. You must return your response in a line with only the score. Do not return answers in any other format. On a separate line, provide your reasoning for the score as well.

Follow these guidelines for scoring:

- Your score has to be between 1 and 5, where 1 is the worst and 5 is the best.
- Use the following criteria for scoring correctness:

1. Score of 1:
   - The generated answer is completely incorrect.
   - Contains major factual errors or misconceptions.
   - Does not address any components of the user query correctly.
2. Score of 2:
   - The generated answer has significant mistakes.
   - Addresses at least one component of the user query correctly but has major errors in other parts.
3. Score of 3:
   - The generated answer is partially correct.
   - Addresses multiple components of the user query correctly but includes some incorrect information.
   - Minor factual errors are present.
4. Score of 4:
   - The generated answer is mostly correct.
   - Correctly addresses all components of the user query with minimal errors.
   - Errors do not substantially affect the overall correctness.
5. Score of 5:
   - The generated answer is completely correct.
   - Addresses all components of the user query correctly without any errors.
   - The answer is factually accurate and aligns perfectly with the reference answer.

A.7.3 Method 3: Custom Prompt 2

You are an expert evaluation system for a question answering

chatbot. You are given the following information:

- a user query,
- a reference answer, and
- a generated answer.

Your job is to judge the correctness of the generated answer. Output a single score that represents a holistic evaluation. You must return your response in a line with only the score. Do not return answers in any other format. On a separate line, provide your reasoning for the score as well. The reasoning must not exceed one sentence.

Follow these guidelines for scoring:

- Your score has to be between 1 and 5, where 1 is the worst and 5 is the best.
- Use the following criteria for scoring correctness:

1. Score of 1:
   - The generated answer is completely incorrect.
   - Contains major factual errors or misconceptions.
   - Does not address any components of the user query correctly.

- Example:
  Query: "What is the capital of France?"
  Generated Answer: "The capital of France is Berlin."

2. Score of 2:
   - Significant mistakes are present.
   - Addresses at least one component of the user query correctly but has major errors in other parts.
   - Example:
     Query: "What is the capital of France and its population?"
     Generated Answer: "The capital of France is Paris, and its population is 100 million."

3. Score of 3:
   - Partially correct with some incorrect information.
   - Addresses multiple components of the user query correctly.
   - Minor factual errors are present.
   - Example:
     Query: "What is the capital of France and its population?"
     Generated Answer: "The capital of France is Paris, and its population is around 3 million."

4. Score of 4:
   - Mostly correct with minimal errors.
   - Correctly addresses all components of the user query.
   - Errors do not substantially affect the overall correctness.
   - Example:
     Query: "What is the capital of France and its population?"
     Generated Answer: "The capital of France is Paris, and its population is approximately 2.1 million."

5. Score of 5:
   - Completely correct.
   - Addresses all components of the user query correctly without any errors.
   - Providing more information than necessary should not be penalized as long as all provided information is correct.
   - Example:
     Query: "What is the capital of France and its population?"
     Generated Answer: "The capital of France is Paris, and its population is approximately 2.1 million. Paris is known for its rich history and iconic landmarks such as the Eiffel Tower and Notre-Dame Cathedral."

Checklist for Evaluation:

- Component Coverage: Does the answer cover all parts of the query?
- Factual Accuracy: Are the facts presented in the answer correct?
- Error Severity: How severe are any errors present in the answer?
- Comparison to Reference: How closely does the answer align with the reference answer?

Edge Cases:

- If the answer includes both correct and completely irrelevant information, focus only on the relevant portions for scoring.
- If the answer is correct but incomplete, score based on the completeness criteria within the relevant score range.
- If the answer provides more information than necessary, it should not be penalized as long as all information is correct.

A.8 Correctness Evaluator Results

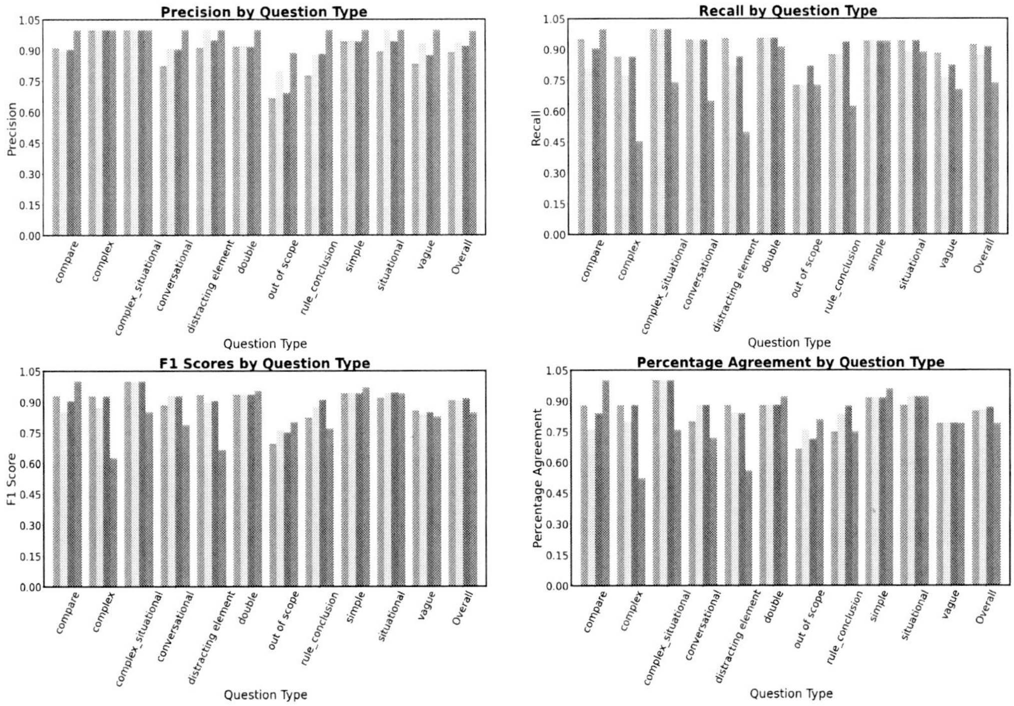

Figure 8: Precision, recall, F1 score, and percentage agreement of the prompt-based (1-5 scale) LLM-as-a-judge correctness evaluation compared to human judgments.

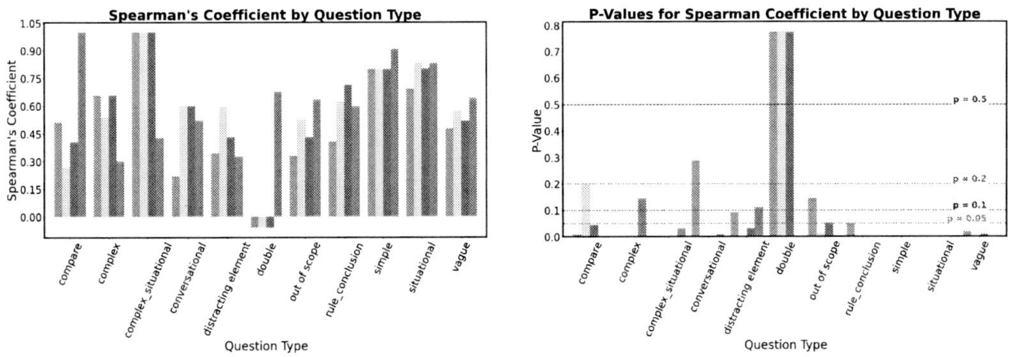

Figure 9: Spearman Coefficient comparing our custom LLM-as-a-judge (1-5 scale) prompts with Giskard's binary correctness evaluator for each question type. The second plot displays the p-values.

A.9 Classifier Data Augmentation Prompts

A.9.1 Vague Prompt

Rewrite the following question to be more vague, but it must still require the same number of pieces of information to answer. For example, a definition is one piece of information. A definition and an explanation of the concept are two separate pieces of information. Do not add or remove any pieces of information, and do not alter the fundamental meaning of the question. Output only the rewritten question, absolutely nothing else: `{question}`

A.9.2 Verbose Prompt

Rewrite the following question to be more verbose, but it must still require the same number of pieces of information to answer. For example, a definition is one piece of information. A definition and an explanation of the concept are two separate pieces of information. Do not add or remove any pieces of information, and do not alter the fundamental meaning of the question. Output only the rewritten question, absolutely nothing else: `{question}`

A.9.3 Concise Prompt

Rewrite the following question to be more concise, but it must still require the same number of pieces of information to answer. For example, a definition is one piece of information. A definition and an explanation of the concept are two separate pieces of information. Do not add or remove any pieces of information, and do not alter the fundamental meaning of the question. Output only the rewritten question, absolutely nothing else: `{question}`

A.10 2-Class Classifier Results

Model	Precision	Recall	F1 Score
Random Labels	0.49	0.49	0.49
facebook/bart-large-mnli	0.55	0.55	0.53
DeBERTa-v3-base-mnli-fever-anli	0.59	0.57	0.56
Logistic Regression (TF-IDF)	0.88	0.88	0.88
SVM (TF-IDF)	0.92	0.92	0.92
distilbert-base-uncased finetuned	0.92	0.92	0.92

Table 8: 2-Class Classification Results

A.11 2-Class Ablation Results

Method	Faithfulness	Answer Relevancy	Absolute Correctness (1-5)	Correctness (Threshold=4.0)
k	0.8111	0.7835	4.0372	0.7546
k, K^*, S^*	0.8725	<u>0.7830</u>	4.1115	<u>0.8216</u>
k, K, S	0.8551	0.7810	4.1487	0.7955
k, K, S + reranker	**0.8792**	**0.7878**	**4.1710**	0.8141
k, K, S + adaptive Q	0.8328	0.7800	4.0558	0.7770
k, K, S + Q + reranker	<u>0.8765</u>	0.7803	<u>4.1636</u>	**0.8253**

Table 9: Ablation study results for different configurations starting from adaptive k. The highest value in each column is highlighted in bold, and the second highest value is underlined.

What Kind of Sourcery is This? Evaluating GPT-4's Performance on Linking Scientific Fact to Citations

Autumn Toney-Wails
Georgetown University
SciTech Strategies, Inc.
autumn.toney@georgetown.edu

Abstract

From document summarization to code generation, chabots have disrupted various aspects of scientific research and writing. While chabots are useful research resources for ideation, information retrieval, and editing, their generative pre-trained transformer (GPT) models' underlying knowledge infrastructure is opaque. This has raised questions about the reliability of generative chatbot responses, as GPT models are known to respond with misleading information that appears to be accurate. Prior research has investigated the utility of OpenAI's public chatbot, ChatGPT, to generate reliable bibliographic information with a focus on small-scale medical-related scientific facts. We present an expanded study that analyzes GPT-4's ability to accurately identify 1,326 scientific facts and link them to academic sources. Using both the API and UI service, we experimented with open-ended and close-ended prompts to establish an understanding of GPT-4's general ability at this domain-specific task, as well as study the real-world scenario of an average user interacting with ChatGPT using its UI. GPT-4 accurately identified 96% of the scientific facts and generated relevant and existent academic citations with 78% accuracy. Using the claims that GPT-4 mislabeled and provided incorrect sources via the API, we prompt two public GPTs customized for academic writing to evaluate if they correctly label the scientific claims and provide accurate sources. We find that these GPTs are able to accurately label 38% of the mislabeled claims, with 95% of the corresponding citations being accurate and relevant.

1 Introduction

With the ability to perform a wide range of natural language generation (NLG) and information retrieval tasks, chatbots have enabled individuals to experiment with the utility of generative pre-trained transformer (GPT) language models in a publicly available, online interface. While chatbots are *generative* AI tools, users often query chatbots in a paired task that includes both NLG and information retrieval; for example, generating new content (e.g., write an introduction for a paper on a given topic) and retrieving information (e.g., provide citations when necessary). However, users often engage with chatbots for a specific task without understanding its utility in the given domain.

Using a chatbot as an information gathering tool is convenient, but comes with caveats. Various studies that analyze a chabot's performance on NLG and information retrieval tasks (e.g., document summarization and code generation) highlight a persistent error in the GPT model's responses—*hallucinations* (Shuster et al., 2021; Ji et al., 2023). Hallucinations refer to factually incorrect responses that often pass as being correct and credible text to a user (Dziri et al., 2022). Hallucinations are harmful to users, particularly in information retrieval-like tasks where the user is not an expert in the prompt topic, because chatbots can respond with well-formatted text that is convincingly accurate, but is completely fabricated.

In this work, we focus on a particular use-case for information gathering—linking scientific facts to sources for citations. Prior research has focused on evaluating GPT models (mainly versions 3 and 3.5) via the online ChatGPT interface in small scale experiments on complex scientific topics for citation generation (Wagner and Ertl-Wagner, 2023; Sebo, 2023; Xames and Shefa, 2023). Our study expands this research to prompt GPT-4 via the API on 1,326 scientific facts from 3rd–5th grade level coursework, covering a range of scientific topics. Specifically, we design an automated prompt framework that includes a close-ended prompt ("is the fact true or false?") and an open-ended prompt ("provide a citation to support your response") to analyze GPT-4's ability to identify scientific facts and accurately link them to academic citations. We then provide human annotation to evaluate the ac-

Proceedings of the 1st Workshop on Customizable NLP: Progress and Challenges in Customizing NLP for a Domain, Application, Group, or Individual (CustomNLP4U), pages 257–268
November 16, 2024 ©2024 Association for Computational Linguistics

curacy of GPT-4's responses, assessing if the provided citation is relevant to the scientific fact and exists (i.e. the source is not hallucinated).

Further assessing GPT-4's ability to generate reliable and accurate bibliographic information, we design a second prompt with two close-ended questions to verify its prior responses on the same criteria as the human annotation: "is the citation relevant to the scientific fact?" (yes or no) and "does the citation exist?" (real or fake). The full experimental design is illustrated in Figure 1.

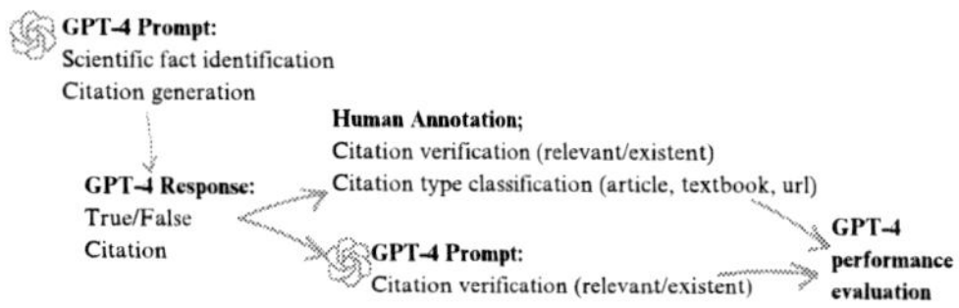

Figure 1: Experimental design framework for GPT-4 API prompts and response evaluation

Evaluating GPT-4's ability to verify scientific fact and provide a corresponding source via the API, we then use two sets of GPT-4 labeled claims for further experimentation: (1) claims that GPT-4 incorrectly labeled as *false* and (2) claims that GPT-4 provided hallucination sources for. We select two public GPTs[1] cusotmized for academic writing to converse with in the online user interface (UI). This experiment captures a real-world chabot interaction, where a customized chatbot is being used as a tool for a domain-specific task, while the API experiment comprehensively evaluates GPT-4's knowledge capacity and retrieval capabilities in an automated pipeline.

Our experimental results show that GPT-4 is capable of identifying scientific fact with 96% accuracy and generating a relevant, existing citation with 78% accuracy. GPT-4 favored providing a textbook citation over a scientific article or website, and only hallucinated 1% of textbook citation responses. We find that GPT-4 performs poorly as an evaluator of generated citations (determining if a source exitst), only correctly identifying 2% of the non-existent citations. In the UI experiments, we find that GPTs customized for academic writing increased the accuracy of scientific claim verification, with 38% of the previously 56 mislabeled claims receiving correct *true* labels. Additionally, the academic GPTs provided accurate and relevant citations with 95% accuracy for this set of claims. Analyzing the GPTs on a sample of 50 of the claims that GPT-4 correctly labeled as *true* but provided hallucination sources, we find that the academic GPTs responded with accurate and relevant citations for all claims when it providing a source.

Our API and UI results demonstrate that GPT-4 is able to provide reliable responses for information retrieval tasks that require scientific knowledge, both for identifying the veracity of a scientific claim and for providing an accurate source to justify its response. However, GPT-4 is stronger at the question answering task (achieving 96% accuracy) than the strict information retrieval task of providing a linked citation (achieving 78% accuracy). Chatbots customized for specific tasks, such as academic writing, improve the reliability of outputs and should be leveraged by users when available.

2 Related Work

Prior work has analyzed ChatGPT models, namely versions 3 and 3.5, in their ability to generate accurate scientific publication references, with the majority of studies focused on medical research (Gravel et al., 2023; Wagner and Ertl-Wagner, 2023; Alkaissi and McFarlane, 2023; Sebo, 2023). Additionally, researchers have analyzed and discussed GPT models' ability to be a reliable tool in scientific communication as an information resource or co-author (Schäfer, 2023; Flanagin et al., 2023; De Angelis et al., 2023; Kasneci et al., 2023; Xames and Shefa, 2023). While researchers acknowledge that GPT models have potential as a resource in academic and scientific writing, several studies highlight its shortcomings on citation generation tasks.

Gravel et al. queried ChatGPT with 20 medical questions derived from research publications, asking for the corresponding citation. ChatGPT's responses contained 59 distinct citations, which were then reviewed by the authors of the original research publications. The authors found that 69% of the citations were fabricated, with 71% of the fabrications having correctly formatted metadata (e.g., year, page numbers, volume number) and known publishers (e.g., MedRxiv and Centers for Disease Control and Prevention) (Gravel et al., 2023). Wagner and Ertl-Wagner prompted ChatGPT-3 with 88 radiology-related questions asking for responses with citations and ChatGPT-3 provided 343 distinct citations across all responses for review. Of

[1] `https://openai.com/index/introducing-gpts/`

the references that could be verified, only 24% related to the question (i.e., the publication could be used to support the response) and 64% of the 343 citations appeared to be fabricated by ChatGPT-3 (Wagner and Ertl-Wagner, 2023). Sebo asked ChatGPT-3.5 to provide 10 references to a set of 10 questions related to internal medicine, resulting in 100 citations for review. Of the 100 ChatGPT-3.5 provided citations, 34% were completely incorrect and 40% were partially correct due to error in metadata (e.g., publication year/publisher/etc. was incorrect) (Sebo, 2023).

While these studies are useful in understanding ChatGPT's performance on citation generation, they are limited in scope due to their topics and number of questions. Additionally, these studies query chatbots with highly specialized domain questions without leveraging a chatbot customized for that domain. Our work focuses on extending these studies to a range of 1,326 well-established scientific facts in a more generalized domain, and includes experiments using domain-specific chatbots.

3 Experimental Design

Here we describe the dataset, prompt design, and response evaluation for our experiments.

We experiment with GPT-4's ability to provide accurate bibliographic information for NLG (open-ended question) and information retrieval (close-ended) tasks. Specifically, our objective is to evaluate GPT-4's ability to identify scientific fact and provide accurate (existing and relevant) sources to support its responses, and compare the general GPT-4 performance to domain-specific ChatGPTs.

3.1 Scientific Fact Data

We use the OpenBookQA dataset from Gravel et al. (2023), which provides a set of 1,326 scientific facts. Designed for question and answering natural language processing tasks, Grave et al. extracted simple, one sentence scientific fact claims from WorldTree (Jansen et al., 2018), a corpus of 3rd–5th grade science questions with explanations. OpenBookQA contains a wide range of scientific facts (e.g., "a deer lives in a forest", "a landslide is when gravity rapidly moves rocks or soil downhill especially after a rain storm", "the moon reflects sunlight towards the Earth") that do not surpass 5th-grade knowledge, thus we consider these facts to be clear, simple, and general for GPT-4 to label as fact and provide an accurate supporting citation.

3.2 Scientific Claim Prompt

Our API experiments requires two different prompts: 1) an initial prompt to elicit a response identifying if a given claim is scientific fact and a citation supporting the fact (or not fact) identification, and 2) a follow-up prompt asking for verification of the citation and its relevancy to the scientific fact. Additionally, for the system prompt, we assign a scientific research persona in order to produce the most optimal results following OpenAI's prompt engineering documentation (OpenAI, 2023). We access GPT-4 programmatically via the API and set `temperature` = 0 for minimal model randomness in GPT-4's output [2].

For the initial prompt of identifying scientific fact and providing a source citation, we give GPT-4 the persona of a scientific researcher who is responsible for verifying scientific facts. In the user prompt, we ask GPT-4 a close-ended question to label a scientific claim as being true or false in order to elicit an automatically parsable response in an information retrieval task; however, we ask an open-ended question to generate a supporting source citation in a NLG task. Figure 2 displays both the system prompt and the user prompt for the first response collection.

system prompt: "You are a scientific researcher working on verifying scientific facts."

user prompt: "Please label the following claim with True or False, indicating whether or not it is a scientific fact: {*claim*}. Please provide a scientific citation supporting your response."

Figure 2: GPT-4 system and user prompts for scientific claim and citation chatbot response.

We alter the persona in the scientific claim and citation verification prompt to include that the system is responsible for verifying scientific fact *and* citations. Figure 3 displays the system and user prompt for this experiment, where two close-ended questions are asked to elicit automatically parsable responses identifying if the citation is relevant to the scientific fact (yes/no) and if the citation exists (real/fake).

We do not implement chain-of-thought prompts in our experiments, but instead treat the validation GPT-4 experiment as a separate task for compari-

[2] https://github.com/autumntoney/GPT4-scifact-citation

system prompt: "You are a scientific researcher working on verifying scientific facts and citations."

user prompt: "Given the scientific fact and citation below please respond with Yes or No indicating whether or not the citation contains information about the scientific fact. Yes indicates that the citation contains relevant information to the scientific fact and No indicates that the citation does not contains relevant information to the scientific fact. Citation: {*citation*}. Scientific Fact: {*claim*}. The citation came from an unreliable source and identifying its validity is important, please search the internet and respond with Real or Fake indicating if the citation is a real publication, document, or website. Real indicates that the publication, document, or website does exist and Fake indicates that the citation is fabricated."

Figure 3: GPT-4 system and user prompts for verification of the scientific claim and citation accuracy.

son via human annotation. Thus, in our citation validation prompt, we do not state that the citation was generated from GPT-4, but rather an "unreliable source", in order to elicit a more considered evaluation. The first prompt contains a closed-ended prompt for citation generation, representing a NLG task, and the second prompt contains a close-ended prompt, representing an information retrieval task to evaluate two use cases of bibliography generation.

For our UI experiments, we manually interact with customized GPT-4 chatbots. We use the API prompt asking for scientific fact verification and citation generation (Figure 2) and we include a third, informal prompt simulating a real-world, conversational chatbot use-case, shown in Figure 4. In this prompt, the scientific fact is explicitly stated as such to the chatbot, and the user is only asking for a corresponding source for a citation. While user interactions vary widely in conversation style and writing level, we chose a simple conversation prompt to analyze the GPTs, similar to the GPT-4 API prompt experiments.

user prompt: I need a citation for the scientific fact: {*claim*}.

Figure 4: GPT-4 system and user prompts for verification of the scientific claim and citation accuracy.

3.3 Response Evaluation

For the initial API prompt (scientific fact identification and citation generation) we parse GPT-4's response for the true or false label and extract the provided citation in order to evaluate its performance. Next, we take the parsed citation as input to the citation verification prompt and we parse GPT-4's response (citation relevance and existence) for further evaluation. Lastly, we manually verify all citations that GPT-4 provided on the following four criteria: 1) Does the cited source exist?, 2) What type of error occurred (e.g., no error, fabricated source, page not found), 3) What type of source was provided (e.g., textbook, article, URL), and 4) Is the source related to the scientific fact?

We are not concerned with evaluating the consistency of GPT-4's citation formatting, as we did not specify citation style in our prompt. Our evaluation criteria are focused on determining if GPT-4 is able to support its scientific fact identification with accurate (existing and relevant) sources.

Due to many of the generated citations being paywalled or textbooks, we determine relevance to a scientific fact by publicly available information. Thus, even if a full paper is available to read we consider only the title, abstract, and publication venue. For a textbook citation, we consider the general topic that is covered and if the scientific fact falls under that topic. The widest variety of material to review are URLs, as GPT-4 provides links to credible sources (e.g., National Geographic, NOAA, the Oxford Dictionary), but also blog posts, articles, and guides. We evaluate a URL as being accurate if the page exists and contains information relevant to the scientific fact—we do not investigate the credibility of the source itself (i.e., if the URL links to a personal blog). We use this annotation framework for both API and UI GPT responses.

4 Results and Discussion

We evaluate GPT-4's ability to accurately identify scientific fact and provide a relevant and existing citation using the API and UI prompts. Each chatbot experiment involves curating a GPT-4 response dataset from the various prompts and analyzing the responses for accuracy and relevancy.

4.1 GPT-4 API

We first evaluate the results from the first GPT-4 prompt (scientific fact identification and citation generation). GPT-4 accurately identified 96% (1,273 in total) of the claims as being scientific fact. The majority of errors were made in the citation information provided. We display the results in Table 1, listing the total count, percentage incorrect, and the most frequent error by citation type. We distinguish page not found errors from fabrication errors, since we did not investigate if a currently broken url was a historical artifact of the training data for GPT-4 (i.e., if the URL provided was previously valid and potentially a part of the model's ingested knowledge).

Type	Count	% Incorrect	Frequent Error
Article	297	13%	Fabrication
Textbook	600	1%	Fabrication
URL	429	42%	Page Not Found

Table 1: GPT-4 citation responses by source type, with the corresponding count, percentage incorrect, and most frequent error by citation type.

GPT-4 most commonly responded with a textbook citation (45% of citations) and URL (32% of citations), however the URL citations had the highest error rate (42%) compared to the textbook citation error rate (1%), which was the lowest. GPT-4 provided scientific articles with the lowest frequency (22%) and a 13% error rate. This result indicates that GPT-4 has the ability to provide accurate and relevant citations for scientific facts, with the most reliable responses involving a textbook citation, followed by an academic publication.

We analyzed the sources that GPT-4 responded with to assess if it used the same textbooks, website domains, or scientific articles for multiple responses since all scientific facts were derived from grade school knowledge. Table 2 displays the top 10 most commonly cited sources in our GPT-4 API experiments.

The most commonly referenced textbooks cover the general subjects of physics, biology, meteorology, and earth science. For URL citations, GPT-4 most frequently provided webpages to the National Aeronautics and Space Administration (NASA), Encyclopedia Britannica, and National Geographic. Additionally, we found that the most commonly referenced sources in the GPT-4 responses are reputable citations and could be selected by a user as an accurate reference. While only several textbooks could have been used repeatedly as sources, GPT-4 varies its response with more specific sources using scientific articles and webpages.

Next, we compared the human annotation results with the second GPT-4 prompt (citation validation) results. Figure 5 displays the co-occurrence

Citation	Count
1. Halliday, David, Robert Resnick, and Jearl Walker. Fundamentals of physics. John Wiley & Sons, 2013.	78
2. National Aeronautics and Space Administration	53
3. Encyclopedia Britannica	44
4. National Geographic	35
5. Raven, Peter H., Ray F. Evert, and Susan E. Eichhorn. Biology of plants. Macmillan, 2005.	33
6. National Oceanic and Atmospheric Administration	33
7. National Weather Service	20
8. Lutgens, Frederick, Edward J. Tarbuck, Redina Herman, and Dennis G. Tasa. The Atmosphere: An Introduction to Meteorology. Pearson, 2017.	13
9. Marshak, Steve. Earth: portrait of a planet: 5th international student edition. WW Norton & Company, 2015.	13
10. Smithsonian Museums	10

Table 2: Top 10 most frequently cited source by GPT-4. The organization name is provided for URLs and the MLA-style citation is provided for textbooks.

matrices for citation relevancy and existence. We consider human annotation as the ground truth label since every generated citation was checked manually, thus the GPT-4 responses that disagree with human annotation are considered incorrect responses from GPT-4.

GPT-4 achieved high performance as an evaluator of citation relevancy, identifying 83% of the irrelevant citations and 93% of the relevant citations correctly. However, GPT-4 did not exhibit the ability to identify citations that were non-existent; it incorrectly claimed that almost all (98%) of the non-existent citations were real. Of the 219 claims that GPT-4 incorrectly identified as being existent 83% were broken URLs. We did not further inves-

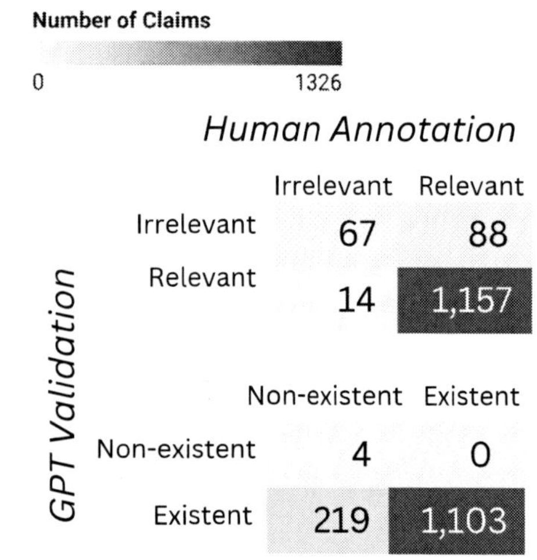

Figure 5: GPT-4 and human annotation citation validation results for relevancy and existence.

tigate if the URL was ever active online and could be a temporal error due to the data that GPT-4 was trained on, as opposed to a true hallucination.

During manual review, we did not discover any topical patterns for the set of facts that GPT-4 did not provide accurate citations. Specifically, there was not a distinct subject area (e.g., biology or chemistry), a claim length, or subject level that caused erroneous generated citations. For example the simple fact, "a balloon contains gas", resulted in the following GPT-4 response with a broken URL citation:

> True.
>
> A balloon typically contains gas, such as helium or air. This is a basic principle of balloon inflation. The gas inside the balloon is less dense than the surrounding air, which allows the balloon to float if the gas is lighter than air, like helium.
>
> Reference: Encyclopedia Britannica. (n.d.). Balloon. In Encyclopedia Britannica online. Retrieved from `https://www.britannica.com/technology/balloon-flight-vehicle`

In this error example we find that GPT-4 provided a similar citation to a correct link (`https://www.britannica.com/technology/balloon-flight`), but included an incorrect third word "vehicle". A source error such as this might be difficult for a user to notice, as the URL appears to be accurate and the Encyclopedia Britannica is a reputable source.

While GPT-4 did not always provide accurate and relevant sources for more simple scientific facts like the example above, we find that GPT-4 correctly generated citations for a more complex facts, such as "using tools is a learned characteristic", responding with the following:

> True.
>
> Using tools is indeed a learned characteristic. This is not only true for humans but also for certain animal species. For example, chimpanzees have been observed to learn tool use from their peers, indicating that this is a learned behavior rather than an innate one.
>
> Reference: Whiten, A., Goodall, J., McGrew, W. C., Nishida, T., Reynolds, V., Sugiyama, Y., ... & Boesch, C. (1999). Cultures in chimpanzees. Nature, 399(6737), 682-685.

In this example, GPT-4 processed the scientific fact, correctly assigning the label *true*, and provided an accurate and relevant citation discussing tool use as a learned behavior for chimpanzees. Linking human behavior to chimpanzee behavior is a more human-like reasoning task, highlighting that GPT-4 has ingested knowledge that enables this type of information retrieval performance.

Our experimental API results establish a baseline understanding of how well GPT-4 performs at the task of correctly answering if a scientific claim is true and linking the claim to an academic citation. While GPT-4 did fabricate citations and provide broken URLs, the majority (78%) of generated citations were relevant and existent. Additionally, GPT-4 did not have an underlying pattern to the incorrect generated citations, supporting prior research indicating its hallucinations are difficult to predict. Furthermore, our results suggest that despite having ingested the appropriate knowledge to respond with an accurate answer in an scientific knowledge information retrieval task, GPT-4 is still prone to hallucinate at random.

4.2 Academic GPT UIs

For the UI experiments we select two public GPTs that are customized for academic writing based on their use rankings and reviews on the OpenAI platform: academic assistant pro and scholar AI pro[3]. These public GPTs reflect the GPT-4 chabot a user might select in a real-world scenario, and they are designed specifically for the research task of academic writing. Here, we evaluate if these GPTs are able to correctly identify scientific fact and provide accurate and relevant corresponding citations using the claims that GPT-4 responded with error in the API experiments.

Using the API experiment prompt (Figure 2) that asks for a *true* or *false* label on the scientific claim and a corresponding citation, we prompt both academic GPTs with the 56 claims that GPT-4 mislabeled in the API experiments (See Appendix for full list of claims). The academic assistant pro GPT labeled 38% of the claims as true and the scholar AI pro GPT labeled 39% as true. We included a third label, *gray*, indicating an indecisive GPT response, which did not occur in the API experiments. For example, when prompted about the claim "veins transport nutrients throughout the body", the academic assistant pro GPT stated:

> The statement "veins transport nutrients throughout the body" can be nuanced in scientific literature because, while veins are a critical component of the circulatory system, their primary function is to return deoxygenated blood back to the heart, from where it is sent to the lungs for oxygenation.

The scholar AI GPT provided 10 gray labels and the academic assistant provided only two.

In the same annotation task as the GPT-4 API responses, we annotate the academic GPTs' source type. Table 3 displays the frequencies of the citation type provided by each GPT. Both academic GPTs aligned with the API experiments, providing majority textbook sources; however, the scholar AI pro GPT did not provide a source for 20 of the prompts (35%). We include a source label of organization, as both GPTs provided the general source of the International Astronomical Union as reference to the scientific fact "Pluto is the planet that is ninth closest to the Sun." Similarly, both customized GPTs only provided three distinct sources that did not exist (hallucinated) per GPT respectively(six sources in total from both GPTs), an improvement from the API results.

Using the informal ask for a source given a scientific fact (Figure 4), we sample 50 claims that GPT-4 correctly labeled as *true*, but provided an incorrect citation for (e.g., hallucination or broken URL); see Appendix for list of claims. Table 4 displays the source counts by type.

The academic assistant GPT did not provide a source for one claim ("as the use of a crop increases, the amount of crops planted will increase"), whereas the scholar AI GPT did not provide a source for the majority (76%) of the claims[4]. All sources provided in this prompt experiment were accurate and relevant from both GPTs. The academic assistant responded with textbook sources for 94% of its responses, wheres the scholar AI responded with 75% URL sources (of the 24% of claims it provided a source for). The chatbot UI results strengthen the API finding that GPT-4 has the most reliable results when providing a textbook citation.

In general, we find that using a customized, public GPT provides improved results from prompting GPT-4 via the API. For the application of our study, this result indicates that in a real-world scenario a user can select a GPT to reliably support bibliography curation.

5 Discussion and Limitations

The inability to study the underling algorithms, codebase, and knowledge infrastructure of a GPT model presents a challenge when studying closed-source chatbots. In this work, our goal is to systematically evaluate GPT-4's API and UI performances as reliable tools for a paired task of natural language generation and information retrieval on a domain-specific task— linking scientific claims to relevant and existent sources. A limitation of our results is the lack of validation that can only be fully achieved with the transparency of an open-source model. Additionally, we only query one chatbot (GPT-4) on scientific facts and sources (limited information types). We highlight our main findings and discuss our interpretations of these results.

GPT-4's apparent knowledge acquisition and reliability mimics the real-world. When evaluating the reliability of sources provided, we found that GPT-4 had the most accurate citations when referencing a textbook and the least accurate citations when referencing a URL. This behavior mimics real-world bibliographic curation—a relevant published piece of knowledge is more

[3] https://awesomegpts.vip/

[4] During experimentation we tested follow-on prompts asking for a citation again, but did not receive any source information.

GPT	Article	Organization	Textbook	URL	No Citation Provided
academic assistant	15	1	38	1	0
scholar AI	12	1	14	10	20

Table 3: Academic GPTs citation responses by source type using the formal prompt asking for scientific fact verification and a corresponding source.

GPT	Article	Organization	Textbook	URL	No Citation Provided
academic assistant	0	0	47	2	1
scholar AI	1	1	1	9	38

Table 4: Academic GPTs citation responses by source type using the informal prompt asking for a source given the scientific fact.

reliable for academic citation than a URL. While we did not further investigate erroneous URLs for their potential historical existence, it appeared that GPT-4 would use a reliable domain name (e.g., `nationalgeographic.com/`) with an incorrect (hallucinated) page reference (e.g., `article/volcanic-landforms-extrusive-intrusive/`). Thus, we hypothesize that GPT-4 has has ingested information on reputable bibliographic sources (e.g., National Geographic) and their corresponding domain, but does not always "retrieve" a correct URL.

Customized GPTs achieve higher performance for the intended (domain-specific) task. OpenAI's description of creating customized GPTs indicates its user-friendly design (no coding required) by stating that all a user needs is to prompt ChatGPT with further instructions or *extra knowledge*. Despite ChatGPT being a closed-source model, it can ingest knowledge via human interaction directly in the UI. Selecting the additional knowledge that a chabot can learn improves the transparency of knowing what the GPT "knows" and also increases the reliability of the chatbot's responses related to the specific information retrieval task. We highlight the fact that GPT models may appear to be poor tools for an information retrieval task like bibliography generation, as discussed in prior research, however GPT models are generative in their nature. Fine-tuning a GPT model with the necessary information for a task will improve its results and reliability, as the knowledge and knowledge sources are identified by the user. Thus, customization for a domain-specific task should be heavily considered when leveraging chatbots as a domain-specific tool.

6 Conclusion

In this paper we evaluated GPT-4's ability to identify scientific fact and generate a citation to support its response. Our experimental design contained two chatbot environments, API and UI, to fully assess GPT-4's performance. We designed prompts that included open-ended (generative) and close-ended (information retrieval) questions in order to test two prompt and response formats. Our experiments are designed to compare how GPT-4 generally performs on a domain-specific task (via the API) and how a GPT-4 chatbot performs (via the UI) when customized for use in the specified domain.

Using the API, we find that in general, GPT-4 performs well on identifying scientific fact and providing reliable sources. For the citation generation task, we find that GPT-4 provided relevant and existent academic citations with 78% accuracy. For the information retrieval tasks, we find that GPT-4 is able to identify scientific fact with 96% accuracy and determine the relevancy of citations with 83% accuracy for irrelevant citaitons and 93% accuracy for relevant citations. GPT-4 had the worst performance when determining if a citation existed, with the majority of its error as labeling broken URLs as existent. In the UI experiments, we find that using public GPTs customized for academic writing improved the API results in both scientific fact identification and source generation. However, we did identify discrepancies in chatbot performances between the two GPTs, with one chatbot's outputs resulting in the majority (76%) not containing a source when being explicitly asked for one.

Overall, we find GPT-4 to be a useful information gathering tool for general scientific knowledge.

Our experiments suggest that a user should select or design a customized chatbot for domain-specific tasks for improved utility.

References

Hussam Alkaissi and Samy I McFarlane. 2023. Artificial hallucinations in chatgpt: implications in scientific writing. *Cureus*, 15(2).

Luigi De Angelis, Francesco Baglivo, Guglielmo Arzilli, Gaetano Pierpaolo Privitera, Paolo Ferragina, Alberto Eugenio Tozzi, and Caterina Rizzo. 2023. Chatgpt and the rise of large language models: the new ai-driven infodemic threat in public health. *Frontiers in Public Health*, 11:1166120.

Nouha Dziri, Sivan Milton, Mo Yu, Osmar Zaiane, and Siva Reddy. 2022. On the origin of hallucinations in conversational models: Is it the datasets or the models? In *Proceedings of the 2022 Conference of the North American Chapter of the Association for Computational Linguistics: Human Language Technologies*, pages 5271–5285, Seattle, United States. Association for Computational Linguistics.

Annette Flanagin, Kirsten Bibbins-Domingo, Michael Berkwits, and Stacy L Christiansen. 2023. Nonhuman "authors" and implications for the integrity of scientific publication and medical knowledge. *Jama*, 329(8):637–639.

Jocelyn Gravel, Madeleine D'Amours-Gravel, and Esli Osmanlliu. 2023. Learning to fake it: limited responses and fabricated references provided by chatgpt for medical questions. *Mayo Clinic Proceedings: Digital Health*, 1(3):226–234.

Peter Jansen, Elizabeth Wainwright, Steven Marmorstein, and Clayton Morrison. 2018. WorldTree: A corpus of explanation graphs for elementary science questions supporting multi-hop inference. In *Proceedings of the Eleventh International Conference on Language Resources and Evaluation (LREC 2018)*, Miyazaki, Japan. European Language Resources Association (ELRA).

Ziwei Ji, Nayeon Lee, Rita Frieske, Tiezheng Yu, Dan Su, Yan Xu, Etsuko Ishii, Ye Jin Bang, Andrea Madotto, and Pascale Fung. 2023. Survey of hallucination in natural language generation. *ACM Computing Surveys*, 55(12):1–38.

Enkelejda Kasneci, Kathrin Seßler, Stefan Küchemann, Maria Bannert, Daryna Dementieva, Frank Fischer, Urs Gasser, Georg Groh, Stephan Günnemann, Eyke Hüllermeier, et al. 2023. Chatgpt for good? on opportunities and challenges of large language models for education. *Learning and individual differences*, 103:102274.

OpenAI. 2023. Tactic: Ask the model to adopt a persona. `https://platform.openai.com/docs/guides/prompt-engineering/tactic-ask-the-model-to-adopt-a-persona`. Accessed: 2023-11-20.

Mike S Schäfer. 2023. The notorious gpt: science communication in the age of artificial intelligence. *Journal of Science Communication*, 22(2):Y02.

Paul Sebo. 2023. How accurate are the references generated by chatgpt in internal medicine? *Internal and Emergency Medicine*, pages 1–3.

Kurt Shuster, Spencer Poff, Moya Chen, Douwe Kiela, and Jason Weston. 2021. Retrieval augmentation reduces hallucination in conversation. In *Findings of the Association for Computational Linguistics: EMNLP 2021*, pages 3784–3803, Punta Cana, Dominican Republic. Association for Computational Linguistics.

Matthias W Wagner and Birgit B Ertl-Wagner. 2023. Accuracy of information and references using chatgpt-3 for retrieval of clinical radiological information. *Canadian Association of Radiologists Journal*, page 08465371231171125.

Md Doulotuzzaman Xames and Jannatul Shefa. 2023. Chatgpt for research and publication: Opportunities and challenges. *Available at SSRN 4381803*.

A GPT-4 UI Scientific Claim Sets

We provide the sets of claims used in the UI experiments, which provide insight into the claims that resulted in error responses from the API experiments. Table 5 lists all scientific claims that GPT-4 incorrectly labeled *false* in the API experiments and Table 6 lists a random sample of 50 claims that GPT-4 correctly labeled as *true* in the API experiments, but provided inaccurate sources for.

Table 5: Set of 56 scientific facts that GPT-4 mislabled as *false* in API experiments and are used in the UI experiments.

limestone is formed by water evaporating from a solution of water and minerals	omnivores are predators
if a weed is pulled then that weed is destroyed	as the time a tool lasts increases, the number of tools discarded will decrease
as water increases in an environment, the population of aquatic animals will increase	hunting requires seeing prey
as ability to preserve food increases, the ability to transport food increases	as the size of the eyes of an animal increases, the ability of that animal to see will usually increase
cold environments are usually white in color from being covered in snow	clear weather means sunny weather
as air pressure decreases, the chance of rain will increase	the increase of something required by an organism has a positive impact on that organism 's survival
as the available water in an environment increases, the populations of organisms in that environment will increase	cold environments contain few organisms
a complete electrical circuit is a source of electrical energy	adding salt to a solid decreases the freezing point of that solid
if a tree falls then that tree is dead	water is in the solid state, called ice, for temperatures between 0 and 0 F
decreasing something negative has a positive impact on a thing	if a cell can not specialize then that cell must perform all life functions
precipitation is when snow fall from clouds to the Earth	as number of organisms in a group increases, the chance of survival of each organism will increase
poisonous darts are used for defense by sea anemones	boiling is when liquids are heated above their boiling point
if an animal relies on plants for food then that animal must store enough food to last through the winter	breathing is when a lung converts from oxygen in air into oxygen in blood
force causes the speed of an object to decrease	as force exerted on an object increases, distance travelled will increase
if a hot object touches a cold substance then that substance will likely cool	an animal usually requires a warm body temperature for survival
as moisture of an object decreases, the friction of that object against another object will increase	a plant requires soil for to grow
as the size of a flower increases, the number of pollinators it will attract increases	as the activity of an animal increases, the amount of water in an animal 's body in that environment will decrease
the Earth revolving around the Sun causes the seasons to change on its axis	if something is outside during the day then that something will receive sunlight
a different moon phase occurs once per week	the moon rising occurs once per day
the sun is located directly overhead at noon	as the weight of an animal decreases, that animal will fly more easily
food is a source of energy for plants	pollination requires pollinating animals
as the number of eggs laid by an animal increases, the number of eggs that hatch will increase	the condition of the parts of an organism are acquired characteristics
if an object is blue then that object reflects only blue light	carnivores only eat animals
bees eat pollen	veins transport nutrients throughout the body
iron is always magnetic	the Earth absorbs more energy than it loses
mountains are formed by volcanoes	as the thickness of an object increases, the resistance to damage of that object will increase
the moon does not contain water	the Earth revolving around the Sun causes the seasons to occur on its axis
cracking something usually has a negative impact on that something	Pluto is the planet that is ninth closest to the Sun

Table 6: Set of 50 randomly sampled scientific facts for UI experiments.

as the use of a crop increases, the amount of crops planted will increase	a scar is an acquired characteristic
magnetism can cause objects to repel each other	a sea turtle lives in the ocean
a spider web is used to capture food by spiders	a renewable resource can be replaced
a greenhouse is used to protect plants by keeping them warm	the tide cycle regularly occurs twice per day
water is an electrical conductor	tectonic plates being pushed together causes earthquakes
crumple means change shape from smooth into	compacted by physical force
sunlight contains ultraviolet light	the Earth revolves around the sun
meters m are a unit used for measuring distance generally used for values between 1 and 1000	the slope of the land causes a river to flow in a particular direction
natural magnetism is used for pointing north by a compass	soil is formed by weathering
if a mineral can be scratched by a fingernail then that mineral is soft	if a substance absorbs solar energy then that substance will increase in temperature
breath contains water vapor	weathering usually occurs over a period of many years
a star is a source of light through nuclear reactions	a star is made of gases
a reflector is used to reflect light especially on vehicles	high means great in altitude
a flashlight requires a source of electricity to produce light	endangered means low in population
a Rotation of the Earth on Earth 's axis takes 1 day	An example of an inherited behavior is a bird building a nest
a balloon contains gas	the sun causes water to evaporate more quickly by adding heat
a bubble contains gas	the sun is the source of solar energy called sunlight
winter in the Northern Hemisphere is during the summer in the Southern Hemisphere	coal mine is a source of coal under the ground
In the food chain process some types of plankton have the role of producer	as time spent taking a shower decreases, water used will decrease
a compass 's needle lines up with Earth 's magnetic poles	a stopwatch is used to measure time
coal is used to produce electricity by burning in coal-fire power stations	arteries transport nutrients throughout the body
An example of a reproductive behavior is salmon returning to their birthplace to lay their eggs	a graduated cylinder is a kind of instrument for measuring volume of liquids or objects
a rainbow is formed by refraction of light by splitting light into all different colors	fossil fuels forming occurs over a period of 300000000 years which is considered a very long time to a human
as lightness in color of an object increases, the ability of that object to reflect light will increase the stars in the night sky are very far away from the Earth	wind causes erosion
the sun is located directly overhead at noon	a solar panel converts sunlight into electricity

“Let’s Argue Both Sides”: Argument Generation Can Force Small Models to Utilize Previously Inaccessible Reasoning Capabilities

Kaveh Eskandari Miandoab[+] and **Vasanth Sarathy**[*]
Tufts University
kaveh.eskandari_miandoab@tufts.edu[+]
vasanth.sarathy@tufts.edu[*]

Abstract

Large Language Models (LLMs), despite achieving state-of-the-art results in a number of evaluation tasks, struggle to maintain their performance when logical reasoning is strictly required to correctly infer a prediction. In this work, we propose *Argument Generation* as a method of forcing models to utilize their reasoning capabilities when other approaches such as chain-of-thought reasoning prove insufficient. Our method involves the generation of arguments for each possible inference result, and asking the end model to rank the generated arguments. We show that *Argument Generation* can serve as an appropriate substitute for zero-shot prompting techniques without the requirement to add layers of complexity. Furthermore, we argue that knowledge-probing techniques such as chain-of-thought reasoning and *Argument Generation* are only useful when further reasoning is required to infer a prediction, making them auxiliary to more common zero-shot approaches. Finally, we demonstrate that our approach forces larger gains in smaller language models, showcasing a complex relationship between model size and prompting methods in foundation models.

1 Introduction

Large Language Models, including state-of-the-art models such as Llama family of LLMs (Touvron et al., 2023), Mistral 7B (Jiang et al., 2023), and Phi-3 (Abdin et al., 2024) have shown to significantly outperform previous generation of models (Wang et al., 2023b) such as BERT (Devlin et al., 2019) in several mainly classification tasks (Chang et al., 2024). However, despite their seemingly human-like auto-regressive behavior, Large Language Models do not perform well when deep reasoning or analysis is required to effectively infer a prediction (Lee et al., 2023; Tao et al., 2023).

In order to bolster the reasoning capabilities of large language models, the research community has done extensive recent work in the form of chain-of-thought reasoning (Kojima et al., 2022; Wang et al., 2023a), Self-Reflection (Madaan et al., 2023), Multi-Agent Debate (Liang et al., 2023; Du et al., 2023), and Socratic prompting (Chang, 2023), demonstrating that prompting the model to generate the reasoning behind its answer, or generating a step-by-step guide to reach its response can help predict better results.

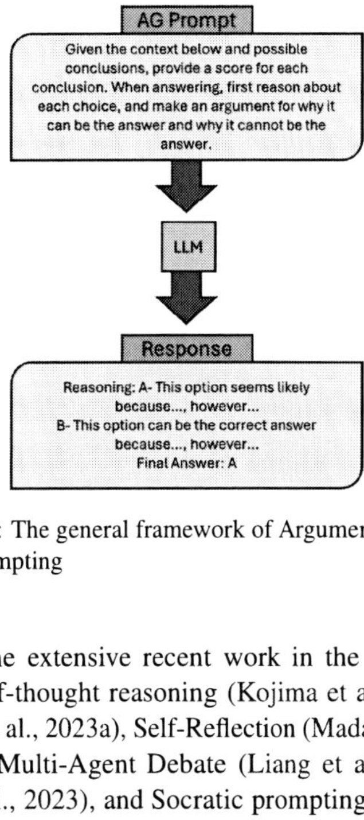

Figure 1: The general framework of Argument Generation Prompting

Taking inspiration from chain-of-thought reasoning, and motivated by the need to develop better prompt techniques with the goal of increasing model performance in reasoning tasks, we introduce *Argument Generation*, a single-pass prompting technique that aims to utilize the reasoning and argumentation capabilities of Large Language Models to generate better responses where deeper consideration of logic or reasoning is required to infer the correct result. *Argument Generation* involves a two-step process. We first prompt the model to generate possible reasoning for the truthfulness of each possible option, and then we ask the model to rank the generated arguments and map

Proceedings of the 1st Workshop on Customizable NLP: Progress and Challenges in Customizing NLP for a Domain, Application, Group, or Individual (CustomNLP4U), pages 269–283
November 16, 2024 ©2024 Association for Computational Linguistics

its ranking to a final output in accordance with the task expectations.

We evaluate our method on a number of openly available state-of-the-art Large Language Models using nine tasks of different natures. We find that *Argument Generation* at its weakest, does not perform significantly worse than chain-of-thought reasoning, and is able to outperform both zero-shot reasoning and chain-of-thought reasoning when a deeper understanding of the task options is required. Furthermore, we note that in comparison to chain-of-thought reasoning, *Argument Generation* can be used as a stronger knowledge probing technique that is useful in instances where such probing is essential, or some level of prior knowledge regarding the task is present (such as possible response candidate). However, our method does not necessarily increase the model performance for inputs that observe acceptable results under more common methods.

We make the following contributions: (1) We introduce *Argument Generation*, a novel prompting technique that aims to access the underlying reasoning capabilities of LLMs. (2) We show through a series of experiments that our method is able to effectively reason under conditions that fail chain-of-thought reasoning. (3) We show that our prompting method is more effective when used with smaller language models, eliciting further investigation into the relationship between prompting approaches and model capabilities.

2 Background and Motivation

Argumentation is the cognitive capability of generating and evaluating "reasons" for deriving a conclusion (Mercier, 2016). It is a central aspect of human intelligence and is omnipresent in natural human communication. It extends the conception of reasoning in LLM-research (Yu et al., 2023a) by including the notion that conclusions drawn must be new. Indeed, it has been suggested that human reasoning evolved for the purposes of enabling humans to persuade each other (Mercier and Sperber, 2011) through arguments.

We hypothesize that many day-to-day arguments are evaluated by humans in an intuitive (fast, system 1) manner, without deep thought or "epistemic vigilance" (Sperber et al., 2010), unless they are from trusted sources and appear to contradict our own beliefs. Thus, because LLMs were pretrained with human communicative interactions, we hypothesize that LLMs are capable of fast argumentative thinking. By triggering argumentative thought, we hypothesize that LLMs can effectively generate reasons and assess conclusions, as well as improve core reasoning capabilities across a variety of domains, including commonsense, logical, and social.

3 Related Work

General argumentation ability of LLMs have begun to be explored by researchers, with a focus on a number of computational argumentation subtasks such as argument mining, claim detection, evidence detection and type classification, argument generation, and summarization (Balikas, 2023; Chen et al., 2023; Holtermann et al., 2022; Ruiz-Dolz and Lawrence, 2023; Thorburn and Kruger; de Wynter and Yuan, 2023). Research suggests that LLMs "exhibit commendable performance" (Chen et al., 2023) in zero-shot and few-shot settings thereby supplying a foundation supporting our approach.

Delving deeper, we can explore two core aspects of argumentation. First, the ability to argue for/against all sides (thinking like a lawyer). Second, the ability to generate implicit assumptions (necessary or sufficient warrants) needed to support the argument.

Arguing all sides is related to "backward reasoning" suggested in (Yu et al., 2023a), where they discuss that it is "better to collect both supportive and opposing knowledge to compare the confidence of different conclusions for defeasible reasoning." Additionally (Wang et al., 2022) discuss the idea of allowing several different reasoning paths and choosing the "most consistent one". Another approach is contrastive chain-of-thought (Chia et al., 2023) where they consider both valid and invalid reasoning demonstrations alongside original prompt – a dual perspective approach. Additionally, work in multiagent debate, for example (Chia et al., 2023) uses a notion of a debate with multiple agents discussing and talking about the problem. However, none of these approaches attempt at *rationalizing* all sides of an argument. That is none of these offer up the best possible argument for/against each choice, and then evaluate the best argument (for example, anticipatory reflection of plans in (Wang et al., 2024)).

Extracting implicit information relates to work in "knowledge-enhanced" (Qiao et al., 2023) strategies in which an implicit model generates knowledge and rationales. Also Yu et al. (2023a) discusses Leap-of-thought reasoning which uses implicit facts to answer questions. A related notion is that of decomposing implicit multi-hop questions down in connection with the general backward reasoning tactic of question-decomposition (see summary in (Yu et al., 2023a)). Work by (Sarathy et al., 2022) suggests extracting implicit assumptions from premise-conclusion pairs, however, that work does not explore how such endeavor influences an LLM's reasoning capability. Although there is a growing body of work in question decomposition, it is unclear to what extent they take implicit assumptions into account.

General LLM reasoning capabilities have been improving over the past several years with numerous datasets targeting different types of reasoning – logical, mathematical, commonsense, argumentation, and social reasoning (Qiao et al., 2023; Yu et al., 2023a; Huang and Chang, 2023; Yu et al., 2023b; Luo et al., 2023; Sahoo et al., 2024a). The methods have involved various techniques to evoke reasoning processes such as having the LLM explicate its chain of thought (Wei et al., 2022a), reflect on its own reasoning process (Wang and Zhao, 2023), decompose complex reasoning processes into simpler problems that can be solved more easily (Khot et al., 2023), explore many different reasoning paths and decide on one that wins a majority vote (Wang et al., 2022), and others. These various methods have shown improvements in various reasoning tasks, but none have shown cross-domain effectiveness. Moreover, their reasoning capabilities are limited when exposed to scenarios in which the model must resolve a disagreement (Lee et al., 2023), distinguish a correct phrase from an incorrect one (Riccardi and Desai, 2023), or assign a nondeterministic gender to a subject (Zakizadeh et al., 2023). Overall, Large Language Models have shown promising results in a variety of reasoning tasks while serious challenges and shortcomings still remain (Chang et al., 2024). What is missing is a cross-domain strategy to improve an LLM's zero-shot reasoning capabilities, which we hypothesize to be enhanced by its latent capability for argumentative thinking.

4 Methodology

We now provide details regarding our approach, including the proposed zero-shot approach and the reasoning behind our choice of *Argument Generation* as a prompting technique.

Argument Generation involves two overall steps. Given an initial input x with possible answers $k_1, k_2, ...k_n$, we first prompt the model to generate arguments supporting and attacking each answer k_i, creating arguments $x'_1, x'_2, ...x'_n$ for each possible answer. We then ask the model to choose the answer with the strongest argument as the final output. More concretely, the Large Language Model is utilized as a proxy for an argument ranking function that chooses the most feasible options among arguments $x'_1, x'_2, ...x'_n$.

The rationale behind our approach is two-fold. First, it has been shown that Large Language Models, when provided with a reasoning context towards the correct output, observe significantly improved performance (Wei et al., 2022b; Kojima et al., 2022), making the reasoning behind each choice an important contributor to model performance. Second, Large Language Models can act as effective rankers when provided with a list-wise input of possible options (Ma et al., 2023), indicating the feasibility of their possible utilization for the effective ranking of arguments. As a result, the proposed technique relies on the assumption that the correct answer k_i to the query x should logically have the strongest argument supporting it, forcing the ranker model to choose the argument that is directly mapped to the correct answer.

Essentially, *Argument Generation* is similar to chain-of-thought reasoning because both focus on the generation of a token chain with the goal of increasing the probability of generating a viable final answer. However, chain-of-thought reasoning operates under the assumption that the generation of supporting steps is sufficient for the final true output. On the other hand, *Argument Generation* aims to take into consideration the possibility of the presence of a counterargument that is statistically more significant than the answer that is generated by pure chain-of-thought. As such, we hypothesize that chain-of-thought can sufficiently generate the most logically intuitive response to the user input, while *Argument Generation* might be better suited for cases where the correct answer is initially unintuitive but may increase in statistical significance as a valid counterargument is presented against the other answer candidates.

5 Evaluation

To empirically evaluate the effectiveness of our proposed method, we have tested the performance of *Argument Generation* in nine datasets and across nine models. For the remainder of this section, we focus on describing our evaluation setting.

5.1 Models

In order to perform a comprehensive evaluation over models of different size and architecture, we test our approach using nine models, including two families of models, and five independent, recently released LLMs. These include Llama 3 family of models (8B and 70B), Gemma family of models (2B and 7B) (Mesnard et al., 2024), Phi-3 3.8B (Abdin et al., 2024), Mistral 7B (Jiang et al., 2023), GPT 4o-mini[1], Qwen2 1.5B (Yang et al., 2024), and Aya 35B (Üstün et al., 2024).

5.2 Datasets

Our choice of datasets includes candidates from nine different tasks, each representing a group of tasks that aim to quantify a specific aspect of a given model. We strive to cover tasks belonging to different domains, including question-answering, argumentation, reasoning, bias evaluation, human-alignment, and autoregressive generation. The tested datasets include CommonSenseQA (Talmor et al., 2019), DiFair (Zakizadeh et al., 2023), IBM-30K (Gretz et al., 2020) TruthfulQA (generation and multiple choice tasks) (Lin et al., 2022), StereoSet (Nadeem et al., 2021), StrategyQA (Geva et al., 2021), Formal Fallacies (Suzgun et al., 2023), and AlpacaEval (human annotation task) (Dubois et al., 2024).

For all tasks, we report the metric proposed by the task's respective paper. The only exceptions to this rule are IBM-30K and the generation task of TruthfulQA. For IBM-30K, we report $1 - MAE$ as the final score to be consistent with others metrics and to showcase the model response quality per individual instance. In the case of TruthfulQA, we use GPT 4o-mini as the judge model as opposed to the fine-tuned GPT-3 utilized by the authors. For the multi-choice TruthfulQA task, we additionally generate 60 questions by randomly sampling 15% of the original dataset and replacing the correct option with 'None of the Answers are Correct'. This is done in order to further evaluate model performance when no clear answer exists.

[1]OpenAI

Observe that *Argument Generation* requires the existence of valid candidate responses in order to correctly reason, and choose a response. However, in the case of Large Language Models, it is often the case that the user does not have a set of candidate responses for their question. In such cases, we prompt the model to generate such responses first, and then use them as the possible answers to the question. This approach is based on the hypothesis that if a model has sufficient knowledge to answer a question, it should also generate that response as a candidate. Similar methods have shown to be effective in prompt ranking approaches (Hu et al., 2024).

5.3 Argument Generation

We perform our evaluations using two different *Argument Generation* settings in order to evaluate both the effect of generation of **implicit assumptions**, as well as the model sensitivity to different *Argument Generation* prompts. In the first approach, given an input x and a possible answer k, we explicitly ask the model to generate an **implicit assumption** under which k is a valid response to x. An implicit assumption is a set of logical propositions P such that every proposition in P must hold in order for the answer to follow logically from x. We then ask the model to rank these implicit assumptions by the feasibility of all $p_i \in P$ to hold simultaneously. We finally take the implicit assumption with the highest feasibility ranking as the final answer to the input.

In the second approach, given an input x and a possible answer k, we ask the model to both generate an argument for accepting k as a correct answer to x and generate an argument for rejecting k as a correct answer to x. We then apply this process to all candidate answers k_1 through k_n such that n tuples of arguments are generated by the model. We finally prompt the model to rank the aforementioned n tuples and generate the final answer to input x.

Algorithm 1 showcases both of the aforementioned techniques, where ASSUMPTION(x, K) refers to the generation of implicit assumptions for each candidate answer, and ranking them via a list-wise ranking technique, and ARGUMENT(x, K) refers to the generation of tuples of arguments for each candidate answer that both support and attack the corresponding candidate answer, and then ranking them via a list-wise ranking approach.

We acknowledge that it is possible to extend

Algorithm 1 Argument Generation

Require: Input x, List of Possible Answers K
Ensure: Final Response k_i

procedure GENERATION(x, K)
  function IMPLICITASSUMPTION(x, K)
    Let $A := \emptyset$
    for all $k_i \in K$ **do**
      $A := A \cup$ ASSUMPTION(x, k_i)
    Let $Ranking :=$ RANKING(A)
    return $Ranking[0]$ ▷ Return the Top Ranking Answer
  function ARGUMENTGENERATION(x, K)
    Let $A := \emptyset$
    for all $k_i \in K$ **do**
      $A := A \cup \{$ARGUMENT(x, k_i), ARGUMENT(x, $\neg k_i$)$\}$
    Let $Ranking :=$ LWR(A)
    return $Ranking[0]$ ▷ Return the Top Ranking Answer

our approach to a multi-agent setting, where the argument generation is done by an external model that is separate from the ranking model. However, we focus on single-pass prompting for the purpose of this study to (i) provide a single-pass, easy-to-implement approach that is comparable to zero-shot chain-of-thought reasoning both in performance, and running time, and (ii) refrain from unnecessarily increasing the computational requirement of the approach, as seen in other multi-agent techniques. However, we hypothesize that generalizing our algorithm to utilize multiple agents is both simple and observes an increase in performance.

6 Evaluation Results

We now showcase our results as tested against the datasets mentioned in section 5. We additionally show that *Argument Generation*, when outperforming zero-shot chain-of-thought reasoning, demonstrates significantly higher performance gain, and suffers smaller losses in cases where it does not result in increased performance. We finally provide a model size analysis to better understand the relationship between prompting methods and the number of parameters present in a given Large Language Model.

6.1 Performance Analysis

Table 1 showcases the evaluation results when using *Argument Generation* against zero-shot chain-of-thought prompting (Kojima et al., 2022) and common zero-shot prompting (Radford et al., 2019).

We observe that our method is able to outperform both zero-shot prompting and chain-of-thought reasoning in 38 of the 81 test settings, amounting to a win rate of 46.91%. Additionally, our approach outperforms chain-of-thought reasoning in 47 of the 81 settings, showcasing that *Argument Generation* yields better results in 58.02% of the test cases. Among the 45 cases where our proposed method performs better, there are 35 cases (77.77%) in which both proposed approaches outperform chain-of-thought reasoning, while *Argument Generation* with implicit assumptions is able to yield better results in 38 cases (84.44%), and *Argument Generation* without implicit assumptions has a better performance in 42 cases (93.33%), showcasing that both methods have similar results while tested against chain-of-thought reasoning.

With respect to individual datasets, we find that our method enjoys a significant performance boost when tested against instances of IBM-30K (Gretz et al., 2020), with both methods showing improved results over the two other baselines in all models. This behavior is expected as IBM-30K measures a model's capability to correctly discern a valid argument from an invalid one, and our approach operates via generating arguments that both support and attack the given input, meaning that invalid arguments will have weaker support, allowing the model to effectively rank the inputs based on their argumentative strength.

Additionally, we observe that *Argument Generation* is able to increase model performance for 10 out of 18 instances (55.55%) against all methods, and for 13 out of 18 instances (72.22%) against chain-of-thought reasoning in DiFair (Zakizadeh et al., 2023) and StereoSet (Nadeem et al., 2021) datasets, showcasing that argumentation might serve as a reliable debiasing method for Large Language Models. Interestingly, the correlation between our approach's improving effects and a given model's general capability is not strictly positive in this case, meaning that it is possible for larger models to observe lower, or no gains when prompted with *Argument Generation*. We attribute this observation to the possibility of more capable models deceiving themselves via supporting an incorrect candidate when the initial knowledge is sufficient to make a prediction, meaning that *Argument Generation* might force an artificial and

Model	Prompt	CommonSenseQA	DiFair	IBM-30K	TruthfulQA	StereoSet	StrategyQA	TruthfulQA Gen	FormalFallacies	AlpacaEval
Gemma 2B	Zero-Shot	**43.24**%	0.0%	59.46%	20.63%	**63.70**%	**55.45**%	34.66%	53.20%	54.39%
	Chain of Thought	41.85%	12.65%	49.98%	18.61%	36.17%	49.34%	**34.77**%	53.20%	57.01%
	Argument Generation w/ Implicit Assumptions	37.18%	34.54%	62.63%	**47.97**%	44.97%	46.28%	29.32%	49.60%	**57.78**%
	Argument Generation	39.80%	**55.39**%	**80.93**%	31.27%	34.3%	50.21%	29.32%	**53.60**%	57.62%
Gemma 7B	Zero-Shot	**69.28**%	0.0%	70.85%	28.93%	**88.87**%	**66.37**%	55.99%	**49.60**%	**62.71**%
	Chain of Thought	69.12%	32.52%	63.14%	**41.48**%	66.98%	58.07%	50.69%	47.20%	61.94%
	Argument Generation w/ Implicit Assumptions	66.33%	47.51%	69.31%	33.05%	64.05%	61.33%	59.59%	47.20%	59.93%
	Argument Generation	66.66%	**55.84**%	**72.94**%	25.21%	73.88%	54.14%	**59.65**%	49.20%	57.62%
Llama3 8B	Zero-Shot	71.33%	22.19%	60.51%	47.97%	42.47%	65.93%	47.52%	53.20%	**58.24**%
	Chain of Thought	**71.41**%	10.80%	66.03%	44.57%	54.36%	**74.23**%	64.65%	**59.20**%	55.00%
	Argument Generation w/ Implicit Assumptions	63.22%	55.88%	71.22%	**51.70**%	**55.73**%	60.26%	78.28%	46.80%	51.30%
	Argument Generation	64.12%	**58.57**%	**73.50**%	33.93%	45.90%	62.88%	**78.88**%	50.00%	46.68%
Llama3 70B	Zero-Shot	79.85%	78.08%	76.04%	69.04%	41.91%	**72.77**%	57.09%	53.20%	**52.22**%
	Chain of Thought	**80.26**%	**82.79**%	64.46%	**70.53%**	39.04%	74.67%	77.80%	**71.60**%	49.36%
	Argument Generation w/ Implicit Assumptions	74.44%	72.45%	**76.98**%	56.91%	**73.44**%	45.41%	82.58%	64.40%	49.52%
	Argument Generation	75.34%	79.16%	76.13%	68.93%	52.05%	72.05%	**82.59**%	62.80%	50.15%
Phi3 3.8B	Zero-Shot	**67.97**%	6%	63.04%	47.55%	56.0%	64.19%	57.33%	53.20%	62.22%
	Chain of Thought	66.66%	**71.59**%	62.57%	51.48%	61.52%	**64.62**%	63.94%	54.80%	61.63%
	Argument Generation w/ Implicit Assumptions	66.91%	57.24%	**69.50**%	51.70%	61.15%	60.26%	73.08%	54.80%	**63.17**%
	Argument Generation	**67.97**%	52.39%	69.17%	**52.12**%	**61.67**%	62.88%	**73.54**%	**55.60**%	57.62%
Mistral 7B	Zero-Shot	67.81%	45.66%	64.83%	8%	46.61%	61.57%	65.74%	**53.20**%	59.93%
	Chain of Thought	**67.89**%	62.19%	59.82%	**55.95**%	41.10%	**65.06**%	**77.91**%	47.20%	**61.01**%
	Argument Generation w/ Implicit Assumptions	64.29%	63.44%	66.58%	50.63%	46.28%	60.26%	77.29%	50.40%	58.08%
	Argument Generation	64.70%	**66.51**%	**66.85**%	51.27%	**49.24**%	60.69%	77.50%	50.00%	54.54%
GPT-4o-Mini	Zero-Shot	82.47%	**83.58**%	55.78%	**66.06**%	75.48%	**77.50**%	66.15%	53.20%	**65.63**%
	Chain of Thought	**82.71**%	79.92%	51.25%	65.53%	86.37%	**77.50**%	82.30%	63.20%	63.63%
	Argument Generation w/ Implicit Assumptions	79.68%	73.15%	**71.96**%	58.29%	86.22%	70.30%	91.83%	**71.20**%	56.70%
	Argument Generation	80.26%	81.10%	71.71%	56.38%	**86.87**%	71.61%	**91.89**%	69.20%	53.77%
Qwen2 1.5B	Zero-Shot	**69.45**%	10.21%	76.04%	29.14%	**50.31**%	54.58%	42.37%	**53.20**%	53.15%
	Chain of Thought	59.95%	22.56%	64.46%	**32.65**%	39.55%	54.58%	**53.76**%	46.40%	61.32%
	Argument Generation w/ Implicit Assumptions	49.95%	50.03%	**76.98**%	11.48%	26.99%	49.34%	44.46%	49.60%	**63.02**%
	Argument Generation	54.79%	**52.57**%	76.13%	14.68%	31.87$	**55.02**%	43.80%	50.00%	62.40%
Aya 35B	Zero-Shot	**85.83%**	69.71%	62.73%	48.82%	**65.28**%	67.68%	**44.44**%	**53.20**%	65.48%
	Chain of Thought	82.39%	**74.02**%	40.06%	43.82%	48.61%	**82.53**%	41.81%	47.60%	63.02%
	Argument Generation w/ Implicit Assumptions	76.16%	61.63%	**72.64**%	**58.19**%	47.33%	72.48%	30.20%	48.40%	63.63%
	Argument Generation	77.31%	66.25%	64.56%	54.25%	47.85%	78.60%	29.84%	47.60%	**66.10**%

Table 1: Prompting results using Argument Generation, Chain of Thought Reasoning, and Zero-Shot Prompting in nine different tasks.

unwanted decrease in model confidence. We provide further details and analysis in section 6.3.

6.2 Performance Difference Analysis

In order to observe the expected performance metric difference, we define Δ_{min} as the mean difference between chain-of-thought reasoning and the worst-performing *Argument Generation* method when chain-of-thought reasoning is performing better than our approach, and Δ_{max} as the mean difference between chain-of-thought reasoning and the best-performing *Argument Generation* method when chain-of-thought reasoning is performing better than our approach. Conversely, we define Γ_{min} and Γ_{max} similarly for cases in which *Argument Generation* is performing better than chain-of-thought reasoning. More concretely, Δ values show the performance decrease of *Argument Generation* with respect to chain-of-thought reasoning when the second approach is able to outperform our method, while Γ values demonstrate the performance increase when *Argument Generation* produces better results in comparison to chain-of-thought reasoning.

Table 2 showcases our empirical results. We find that except for the Phi3 3.8B model, all LLMs demonstrate significantly higher performance in instances where our method outperforms zero-shot chain-of-thought reasoning. Most significantly, Llama3 8B has a mean performance difference of 21.29% between the worst-performing *Argument Generation* approach and zero-shot chain-of-thought reasoning (Γ_{min}) in tasks that our method performs better. Looking at Γ_{max}, the best-performing proposed method is able to boost Gemma 2B model performance by 25.95%, and Llama3 8B performance by 23.15%, showcasing that overall when such an increase in model performance is observed, the increase is significant.

Model Name	Δ_{min}	Δ_{max}	Γ_{min}	Γ_{max}
Gemma 2B	5.06	3.75	**11.95**	**25.95**
Gemma 7B	7.79	4.30	**10.02**	**14.02**
Llama3 8B	10.72	7.88	**21.29**	**23.15**
Llama3 70B	**13.56**	3.99	**7.40**	13.12
Phi3 3.8B	**11.78**	**8.04**	4.05	4.62
Mistral 7B	4.16	3.11	**3.99**	**5.67**
GPT-4o-Mini	8.39	5.45	**17.08**	**17.82**
Qwen2 1.5B	**13.42**	10.02	**10.85**	11.95
Aya 35B	8.38	5.83	**11.84**	**16.67**
Overall	10.33	7.03	**11.48**	**15.35**

Table 2: Observed results of Δ_{min}, Δ_{max}, Γ_{min}, and Γ_{max} for all tested models. We find that in cases where our method performs better, it generally holds that it has a larger performance gain in comparison to the instances where Chain-of-Thought reasoning is the best method.

Conversely, Phi3 3.8B, when prompted using our method, only has an increased output value of 4.62% at best, while performing 11.78% better than the worst-performing *Argument Generation* approach, and 8.04% better than the best-performing approach in instances that chain-of-thought reasoning yields better results. We attribute this behavior to the model's lower argument ranking capabilities, meaning that Phi3 cannot effectively rank the arguments based on their validity. This notion is further bolstered by the model's relatively low performance in the IBM-30K task when using our proposed method, as seen in Table 1. Additionally, Phi family of models enjoy a significant performance boost when paired with chain-of-thought reasoning [2], which we believe contributes to the observation that our approach does not significantly increase the model performance in this instance relative to other models. Overall, our observations suggest that the effectiveness of prompting techniques might be as much model-dependent as they are task-dependent.

Finally, in order to better understand the model sensitivity to the presence or absence of implicit assumptions in the designed prompts, we report the average performance difference between the two *Argument Generation* methods. We find an absolute performance difference of 4.09% between the two approaches, the lowest amount among every other possible pair, with the closest pair being chain-of-thought reasoning and normal *Argument Generation* with an absolute performance difference of 8.56%. Similarly, the two *Argument Generation* methods have a Spearman correlation coefficient of 0.8351, with the closest pair having a correlation coefficient of 0.6685. Overall, our tests show that different models are generally resilient to variations in the prompt design as long as they are bound by the general procedure as provided in algorithm 1.

6.3 Model Size Analysis

We now provide our results on the effects of prompting on models of different sizes. In order to conduct our evaluation, we divide the models under test into three subcategories. The first category constitutes Gemma 2B, Phi3 3.8B, and Qwen2 1.5B and is demonstrative of small language models (below 7 billion parameters). The second category contains Gemma 7B, Llama3 8B, Mistral 7B, and GPT4o mini and showcases language models of medium size. Finally, Llama 3 70B and Aya 35B are members of the third category and act as sample members for the largest of language models by parameter count.

Figure 2 demonstrates the mean performance of the four prompting methods across different sizes, grouped by the aforementioned categorization where ZS, COT, AGIP, and AG stand for zero-shot, chain-of-thought, Argument Generation with Implicit Assumptions, and Argument Generation, respectively. Our findings show that generally, models experience a performance increase when prompted either with chain-of-thought reasoning, or *Argument Generation* with Aya 35B being the only significant exception. We observe that models of smaller sizes (medium and small) experience a significant performance boost when prompted via *Argument Generation* (for 100% of the models) and chain-of-thought reasoning (for 62% of the models).

Furthermore, smaller models show a higher performance gain when compared to the largest Llama 3 and Aya instances. More specifically, the mean performance gain when utilizing *Argument Generation* compared to chain of thought prompting is 3.18% for small models, and 2.72% for medium models, while the performance gain for the large models is 0.95%. We hypothesize that the reason behind the lower performance gain in larger models is due to their already impressive capability to infer the correct results without the requirement to introduce further information probing techniques such as chain-of-thought reasoning and *Argument Generation*. More concretely, forcing the model to perform self-reasoning or rank the validity of arguments and responses does not expose the model to previously hidden information, and does not necessarily increase the performance when additional information is not strictly required to respond to the input. This phenomenon is especially observable in CommonSenseQA and TruthfulQA as seen in table 1, where the introduction of prompting does not improve the model performance in all instances. These observations are in line with those reported by Kojima et al. (2022) and lead us to believe that knowledge probing prompting methods are only useful in cases where this additional information is required to make strong predictions and might additionally depend on model architecture.

To further investigate the effects of prompting on model performance, and its relationship with

[2] Open COT Leaderboard

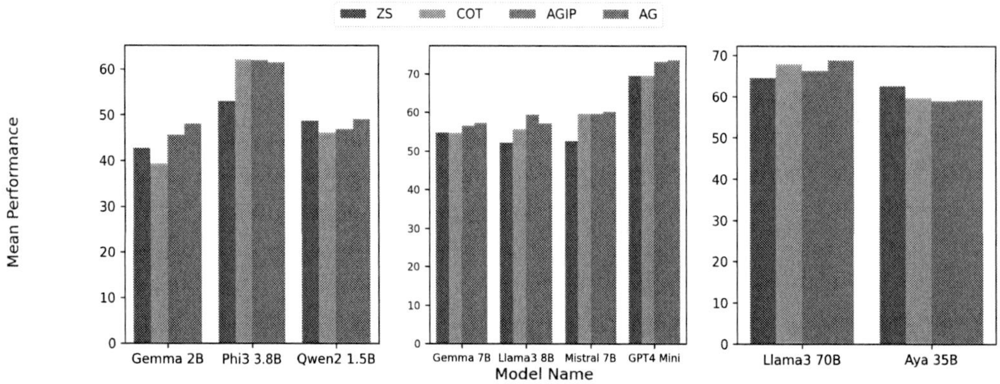

Figure 2: Mean Performance in models of different size

the number of model parameters, we report the mean performance across the number of parameters in figure 3. We find that although both our proposed method and chain-of-thought reasoning provide improved performance in models of larger size, their impact diminishes as the models grow larger. More specifically, we find that the mean difference between zero-shot prompting and *Argument Generation* methods is 4.66% for models with less than 7 billion parameters, 4.94% for models of 7 billion to 8 billion parameters, and 0.45% for the largest models. Further investigation is required to fully confirm our observations, however, this finding bolsters the previous hypothesis that *Argument Generation* as a prompting technique, is more effective in increasing the performance of smaller models. This behavior may stem from the fact that large models are able to generate convincing arguments for incorrect options, making the task of discerning an invalid argument from a valid one difficult. Conversely, smaller models are not able to generate arguments of high quality for incorrect candidates, thus goading the model to rank the valid argument over the incorrect one. Similarly, the observed mean differences between *Argument Generation* and chain-of-thought reasoning are 2.92%, 2.33%, and 0.95% respectively for models of small (<7B), medium (7B and 8B), and large (>8B) sizes.

Based on the above observation, a multi-agent technique to increase performance might be to generate arguments using a less capable model, while utilizing a more performant model to rank the arguments. We delegate these additional analyses to future work.

7 Discussion and Future Work

Prompting has been proposed as a method of improving model performance in either task-specific settings or broader, task-agnostic environments (Sahoo et al., 2024b). Despite the visible gains of employing prompting to yield better model results, the literature showcasing how, and when prompting works is limited (Petrov et al., 2024). We observe that the proposed method is able to significantly boost the model performance in smaller models while gaining marginal improvements as the model size increases, which is contrary to the previous work showing that larger models have higher gains through prompting (Wei et al., 2022b). This leads us to believe that the relationship between prompting and the nature of the model is complex, and might be affected both by the model size, and its relative task-specific knowledge and capabilities. Further work is required to demonstrate the effects of prompting when models hold knowledge of varying degrees with respect to a task description. Investigation of the learning resources used in model training can provide invaluable insight into the relationship between prompting and model reasoning.

8 Conclusion

In this work, we have proposed *Argument Generation* as a novel, zero-shot prompting technique. Through empirical evaluation using a number of datasets, we observe that our method is able to outperform both zero-shot prompting and zero-shot chain-of-thought reasoning in the majority of the conducted tests, making it a likely candidate when improving the model performance in a zero-shot setting is required. Furthermore, we show that

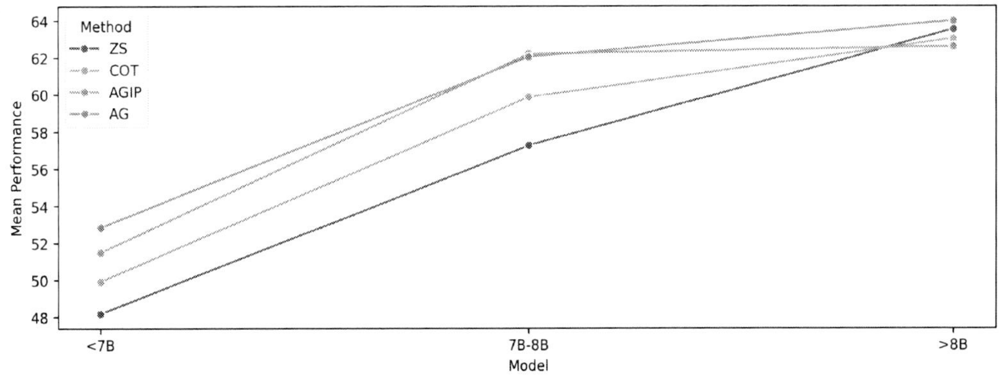

Figure 3: Mean Performance trend across model parameters

our approach yields larger gains in smaller models, both offering an effective method that can be used in small models and providing a possible future direction to better understand the relationship between model capabilities and prompting.

9 Limitations

Despite the observation that *Argument Generation* is able to generally outperform other common zero-shot prompting methods, its reliance on the existence of a predefined number of options from which the model can arguments is an inherent limitation of our work. While it is true that all questions can be modified to behave as either a multi-choice question or a yes-no question, this conversion relies on the background knowledge of the user that is interacting with the model, meaning that in cases where the user has no information regarding the possible answer for an open question, the correct formulation of the input to fit our criteria can only be delegated to the model itself.

In addition, while we have made the best effort to cover datasets pertaining to different tasks that evaluate various model capabilities, it is possible that other task-agnostic prompting methods outperform our approach in a number of yet untested metrics. Further investigation is required to fully confirm the effects of our approach on different models and tasks.

10 Ethical Considerations

Previous work has shown that Large Language Models are limited in their capability to understand their own lack of knowledge (Yin et al., 2023). As such, it is possible to generate prompts that exacerbate model hallucinations, and even force models to generate misinformation. The proposed method can especially be prone to attacks of a similar kind as a malicious agent can force the model to showcase generally unwanted behavior by providing the model with incorrect, and even dangerous options. Based on this observation, we encourage the research community to continue the work in hallucination reduction and use all prompting methods both responsibly and skeptically.

11 Acknowledgments

This research was supported in part by Other Transaction award HR00112490378 from the U.S. Defense Advanced Research Projects Agency (DARPA) Friction for Accountability in Conversational Transactions (FACT) program.

References

Marah Abdin, Sam Ade Jacobs, Ammar Ahmad Awan, Jyoti Aneja, Ahmed Awadallah, Hany Awadalla, Nguyen Bach, Amit Bahree, Arash Bakhtiari, Jianmin Bao, Harkirat Behl, Alon Benhaim, Misha Bilenko, Johan Bjorck, Sébastien Bubeck, Qin Cai, Martin Cai, Caio César Teodoro Mendes, Weizhu Chen, Vishrav Chaudhary, Dong Chen, Dongdong Chen, Yen-Chun Chen, Yi-Ling Chen, Parul Chopra, Xiyang Dai, Allie Del Giorno, Gustavo de Rosa, Matthew Dixon, Ronen Eldan, Victor Fragoso, Dan Iter, Mei Gao, Min Gao, Jianfeng Gao, Amit Garg, Abhishek Goswami, Suriya Gunasekar, Emman Haider, Junheng Hao, Russell J. Hewett, Jamie Huynh, Mojan Javaheripi, Xin Jin, Piero Kauffmann, Nikos Karampatziakis, Dongwoo Kim, Mahoud Khademi, Lev Kurilenko, James R. Lee, Yin Tat Lee, Yuanzhi Li, Yunsheng Li, Chen Liang, Lars Liden, Ce Liu, Mengchen Liu, Weishung Liu, Eric Lin, Zeqi Lin, Chong Luo, Piyush Madan, Matt Mazzola, Arindam Mitra, Hardik Modi, Anh Nguyen, Brandon Norick, Barun Patra, Daniel Perez-Becker, Thomas

Portet, Reid Pryzant, Heyang Qin, Marko Radmilac, Corby Rosset, Sambudha Roy, Olatunji Ruwase, Olli Saarikivi, Amin Saied, Adil Salim, Michael Santacroce, Shital Shah, Ning Shang, Hiteshi Sharma, Swadheen Shukla, Xia Song, Masahiro Tanaka, Andrea Tupini, Xin Wang, Lijuan Wang, Chunyu Wang, Yu Wang, Rachel Ward, Guanhua Wang, Philipp Witte, Haiping Wu, Michael Wyatt, Bin Xiao, Can Xu, Jiahang Xu, Weijian Xu, Sonali Yadav, Fan Yang, Jianwei Yang, Ziyi Yang, Yifan Yang, Donghan Yu, Lu Yuan, Chengruidong Zhang, Cyril Zhang, Jianwen Zhang, Li Lyna Zhang, Yi Zhang, Yue Zhang, Yunan Zhang, and Xiren Zhou. 2024. Phi-3 technical report: A highly capable language model locally on your phone. *Preprint*, arXiv:2404.14219.

Georgios Balikas. 2023. John-arthur at semeval-2023 task 4: Fine-tuning large language models for arguments classification. In *Proceedings of the 17th International Workshop on Semantic Evaluation (SemEval-2023)*, page 1428–1432, Toronto, Canada. Association for Computational Linguistics.

Edward Y. Chang. 2023. Prompting large language models with the socratic method. In *2023 IEEE 13th Annual Computing and Communication Workshop and Conference (CCWC)*, pages 0351–0360.

Yupeng Chang, Xu Wang, Jindong Wang, Yuan Wu, Linyi Yang, Kaijie Zhu, Hao Chen, Xiaoyuan Yi, Cunxiang Wang, Yidong Wang, Wei Ye, Yue Zhang, Yi Chang, Philip S. Yu, Qiang Yang, and Xing Xie. 2024. A survey on evaluation of large language models. *ACM Trans. Intell. Syst. Technol.*, 15(3).

Guizhen Chen, Liying Cheng, Luu Anh Tuan, and Lidong Bing. 2023. Exploring the potential of large language models in computational argumentation. (arXiv:2311.09022). ArXiv:2311.09022 [cs].

Yew Ken Chia, Guizhen Chen, Luu Anh Tuan, Soujanya Poria, and Lidong Bing. 2023. Contrastive chain-of-thought prompting. (arXiv:2311.09277). ArXiv:2311.09277 [cs].

Adrian de Wynter and Tommy Yuan. 2023. I wish to have an argument: Argumentative reasoning in large language models. (arXiv:2309.16938). ArXiv:2309.16938 [cs].

Jacob Devlin, Ming-Wei Chang, Kenton Lee, and Kristina Toutanova. 2019. BERT: Pre-training of deep bidirectional transformers for language understanding. In *Proceedings of the 2019 Conference of the North American Chapter of the Association for Computational Linguistics: Human Language Technologies, Volume 1 (Long and Short Papers)*, pages 4171–4186, Minneapolis, Minnesota. Association for Computational Linguistics.

Yilun Du, Shuang Li, Antonio Torralba, Joshua B Tenenbaum, and Igor Mordatch. 2023. Improving factuality and reasoning in language models through multiagent debate. *arXiv preprint arXiv:2305.14325*.

Yann Dubois, Balázs Galambosi, Percy Liang, and Tatsunori B Hashimoto. 2024. Length-controlled alpacaeval: A simple way to debias automatic evaluators. *arXiv preprint arXiv:2404.04475*.

Mor Geva, Daniel Khashabi, Elad Segal, Tushar Khot, Dan Roth, and Jonathan Berant. 2021. Did aristotle use a laptop? a question answering benchmark with implicit reasoning strategies. *Transactions of the Association for Computational Linguistics*, 9:346–361.

Shai Gretz, Roni Friedman, Edo Cohen-Karlik, Assaf Toledo, Dan Lahav, Ranit Aharonov, and Noam Slonim. 2020. A large-scale dataset for argument quality ranking: Construction and analysis. *Proceedings of the AAAI Conference on Artificial Intelligence*, 34(05):7805–7813.

Carolin Holtermann, Anne Lauscher, and Simone Paolo Ponzetto. 2022. Fair and argumentative language modeling for computational argumentation. (arXiv:2204.04026). ArXiv:2204.04026 [cs].

Chi Hu, Yuan Ge, Xiangnan Ma, Hang Cao, Qiang Li, Yonghua Yang, Tong Xiao, and Jingbo Zhu. 2024. RankPrompt: Step-by-step comparisons make language models better reasoners. In *Proceedings of the 2024 Joint International Conference on Computational Linguistics, Language Resources and Evaluation (LREC-COLING 2024)*, pages 13524–13536, Torino, Italia. ELRA and ICCL.

Jie Huang and Kevin Chen-Chuan Chang. 2023. Towards reasoning in large language models: A survey. (arXiv:2212.10403). ArXiv:2212.10403 [cs].

Albert Q. Jiang, Alexandre Sablayrolles, Arthur Mensch, Chris Bamford, Devendra Singh Chaplot, Diego de las Casas, Florian Bressand, Gianna Lengyel, Guillaume Lample, Lucile Saulnier, Lélio Renard Lavaud, Marie-Anne Lachaux, Pierre Stock, Teven Le Scao, Thibaut Lavril, Thomas Wang, Timothée Lacroix, and William El Sayed. 2023. Mistral 7b. *Preprint*, arXiv:2310.06825.

Tushar Khot, Harsh Trivedi, Matthew Finlayson, Yao Fu, Kyle Richardson, Peter Clark, and Ashish Sabharwal. 2023. Decomposed prompting: A modular approach for solving complex tasks. (arXiv:2210.02406). ArXiv:2210.02406 [cs].

Takeshi Kojima, Shixiang Shane Gu, Machel Reid, Yutaka Matsuo, and Yusuke Iwasawa. 2022. Large language models are zero-shot reasoners. In *Proceedings of the 36th International Conference on Neural Information Processing Systems*, NIPS '22, Red Hook, NY, USA. Curran Associates Inc.

Noah Lee, Na Min An, and James Thorne. 2023. Can large language models capture dissenting human voices? In *Proceedings of the 2023 Conference on Empirical Methods in Natural Language Processing*, pages 4569–4585, Singapore. Association for Computational Linguistics.

Tian Liang, Zhiwei He, Wenxiang Jiao, Xing Wang, Yan Wang, Rui Wang, Yujiu Yang, Zhaopeng Tu, and Shuming Shi. 2023. Encouraging divergent thinking in large language models through multi-agent debate. *Preprint*, arXiv:2305.19118.

Stephanie Lin, Jacob Hilton, and Owain Evans. 2022. TruthfulQA: Measuring how models mimic human falsehoods. In *Proceedings of the 60th Annual Meeting of the Association for Computational Linguistics (Volume 1: Long Papers)*, pages 3214–3252, Dublin, Ireland. Association for Computational Linguistics.

Man Luo, Shrinidhi Kumbhar, Ming shen, Mihir Parmar, Neeraj Varshney, Pratyay Banerjee, Somak Aditya, and Chitta Baral. 2023. Towards logiglue: A brief survey and a benchmark for analyzing logical reasoning capabilities of language models. (arXiv:2310.00836). ArXiv:2310.00836 [cs].

Xueguang Ma, Xinyu Crystina Zhang, Ronak Pradeep, and Jimmy J. Lin. 2023. Zero-shot listwise document reranking with a large language model. *ArXiv*, abs/2305.02156.

Aman Madaan, Niket Tandon, Prakhar Gupta, Skyler Hallinan, Luyu Gao, Sarah Wiegreffe, Uri Alon, Nouha Dziri, Shrimai Prabhumoye, Yiming Yang, Shashank Gupta, Bodhisattwa Prasad Majumder, Katherine Hermann, Sean Welleck, Amir Yazdanbakhsh, and Peter Clark. 2023. Self-refine: Iterative refinement with self-feedback. In *Advances in Neural Information Processing Systems*, volume 36, pages 46534–46594. Curran Associates, Inc.

Hugo Mercier. 2016. The argumentative theory: Predictions and empirical evidence. *Trends in Cognitive Sciences*, 20(9):689–700.

Hugo Mercier and Dan Sperber. 2011. Why do humans reason? arguments for an argumentative theory. *Behavioral and Brain Sciences*, 34(2):57–74.

Gemma Team Thomas Mesnard, Cassidy Hardin, Robert Dadashi, Surya Bhupatiraju, Shreya Pathak, L. Sifre, Morgane Riviere, Mihir Kale, J Christopher Love, Pouya Dehghani Tafti, L'eonard Hussenot, Aakanksha Chowdhery, Adam Roberts, Aditya Barua, Alex Botev, Alex Castro-Ros, Ambrose Slone, Am'elie H'eliou, Andrea Tacchetti, Anna Bulanova, Antonia Paterson, Beth Tsai, Bobak Shahriari, Charline Le Lan, Christopher A. Choquette-Choo, Cl'ement Crepy, Daniel Cer, Daphne Ippolito, David Reid, Elena Buchatskaya, Eric Ni, Eric Noland, Geng Yan, George Tucker, George-Christian Muraru, Grigory Rozhdestvenskiy, Henryk Michalewski, Ian Tenney, Ivan Grishchenko, Jacob Austin, James Keeling, Jane Labanowski, Jean-Baptiste Lespiau, Jeff Stanway, Jenny Brennan, Jeremy Chen, Johan Ferret, Justin Chiu, Justin Mao-Jones, Katherine Lee, Kathy Yu, Katie Millican, Lars Lowe Sjoesund, Lisa Lee, Lucas Dixon, Machel Reid, Maciej Mikula, Mateo Wirth, Michael Sharman, Nikolai Chinaev, Nithum Thain, Olivier Bachem, Oscar Chang, Oscar Wahltinez, Paige Bailey, Paul Michel, Petko Yotov, Pier Giuseppe Sessa, Rahma Chaabouni, Ramona Comanescu, Reena Jana, Rohan Anil, Ross McIlroy, Ruibo Liu, Ryan Mullins, Samuel L Smith, Sebastian Borgeaud, Sertan Girgin, Sholto Douglas, Shree Pandya, Siamak Shakeri, Soham De, Ted Klimenko, Tom Hennigan, Vladimir Feinberg, Wojciech Stokowiec, Yu hui Chen, Zafarali Ahmed, Zhitao Gong, Tris Brian Warkentin, Ludovic Peran, Minh Giang, Cl'ement Farabet, Oriol Vinyals, Jeffrey Dean, Koray Kavukcuoglu, Demis Hassabis, Zoubin Ghahramani, Douglas Eck, Joelle Barral, Fernando Pereira, Eli Collins, Armand Joulin, Noah Fiedel, Evan Senter, Alek Andreev, and Kathleen Kenealy. 2024. Gemma: Open models based on gemini research and technology. *ArXiv*, abs/2403.08295.

Moin Nadeem, Anna Bethke, and Siva Reddy. 2021. StereoSet: Measuring stereotypical bias in pretrained language models. In *Proceedings of the 59th Annual Meeting of the Association for Computational Linguistics and the 11th International Joint Conference on Natural Language Processing (Volume 1: Long Papers)*, pages 5356–5371, Online. Association for Computational Linguistics.

Aleksandar Petrov, Philip H. S. Torr, and Adel Bibi. 2024. When do prompting and prefix-tuning work? a theory of capabilities and limitations. *Preprint*, arXiv:2310.19698.

Shuofei Qiao, Yixin Ou, Ningyu Zhang, Xiang Chen, Yunzhi Yao, Shumin Deng, Chuanqi Tan, Fei Huang, and Huajun Chen. 2023. Reasoning with language model prompting: A survey. In *Proceedings of the 61st Annual Meeting of the Association for Computational Linguistics (Volume 1: Long Papers)*, pages 5368–5393, Toronto, Canada. Association for Computational Linguistics.

Alec Radford, Jeff Wu, Rewon Child, David Luan, Dario Amodei, and Ilya Sutskever. 2019. Language models are unsupervised multitask learners.

Nicholas Riccardi and Rutvik H. Desai. 2023. The two word test: A semantic benchmark for large language models. *Preprint*, arXiv:2306.04610.

Babak Rokh, Ali Azarpeyvand, and Alireza Khanteymoori. 2023. A comprehensive survey on model quantization for deep neural networks in image classification. *ACM Trans. Intell. Syst. Technol.*, 14(6).

Ramon Ruiz-Dolz and John Lawrence. 2023. Detecting argumentative fallacies in the wild: Problems and limitations of large language models. In *Proceedings of the 10th Workshop on Argument Mining*, page 1–10, Singapore. Association for Computational Linguistics.

Pranab Sahoo, Ayush Kumar Singh, Sriparna Saha, Vinija Jain, Samrat Mondal, and Aman Chadha. 2024a. A systematic survey of prompt engineering in large language models: Techniques and applications. (arXiv:2402.07927). ArXiv:2402.07927 [cs].

Pranab Sahoo, Ayush Kumar Singh, Sriparna Saha, Vinija Jain, Samrat Mondal, and Aman Chadha. 2024b. A systematic survey of prompt engineering in large language models: Techniques and applications. *Preprint*, arXiv:2402.07927.

Vasanth Sarathy, Mark Burstein, Scott Friedman, Robert Bobrow, and Ugur Kuter. 2022. A neuro-symbolic cognitive system for intuitive argumentation. In *Advances in Cognitive Systems (ACS)*.

Dan Sperber, Fabrice Clement, Christophe Heintz, Olivier Mascaro, Hugo Mercier, Gloria Origgi, and Deirdre Wilson. 2010. Epistemic vigilance. *Mind & Language*, 25(4):359–393.

Mirac Suzgun, Nathan Scales, Nathanael Schärli, Sebastian Gehrmann, Yi Tay, Hyung Won Chung, Aakanksha Chowdhery, Quoc Le, Ed Chi, Denny Zhou, and Jason Wei. 2023. Challenging BIG-bench tasks and whether chain-of-thought can solve them. In *Findings of the Association for Computational Linguistics: ACL 2023*, pages 13003–13051, Toronto, Canada. Association for Computational Linguistics.

Alon Talmor, Jonathan Herzig, Nicholas Lourie, and Jonathan Berant. 2019. CommonsenseQA: A question answering challenge targeting commonsense knowledge. In *Proceedings of the 2019 Conference of the North American Chapter of the Association for Computational Linguistics: Human Language Technologies, Volume 1 (Long and Short Papers)*, pages 4149–4158, Minneapolis, Minnesota. Association for Computational Linguistics.

Zhengwei Tao, Zhi Jin, Xiaoying Bai, Haiyan Zhao, Yanlin Feng, Jia Li, and Wenpeng Hu. 2023. Eveval: A comprehensive evaluation of event semantics for large language models. *Preprint*, arXiv:2305.15268.

Luke Thorburn and Ariel Kruger. Optimizing language models for argumentative reasoning.

Hugo Touvron, Louis Martin, Kevin Stone, Peter Albert, Amjad Almahairi, Yasmine Babaei, Nikolay Bashlykov, Soumya Batra, Prajjwal Bhargava, Shruti Bhosale, Dan Bikel, Lukas Blecher, Cristian Canton Ferrer, Moya Chen, Guillem Cucurull, David Esiobu, Jude Fernandes, Jeremy Fu, Wenyin Fu, Brian Fuller, Cynthia Gao, Vedanuj Goswami, Naman Goyal, Anthony Hartshorn, Saghar Hosseini, Rui Hou, Hakan Inan, Marcin Kardas, Viktor Kerkez, Madian Khabsa, Isabel Kloumann, Artem Korenev, Punit Singh Koura, Marie-Anne Lachaux, Thibaut Lavril, Jenya Lee, Diana Liskovich, Yinghai Lu, Yuning Mao, Xavier Martinet, Todor Mihaylov, Pushkar Mishra, Igor Molybog, Yixin Nie, Andrew Poulton, Jeremy Reizenstein, Rashi Rungta, Kalyan Saladi, Alan Schelten, Ruan Silva, Eric Michael Smith, Ranjan Subramanian, Xiaoqing Ellen Tan, Binh Tang, Ross Taylor, Adina Williams, Jian Xiang Kuan, Puxin Xu, Zheng Yan, Iliyan Zarov, Yuchen Zhang, Angela Fan, Melanie Kambadur, Sharan Narang, Aurelien Rodriguez, Robert Stojnic, Sergey Edunov, and Thomas Scialom. 2023. Llama 2: Open foundation and fine-tuned chat models. *Preprint*, arXiv:2307.09288.

Ahmet Üstün, Viraat Aryabumi, Zheng Yong, Wei-Yin Ko, Daniel D'souza, Gbemileke Onilude, Neel Bhandari, Shivalika Singh, Hui-Lee Ooi, Amr Kayid, Freddie Vargus, Phil Blunsom, Shayne Longpre, Niklas Muennighoff, Marzieh Fadaee, Julia Kreutzer, and Sara Hooker. 2024. Aya model: An instruction finetuned open-access multilingual language model. In *Proceedings of the 62nd Annual Meeting of the Association for Computational Linguistics (Volume 1: Long Papers)*, pages 15894–15939, Bangkok, Thailand. Association for Computational Linguistics.

Haoyu Wang, Tao Li, Zhiwei Deng, Dan Roth, and Yang Li. 2024. Devil's advocate: Anticipatory reflection for llm agents. (arXiv:2405.16334). ArXiv:2405.16334 [cs].

Xuezhi Wang, Jason Wei, Dale Schuurmans, Quoc Le, Ed Chi, Sharan Narang, Aakanksha Chowdhery, and Denny Zhou. 2022. Self-consistency improves chain of thought reasoning in language models. (arXiv:2203.11171). ArXiv:2203.11171 [cs].

Xuezhi Wang, Jason Wei, Dale Schuurmans, and Quoc V Le. 2023a. H. chi, sharan narang, aakanksha chowdhery, and denny zhou. self-consistency improves chain of thought reasoning in language models. In *The Eleventh International Conference on Learning Representations*, volume 1.

Yuqing Wang and Yun Zhao. 2023. Metacognitive prompting improves understanding in large language models. (arXiv:2308.05342). ArXiv:2308.05342 [cs].

Zengzhi Wang, Qiming Xie, Zixiang Ding, Yi Feng, and Rui Xia. 2023b. Is chatgpt a good sentiment analyzer? a preliminary study. *arXiv preprint*.

Jason Wei, Xuezhi Wang, Dale Schuurmans, Maarten Bosma, Ed Chi, Quoc Le, and Denny Zhou. 2022a. Chain of thought prompting elicits reasoning in large language models. (arXiv:2201.11903). ArXiv:2201.11903 [cs].

Jason Wei, Xuezhi Wang, Dale Schuurmans, Maarten Bosma, Brian Ichter, Fei Xia, Ed H. Chi, Quoc V. Le, and Denny Zhou. 2022b. Chain-of-thought prompting elicits reasoning in large language models. In *Proceedings of the 36th International Conference on Neural Information Processing Systems*, NIPS '22, Red Hook, NY, USA. Curran Associates Inc.

An Yang, Baosong Yang, Binyuan Hui, Bo Zheng, Bowen Yu, Chang Zhou, Chengpeng Li, Chengyuan Li, Dayiheng Liu, Fei Huang, Guanting Dong, Haoran Wei, Huan Lin, Jialong Tang, Jialin Wang, Jian Yang, Jianhong Tu, Jianwei Zhang, Jianxin Ma, Jianxin Yang, Jin Xu, Jingren Zhou, Jinze Bai, Jinzheng He, Junyang Lin, Kai Dang, Keming Lu, Keqin Chen, Kexin Yang, Mei Li, Mingfeng Xue, Na Ni, Pei Zhang, Peng Wang, Ru Peng, Rui Men, Ruize Gao, Runji Lin, Shijie Wang, Shuai Bai, Sinan Tan, Tianhang Zhu, Tianhao Li, Tianyu Liu, Wenbin Ge, Xiaodong Deng, Xiaohuan Zhou, Xingzhang Ren,

Xinyu Zhang, Xipin Wei, Xuancheng Ren, Xuejing Liu, Yang Fan, Yang Yao, Yichang Zhang, Yu Wan, Yunfei Chu, Yuqiong Liu, Zeyu Cui, Zhenru Zhang, Zhifang Guo, and Zhihao Fan. 2024. Qwen2 technical report. *Preprint*, arXiv:2407.10671.

Zhangyue Yin, Qiushi Sun, Qipeng Guo, Jiawen Wu, Xipeng Qiu, and Xuanjing Huang. 2023. Do large language models know what they don't know? In *Findings of the Association for Computational Linguistics: ACL 2023*, pages 8653–8665, Toronto, Canada. Association for Computational Linguistics.

Fei Yu, Hongbo Zhang, Prayag Tiwari, and Benyou Wang. 2023a. Natural language reasoning, a survey. (arXiv:2303.14725). ArXiv:2303.14725 [cs].

Zihan Yu, Liang He, Zhen Wu, Xinyu Dai, and Jiajun Chen. 2023b. Towards better chain-of-thought prompting strategies: A survey. (arXiv:2310.04959). ArXiv:2310.04959 [cs].

Mahdi Zakizadeh, Kaveh Miandoab, and Mohammad Pilehvar. 2023. DiFair: A benchmark for disentangled assessment of gender knowledge and bias. In *Findings of the Association for Computational Linguistics: EMNLP 2023*, pages 1897–1914, Singapore. Association for Computational Linguistics.

A Model Details

We utilize the Ollama framework [3] to conduct all evaluations described in the paper. Generally, we make use of the 4-bit quantized (Rokh et al., 2023) versions of the tested models to maintain consistency, and due to hardware limitations. Table 3 demonstrates all the tested models, their Ollama hub links, as well as their quantization methods. In the cases that an Ollama model is not available, or the model is closed-source, we use the associated Huggingface[4] instance of the model, or use an API to access the model.

Model Name	Hub Link	Quantization Method
Gemma 2B	Link	Q4
Gemma 7B	Link	Q4
Llama3 7B	Link	Q4
Llama3 80B	Link	Q4
Phi3 3.8B	Link	Q5
Mistral 7B	Link	Q4
GPT-4o-Mini	Link	N/A
Qwen 2 1.5B	Link	FP16
Aya 35B	Link	Q4

Table 3: All model sources as well as their quantization method.

Additionally, in order to minimize output variance and generate reproducible evaluations, all tests were performed with a model temperature of 0 and a random seed of 42. Furthermore, our test setting involved a workstation containing an Nvidia A6000, and an Nvidia RTX 4090, with 128 GB of available RAM. All testing code will be made publicly available upon the publication of the work.

B Evaluation Method and Prompt Strings

Table 4 lists the tested prompting methods as well as the special instruction used for each prompt. A special instruction is a text string that is appended to the end of the input question and aims to guide the model behavior while responding to that specific input.

For the case of zero-shot prompting, we simply ask the model to only respond with the correct answer without providing any instructions to reason about the input. Chain-of-thought reasoning is additionally employed via the guidelines provided by Kojima et al. (2022). Finally, we showcase the special instructions for the proposed method, both containing the implicit assumption generation, and common argument generation.

[3] https://github.com/ollama/ollama-python

[4] https://huggingface.co/

Prompting Method	Special Instruction
Zero-Shot	Only respond with the correct answer
Chain-of-Thought	Let's think about each option step by step
Argument Generation w/ Implicit Assumptions	When answering, first reason about each choice, and make an argument for why it can be the answer and why it cannot be the answer. Then identify, for each choice, what implicit assumptions you might be making for each of your arguments. By implicit assumption, we mean those propositions that are necessary so that the choice logically follows the question. Then select one of the choices based on the strongest argument
Argument Generation	When answering, first reason about each choice, and make an argument for why it can be the answer and why it cannot be the answer. Then select one of the choices based on the strongest argument.

Table 4: Special model instructions corresponding to each prompting method.

LLM-as-a-tutor in EFL Writing Education: Focusing on Evaluation of Student-LLM Interaction

Jieun Han, Haneul Yoo, Junho Myung, Minsun Kim, Hyunseung Lim, Yoonsu Kim, Tak Yeon Lee, Hwajung Hong, Juho Kim, So-Yeon Ahn, Alice Oh
KAIST, South Korea
{jieun_han, haneul.yoo, junho00211, 9909cindy, charlie9807, yoonsu16, takyeonlee, hwajung, juhokim, ahnsoyeon}@kaist.ac.kr, alice.oh@kaist.edu

Abstract

In the context of English as a Foreign Language (EFL) writing education, LLM-as-a-tutor can assist students by providing real-time feedback on their essays. However, challenges arise in assessing LLM-as-a-tutor due to differing standards between educational and general use cases. To bridge this gap, we integrate pedagogical principles to assess student-LLM interaction. First, we explore how LLMs can function as English tutors, providing effective essay feedback tailored to students. Second, we propose three criteria to evaluate LLM-as-a-tutor specifically designed for EFL writing education, emphasizing pedagogical aspects. In this process, EFL experts evaluate the feedback from LLM-as-a-tutor regarding (1) quality and (2) characteristics. On the other hand, EFL learners assess their (3) learning outcomes from interaction with LLM-as-a-tutor. This approach lays the groundwork for developing LLMs as a tutor tailored to the needs of EFL learners, advancing the effectiveness of writing education in this context.

1 Introduction

Personalized feedback is known to significantly enhance student achievement (Bloom, 1984). However, providing real-time, individualized feedback at scale in traditional classroom settings is challenging due to limited resources. Large language models (LLMs) can be particularly beneficial to address this challenge by enabling real-time feedback in educational settings (Kasneci et al., 2023; Wang and Demszky, 2023; Yan et al., 2024). However, LLMs often struggle to generate constructive feedback within educational contexts. Unlike human feedback, which consistently identifies areas for improvement, LLM-generated feedback frequently fails to effectively highlight students' weaknesses (Behzad et al., 2024). Therefore, it is essential to identify the advantages and limitations of LLMs as English writing tutors and to develop methods for providing effective feedback for students.

The evaluation of LLMs for educational purposes differs significantly from their general-purpose evaluation. General-purpose LLM evaluation primarily focuses on assessing the quality of responses (Wang et al., 2023; Zheng et al., 2023; Chang et al., 2024). However, as Lee et al. (2023) emphasize, merely evaluating the final output quality is insufficient to capture the full dynamics of human-LLM interactions. In particular, educational feedback needs a more nuanced consideration of factors beyond traditional metrics. It also requires the expertise of education professionals to evaluate the learning process and outcomes due to its inherent challenges. Our work incorporates metrics specifically tailored to pedagogical considerations by involving real-world education stakeholders to better assess student-LLM interactions.

In summary, the main contributions of this work are as follows:

1. We explore the role of LLM as tutors in generating essay feedback.
2. We introduce an educational evaluation metric customized for EFL writing education.
3. We assess student-LLM interactions by involving real-world educational stakeholders.

2 LLMs as EFL Tutors: Early Insights

In this section, we report preliminary findings that display both the advantages and limitations of LLM-as-a-tutor.

2.1 Advantage of LLM-as-a-tutor

We conduct a group interview with six EFL learners and a written interview with three instructors to explore the needs for LLM-as-a-tutor. To reflect the perspectives of key stakeholders in EFL writing education, we recruit undergraduate EFL

Proceedings of the 1st Workshop on Customizable NLP: Progress and Challenges in Customizing NLP for a Domain, Application, Group, or Individual (CustomNLP4U), pages 284–293
November 16, 2024 ©2024 Association for Computational Linguistics

learners and instructors from a college EFL center. The use of LLM-as-a-tutor presents a significant opportunity for EFL learners by enabling real-time feedback at scale. While all students expressed a strong need for both rubric-based scores and feedback, only two of them had previously received feedback from their instructors. Students are particularly interested in receiving immediate scores and feedback, allowing them to identify weaknesses in their essays and refine them through an iterative process.

2.2 Limitation of LLM-as-a-tutor

We conduct an experiment using `gpt-3.5-turbo` to generate essay feedback on standard setting. The model is configured to act as an English writing teacher and provide feedback based on an EFL writing scoring rubric (Cumming, 1990; Ozfidan and Mitchell, 2022). Detailed experimental settings and prompts are described in Appendix §A. We ask 21 English education experts to evaluate the feedback on a 7-point Likert scale, focusing on feedback tone (positiveness, directness) and helpfulness. The experts rate the feedback's positiveness at 5.93 and directness at 3.72. This result indicates `gpt-3.5-turbo`'s inherent tendency to generate positive feedback. However, previous research and our qualitative interviews suggest that EFL learners prefer direct and negative feedback (Ellis, 2008; Saragih et al., 2021). Moreover, the experts found the feedback from `gpt-3.5-turbo` less helpful, with an average helpfulness rating of 3.41 out of 7.

2.3 Mitigating Limitation

To address the limitations of standard prompting in generating effective feedback for EFL learners, we propose a score-based prompting method that involves informing the model of a student's essay weakness using rubric-based scores. While models like `gpt-3.5-turbo`, trained with reinforcement learning from human feedback, generally align with human preferences in broad contexts, they may not always provide the most constructive feedback for EFL learners who need more targeted guidance. These models tend to generate positive and indirect feedback, which, though satisfactory in general contexts, may not be as effective for learners who need more targeted and constructive guidance. Therefore, we suggest score-based prompting method, leveraging rubric-based scores for LLM self-refinement of feedback generation (Pan et al., 2024).

Score-based prompting method uses predicted scores and rubric explanations to generate feedback on students' essays. Student's essays are scored by the state-of-the-art automated essay scoring model (Yoo et al., 2024) under three rubrics: content, organization, and language (Table 2). We assume this scoring information can guide the model in generating feedback that is more aligned with students' needs. The exact prompting setup is described in Appendix §A.

3 Student-LLM Interaction Evaluation

In this section, we introduce evaluation methods for student-LLM interaction. We provide feedback generated with score-based prompting to student. English experts then evaluate LLM-generated feedback with our evaluation metrics on a 7 point Likert scale.

3.1 Annotator Details

We explore student-LLM interaction of 33 EFL learners and gather evaluations from 21 English education experts, who are key stakeholders in EFL writing education. These experts hold Secondary School Teacher's Certificates (Grade II) for English, licensed by the Ministry of Education, Republic of Korea. The student cohort comprises 32 Korean students and one Italian student, with a gender distribution of 12 females and 21 males. While participating in EFL writing courses, students independently write their essays, which are then subjected to LLM-generated feedback. This feedback is produced by `gpt-3.5-turbo` using score-based prompting, and is delivered through the RECIPE (Han et al., 2023) platform as part of their coursework.

3.2 Evaluation Details

We introduce educational metrics specifically designed to assess student-LLM interactions within the context of EFL writing education (Table 1). These metrics are constructed by adapting Lee et al. (2023)'s framework to fit the EFL writing settings, focusing on targets, perspectives, and criteria.

Targets We identify two primary aspects for evaluating student-LLM interactions: *output* and *process*. *Output* refers to the LLM's generated feedback that students receive, while *process* encompasses the development of students' essays, com-

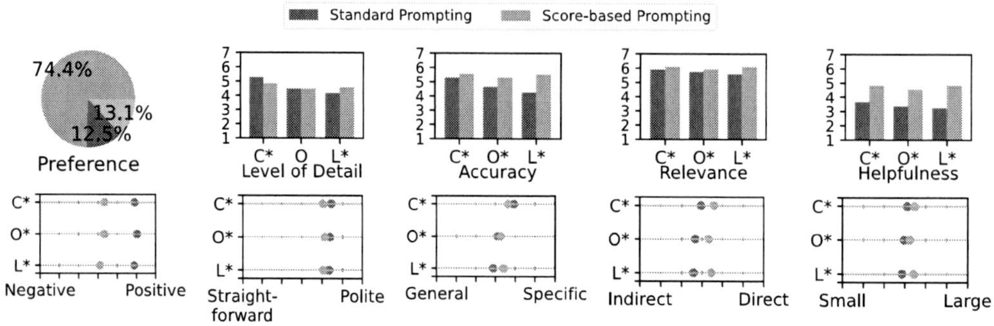

Figure 1: Evaluation results on quality and characteristic of two rubric-based feedback with standard prompting and score-based prompting in a 7-point Likert scale. C, O, and L denote Content, Organization, and Language, respectively. Asterisk denotes statistical significance tested by the paired T-test at p level of < 0.05.

Criteria	Target	Perspective	Metric
1. Quality	Output	Teacher	Level of detail, Accuracy, Relevance, Helpfulness
2. Characteristic	Output	Teacher	Negative-Positive, Straightforward-Polite, General-Specific, Indirect-Direct, Small-Large
3. Learning outcome	Process	Student	Essay quality improvement, Understanding

Table 1: Evaluation metrics constructed upon targets, perspectives, and criteria

prehension, and overall progress during the interaction.

Perspectives The evaluation involves the two main stakeholders in EFL education: *students* and *teachers*. While students may favor LLMs that provide immediate, correct answers, this approach may not be pedagogically optimal. Therefore, it is crucial to incorporate *teachers'* perspectives when assessing the *quality* and *characteristics* of LLM-generated feedback.

Criteria We first evaluate student-LLM interactions using three key criteria: *quality*, *characteristics*, and *learning outcomes.*

For *quality* assessment, we adapt evaluation criteria from LLM response assessments (Zheng et al., 2023), re-defining those criteria to suit our domain of feedback generation: level of detail, accuracy, relevance, and helpfulness (Appendix §B.1).

For *characteristics* assessment, we propose five characteristics to analyze the type of feedback, building on previous studies in English writing education. These criteria include: negative ↔ positive (Cheng and Zhang, 2022), straightforward ↔ polite (Lysvåg, 1975; Danescu-Niculescu-Mizil et al., 2013), general ↔ specific (Leibold and Schwarz, 2015), indirect ↔ direct (Van Beuningen et al., 2012; Eslami, 2014), small ↔ large (Liu and Brown, 2015). See Table 3 for more detailed explanations and examples. Since these five criteria are grounded in pedagogical theory and research, the analysis of feedback requires the involvement of educational experts who can interpret subtle distinctions in feedback in alignment with instructional objectives.

For *learning outcome* assessment, We assess the impact of student-LLM interaction. Students assess their own learning progress by comparing their improvement before and after receiving feedback from the LLM. After engaging with LLM-as-a-tutor to revise their essays, students reflect on their learning process through a questionnaire. The detailed questions are provided in Appendix §C.

- **Negative ↔ Positive**: Is the tone of feedback positive?
- **Straightforward ↔ Polite**: Is the feedback polite?
- **General ↔ Specific**: Is the feedback specific?
- **Indirect ↔ Direct**: Is the feedback direct?
- **Small ↔ Large**: How extensive is the quantity of feedback provided?

3.3 Results

In this section, we report the results of standard and score-based prompting across three criteria: *quality*, *characteristic*, and *learning outcome*.

Quality Four figures in the top row in Figure 1 present the quality evaluation results for the two types of feedback. Score-based prompting outperforms standard prompting in terms of accuracy, relevance, and helpfulness, achieving statistical significance across all rubrics. Feedback generated by standard prompting varies in the level of detail (4.16 – 5.28), while score-based prompting produces consistently detailed feedback (4.48 – 4.86). Moreover, feedback from standard prompting tends to be overly detailed in summarizing the essay, which is not perceived as constructive (see examples in Table 4). Further qualitative analysis is described in Appendix §B.2.1.

Characteristic We evaluate feedback using five metrics tailored to English writing education. Score-based prompting generates more negative, straightforward, direct, and extensive feedback compared to standard prompting across all rubrics (see the figures located in the lower section of Figure 1). Specifically, feedback from standard prompting tends to generate general compliments rather than constructive criticism. In contrast, feedback from score-based prompting is notably more concise, delivering more content in significantly fewer tokens (70.46 vs. 79.19) and sentences (4.20 vs. 5.04). To further support the results, we also conduct a qualitative analysis of the feedback characteristics on Negative ↔ Positive and Straightforward ↔ Polite (Appendix §B.2.2).

As a result, 74.38% of teacher annotators prefer feedback from score-based prompting, compared to only 12.50% who favor feedback from standard prompting (Pie chart in Figure 1). The remaining 13.12% report no difference between the two feedback types. This is statistically significant at a p level of < 0.05 using the Chi-squared test, with a fair agreement (Fleiss Kappa 0.22).

Learning Outcome The feedback provided through score-based prompting leads to a significant improvement in students' confidence regarding the quality of their essays and their understanding of each rubric (Figure 2). On average, EFL learners express high satisfaction with the LLM-generated feedback, rating 6.0 for *quality* and 6.03 for *characteristics* on a 7.0 scale. These results

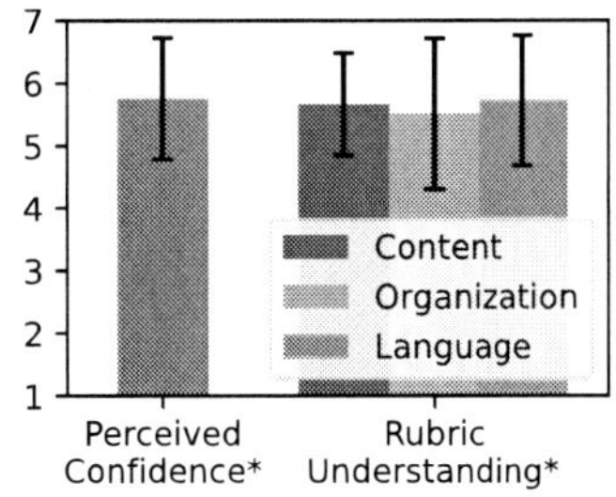

Figure 2: Learning outcome

are statistically significant, tested by the Wilcoxon test at p value of < 0.05. Such a strong positive response underscores the potential of score-based prompting on both student confidence and satisfaction, highlighting its potential to enhance writing instruction in EFL contexts.

4 Conclusion

This paper advances EFL writing education by generating and evaluating feedback tailored to students' needs, incorporating pedagogical principles, and involving real-world educational stakeholders. Our focus on essay feedback through LLM-as-a-tutor aims to more effectively support EFL students in their writing process. In the future, we plan to customize the LLM-as-a-tutor to provide individualized support. For instance, our evaluation metric and dataset can be utilized to personalize feedback, aligning with students' varying preferences. This customization would allow LLM-as-a-tutor to adapt to the specific needs and desires of each student, thereby enhancing the learning experience. Ultimately, we envision personalized LLM agents in EFL education, offering tailored support to each learner based on their unique needs.

Limitations

We utilize ChatGPT, a black-box language model, for feedback generation. This results in a lack of transparency in our system, as it does not provide explicit justifications or rationales for the generated feedback. We acknowledge the importance of and the need for continued research aimed at developing models that produce more explainable feedback, thereby opening avenues for future exploration.

Ethics Statement

We expect that this paper will make a significant contribution to the application of NLP for good, particularly in the domain of NLP-driven assistance in EFL writing education. All studies are conducted with the approval of our institutional review board (IRB). We ensured non-discrimination across all demographics, including gender and age. We set the wage per session to be above the minimum wage in the Republic of Korea in 2023 (KRW 9,260 $\approx$ USD 7.25) [1]. Participation in the experiment was entirely voluntary, with assurance that their choice would not influence their academic scores or grades.

Acknowledgements

This work was supported by Institute for Information & communications Technology Promotion(IITP) grant funded by the Korea government (MSIP) (No. RS-2024-00443251, Accurate and Safe Multimodal, Multilingual Personalized AI Tutors)

References

Shabnam Behzad, Omid Kashefi, and Swapna Somasundaran. 2024. Assessing online writing feedback resources: Generative AI vs. good samaritans. In *Proceedings of the 2024 Joint International Conference on Computational Linguistics, Language Resources and Evaluation (LREC-COLING 2024)*, pages 1638–1644, Torino, Italia. ELRA and ICCL.

Benjamin S. Bloom. 1984. The 2 sigma problem: The search for methods of group instruction as effective as one to one tutoring. *Educational Researcher*, 13(6):4–16.

Yupeng Chang, Xu Wang, Jindong Wang, Yuan Wu, Linyi Yang, Kaijie Zhu, Hao Chen, Xiaoyuan Yi, Cunxiang Wang, Yidong Wang, Wei Ye, Yue Zhang, Yi Chang, Philip S. Yu, Qiang Yang, and Xing Xie. 2024. A survey on evaluation of large language models. *ACM Trans. Intell. Syst. Technol.*, 15(3).

Xiaolong Cheng and Lawrence Jun Zhang. 2022. Teachers helping efl students improve their writing through written feedback: the case of native and non-native english-speaking teachers' beliefs. *Frontiers in Psychology*, 13:804313.

Alister Cumming. 1990. Expertise in evaluating second language compositions. *Language Testing*, 7(1):31–51.

Cristian Danescu-Niculescu-Mizil, Moritz Sudhof, Dan Jurafsky, Jure Leskovec, and Christopher Potts. 2013. A computational approach to politeness with application to social factors. In *Proceedings of the 51st Annual Meeting of the Association for Computational Linguistics (Volume 1: Long Papers)*, pages 250–259, Sofia, Bulgaria. Association for Computational Linguistics.

Rod Ellis. 2008. A typology of written corrective feedback types. *ELT Journal*, 63(2):97–107.

Elham Eslami. 2014. The effects of direct and indirect corrective feedback techniques on efl students' writing. *Procedia - Social and Behavioral Sciences*, 98:445–452. Proceedings of the International Conference on Current Trends in ELT.

Jieun Han, Haneul Yoo, Yoonsu Kim, Junho Myung, Minsun Kim, Hyunseung Lim, Juho Kim, Tak Yeon Lee, Hwajung Hong, So-Yeon Ahn, and Alice Oh. 2023. Recipe: How to integrate chatgpt into efl writing education. In *Proceedings of the Tenth ACM Conference on Learning @ Scale*, L@S '23, page 416–420, New York, NY, USA. Association for Computing Machinery.

Fiona Hyland and Ken Hyland. 2001. Sugaring the pill: Praise and criticism in written feedback. *Journal of Second Language Writing*, 10(3):185–212.

Enkelejda Kasneci, Kathrin Sessler, Stefan Küchemann, Maria Bannert, Daryna Dementieva, Frank Fischer, Urs Gasser, Georg Groh, Stephan Günnemann, Eyke Hüllermeier, Stephan Krusche, Gitta Kutyniok, Tilman Michaeli, Claudia Nerdel, Jürgen Pfeffer, Oleksandra Poquet, Michael Sailer, Albrecht Schmidt, Tina Seidel, Matthias Stadler, Jochen Weller, Jochen Kuhn, and Gjergji Kasneci. 2023. Chatgpt for good? on opportunities and challenges of large language models for education. *Learning and Individual Differences*, 103:102274.

Mina Lee, Megha Srivastava, Amelia Hardy, John Thickstun, Esin Durmus, Ashwin Paranjape, Ines Gerard-Ursin, Xiang Lisa Li, Faisal Ladhak, Frieda Rong, Rose E Wang, Minae Kwon, Joon Sung Park, Hancheng Cao, Tony Lee, Rishi Bommasani, Michael S. Bernstein, and Percy Liang. 2023. Evaluating human-language model interaction. *Transactions on Machine Learning Research.*

Nancyruth Leibold and Laura Marie Schwarz. 2015. The art of giving online feedback. *Journal of Effective Teaching*, 15(1):34–46.

Qiandi Liu and Dan Brown. 2015. Methodological synthesis of research on the effectiveness of corrective feedback in l2 writing. *Journal of Second Language Writing*, 30:66–81.

Per Lysvåg. 1975. Verbs of hedging. In *Syntax and Semantics volume 4*, pages 125–154. Brill.

Burhan Ozfidan and Connie Mitchell. 2022. Assessment of students' argumentative writing: A rubric development. *Journal of Ethnic and Cultural Studies*, 9(2):121–133.

[1] `https://www.minimumwage.go.kr/`

Liangming Pan, Michael Saxon, Wenda Xu, Deepak Nathani, Xinyi Wang, and William Yang Wang. 2024. Automatically correcting large language models: Surveying the landscape of diverse automated correction strategies. *Transactions of the Association for Computational Linguistics*, 12:484–506.

Novilda Angela Saragih, Suwarsih Madya, Renol Aprico Siregar, and Willem Saragih. 2021. Written corrective feedback: Students' perception and preferences. *International Online Journal of Education and Teaching*, 8(2):676–690.

Catherine G. Van Beuningen, Nivja H. De Jong, and Folkert Kuiken. 2012. Evidence on the effectiveness of comprehensive error correction in second language writing. *Language Learning*, 62(1):1–41.

Hongru Wang, Rui Wang, Fei Mi, Yang Deng, Zezhong Wang, Bin Liang, Ruifeng Xu, and Kam-Fai Wong. 2023. Cue-CoT: Chain-of-thought prompting for responding to in-depth dialogue questions with LLMs. In *Findings of the Association for Computational Linguistics: EMNLP 2023*, pages 12047–12064, Singapore. Association for Computational Linguistics.

Rose Wang and Dorottya Demszky. 2023. Is ChatGPT a good teacher coach? measuring zero-shot performance for scoring and providing actionable insights on classroom instruction. In *Proceedings of the 18th Workshop on Innovative Use of NLP for Building Educational Applications (BEA 2023)*, pages 626–667, Toronto, Canada. Association for Computational Linguistics.

Lixiang Yan, Lele Sha, Linxuan Zhao, Yuheng Li, Roberto Martinez-Maldonado, Guanliang Chen, Xinyu Li, Yueqiao Jin, and Dragan Gašević. 2024. Practical and ethical challenges of large language models in education: A systematic scoping review. *British Journal of Educational Technology*, 55(1):90–112.

Haneul Yoo, Jieun Han, So-Yeon Ahn, and Alice Oh. 2024. Dress: Dataset for rubric-based essay scoring on efl writing. *Preprint*, arXiv:2402.16733.

Lianmin Zheng, Wei-Lin Chiang, Ying Sheng, Siyuan Zhuang, Zhanghao Wu, Yonghao Zhuang, Zi Lin, Zhuohan Li, Dacheng Li, Eric Xing, Hao Zhang, Joseph E Gonzalez, and Ion Stoica. 2023. Judging llm-as-a-judge with mt-bench and chatbot arena. In *Advances in Neural Information Processing Systems*, volume 36, pages 46595–46623. Curran Associates, Inc.

Appendix

A Essay Feedback Generation Model

The essay feedback generation experiments were conducted with `gpt-3.5-turbo` (0301 version) with Azure OpenAI API. To provide consistent feedback among students, we opted for a temperature setting of 0. This deterministic approach ensures that our system remains uniform, akin to evaluations from a single, consistent instructor. Below is the prompt template we used for feedback generation.

Standard Prompting

You are an English writing teacher;
give feedback on this argumentative essay with three rubrics: content, organization, and language.
`${rubric explanation}`
`${essay prompt}`
`${student's essay}`

Score-based Prompting

You are an English writing teacher;
according to the provided score , give feedback on this argumentative essay with three rubrics: content, organization, and language.
`${rubric explanation}`
`${essay prompt}`
`${student's essay}`

Score
`${rubric-based essay scores}`

B Essay Feedback Evaluation Details

B.1 Quality Assessment Explanation

- **Level of detail**: The feedback is specific, supported with details.
- **Accuracy**: The feedback content provides accurate information according to the essay.
- **Relevance**: The feedback is provided according to the understanding of the essay criteria.
- **Helpfulness**: The feedback is helpful for students to improve the quality of writing.

Table 2: Rubric explanations

Rubric	Description
Content	Paragraph is well-developed and relevant to the argument, supported with strong reasons and examples.
Organization	The argument is very effectively structured and developed, making it easy for the reader to follow the ideas and understand how the writer is building the argument. Paragraphs use coherence devices effectively while focusing on a single main idea.
Language	The writing displays sophisticated control of a wide range of vocabulary and collocations. The essay follows grammar and usage rules throughout the paper. Spelling and punctuation are correct throughout the paper.

B.2 Sample-level Analysis on Essay Feedback Evaluation

B.2.1 Quality

Table 5 shows two different language feedback examples for the same essay with a score of 2.5 out of 5.0. These examples are generated using different prompts: a standard prompt and a score-based prompt. The green text indicates detailed support and examples provided by the essay (level of detail), and the blue text describes the overall evaluation of the essay regarding the language criterion. By comparing blue text, score-based prompting suggests the improvements (helpfulness) such as *'errors and awkward phrasing'* and *'punctuation and capitalization'*, while standard prompting only praises language use such as *'vocabulary and collocations'*. Considering that the language score of the essay is 2.5 out of 5.0, the feedback generated by score-based prompting appears to be more accurate. The orange text in the feedback generated by the standard prompt is irrelevant to the language criterion (relevance) and has similar expressions to an organization explanation in Table 2. We assume that score-based prompting, providing more detailed, relevant, and accurate feedback, will be more helpful to EFL students in improving their

Type	Explanation	Example
Negative	Teachers' comments indicate that there are some errors, problems, or weaknesses in students' writing.	The essay lacks depth and development in its content.
Positive	The former refers to comments affirming that students' writing has met a standard such as "good grammar", "clear organization", and "the task is well achieved".	The essay is very well-organized and effectively structured.
Polite	Politeness includes hedge expressions, modal verbs, positive lexicon, and 1st person pronouns.	However, the essay could benefit from more elaboration and development of each point.
Straightforward	Straightforward includes factuality expression and negative lexicon	The essay lacks depth and analysis.
Vague	Feedback is vague in its suggestions for ways a student can enhance their work.	There are some grammar errors.
Specific	Feedback is specific in its suggestions for ways a student can enhance their work.	There are some split infinitives in the paper. Check out more information about split infinitives in the courseroom folder titled Writing Resources.
Indirect	The teacher indicates in some way that an error exists but does not provide the correction, thus leaving it to the student to find it.	However, the essay could benefit from more examples and evidence to further strengthen the argument ...
Direct	The teacher provides the student with the correct form.	In the third paragraph, the phrase 'unsatisfied things' could be more specific and descriptive.
Small	Feedback with a small quantity contains less content.	The essay provides a clear argument and supports it with well-developed paragraphs that are relevant to the topic. The reasons and examples provided are strong and effectively demonstrate the writer's opinion. The essay effectively addresses the prompt and provides a well-rounded argument.
Large	Feedback with a large quantity contains more extensive content in the feedback.	The essay provides a clear and well-supported argument on the topic of whether young children should spend most of their time playing or studying. The writer presents two strong reasons for their opinion that playing is better for young children. The first reason is that playing is a way of studying, as it helps children learn how to communicate and collaborate with others. The second reason is that young children are not yet mature enough for formal education, and forcing them to learn before they are ready can lead to a decline in their interest in learning. The writer supports their argument with specific examples and uses clear and concise language throughout the essay.

Table 3: Explanation and example of feedback types

essays. This again highlights the necessity of the score-based prompting process.

The green text in Table 4 represents detailed support and examples, while the blue text suggests improvements for the essay, which align with level of detail and helpfulness criteria, respectively. Feedback generated with standard prompting describes specific details of the content of the essay. However, it only summarizes the content of the essay and provides praise, instead of suggestions or criticism. On the other hand, feedback with score-based prompting points out that *'the essay lacks depth and analysis'* and *'could benefit from expanding on their ideas and providing more specific examples'*.

B.2.2 Characteristics

Table 6 presents two different content feedback examples for the same essay, scored 2.0 out of 5.0. Positive feedback is highlighted in blue text, while negative feedback is in orange. Negative feedback identifies errors in the essay, helping students recognize and address their weaknesses. Positive feedback, on the other hand, affirms that students' writing meets certain standards through praise (Cheng and Zhang, 2022; Hyland and Hyland, 2001). When comparing feedback generated by the two prompting methods, score-based prompting focuses more on negative feedback, while standard prompting only emphasizes positive aspects. Since overuse of negative feedback may discourage students' self-efficacy, teachers often precede negative feedback with positive feedback or tone down the negative feedback (Hyland and Hyland, 2001) with hedge expressions such as 'could', which is written as green text in Table 6.

C Questionaire for Learning Outcome

Please answer these questions AFTER finishing the main exercise.

1. My confidence in the quality of the essay increased after the exercise.
2. My understanding of the content criteria increased after the exercise.
3. My understanding of the organization criteria increased after the exercise.
4. My understanding of the language criteria increased after the exercise.
5. Please rate the appropriateness of the style or tone of the AI-based feedback.
6. Please rate the overall performance of AI-based scoring.
7. Please rate the overall quality of AI-based feedback.
8. Please freely share your thoughts regarding the exercise.

Standard Prompting	Score-based Prompting
The content of the essay is well-developed and relevant to the argument. The writer has identified three major problems in their country and has provided specific reasons and details to support their opinion. The writer has effectively highlighted the gender problem, inequality problem, and offensive replying culture in some communities. The writer has also provided examples of how these problems are threatening their society and splitting people up. Overall, the content of the essay is strong and persuasive.	The essay has some relevant points, but the content is not well-developed. The writer mentions three problems in Korea, but only briefly touches on each one without providing strong reasons or examples to support their argument. The essay lacks depth and analysis, and the writer could benefit from expanding on their ideas and providing more specific details.

Table 4: Example of quality evaluation on content feedback. The feedback is generated based on the student's essay, whose content score is 2.5 out of 5.0. The colors of the texts stand for quality evaluation criteria as follows: green (level of detail), and blue (helpfulness).

Standard Prompting	Score-based Prompting
The language used in the essay is sophisticated and displays a wide range of vocabulary and collocations. The writer follows grammar and usage rules throughout the paper, and spelling and punctuation are correct. The essay is well-written and easy to read. Overall, the language used in the essay is strong and effectively communicates the writer's argument.	The essay displays some control of vocabulary and grammar, but there are also several errors and awkward phrasings throughout. For example, the writer uses the phrase ('now-days' instead of 'nowadays'), and there are several instances of awkward phrasing and word choice. Additionally, there are several errors in punctuation and capitalization. The essay would benefit from more careful proofreading and editing, as well as more attention to precise and effective language use.

Table 5: Example of quality evaluation on language feedback. The feedback is generated based on the student's essay, whose language score is 2.5 out of 5.0. The colors of the texts stand for quality evaluation criteria as follows: green (level of detail), blue (helpfulness), and orange (relevance).

Standard Prompting	Score-based Prompting
The essay effectively addresses the prompt by discussing three qualities of a good friend: honesty, sharing, and competition. Each quality is well-developed and supported with specific reasons and examples. The writer's argument is clear and persuasive, making a strong case for why these qualities are important in a friendship. Overall, the content is well-organized and relevant to the topic at hand.	The essay provides a clear and concise argument about the qualities of a good friend. The writer has identified three key qualities - honesty, sharing, and competition - and has provided specific reasons and examples to support each point. However, the essay could benefit from more elaboration and development of each point. For example, the writer could provide more specific examples of how honesty is important in a friendship, or how competition can lead to personal growth. Additionally, the essay could benefit from a stronger conclusion that summarizes the main points and provides a final thought on the topic.

Table 6: Example of characteristics analysis on language feedback. The feedback is generated based on the student's essay, whose language score is 2.0 out of 5.0. The colors of the texts stand for feedback type as follows: blue (positive), green (polite), and orange (negative).

E-Commerce Product Categorization with LLM-based Dual-Expert Classification Paradigm

Zhu Cheng* **Wen Zhang*** **Chih-Chi Chou** **You-Yi Jau**
Archita Pathak **Peng Gao** **Umit Batur**
Amazon, Seattle, WA, USA
{zzcheng, wenzhaw, jimmchou, jauyouyi, arcpatha, gaope, baturab}@amazon.com

Abstract

Accurate product categorization in e-commerce is critical for delivering a satisfactory online shopping experience to customers. With the vast number of available products and the numerous potential categories, it becomes crucial to develop a classification system capable of assigning products to their correct categories with high accuracy. We present a dual-expert classification system that utilizes the power of large language models (LLMs). This framework integrates domain-specific knowledge and pre-trained LLM's general knowledge through effective model fine-tuning and prompting techniques. First, the fine-tuned domain-specific expert recommends top K candidate categories for a given input product. Then, the more general LLM-based expert, through prompting techniques, analyzes the nuanced differences between candidate categories and selects the most suitable target category. We introduce a new in-context learning approach that utilizes LLM self-generated summarization to provide clearer instructions and enhance its performance. Experiments on e-commerce datasets demonstrate the effectiveness of our LLM-based Dual-Expert classification system.

1 Introduction

Accurate product categorization on e-commerce sites is the foundation of a structured catalog system to better meet customer needs. A catalog with accurate categorization helps fuel the search engine, which scopes and ranks the search results from queries efficiently. The buyers can find relevant products through the query or browse directly from the targeted categories. The customer behavior can further enhance the downstream personalized tasks like advertisement and item recommendations. Eventually the accurate catalog leads to customer satisfaction as well as the revenue.

Assigning the category for every single product in the world is far from simple. The problem is to map the product description to the label under a well-defined category taxonomy, which includes over thousands of labels. The category selected by the sellers can be noisy due to the vast number of labels and different interpretation of the categories. Reviewing and fixing the wrongly assigned items manually is not feasible. Therefore, the catalog relies on a categorization system, which utilizes a classification model with high accuracy and coverage to improve the catalog quality.

Although the classification problems have been researched for years, e-commerce product categorization differs from classical ones. This is due to the vast volume of products with noisy and incomplete signals in both product description and categorical labels. Besides, subjective customer opinions about multi-functional products add the complexity, as these opinions can influence product descriptions and optimal category assignment. It is non-trivial to train machine learning models to discern consistent categorical patterns that meet customer expectations for a large population of catalog.

We approach product categorization as a text classification problem, since most product items in e-commerce platform are represented through structured or unstructured textual features. Recently, pre-trained models (PTMs) have shown substantial benefits in capturing universal language representations and strong reasoning capability with RLHF (Ziegler et al., 2019; Lampinen et al., 2022). Two prominent PTM frameworks are: 1) discriminative models with the encoder structure, like BERT (Bidirectional Encoder Representations from Transformers) (Devlin et al., 2018; Conneau and Lample, 2019; Conneau et al., 2019), and 2) generative models with the decoder structure, like OpenAI's GPT series (Generative Pre-trained Transformer) (Radford et al., 2018, 2019; Brown

*Equal contribution.

Proceedings of the 1st Workshop on Customizable NLP: Progress and Challenges in Customizing NLP for a Domain, Application, Group, or Individual (CustomNLP4U), pages 294–304

et al., 2020; Ouyang et al., 2022). Though some efforts have unified discriminative and generative tasks within a single framework, discriminative language models are generally preferred for sentence understanding, while generative language models are more commonly used for text generation and reasoning. With the increasing parameter sizes and extensive pre-training on vast datasets and various learning tasks, these language models have consistently attained state-of-the-art (SOTA) performance across numerous NLP benchmarks. Given the overlap between pretrained knowledge and e-commerce catalog, we believe that PTMs possess the domain knowledge that is necessary to differentiate the nuances between categories.

In this study, we introduce an innovative dual-expert framework that integrates both discriminative and generative large language models (LLM) in a cascading approach to achieve precise product categorization. Initially, the discriminative language model is fine-tuned with domain data, acting as a domain expert to recommend the top K candidate classes for each product. Subsequently, an off-the-shelf LLM selects the optimal target from the top K suggestions based on certain criteria via prompting. The LLM in our framework serves as the general expert due to its capability acquired through pre-training on a large corpus of general data and well alignment with human instructions. The major contribution of this study can be summarized in 3 folds:

- 1) We propose a novel LLM-based dual-expert categorization system, which is designed to achieve accurate product classification in e-commerce and output reasons for hard cases.
- 2) We introduce the key components of domain-specific and general experts, and describe the strategies to inject domain knowledge into the decision-making process of each expert.
- 3) We compare the performance of this dual-expert framework against the popular text classification models as well as the SOTA model in two e-commerce catalog datasets, proved its superiority on e-commerce categorization.

2 E-commerce Product Categorization

In e-commerce, product categorization involves assigning one or more optimal categories from thousands of labels based on product features. This task is challenging due to noisy and incomplete catalog data. E-commerce sites generally define a taxonomy (a hierarchical structure) as the target label space for categorization. As this taxonomy becomes more granular, categories can become very similar, with only subtle differences distinguishing them.

Output Label Space Online e-commerce sites pre-define the semantic structure of item categories (known as taxonomy) according to business purpose. This taxonomy serves as the target label space for categorization, and is constructed as hierarchical trees. As the taxonomy tree becomes fine and granular, the categories may appear similar to each other, with only subtle differences separating them. Extreme multi-label text classification aims to identify relevant labels from an extremely large set of labels, making it a challenging task (Zhang et al., 2021a; Chang et al., 2020). Accuracy of classification models can vary depending on the complexity and dimensionality of the label space. Additionally, catalog data inherently suffers from label imbalance, which is widely known as the long tail issue. Classification models may struggle to learn patterns for the underrepresented, smaller categories in the skewed distribution.

Catalog Noise and Incompleteness The training data for our ML-based categorization model is mainly derived from samples of catalog data, which often includes noisy labels and incomplete information. A key challenge for e-commerce categorization systems is to extract meaningful signals about customer preferences from this low-quality data. We classify the quality of the model training data into two types:

- **Noise Signals.** Item features and labels often contain noise, leading to unstable learning. This noise can be soft (exaggerated properties) or hard (misleading/irrelevant descriptions) and is common in popular categories. Meanwhile, label assignments can be noisy due to outdated categorization systems, internal biased corrections, and incorrect label suggestions from sellers. These are the major sources of label noise.
- **Incomplete Information.** Incomplete information often arises from the subjective opinions of sellers and customers. For instance, sellers in an automobile store might omit

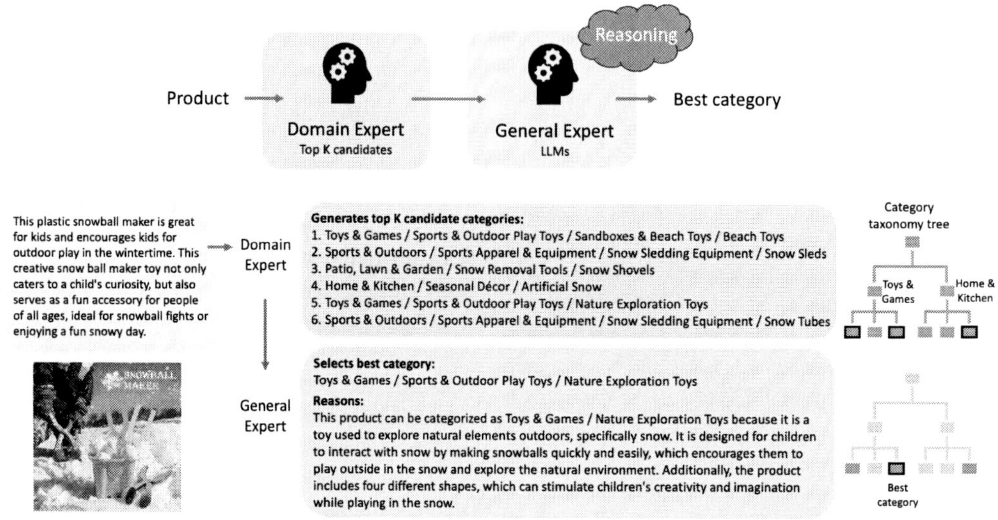

Figure 1: LLM-based Dual-Expert e-commerce categorization framework. The system comprises two key components that operate sequentially: a Domain Expert that identifies the top K categories, followed by a General Expert that decides the optimal category from the top candidates by applying reasoning. We inject the domain knowledge to each expert through model fine-tuning (domain expert) and prompting (LLM-based general expert).

keywords and only provide brand and series numbers, resulting in very brief item descriptions. This limited information confuses general buyers. Additionally, catalog labels are incomplete because selling items may be multi-functional, yet sellers typically provide only a single label which may not align with how different buyers perceive or intend to use the product. In this scenario, our task is to find the most favored category, even when multiple options are acceptable.

To overcome the issues, we propose a novel LLM based Dual-Expert approach for product classification.

3 LLM Based Dual-Expert System

LLM-based multi-agent systems have emerged as a novel technology with advanced capabilities. These systems specialize LLMs into various distinct agents, each with different expertise (Wu et al., 2023; Qian et al., 2024; Yue et al., 2024). Our domain-specific and general expert system has two language models cooperating with each other and each has a specialty. Specifically, we have designed two expert models that work sequentially to assign the optimal category to a given product. The whole pipeline is shown in Figure 1. First, a discriminative model work as the domain expert to find top K candidate categories for the selling product given its item data. Then, an off-the-shelf LLM serves as the general expert, evaluating which categories from the top K candidates are most suitable and accurate for the selling product in question. The LLM outputs its decision and the reasoning behind its selection.

3.1 Domain Expert

The primary objective of the domain expert is to identify the top K most relevant leaf categories for a given product, with relevance determined by similar patterns observed in the training data. Simultaneously, the domain expert ensures a highly accurate top 1 prediction to support the online inference pipeline. The backbone of the domain expert is XLM-R (Conneau et al., 2019), a Transformer model that is pre-trained on monolingual data using the multilingual masked language modeling (MLM) objective.

3.1.1 Label Semantic Capture via Label Augmentation

Discriminative models face a limitation in explicitly lacking semantic knowledge about the labels. Our in-depth study observed a high frequency of label-related keywords in the item data written by sellers, indicating that keyword matching could benefit semantic understanding in our domain tasks. Therefore, we strategically expose the label names to the model, aiding its few-shot and zero-shot learning capabilities. To enhance the training data with label names, we use the full path of labels, i.e., a path in a taxonomy tree. We randomly mask the branch along this path and replace the title or description of sampled training data with the masked path (Figure 2). These synthetic training samples are then added to the original data.

3.1.2 Two-phase Learning

Learning from large, noisy catalog data is difficult due to label imbalance and errors in signals. To tackle this, we split model training into two phases. In the first phase, the domain expert reviews challenging cases and uses focal loss to handle imbalance. In the second phase, the model focuses on major patterns, reinforcing the initial phase with bootstrap loss. Further details are in the following sections.

Phase 1: Exploration of Category Relationship The catalog data inherently suffers from label imbalance, commonly referred to as the long tail issue. To address this, we incorporate focal loss (Lin et al., 2017) into our objectives as a dynamic learning approach to better capture challenging cases in smaller categories. The mathematics definition of focal loss for classification can be defined as:

$$L_{FL} = -\sum_{k=1}^{N} \alpha_k \left(1 - q_k\right)^{\gamma} \log\left(q_k\right), \quad (1)$$

where q_k is the predicted probability of the true label k by model. α_k is the corresponding class weight of the true label. It is predefined based on the desired label distribution, e.g., popularity score of the product in catalog. γ is a hyperparameter controlling the learning weight of hard examples. The higher the value of γ, the lower the loss for well-classified examples.

Phase 2: Self-Exploitary The second phase of training employs a self-justifying learning mechanism that accounts for knowledge consistency during training (Reed et al., 2014). It augments the usual prediction objective with a notion of perceptual consistency, which allows the model to disagree with a perceptually-inconsistent training label and effectively relabel the data while training. The assumption behind this idea is that incorrect labels are likely to be eventually highly inconsistent with other data points predicted to the same label by the model. Therefore, it acts in a manner of self label clean-up and bootstraps itself until convergence to stable knowledge. Here, we incorporate this idea into the cross-entropy training loss:

$$L_{BT\_BCE}(p, q) = -\sum_{k=1}^{N} \beta p_k log(q_k) + \beta(1 - p_k) log(1 - q_k) + \sum_{k=1}^{N} (1 - \beta) q_k log(q_k), \quad (2)$$

where p_k, q_K are ground truth label and model prediction, respectively. N is the size of target labels. Parameter $0 \leq \beta \leq 1$ balances bootstrap learning and supervised classification. It is empirically set in the range $[0.8, 0.95]$. Due to the large batch training steps (t_{batch}), we can set a delta activation $\hat{\beta}$ that adaptively turns on/off the bootstrap loss at a given global step T_{gate}:

$$\hat{\beta} = \begin{cases} 1, & \text{if } t_{batch} < T_{gate} \\ \beta, & \text{if } t_{batch} \geq T_{gate} \end{cases} \quad (3)$$

Figure 2: Example of synthetic data for capturing label semantics.

3.2 General Expert

After the Domain Expert produces top K candidate categories, the LLM-based General Expert then reasons about the top candidate categories via proper prompting strategies, and selects optimal category among the candidates.

3.2.1 Zero-shot

Product category names often carry rich semantic meaning. For instance, hierarchical path of category "Toys and Games / Sports & Outdoor Play Toys / Sandboxes & Beach Toys / Beach Toys" self explains that "Beach Toys" is for outdoor play and is under Toys and Games department. Thus, we directly prompt the LLM-based General Expert with product item data and candidate categories' path names.

3.2.2 In-context learning via LLM self-generated summarization

LLMs demonstrate remarkable capabilities in in-context learning (ICL), they can learn to do a specific task by conditioning on a prompt consisting of input-output examples (Brown et al., 2020). LLMs can generalize to previously unseen data by using few-shot examples provided in the prompt, without explicit pre-training for the specific task (Xie et al., 2021). ICL are recently used in text classification(Milios et al., 2023; Zhu and Zamani, 2023; Simig et al., 2022; D'Oosterlinck et al., 2024a).

In e-commerce product categorization task, there are a vast number of different categories in the taxonomy tree, each with numerous products associated with it. In the traditional approach of few-shot in-context learning, we need to select example products for each candidate category in the prompt. However, the selected products may contain information irrelevant to the candidate category, and may not adequately represent the candidate category.

To address these issues, we propose a novel in-context learning approach. Rather than providing a few products and their associated categories as few-shot examples in the prompts, we provide clear definitions of the candidate categories to the LLM-based General Expert, where the category definition is self-generated by LLMs. The self-generation process is as follows. For each category, we curated a collection of data points that have been previously labeled as belonging to that particular category, then LLMs were instructed to summarize from the pool of data and generate a clear definition for the category based on the provided data. To ensure diversity in the summarizing samples, we include multi-source data from both popular selling products and catalog representatives of each category via unsupervised learning. Consequently, a summarized definition of each category was self-generated by LLMs. We then feed these LLM-generated category definitions to the LLM-based General Expert, aiding in more accurate category selection (Figure 3b, Figure 6).

(a) *Zero-shot:*
You will try to classify a product in the catalog of an e-commerce site to a product category. Below is the data for the product: {product information}
Can this product be categorized to any of the categories listed below?
Category 0: …, Category 1: …, Category 2: …
If this product belongs to none of them, answer none. If the product information is not provided enough for you to make judgement, answer "cannot decide". If this product is multi-functional, answer the categories with its primary function.

(b) *Representation of the categories:*
- Leaf node only: Category 0: Shorts, …
- Full path: Category 0: Fashion / Women / Clothing / Active / Base Layers & Compression / Shorts, …
- Descriptive name: Category 0: Women's Base layers & Compression Shorts, …
- Descriptive name with In-Context Learning via LLM self-generated summarization/definition:

Category 0: Women's Base layers & Compression Shorts, Women's Base Layer Shorts are designed for various activities such as gym workouts, cycling, running. They are typically made of stretchy, breathable, and moisture-wicking materials that provide support, comfort, and flexibility. They are shorts or tights that cover the upper part of the legs …

(c) *Enhanced reasoning via ranking:* This product can be possibly categorized to the categories listed below. Can you rank the relevant categories for this product in order of likelihood, starting with the most probable and ending with the least probable.

(d) *Enhanced reasoning via CoT and ranking:* Let's think step by step. First, find clues in the product data sources and candidate category data, then think of who may be the users of this product and under what scenarios will this product be used, finally rank the candidate categories. Your thinking process should be in the <reasons> section.

Figure 3: Prompting strategies. (a) LLM is prompted to directly select an optimal category. (b) Categories are represented by various levels of information, including in-context learning via summarization. (c) LLM is enforced to rank in order to reason. (d) LLM is encouraged to execute CoT before ranking.

3.2.3 Enhanced reasoning

To boost LLM's decision-making capabilities, we employed prompts that are designed to enhance the reasoning processes within LLMs. We instructed LLMs to identify the categories that match the main functionality or intended usage of the product (Figure 3a). A product category consists of a root level node (typically a Department) and intermediate nodes, followed by a fine-grained leaf node. We experiment with prompts containing various levels of information from the categories (Figure 3b).

Think step by step enables LLMs to generate task reasoning processes (Kojima et al., 2022). Chain-of-thought (CoT) prompting significantly enhances reasoning abilities of LLMs through chained reasoning steps (Wei et al., 2022, 2021). CoT prompting, which involves the presentation of intermediate reasoning steps, has proven effective in zero-shot (Kojima et al., 2022) and in-context learning (Wei et al., 2022) settings. To enhance LLM's reasoning capability on product classification task, we instructed LLMs to rank the relevant candidate categories from the most likely to the least likely for a given product (Figure 3c). Furthermore, LLM is encouraged to find clues in the product item data, think of a potential user and a use case for the product, then finally proceed to perform the ranking task (Figure 3d).

4 Experiments

4.1 Dataset

We evaluate our Dual-Expert framework on two benchmark datasets.

RetailProducts2023. This dataset contains 95,526 products that potentially belong to 2,214 categories from an E-commerce site. The dataset contains categories that have limited number of data entries. Each category has at least 10 associated data points to guarantee sufficient data for training and testing.

E-commerceCatalog. For curating this data, we select the e-commerce catalog data of 3 locales in different languages to assess the robustness of our

Table 1: Model performance on RetailProducts2023 dataset.

	Precision*	Recall*	F1 score*	F1 score (macro)
fastText	0.857	0.837	0.836	0.716
BERT	0.901	0.890	0.891	0.779
XLM-R	0.902	0.910	0.899	0.782
Domain Expert alone	0.925	0.929	0.921	0.825
Dual-Expert	**0.972**	**0.969**	**0.968**	**0.925**

*Weighted average.

Table 2: Classification accuracy on the E-commerceCatalog dataset.

	Locale 1	Locale 2	Locale 3
DHPC (Zhang et al., 2021b) (baseline)	+0%	+0%	+0%
Domain Expert alone	+1.01%	+1.33%	+1.57%
Domain Expert w/ XLM-R Selector	+1.12%	+1.05%	+1.31%
Dual-Expert	**+3.81%**	**+4.01%**	**+3.14%**

dual-expert approaches. In each locale, we collect an evaluation dataset of 10K products. This dataset was curated through multiple iterations of human review to provide a fair evaluation of all models compared. The Domain Expert is fine-tuned on millions of sampled catalog data per locale and we pick $K = 10$ as the number of suggested candidate categories for the LLM-based General Expert. The SOTA model Deep Hierarchical Product Classifier (DHPC) (Zhang et al., 2021b) is used as the baseline for comparison.

We leverage Mixtral from mistral.ai, a high-quality sparse mixture of experts model (SMoE) as the General Expert. Unless otherwise stated, we perform experiments with a temperature of 0.

4.2 Results

4.2.1 Dual-Expert model achieves better classification performance compared to the baseline

The results indicate that Dual-Expert model achieves higher classification performance consistently across RetailProducts2023 and E-commerceCatalog datasets compared to baseline models (Tables 1 and 2). On the RetailProducts2023 dataset, many categories have limited number of data points, consequently, vanilla XLM-R models exhibit poor performance on these minority classes, as evidenced by the significantly lower macro F1 score of 0.782, when compared to our Dual-Expert model (0.925). Similarly, fastText (Joulin et al., 2017) and BERT models exhibit relatively poor performance (Table 1). The Domain Expert model, which is a specialized version of XLM-R, has improved classification performance, although it requires relatively large amount of training data to accurately learn and distinguish between different categories. The Dual-Expert model demonstrates generalization capabilities on minority classes, showcasing its remarkable zero-shot and few-shot capabilities (Table 1). This is powered by the extensive knowledge gained during pretraining and alignment stages of the LLMs.

On the E-commerceCatalog dataset (Table 2), Dual-Expert model demonstrates significant accuracy improvement in 3 locales compared to the baseline SOTA model DHPC and Domain-specific Expert alone (Table 2). These results demonstrate that collaboration between the two experts, where the Domain Expert provides relevant categories and the LLM-based General Expert applies its reasoning capability to distinguish among categories and select the optimal one, leads to increased classification performance. Of note, we trained a XLM-R based binary classification model that makes binary predictions for (product, category) pairs. We used this model as a selector, substituting the General Expert. The overall accuracy was comparable or inferior to Domain Expert, suggesting these models likely learned the same noise in the training data.

Dual-Expert achieves higher classification accuracy partially due to its ability to address noisy mislabeled data in the training set. Consider the product shown in Figure 1, there are snowball clippers that are incorrectly labeled as beach toys in training data, a BERT-based discriminative model would learn this inaccurate classification during fine-tuning. In contrast, LLMs have the extensive general knowledge to recognize that such product is not a beach toy, but rather a snow exploration toy. Consequently, this approach effectively mitigates the issue of incorrect labeling in training data.

4.2.2 Impact of domain expert training strategies

We conduct ablation study to assess the impact of removing the proposed components of domain expert's training strategies. As shown in Table 3, removing any of these strategies causes performance drop. The bootstrap learning in phase 2 has the most significant impact on the accuracy of domain-expert's top1 prediction, as it stabilizes the later stages of model training and prevent over-fitting. For the entire dual-expert system, label augmentation and phase 1 training play a more crucial role than phase 2 since they enhance model's learning from the few-shot knowledge and improves topK retrieval performance of the domain expert.

4.2.3 Clear category definitions through LLM self-generated summarization enhance Dual-Expert's decision-making capabilities

Table 4 summarizes Dual-Expert's performance when using prompts that provide clear category definitions and enhance its reasoning capabilities. We observed that the prompts employing short phrases to represent categories achieved relatively low classification accuracy (Table 4, with ambiguous category definition). This is expected, as short phrases encode limited category information. For example, 'accessory' as a category name is ambiguous, therefore LLM misunderstands the category and makes errors.

To make the category definitions more clear, we propose a novel in-context learning approach via LLM self-generated summarization. For each category, we first instructed LLMs to summarize from the pool of data and generate a clear definition for the category based on the provided data. Then, instead of providing products and their associated categories as few-shot examples directly in the prompts, we provide the LLM with self-generated category summary, and instruct the LLM to select the most appropriate category among the candidates. As a result, the Dual-Expert model achieves the highest classification accuracy improvement of 3.8%, 4.0%, 3.1% for the 3 locales, respectively (Table 4, descriptive category name with ICL summarization). The findings suggest that LLMs excel at summarizing the core characteristics of a particular category. By leveraging the summarizations of categories generated by LLMs themselves, the models are equipped with more precise and well-defined descriptions of the categories, enabling them to make more accurate classification predictions (Figure 6).

4.2.4 Classification accuracy of the LLM-based Dual-Expert improves via enhanced reasoning

Our baseline prompting strategy involves instructing the LLM to directly choose optimal category from candidate classes (Table 4, zero-shot). LLM often states that "category A is correct" and that "categories B, C, and D are incorrect" without further explanations and reasoning. LLMs likely did not engage in extensive reasoning, classification accuracy was relatively low. When prompted to rank all relevant candidate categories in descending order, from the most likely to the least likely, LLM enhanced its reasoning capabilities. As a result, we observe classification accuracy improvement by 3.85%, 3.55% and 2.26% in the 3 locales, respectively (Table 4).

Table 3: Ablation Study: Impact of training strategies on Domain Expert's classification accuracy, i.e. Label Augmentation (LA), Phase 1&2 training.

Training Method	Domain Expert Acc (top 1)	Dual-Expert Acc (top k -> 1)
Domain Expert w/o LA	-0.7%	-1.5%
Domain Expert w/o Phase1	-0.2%	-0.5%
Domain Expert w/o Phase2	-1.4%	-0.25%

Table 4: Comparison of LLM prompting strategies on Dual-Expert's classification accuracy. Baseline is DHPC (Zhang et al., 2021b)

Prompt Strategy	Locale 1	Locale 2	Locale 3
with ambiguous category definition	+0.85%	+0.53%	-0.68%
descriptive category name	+1.23%	+0.80%	+2.06%
descriptive category name with ICL summarization*	**+3.81%**	**+4.01%**	**+3.14%**
enhanced reasoning via rank	**+3.85%**	+3.55%	+2.26%
enhanced reasoning via CoT and rank	+3.32%	**+3.59%**	**+2.86%**

*Proposed prompt strategy in Dual-Expert

4.3 Discussion

4.3.1 Inference cost

Inference cost is crucial for the practical application of this work to large-scale e-commerce product categorization. Consider the online/offline traffic of practical categorization system, we utilized the thresholding within the domain expert to regulate the traffic flowing into the general expert. In our practice, this approach reduces total traffic by 80% while maintaining overall accuracy improvements, as the 20% of data that passed through the entire workflow are typically cases the Domain Expert alone struggles to classify correctly (Figure 4). Furthermore, the Dual-Expert system (Table 1), in return, can act as a reliable auditor for determining the appropriate threshold for the Domain Expert model, further dynamically optimizing the tradeoff between performance and computational cost.

4.3.2 Probing framework feasibility

From our experiments, we found that for classification tasks with fine-grained categories and limited number of data points per category, LLMs demonstrate robust zero-shot and few-shot capabilities. As shown in Figure 5, when minimum number of data points per category is small, Dual-Expert outperforms the Domain Expert with larger margin. E-commerce categorization task falls under this regime, since catalog data inherently exhibits long

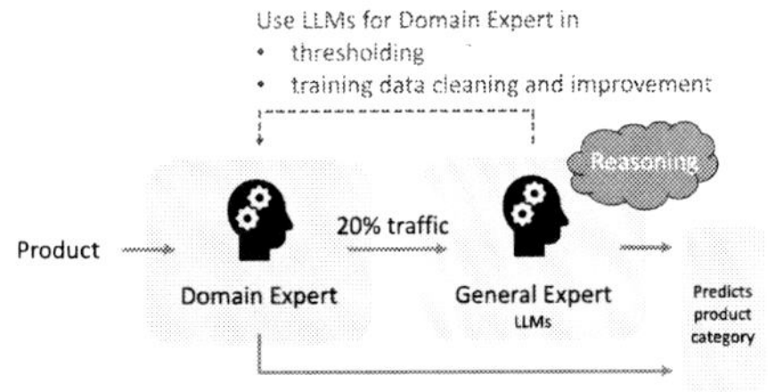

Figure 4: Modified framework that utilizes both Dual-Expert and Domain Expert alone for large scale applicability.

tail distribution, and the categories are fine-grained with subtle differences, such example categories are shown in Figure 6. As the categories become larger with sufficient amount of training data per category, and categories are well-separated with no conceptual overlap or nuanced difference, discriminative classification models tend to provide on-par classification performance compared to the LLM-based Dual-Expert (Figure 5).

5 Related Work

When the label space is vast with thousands of labels, a typical approach towards classification based on ICL is reducing the label space by identifying most relevant candidates for a given input (Milios et al., 2023). In this regards, research community has worked with both generative and non-generative techniques to narrow down to most relevant labels. Simig et al. (2022) explored generating candidate labels in the setting where task involves classification in unseen labels. Zhu and Zamani (2023) uses a set of labels and map the LLM generated candidates to actual labels by using semantic similarity. D'Oosterlinck et al. (2024b) takes a step further and ranks the retrieved labels by using an additional LLM. Semantic similarity works well when there is direct mapping between input and output. In our work, we target e-commerce data where the direct mapping between input to leaf categories does not work because a large number of leaf categories can have semantically similar definition which defeats the purpose of classifying the product in a single leaf category. Further, using multiple LLMs and making several calls to them is expensive. We reduce that cost by using only one LLM that processes the relevant labels selected by a non-generative model. In the non-generative approaches, Jain et al. (2019) considered building an approximate nearest neighbor (ANN) graph as an indexing structure over the labels by relying on sparse features engineered from the text. The relevant labels for a given text were then found quickly from the nearest neighbors of the instance via the ANN graph. With the introduction of PLMs, classification performance on several tasks improved significantly through PLMs' ability of learning better text representation from the raw, unstructured text. In our work, we explore LLM's capability for classification in different situations that occur in e-commerce domain - when product text is noisy, and when classification labels are fine-grained and conceptually overlapping. Each situation has their own challenges. We show that the Dual-Expert paradigm overcomes these challenges and outperforms the discriminative classification model in selecting the optimal category. We also show that enhancing the LLM prompt with self-generated summarization outperforms other prompt-tuning techniques experimented in this paper.

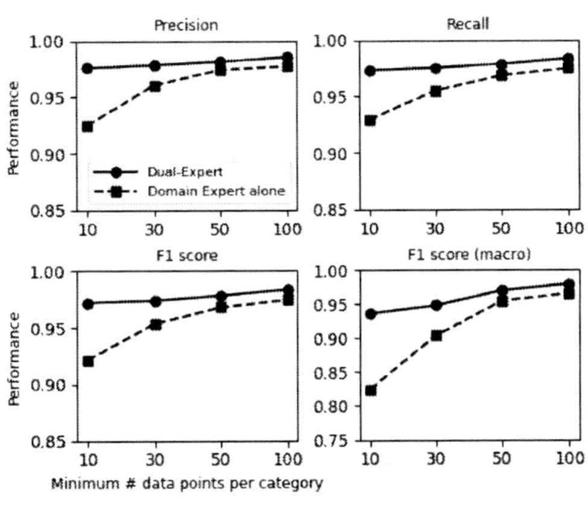

Figure 5: Framework feasibility on RetailProducts2023.

6 Conclusion

In this study, we propose a Dual-Expert classification workflow, which leverages the pre-trained LLMs for accurate e-commerce product categorization. It comprises two experts: a domain-specific expert, trained on a large e-commerce domain data, identifies relevant candidate classes; and a general expert, powered by a LLM with In-Context Learning, that handles nuanced reasoning and decision-making. This dual-expert architecture leverages the complementary strengths of each expert, blending specialized domain knowledge with general reasoning capabilities from pre-training, to achieve high classification accuracy in e-commerce categorization.

References

Tom Brown, Benjamin Mann, Nick Ryder, Melanie Subbiah, Jared D Kaplan, Prafulla Dhariwal, Arvind Neelakantan, Pranav Shyam, Girish Sastry, Amanda Askell, et al. 2020. Language models are few-shot learners. *Advances in neural information processing systems*, 33:1877–1901.

Wei-Cheng Chang, Hsiang-Fu Yu, Kai Zhong, Yiming Yang, and Inderjit S Dhillon. 2020. Taming pre-trained transformers for extreme multi-label text classification. In *Proceedings of the 26th ACM SIGKDD international conference on knowledge discovery & data mining*, pages 3163–3171.

Alexis Conneau, Kartikay Khandelwal, Naman Goyal, Vishrav Chaudhary, Guillaume Wenzek, Francisco Guzmán, Edouard Grave, Myle Ott, Luke Zettlemoyer, and Veselin Stoyanov. 2019. Unsupervised cross-lingual representation learning at scale. *arXiv preprint arXiv:1911.02116*.

Alexis Conneau and Guillaume Lample. 2019. Cross-lingual language model pretraining. *Advances in neural information processing systems*, 32.

Jacob Devlin, Ming-Wei Chang, Kenton Lee, and Kristina Toutanova. 2018. Bert: Pre-training of deep bidirectional transformers for language understanding. *arXiv preprint arXiv:1810.04805*.

Karel D'Oosterlinck, Omar Khattab, François Remy, Thomas Demeester, Chris Develder, and Christopher Potts. 2024a. In-context learning for extreme multi-label classification. *arXiv preprint arXiv:2401.12178*.

Karel D'Oosterlinck, Omar Khattab, François Remy, Thomas Demeester, Chris Develder, and Christopher Potts. 2024b. In-context learning for extreme multi-label classification. *arXiv preprint arXiv:2401.12178*.

Himanshu Jain, Venkatesh Balasubramanian, Bhanu Chunduri, and Manik Varma. 2019. Slice: Scalable linear extreme classifiers trained on 100 million labels for related searches. In *Proceedings of the twelfth ACM international conference on web search and data mining*, pages 528–536.

Armand Joulin, Edouard Grave, Piotr Bojanowski, and Tomas Mikolov. 2017. Bag of tricks for efficient text classification. In *Proceedings of the 15th Conference of the European Chapter of the Association for Computational Linguistics: Volume 2, Short Papers*, pages 427–431, Valencia, Spain. Association for Computational Linguistics.

Takeshi Kojima, Shixiang Shane Gu, Machel Reid, Yutaka Matsuo, and Yusuke Iwasawa. 2022. Large language models are zero-shot reasoners. *Advances in neural information processing systems*, 35:22199–22213.

Andrew Lampinen, Ishita Dasgupta, Stephanie Chan, Kory Mathewson, Mh Tessler, Antonia Creswell, James McClelland, Jane Wang, and Felix Hill. 2022. Can language models learn from explanations in context? In *Findings of the Association for Computational Linguistics: EMNLP 2022*, pages 537–563, Abu Dhabi, United Arab Emirates. Association for Computational Linguistics.

Tsung-Yi Lin, Priya Goyal, Ross Girshick, Kaiming He, and Piotr Dollár. 2017. Focal loss for dense object detection. In *Proceedings of the IEEE international conference on computer vision*, pages 2980–2988.

Aristides Milios, Siva Reddy, and Dzmitry Bahdanau. 2023. In-context learning for text classification with many labels. In *Proceedings of the 1st GenBench Workshop on (Benchmarking) Generalisation in NLP*, pages 173–184.

Long Ouyang, Jeffrey Wu, Xu Jiang, Diogo Almeida, Carroll Wainwright, Pamela Mishkin, Chong Zhang, Sandhini Agarwal, Katarina Slama, Alex Ray, et al. 2022. Training language models to follow instructions with human feedback. *Advances in neural information processing systems*, 35:27730–27744.

Chen Qian, Wei Liu, Hongzhang Liu, Nuo Chen, Yufan Dang, Jiahao Li, Cheng Yang, Weize Chen, Yusheng Su, Xin Cong, Juyuan Xu, Dahai Li, Zhiyuan Liu, and Maosong Sun. 2024. ChatDev: Communicative agents for software development. In *Proceedings of the 62nd Annual Meeting of the Association for Computational Linguistics (Volume 1: Long Papers)*, pages 15174–15186, Bangkok, Thailand. Association for Computational Linguistics.

Alec Radford, Karthik Narasimhan, Tim Salimans, Ilya Sutskever, et al. 2018. Improving language understanding by generative pre-training.

Alec Radford, Jeffrey Wu, Rewon Child, David Luan, Dario Amodei, Ilya Sutskever, et al. 2019. Language models are unsupervised multitask learners. *OpenAI blog*, 1(8):9.

Scott Reed, Honglak Lee, Dragomir Anguelov, Christian Szegedy, Dumitru Erhan, and Andrew Rabinovich. 2014. Training deep neural networks on noisy labels with bootstrapping. *arXiv preprint arXiv:1412.6596*.

Daniel Simig, Fabio Petroni, Pouya Yanki, Kashyap Popat, Christina Du, Sebastian Riedel, and Majid Yazdani. 2022. Open vocabulary extreme classification using generative models. *arXiv preprint arXiv:2205.05812*.

Jason Wei, Maarten Bosma, Vincent Y Zhao, Kelvin Guu, Adams Wei Yu, Brian Lester, Nan Du, Andrew M Dai, and Quoc V Le. 2021. Finetuned language models are zero-shot learners. *arXiv preprint arXiv:2109.01652*.

Jason Wei, Xuezhi Wang, Dale Schuurmans, Maarten Bosma, Fei Xia, Ed Chi, Quoc V Le, Denny Zhou, et al. 2022. Chain-of-thought prompting elicits reasoning in large language models. *Advances in neural information processing systems*, 35:24824–24837.

Qingyun Wu, Gagan Bansal, Jieyu Zhang, Yiran Wu, Shaokun Zhang, Erkang Zhu, Beibin Li, Li Jiang, Xiaoyun Zhang, and Chi Wang. 2023. Autogen: Enabling next-gen llm applications via multi-agent conversation framework. *arXiv preprint arXiv:2308.08155*.

Sang Michael Xie, Aditi Raghunathan, Percy Liang, and Tengyu Ma. 2021. An explanation of in-context learning as implicit bayesian inference. *arXiv preprint arXiv:2111.02080*.

Murong Yue, Jie Zhao, Min Zhang, Liang Du, and Ziyu Yao. 2024. Large language model cascades with mixture of thought representations for cost-efficient reasoning.

Jiong Zhang, Wei-Cheng Chang, Hsiang-Fu Yu, and Inderjit Dhillon. 2021a. Fast multi-resolution transformer fine-tuning for extreme multi-label text classification. *Advances in Neural Information Processing Systems*, 34:7267–7280.

Wen Zhang, Yanbin Lu, Bella Dubrov, Zhi Xu, Shang Shang, and Emilio Maldonado. 2021b. Deep hierarchical product classification based on pre-trained multilingual knowledge. *IEEE - The Bulletin of the Technical Committee on Data Engineering*.

Yaxin Zhu and Hamed Zamani. 2023. Icxml: An in-context learning framework for zero-shot extreme multi-label classification. *arXiv preprint arXiv:2311.09649*.

Daniel M Ziegler, Nisan Stiennon, Jeffrey Wu, Tom B Brown, Alec Radford, Dario Amodei, Paul Christiano, and Geoffrey Irving. 2019. Fine-tuning language models from human preferences. *arXiv preprint arXiv:1909.08593*.

A Appendix

A.1 Example that showcases the effectiveness of in-context learning via LLM self-generated summarization/definition

LLM self-generated summarization/definition of the categories helps clarify the category definitions to the LLM, which in turn improves LLM's product categorization capability (Figure 6).

Black Glitter Level 16 Unlocked Game Birthday Cake Topper - Boy's 16th Birthday Cake Decorations. The cake toppers are approx 5.9" wide and 5.6" high. This unique decoration is the perfect centerpiece for a truly epic birthday bash. The bottom of the cake topper is made of wooden sticks, please pay attention to your child to avoid accidents.

Candidate categories produced by Domain Expert that have nuanced difference:

- Grocery / Pantry Staples / Cooking & Baking Grocery Supplies / Frosting, Icing & Decorations / Cake Toppers (denoted as cake toppers 1)
- Toys & Games / Kids' Party Supplies / Kids' Party Decorations / Cake & Cupcake Toppers / Cake Toppers (denoted as cake toppers 2)
- ...

LLM self-generated summarization/definition:

- Cake toppers 1: Cake toppers are ***edible*** decorative elements used to decorate cakes. They are typically made from sweet ingredients like sugar, chocolate, or marzipan. These decorative pieces are placed directly on top of the cake.
- Cake toppers 2: Cake toppers are ***non-edible*** decorative elements used to embellish cakes. They are typically made of materials like plastic or cardboard and fashioned into various figures or shapes. These decorative pieces are usually made of plastic or made of cardboard attached to toothpicks.

Optimal category selected by the LLM-based General Expert:
Cake toppers 2.

Reasoning:
Based on the product information, this product is made of glittery card-stock with wooden stick to insert into the cake. The dimensions of 5.9" wide and 5.6" high are suitable for most cake sizes. All these details indicate that this product is meant to decorate cakes. This product is a ***non-edible*** cake topper made of glittery card-stock and wooden sticks. Therefore, it belongs to the category of ***non-edible*** decorative cake toppers.

Figure 6: An example product that showcases the effectiveness of LLM self-generated summarization/definition. Two candidate categories are similar with subtle differences. LLM self-generated summarization identifies the key features that separate them: one is edible cake topper, the other is non-edible.

Adapting LLM Predictions in In-Context Learning with Data Priors

Javier Chiyah-Garcia[*] Heriot-Watt University Edinburgh, UK fjc3@hw.ac.uk

Prasoon Goyal Amazon New York, USA prasog@amazon.com

Michael Johnston Amazon New York, USA mjohnstn@amazon.com

Reza Ghanadan University of Maryland College Park, USA rezag@umd.edu

Abstract

In-Context Learning (ICL) has enabled Large Language Models (LLMs) to excel as general-purpose models in zero and few-shot task settings. However, since LLMs are often not trained on the downstream tasks, they lack crucial contextual knowledge from the data distributions, which limits their task adaptability.

This paper explores using data priors to automatically customize prompts in ICL. We extract these priors in a dataset-agnostic way based on historical information, enabling LLMs to personalize their output towards users or tasks at inference time. We find that they improve LLM's output by injecting latent dataset-specific information for the task of rating prediction. Throughout a series of experiments, we show replicable results across LLMs and datasets on what information and methods are most effective for adapting ICL outputs with priors. Our findings offer a systematic approach to customizing prompts with additional information in a privacy-friendly manner, requiring only aggregated data that is computationally efficient.

1 Introduction

The field of NLP has progressed significantly towards generalizing to unseen tasks and inputs with pre-trained Large Language Models (LLMs). With In-Context Learning (ICL) (Brown et al., 2020; Liu et al., 2023), models are conditioned with task instructions and a few examples to generate text predictions, without task-specific training in zero and few-shot settings (Wei et al., 2022; Chowdhery et al., 2022). Thus, LLMs are increasingly used as all-purpose models for tasks beyond text generation, such as classification and regression (Zhu and Zamani, 2024; Salemi et al., 2024).

ICL enables the personalization of LLM outputs by incorporating relevant context in the prompt, without fine-tuning individual models (Salemi et al., 2024). Recent approaches focus on retrieving and incorporating relevant information in the prompt (Mireshghallah et al., 2022; Andreas, 2022) or building personal user profiles (Mazaré et al., 2018; Naumov et al., 2019; Li and Tuzhilin, 2019). However, these methods have challenges, such as identifying relevant information, impracticality of fine-tuning models or parameters for each user, computational constraints with large prompts, and avoiding over-personalization (i.e., profiling).

In this paper, we focus on knowledge personalization (Kirk et al., 2023) of outputs based on historical data (i.e., previous interactions with the system), and argue that LLMs benefit from explicitly providing information about the data distribution in ICL prompts. We initially experiment with the use of data priors as supplementary context in prompts for rating prediction, automatically synthesized based on previous behavior, e.g., "*Consider that this product is rated on average with a 4*". Secondly, we probe LLMs with modifications of these priors to analyze their benefits and limitations.

We find that LLMs leverage this information to adapt to the input and calibrate their predictions within ranges that align with the underlying dataset distribution. Our findings also indicate that LLMs are generally resilient to inaccurate priors, and that their benefits are more significant when task demonstrations are absent from the prompts, potentially benefiting resource-constrained scenarios. Data priors offer a computationally efficient alternative to methods that depend on large volumes of data, retrieval algorithms or fine-tuned LMs.

Our contributions in this paper are as follows:

1. We demonstrate how incorporating data priors in prompts enhances the ICL performance of LLMs by better aligning with a particular user/element.

2. We probe LLMs with a range of alterna-

[*]Research conducted during an internship at Amazon. Correspondence to fjc3@hw.ac.uk and prasog@amazon.com

Proceedings of the 1st Workshop on Customizable NLP: Progress and Challenges in Customizing NLP for a Domain, Application, Group, or Individual (CustomNLP4U), pages 305–316

tive prior values, including upper and lower bounds, and analyze their role in downstream task adaptation.

3. We present experiments and prompt samples to facilitate the reproduction of our results and to adapt our method to other datasets.

2 Background

ICL relies on an LLM's ability to transfer and generalize to unseen tasks, without updating or training its parameters (see Dong et al. (2023) for a comprehensive survey and definition). The initial instruction conditions models to the task, whilst the demonstration examples, henceforth *demonstrations*, provide both the task format and useful input knowledge (i.e., label space) (Min et al., 2022).

ICL is highly sensitive to the prompt context and its demonstrations for downstream task adaptation (Jiang et al., 2020; Zhao et al., 2021; Mishra et al., 2022), thus prior works have explored selecting optimal demonstrations (Liu et al., 2022) and ordering them (Li and Qiu, 2023; Zhang et al., 2022; Lu et al., 2022). They have also proposed LMs to generate demonstrations (Kim et al., 2022; Zemlyanskiy et al., 2022) and unsupervised or supervised retrievers (Rubin et al., 2022; Agrawal et al., 2023). However, most of these methods rely on resource-intensive training or pre-processing (e.g., SBERT (Reimers and Gurevych, 2019) or BM25 (Robertson and Zaragoza, 2009) for similarity), which limits their scope to small pre-fixed data subsets. Our method, in contrast, relies solely on context (Dudy et al., 2021) from population-wide statistics as an alternative to training or retrievers.

Previous NLP personalization efforts have focused on creating user-specific representations (Mazaré et al., 2018; Wu et al., 2021) by inferring user attributes (Mireshghallah et al., 2022) or personas (Zhang et al., 2018) from narratives (Vincent et al., 2024) or public reviews (Li and Tuzhilin, 2019). These representations are then used to condition the input and generate more personalized outputs (Mairesse and Walker, 2011; Zhang et al., 2018; Li and Tuzhilin, 2019; Majumder et al., 2019). While these approaches target user-specific adaptation (e.g., chatty vs. terse (Mairesse and Walker, 2011)), we propose adapting to users or other elements by leveraging the data distribution, without training user-specific modules (e.g., user-specific vectors (Zhong et al., 2021)), which require substantial computational resources.

3 Contextual Data Priors

This section explores how including priors into prompts enhances LLM adaptation and predictions. Data priors represent population characteristics (e.g., averages) and thus can be leveraged to personalize outputs beyond users (e.g., products).

3.1 Experimental Setup

Task We evaluate our approach on numeric rating prediction based on review text (Baccianella et al., 2009) with several LLMs. Given an input review text t for an element, these models predict a rating $r^{\text{pred}} \in [1, 5] \cap \mathbb{R}$. This task is similar to personalized sentiment prediction (Zhong et al., 2021; Mireshghallah et al., 2022) and LAMP-3 (Salemi et al., 2024); however we use considerably larger test datasets and allow floating-point rating predictions rather than restricting to integers.

Datasets We use two large-scale online review datasets: **Amazon Product Reviews (APR)** (Ni et al., 2019), 233 million reviews divided into 29 product categories; and **Google Local Reviews (GLR)** (Li et al., 2022), with 666 million Google Maps reviews of USA businesses and landmarks split by state. Both datasets use ratings from 1 (*bad*) to 5 (*good*) stars and feature many-to-many relationships between users and reviewed items.

Given the large size of APR and GLR datasets, we limit our experiments to sub-categories. We further reduce these to dense K-core subsets, as sampled by the APR authors, where each user and element has at least K reviews. We aim to balance dataset size and reproducibility after extracting K-core subsets, yielding substantial subsets of dense data. Our final test subsets have the following entries: APR-Games (19K), APR-Clothing (17K), GLR-Montana (7.5K) and GLR-Vermont (15K). Since we use ICL and our method does not require training, we do not have training subsets. Previous works applying ICL to these datasets restrict their test sets to 2K (Li and Qiu, 2023) and 2.5K (Salemi et al., 2024) randomly sampled entries, and over 20K entries for training. Appendix D provides further dataset details.

Models We test with the following models[1]: LaMini-GPT (Wu et al., 2023), FLAN-T5-XL (Chung et al., 2022), Instruct-GPT-J (NLP Cloud, 2023), and Alexa Teacher Model (AlexaTM) (Soltan et al., 2022; FitzGerald et al., 2022).

[1]See Appendix A for further model details.

Metrics Following recent works (Salemi et al., 2024), we use **Root Mean Squared Error (RMSE)** to measure the distance between predicted r^{pred} and true r^{true} ratings (1 to 5) for n test entries (Eq. (1)). As a distance, lower numbers are closer to the target and thus better. We additionally calculate the **Percentage Change (Δ %)** to facilitate comparisons across experiments, models and datasets with the baseline (No priors); see Eq. (2).

$$\text{RMSE} = \sqrt{\frac{1}{n}\sum_{i=1}^{n}(r^{true} - r^{pred})^2} \quad (1)$$

$$\Delta\% = \frac{\text{RMSE}_x - \text{RMSE}_{\text{baseline}}}{\text{RMSE}_{\text{baseline}}} \times 100 \quad (2)$$

Implementation To evaluate performance in review prediction, we prompt the LLMs to generate up to 5 tokens (or end of sequence) and parse the predicted rating. While both APR and GLR datasets use integer scores, we allow outputs between 1.0 and 5.0 (1.3, 4.4...) since it is commonly treated as a regression task. Predictions outside this range or with additional text (e.g., "*3 stars*") are marked as out of distribution and removed[2]. We use custom prompts adapted to each LLM's prompting strategy[3] and provide 3 random reviews demonstrations in the prompt.

3.2 Experiment 1: ICL Adaptation

To understand how data priors influence LLM outputs, we compare the following conditions, where we add a sentence containing the prior value in natural language (refer to Table 1 for examples):

- `None`: default ICL prompt without priors.
- `Object`: sentence with the prior P^{obj} for an object or site as its mean rating from previous reviews.

$$P_n^{obj} = \frac{1}{n-1}\sum_{i=1}^{n-1} Rating_i^{obj}$$

- `User`: sentence with the prior P^{usr} for a user calculated from the user's mean historical ratings.

$$P_n^{usr} = \frac{1}{n-1}\sum_{i=1}^{n-1} Rating_i^{usr}$$

- `Object+User`: both priors combined into a single sentence.

[2]Fewer than 0.5% entries.

[3]Full prompts are provided in Appendix B.

Prior	Example Prompt
`None`	Give a rating between 1 to 5: <demonstrations> Input: Loved it! Review:
`Object`	Give a rating between 1 to 5: <demonstrations> Consider this product is rated on average with a 3.5 Input: Loved it! Review:
`User`	Give a rating between 1 to 5: <demonstrations> Consider this reviewer rates on average with a 4.1 Input: Loved it! Review:
`Object + User`	Give a rating between 1 to 5: <demonstrations> Consider that this product is rated on average with 3.5 and that this reviewer rates on average with 4.1 Input: Loved it! Review:

Table 1: Sample prompts for each data prior with task instruction, demonstrations, data prior and input query.

3.3 Experiment 2: Control Conditions

Along with exploring the enhancements that data priors provide, we also test if these improvements arise due to other factors, such as priors being a good approximation of the target output, which LLMs can use as predictions. We compare our results with baselines and isolate confounding factors through several control conditions with priors.

Prior baselines We first evaluate how close the synthesized priors are from the target output by using each prior as the prediction, without the ICL prompt or LLMs. We experiment with two: `Baseline`$^{\texttt{Object}}$ and `Baseline`$^{\texttt{User}}$.

Oracle (or upper bound) We evaluate whether providing the gold target output as the prior in the prompt pushes LLMs towards better results. We would expect that models that merely carry over priors as a prediction would also reach perfect scores. We substitute the calculated priors from § 3.2 with the gold output value $P^{Oracle} = r^{true}$ (keeping prompt text intact) in these experiments: `Oracle`$^{\texttt{Object}}$ and `Oracle`$^{\texttt{User}}$.

Distractor (or lower bound) Similarly, we test whether wrong or inaccurate data priors may hinder the LLM's performance. Thus we introduce "distractor" conditions, whereby we substitute the prior with a value far from the true output whilst keeping prompts intact. Since outputs range from 1 to 5, and a random baseline has a mean RMSE $\approx$ 2.0 across datasets, we calculate the distractor value D_n as 2 points away from the true gold output, $D_n = (r_n^{true} - 2)$ if $r_n^{true} \geq 3$, else $(r_n^{true} + 2)$, in: `Distract`$^{\texttt{Object}}$ and `Distract`$^{\texttt{User}}$.

We discuss other types of priors in Appendix C.

3.4 Results

We evaluate the impact of priors by comparing each condition to the performance of each model's prompt without priors (None) using **Percentage Change** Δ %. Specifically, we calculate:

$$\Delta\% = \frac{\text{RMSE}_x - \text{RMSE}_{pNone}}{\text{RMSE}_{pNone}} \times 100$$

This section discusses results from comparing PC Δ %, refer to Appendix E for extended results.

ICL Improvements Table 2 shows the benefits that data priors provide to LLMs, with similar gains when using `Object` or `User` priors, and larger when these are combined in `Object+User`. We see that the historic ratings help models anchor their output towards a rating, likely exploiting the propensity that some users and objects may have around a particular rating.

We also see that all but one LLM reach their best scores when combining `Object+User` priors, despite the relatively increased noise in the prompt from a longer sentence and two conflicting values. The relative improvement is often greater than both `Object` or `User` separately, suggesting that this may be further used as a balancing between a range of ratings. All LLMs benefit from priors, although we see variance as some favor either `Object` or `User`.

Control Conditions Due to space constraints, we provide all results in Appendix E (Table 8). Firstly, we observe that the prior baselines are not good approximations of the gold output, usually with a RMSE of ≈ 1 and higher (worse) than most out-of-the-box LLMsPredicting (copying) the same prior number would deteriorate results, suggesting their usefulness extends beyond a numerical value.

Model	Object Δ %	User Δ %	Object+User Δ %
LaMini-GPT	-8.59	-9.35	-11.88
FLAN-T5-XL	-8.10	-7.74	-9.72
Instruct-GPT-J	-12.09	-20.70	-15.41
AlexaTM	-2.40	-5.36	-10.51
Mean Δ %	-7.79	-10.79	-11.88

Table 2: Relative improvements from § 3.2 experiments compared to not using priors (None), averaged across datasets (lower is better ↓). Refer to Table 8 (Appendix E) for baselines and absolute results.

In the **Oracle** setting, LLMs consistently reach their best results and largest improvements (see Table 3), yet they are far from perfect scores. This reaffirms that LLMs are not copying these priors and instead use them to tune or guide their output.

Regarding the **Distractor** setting, the tests yield a mix of effects. Depending on the condition and LLM, we get slightly worse or better results than not having priors (None), $\pm 1.5\%$. The results far exceed a random baseline and are not substantially compromised by inaccurate information, which reinforces the notion that priors balance or tune models closer to a dataset with insight that is not present in demonstrations alone.

Model	Oracle Object Δ %	Oracle User Δ %	Distract Object Δ %	Distract User Δ %
LaMini-GPT	-25.07	-13.60	+9.01	+0.31
FLAN-T5-XL	-7.62	-7.10	-0.74	+0.47
Instruct-GPT-J	-20.93	-28.52	+0.16	-4.09
AlexaTM	-14.86	-12.15	-2.06	-2.36
Mean Δ %	-17.12	-15.34	+1.59	-1.42

Table 3: Summary of § 3.3 experiments, negative results show improvement. Refer to Appendix E for all results.

Priors without Demonstrations The gains in Distractor settings suggest that priors may be useful beyond providing a value to anchor outputs, and may play a role in helping LLMs adapt to the task. Therefore, we repeat all previous experiments with no demonstrations in the prompt to analyze their role (see Appendix E, Table 9).

Under these settings, we observe a stronger prior effect (larger Δ %) across most conditions. Models less reliant on demonstrations exhibit the greatest impact, with most LLMs achieving their best results under the `Object+User` and `Oracle` prior conditions. In the absence of demonstrations, models seem to heavily rely on priors, which can serve as a suitable alternative even when they poorly approximate the target output. This mirrors the effectiveness of demonstrations even with incorrect labels (Min et al., 2022).

4 Discussion and Conclusion

This paper explores the adaptation of LLM outputs in ICL using easily-calculable data priors as contextual information. We demonstrate that incorporating user- or object-specific context in prompts helps LLMs to customize outputs, consistently improving results.

Secondly, we test isolating factors responsible for these improvements and find that LLMs do not simply reproduce the provided priors in their outputs. Instead, higher-quality priors – those closer to the latent dataset distribution or ground truth – lead to enhanced outcomes, particularly in the absence of demonstrations. Results show that inaccurate data prior values have minor negative impact and may even provide benefits. This reveals LLMs may leverage priors for more than tuning their predictions. Our findings suggest that **priors serve a dual purpose**: anchoring predictions around specific values and facilitating downstream task adaptation. This could be similar to the role of demonstrations, which extends beyond format examples (Min et al., 2022).

While priors may have limited utility in tasks lacking clear numeric population traits (e.g., reasoning), we anticipate this work paves the way towards further exploring the role of additional context in ICL. Future work will explore tasks with unbalanced datasets, such as categorical classification with majority labels, where providing mode rather than mean may prove beneficial.

These conceptually straightforward data priors offer complementary benefits to demonstrations for task or user adaptations, while being significantly more computationally efficient and easier to implement than training demonstration retrievers or models, which could be intractable for user-specific modules. Their aggregate nature also helps mitigate some of the drawbacks typically associated with personalization in NLP (Flek, 2020; Dudy et al., 2021; Kirk et al., 2023).

5 Limitations

Our work has several limitations: 1) we only investigate the task of rating review prediction, which has a numeric output and thus allows to calculate averages to use as priors. Further investigation would be required as to determine whether there is task-agnostic context that we can consistently extract to improve ICL in other domains, i.e., classification. 2) We use subsets of two large datasets, but these categories could be biased or provide limited transferable evidence of the benefits of priors. We aimed to balance dataset size versus reproducibility, as larger subsets would be more difficult to evaluate. Our work contributes an initial step into understanding how context in the prompt, different from task demonstrations, could be useful across models and datasets in ICL. 3) We use models of different sizes that we think are representative of the ICL research field, from a small 1.5B parameter model, LaMini-GPT, to a large LLM with 20B parameters, AlexaTM. However, we were not able to test all models that may also be relevant, such as GPT-4/ChatGPT (OpenAI, 2023), LLama 2 (Touvron et al., 2023) or OPT-IML (Iyer et al., 2023). 4) We did not test whether retrieving optimal demonstrations rather than randomly choosing them, had any effects on the benefits of data priors. Instead, this paper focused on exploring complementary information in the prompts that could be useful when a retriever is not practical or in data-scarce settings. Finally, 5) we did not exhaustively test alternative priors, e.g., random numbers. We use personalized priors for users/objects as a way of adapting to the input and providing some useful information. We discuss alternative data priors in Appendix C and why they were not included, but ultimately leave the study of alternative data priors for future work as this may be dataset-dependent.

Acknowledgments

We thank the anonymous reviewers for their insightful comments that helped improve this paper.

References

Sweta Agrawal, Chunting Zhou, Mike Lewis, Luke Zettlemoyer, and Marjan Ghazvininejad. 2023. In-context examples selection for machine translation. In *Findings of the Association for Computational Linguistics: ACL 2023*, pages 8857–8873, Toronto, Canada. Association for Computational Linguistics.

Jacob Andreas. 2022. Language models as agent models.

Stefano Baccianella, Andrea Esuli, and Fabrizio Sebastiani. 2009. Multi-facet rating of product reviews. In *Proceedings of the 31th European Conference on IR Research on Advances in Information Retrieval*, ECIR '09, page 461–472, Berlin, Heidelberg. Springer-Verlag.

Tom B. Brown, Benjamin Mann, Nick Ryder, Melanie Subbiah, Jared Kaplan, Prafulla Dhariwal, Arvind Neelakantan, Pranav Shyam, Girish Sastry, Amanda Askell, Sandhini Agarwal, Ariel Herbert-Voss, Gretchen Krueger, Tom Henighan, Rewon Child, Aditya Ramesh, Daniel M. Ziegler, Jeffrey Wu, Clemens Winter, Christopher Hesse, Mark Chen, Eric Sigler, Mateusz Litwin, Scott Gray, Benjamin Chess, Jack Clark, Christopher Berner, Sam McCandlish, Alec Radford, Ilya Sutskever, and Dario Amodei. 2020. Language models are few-shot learners. In

Proceedings of the 34th International Conference on Neural Information Processing Systems, NIPS'20, Red Hook, NY, USA. Curran Associates Inc.

Aakanksha Chowdhery, Sharan Narang, Jacob Devlin, Maarten Bosma, Gaurav Mishra, Adam Roberts, Paul Barham, Hyung Won Chung, Charles Sutton, Sebastian Gehrmann, Parker Schuh, Kensen Shi, Sasha Tsvyashchenko, Joshua Maynez, Abhishek Rao, Parker Barnes, Yi Tay, Noam Shazeer, Vinodkumar Prabhakaran, Emily Reif, Nan Du, Ben Hutchinson, Reiner Pope, James Bradbury, Jacob Austin, Michael Isard, Guy Gur-Ari, Pengcheng Yin, Toju Duke, Anselm Levskaya, Sanjay Ghemawat, Sunipa Dev, Henryk Michalewski, Xavier Garcia, Vedant Misra, Kevin Robinson, Liam Fedus, Denny Zhou, Daphne Ippolito, David Luan, Hyeontaek Lim, Barret Zoph, Alexander Spiridonov, Ryan Sepassi, David Dohan, Shivani Agrawal, Mark Omernick, Andrew M. Dai, Thanumalayan Sankaranarayana Pillai, Marie Pellat, Aitor Lewkowycz, Erica Moreira, Rewon Child, Oleksandr Polozov, Katherine Lee, Zongwei Zhou, Xuezhi Wang, Brennan Saeta, Mark Diaz, Orhan Firat, Michele Catasta, Jason Wei, Kathy Meier-Hellstern, Douglas Eck, Jeff Dean, Slav Petrov, and Noah Fiedel. 2022. Palm: Scaling language modeling with pathways.

Hyung Won Chung, Le Hou, Shayne Longpre, Barret Zoph, Yi Tay, William Fedus, Eric Li, Xuezhi Wang, Mostafa Dehghani, Siddhartha Brahma, Albert Webson, Shixiang Shane Gu, Zhuyun Dai, Mirac Suzgun, Xinyun Chen, Aakanksha Chowdhery, Sharan Narang, Gaurav Mishra, Adams Yu, Vincent Zhao, Yanping Huang, Andrew Dai, Hongkun Yu, Slav Petrov, Ed H. Chi, Jeff Dean, Jacob Devlin, Adam Roberts, Denny Zhou, Quoc V. Le, and Jason Wei. 2022. Scaling instruction-finetuned language models.

Qingxiu Dong, Lei Li, Damai Dai, Ce Zheng, Zhiyong Wu, Baobao Chang, Xu Sun, Jingjing Xu, Lei Li, and Zhifang Sui. 2023. A survey on in-context learning.

Shiran Dudy, Steven Bedrick, and Bonnie Webber. 2021. Refocusing on relevance: Personalization in NLG. In *Proceedings of the 2021 Conference on Empirical Methods in Natural Language Processing*, pages 5190–5202, Online and Punta Cana, Dominican Republic. Association for Computational Linguistics.

Jack FitzGerald, Shankar Ananthakrishnan, Konstantine Arkoudas, Davide Bernardi, Abhishek Bhagia, Claudio Delli Bovi, Jin Cao, Rakesh Chada, Amit Chauhan, Luoxin Chen, Anurag Dwarakanath, Satyam Dwivedi, Turan Gojayev, Karthik Gopalakrishnan, Thomas Gueudre, Dilek Hakkani-Tur, Wael Hamza, Jonathan J. Hüser, Kevin Martin Jose, Haidar Khan, Beiye Liu, Jianhua Lu, Alessandro Manzotti, Pradeep Natarajan, Karolina Owczarzak, Gokmen Oz, Enrico Palumbo, Charith Peris, Chandana Satya Prakash, Stephen Rawls, Andy Rosenbaum, Anjali Shenoy, Saleh Soltan, Mukund Harakere Sridhar, Lizhen Tan, Fabian Triefenbach, Pan Wei, Haiyang Yu, Shuai Zheng, Gokhan Tur, and Prem Natarajan. 2022. Alexa teacher model: Pretraining and distilling multi-billion-parameter encoders for natural language understanding systems. In *Proceedings of the 28th ACM SIGKDD Conference on Knowledge Discovery and Data Mining*, KDD '22. ACM.

Lucie Flek. 2020. Returning the N to NLP: Towards contextually personalized classification models. In *Proceedings of the 58th Annual Meeting of the Association for Computational Linguistics*, pages 7828–7838, Online. Association for Computational Linguistics.

Srinivasan Iyer, Xi Victoria Lin, Ramakanth Pasunuru, Todor Mihaylov, Daniel Simig, Ping Yu, Kurt Shuster, Tianlu Wang, Qing Liu, Punit Singh Koura, Xian Li, Brian O'Horo, Gabriel Pereyra, Jeff Wang, Christopher Dewan, Asli Celikyilmaz, Luke Zettlemoyer, and Ves Stoyanov. 2023. Opt-iml: Scaling language model instruction meta learning through the lens of generalization.

Zhengbao Jiang, Frank F. Xu, Jun Araki, and Graham Neubig. 2020. How Can We Know What Language Models Know? *Transactions of the Association for Computational Linguistics*, 8:423–438.

Hyuhng Joon Kim, Hyunsoo Cho, Junyeob Kim, Taeuk Kim, Kang Min Yoo, and Sang goo Lee. 2022. Self-generated in-context learning: Leveraging autoregressive language models as a demonstration generator.

Hannah Rose Kirk, Bertie Vidgen, Paul Röttger, and Scott A. Hale. 2023. Personalisation within bounds: A risk taxonomy and policy framework for the alignment of large language models with personalised feedback.

Jiacheng Li, Jingbo Shang, and Julian McAuley. 2022. UCTopic: Unsupervised contrastive learning for phrase representations and topic mining. In *Proceedings of the 60th Annual Meeting of the Association for Computational Linguistics (Volume 1: Long Papers)*, pages 6159–6169, Dublin, Ireland. Association for Computational Linguistics.

Pan Li and Alexander Tuzhilin. 2019. Towards controllable and personalized review generation. In *Proceedings of the 2019 Conference on Empirical Methods in Natural Language Processing and the 9th International Joint Conference on Natural Language Processing (EMNLP-IJCNLP)*, pages 3237–3245, Hong Kong, China. Association for Computational Linguistics.

Xiaonan Li and Xipeng Qiu. 2023. Finding support examples for in-context learning. In *Findings of the Association for Computational Linguistics: EMNLP 2023*, pages 6219–6235, Singapore. Association for Computational Linguistics.

Jiachang Liu, Dinghan Shen, Yizhe Zhang, Bill Dolan, Lawrence Carin, and Weizhu Chen. 2022. What makes good in-context examples for GPT-3? In *Proceedings of Deep Learning Inside Out (DeeLIO*

2022): The 3rd Workshop on Knowledge Extraction and Integration for Deep Learning Architectures, pages 100–114, Dublin, Ireland and Online. Association for Computational Linguistics.

Pengfei Liu, Weizhe Yuan, Jinlan Fu, Zhengbao Jiang, Hiroaki Hayashi, and Graham Neubig. 2023. Pre-train, prompt, and predict: A systematic survey of prompting methods in natural language processing. *ACM Comput. Surv.*, 55(9).

Yinhan Liu, Myle Ott, Naman Goyal, Jingfei Du, Mandar Joshi, Danqi Chen, Omer Levy, Mike Lewis, Luke Zettlemoyer, and Veselin Stoyanov. 2019. Roberta: A robustly optimized bert pretraining approach. *arXiv preprint arXiv:1907.11692*.

Yao Lu, Max Bartolo, Alastair Moore, Sebastian Riedel, and Pontus Stenetorp. 2022. Fantastically ordered prompts and where to find them: Overcoming few-shot prompt order sensitivity. In *Proceedings of the 60th Annual Meeting of the Association for Computational Linguistics (Volume 1: Long Papers)*, pages 8086–8098, Dublin, Ireland. Association for Computational Linguistics.

François Mairesse and Marilyn A. Walker. 2011. Controlling User Perceptions of Linguistic Style: Trainable Generation of Personality Traits. *Computational Linguistics*, 37(3):455–488.

Bodhisattwa Prasad Majumder, Shuyang Li, Jianmo Ni, and Julian McAuley. 2019. Generating personalized recipes from historical user preferences. In *Proceedings of the 2019 Conference on Empirical Methods in Natural Language Processing and the 9th International Joint Conference on Natural Language Processing (EMNLP-IJCNLP)*, pages 5976–5982, Hong Kong, China. Association for Computational Linguistics.

Pierre-Emmanuel Mazaré, Samuel Humeau, Martin Raison, and Antoine Bordes. 2018. Training millions of personalized dialogue agents. In *Proceedings of the 2018 Conference on Empirical Methods in Natural Language Processing*, pages 2775–2779, Brussels, Belgium. Association for Computational Linguistics.

Sewon Min, Xinxi Lyu, Ari Holtzman, Mikel Artetxe, Mike Lewis, Hannaneh Hajishirzi, and Luke Zettlemoyer. 2022. Rethinking the role of demonstrations: What makes in-context learning work? In *Proceedings of the 2022 Conference on Empirical Methods in Natural Language Processing*, pages 11048–11064, Abu Dhabi, United Arab Emirates. Association for Computational Linguistics.

Fatemehsadat Mireshghallah, Vaishnavi Shrivastava, Milad Shokouhi, Taylor Berg-Kirkpatrick, Robert Sim, and Dimitrios Dimitriadis. 2022. UserIdentifier: Implicit user representations for simple and effective personalized sentiment analysis. In *Proceedings of the 2022 Conference of the North American Chapter of the Association for Computational Linguistics: Human Language Technologies*, pages 3449–3456, Seattle, United States. Association for Computational Linguistics.

Swaroop Mishra, Daniel Khashabi, Chitta Baral, Yejin Choi, and Hannaneh Hajishirzi. 2022. Reframing instructional prompts to GPTk's language. In *Findings of the Association for Computational Linguistics: ACL 2022*, pages 589–612, Dublin, Ireland. Association for Computational Linguistics.

Maxim Naumov, Dheevatsa Mudigere, Hao-Jun Michael Shi, Jianyu Huang, Narayanan Sundaraman, Jongsoo Park, Xiaodong Wang, Udit Gupta, Carole-Jean Wu, Alisson G. Azzolini, Dmytro Dzhulgakov, Andrey Mallevich, Ilia Cherniavskii, Yinghai Lu, Raghuraman Krishnamoorthi, Ansha Yu, Volodymyr Kondratenko, Stephanie Pereira, Xianjie Chen, Wenlin Chen, Vijay Rao, Bill Jia, Liang Xiong, and Misha Smelyanskiy. 2019. Deep learning recommendation model for personalization and recommendation systems.

Jianmo Ni, Jiacheng Li, and Julian McAuley. 2019. Justifying recommendations using distantly-labeled reviews and fine-grained aspects. In *Proceedings of the 2019 Conference on Empirical Methods in Natural Language Processing and the 9th International Joint Conference on Natural Language Processing (EMNLP-IJCNLP)*, pages 188–197, Hong Kong, China. Association for Computational Linguistics.

NLP Cloud. 2023. An Instruct Version Of GPT-J Using Stanford Alpaca's Dataset. [Last Accessed 18-11-2023].

OpenAI. 2023. Gpt-4 technical report.

Alec Radford, Jeff Wu, Rewon Child, David Luan, Dario Amodei, and Ilya Sutskever. 2019. Language models are unsupervised multitask learners.

Colin Raffel, Noam Shazeer, Adam Roberts, Katherine Lee, Sharan Narang, Michael Matena, Yanqi Zhou, Wei Li, and Peter J. Liu. 2020. Exploring the limits of transfer learning with a unified text-to-text transformer. *J. Mach. Learn. Res.*, 21(1).

Nils Reimers and Iryna Gurevych. 2019. Sentence-BERT: Sentence embeddings using Siamese BERT-networks. In *Proceedings of the 2019 Conference on Empirical Methods in Natural Language Processing and the 9th International Joint Conference on Natural Language Processing (EMNLP-IJCNLP)*, pages 3982–3992, Hong Kong, China. Association for Computational Linguistics.

Stephen Robertson and Hugo Zaragoza. 2009. The probabilistic relevance framework: Bm25 and beyond. *Found. Trends Inf. Retr.*, 3(4):333–389.

Ohad Rubin, Jonathan Herzig, and Jonathan Berant. 2022. Learning to retrieve prompts for in-context learning. In *Proceedings of the 2022 Conference of the North American Chapter of the Association for*

Computational Linguistics: Human Language Technologies, pages 2655–2671, Seattle, United States. Association for Computational Linguistics.

Alireza Salemi, Sheshera Mysore, Michael Bendersky, and Hamed Zamani. 2024. LaMP: When large language models meet personalization. In *Proceedings of the 62nd Annual Meeting of the Association for Computational Linguistics (Volume 1: Long Papers)*, pages 7370–7392, Bangkok, Thailand. Association for Computational Linguistics.

Saleh Soltan, Shankar Ananthakrishnan, Jack FitzGerald, Rahul Gupta, Wael Hamza, Haidar Khan, Charith Peris, Stephen Rawls, Andy Rosenbaum, Anna Rumshisky, Chandana Satya Prakash, Mukund Sridhar, Fabian Triefenbach, Apurv Verma, Gokhan Tur, and Prem Natarajan. 2022. Alexatm 20b: Few-shot learning using a large-scale multilingual seq2seq model.

Hugo Touvron, Louis Martin, Kevin Stone, Peter Albert, Amjad Almahairi, Yasmine Babaei, Nikolay Bashlykov, Soumya Batra, Prajjwal Bhargava, Shruti Bhosale, Dan Bikel, Lukas Blecher, Cristian Canton Ferrer, Moya Chen, Guillem Cucurull, David Esiobu, Jude Fernandes, Jeremy Fu, Wenyin Fu, Brian Fuller, Cynthia Gao, Vedanuj Goswami, Naman Goyal, Anthony Hartshorn, Saghar Hosseini, Rui Hou, Hakan Inan, Marcin Kardas, Viktor Kerkez, Madian Khabsa, Isabel Kloumann, Artem Korenev, Punit Singh Koura, Marie-Anne Lachaux, Thibaut Lavril, Jenya Lee, Diana Liskovich, Yinghai Lu, Yuning Mao, Xavier Martinet, Todor Mihaylov, Pushkar Mishra, Igor Molybog, Yixin Nie, Andrew Poulton, Jeremy Reizenstein, Rashi Rungta, Kalyan Saladi, Alan Schelten, Ruan Silva, Eric Michael Smith, Ranjan Subramanian, Xiaoqing Ellen Tan, Binh Tang, Ross Taylor, Adina Williams, Jian Xiang Kuan, Puxin Xu, Zheng Yan, Iliyan Zarov, Yuchen Zhang, Angela Fan, Melanie Kambadur, Sharan Narang, Aurelien Rodriguez, Robert Stojnic, Sergey Edunov, and Thomas Scialom. 2023. Llama 2: Open foundation and fine-tuned chat models.

Sebastian Vincent, Rowanne Sumner, Alice Dowek, Charlotte Prescott, Emily Preston, Chris Bayliss, Chris Oakley, and Carolina Scarton. 2024. Reference-less analysis of context specificity in translation with personalised language models. In *Proceedings of the 2024 Joint International Conference on Computational Linguistics, Language Resources and Evaluation (LREC-COLING 2024)*, pages 13769–13784, Torino, Italia. ELRA and ICCL.

Ben Wang and Aran Komatsuzaki. 2021. GPT-J-6B: A 6 Billion Parameter Autoregressive Language Model. `https://github.com/kingoflolz/mesh-transformer-jax`.

Jason Wei, Maarten Bosma, Vincent Y. Zhao, Kelvin Guu, Adams Wei Yu, Brian Lester, Nan Du, Andrew M. Dai, and Quoc V. Le. 2022. Finetuned language models are zero-shot learners.

Minghao Wu, Abdul Waheed, Chiyu Zhang, Muhammad Abdul-Mageed, and Alham Fikri Aji. 2023. Lamini-lm: A diverse herd of distilled models from large-scale instructions. *CoRR*, abs/2304.14402.

Yuwei Wu, Xuezhe Ma, and Diyi Yang. 2021. Personalized response generation via generative split memory network. In *Proceedings of the 2021 Conference of the North American Chapter of the Association for Computational Linguistics: Human Language Technologies*, pages 1956–1970, Online. Association for Computational Linguistics.

Yury Zemlyanskiy, Michiel de Jong, Joshua Ainslie, Panupong Pasupat, Peter Shaw, Linlu Qiu, Sumit Sanghai, and Fei Sha. 2022. Generate-and-retrieve: Use your predictions to improve retrieval for semantic parsing. In *Proceedings of the 29th International Conference on Computational Linguistics*, pages 4946–4951, Gyeongju, Republic of Korea. International Committee on Computational Linguistics.

Rongzhi Zhang, Yue Yu, Pranav Shetty, Le Song, and Chao Zhang. 2022. Prompt-based rule discovery and boosting for interactive weakly-supervised learning. In *Proceedings of the 60th Annual Meeting of the Association for Computational Linguistics (Volume 1: Long Papers)*, pages 745–758, Dublin, Ireland. Association for Computational Linguistics.

Saizheng Zhang, Emily Dinan, Jack Urbanek, Arthur Szlam, Douwe Kiela, and Jason Weston. 2018. Personalizing dialogue agents: I have a dog, do you have pets too? In *Proceedings of the 56th Annual Meeting of the Association for Computational Linguistics (Volume 1: Long Papers)*, pages 2204–2213, Melbourne, Australia. Association for Computational Linguistics.

Zihao Zhao, Eric Wallace, Shi Feng, Dan Klein, and Sameer Singh. 2021. Calibrate before use: Improving few-shot performance of language models. In *Proceedings of the 38th International Conference on Machine Learning*, volume 139 of *Proceedings of Machine Learning Research*, pages 12697–12706. PMLR.

Wanjun Zhong, Duyu Tang, Jiahai Wang, Jian Yin, and Nan Duan. 2021. UserAdapter: Few-shot user learning in sentiment analysis. In *Findings of the Association for Computational Linguistics: ACL-IJCNLP 2021*, pages 1484–1488, Online. Association for Computational Linguistics.

Yaxin Zhu and Hamed Zamani. 2024. ICXML: An in-context learning framework for zero-shot extreme multi-label classification. In *Findings of the Association for Computational Linguistics: NAACL 2024*, pages 2086–2098, Mexico City, Mexico. Association for Computational Linguistics.

A Model and Compute Details

Models We run our experiments with models that have been Instruction-Tuned (IT) with varied prompts and datasets to augment their transferability (Chowdhery et al., 2022; Wei et al., 2022). These models usually have a superior performance in ICL and have an easier time adapting to tasks. We test with these popular models of different sizes (refer to Table 4 for number of parameters):

- **LaMini-GPT** (Wu et al., 2023), distilled IT version of GPT-2 (Radford et al., 2019).
- **FLAN-T5-XL** (Chung et al., 2022), IT version from T5-XL (Raffel et al., 2020).
- **Instruct-GPT-J** (NLP Cloud, 2023), IT version of GPT-J (Wang and Komatsuzaki, 2021).
- **Alexa Teacher Model (AlexaTM)**, further IT from (Soltan et al., 2022; FitzGerald et al., 2022).

A.1 Other Baselines

Random Baseline We randomly select an integer out of 5 as the output.

Fine-tuned RoBERTa We fine-tune a RoBERTa (Liu et al., 2019) model trained to predict a number out of 5 as a classification task. This resembles previous works that treat the task as sentiment prediction from a few pre-determined labels. We train this model for 3 epochs using only the review text as input.

Model	# of Parameters
LaMini-GPT-1.5B (Wu et al., 2023)	1.5B
FLAN-T5-XL (Chung et al., 2022)	3B
Instruct-GPT-J (NLP Cloud, 2023)	6B
AlexaTM (Soltan et al., 2022; FitzGerald et al., 2022)	20B

Table 4: LLMs used in experiments with their approximate number of parameters.

Experiments We used a machine with 4 NVIDIA V100 GPUs with 16G of RAM each, with a maximum sequence length of 1024 tokens. We used the LLM's HuggingFace versions when available. A full range of experiments, as in i.e., Table 8, takes approximately 3-4 days.

B Model Prompts

We provide full sample prompts in Table 5. Prior sentences would change to reflect more accurate descriptions of the items reviewed per dataset: "product" for APR and "location/place" for GLR.

C Additional Data Priors

The data priors evaluated in the paper are not an exhaustive list of dataset statistics that could be extracted. We limited our experiments to priors that were easy to understand but also provided a wide (and scoped) range of interesting results. Mean values are a representation of the underlying data distribution (i.e. the mean of a product rating conveys a rough summary of the data), and thus enable adaptation based on available information: a general dataset mean compared to a lower-level personalized mean for users or objects (mean of previous user/item ratings).

This paper aims to demonstrate that using these prior values aids LLM adaptation to tasks in ICL, yet the exact choice of prior would depend on the specific setting (task/dataset/model).

We considered the following priors before deciding to only include mean and the oracle/distractor variants:

- **Mode/Median:** alternative user or object-specific metrics, such as mode and median, may be too dataset-dependent and provide poor approximations. Our proposed data priors aim to convey distribution tendencies, which we believe the mean better represents in these datasets. Both APR and GLR datasets have slightly skewed distributions towards 1 and 5 stars (more 1 and 5 star reviews than others), and thus the arithmetic mean can capture distribution shifts in the underlying distribution with decimal precision, unlike median or mode. Datasets with a different distribution should consider these alternatives.
- **Random:** use a random value as the prior. We believe that the `Distractor` conditions better demonstrate the impact of incorrect values without the unpredictability of randomness. In practice, we observed results that were slightly better than the `Distractor` conditions.
- **Consistent values:** using the same value across all dataset priors as a control condition. Similar to the random values as priors,

Model	Sample Prompt
LaMini-GPT + None prior	Below is an instruction that describes a task. Write a response that appropriately completes the request.\n ### Instruction: Choose the rating between 1.0 (bad) and 5.0 (good) for this review.\n Here are some examples: \n <demonstrations> Review: Loved it! \n Rating:
FLAN-T5-XL + Object prior	Given a product review, you MUST choose the most likely rating from 1.0 (bad) to 5.0 (good). Here are several cases for your reference: \n <demonstrations> Consider this product is rated on average with a 3.5 \n Review: Loved it! \n Rating:
Instruct-GPT-J + User prior	Given a product review, you MUST choose the most likely rating from 1.0 (bad) to 5.0 (good). Here are several cases for your reference: \n <demonstrations> Consider this reviewer rates on average with a 4.1 \n Review: Loved it! \n Rating:
AlexaTM + Object+User prior	Below is an instruction that describes a task. Write a response that appropriately completes the request.\n ### Instruction: Choose the rating between 1.0 (bad) and 5.0 (good) for this review.\n ### Here are some examples:\n <demonstrations> Consider that this product is rated on average with a 3.5 and that this reviewer rates on average with a 4.1 \n Review: Loved it! \n Rating:

Table 5: Sample prompts for each model with task instruction, demonstrations, data prior and input query. We tested several prompts but we settled on these as they seemed to work well across LLMs. Demonstrations have the same format as the input query (Review-Rating) and are selected at random from an unrelated subset (different object and user).

we think that this does not provide further relevant results. We think that experimenting `Oracle` (always correct) and `Distractor` (always incorrect) provide better insights into the mechanisms that makes data priors work.

D Datasets

Table 6 summarizes the test entries used after filtering with the K-core process described in § 3.1. Since our method does not require training, we only use test data.

Dataset	Category	Test Set
Amazon Product Reviews (Ni et al., 2019)	Games	18,802
	Clothing	17,084
Google Local Reviews (Li et al., 2022)	Montana	7,473
	Vermont	14,919

Table 6: Test entries per subset used in our experiments.

We compare the train/test dataset sizes with previous works in ICL in Table 7. These works also used other datasets and tasks in their experiments but treated each separately, hence we only report the sizes for the Amazon Product Review dataset that we have in common.

Work	Sampling	#Classes	#Train	#Test
Li and Qiu (2023)	Random	2	30000	2000
Salemi et al. (2024)	Random	5	20000	2500
Our work	K-core dense	-	0	35800

Table 7: Comparison of previous ICL works using the Amazon Product Reviews dataset.

E Additional Experiment Results

Table 8 shows extra results from § 3.2 and § 3.3. Table 9 shows the results from running the same experiments without demonstrations in the prompts.

Notably, the $\texttt{Baseline}^{\texttt{User}}$ prior has a 0.0 RMSE for the APR-Clothing dataset in experiments, with the fine-tuned RoBERTa (Liu et al., 2019) closely following at 0.07 RMSE. This suggests that this particular data split may be exceptionally predictable.

Demonstration Selection When using demonstrations (Table 8), we randomly sample 3 entries from the same data subset to use as examples in the prompt. We ensure that these entries are not from the same user, product or location as the test review to avoid biases.

Model	Datasets								
	APR-Games		APR-Clothing		GLR-Montana		GLR-Vermont		Mean
	RMSE ↓	Δ %	RMSE ↓	Δ %	RMSE ↓	Δ %	RMSE ↓	Δ %	Δ %
Random Baseline	2.159		2.058		1.956		1.973		
Fine-tuned RoBERTa	0.724		0.073		0.780		0.749		
Priors									
Baseline^{Object}	0.880		1.372		1.007		0.985		
Baseline^{User}	0.781		0.000		0.919		0.932		
LaMini-GPT									
None	0.761		1.000		0.909		0.882		
Object	0.661	-13.15	0.942	-5.74	0.840	-7.53	0.812	-7.92	-8.59
User	0.700	-7.99	0.872	-12.81	0.832	-8.51	0.811	-8.07	-9.35
Object+User	0.657	-13.56	0.850	-14.94	0.821	-9.66	0.800	-9.34	-11.88
Oracle^{Object}	0.582	-23.50	0.784	-21.57	0.662	-27.11	0.634	-28.10	-25.07
Oracle^{User}	0.674	-11.35	0.872	-12.82	0.776	-14.67	0.745	-15.54	-13.60
Distract^{Object}	0.849	11.62	1.083	8.31	0.977	7.46	0.959	8.65	9.01
Distract^{User}	0.776	2.08	1.034	3.42	0.893	-1.76	0.860	-2.49	0.31
FLAN-T5-XL									
None	0.7156		1.0490		1.0075		0.966		
Object	0.6741	-5.80	0.906	-13.66	0.9454	-6.16	0.900	-6.77	-8.10
User	0.6701	-6.36	0.9447	-9.94	0.9355	-7.15	0.8932	-7.50	-7.74
Object+User	0.6539	-8.62	0.9046	-13.77	0.9253	-8.16	0.8853	-8.32	-9.72
Oracle^{Object}	0.6606	-7.69	0.9259	-11.73	0.9555	-5.16	0.9085	-5.91	-7.62
Oracle^{User}	0.6609	-7.64	0.9447	-9.94	0.9577	-4.94	0.9091	-5.85	-7.10
Distract^{Object}	0.7115	-0.57	0.9994	-4.73	1.0226	1.50	0.9738	0.85	-0.74
Distract^{User}	0.7128	-0.39	1.0595	1.00	1.0191	1.15	0.9666	0.10	0.47
Instruct-GPT-J									
None	0.9530		1.2353		1.1310		1.1182		
Object	0.821	-13.85	1.2011	-2.77	0.9544	-15.61	0.9379	-16.12	-12.09
User	0.8061	-15.41	0.8782	-28.91	0.9122	-19.35	0.9044	-19.12	-20.70
Object+User	0.7976	-16.31	1.1488	-7.00	0.9101	-19.53	0.9082	-18.78	-15.41
Oracle^{Object}	0.7788	-18.28	1.0009	-18.98	0.8467	-25.14	0.8798	-21.32	-20.93
Oracle^{User}	0.7202	-24.43	0.8782	-28.91	0.7646	-32.40	0.8014	-28.33	-28.52
Distract^{Object}	0.9575	0.47	1.3672	10.68	1.0662	-5.73	1.0648	-4.78	0.16
Distract^{User}	0.9673	1.50	1.2951	4.84	0.9934	-12.17	1.0005	-10.53	-4.09
AlexaTM									
None	0.6195		0.8757		0.8386		0.8490		
Object	0.6318	1.99	0.8279	-5.46	0.829	-1.14	0.8067	-4.98	-2.40
User	0.6265	1.13	0.7139	-18.48	0.8163	-2.66	0.8367	-1.45	-5.36
Object+User	0.605	-2.34	0.6274	-28.35	0.789	-5.91	0.803	-5.42	-10.51
Oracle^{Object}	0.5753	-7.13	0.6743	-23.00	0.7047	-15.97	0.7359	-13.32	-14.86
Oracle^{User}	0.5689	-8.17	0.7139	-18.48	0.7367	-12.15	0.7657	-9.81	-12.15
Distract^{Object}	0.6342	2.37	0.8012	-8.51	0.8374	-0.14	0.8324	-1.96	-2.06
Distract^{User}	0.6408	3.44	0.7957	-9.14	0.8257	-1.54	0.8303	-2.20	-2.36

Table 8: Results from experiments with data priors. We compare LLMs across datasets and under 8 conditions: the initial 4 with distinct prior prompts (§ 3.2); followed by 4 highlighted rows with altered prior values (§ 3.3). We provide a supervised fine-tuned RoBERTa (Liu et al., 2019) baseline for comparison and the prior baselines from § 3.3. Lower is better for RMSE and percentage change Δ % (refer to § 3.1). We average the results of 3 runs, and provide prompts with 3 randomly-selected task demonstrations each.

Experiments with 0 Demonstrations in Prompts									
	Datasets								
Model	**APR-Games**		**APR-Clothing**		**GLR-Montana**		**GLR-Vermont**		**Mean**
	RMSE ↓	Δ %	**RMSE** ↓	Δ %	**RMSE** ↓	Δ %	**RMSE** ↓	Δ %	Δ %
Random Baseline	2.159		2.058		1.956		1.973		
Fine-tuned RoBERTa	0.724		0.073		0.780		0.749		
Priors									
`Baseline`$^{\texttt{Object}}$	0.880		1.372		1.007		0.985		
`Baseline`$^{\texttt{User}}$	0.781		0.000		0.919		0.932		
LaMini-GPT									
`None`	0.742		0.874		0.837		0.784		
`Object`	0.654	-11.84	0.883	1.08	0.796	-4.85	0.747	-4.69	-5.08
`User`	0.663	-10.67	0.801	-8.31	0.783	-6.44	0.735	-6.23	-7.91
`Object+User`	0.629	-15.28	0.798	-8.71	0.745	-11.02	0.715	-8.85	-10.96
`Oracle`$^{\texttt{Object}}$	0.483	-34.94	0.645	-26.15	0.553	-33.95	0.502	-36.00	-32.76
`Oracle`$^{\texttt{User}}$	0.620	-16.45	0.801	-8.31	0.720	-13.93	0.655	-16.49	-13.80
`Distract`$^{\texttt{Object}}$	0.957	28.87	1.191	36.32	0.921	10.06	0.873	11.34	21.65
`Distract`$^{\texttt{User}}$	0.775	4.42	0.979	12.04	0.850	1.59	0.799	1.91	4.99
FLAN-T5-XL									
`None`	0.7124		1.0646		1.0367		0.986		
`Object`	0.6724	-5.61	0.908	-14.70	0.9691	-6.52	0.929	-5.84	-8.17
`User`	0.6716	-5.73	0.9422	-11.50	0.9795	-5.52	0.9316	-5.53	-7.07
`Object+User`	0.63	-11.57	0.8055	-24.34	0.89	-14.15	0.8589	-12.90	-15.74
`Oracle`$^{\texttt{Object}}$	0.6511	-8.60	0.8721	-18.08	0.9635	-7.06	0.9176	-6.95	-10.17
`Oracle`$^{\texttt{User}}$	0.6574	-7.72	0.9422	-11.50	0.9744	-6.01	0.9257	-6.13	-7.84
`Distract`$^{\texttt{Object}}$	0.685	-3.85	0.9738	-8.53	1.0182	-1.78	0.9591	-2.74	-4.22
`Distract`$^{\texttt{User}}$	0.693	-2.72	1.0629	-0.16	1.0226	-1.36	0.9667	-1.97	-1.55
Instruct-GPT-J									
`None`	1.0336		1.2638		1.0345		1.0230		
`Object`	0.9011	-12.82	1.2251	-3.06	1.0608	2.54	1.048	2.44	-2.72
`User`	0.8666	-16.16	1.0541	-16.59	1.0461	1.12	1.028	0.49	-7.78
`Object+User`	0.902	-12.73	1.1743	-7.08	1.0459	1.10	1.0301	0.69	-4.50
`Oracle`$^{\texttt{Object}}$	0.8251	-20.17	1.102	-12.80	0.9081	-12.22	0.9208	-9.99	-13.80
`Oracle`$^{\texttt{User}}$	0.7634	-26.14	1.0539	-16.61	0.8164	-21.08	0.8217	-19.68	-20.88
`Distract`$^{\texttt{Object}}$	0.9498	-8.11	1.2156	-3.81	1.0277	-0.66	1.017	-0.59	-3.29
`Distract`$^{\texttt{User}}$	0.9912	-4.10	1.2501	-1.08	1.0016	-3.18	0.9962	-2.62	-2.75
AlexaTM									
`None`	0.6306		0.9793		0.8706		0.8583		
`Object`	0.6183	-1.95	0.7565	-22.75	0.8067	-7.34	0.7654	-10.82	-10.72
`User`	0.6126	-2.85	0.6285	-35.82	0.7509	-13.75	0.7476	-12.90	-16.33
`Object+User`	0.5977	-5.22	0.5086	-48.06	0.7631	-12.35	0.7249	-15.54	-20.29
`Oracle`$^{\texttt{Object}}$	0.5461	-13.40	0.6743	-31.14	0.7331	-15.79	0.6797	-20.81	-20.29
`Oracle`$^{\texttt{User}}$	0.5507	-12.67	0.6285	-35.82	0.7304	-16.10	0.6771	-21.11	-21.43
`Distract`$^{\texttt{Object}}$	0.6511	3.25	0.782	-20.15	0.8269	-5.02	0.7845	-8.60	-7.63
`Distract`$^{\texttt{User}}$	0.6649	5.44	0.8566	-12.53	0.8168	-6.18	0.7925	-7.67	-5.23

Table 9: Results from experiments with data priors without task demonstrations in the prompts. Note that Δ % in this table references the respective `None` prior condition, and thus cannot be compared directly with Table 8. Lower is better for RMSE and percentage change Δ %.

V-GlórIA:
Customizing Large Vision and Language Models to European Portuguese

Afonso Simplício, David Semedo, João Magalhães
NOVA LINCS, NOVA School of Science and Technology, Portugal
{am.simplicio}@campus.fct.unl.pt
{df.semedo, jmag}@fct.unl.pt

Abstract

Generative Vision and Language models have obtained remarkable results recently, thanks to the use of robust pre-trained Visual encoders and Large Language Models (LLMs), together with efficient model adaptation training strategies, requiring minimal architectural modifications, while preserving LLMs' original capabilities. With these advances focusing mainly on the English language, there is a gap in customization methodologies for other languages. In this paper, we propose a customization methodology that adapts existing state-of-the-art vision and language architectures to European Portuguese (PT-PT). As a result of applying this methodology, we introduce V-GlórIA , the first Large Vision and Language generative model specifically customized for European Portuguese. V-GlórIA supports multimodal tasks such as image captioning, retrieval, and dialogue. To deliver V-GlórIA, we leverage state-of-the-art V&L architectures, and contribute with PT-PT machine translated pre-training (CC3M PT-PT) and benchmark (MSCOCO PT-PT and VisDial PT-PT) datasets. Our experiments show that V-GlórIA delivers promising performance in text-image retrieval and downstream tasks in a zero-shot setting, such as image captioning and visual dialogue tasks, highlighting the effectiveness of our customization approach. [1]

1 Introduction

Vision and Language are two of the main communication and information perception mediums, serving as fundamental channels through which humans interpret and interact with the world around them. Devising Vision and Language (V&L) models that can seamlessly combine these two modalities is paramount to delivering AI systems capable of addressing tasks such as image captioning and visual question-answering, essential tasks to aid visually impaired individuals, and Image-to-Text and Text-to-Image retrieval, for general multimodal information seeking. Recently, there have been notable advances in vision and language models (Liu et al., 2023; Koh et al., 2023; Kim et al., 2021), which leverage Large Language Models as backbones (Touvron et al., 2023; Brown et al., 2020; Zhang et al., 2022) (LLMs). Most of these advances have been made with models in English or other high-resource languages, leaving behind other lower-resource languages, as is the case of European Portuguese (PT-PT). This evidences the urgent need of having effective customization methologies to deliver V&L LMs, openly available, for PT-PT speakers. This customization process raises two complementary challenges: 1) how to overcome the limited availability of PT-PT multimodal datasets and resources, and 2) how to train a Large Visiwon and Language model, capable of addressing multiple V&L tasks, in PT-PT.

Most LLMs are trained with text-only web scraped data, achieving great performance on a myriad of natural language tasks, but lack an overall understanding of images, thus not having visual reasoning capabilities. Pioneering vision and language models, adopted fully multimodal Transformer-based models (Lu et al., 2019; Yu et al., 2022; Wang et al., 2022), with either single-stream or dual-stream architectures (Bugliarello et al., 2021), pre-trained on image-text pairs. More recently, towards generalizing high-performing large LMs to the visual domain, it is common practice to leverage text-only LLMs as the backbone and equip them with a visual encoder (Radford et al., 2021; Dosovitskiy et al., 2021). Then, LLMs are augmented with a visual projection component that aligns visual tokens with the LLM token-space (Koh et al., 2023; Liu et al., 2023).

In this paper, we seek to establish a V&Lcustomization methodology to European Portuguese, and as a result, deliver the first European

[1] Code and data are available in https://github.com/amsimplicio/V-GlorIA.

Proceedings of the 1st Workshop on Customizable NLP: Progress and Challenges in Customizing NLP for a Domain, Application, Group, or Individual (CustomNLP4U), pages 317–326
November 16, 2024 ©2024 Association for Computational Linguistics

Portuguese vision and language LM, **V-GlórIA**. To this extent, we make two major contributions: **1)** we create and make available both large-scale image-text pre-training datasets as well as well-known V&L benchmarks in European Portuguese. In particular, CC3M (Sharma et al., 2018a) PT-PT (3 million image-caption pairs) for pre-training, MSCOCO (Lin et al., 2014) PT-PT (image-caption pairs) and VisDial (Das et al., 2017) PT-PT (visual dialogs) for benchmarking on downstream V&L tasks. An extensive assessment of available machine translation approaches is carried out. **2)** following the V&L LMs state-of-the-art, we adapt the FROMAGe (Koh et al., 2023) model to support PT-PT. Its flexible decoder-based architecture, augmented with multimodal specialized layers, gives the model the capacity to process and produce interleaved multimodal inputs and outputs. Given that a key step is to replace the original LLM by a PT-PT LLM, we leverage a recent PT-PT text-only decoder, GlórIA (Lopes et al., 2024), and conduct extensive experiments, in a zero-shot setting, on image caption and visual dialog tasks.

2 Related Work

Most Generative Vision and Language models consist of decoder-only Transformers. GPT-3 (Brown et al., 2020) showed that when trained with a lot of data, language models can generalize and solve new (unseen) tasks. This is very useful since although the training is expensive and requires a lot of data, once they are pre-trained, they can be applied to a myriad of tasks with reduced adaptation costs. LLaVA (Liu et al., 2023) takes advantage of this by creating a general Vision and Language model using a frozen LLM as decoder and a frozen visual encoder to encode the images, training a linear layer that transforms the image embeddings into the LLM embedding space. This simple linear transformation has the advantage of introducing a very small number of parameters to be learned, allowing for efficient large-scale training, while leveraging the generalization capabilities of the backbone text LLM. Different ways of mapping image embeddings to the LLM token subspace have been tried, such as a Q-Former (Li et al., 2022) consisting of a Query transformer that learns query embeddings that will interact with the image encoding through cross attention, and CogVLM (Wang et al., 2024) where although the part of the LLM that processes the text input will still be frozen, it trains the weights used to compute the queries, keys, and values relative to the image embeddings. FROMAGe (Koh et al., 2023) takes a step further by extra linear transformations that enable to model to generatively retrieve images/texts. This is accomplished by introducing a special retrieval token, that is then trained under a multimodal contrastive learning of cross-modal mappings.

Most of these models are in English or other high-resource languages. Very recently, open European Portuguese LLMs have been made available. In particular, GlórIA (Lopes et al., 2024) is a European Portuguese LLM Decoder based on GPT-Neo (Black et al., 2021) - which approximates the GPT3 architecture - trained on a 35B token corpus, from a diverse set of domains, including web content, news pieces, encyclopedic knowledge, news articles, and dialogs. Gervásio (Santos et al., 2024) is another relevant European Portuguese LLM decoder which is based on a pre-trained LLaMA 2 7B (Touvron et al., 2023) model, fine-tuned on Portuguese instruction datasets, comprising around 83M tokens. Regarding V&L approaches, literature is scarce. CAPIVARA (dos Santos et al., 2023) trains a Brazilian Portuguese CLIP model, while performing data augmentation through image captioning and machine translation. In this work, and using recent developments in the LLM PT-PT, we seek to narrow this gap, by introducing a European Portuguese V&L model.

3 PT-PT Datasets for Vision and Language AI

Due to the lack of European Portuguese V&L datasets, we embraced the task of translating core vision and language datasets from English into European Portuguese. Given the size of existing datasets (millions scale), translating the datasets with human experts would be too costly, hence we considered three distinct automatic machine translation models: first, we considered a) **MADLAD-400** (Kudugunta et al., 2023), a model trained on a 3T token dataset based on CommonCrawl, created by Google, covering text data from over 400 languages; b) **Narrativa**[2], which is an mBART-50 (Tang et al., 2020) model fine-tuned on the opus-100 (Zhang et al., 2020) dataset for English to Portuguese Translation, c) **DeepL**[3] a

[2] https://huggingface.co/Narrativa/mbart-large-50-finetuned-opus-en-pt-translation

[3] https://www.deepl.com/translator

Table 1: Translation statistics, for CC3M and COCO, with different machine translation approaches. # Samples - total number of samples, # Tokens - total number of tokens, # Avg. Tokens/Sample - average number of tokens per sample. * Stands for the original captions.

	Statistic	English*	MADLAD	Narrativa	DeepL
CC3M	# Samples	2 709 383	2 709 383	2 287 769	2 709 383
	# Tokens	27 919 393	26 558 075	24 257 997	29 844 147
	# Tokens/Sample	10.30	9.80	10.60	11.02
COCO	# Samples	25 014	25 014	23 614	25 014
	# Tokens	282 297	282 172	267 893	292 626
	# Tokens/Sample	11.29	11.28	11.34	11.70

Original*: plenty of space : at square feet the property would have ample room for actor and her daughter

MADLAD-400: abundância de espaço: em pés quadrados a propriedade teria amplo espaço

Narrativa: plenty of space : at square feet the property would have ample room for actor and her daughter

DeepL: muito espaço: em metros quadrados, a propriedade teria muito espaço para o ator e a sua filha

Original*: people waiting for the bus in snow storm

MADLAD-400: pessoas à espera do ônibus na tempestade de neve

Narrativa: Pessoas à espera do autocarro em tempestade de neve

DeepL: pessoas à espera do autocarro numa tempestade de neve

Original*: person serves lunch to two of her daughters at their farm.

MADLAD-400: uma mulher serve o almoço para duas de suas filhas em sua fazenda

Narrativa: A pessoa serve o almoço a duas filhas da fazenda dela.

DeepL: uma pessoa serve o almoço a duas das suas filhas na sua quinta.

Figure 1: Translation results of sample captions from the CC3M dataset, using each of the three considered translation approaches. The original caption is shown for reference.

commercial translation service.

We started by pre-assessing the performance of each of the three approaches, using a subset of CC3M, comprising both shorter and longer captions. Table 1 illustrates some of the translated examples of the CC3M dataset (Sharma et al., 2018a). First, although **MADLAD-400** seems to give good translations, most are in Brazilian Portuguese. **Narrativa** translations are in European Portuguese, but for many captions, the model output is the original English caption, rather than its translation. **DeepL** seems to solve these problems, by providing high-quality European Portuguese translations, with the disadvantage of being a commercial solution. For example, for the first image, Narrativa outputted the original caption, and in the second image MADLAD-400 uses a Brazilian Portuguese lexicon in its translations (e.g. "ônibus" instead of "autocarro", the word bus). Something we also notice is that MADLAD-400 often does not translate the full caption (as in the first image).

Given these observations, we translated the CC3M (Sharma et al., 2018b), MSCOCO (Lin et al., 2014), and VisDial (Das et al., 2017) datasets, using **DeepL** and MADLAD-400(Kudugunta et al., 2023). Given the higher effectiveness of DeepL, we will take them as the main datasets/benchmarks, and refer to them as CC3M PT-PT, MSCOCO PT-PT and VisDial PT-PT, respectively. The CC3M PT-PT dataset was used as the pre-training dataset, and both MSCOCO PT-PT and VisDial PT-PT were used for benchmarking retrieval, image-captioning and visual dialog tasks. Table 1 shows the aggregated statistics of these datasets. It is important to note that the lower number of total tokens in the Narrativa translation stems from the fact that some captions are not actually translated. DeepL translations have higher token numbers than the original

English dataset, which despite corroboration with the increased verbosity of Portuguese vs. English, will have an impact on the models' performance.

4 Method

In this section we present V-GlórIA, an European Portuguese Large V&L model, capable of flexibly interleaving the two modalities, images and text, and therefore generalize to different NLP and CV tasks such as multimodal retrieval, image captioning, and visual dialog. Therefore, we adapt the FROMAGe model (Koh et al., 2023) architecture, which leverages a text LLM and adds a set of projection layers to align images with the LLM input subspace, and support generative retrieval. Specifically, it allows us to use an European Portuguese LLM, that will be frozen during training, with lightweight training strategies aimed at equip V-GlórIA with visual and linguistic reasoning capabilities.

4.1 V-GlórIA Architecture

4.1.1 PT-PT Language Model Backbone.

V-GlórIA uses a Portuguese large language model decoder originally trained with text-only data with a causal language modeling task. V-GlórIA is based on a PT-PT open and top performing LLM, GlórIA (Lopes et al., 2024). In the experiments, we compare it with alternative LLM backbones, such as Gervásio (Santos et al., 2024).

4.1.2 Visual Encoder Model.

Images are encoded using a pre-trained CLIP ViT-L/14 (Radford et al., 2021), such that given an image y, the visual model outputs $v(y) \in \mathbb{R}^m$, corresponding to the [CLS] token embedding. Both θ and ϕ, both LLM and visual encoder parameters will be frozen.

4.1.3 Visual Projection Layer.

With the LLM and the visual encoder frozen, a projection layer is used to map the encoded images to the embedding subspace of the LLM token. Namely, a linear layer, $v(y)^T \cdot \mathbf{W}_c \in \mathbb{R}^d$, where d corresponds to the LLM hidden dimension. This transformation makes it possible for our Portuguese decoder to understand the contents of the image it receives.

4.1.4 Multimodal Retrieval.

In order to support retrieving images, conditioned either on text or images, a special token [RET] is added to the model vocabulary, so that at any point in the decoding, the model can decode this token and its embedding (which will be learned) can be used for retrieval. During training, a [RET] token is appended to the end of the input captions. In practice, two linear mappings are trained, $\mathbf{W}_t \in \mathbb{R}^{d \times q}$ and $\mathbf{W}_i \in \mathbb{R}^{m \times q}$, which will map the hidden representation of [RET] obtained from the last hidden layer of the LLM and the visual embeddings, respectively, into a common q dimensional space.

4.2 Training

The training tasks are specifically designed to equip the model vision and language reasoning capabilities: describing visual content; processing intervealed images and text in its context; and third matching images to text and vice versa. The model is trained with a multitask objective $\mathcal{L}$ comprising image captioning and image-text retrieval, with

$$\mathcal{L} = \lambda_c \mathcal{L}_c + \lambda_r (\mathcal{L}_{i2t} + \mathcal{L}_{t2i}), \tag{1}$$

with $\lambda_c = \lambda_r = 0.5$, as illustrated in Figure 2.

4.2.1 Image Captioning.

For captioning, the model is trained to autoregressively predict the next token, with a Cross-entropy loss conditioned on the image representation, i.e.

$$l_c(x, y) = \sum_{t=1}^{T} \log p_\theta(s_t | v(y)^T \mathbf{W}_c, s_1, \dots, s_{t-1}), \tag{2}$$

where s_t represents the t-th token of the caption x, $\mathbf{W}_c$ the weights of the visual projection layer, and θ the frozen parameters of the LLM.

4.2.2 Image-text Retrieval.

For bidirectional multimodal retrieval, given a caption x_i and its corresponding image y_i[4], the InfoNCE (van den Oord et al., 2018) loss for multimodal contrastive learning is used as

$$\mathcal{L}_{t2i} = -\frac{1}{N} \sum_{i=1}^{N} \left(\log \frac{\exp(x_i \cdot y_i / \tau)}{\sum_{j=1}^{N} \exp(x_j \cdot y_j / \tau)} \right), \tag{3}$$

where $x_i \cdot y_i$ corresponds to the cosine similarity between embeddings. The loss in the opposite direction, $\mathcal{L}_{i2t}$, is defined reciprocally, with x_i and y_i swapped.

[4] For the sake of notation simplification, $x_i \in \mathbb{R}^q$ and $y_i \in \mathbb{R}^q$ correspond to the [RET] token output of the retrieval mapping $\mathbf{W}_t \in \mathbb{R}^{d \times q}$, and to the outputs of the visual mapping $\mathbf{W}_i \in \mathbb{R}^{m \times q}$, respectively.

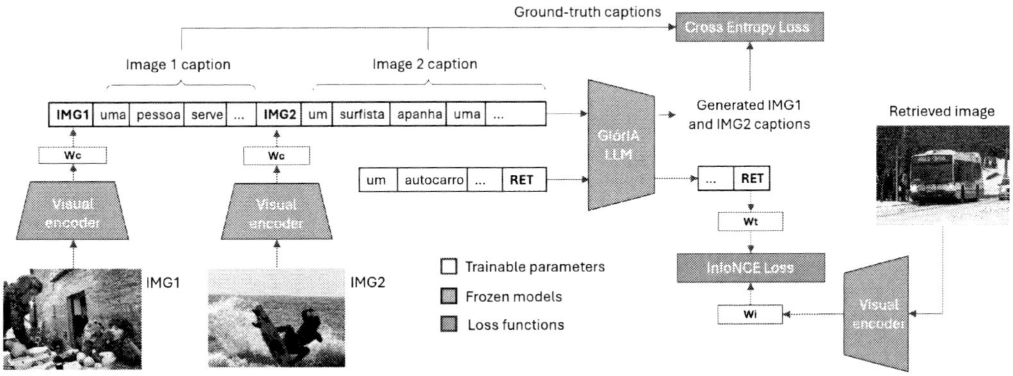

Figure 2: Overview of the V-GlórIA architecture. The model is trained on image-text pairs for image captioning and image-text retrieval. The LLM and visual encoder are frozen, while the three projection layers (in yellow), with weight matrices $\mathbf{W}_c$, $\mathbf{W}_i$, and $\mathbf{W}_t$, are learned.

5 Experimental Setup

We assess the performance of our model in both image retrieval and image-and-text generation tasks. The models were trained on the CC3M PT-PT dataset, originally comprising 3.3 million image-text pairs, which after filtering out missing and corrupted images resulted in a total of 2.7M samples. We consider both GlórIA 1.3B [5] and Gervásio 7B [6] as the PT-PT LLM backbones.

Multimodal retrieval and image captioning are evaluated in both the CC3M PT-PT (full-shot) and MSCOCO PT-PT (zero-shot) evaluation sets. Models are also evaluated in the Visual Dialog task (Das et al., 2017), in a zero-shot setting. To establish a comparison between English and European Portuguese, we consider the architectural twin of GlórIA 1.3B, GPTNeo 1.3B (Black et al., 2021), an English-only LLM.

Training details. For training, we set a batch size of 180 and train for a total of 20000 iterations, taking about 24 hours on 1x NVIDIA A100 40GB GPU. We used the Adam optimizer (Kingma and Ba, 2015) with a learning rate of 0.0003 and a warmup of 100 steps.

The loss weight λ_c and λ_r are set to 1, the visual prefix length of $k = 1$. As for the embedding dimensions, we set the retrieval embedding dimension to $q = 256$, and model inner embedding dimension to $d = 2048$.

As most of the model parameters are frozen, our method is memory and compute-efficient: we backpropagate through the frozen LLM and visual model but only compute gradient updates for the 3 trainable linear mappings and [RET] embedding.

[5]https://huggingface.co/NOVA-vision-language/GlorIA-1.3B

[6]https://huggingface.co/PORTULAN/gervasio-7b-portuguese-ptpt-decoder

6 Results and Discussion

In this section, we discuss the experimental results in the image captioning and cross-modal retrieval tasks. We start by evaluating our model in cross-modal retrieval, in both Image to Text (I2T) and Text to Image (T2I) settings, and then in image captioning. We follow related work, and for cross-modal retrieval experiments adopt as metrics Recall@5 (R@5), and Recall@10 (R@10), and for image captioning BLEU and METEOR. Finally, we consider the challenging task of Visual Dialog, in a zero-shot setting. For the three tasks, we follow the established task evaluation protocols.

6.1 Cross-Modal Retrieval Results

The cross-modal retrieval results are shown in Table 2, where, for reference, we show (in gray) the performance of an English model (GPT-Neo 1.3B), trained and evaluated on the corresponding original English datasets. We can observe that V-GlórIA, using GlórIA as LLM, trained with data translated with DeepL, has the best results, significantly outperforming Gervásio in both directions, although the latter has more than five times the number of GlórIA parameters. In the MSCOCO validation set (unseen data), we observe a similar trend, where GlórIA shows to be preferable to Gervásio. However, in MSCOCO, we observe that higher performance is achieved when training

Table 2: Cross-modal Retrieval results for CC3M PT-PT and MSCOCO PT-PT datasets.

	LLM Backbone	Data Language	I2T R@5	I2T R@10	T2I R@5	T2I R@10
CC3M	GPT-Neo 1.3B	English	13.7	31.3	11.9	29.0
	GlórIA 1.3B	PT-PT MADLAD-400	22.5	44.9	22.0	44.1
	GlórIA 1.3B	PT-PT DeepL	**23.4**	**45.9**	**23.3**	**45.9**
	Gervásio 7B	PT-PT MADLAD-400	15.5	33.8	15.3	34.4
	Gervásio 7B	PT-PT DeepL	16.6	34.8	16.1	35.5
MSCOCO	GPT-Neo 1.3B	English	21.0	30.7	21.1	29.6
	GlórIA 1.3B	PT-PT MADLAD-400	**34.7**	**46.8**	**35.7**	**47.2**
	GlórIA 1.3B	PT-PT DeepL	30.2	41.1	30.1	40.7
	Gervásio 7B	PT-PT MADLAD-400	16.6	25.5	16.5	24.2
	Gervásio 7B	PT-PT DeepL	16.7	24.5	15.7	22.3

Table 3: Image Captioning results on the validation split of the CC3M PT-PT and MSCOCO PT-PT datasets.

	LLM Backbone	Data Language	BLEU1	BLEU2	BLEU3	BLEU4	METEOR
CC3M	GPT-Neo 1.3B	English	18.5	9.9	6.0	4.0	17.6
	GlórIA 1.3B	PT-PT MADLAD-400	11.9	6.0	3.5	2.3	13.9
	GlórIA 1.3B	PT-PT DeepL	11.8	5.7	3.3	2.2	13.7
	Gervásio 7B	PT-PT MADLAD-400	9.6	5.4	3.4	2.3	12.3
	Gervásio 7B	PT-PT DeepL	10.8	6.1	3.8	2.6	13.1
MSCOCO	GPT-Neo 1.3B	English	42.8	24.1	12.9	7.0	13.1
	GlórIA 1.3B	PT-PT MADLAD-400	29.7	16.2	8.8	4.7	13.8
	GlórIA 1.3B	PT-PT DeepL	25.8	12.7	6.8	3.6	12.1
	Gervásio 7B	PT-PT MADLAD 400	21.6	12.3	7.0	3.9	13.4
	Gervásio 7B	PT-PT DeepL	23.8	13.3	7.9	4.7	12.9

and evaluating using the dataset translations obtained with MADLAD-400. This might be because although these models are European Portuguese LLMs, some of the data they were trained on may be in Brazilian Portuguese allowing the model to better understand the latter variety present in the MADLAD-400 translation.

When comparing the performance between the two languages, i.e. PT-PT (GlórIA 1.3B) and English (GPT-Neo 1.3B), we observe that performance is higher in PT-PT. This shows the robustness of our training procedure and hints at the promising capabilities of PT-PT vision and language models.

Table 4: Zero-shot results on VisDial (Das et al., 2017), for image-and-text-to-text (IT2T) and text-to-image (T2I) retrieval. Unlike previous methods, is capable of generating free-form text interleaved with image outputs through text-to-image retrieval.

Backbone	IT2T R@5	IT2T R@10	T2I R@5	T2I R@10
GlórIA 1.3B	**4.2**	**14.1**	**17.3**	**25.2**
Gervásio 7B	4.0	13.9	8.2	14.0

6.2 Image Captioning Results

Table 3 shows the results of the image captioning. Again, for reference, we show (in gray) the performance of an English model (GPT-Neo 1.3B), trained and evaluated on the corresponding original English datasets.

Query: *"Uma mota Honda preta estacionada em frente a uma garagem."*
Query in English - *"A dark Honda motorbike parked in front of a garage."*

Retrieved images:

(a) Image retrieval

Ground truth:
Um homem numa prancha de surf na água.

V-GlórIA generated caption:
Um surfista a surfar a onda!

Gervásio generated caption:
um surfista a saltar de uma onda[RET] surfista a saltar de uma onda[RET] surfista ...

Ground truth caption:
Várias pessoas caminham pelo aeroporto enquanto esperam pelas suas malas.

V-GlórIA generated caption:
A fila de pessoas que se encontram a caminho do aeroporto.

Gervásio generated caption:
pessoas a descer a passagem de nível.

(b) Image captioning.

Question: Quantas pessoas estão na foto?
Answer (GT): 5
Answer (V-GlórIA): 13

Question: Estão virados para a câmara?
Answer (GT): sim
Answer (V-GlórIA): sim

Question: Estão a usar casacos?
Answer (GT): sim
Answer (V-GlórIA): sim

Question: Existem árvores visíveis?
Answer (GT): sim
Answer (V-GlórIA): branco

(c) Visual dialog.

Figure 3: V-GlórIA can solve core vision and language tasks.

First, we observe the same trend in which our model, V-GlórIA, using GlórIA 1.3B as its LLM backbone, consistently achieves superior performance, compared to the Gervásio LLM backbone. Second, it can be seen that the task is much more challenging on CC3M-PT, with all models obtaining a lower performance. These low BLEU scores on CC3M, might be explained by the fact that since CC3M captions are collected from the web, and not manually annotated like in MSCOCO, making them more prone to being unaligned with the image. This is evidenced in the first example of Table 1, where the caption mentions "actor and her daughter" which cannot be guessed from the picture. However, in MSCOCO, higher BLEU and METEOR scores are obtained. This is explained by three aspects: 1) the captions' lexicon diversity in MSCOCO is significantly lower when compared to CC3M, and 2) the connection between images and the captions is much tighter in MSCOCO, and 3) captions have a more predictable format. It should be noted that for MSCOCO, models are evaluated in a zero-shot setting, evidencing that V-GlórIAis capable of generalizing to unseen data.

When comparing a full English setup (gray lines) vs. a PT-PT model trained on PT-PT data, we observe that the former achieves higher performance in both datasets. Given the proximity of the image captioning task to the original LLM loss, and the fact that GPT-Neo 1.3B was pre-trained on a significantly larger text corpus, compared to GlórIA and Gervásio, this is not surprising, and we believe that this can be countered with an improved PT-PT LLM.

6.3 Visual Dialog Results

To assess our model performance on a more challenging vision and language task, we evaluate it on the Visual Dialog (VisDial) (Das et al., 2017) task, in zero-shot, in two different settings: **a)** IT2T (image and text to text) where given an image, a dialog about it, and a question, the model has to select the correct answer from a pool of 100 candidate answers, and **b)** T2I (text to image), where given a dialog about an image, the model has to retrieve the correct image. Given that V-GlórIA is an autoregressive decoder, we follow the protocol of (Koh et al., 2023) for IT2T, and given a question and answer sequence, we select the answer with the lowest perplexity, among the candidate answer options.

Table 4 shows the results. We observe that all models exhibit low performance, regardless of the PT-PT LLM backbone. Performance is, however, higher in T2I, compared to IT2T, which is consistent with the fact that the T2I task is closer to the vision and language tasks considered in training. Notwithstanding, V-GlórIA , using the GlórIA PT-PT LLM, demonstrates better generalization capabilities to new tasks, significantly outperforming the model using the Gervásio PT-PT LLM. We believe that part of these results can be dramatically improved by using a stronger PT-PT LLM. That is, despite the higher effectiveness of the GlórIA PT-PT LLM, it was not trained on instructions. This makes the model struggle when instructed to answer questions.

7 Conclusions

In this paper, we proposed a methodology to efficiently customize a Vision and Language LLM to European Portuguese. In particular, we introduced V-GlórIA, the first European-Portuguese Vision and Language model, capable of addressing multimodal tasks such as retrieval, image captioning, and visual dialogs illustrated in Figure 3. Experiments, leveraging current best performing open PT-PT LLMs as backbones, reveal performances that are competitive with the English counterpart setting (i.e. English pre-training and benchmarks), on these tasks. V-GlórIA demonstrated to be capable of generalizing to unseen data, especially in multimodal retrieval. For more challenging tasks, such as Visual Dialog, the proposed approach is still not on par with English models. However, we believe that as better PT-PT models arise, including instruction-tuned ones, the performance gap can be narrowed down by employed our devised customization methodology, and leveraging our contributed PT-PT data resources. We will release the PT-PT high-quality translations of the most popular V&L datasets to foster research in this area.

8 Ethical Considerations

This research presents a methodology for customizing and adapting vision and language models to European Portuguese. In alignment with principles of transparency and ethical responsibility, we exclusively utilized publicly available research datasets and benchmarks. No private or sensitive information, whether personal or proprietary, was used in this work.

Acknowledgements

This work has been partially funded by the FCT project NOVA LINCS Ref. UIDP/04516/2020, by CMU|Portugal project iFetch, Ref. CMUP LISBOA-01-0247-FEDER-045920, and by the Google Cloud Grant Ref. Nº CPCA-IAC/AV/594875/2023.

References

Sid Black, Gao Leo, Phil Wang, Connor Leahy, and Stella Biderman. 2021. GPT-Neo: Large Scale Autoregressive Language Modeling with Mesh-Tensorflow.

Tom B. Brown, Benjamin Mann, Nick Ryder, Melanie Subbiah, Jared Kaplan, Prafulla Dhariwal, Arvind Neelakantan, Pranav Shyam, Girish Sastry, Amanda Askell, Sandhini Agarwal, Ariel Herbert-Voss, Gretchen Krueger, Tom Henighan, Rewon Child, Aditya Ramesh, Daniel M. Ziegler, Jeffrey Wu, Clemens Winter, Christopher Hesse, Mark Chen, Eric Sigler, Mateusz Litwin, Scott Gray, Benjamin Chess, Jack Clark, Christopher Berner, Sam McCandlish, Alec Radford, Ilya Sutskever, and Dario Amodei. 2020. Language models are few-shot learners. *Preprint*, arXiv:2005.14165.

Emanuele Bugliarello, Ryan Cotterell, Naoaki Okazaki, and Desmond Elliott. 2021. Multimodal pretraining unmasked: A meta-analysis and a unified framework of vision-and-language berts. *Preprint*, arXiv:2011.15124.

Abhishek Das, Satwik Kottur, Khushi Gupta, Avi Singh, Deshraj Yadav, José M.F. Moura, Devi Parikh, and Dhruv Batra. 2017. Visual Dialog. In *Proceedings of the IEEE Conference on Computer Vision and Pattern Recognition (CVPR)*.

Gabriel Oliveira dos Santos, Diego Alysson Braga Moreira, Alef Iury Ferreira, Jhessica Silva, Luiz Pereira, Pedro Bueno, Thiago Sousa, Helena Maia, Nádia Da Silva, Esther Colombini, Helio Pedrini, and Sandra Avila. 2023. CAPIVARA: Cost-efficient approach for improving multilingual CLIP performance on low-resource languages. In *Proceedings of the 3rd Workshop on Multi-lingual Representation Learning (MRL)*, pages 184–207, Singapore. Association for Computational Linguistics.

Alexey Dosovitskiy, Lucas Beyer, Alexander Kolesnikov, Dirk Weissenborn, Xiaohua Zhai, Thomas Unterthiner, Mostafa Dehghani, Matthias Minderer, Georg Heigold, Sylvain Gelly, Jakob Uszkoreit, and Neil Houlsby. 2021. An image is worth 16x16 words: Transformers for image recognition at scale. In *International Conference on Learning Representations*.

Wonjae Kim, Bokyung Son, and Ildoo Kim. 2021. Vilt: Vision-and-language transformer without convolution or region supervision. In *Proceedings of the 38th International Conference on Machine Learning*, volume 139 of *Proceedings of Machine Learning Research*, pages 5583–5594. PMLR.

Diederik P. Kingma and Jimmy Ba. 2015. Adam: A method for stochastic optimization. In *3rd International Conference on Learning Representations, ICLR 2015, San Diego, CA, USA, May 7-9, 2015, Conference Track Proceedings*.

Jing Yu Koh, Ruslan Salakhutdinov, and Daniel Fried. 2023. Grounding language models to images for multimodal inputs and outputs. In *Proceedings of the 40th International Conference on Machine Learning*, volume 202 of *Proceedings of Machine Learning Research*, pages 17283–17300. PMLR.

Sneha Kudugunta, Isaac Caswell, Biao Zhang, Xavier Garcia, Derrick Xin, Aditya Kusupati, Romi Stella, Ankur Bapna, and Orhan Firat. 2023. MADLAD-400: A multilingual and document-level large audited dataset. In *Advances in Neural Information Processing Systems 36: Annual Conference on Neural Information Processing Systems 2023, NeurIPS 2023, New Orleans, LA, USA, December 10 - 16, 2023*.

Junnan Li, Dongxu Li, Caiming Xiong, and Steven Hoi. 2022. BLIP: Bootstrapping language-image pre-training for unified vision-language understanding and generation. In *Proceedings of the 39th International Conference on Machine Learning*, volume 162 of *Proceedings of Machine Learning Research*, pages 12888–12900. PMLR.

Tsung-Yi Lin, Michael Maire, Serge Belongie, James Hays, Pietro Perona, Deva Ramanan, Piotr Dollár, and C. Lawrence Zitnick. 2014. Microsoft coco: Common objects in context. In *Computer Vision – ECCV 2014*, pages 740–755, Cham. Springer International Publishing.

Haotian Liu, Chunyuan Li, Qingyang Wu, and Yong Jae Lee. 2023. Visual instruction tuning. In *Thirty-seventh Conference on Neural Information Processing Systems*.

Ricardo Lopes, Joao Magalhaes, and David Semedo. 2024. GlórIA: A generative and open large language model for Portuguese. In *Proceedings of the 16th International Conference on Computational Processing of Portuguese*, pages 441–453, Santiago de Compostela, Galicia/Spain. Association for Computational Linguistics.

Jiasen Lu, Dhruv Batra, Devi Parikh, and Stefan Lee. 2019. Vilbert: Pretraining task-agnostic visiolinguistic representations for vision-and-language tasks. In *Advances in Neural Information Processing Systems*, volume 32. Curran Associates, Inc.

Alec Radford, Jong Wook Kim, Chris Hallacy, Aditya Ramesh, Gabriel Goh, Sandhini Agarwal, Girish Sastry, Amanda Askell, Pamela Mishkin, Jack Clark, Gretchen Krueger, and Ilya Sutskever. 2021. Learning transferable visual models from natural language supervision. In *Proceedings of the 38th International*

Conference on Machine Learning, volume 139 of *Proceedings of Machine Learning Research*, pages 8748–8763. PMLR.

Rodrigo Santos, João Silva, Luís Gomes, João Rodrigues, and António Branco. 2024. Advancing generative ai for portuguese with open decoder gervásio pt*. *Preprint*, arXiv:2402.18766.

Piyush Sharma, Nan Ding, Sebastian Goodman, and Radu Soricut. 2018a. Conceptual captions: A cleaned, hypernymed, image alt-text dataset for automatic image captioning. In *Proceedings of the 56th Annual Meeting of the Association for Computational Linguistics (Volume 1: Long Papers)*, pages 2556–2565, Melbourne, Australia. Association for Computational Linguistics.

Piyush Sharma, Nan Ding, Sebastian Goodman, and Radu Soricut. 2018b. Conceptual captions: A cleaned, hypernymed, image alt-text dataset for automatic image captioning. In *Proceedings of ACL*.

Yuqing Tang, Chau Tran, Xian Li, Peng-Jen Chen, Naman Goyal, Vishrav Chaudhary, Jiatao Gu, and Angela Fan. 2020. Multilingual translation with extensible multilingual pretraining and finetuning. *Preprint*, arXiv:2008.00401.

Hugo Touvron, Louis Martin, and et. al. 2023. Llama 2: Open foundation and fine-tuned chat models. *Preprint*, arXiv:2307.09288.

Aäron van den Oord, Yazhe Li, and Oriol Vinyals. 2018. Representation learning with contrastive predictive coding. *ArXiv*, abs/1807.03748.

Peng Wang, An Yang, Rui Men, Junyang Lin, Shuai Bai, Zhikang Li, Jianxin Ma, Chang Zhou, Jingren Zhou, and Hongxia Yang. 2022. Ofa: Unifying architectures, tasks, and modalities through a simple sequence-to-sequence learning framework. In *International Conference on Machine Learning*.

Weihan Wang, Qingsong Lv, Wenmeng Yu, Wenyi Hong, Ji Qi, Yan Wang, Junhui Ji, Zhuoyi Yang, Lei Zhao, Xixuan Song, Jiazheng Xu, Bin Xu, Juanzi Li, Yuxiao Dong, Ming Ding, and Jie Tang. 2024. Cogvlm: Visual expert for pretrained language models. *Preprint*, arXiv:2311.03079.

Jiahui Yu, Zirui Wang, Vijay Vasudevan, Legg Yeung, Mojtaba Seyedhosseini, and Yonghui Wu. 2022. Coca: Contrastive captioners are image-text foundation models. *Transactions on Machine Learning Research*.

Biao Zhang, Philip Williams, Ivan Titov, and Rico Sennrich. 2020. Improving massively multilingual neural machine translation and zero-shot translation. *Preprint*, arXiv:2004.11867.

Susan Zhang, Stephen Roller, Naman Goyal, Mikel Artetxe, Moya Chen, Shuohui Chen, Christopher Dewan, Mona Diab, Xian Li, Xi Victoria Lin, Todor Mihaylov, Myle Ott, Sam Shleifer, Kurt Shuster, Daniel Simig, Punit Singh Koura, Anjali Sridhar, Tianlu Wang, and Luke Zettlemoyer. 2022. Opt: Open pre-trained transformer language models. *Preprint*, arXiv:2205.01068.

Author Index

Association for Computational Linguistics
209 N. Eighth Street
Stroudsburg, Pennsylvania 18360

ISBN 979-8-3313-0844-5

9 798331 308445